AMERICAN MURDERS

GARLAND REFERENCE LIBRARY OF
THE HUMANITIES (VOL. 610)

AMERICAN MURDERS

11 Rediscovered Short
Novels from the
American Magazine
1934–1954

Edited by JON L. BREEN
& RITA A. BREEN

Garland Publishing, Inc.
New York & London 1986

M
STORIES
AME
9-86 BT 1900

LIBRARY OF CONGRESS
CATALOGING-IN-PUBLICATION DATA
Main entry under title:
American murders.

(Garland reference library of the humanities ;
vol. 610)
1. Detective and mystery stories, American.
2. American fiction—20th century.
I. Breen, Jon L., 1943–
II. Breen, Rita A., 1946–
III. Series: Garland reference library of the
humanities ; v. 610.
PS648.D4A46   1986   813'.0872'08
85-45120
ISBN 0-8240-8672-4 (alk. paper)

Design by Jonathan Billing

Printed on acid-free, 250-year-life paper
Manufactured in the United States of America

For our parents,
who knew these times
better than we

CONTENTS

INTRODUCTION

Between the early 1930's and the middle 1950's, there were three print markets available to fiction writers. The book market had the greatest prestige, for books would be reviewed in newspapers and magazines; they would line the shelves of public libraries; and they would have a feel of permanence about them, bound in hard covers (until paperback originals came on the scene in the fifties) and on good paper (at least until the World War II paper shortages came along). But books, at least for writers of genre fiction, paid surprisingly poorly to all but the most popular and successful. In her pioneering technical manual, Mystery Fiction: Theory and Technique (Duell, Sloan, and Pearce, 1943), Marie F. Rodell reported that the "average mystery writer makes from the sale of his book in book form no more than five hundred dollars."

Then there were the pulps, with specialized titles for every genre. Printed on cheap paper, offering mostly low rates (starting at 1¢ or even ½¢ a word), decisively impermanent, they were a training ground for new writers, and only the very prolific, those who could turn out a million or more words per year, could make a reasonable living writing to their specifications.

Finally, there were the slicks, popular magazines like Saturday Evening Post, Collier's, Cosmopolitan, and others of that ilk. Slick writers tended to write to formula as surely as did the pulp writers, but their style was smoother and their products geared to a family audience. And the slicks in those days bought great amounts of fiction and paid well. Writers of short stories and novelettes for the slicks could use these markets to support their lesser paying but more prestigious book publications. Slick paper fiction in many ways served the same needs as network TV today-- certainly series like Arthur Train's Mr. Tutt stories and Clarence Budington Kelland's Scattergood Baines saga were comparable to today's situation comedies and human-interest dramas, though they may have been slightly less likely to insult the intelligence of their audience.

Today, the pulps are gone, victims initially of wartime paper shortages, later of TV and paperback books, with only a few digest-sized mystery and science fiction magazines to take their place as markets for short stories in popular categories. Many of the best-known slicks have died, and the magazines that remain publish little fiction, though those that do continue to pay excellent rates. The book market remains, with the paperback original field in some degree taking up the fictional slack for both pulps (e.g., the Executioner) and slicks (e.g., Harlequin romances). Hard covers still carry the most prestige, but authors of fiction who write in popular genres or who don't regularly make the best-seller lists continue to be paid surprisingly poorly.

The American Magazine was one of the best and most popular of the general slicks, home to the glossiest ads of the richest advertisers of the day, full of fiction short and long, articles on current events and personalities. Both fiction and non-fiction in the American offered viewpoints that reflected the concerns, the attitudes, and often the prejudices of its readers. The July 1934 issue includes, besides the Philip Wylie novelette that leads off the present collection, short stories by Roland Pertwee, Max Brand, Octavus Roy Cohen, and others; serials at various stages of completion by Edward Hope, Ursula Parrott, and Channing Pollock; a humorous article on playing golf by Paul Gallico; pieces by and about Vice President John Nance Garner; an interview with Secretary of Agriculture Henry Wallace; a feature called "From a Doctor's Notebook" by Maurice Chideckel, M.D.; "A City Fellow Goes Rustic" by composer Deems Taylor; and photo-portraits of song-writer Dorothy Fields, undersea artist Chris Emile Olsen, tennis player Sarah Palfrey, Federal Judge Florence E. Allen, and several other personalities of the day. As time went on, the mix of fiction and non-fiction would remain about the same, but American would differentiate itself from its most similar competitors, Saturday Evening Post and Collier's, by running fewer and fewer serials and finally none at all, relying on complete-in-one-issue material.

The short mystery novel became an occasional feature starting with the March 1934 issue and a tale called "Eyes at the Window" by the intriguingly named but otherwise obscure Mrs. Wilson Woodrow. At first appearing bimonthly, the mystery novel became a monthly feature throughout 1936 and 1937. For the next few years, the series appeared in most issues, with occasional gaps. From the beginning of 1944 to the magazine's final issue in August 1956, the feature appeared in every single issue of the magazine. For most of that period, there was a monthly romantic novel as well.

How well did American pay its contributors? Rex Stout, according to biographer John McAleer, received $2500 for serialization rights to Fer-de-Lance, the first Nero Wolfe novel, in 1934, the depths of the Great Depression. It appeared in abridged form, as "Point of Death," only two days before book publication. In his article "The Dollars and Cents of Mystery Writing," in The Mystery Writer's Handbook (Harper, 1956), literary agent Paul Reynolds reported that the American paid an average price of $3500 to "unknown" mystery writers in 1955, a larger sum than some mystery writers receive for a hardcover advance thirty years later. Presumably it was much more for big-name regulars. Gordon Gordon, who collaborated with the late Mildred Gordon and more recently with second wife Mary Dorr as the Gordons, writes, "I remember so vividly our first sale, 'The Case of the Talking Bug.' The magazine paid us $4500.00 which at that time was a fantastic sum! This was more money we had ever seen before and as I remember we didn't even have enough cash in our pockets to go out for a car drive much less celebrate in any other way."

Many of the American mysteries appeared as full-length novels after magazine publication. The obvious question: which came first? Were the magazine stories condensed novels or were the novels expanded (and sometimes padded) magazine stories? Originally, as with Fer-de-Lance, the novel versions generally came first. But soon writers were writing specifically to the magazine's length requirement. Hugh Pentecost (Judson P. Philips) writes, "I didn't think there was that much 'fat' in my book length stories and finally persuaded them to let me do them at the length they wanted to publish." Pentecost came to specialize in the novelette length and usually did not expand his American contributions for later book publication. The same was true of Rex Stout and Phoebe Atwood Taylor, who published book collections of their novelettes, usually three to a volume. The late George Harmon Coxe's American stories all exist in both short and long forms, but as he wrote us shortly before his death, "the novelettes came first but always with a book length in mind." Sometimes the book-length version did not appear until years later. After the Kelley Roos team's first two contributions, condensed from the novels If the Shroud Fits and The Frightened Stiff, William Roos (who collaborated on the stories with his late wife Audrey) writes, "we always cleared our ideas with our editors, then when the American bought them, we stretched them into books."

The American editors loved to publish mysteries with unusual backgrounds. Ellery Queen writes in the essay collection In the Queens' Parlor (Simon and Schuster, 1957) that "the editors...capitalized on the dramatic values of a carefully chosen scene by actually assigning backgrounds to the authors of 'American' novelettes," citing examples in the works of Lawrence G. Blochman, Kelley Roos, Rex Stout, Hugh Pentecost, and Philip Wylie. William Roos verifies Queen's statement, writing that American editor Henry La Cossitt suggested the background of "the adult sailors and their model sailboats on a lake in Central Park" ("The Toy-Boat Murder," November 1943, later expanded to novel form as Sailor Take Warning, 1944) and of Columbia University's rare book library ("Murder by Degrees," September 1944, novelized as There Was a Crooked Man, 1944).

Roos also recalls that each story had to have exactly four suspects and run ninety typed pages.

The editors of the series varied. John McAleer writes in his Rex

Stout biography that editor-in-chief Sumner Blossom acquired Fer-de-Lance and that Albert J. Benjamin III was the editor who abridged all Stout's appearances in American between 1934 and 1941, presumably excepting "Bitter End" (see below). The Kelley Roos team worked with four different editors: Hubert Kelley (briefly), Henry La Cossitt, John K.M. McCaffrey, and J. Robert Meskill. Many of the other editors who appeared on American's masthead over the years probably also worked on the mystery novel series.

While it would be an exaggeration to claim every important American mystery writer of the time contributed to the series, certainly a majority of the best known did. Among those who made one-shot appearances were Graham Greene (one of the few non-American writers to contribute), Kenneth Millar (later to become Ross Macdonald), Charlotte Armstrong, Dorothy B. Hughes, and Donald Hamilton. Erle Stanley Gardner's name turned up on occasion, with the only two Perry Mason novelettes as well as some non-series pieces. Leslie Charteris and the Saint appeared several times early in the series, as did the various sleuths of Zenith Brown, writing as Leslie Ford or David Frome.

There were certain bylines, though, that appeared with such regularity they seemed to dominate the series. Hugh Pentecost writes, "I used to think that Rex Stout and I had done about half of them. Not so, of course." Actually, Pentecost and Stout tied for first place in frequency of appearance with thirty contributions each, nearly twice the total of their nearest competitor, Kelley Roos with sixteen. George Harmon Coxe made fifteen appearances. The only other contributor in double figures (with ten) is the team of Richard Webb and Hugh Wheeler, who wrote first as Q. Patrick and later as Patrick Quentin.

Of the American novelettes that were not expanded into novels, some have been reprinted in book form again and again, whether in single-author collections or multi-author anthologies. Others have been reprinted in Ellery Queen's Mystery Magazine or one of the other digests. Some have even seen separate paperback publication in their original short form in Dell's short-lived (and highly collectible) 10¢ series of the early fifties. Richard Powell's "Death Talks Out of Turn" (March 1944) had sufficient loose-lips-sink-ships propaganda value to be issued as a Government Printing Office pamphlet, as well as in book-length form as All Over But the Shooting (1944). Many more of the novelettes, though, including some by formidable names, have never been reprinted since they first appeared in American's pages, and it is from these that we have chosen the contents of this volume. Of the stories included here, only Mignon G. Eberhart's "Murder Goes to Market" has appeared in book form to our knowledge-- and that in a collection of her shorter work published only in Great Britain.

Thus, the most famous American series sleuth of them all, Rex Stout's Nero Wolfe, does not appear in these pages. All his cases have been reprinted in hard and soft covers, so they are readily available to readers. The closest thing to an unknown Wolfe story is "Bitter End" (November 1940), originally written as the novel Bad for Business (1940), starring Stout's second-string detective Tecumseh Fox. American offered to double their offer for the novel if Stout would put Wolfe into the abridged version. He complied. For obvious reasons, the novelette was never included in any of Stout's three-in-one Wolfe collections, but it was reprinted in the limited edition Corsage (James A. Rock, 1977) and was unavailable for inclusion in the present book.

The stories gathered here have not been changed in any way from their original magazine form, aside from the correction of obvious typographical errors, which (in those lost days of careful proof-reading) were relatively rare. Some sequences, the treatment of the Japanese passenger in Philip Wylie's "Death Flies High," for example, and the stereotyped black porters of H.W. Roden's "Death on the Pegasus," seem racist by today's standards, though by the standards of their day they are relatively mild. To give a true picture of the prejudices of the era that produced them, they have been left intact.

Selections were made on the basis of quality, unfamiliarity, and the unusualness of the background. In these pages, murder strikes an early cross-country passenger flight, a super market, a car dealership, a jet plane factory, an enemy aircraft spotting unit, a luxury passenger train, a small-town centennial celebration, the Smithsonian Institution, and a television studio. Appearing in chronological order, the stories cover a twenty-one-year span, 1934-1954, and in addition to pure entertainment provide a view of the concerns and attitudes, the pleasures and pains of American life over that period. These are American murders in more ways than one.

ACKNOWLEDGEMENTS

"Death Flies East," copyright 1933 by Crowell Publishing Co.; renewed 1961 by Columbia Pictures; reprinted by permission of Harold Ober Associates.

"The Corpse was Beautiful," copyright 1942 by Judson Philips; renewed 1970; reprinted by permission of Brandt and Brandt Literary Agents Inc.

"Murder Goes to Market," copyright 1943 by Mignon G. Eberhart; renewed 1971; reprinted by permission of Brandt and Brandt Literary Agents Inc.

"The Disappearing Hermit," copyright 1946 by Phoebe Atwood Taylor; renewed; reprinted by permission of McIntosh and Otis, Inc.

"Death on the Pegasus," copyright 1947 by Crowell-Collier Publishing Co. Rights reverted to author H.W. Roden; current holder of copyright unknown.

In gathering the novelettes for this volume, as well as information for the introduction and checklist, we have been aided by many individuals and institutions. Special thanks are due the late George Harmon Coxe, Gordon Gordon, Paul M. James, Lou Kannenstine, Brian KenKnight, John McAleer, Francis M. Nevins, Jr., Judson Philips, William Roos, Robert Samoian, and the public libraries of Fullerton and Santa Ana, California.

Death flies east

By Philip Wylie

Philip Wylie (1902-1971) was among the most versatile authors of this century, known for fiction both slick and literary, including frequent ventures into mystery and science fiction. He is probably best remembered as a popular social critic, his A Generation of Vipers (1942) having added the term "Momism" to the American vocabulary.

By 1934, passenger air travel was an established feature of twentieth-century life but one that seemed exotic, adventurous, and vaguely dangerous to the average person. Conveyances like ships and trains have long provided an ideal setting for detective stories and thrillers. Planes, superficially at least, seem less attractive by the virtue of their greater speed. But when this novelette was written, a cross-country flight from Los Angeles to New York involved numerous stops along the way, and there was plenty of time to develop a whodunit plot among the passengers, all (hero and heroine especially) shrouded in mystery.

DEATH FLIES EAST by Philip Wylie

Fog at daybreak is not unusual over the flying fields that lie on the outskirts of Los Angeles. Veteran travelers of the air are accustomed to its clinging chill as they drive over the desert hills past rows of street lamps made wan by morning.

It was not the fog.

On this particular morning there was a subtler and more sinister threat, an emanation from human beings as frigid and deceiving as the mist, but even more treacherous.

Evelyn felt it. She shivered with excitement-- and with a little fear. Through her tinted sunglasses she peered at the people in the waiting-room of the airport. She pulled her hat farther over her hair. She hugged her suitcase.

A man was buying his ticket. In the spacious, echoing room she heard him give his name: "Leslie Evans. I'm an insurance broker. Bad risk in my own business, eh?" He laughed and the clerk laughed. "Well-- I'm in a hurry." He was a fat man with red cheeks and a small, irritable mouth.

Another man stood near the gate. Evelyn had already made up her mind about him. The tilted derby, the big feet, the toothpick, the stiff posture. A detective. He did not seem to be paying attention to her.

And yet, she thought, he was possibly looking for her.

Outside, propellers tore the air with a throbbing sound. No. 60 taxied ponderously to the canopy.

Evelyn smiled nervously. The detective was exactly like the ones in stories. She walked to the clerk.

"I telephoned for reservations."

"Your name?"

"Dorothy Jones."

"Oh, yes-- Miss Jones." He commenced to stamp the ticket just as they do in railroad stations.

A short, gray-haired man in a gray coat and a gray hat showed his ticket and walked through the gate. Outside, at the front doors of the building, a taxi stopped. Evelyn, waiting anxiously, saw a Chinaman, or a Jap, walk blandly to another clerk. She could not tell the Chinese from the Japanese. Many people could. She wondered how. Her mind began to hum a refrain that the orchestra had been playing early the evening before.

A red-headed man, past middle age, stepped nimbly from a limousine, walked across the station, and entered a plane.

She could see him through the window, crouching so that he would not bump his head.

Her eyes rested on the ship itself. Seen in the sky from the ground, transcontinental air-liners seem small. But at this distance the plane was gigantic. Sleek, its metal body clammy with fog, its motors now still, it did not associate itself with flight. She shivered in anticipation.

Her ticket was presented to her. She glanced at the detective. But he was obviously not going to stop her. He was intently looking the other way.

Evelyn looked in the same direction.

A man of about thirty was entering the waiting-room from the avenue side. In a glance the girl saw a great deal. He was tall. He had a high forehead. His eyes were black and extraordinarily brilliant. He seemed excited and he walked with long, easy strides.

She turned away, then, and once more eyed the detective. He was staring at the young man with the utmost concentration and upon his face was a faintly veiled expression of satisfaction.

The man gave his name: "John Robinson."

His ticket was stamped. He went to the canopy. He had surrendered his suitcase. But he still carried a locked, black leather brief-case. He had run his wrist through its handle and was holding it by a strap.

He had said, "All the way," to the clerk. That meant he was going to New York.

So was Evelyn-- who had given her name as Dorothy Jones.

And it was in the young man that the detective was interested. Why? She wondered. He looked extraordinarily unlike a criminal.

Odd. But everything was odd that morning.

She started toward the plane. Behind her, the detective went to the ticket window. "All the way," she heard him say.

She had never before been inside an airplane. Its compactness, its up-slanted rows of seats, its chintz curtains and blue rug, held her unconscious attention.

She trembled. She was going to make it.

There was an empty chair beside the tall, young man. Almost against her will, she sat in it.

A pretty blond girl in a smartly cut uniform hung up Evelyn's coat.

The others were seated; the fat man was squirming into a comfortable position. The gray-coated man also wore a gray suit. The red-headed man who looked like a Scotchman was reading. The Jap was grinning at nothing.

She heard the detective enter. Faces turned back to look at the new passenger-- blank, incurious faces, pale from rising at so early an hour.

"First flight?"

The young man had spoken to her. She nodded uncertainly. She had determined not to speak to anyone. He was smiling. She thought that he looked unusually intelligent.

He peered past her and out of the window. She followed his gaze. Fog floated along the field. The vast main building of the airport dimmed away to nothing.

"Won't be bad," he said reassuringly. "I mean the fog. We'll be out of it in a minute."

"Yes," she said.

Someone bumped her. It was the man in the gray suit. He stepped from the plane and she saw him go into the waiting room. Motors throbbed. The cabin vibrated. They had told her that this plane was equipped with the new quiet engines, but the sound was louder than she had expected. It was a broken stutter, as if the propellers were jumping through the air instead of spinning steadily.

The gray-haired man ran back and reentered the ship with an armful of magazines and newspapers, which he piled in a rack with those he had already bought.

An official was yelling at the pilots, who sat forward in their lofty cockpit.

Evelyn felt hot and cold in turns. She was almost praying that they would start. At any moment someone might come out of the mist and detain her.

The engines raced faster.

Then she saw a man running through the canopy. The door into the rear compartment of the plane slammed and was reopened. The runner bounced into the plane and took one of the seats. He, also, carried a suitcase. He was grinning strangely and panting. He was quite young, and pallid. He possessed a herculean pair of shoulders.

He sat down, breathing hard.

Presently he addressed the dark Mr. Robinson:

"Just made it, eh?"

"You did."

"Hope it didn't hold you up."

"Guess not."

The motors suddenly split the air. The stewardess snapped around each passenger a wide safety belt. It was to be worn, she explained, only while taking off and landing. The ship bulged forward. Evelyn gathered herself for the plunge into the sky, but instead, after running along the field for some distance, the plane stopped, turned heavily at a right angle, and stood with braked wheels while the propellers sent a mighty cloud of dust into the fog.

Then the race began.

Evelyn's heart was in her mouth. Faster and faster they shot forward, bumping and roaring. The earth streaked under the window. The fog moved in a whirlwind. They approached the slim bulk of a hangar.

And they went right over the hangar.

She had never been more astonished in her life. They were flying!

John Robinson gazed covertly at the girl. Thoughts poured through his mind-- some of them alarming, all of them exciting. And underneath that emotional medley he made notes on her. Funny that she had been wearing sunglasses. They were often worn in California, of course-- but not on foggy mornings. She was quite tall and slender. She had blue eyes. Those characteristics he liked. But she had blond hair, and John Robinson did not care especially for blondes. If he had been a woman he would have noticed that her clothes, although unpretentious, were fashionable and expensive.

As he looked, he received a shock. She took off her hat-- and the blond hair came with it. She hastily concealed the hat, the two golden, artificial buns attached to it. Her own hair was very dark, cut just below her ears, and it curled in the easy waves of nature-- not the tight spirals of beauty parlors.

Then she glanced at him in a startled way.

He tried to behave as if he had not noticed. But he knew that she had caught him. She picked up one of the illustrated maps supplied by the airline and pretended to study it. She felt amused, and at the same time agitated. At least, she had been successful in getting away. But there was a detective on the plane who was most certainly following Mr. Robinson.

The fat man was talking to the small man in the gray suit: "Soon be out of it."

The small man smiled. "Hope so. Lots of mountains around here."

"My name's Evans."

"Mine's Baker."

They shook hands across the aisle.

Evelyn looked out of the window. Around them was a sea of fog. They were floating on it and submerged in it. She felt giddy for an instant. She thought of airsickness. With an almost childish fright, she hoped that she would not get sick in the presence of the good-looking dark young man.

Then a miracle happened.

In one second the plane emerged from the fog. Sun burst upon them. The sky overhead was bright blue. And below was a floor of white vapor rolling out toward the sea. Islands of land-- mountains, she realized-- stood up in it. And the fog seemed substantial, like mashed potatoes.

Far away, snow-capped peaks, rose and gold in dawn, cut themselves against the blue.

"Oh!" she exclaimed involuntarily.

Mr. Robinson, with the dark and blazing eyes, agreed with her. "It's magnificent!"

"Isn't it!"

"No one who hasn't flown can have the remotest imaginative notion of the grandeur of air scenery."

A criminal, she thought, wouldn't say a thing like that. She looked back at the detective. He was sleeping under his derby. She decided to ask Mr. Robinson why he was being followed. It would be rude and might make trouble, but Evelyn felt entitled to both. Before she had framed a satisfactory question, he spoke again, leaning toward her:

"Tell me-- are you a fugitive from justice? Are you running away from an undesirable marriage? Are you a mysterious Belgian spy?"

"What are you talking about?"

"People," he said calmly, "simply do not get jitteringly onto airplanes at dawn disguised to the ears, when they are merely on normal junkets around the country."

She was going to retort that people also do not board planes with toothpick-chewing detectives on their trails-- just for the love of the thing. But she did not. No one in the cabin seemed to be paying attention to them. She had an impulse to tell him the truth, and she thought she was an errant fool for considering it. The impulse was in any case checked when the co-pilot, in a brown uniform, with a revolver at his hip, opened the door into the cockpit and went through the cabin examining tickets.

He smiled at Evelyn. "Everything all right, Miss Jones?"

"Marvelous, thank you."

He went away.

"Everything," said the persistent Mr. Robinson, "is fishy. Tell me about yourself."

"Tell me about yourself."

His smile faded and returned. "I'm afraid I can't-- just at the moment. But will some other time suffice?"

"Don't you think," she said coolly, "that you're a trifle presumptuous?"

"I'm sorry."

He sounded extremely apologetic. He immediately opened a morning paper and began to read. Evelyn was left to her own resources, which consisted of watching the scenery, of which there was an immense amount. They were flying east over the foothills of a range of mountains, rising steadily. Below was a fixed ocean of turbulent, barren earth and on the sides of sheer mountains that earth was broken away, leaving many-hued cliffs.

The fat man and the small man were talking about baseball. The red-headed man was obviously annoyed by their loud voices. The Jap was asleep, as was the young man who had arrived late.

Evelyn felt lonesome, in spite of the proximity of so many people. And she felt inside herself a premonition of peril. Perhaps, she thought, the ship was going to crash. But she realized that she was not in the least afraid of that possibility or concerned with it.

By and by she dozed.

She was surprised when she opened her eyes to see a toy town on the desert far below. The ship was winding down toward it.

"We're going to land," said Mr. Robinson.

"Is anything the matter?"

"Nothing. This is our regular stop."

"Oh."

Five minutes later they were on the ground again. In another state. All of the passengers rose and filed out. It had been comfortable in the airplane, but on the ground in the outdoors it was furnace hot. The desert airport was baked by a relentless sun.

Evelyn walked aimlessly by herself. The young man who had arrived late spoke to her politely, but she replied with such studied aloofness that he went away. Mr. Robinson stepped into the waiting-room on the field. The detective, apparently in the most idle manner, followed.

When Mr. Robinson came out he walked toward her, not as if he were going to speak of his own accord, but as if he wished to speak.

The detective was standing on the porch in the shade, smoking and watching in a slack-faced, heavy-eyed silence.

"It's fun," she said.

"Flying?"

"Yes."

"I enjoy it."

"You've flown a lot?"

"Not recently. Not for years. I flew in the war."

"Really?"

He nodded. "Really. And now suppose you tell me about the goggles and the false hair. My dear Miss Jones, I am devoured by curiosity. Eaten, ravaged by it."

She looked directly at him. Why not? Common sense indicated that it would be a foolish thing to do. But her private wishes offered an excuse. If she told him about herself, he would undoubtedly explain his own unconventional circumstances. And she was as curious about him as he about her.

"All right," she said. "I'll tell you. But it's got to be kept in the strictest confidence."

"From my cradle days," Mr. Robinson replied soberly, "I've had a reputation for confidential behavior. I'm so close-mouthed and mum, in fact, that I had difficulty in getting through school, because I would not answer the teachers' questions."

"You sound reliable. Well-- have you ever heard of the Vale millions? Of Thomas Vale?"

He kept an impassive face and nodded. "Certainly. The redoubtable copper king. The great philanthropist. The gentleman whose untimely death left his daughter the fifth or sixth largest fortune in America. Your acquaintance, Miss Vale-- or shall I say Miss Jones?-- is a privilege."

"You've recognized me all the time?"

He shook his head. "A chance thrust. Aren't you supposed to be the most difficult girl to meet or even to photograph in America?"

They walked side by side in the broiling sun, a little distance from the others.

"You shouldn't have guessed so quickly. I wanted to build up a fine story--"

He chuckled. "You can still do so. The story will be about why the nation's richest and handsomest girl is traveling around in transcontinental airplanes, disguised. Or-- shall we say?-- incognito."

"That's quite long. And quite short, too. I suppose," she continued blandly, "that you've never been known as America's millionaire princess."

"Now that I think of it-- I never have," he answered.

"Well-- wherever you go, thousands of people pursue you. People who want your money and people who want to meet you and people who would like to get a snip of your hair. That is very embarrassing. So you stop going places, as a general rule. When you do go places, you are usually accompanied by from two to four detectives, who more or less spoil your fun. If you go automobile riding with a boy you like, they turn out State Police in thousands. Last night, I went to a ball in Los Angeles, and my fastidious and careful brother had no less than three plain-clothes men here and there to guard me.

"I got sick of it. The more I thought of it, the more irritated I became. I drank a cocktail, and when I sent an emissary for another, a detective asked him to take no more to me. So I bolted. I sneaked out of the party. I hired a cab. I changed my clothes at my palatial hotel suite and bribed my maid to tell phone callers I had not appeared. I took a reservation on a plane through an agency under a wrong name. And I provided myself with smoked glasses in case the customary cordon was formed to watch the ships and trains. On my way here I passed a store that was selling Halloween costumes. I stopped my cab and banged on the door till I woke the man up, and I bought some false whiskers. Yellow ones. I made them into buns and pinned them on my hat.

"I think now that I was more or less nutty, but you do get sick of the pitter-patter of flat feet always behind you. I get those descriptive terms from reading-- that's about all I'm allowed to do. Read. I can even read thrillers. But I know the detective clan from experience. I haven't any idea what I'll do when I get to New York. But I should have a couple of days of magnificent privacy. That's all."

"A very sad story," said Mr. Robinson.

"Now-- about yourself."

He frowned unhappily. "I'm extremely sorry, Miss Vale--"

"Call me Miss Jones."

"Miss Jones-- but I'm afraid I can't tell much. I'm just a business man going to Wash-- to New York-- on business."

The unhappy multimillionairess was provoked. She had thought that her recital would be met by equal candor. What she had told was the precise truth. But Mr. Robinson had replied unsatisfactorily. She tried a new tack.

"I know detectives so well," she said, watching him closely, "that I know there is one on this plane."

"Really?" Either he had nothing to hide, or else he was a gifted actor. "Who?"

"The man standing on the porch there."

He looked. "By George! He does have a sort of policeman aspect."

"I'm sure he's a plain-clothes man."

"Going to a distant city," said Mr. Robinson. "In search of gangsters, kidnappers, or other felons."

Evelyn watched the tall, dark man narrowly. "Or else following someone on this plane," she said.

"You're romantic," he answered. "Look at the passengers. Are they hard-faced? Are they the rat type? Are they slinking and sinister? A thousand times, no, Miss-- Jones. A bunch of business men about their normal affairs. The Scotchman is undoubtedly a banker. The fat man sells something. The little chap in the natty gray is a retired tailor. The young man is-- well-- he looks like a gymnasium instructor. The Jap is a Jap pure and simple. His father probably owns hundreds of acres of Tokyo silk mills. I grant you the detective. That leaves me. Now-- do I look like an anarchist, an incendiary, a pickpocket, or a burglar?"

"You have a sort of Jimmy Valentine air," she replied.

He laughed buoyantly, bent toward her with merry eyes, and whispered, "Hist!"

"All aboard!" a voice called.

He helped her up the portable steps.

He had not given himself away, she reflected. But when he had stepped from the plane, and while he was in the waiting-room, and during his short walk with her, he had carried the locked brief-case-- with his wrist through the handle and his long fingers wrapped around a strap.

Evelyn Vale, alias Dorothy Jones, would have given a great deal to know what that frantically clutched brief-case contained.

The second take-off was less startling than the first. As the huge plane gathered speed Evelyn felt that she was already past the neophyte stage. She was an air tourist now. She looked calmly at the rushing earth, and her heart did not sink when she perceived they were off the ground.

At the forward end of the cabin was a printed sign which said, "J. L. Anderson, Pilot. R. F. Blackley, Co-pilot. Myra Sayre, R. N., Stewardess."

Evelyn wondered what "R. N." meant, and presently she guessed correctly: "Registered nurse."

The blond registered nurse and stewardess appeared with cups of cold tomato juice. Everyone drank. The four men in the four front seats were talking: Mr. Evans, Mr. Baker, the red-headed man, and the young man with the big shoulders.

The dark young man leaned back in his seat. His face wore a slight smile. He was thinking about Evelyn Vale. Funny thing for a girl to do. And yet-- she seemed to have a quantity of latent spirit. She was just the sort of person who would submit quietly and for years to all sorts of chaperonage and surveillance and then suddenly break away. He wondered how old she was. Twenty-two, possibly.

The co-pilot came from the cockpit and smiled with professional assurance at the passengers. None of them needed encouragement, however. The sun was bright and, although the air was somewhat bumpy, no one was sick.

He spoke to the four conversing men and walked past Mr. Robinson and Evelyn Vale. At the seat of the detective, which was last in the row, he paused and bent over. He spoke in a voice no one could hear:

"Something big, Lieutenant?"

"I don't know-- exactly."

"Going all the way, eh?"

"I think so."

"Oh-- oh!" The co-pilot looked at the passengers with a queer expression. "You aren't sure, eh?"

Lieutenant O'Brien shook his head. "The chief didn't give me any details. Just instructions. And I may be getting off any time. Can't say."

"Well-- if we can do anything for you--" The co-pilot's hand unconsciously touched the revolver at his side.

"I'll yell."

"Right."

The detective smiled at the co-pilot and sank back into his torpid reverie. After a long time he opened his eyes and stared thoughtfully at the back of the head of the young man in front of him. At last he whispered softly to himself, "John Robinson, eh?"

It was while he stared at the man in the seat ahead that Evelyn again regarded him. She tried to weigh the detective's expression. It was pensive, speculative, and very somber. Then a new element in the behavior of her fellow passengers attracted her interest.

She realized abruptly that for the third time the Jap had made an abnormal attempt to stare at John Robinson. And she recalled that at the stop in the desert the Jap had been on the heels of the detective when he followed Mr. Robinson into the waiting-room.

The black brief-case, Evelyn thought. He still held it-- tightly.

While she watched the Jap, she saw his eyes stray to the brief-case and remain fixed upon it. However, with the quick and incomprehensible sensitivity of his race, he seemed to feel her scrutiny, for he turned his head away after regarding her for a brief instant.

She looked out of the window and down at the earth. The ship was flying fast and high over smooth-crested mountains, in the valleys and crevices of which were broad areas of vividly colored flowers-- red, yellow, and orange. Far away she saw a level horizon that was gray-blue, and she knew it was a vast expanse of water. She was astonished that any body of water so large existed in this arid region, and then she remembered Great Salt Lake.

The land under the plane began to be regularly broken into square patterns on the corners of which were diminutive farmhouses. Then the great city became visible.

"Elegant!" Mr. Robinson said.

"I thought you were asleep."

He shook his head. "I wasn't. I was sitting here wondering if you had told me the truth about yourself."

"I'm complimented."

"I didn't actually doubt it. But it does seem a trifle strange. Your family will think--"

"My family consists of a brother. And it will do him good to worry a little in his life. He never has. Besides, I left a note for him."

"What did you say?"

Evelyn made a sound that, for so patrician a lady, was not unlike a giggle. "I said that I was free, white, and twenty-one, and that I hadn't been kidnapped; and that I was going to become a missionary in Asia-- as was my right if I wished."

"Well," Mr. Robinson replied judiciously, "that ought to insure him the worry you believe will be so beneficial."

"It should," said the girl.

The plane banked and wound its way toward a flying field that was some distance from the majestic city near the inland salt sea.

"We will have lunch here," he said.

"We?"

"You and I."

"Very well. We shall have lunch."

There is something in the adventure of flying that is conducive to companionship. Utter strangers, who remain habitually wrapped in snobbish silence on boats and trains, will, on an air-liner, communicate the intimate details of their lives to each other.

This is partly due, no doubt, to the fact that most of the travelers do not read the statistics of commercial air travel. They do not realize that they are extremely safe in the air and that with every passing month their security is increased. They have learned of the occasional dramatic disasters, and they think of themselves as brave and doughty persons-- although the pilot forward may be far calmer and more sure of himself than the driver of a cross-country bus.

In explaining her acute interest in Mr. Robinson, Evelyn Vale employed that theory. She furthermore told herself that she had justifiably thrown a certain portion of caution to the winds. She was out for a lark. She was hungry for excitement. She felt perfectly safe, although Mr. Robinson was unquestionably a suspicious character. There was a detective on the plane. The co-pilot was armed, and both he and the pilot, as well as the stewardess, looked like persons of resource and nerve. Besides that, the red-headed Scotchman was obviously a sturdy citizen, and so was the fat man, and so were the other two Americans on the ship-- the youth with broad shoulders and the gray, quiet man who told anecdotes to the other passengers.

Evelyn Vale went so far in her mind as to admit that Mr. Robinson was excessively attractive. He had had a remarkable education and his manners were superlative. If he were doing something criminal, she thought, he had an interesting motive. And if he were in trouble, it was doubtless through no fault of his own.

At Salt Lake City, in the airport restaurant, they had lunch.

There they changed planes.

They found that Mr. Robinson, free from the handicap of talking against the roar of the motors, was a distinguished conversationalist. He had been in many places in the world. He was reluctant to discuss his friends and associates, but delighted to converse on any topic.

Once she spoke about the brief-case he carried: "You must have something very valuable in that."

"Something," he had answered gravely, "of inconceivable value."

"If the plane crashed and the baggage were sold at auction," she asked innocently, "and I bought the brief-case blind-- would its contents be worth anything to me?"

He grinned at her. "You're extremely prying," he said. "The contents of this brief-case would be worth more than your fortune."

A fresh ship with a new stewardess and new pilots took them aloft.

The young man with big shoulders came from his seat to talk to them after a while.

"Going to New York?" he asked.

"Yes."

He had a broad, frank face, with gleaming blue eyes, and his hands were the largest Evelyn had ever seen. "Well-- we'll have some fun before we get there."

"Meaning what?" Mr. Robinson asked.

"Weather."

"Is it going to be bad?"

"Pretty bad. Fog around the Great Lakes. Thunderstorms in Pennsylvania. And a high wind between."

Mr. Baker, the man in gray, walked to the rear end of the cabin. He addressed Mr. Robinson: "Would you care to join Mr. Evans and Mr. Macavendish and myself in a game of bridge?"

"I'm sorry," said Mr. Robinson, "but I don't play."

"And you, Mr. Winter?"

The athletic young man shook his head. "Pinochle's my game." He nodded to Evelyn and her companion and went back to his seat. Mr. Baker withdrew along the aisle and his sleeve was touched by the Jap. "Your pardon-- I play commendable game."

"Splendid!"

The afternoon began to pass. Twice the plane descended for gasoline, brief stops in small mid-Western towns. Mail and greetings were exchanged. A swift airport crew fueled the ship. Then the take-off again.

The mountains were far behind.

Hundreds upon hundreds of miles of prairies had been crossed.

The moon showed full and yellow on the horizon. Night descended.

The bridge game continued. Occasionally passengers walked through the ship. Towns, glittering like platters of jewelry, passed underneath them. And at last, on the horizon, the aura of Chicago showed.

Through all that time Evelyn and Mr. Robinson had been talking. And his conversation, drifting from boyhood days through the war to a nebulous and unexplained present, had held her spellbound.

At Chicago, in a dazzling station-restaurant, they dined. Evelyn did not feel tired. Mr. Robinson showed no signs of fatigue. After some delay and a trip to the weather offices, where Mr. Robinson expertly explained the maps and the bulletins, they were in the air again.

It was quite late.

Dawn would see them in New York.

They rose in shredded mist over the vast city. For a long while everyone sat with eyes glued to the window, staring at the myriad lights: the red neon signs and the lights on the lake; blue revolving lights, and beacons; roads filled with automobiles whose headlamps made a parade of double diamonds, and street lights in straight rows bisecting each other at right angles.

Then the ground below darkened. Here and there the flame of blast furnaces showed evanescently. And the moon rode high overhead.

Lights in the cabin were turned out by the stewardess. The seats were tilted back. Slumber overtook many of the passengers.

Evelyn tried to sleep. Her thoughts were riveted first upon the dark and handsome man at her side. A strange, fascinating man. Perhaps, after all, he was a fugitive and a criminal. Perhaps there were such criminals as one read about in fictitious romances-- desperate, chivalrous, handsome men without character or remorse.

The thought chilled her. She began to feel the strangeness of her predicament. Suppose, she thought, the whole trip had been framed? Suppose all those on board the plane were kidnappers. Suppose that instead of landing in the morning at Newark she would be taken to some far-off and hidden place. The emotion which had made her shiver in the early morning of that day returned powerfully to her as she half reclined in the dark.

She forgot the detective, sitting behind Mr. Robinson. She thought only of the folly of exposing such a person as herself to the sort of thing from which she had been protected all her life. The ship bumped and dropped, lurched and swayed. The interior of its cabin became a throbbing, shadowed, sinister place, and the strange men in it potential enemies.

She dozed uneasily and had a nightmare. She woke, startled. The ship was swaying oddly.

She saw the silhouette of Mr. Robinson sit up.

The door to the cockpit opened. The stewardess in her chair turned on the cabin lights. Evelyn could imagine the effect from the ground-- a huge and droning bird suddenly becoming illuminated like a ship at sea or a deep-water fish.

The co-pilot walked into the cabin and looked up and down the rows of seats. Then he moved to the rear door, beyond which was the wash-room and the entrance vestibule. He was gone only for a moment. The Jap, Evelyn noticed, was watching him. So was Mr. Robinson.

When he returned, his face was white. He hurried to the stewardess, bent over her, and then fairly leaped into the cockpit. The stewardess rose, startled. She spoke to Mr. Baker first, then to the Jap, then to Mr. Robinson and Evelyn.

"Somebody," she said, "jacked open the door against the slip stream and Mr. Winter jumped overboard-- or fell-- or was thrown."

Mr. Winter, Evelyn's curdled mind reflected, was the broad-shouldered young man who had almost missed the plane at Los Angeles.

It had happened-- the thing which had caused that early-morning incubus, that feeling of threat and dread.

Fearfully, she looked at Mr. Robinson.

He was sitting in his chair with a knitted brow, looking at no one, but thinking hard. As soon as he was conscious of her eyes upon him, he turned toward her.

"That's bad," he said.

Evelyn did not know what reply to make.

"Bad," he repeated. "We'll probably be held up for an investigation."

The door to the cockpit remained open. Inside, one of the flyers was talking rapidly into a radio telephone.

After a few minutes the co-pilot appeared and made an announcement to those passengers who were awake. He shouted it:

"Mr. Winter apparently jumped overboard after jacking open the door. The jack he used is still in place, braced against the ship's frame. It will be left, although the door is now closed. This is a matter for federal investigation. We will proceed to Newark. There is no evidence of foul play. However, no one will be allowed to leave the ship when we come down for fuel in Cleveland. Please keep your places."

In the forward part of the plane a babble of conversation arose at once. Mr. Robinson, having apparently completed whatever mental considerations were necessary to him, gave his full attention to Evelyn.

"It's unfortunate, and I'm terribly sorry," he said. "Most of all because I'm afraid you'll have to give your right name when we reach Newark."

"Why do you think he did it?" Evelyn asked.

"I presume," said Mr. Robinson, "he was one of those people who pick insane ways of committing suicide."

"Suppose he didn't commit suicide." She said it so flatly that he was startled.

"What?"

"He didn't seem crazy."

"Some maniacs," said the dark-eyed man, "are deceptive."

"Did you see him go to the rear compartment?"

He shook his head. "Several people went, at different times."

"Were any two out there at once?"

"There's hardly room."

"But there is enough room."

He leaned forward and touched her arm.   "Please don't get yourself abnormally excited," he said.   "I can't possibly tell you how sorry I am.   If we're investigated, I earnestly urge you to tell the exact truth at once.   I'd give my right arm to have had you have your fun without anything like this.   It embarrasses me, too, in a way. Honestly"-- his tone became less impersonal and more kindly-- "I think you ought to try not to think about it and to sleep, if you can."

She said nothing.

Through the excitement of the discovery, Lieutenant O'Brien, at the rear end of the plane and nearest to the door through which Mr. Winter had vanished, remained sound asleep. He did not stir. His hat was halfway over his face.

Evelyn thought of waking him. She was on the verge of crossing the aisle to do it when the plane dived rapidly downward and walking became momentarily impossible. She wanted to suggest the idea to Mr. Robinson, but he had been so preoccupied with his own unimaginable difficulties that she did not.   Instead, she automatically strapped around herself the belt fixed on her seat. The plane swept over a cluster of buildings and dropped bumpily onto the rectangle of lights that marked the field.

The co-pilot went to the door in the rear vestibule and officially stood guard.   Outside in the night there were shouted communications. The motors bumbled softly. Confinement under such conditions was almost unbearable. To know so little and be unable to talk about it filled Evelyn with alarm.

A few moments after it had landed, the plane took off and turned toward its last destination, Newark.

Mr. Macavendish and Mr. Evans and Mr. Baker were talking in the forward part of the cabin. She could catch a note of indignant protest in the haughty voice of the Scotchman. The co-pilot took one of the empty seats in the plane. The detective still slept.   Mr. Robinson seemed not to want to talk and his last words had not mollified her. The Jap sat silently.

Evelyn Vale, in spite of her millions, had been brought up normally.   She had been taught to be resourceful and cool.   Now, however, she was uncertain of herself. When the newspapers found out that she had been running away under an assumed name on an airplane upon which a man had committed suicide, there would be a frenzied uproar. She could envisage the angry telegrams her brother would send, but that prospect did not terrify her so much as the immediate present.

The plane had flown for perhaps ten minutes after leaving Cleveland when the co-pilot made another announcement:

"I have a radio message that the investigation at Newark will be conducted as quickly as possible. I suggest that you all make every effort to be comfortable and if possible to sleep."

Soon after that he turned out the lights.

Before darkness again enveloped them, Evelyn once more considered waking the detective. She looked back at him. He was apparently deeply asleep.

In the ensuing gloom, she sat and thought.

The moon was on Mr. Robinson's side and she could see his sharp profile against its light whenever the wing lifted. Handfuls of stars showed through. The plane climbed steadily. It was bucking a powerful head wind, but Evelyn did not know that. She slipped back into her irrational nightmare about kidnapping and imagined that she was being carried away by six men and a stewardess and two pilots, to be held for a high ransom from her enormous fortune.

Once she leaned over hopefully in an effort to attract the attention of Mr. Robinson. But he appeared to be sound asleep. Everyone on the plane had been up since daylight, and a new dawn was only two hours away, so that even in the face of tragedy sleep overtook most of them, a fitful, jostled sleep.

It claimed Evelyn, at last. She half felt three or four men brush past her as they walked the length of the cabin and returned to their night-shrouded chairs, but she did not rouse.

The ship flew south and east.

An hour passed.

Evelyn jumped into consciousness.

Nothing had changed. Yet she felt there was a difference. She thought that probably a lost and dreadful nightmare had awakened her. But she rejected that thought. For one horrible instant she believed that she saw someone crawling down the aisle of the plane between the parallel rows of seats. But it was only a shapeless shadow which slid into the ship through its small windows from the eerie moonlight outside.

She sat up stiffly.

The plane was pitching and tossing. Her belt was still around her, snapped shut. Ahead in the cabin, a single dim light burned, and by leaning out she could see that Mr. Evans, the plump man, was using it for a reading lamp. He had a magazine in his hands and his head bent over it. The idea that anyone in that silent space was reading reassured Evelyn.

"Awake?" a voice asked.

"Yes."

Mr. Robinson leaned toward her. "Look, Evelyn," he said earnestly. "I was rude to you a while ago. I regret it. I was worried by my own responsibilities."

She felt warmed and grateful. "It's quite all right."

He continued in a low voice that disturbed no one: "I'm ashamed of myself. I've been thinking about you nearly all night. You're a fine girl. I'm sorry I have to appear in so bad a light at the moment. If I clear it up satisfactorily-- may I presume--?"

"Why-- certainly," she said.

"You'd really better try to sleep."

"I shall. I'm glad you said that."

She settled back on her pillow. But she could not sleep. As soon as her mind strayed from the fact that Mr. Evans was reading or from Mr. Robinson's kindness-- she though of it as kindness-- she began to fidget and prickle.

She looked at the men forward.

She looked at Mr. Robinson. His head nodded.

Then she looked at the detective. He still slept, a poor example of the vigilance of the law. He had apparently not wakened at Cleveland, and Mr. Robinson might easily have escaped from him if it had not been for the accident of their imprisonment in the ship, an accident about which the Los Angeles plain-clothes man knew nothing.

As she looked at him, she realized that he had not moved at all for a long time.

A very long time.

She bit her lip in the dark and twisted so that she would have a better view of him.

Then a strange thing happened. A frightful thing.

The plane lifted. Moonlight streamed in upon the detective. For a fraction of a second Evelyn saw him clearly. He was sprawled back on his seat. His hat was over his face. Protruding from the center of his chest was the hilt of a knife, and running down from that knife over his waistcoat was a darker course which was not fabric.

The sight was obliterated.

The plane heeled in the opposite direction.

Evelyn opened her mouth to scream. But no sound came from her parted lips.

The realization that she could not scream still further appalled her. She sat for three or four seconds in locked paralysis.

"I won't scream," she said finally to herself. "I won't."

Shakily she leaned toward the man at her side. "Mr. Robinson," she said in a high-pitched voice.

He sat up instantly. "Yes."

"Please." She gulped. "Listen. That man behind you has been stabbed. There's a knife in his chest."

"What?" Robinson spun around in his seat. He stared through the gloom at the figure beside him. "Can't see."

Evelyn watched and shook.

"Stewardess!" Robinson called. "Let's have the lights."

His hand was fumbling for the dim individual bulb in the seat behind. He found it as the stewardess switched on the cabin lights.

What Evelyn had seen was fact.

The detective lay dead, a knife through his heart. Blood covered his waistcoat.

The men forward were looking back.

Robinson swore softly.

The stewardess blanched. Then she ran jerkily toward the cockpit doors. Evelyn started to fall forward in her safety belt. Robinson caught her.

Mr. Baker stepped toward them. "What's happened?"

"See for yourself," said Robinson briefly.

Mr. Baker looked, and then went back sickened to his own seat. He sat down and wiped his face over and over with his handkerchief.

"What is it?" the fat insurance salesman asked noisily.

Mr. Baker did not reply.

Robinson lifted Evelyn back on her seat and commenced to rub her hands. The co-pilot leaped down from the cockpit and banged into him as he passed.

Mr. Macavendish woke. "Coming down?" he asked. Then he saw the commotion in the rear of the plane.

Evelyn murmured, "I'll be all right."

"Swell!" said Robinson. He turned to the stewardess, who was pallidly waiting orders from the co-pilot. "Get water. And get coffee ready. Nobody's going to try to sleep any more tonight."

The co-pilot turned to Robinson. "Keep everybody away from the seat for a minute, will you?"

"I will."

The stewardess came with water. Then she put a blanket over the body of the detective.

Evelyn drank. She was trembling.

Mr. Macavendish walked down the aisle. "Look here," he said to Robinson; "I'm the president of the Midcoast Trust. This is my card. We're in something a lot more serious than a suicide now."

Robinson nodded. Evelyn looked at him hopefully. "Yes."

"What's your name?"

"Robinson."

"What's your line?"

"None in particular."

Mr. Macavendish was joined by the other men. The Jap was on the fringe of the group. The Scotch banker did not appear to like Mr. Robinson's blank answers, but he continued: "Mr. Evans here is an insurance underwriter. Mr. Baker is a retired dress manufacturer. You and Miss Jones haven't been very sociable on this trip, but we can understand that. We might as well all be friends, since we'll surely be hung up together for a while now." He partly overcame an undoubted racial prejudice. "This is Mr. Suka-something or other. Father's some sort of a banker in Tokyo." He smiled tightly.

"He's excited," Evelyn thought. "And he wants to manage things."

Robinson shook hands with the men as they were introduced. He glanced back at the shrouded body.

"The fellow that jumped," said Macavendish positively, "killed him and then himself. Or, maybe-- say-- that bird had a suitcase, didn't he?"

"Yes, he did," said Baker.

"Maybe there was a parachute in!"

"Good heavens!" Baker exclaimed.

The co-pilot reappeared from the cockpit. "Sit down, everybody," he said.

The revolver at his hip was unstrapped.

The banker looked at the flyer for a moment and then shrugged his shoulders. Everyone went to his own seat.

The stewardess brought coffee first to Evelyn.

It seemed to her that the speed of the motors was being increased. She drank the coffee.

Robinson took his cup.

Evelyn smiled wanly at him. He smiled in return.

"Now," she said, "I am in trouble. My brother will raise the roof! He'll say that it all serves me right--"

"Don't worry," said Robinson; "you'll pull through."

"You were nice when I-- fainted."

"Nothing else to do. Lady faints. Water."

"I wish we could-- move him somewhere."

He threw a glance over his shoulder. "Not pleasant," he agreed.

She looked at him for a long time, then. Her eyes slowly widened and afterward narrowed. She did not seem in that instant like a pampered daughter of the rich but like an exceedingly shrewd and calculating woman. Finally she averted her face.

"Why the scrutiny?"

"No reason."

"Why?"

"You're something of a mystery yourself," she said. "I'll be eager to hear how you answer the questions of the police, since you won't tell me anything about yourself."

"I told you lots. Chapters of my life."

"Not the right ones. Maybe, too, maybe they'll open that bag."

She was astonished at the suddenness and force with which his lips locked. He laughed. "I'm afraid not. I'm afraid you'll have to go on being curious."

The cockpit door opened again. The co-pilot entered and walked back. "We've radioed the exact position where Mr. Winter jumped; we have it fairly accurately because opening the door was detectable. Searching parties are going out. Winter is being looked up."

Robinson addressed the co-pilot: "Did you consider the possibility of his using a 'chute?"

"No."

"You'd better. He had a suitcase that wasn't in the baggage section."

The man in uniform went to the radiophones with that information after saying, "He probably carried the jack in that. Slick, if he had a 'chute, too."

A few moments later he stepped into the cabin, his face aghast.

Mr. Macavendish stopped him. "What is it?"

Robinson rose from his seat and went forward to hear the words of the pilot.

He stood there, fingering his gun. "You're probably mistaken about thinking Winter killed O'Brien," he said. "They got all the dope on him. A Los Angeles fellow. Been trying to get into pictures for a year and a half. Couldn't. Had girl trouble, too. Yesterday she got married. He's been threatening to kill himself for weeks. He used to be a stunt flyer and that probably gave him the idea of taking this way out. But he hasn't any kind of police record. The captain in L.A. told us to look for somebody else. Of course, it's possible, but--"

"If Winter didn't kill O'Brien," said Baker, looking slowly from one face to another, "then somebody here did."

The co-pilot nodded slowly.

Macavendish, Evans, and the Jap sat down. Mr. Baker walked to the rear of the plane, entered the vestibule, and stared at the jack with which the outer door had been pushed open against the force of the air rushing along the plane's side. No man would have been strong enough to open the door with his unassisted muscles.

Then Baker returned, studiously keeping his eyes from the figure covered by the blanket.

Robinson resumed his place. The co-pilot took one of the empty rear seats.

"What did they say?" Evelyn asked.

Robinson told her.

"In other words, the man who jumped didn't do the murder?"

"That's a possibility."

Evelyn felt again an intense doubt of the man at her side. The lights seemed to grow dim and bright. The shock of the glimpse of Lieutenant O'Brien with a knife in his heart made her disbelieve the record of her senses. She reflected against her will that anyone who stabbed the detective would have been compelled to do so hastily while walking past him, except Mr. Robinson, who could easily have turned on the sleeping man and measured his thrust carefully.

Mr. Robinson could have done it, and Mr. Robinson had a motive. The detective had been following him. Shadowing him. And if he were engaged in a desperate effort to make a get-away with the contents of the brief-case--

From that thought she turned to speculation on her own predicament. As good a case could be made against herself. She could imagine the words of a police officer at Newark after she had finished her story: "Evelyn Vale, you say you are, eh? And your hand bag chock-full of five-hundred-dollar bills. Suppose I choose to assume that you aren't Evelyn Vale, but her maid, say, and that you robbed her and ran off with the money. Then suppose I choose to think you realized Lieutenant O'Brien was on your trail, so you got scared and ran a knife through him--"

It would not be pleasant, the telling of her story. Of course, in a very short time she would be able to establish her identity.

There were many things to think about. With astonishment at her own rapidly returning self-possession, she began to consider them. Presently she beckoned to the co-pilot. He rose and bent over her.

"I don't suppose," she said, "that there would be anyone on the plane who could determine just when that detective was stabbed. When he died, I mean?"

He shook his head. "No doctor on board, and I couldn't tell."

"Did you know the detective?"

The co-pilot nodded. "Sure. Name was Lieutenant William O'Brien. Los Angeles. He was flying somewhere tonight on a big job. Shadowing somebody, I think."

Evelyn once again looked closely at Robinson, who was listening.

"Did you look at the body?" she asked with a calmness that startled Robinson and shocked herself.

"Certainly," said the flyer.

"Did he die instantly?"

"He must have died at once."

"What sort of knife killed him?"

Robinson looked at the girl in admiration.

The co-pilot was startled. "I didn't notice."

"Why don't you look?"

The man hesitated. Finally, without speaking, he walked to the form under the blanket, lifted an edge, and stared.

"Well?" Evelyn asked.

"It is a long, thin-bladed carving knife, or maybe a bread knife."

Evelyn thought. "Could it have been stolen in an airport restaurant? Why not find out? A meat knife, or one they use to cut up sandwiches. People don't carry carving knives around."

The co-pilot stared at her and started toward the entrance of the control cabin. All of the four men who sat forward in the ship waylaid him with questions, but he turned his back on them and shut the door.

Robinson spoke to Evelyn. "Why did you want to know those things?"

"I can't say. It seems that if someone has been killed, someone else ought to make sure what did it."

Robinson grinned faintly. "It does seem so."

"I mean, if someone here on this plane-- one of you five men, in fact-- killed that detective-- well--"

"One of us," Robinson repeated.

"Certainly. The stewardess wasn't back here. You could have turned around and done it. Several men passed me in the last hour from up front. I don't know which ones. You were asleep. It was so dark you couldn't see your hand in front of your face."

Robinson nodded. "That's true. Of course, you're counting yourself out."

"I'm counting myself out," she said almost complacently, "because I, at least, know that I didn't do it."

"Do you believe I did?"

"Did you?" asked the girl. "I won't tell."

"No. I didn't."

"Good."

He smiled at her. "Don't you think you're being a little hysterical trying to be so calm?"

"Don't you think," she responded, "that you're pushing yourself a trifle to sit quietly when there's a murdered man about eighteen inches behind your back?"

"Possibly. But what is the proper behavior for such a circumstance. I've never been in it before. Except--"

"Except what?" she asked.

His face had clouded. "Let it pass. I was thinking of a war-- not a murder."

"Oh."

The co-pilot reappeared. He stood at the forward end of the cabin and shouted. "I will have to put you all under a sort of arrest," he said.

Macavendish jumped to his feet. "This is an outrage!"

Mr. Baker, the retired dress manufacturer, said in as loud a voice as he could muster, "This will be bad for your airline."

The flyer did not reply directly. "I'll have to search you for weapons."

With the stewardess he started down the aisle. The men permitted themselves to be searched. Macavendish was furious. Mr. Baker was coldly resentful. Mr. Evans, the insurance man, was seemingly amused. The Jap was flustered. His face reddened as the co-pilot went through his pockets.

Evelyn came next. Nothing of interest or value in the matter of the murder could be discovered.

Robinson was last to be searched. The co-pilot took out his wallet and did not open it. He felt his other pockets. Then he noticed the brief-case. "What's in that?"

"Private papers."

"Open it."

"I'm sorry. I haven't the key."

"Where is it?"

"I've lost it. I'll have to have it opened by a locksmith."

The co-pilot squeezed the brief-case. "No gun in it, at any rate."

Robinson smiled urbanely. "No. No gun."

The co-pilot faced all the passengers. "I'll sit in the last seat. I regret the necessity-- but there may be a murderer among you."

Robinson reseated himself. He turned to the co-pilot: "Can, or rather, may we talk?"

"Why not?"

"I'll talk to you, then," Robinson said to Evelyn.

"Good. I was starting to weaken again."

"You mustn't."

"How can I help it! Think of the papers when they find out what I've done."

"It's a rotten break."

"Do you know that you're the first man I've ever spoken to in my life to whom I hadn't been properly introduced?"

"Good Lord!" Robinson exclaimed. He looked forward in the cabin. The men there were in a huddle. One or two of them glanced back at him with suspicious expressions. He nodded toward them and said to Evelyn, "They're telling each other that I killed Mr. O'Brien, because I was nearest."

While he said that, Mr. Macavendish was rising to his feet. He started to walk down the aisle, but a sudden lurch of the plane, which was flying now at top speed, threw him off balance. That ruffled his overweening dignity, and when he reached Robinson's seat he was in a white heat. He waved his long right arm at the co-pilot.

"There's no need of carrying this dramatic charade any farther," he said. "Here's your man."

The co-pilot stood up. "What do you base that on?"

"Lieutenant O'Brien was following this man. Shadowing him. Mr. Evans noticed it from the walk outside the station in Los Angeles; Lieutenant O'Brien was waiting at the airport when Mr. Evans arrived. The lieutenant did not buy a ticket until this gentleman appeared. He took a seat directly behind him. He followed him into the station in Nevada. He ate lunch in plain sight of Mr. Robinson. At three other stops, we're all agreed, he made sure that Mr. Robinson did not get out of his sight. The whole thing's obvious. Mr. Robinson knew he was being followed-- so he killed the man who was on his trail."

The co-pilot nodded. "O'Brien said he was dogging somebody on the ship. Los Angeles has not yet told us who it is. In any event, you'll have to save your charges for the federal men when we reach Newark."

Macavendish was not mollified. He wheeled ferociously on Robinson. "What have you to say?"

Evelyn, who had been listening with bated breath to the conversation, dug her nails in her palms.

Robinson stared coldly at the banker. "Nothing."

Macavendish addressed the co-pilot: "How soon will we be in?"

The flyer consulted a wrist watch. "In about an hour."

Macavendish's belligerent red head swung as he stalked back to his seat. The co-pilot bent over Robinson. "How about it?"

"That gent will raise the devil with the airline," Robinson said. "What about it? I'll make my statement in Newark."

The co-pilot nodded uneasily. "They asked me to find out all I could. This is going to be pretty sensational. The first murder on one of the commercial planes. Or any plane-- as far as I know."

"I can't help you I'm afraid," Robinson answered. "People who take planes do so because their business is urgent. Urgent business is often confidential. Mine is."

"You didn't notice who passed you during that hour following our departure from Cleveland?"

"I paid no attention. Several men. But nobody spoke to Lieutenant O'Brien. I'd have heard that."

The stewardess came wanly and tremulously from her tiny buffet with sandwiches. The fat insurance man took two and stuffed one in his mouth. Mr. Baker thanked her politely and began to nibble one. The banker merely snorted at her. Evelyn and Robinson refused.

Presently the stewardess spoke to the co-pilot, and he left his post at the rear of the plane.

Evelyn looked through the windows and was surprised to see that a feeble light was spreading over the slate-gray metallic wings of the ship. It passed through her mind that she was more concerned with the possible fate of Mr. Robinson than she was with her own. The admission that she was not Miss Dorothy Jones would doubtless cause trouble. But she had had too much experience with the magic of the name of Vale to think that she would suffer any real tribulation. No one would imagine for an instant that Evelyn Vale, the "millionaire princess" of America, would murder a police officer who chanced to be on the same plane.

"I'm glad," said Mr. Robinson's familiar and friendly voice close to her ear, "that the noble and confused pilot has left us."

When she turned she saw that his face already visible in the dun light of morning. And once again she noticed that it was an intelligent face, a face with strength and imagination and humor.

"So am I," she said. "It was like being chaperoned. Though I'm used to that." She hesitated. "You didn't know you were being followed by a detective?"

"I did not. I realize it now."

"Why?"

"A fair question." He chuckled.

"You don't seem to be very much worried by it."

"And you aren't worried either. What will you do when you have to explain that you are traveling under a false name and that you boarded the plane in disguise?"

"Tell them my right name."

He nodded. "It must be stimulating to have such influence."

"It's a nuisance."

"I suppose." He paused and continued carelessly, "I wonder what they'll think when I tell them my name isn't Robinson."

Evelyn was startled. "Isn't it?"

"No. It's the name you happened to adopt this morning."

"Jones?"

"Jones."

She sat for a moment in stunned stillness. For almost three

thousand miles and almost twenty-four hours she had been continually building up her confidence in the dark stranger, only to have it dashed. And yet she felt that she could have confidence in him. His own self-possession was like a guarantee of that. She rallied herself.

"Are you going to shoot your way out?"

"I didn't do it. I told you that. The poor gentleman behind me who lost his life in the line of duty did so through no fault of mine. Don't you believe me?"

"I'm afraid I do."

"Splendid. I believe you, too."

"What do you mean?"

"I mean, I believe you're Evelyn Vale."

"I'd forgotten." She laughed a little.

She stared through the window. Clouds around them were being delicately tinted with orange. It astounded her to observe that even when you were among the clouds, flying straight through them, the colors of sunrise did not recede and melt. The plane forged into a veritable mountain of color and the mist outside was like gilded gauze. . . . So he believed her. And she had forgotten-- forgotten that he had to take her statement on faith. She was ashamed of doubting his scant but definite pronouncements about himself.

"I feel extraordinarily flattered," she finally said, "that you believe me. And I can't imagine why-- because I really ought not to care whether you do or not."

"Good," he answered. "You feel that way because you like me. I like you-- tremendously. This is not the place"-- he grimaced-- "and these are not the circumstances-- for saying such a thing. But the time is getting short. It's odd, because I'd never thought of girls like yourself-- I mean inordinately rich girls-- as human beings at all. I've never met one before. You have nobody knows how many million dollars. But you also have very fine direct blue eyes and an elegant profile, and you are girl through and through. You don't mind my being grossly and inopportunely naive?"

"I guess I don't."

"Very well. What I'm getting at is this: My name is John Robinson Jones. I'm a scientist. A nuclear physicist. I do experimental work at California College of Science. Your millions, as you may or may not know, have, by coincidence, made that school's high-tension laboratories possible."

"I do know," she said. "I'm interested in science."

"Good. Now, I've been working on the structure of metals. The atomic structure."

"That's it!" She looked at him excitedly. "I've seen your name. Doctor J.R. Jones. I read everything. I said that-- didn't I? You're the man who said that alchemy would soon be possible. Changing lead into gold--"

He smiled. "Not lead into gold, but-- say, beryllium into some other metal. I'm that bird. Well, by chance at the college, some other chaps and I ran across a system of increasing the hardness of metals. Not a little-- a lot. We could make metals perhaps a hundred times as tough as they are now. The system seemed very important. It'll change all kinds of steel construction, and battleships, and guns-- everything. When we were sure of it, we decided-- that is, R.M. Grayson, the president of the college, decided-- that the thing ought to be put directly into the hands of the government."

"That's why you started to say you were going to Washington and changed it to New York!"

He grinned. "You don't miss much. That's why. But what we accomplished leaked out. We had to be careful. A good many governments wouldn't mind knowing about our process. Doctor Grayson decided to send me with the equations and formulae. He steamed me up so with the idea of caution that I was fool enough to think the fact I was going East might be noticed. So I gave just part of my name. It wasn't much of an idea."

"Wouldn't you be recognized from that part of your name?"

"Not many people know my middle name. John R. Jones is what I use. I told Doctor Grayson I'd taken an assumed name, over the phone the night before I left. Now what I think is this: He must have sent along Lieutenant O'Brien as an afterthought, a bodyguard."

Evelyn sat back in her seat and sighed with relief. They were flying now in the full light of day through a ceaseless glory of the colors of dawn. It was all right. He was all right. She was exultant, then, that she had escaped from the vigilance of her brother and his plain-clothes men. The hideous night was ended.

She smiled at him. "Thank you for telling me."

"I've wanted to all night. I should have. I guess the strain of work and the trouble of the last few days has shattered my usual academic calm. You see-- the safe at the college was rifled one night. And on another the laboratory was broken into. Night before last my associate, Doctor Weston, was held up. I began to think my mission was really fairly hazardous and," he added lightly, "enormous fun."

His brief gayety vanished. "Evelyn-- we're not going to have much difficulty getting out of this."

"No."

"But that poor devil has been killed."

"Yes. I was thinking--"

"That if it wasn't done by the man who jumped, but by some one of us, we should try to help?" he said.

"Yes."

"And how?"

"By trying to think why anybody here would do it."

"We can't do that," he answered, "because we don't know anything about the people here."

The girl smiled. "No. But why would anyone kill a detective? I can think of only two reasons: For revenge for something the

detective had done; or because the detective appeared to be following someone who didn't want to be followed."

Robinson-- John Robinson Jones, if his story was correct--
looked appreciatively at Evelyn Vale-- Evelyn Vale, if she had told
the truth about herself. He was sure she had. "Of course," he said.

Then the co-pilot emerged from a trip to the control cabin.
"They have found the body of Mr. Winter," he half-shouted, so that all
could hear. "In a field. On the body was a note. It apologized for
jumping from one of the company's planes and explained the act by
stating that it had been planned for a long time. More information on
Mr. Winter has come from Los Angeles. The police there feel that he
had nothing to do with the murder of Lieutenant O'Brien. That means
you are all unfortunately under a temporary but most serious
suspicion."

He walked past the renewed protests of the men in the forward
part of the ship to the place where the dark young man was sitting.
"I would like to ask you a few questions."

Evelyn strained to hear, although she pretended to pay no
attention.

"Sure," said the young man.

"We have a report that you boarded the ship under an assumed
name."

"Well?"

"And that O'Brien was following you."

"And what else have you in your report?"

"That's all," said the co-pilot. "It's a lot."

"It's not enough," the dark man replied.

"You still believe that Winter killed the man who was shadowing
you?"

"It seems the only possibility-- so far."

"What is your real name?"

"Why don't you get that from Los Angeles?"

The flyer looked at his watch, shrugged, and sat down two seats
behind Robinson.

Evelyn had overheard the conversation with some misgivings.
She spoke now: "Why didn't you tell the facts to him?"

"Because I didn't want them known," he answered

Then he looked away from her and out of the window.

The girl in the third from the last seat again felt the creeping
agitation she had known for eighteen hours. Was this man honest?
Or was he merely glib? And if he was lying to her-- why was he
lying? Was it not infinitely more probable that Winter had stabbed
the detective for some reason which would eventually become clear
to the whole world? Or could a man's appearance, his attractiveness,
make her lose her senses entirely?

She glanced back at the aviator. He was doing police duty now,
and the man he was guarding was the man who sat beside her. Out of
the corner of her eye she caught a glimpse of the blanket-wrapped

body. She shuddered. But in the same glimpse she had inadvertently noticed that the air-route map which had belonged to the detective lay on the floor under the corner of John Robinson Jones's chair. It was across the aisle from her seat, less than two feet from where her hand normally fell. She looked at it again. What she had thought she had seen at first she verified: There was writing on the map.

She grasped the little handle under her seat which let it back and cranked herself into a half-reclining posture. Then after a rapid glance at the men forward, the co-pilot, and Mr. Jones, she retrieved the map.

She did not know what she had expected to find written upon it, and what she did find disappointed her. No names. No notes. It was a map that unfolded like a time-table and revealed an illustrated United States with the route line across it and the stops marked in red.

The detective, evidently to help speed the monotony of the journey, had merely ringed each stop in pencil as it was made and set down the times of arrival and departure.

Then Evelyn drew her breath.

There was a ring around Cleveland. And scribbled beside the ring was, "Arr. 3:12. Lft. 3:16."

She knew then that, for a little while, the detective had been awake in Cleveland. He had probably roused when they landed and methodically set down the times. He had, after all, kept his watch over John Robinson Jones at each stop. At Cleveland the passengers had sat in semi-darkness for a few minutes while the plane was re-fueled. The detective had undoubtedly gone back to sleep as soon as they were in the air again.

His brief vigilance had gone unnoticed. Everyone was thinking about Winter.

But the map in Evelyn's hand made one fact positive. Winter had leaped between Chicago and Cleveland. O'Brien had been alive at Cleveland and awake for a few minutes.

Someone still on the ship had killed him.

She wanted to tell the man at her side. After all, his business was not hers. Perhaps, she thought, he had a motive, a good motive. And perhaps he did not do it.

But she decided not to tell. She put the map in her hand bag. Miserably she stared out of the window. Below were fast-moving marshes and blocks of streets crammed with houses, trucks, milk wagons. In the distance, rising magically, were the towers of Manhattan.

"Soon be down," John Robinson Jones said pleasantly.

"Yes." She stared at him. It could not be-- and yet--

The plane began to drop rapidly. Both Jones and Evelyn automatically fastened their safety belts. Houses and buildings hurtled up to meet their descent. They skimmed over a long stretch of marsh land and a vast dump. The cinder field at Newark fled beneath their wheels. They touched earth, bounced, touched again, and began to taxi toward the hangars.

A dozen policemen were waiting for them at the edge of the field. They ran forward.

"Fun!" said Jones sardonically.

When they stepped out of the plane they were stiff and cramped. The motion of the ship through the air remained in their brains and their limbs. The police immediately surrounded them, and they were led to a bare, cement-floored room, where they were told to wait.

There were long benches in the room. Evans, Macavendish, Baker, and the Jap sat down.

An airport official and a police officer entered.

"We regret this incident," said the field official, "exceedingly."

"Incident," Evelyn murmured to Jones.

"You will be detained her for preliminary questioning," the man continued.

Macavendish looked at his watch. "How long?"

"I cannot say. We will act as quickly as possible."

"I protest," the banker said loudly. "I shall have lawyers here in twenty minutes. I want to telephone."

"I'm sorry--"

The pilots came in and sat down. Then the stewardess. They had evidently made reports.

Evelyn walked to the co-pilot. "Did you start an investigation at the stops we made about who stole a big knife?"

"I radioed at once. There was a knife missing from the sandwich board at the lunch-room in Los Angeles. Probably the one that killed O'Brien."

She nodded. "That's what I thought."

Mr. Baker addressed the police officer: "Couldn't we be liberated on our own recognizance? Or on bail? Something?"

"I'm sorry. Captain Humberstone will be here within an hour."

"An hour!"

"I think so. This is a matter which comes under federal jurisdiction. Now."

He looked toward the entrance, where another man was being passed into the room by the guard. He raised his voice: "If all of you will be good enough to make your statements in turn to the stenographer-- I'll take you one at a time in the room to the left. Miss Jones first, if you please. I want each person to give me full information concerning himself."

John Robinson Jones waited anxiously while the girl was in the room with the police officer. As he waited he saw the flash made by the photographers' lamps inside the plane which had brought them to Newark. Then, some time later, he saw the body of the murdered detective carried from the fuselage of the ship. They were questioning the girl at length, evidently.

In the anteroom, Evelyn's story had caused immense consternation. But the police officer had been partially convinced by her frankness. Investigation by telephone quickly made that conviction complete. After twenty minutes of discussion with authorities on the west coast, with Evelyn's brother, and with lawyers in New York, he said, "I'm sorry that even for a moment I doubted you, Miss Vale. You shouldn't do such a thing, however. It's dangerous. And I'm very grateful for the map."

She nodded. "As soon as you can demonstrate that the time schedule was in the detective's handwriting, you can be sure that one of the men in the room outside was his murderer."

He nodded. "You should be in my business." Then he smiled. "Of course, you're free to go now."

Evelyn had not paid much attention to his last remark. "One of the men in the room outside," she repeated. "I wonder if I may make a long-distance call now-- before I leave."

The officer passed across the desk the telephone he had been using.

Evelyn asked for Doctor Grayson, president of the California College of Science, at his home in Pasadena. She waited for two or three minutes. Then she heard a telephone ringing. A sleepy and haughty voice said, "Hello! Newark? What is it."

"This," she said, "is Evelyn Vale. I want to ask you a question."

"Evelyn Vale? Vale!" There was a pause. Then the voice of the learned man said, "What did you wish to ask?"

"I want a description of Doctor John Robinson Jones."

The next pause was longer. Evidently the scientist, awakened from his sleep by a long-distance call, was not at the peak of his mental powers. Finally he said, "Doctor Jones is short and bald and blue-eyed. He-- he stutters, and he has a scar on his chin." The phone was hung up.

Evelyn's face was pale. She turned to the police officer. "I'd like to stay in the room outside for a moment," she said. "You may want to ask me some more questions. I may think of something that will be useful."

"Why-- certainly." He ushered her to the door and beckoned to Macavendish.

The man who called himself Jones hurried toward her. "Are you all right?"

"Quite," she said.

"You identified yourself?"

"I did."

"I'm glad. Extraordinarily glad."

She motioned toward an empty bench. "Let's sit down a minute. I want to talk to you."

Her manner evidently puzzled him.

"I called Doctor Grayson at California College," she said slowly. "I think you'd better give yourself up."

He looked at her in frank amazement. "Evelyn, you've gone

squiffy."

Her dark-blue eyes blazed into his brown, perplexed ones. "He told me that Doctor Jones was bald and short and had a scar on his chin."

Complete amazement spread over his features. And suddenly he began to roar with laughter.

"Golly!" he said at last.

"You think it's funny?"

"I do. Don't you see what happened? Grayson's been making a melodrama of my trip. Sent a detective to look after my health. Suddenly a voice calling itself Miss Vale waked him from Newark. Grayson's not a worldly man. He thinks the whole nation is full of spies and foreign agents attempting to get this." He tapped the brief-case. "He thought you were one-- trying to identify me in order to rob or murder me. So he did what he thought was a bit of master-minding. He gave a wrong description. A diametrically opposite one. Don't you see that?"

Evelyn looked away. She sighed and slowly shook her head. "Either you're right-- or you're the most magnificent and efficient and rapid liar alive."

He put his hand on her shoulder and turned her toward himself.

"Listen," he said, looking directly at her, "I don't care what anyone thinks but you. And you've got to make up your mind what you think. I couldn't stand to have you doubt me any longer. Do you believe me, Evelyn-- or don't you?"

A long moment passed. The girl shivered slightly under the intensity of his gaze. " I guess-- I do," she said.

"That's all I wanted to know."

Tears filled her eyes. She might have wept, but at that moment the Jap approached the place where they were sitting.

"Pardon me," he said.

"What?" John Robinson Jones was curt.

"Before I speak to police questioning, may I speak to you?"

"Of course."

"I am the brother of Salaki Minu Sakuliiti."

"Good heavens!"

"He is, I believe, an associate of yours in the college."

"He certainly is! Salaki and I have worked out a good many problems together. But--"

"I would like to explain to you. The secret you carry is precious. Many persons-- perhaps even some countrymen of mine-- would go far to obtain it. Salaki knew this. Day before yesterday he telephoned to ask me to quietly accompany and escort you to Washington, taking personal care no harm came to your highly estimated person. I have done so until now, when I feel I must speak of it. I had the revolver hidden in my blanket when we were searched. In my embarrassment I later threw it overboard from the washroom. I trust it fell upon nobody. I am at your service for my brother."

Jones nodded.   A grin twitched at the corners of his mouth. He looked at Evelyn, who was staring, wide-eyed.

"I am grateful," he said, "very grateful. And I would like to ask how you knew that I was Mr. John Robinson Jones, and not someone else--"

The Jap reached into his pocket, took out his wallet, opened it, and handed to Jones a picture of himself clipped from a scientific review.   Under the picture was the caption, "John R. Jones, noted nuclear physicist."

Without any comment, Jones passed the picture to Evelyn.

Then she did burst into tears. But, as she wept, she laughed. She laughed and cried, until Jones said in a strong, quiet tone, "You had better stop, Evelyn."

She stopped then and looked up. "We've got to do something right away-- John. At once. We've got to find out who-- why-- oh-- for a long time I've been on the point of remembering something-- some little thing-- that would point to the right person. Every time I think of the knife and where it came from-- I feel on the verge of knowing--"

Jones nodded grimly. "I'd like to pick the man who did it. The police probably will, but by that time everyone may have been released. That detective was doing me a favor--"

"Wait!" she said suddenly. "I think--"

"You think what?"

"Look. Would you mind if I did something alone-- when the examination is over? Or rather-- with that police officer. He's intelligent. And I have an idea. You didn't kill O'Brien. This Japanese gentleman didn't. I didn't. That leaves Macavendish, Baker, and Evans."

Half an hour passed. Captain Humberstone had not yet arrived. All the statements had been dictated. The officer temporarily in charge came from the anteroom.

Evelyn Vale walked up to him. "Have you checked everyone?"

"Not completely. Of course, we went to work while you were flying in. Macavendish is positive. Mr. Baker was a dress manufacturer, all right. Bachelor. Mr. Evans seems to be O.K. We routed out his boss, and the description tallies."

"I see. Look--" She commenced to talk to the officer.

Presently, side by side, they began to walk around the waiting-room.

They passed Macavendish. "I saw it with my own eyes," the banker heard her say. "He picked it up when he was buying papers."

Macavendish snorted and stomped away.

In front of Mr. Evans, she repeated the phrase. He merely peered confusedly at them and looked back toward the flying field.

Their aimless stroll took them past Mr. Baker. He glanced as they drew near, and went on reading his paper.

"I saw it," Evelyn said in pretended confidence to the officer. "He hurried out of the ship at Los Angeles the minute he saw Lieutenant O'Brien come aboard. I watched him through the windows." Out of the corner of her eye she thought that she saw Mr. Baker move. "He went in to buy papers and magazines. He peered around, and then picked up something from the lunch counter and put it in the papers. It glittered--"

She got no farther.

Mr. Baker was on his feet.

In a holster, on his hip, the police officer had worn a revolver. It had been very near to the face of the man reading the paper.

Now it was in Baker's hand.

Everyone was suddenly standing and staring.

John rushed forward.

"Back. Step back," said Baker. His eyes were like sparks.

He glanced toward the door. A single policeman was standing with his back turned.

"You won't ever repeat that," Baker half whispered to the girl.

Jones leaped in front of her.

Baker had pointed the gun, and now he fired.

The first chamber missed.

So did the second.

Baker stared at the weapon.

His face went white.

"Swell!" said the police officer. He started toward the man in the gray suit. Baker lashed out with the revolver butt. It hit the policeman beside the ear. Jones jumped forward and swung his long arm. Baker fell on the floor. The police officer was on his knees, shaking his head. . . .

"Oatmeal and cream," Evelyn said, "and griddle cakes, and coffee. I love these chain restaurants."

John Robinson Jones, still clutching his brief-case, smiled in a manner that was warm and more than friendly.

"Gee!" said America's multimillionaire princess. "I was excited."

"Why didn't you tell them sooner what you'd seen?"

"I didn't see it. But I just remembered that when O'Brien entered the plane, Baker had made a quick trip to the station and came back with a lot of stuff. Besides, for one horrible second"-- she looked at him earnestly-- "I was afraid, after Doctor Grayson had refused to identify you, that all you had said was-- Do you mind?"

"Not a bit. I could only really believe your story when I looked at you."

"That's how I felt."

"Let's look at each other."

They did. "When are you going to Washington?" she asked.

"At noon."

"And when will you return?"

He grinned. "I might be able to make it at ten tonight."

"You'll be very tired."

"Not now. I wonder why that bird Baker stabbed--?"

"Extra!" a voice on the street yelled. "Sensational air murder! Read all about it!"

John Jones ran for a paper.

He began to read:

"MILLIONAIRE VALE DAUGHTER SOLVES SENSATIONAL AIR MURDER

"'Evelyn Vale'-- That's you," he said-- "'solved early this morning the murder of Lieutenant William O'Brien, which took place on the transcontinental air-liner on which she was a passenger last night, and the murderer, Orville Baker, alias Samuel Ponti, is behind bars, although he almost succeeded in making a getaway from California where, it is alleged, he killed Judge Rollin Klein in revenge for a sentence imposed upon him in 1931 for embezzlement. The murder of the noted jurist was discovered late last night. Miss Vale was traveling incognito'-- They're letting you off easy," John grinned-- "'and was assisted by the celebrated scientist--'"

"You," said Evelyn.

"'--John Robinson Jones, who was flying east on an important mission for the Government. Just before the plane took off from Los Angeles, Lieutenant William O'Brien, sent as a bodyguard for Jones, was evidently recognized by Baker; and the alleged slayer of Judge Klein, apparently believing he was being shadowed, determined to slay the detective. It was Lieutenant O'Brien who arrested Baker in 1931. His fragmentary confession reveals that he hurried from the plane, stole a long bread knife from the lunch counter at the airport, and stabbed O'Brien as he walked through the darkened ship after it had taken off from Cleveland.'"

"And so," said Evelyn, as John paused.

"And so," he repeated, smiling.

There was a bustle at the door of the restaurant. Evelyn looked up. She saw a man with a camera.

"Reporters!" she whispered. "They must have followed the car from the flying field. It's like that all the time."

"Do we stand our ground, or run?" John asked.

The reporters were scanning the people in the restaurant.

"What do you think? I've always run."

"They've spotted us!" he said. "We'll have to sit tight. Listen. Why don't you marry somebody inconspicuous and settle down? You'd have any amount of privacy by doing that. The most inconspicuous people in the world are scientists--"

"I'll consider it," she said, as she prepared to greet the nearest reporter. "It sounds like a good emergency measure."

THE CORPSE
WAS BEAUTIFUL

Charity drew back. Her eyes widened with horror

HUGH PENTECOST

Judson Pentecost Philips, born in Northfield, Massachusetts in 1903, has one of the most amazing longevity records among writers of mystery fiction-- or any other kind. Under the Philips name and his better-known pseudonym Hugh Pentecost, he has contributed to the field since "Room Number Twenty-three," a locked-room mystery written while the author was a student at Columbia University, appeared in a 1925 issue of Detective Fiction Weekly. His first novel as Philips was Red War (Double-day, 1936), written with Thomas M. Johnson, while his first as Pentecost, Cancelled in Red (Dodd, Mead, 1939), won the pub-lisher's annual Red Badge Mystery Prize. More than one hundred novels have followed, along with countless magazine short stories and novelettes. In recent years, he has produced three or four new books annually, and Dodd, Mead's Fall 1985 catalogue lists more to come. Thus, Philips/Pentecost has completed a full six decades as a mystery writer.

Among other achievements, Pentecost has probably created more series characters than any other writer. Among the better known are hotel manager Pierre Chambrun, artist John Jericho, psychiatrist Dr. John Smith, police detectives Luke Bradley and Lt. Pascal, small-town ex-lawyer Uncle George Crowder, and (as Philips) columnist Peter Styles. Many of his American novelettes, however, feature no continuing character. The stars are the unique and varied backgrounds, among them an aircraft factory, a U.S. Navy ship in the Pacific, a carnival, a military school, a cattle auction, a coal mine, and various sports (harness racing, golf, boxing, stock car racing.) The present story, one of his best, concerns civilian aircraft spotting and gives a feel of the mood on the homefront during the early days of World War II. It appeared in the May 1942 issue.

THE CORPSE WAS BEAUTIFUL by Hugh Pentecost

"Speed in reporting an observed flight is of extreme importance. If you can do your part in fifteen seconds or less we can depend on a very short over-all time from Observation to the Army

Plotting Board." Instructions for Aircraft Warning Service
Observers.

The colonel sat behind a desk on a raised platform overlooking
the room. The British staff captain sat beside him, tapping polished
cordovan boots with a bamboo swagger stick. There was a grim look
on the colonel's face.

"You were hoping for action, Captain," he said. "Looks like you'd
get it."

"What's up, sir?"

"One of our seaplane patrols has spotted an Axis carrier about
six hundred miles off the New England coast. Her decks are clear of
planes, which means we can look for trouble. Alert signal has been
sounded from Maine to Virginia."

The room below them was strangely still, although there were at
least fifty men in it. Some thirty of them were grouped around a
table, about four times the size of a billiard table. The whole of its
surface area was covered by a relief map of New England. Lying at
various points on top of the map were flat wooden replicas of
airplanes. Whenever orderlies came up with reports from the dozen
or more switchboard and telephone operators at the far end of the
room, these replicas were moved into new positions by officers
holding long-handled pushers that did not look unlike croupier's rakes.

"Where would you expect enemy planes to strike?" the staff
captain asked.

The colonel shrugged indicating a smaller map on the desk in
front of him. "There are Navy Yards at Portsmouth, Boston, here in
Rhode Island. All of this section, including Bridgeport, Hartford,
New Haven, Springfield...all industrial centers...is my area."

"Navy patrols and Coast Guard keep you posted?"

"Of course, but that's often misleading. Planes may make a feint
at one point on the coast, then come up over land...say, through rural
areas in New York, Vermont, New Hampshire...strike at Boston or
Portsmouth from the rear."

"You have air-raid warning services in these areas?"

"You bet," said the colonel. "But half of 'em never had a chance
for practice maneuvers before the real thing hit us amidships."

"How are they set up?" the staff captain asked.

"Each observation post is supposed to be within fifteen seconds
reach of a telephone. The moment a plane or planes are spotted, the
observer goes to a phone and puts in an Army-Flash call. It reaches
one of those operators down there. As soon as the observer is
connected he reports, using this Flash Message Form."

The colonel handed the staff captain a slip of paper.

"As you see," the colonel continued, "the message can be
condensed to eight words. Once you have a series of these messages
from a series of O.P.'s, the direction the enemy planes are taking
becomes apparent."

"How about the accuracy of these civilian observers?"

"They're unflaggingly conscientious," said the colonel. "They stand watch every night and during the daytime are ready to take over the instant an alert sounds. I'd count on them any time."

An orderly approached the desk, saluted, and handed the colonel a message. The colonel unfolded it and read, his forehead contracted in a scowl. "Here's an odd one," he said, and handed the dispatch to the Britisher.

Army Operator 14 had scrawled a note on the back of a message form. "Flash Call from Post 66B at 3:26 A.M. by a woman observer. Instead of regulation message she said quote How do you stop a person who is bleeding to death from bleeding to death? unquote. I disconnected at once to keep wires clear."

The colonel located Post 66B on his map. "There it is. Southern corner of Vermont."

"Any reason to believe planes might be near there?" asked the Britisher.

"Positive they're not," said the colonel. "We'd have had fifty reports before they could get that far inland." He turned to the orderly. "Go to an outside wire and flash the operator at Fairview, Vermont. Have her find out what's wrong at Post 66B."

"Yes, sir."

The colonel shook his head. "Some of these country women still must think the telephone's an arm of God. Disrupt the whole warning service for a cut finger and expect the Army to do something about it."

"And the Army apparently intends to do just that," the Britisher grinned.

Tired lines in the colonel's face deepened. "These litle people are fighting the war just as hard as a pilot in a pursuit ship, Captain. We try to let them know how the Army feels about it whenever we get the chance."

"It is not necessary that a Chief or Assistant Chief Observer remain at the Observation Post throughout the hours of scheduled air operations." Instructions for Chief Observers.

Paul Haviland glanced at the radium dial of his bedside clock and moaned. Then he reached out to touch Charity, found she wasn't there, and moaned again. Charity was up on the mountain-side standing watch at the Observation Post. A fine thing! You learn to sleep double and it's a fine thing, and then suddenly you don't sleep double and it's not a fine thing.

Then he sat bolt upright in bed. The telephone had awakened him. For a moment he strained his ears for the sound of motors. They would call him from the Post if there were aircraft over the area. The cold March night was as still as a tomb. No planes.

He dived back under the covers. There were only two other

reasons for people to telephone you at four o'clock in the morning, with the thermometer registering a good, rousing 28. They are drunk or there has been an accident. Haviland decided it would be pleasanter to assume that they were drunk. He rolled over on his side and pulled the blankets up tight around his neck.

The telephone operator put her finger on the button and just held it there. Haviland drew a deep breath and said, "<u>Shudder</u>!" He had picked that up from a gentleman of the cloth who <u>had a</u> prejudice against profanity when he missed a three-foot putt.

Reluctantly Haviland decided it must be the Aircraft Warning Service, after all. He had joined it against his better judgement. Perhaps that wasn't quite accurate, because anything Charity got him to do was never entirely against his will. Whenever he did something that pleased her he felt good about it, even if doing the thing itself griped him.

The truth was, Haviland couldn't explain Charity. Before he had married her his best friend had asked him what he saw in her.

"Well, she's tiny and she's cute," Haviland said.

"Uh-huh," said his friend.

"She wears bracelets with little bangles that bangle," Haviland said.

"Uh-huh," said his friend.

"It's like owning a permanent Christmas-tree ornament that never tarnishes," Haviland tried again.

The friend said that all this seemed an ideal basis on which to build a life's happiness.

It was funny about Charity. Things that would have annoyed him in someone else amused him in her. She was always taking a hand in other people's affairs. She would stop the taxi in which they were riding to tell a mounted cop the curb chain on his horse was too tight. She would stop dog owners on the street and advise them about the proper diet for their animals. She was always up to her ears in organizations, for which she had an endless enthusiasm.

The Aircraft Warning Service was one of them.

They had come to Vermont a few months back. Haviland had turned over the management of his own successful but nonessential factory to subordinates in order to become head man in a machine-tool works. He and Charity had rented a house in Fairview about seven miles from North Johnsbury and the plant.

It took Charity less than a week to get into the social swim. The house swarmed with people like David and Lois Kelcey, who lived on Glendon Mountain; Diana Phelps, whom Haviland put down in his books as concentrated trouble; Ray Allen, Lois Kelcey's brother; Bill Barnum, a tall, Fred MacMurray kind of guy; and half a dozen others, including Major Wilmot, retired, Dr. Graves, the local G.P., and Professor Coleridge, the high-school superintendent.

Dr. Graves and Professor Coleridge were organizers of the Fairview Observation Post, but it was Charity who became the moving spirit. This was before the outbreak of the war, when it was hard to get people to take it seriously. Somehow she had bullied and brow-beaten about seventy-five people into enlisting as observers.

But the real headache had come when she insisted that Haviland volunteer as Chief Observer. "When a man who is already doing something for defense is willing to do even more for defense it gives prestige," she explained.

"But darling, I'm a working man...seven days a week a working man," Haviland protested.

"You don't have to be there all the time," she said. "It says so on the instruction sheet." She waved it at him, a long, legal-looking affair.

"But..."

"You only have to sort of supervise," she said, "and maybe watch for a couple of hours one day a week. And you could go on at, say, from six to eight in the evening, so it wouldn't interfere with your getting your proper rest...and, please, Paul."

It had seemed like something of a joke, then. There were to be a couple of test maneuvers and then his responsibility would end.

"And that's nothing, darling!" Charity said.

He grinned at her, fatuously. "Okay, baby. We'll compromise. I'll take the job."

It ran into weeks before the day for the maneuvers was announced. They set up an observation post in the summerhouse in the Kelceys' garden. Watchers were assigned for two-hour periods over the whole twenty-four hours, with alternates in case someone was sick or away when the day came. Charity took a hand in this, too.

"You better fix it so Diana and I watch together," she said. "On the grounds that from two to four in the morning is the worst time, and the men need sleep or something, because if you assign Diana to watch with any man some other woman is going to be simply miserable."

"Why doesn't Diana get herself a guy who isn't tied up with someone else?" Haviland asked.

"Who is there, excepting Bill Barnum?-- And he simply despises her!"

"Why?"

"Really, Paul, I don't go around asking people about their private lives."

"The hell you don't," he said.

"Paul, I think I hate you for that!"

"I know, baby, and I hate you, too," he said, and kissed her on the top of her upturned nose.

Then war had hit them like a stunning blow in the pit of the stomach. It was no longer a lark. Three nights a week Charity went up the mountain to watch with Diana from 2 to 4 A.M....

The telephone bell kept ringing.

Once more he strained his ears for the sound of plane motors.

Nothing. Muttering to himself, he swung his feet over the side of the bed and into fur slippers. He pulled on his robe and stumbled out to the phone in the hall.

"This better be good," he said, as he picked up the receiver.

"Paul, this is Lois Kelcey."

"Look, chum, if this is some kind of a gag--" Haviland began.

"Paul, you must come up here right away."

"You feeling okay and in your right mind?" Haviland asked.

"You've got to come at once, Paul. Something's gone wrong."

"What?"

"I don't want to talk over the phone, but--"

"Look," said Haviland, "if you've pulled some kind of boner get in touch with Air Commmand at once and straighten it out. You know as much about this warning service as I do."

"It has nothing to do with the warning service, Paul. Please stop arguing and come at once. Charity needs you."

"Charity?" His voice changed quality. "Is she sick? Is she hurt?"

"Charity's all right. But she needs you, Paul. Right away."

Definitely no gag. He could tell that now from Lois's voice. "Fifteen minutes to get there," he said, and hung up.

"It has been learned that blind persons are well adapted to assist observers because of their well-developed hearing and sensing faculties. It is hoped that an opportunity to serve will be accorded to the blind who live near the Observation Post." Instructions for Chief Observers.

The road up Glendon Mountain to the Kelceys' place was winding, and the frost, glazed over spring mud, made it treacherous. Haviland chafed at the slowness of his progress, while a dozen explanations of Lois's call occurred to him. A practical joke. If it had been anyone else, maybe. But Lois was a pretty level-headed dame.

He looked at his watch. Four-ten. Bill Barnum and Ray Allen were supposed to have relieved Charity and Diana at the Post ten minutes ago. Why hadn't Charity talked to him herself? He felt pin points of cold sweat on his forehead. Diana had been going to drive Charity home, and Diana always drove like hell. On the slippery road....

But he came upon no smashed automobiles.

About a hundred yards below the driveway his headlights picked up two familiar walking figures. Major Thatcher Wilmot was the Kelceys' closest neighbor. With him was Mason, a native who worked the major's farm. They both turned as Haviland drew alongside.

Wilmot, a veteran of the first World War, was a well-set-up, ruddy-faced man with close-cut iron-gray hair. The black glasses he wore over his blinded eyes gave him a curious, expressionless look, alleviated only by a pleasant smile when he was amused. He ran to tweeds, invariably had a pipe between his teeth, and carried a knobby blackthorn stick.

Mason looked what he was-- a Vermont farmer. Haviland had never heard him say more than "yes" or "no."

"That you, Haviland?" the major asked.

"Yes, sir."

"Gotten to know the sound of your motor in the last few weeks," the major said.

"Hop on and I'll take you the rest of the way," Haviland said. "What's wrong?"

"Don't know," said the major. Mason helped him into the back of the car. "But I'm glad you're here. Lois sounded really upset."

"She called you, too?"

"No. I called her. You know, Haviland, I don't sleep well. Been awake all night. Three quarters of an hour ago I heard a couple of shots. I wasn't paying much attention because there was a plane going over. But I heard them quite distinctly...somewhere up the line here. At first I thought it was a native boy doing a little out-of-season work to replenish his larder. Mason tells me there are deer about, looking for spring shoots. A moment or two later I heard a car drive down the mountain, and I took it for granted my poacher, having missed his deer, was making tracks in case somebody'd heard the shots."

"That's probably what it was," said Haviland, trying to wrench his front wheels out of a rut.

"It bothered me, though," said the major, "because it wasn't a shotgun or a rifle, but definitely a .45 automatic."

"That's a hell of a thing for a deer," said Haviland.

"Yes," said the major. "The more I thought about it the more nervous it made me. I decided to call the Kelceys'. When I picked up my bedside phone I heard Lois talking to you. I'm on the same line, you know. As soon as she'd finished I rang her back. She wouldn't tell me what it was except that there'd been an accident. Asked me to come up."

Again Haviland felt moisture on his forhead. "Are you sure it was a .45?"

An air of the parade ground was in the major's voice. "My hearing faculties are more acute than most, Haviland."

"Sorry, sir. Of course," said Haviland, embarrassed.

As they swung into the Kelceys' driveway at the top of the climb Haviland saw that there were lights in every window. He got out and gave Wilmot a hand.

Bill Barnum, the collar of a sheepskin jacket up around his ears, hailed them from the garden path. "Paul! Major!"

They joined him. Bill was usually full of wisecracks, but he was serious now.

"What gives?" Haviland said.

"Watching from here," Bill said. "David's waiting for you at the

Post."

"Where's Lois?" the major asked.

"In the house," said Barnum. "And she could use a strong right arm to lean on."

Wilmot didn't stay to learn more.

"But what's up?" Haviland wanted to know.

"Better see for youself," Bill said. He struck a match to light a cigarette, and Haviland saw that his hand was shaking.

"What the hell is this?" Haviland demanded. "Everybody's so damned secretive!" But he went on down the path to the summerhouse.

David Kelcey's lean figure was visible in the door as his flashlight winked. "This is a bad business, Paul," he said somberly. "Damn' bad." He swung the flashlight around the interior of the summerhouse.

Haviland sucked in his breath. Lying on the slate floor was the body of a woman, wrapped in a mink coat. Through a torn, charred hole in the coat he could see a gaping wound in her back. He whirled on Kelcey.

"You dirty louse!" he cried. "Lois said Charity was all right. Lois said--"

"For God's sake, man, it's not Charity!" David said. "Look!"

Then Haviland saw the hair, red instead of yellow; the outstretched hand with an unfamiliar ring on the finger. It was Diana Phelps. "God, what a turn!" he said. "You see, David, that's Charity's coat!"

There was a little cry from behind him, and Charity was running down the path. It seemed to Haviland that it took forever for her to reach him. He held her close. He was still trembling. "Baby! Baby!" he whispered. His lips touched one pink ear. "You certainly scared the pants off me."

"The procedure to be followed by the Chief Observer in accomplishing the tasks with which he is charged is entirely a matter for him to decide." Instructions for Chief Observers.

It was then that Haviland heard the distant but steady drone of airplane motors.

"Where's Ray?"

"At the phone," David Kelcey said. "Trying to locate Dr. Graves."

"Good God, you mean--?"

"Diana is quite dead," said David in a flat voice. "Dr. Graves is also the coroner."

"How did it happen, David?"

"We don't know. But it's murder, Paul."

The planes came on.

"Bill!" Haviland called. "You'd better get on the job here."

Bill Barnum walked reluctantly down the path toward the summerhouse. Along the rim of the hills in the east was the first light of
morning. Suddenly, into this light spot, came the planes, eight or ten
of them, flying in formation.

"Step lively, Bill," Haviland said. He gave Charity's shoulder a
pat. "Scram for the house and tell Ray to cut whatever call he's
making and put through an Army Flash."

"Oh, Paul!"

"Hurry!" Haviland's voice was crisp. "And get going, Bill."

Barnum smiled a crooked little smile. "Okay, Chief," he said.
He took a message form from his pocket and began filling it in. "I'm
not going in there to look at the orientation card," he said, nodding
toward the summerhouse.

"They're flying approximately southeast," Haviland said.

"Okay." Barnum started for the house.

Haviland looked up again at the planes. He'd seen them like this
before, while it was still a game. Even then they'd had a compelling
quality. Now they sent a cold chill along his spine. It was too dark to
identify them, but they must be defense planes, since there had been
no alert, no warning over the radio.

Diana was dead with a hole in her back. Vaguely the implica-
tions of the word "murder" were beginning to filter into Haviland's
mind. Yet the planes held his attention. They came on and on
relentlessly till they were directly overhead, their motors roaring, so
they seemed to rock the ground under his feet. Those kids up there
were searching through the gray light of dawn for an enemy.

"Nice going, Paul," said David Kelcey, breaking in on Haviland's
thoughts. "We needed someone to get us functioning while we wait
for the police. You see, as far as we know, the only people here when
this happened were Lois and Charity and myself and Mrs. Watson, our
housekeeper. It's put us all in rather a spot."

"When did it happen?" Haviland asked.

Kelcey looked down at the toe of his ski boot. "Perhaps you'd
better talk to Charity," he said. "She and Diana were on watch
together." He raised his eyes to Haviland's. "The rest of us were
asleep."

Haviland felt the equivalent of hackles rising on the back of his
neck. So that was going to be the line!

"You've telephoned for the police?" he asked.

"I telephoned Hiram," said Kelcey. "He's on his way."

"Oh, Lord!" Haviland said. He thought if you were to hunt the
countryside for the person least well equipped to handle this emergency Hiram Hargrove would be your choice. He was the R.F.D.
mail carrier, operated the lone taxi in Fairview, and was sheriff, for
good measure. He was what summer people call a "character." "How
about State Troopers?"

"They're only highway patrol up here."

Haviland's breath made clouds in the cold air. "Someone should stay here with Diana till the proper authorities have looked over the situation. Dr. Graves will probably be more use than anyone."

"It's not likely anyone would want to touch her," David said. Again he looked down at the toe of his boot. "Of course, Charity messed around when she first found her."

"I'll get that from her," Haviland said.

As he and David approached the house Bill and Ray Allen came out. "Got it through okay," Bill said.

Ray Allen, short and stocky, looking like a perennial sophomore despite his thirty-eight years, nodded to Haviland. "There was an in-call a few moments ago. Orderly for the C.O. at Air Command. Seems Charity asked them what to do about Diana. They cut her off to keep commmunications open. But they wanted to know what was up. I told them."

"What did they say?" Haviland asked.

"They said 'thank you,'" said Allen laconically.

"You fellows keep watching from the garden," Haviland instruct-ed them. "And don't let anyone go monkeying around the summer-house till Dr. Graves gets here."

"I don't think you need worry about that," Allen said....

In the low-ceilinged living-room Charity and Lois Kelcey sat on the lounge facing the fireplace. Charity, in gabardine ski pants, a red jacket, and fur-topped galoshes, had pulled a toque off her yellow hair and was twisting it in her fingers.

Lois Kelcey wore a quilted mandarin coat. She was tall and dark; one of those plain women who can be beautiful in moments of animation. Haviland had seen her that way on occasion when she looked at David.

Major Wilmot stood to one side of the fireplace, where a hatchet-faced woman in a flannel robe, her stringy hair done up in old-fashioned curlpapers, knelt, working a pair of hand bellows. This was Mrs. Watson.

Kelcey stopped in the doorway as he caught sight of the major. "Oh, it's you," he said.

"Hello, David."

"Surprised to see you," said Kelcey.

"I heard the commotion and called Lois," Wilmot said. "Thought I might be of use."

"Very thoughtful of you," said David.

Haviland wondered at David's tone. He remembered a rumor that before blindness had overtaken the major he had been a suitor of Lois's. It was a strange time for David to resent it.

Mrs. Watson got up from the fireplace. "It's about time you two come in out of the cold," she said. "I've got coffee on the stove. I suppose there's no doubt about it? I suppose I'll have that Hiram Hargrove tramping all over my kitchen?"

"I'm afraid there's no doubt about it, Mrs. Watson," Haviland said.

Mrs. Watson gave her robe a hitch across her flat chest. "Well, all I can say is, whoever done it must have been awfully provoked!" With which masterpiece of understatement she went off to the kitchen.

Haviland sat down on the arm of the couch beside Charity. He spoke over the top of her head to Lois: "Sorry I was so dense over the phone."

"It's all right, Paul. You got here."

He looked down at the bright-colored child who was his wife. "Can you tell me exactly what happened, kitten?"

Charity's fingers tightened around his. "Oh, Paul, I messed everything up," she said. "Because I asked them how you stop a person who was bleeding to death from bleeding to death, and I never reported the plane because I guess I was rattled and..."

"Hold it," said Haviland gently. "You and Diana were in the summerhouse together. You came on at two o'clock. Right?"

"That's right, darling. Diana came by for me and you never even woke up when I left and pulled an extra blanket over you because I thought maybe you'd be cold alone, and..."

"Look, kitten, would you mind very much telling me what happened here?"

"Darling, I am telling you. But it began then, because Diana stopped for me, and she didn't blow the horn because she didn't want to wake you, and she just blinked the lights on and off, and so I went out and we drove off together. It was about ten minutes ahead of time, and Professor and Mrs. Coleridge were at the Post, and they said Mrs. Watson had left coffee on the stove and we'd better get some. So we did."

"Get the coffee?" said Haviland helpfully.

"Yes. And then at exactly two o'clock Diana and I took over, and we signed the little book you are supposed to sign when you take over, and then we just watched, and there weren't any planes at all...at least, not until the plane which I didn't report because I was so excited, and I suppose that will give our post a black mark."

"Charity, for God's sake get to the point!" David said.

"I am getting to the point, David, which is that Diana was wearing a silk dress and silk stockings under a light coat and she wasn't half warm enough, and I was roasting to death because I had on all this truck and my mink coat. So I traded coats with Diana, and that's what's killing me, Paul, because I can't remember about the policies."

"The policies?" Haviland was patient. He knew the futility of trying to hurry her.

"I can't remember where the policy is that covers the fur coat, Paul, and whether it had a suicide clause in it and..."

"A suicide clause!"

"Well, if it was suicide maybe the policy on the coat becomes null and void, because I have often read about suicide clauses in insurance policies and..."

"It wasn't suicide, kitten," said Haviland, with a straight face, "so you needn't worry about that. You and Diana were watching and you had traded coats?"

"You know the system you worked out, Paul. As soon as you heard or saw a plane one of the watchers was to go at once to the telephone. The other one waited a minute or so, marking off the information on the message form, and then joined the other one at the telephone. Darn it, that sounds kind of mixed up, but you know how it is."

"Yes, angel."

"Well, I was the other one," Charity said.

"Uh-huh. The one who went to the telephone."

"Yes. This one plane came up the valley flying south, or almost south, and I ducked right into the house and said, 'Army Flash, Fairview 163,' and waited. Diana should have come at once but she didn't; and then I heard the man say, 'Army. Go ahead, please.' And I couldn't go ahead because Diana hadn't come with the information. So I hung up. Then I opened the door and looked down the path, and I couldn't see Diana, so I called to her and she didn't answer. So I ran back down the path to the summerhouse. Oh, Paul!"

"Take it easy, baby."

"At first I thought she wasn't there, and then I saw her lying on the floor, and I thought she had tripped over something and knocked her head against the table maybe, so I called her; and then I picked up the flashlight which was on the table right next to the field glasses Major Wilmot loaned us and I turned it on, and..."

"Go ahead."

"Well, I saw right away she hadn't knocked herself out, because there was a big hole in her back and it was all bl-blood and I didn't know what to do, so I ran back to the phone and said, 'Army Flash,' even though I knew I shouldn't; and when they answered I asked them how to stop bleeding, and they just hung up. And that's positively every word of the story, Paul."

"I'm sure of it, baby. Now, it's about a hundred feet to the summerhouse. You probably closed the door when you came in the house."

"Of course, I did, because if you leave the door open the temperature goes down, and that does something to the thermostat and the oil heater..."

"Just a minute, kitten. The point is, how about the noise of the shot? Did you hear it before you put in the call, or while you were waiting for the Army operator to answer?"

"But I didn't hear it at all!" Charity said.

"Now, look, baby, even with the door closed..."

Charity glanced at David. "He asked me that too, Paul, and I swear I didn't hear it, but the plane was flying very low and making a great deal of noise and..."

"How about you, David?" Haviland asked.

"I was asleep," David said levelly.

"And you, Lois?"

"The plane woke me," said Lois. "At least I thought it did. It was still quite close when I opened my eyes. It might have been the shot that woke me, but I didn't consciously hear it."

"How about Mrs. Watson?"

"Dead to the world," said David. "Lois had to shake her to wake her up."

Haviland was frowning. "Yet you heard the shots over two hundred yards down the road, Major?"

"That's not so surprising," said Wilmot. "That southbound plane was just about over the Post, I should judge, when I heard the shots. It's quite understandable that Charity didn't hear them...or perhaps I should say, didn't distinguish them from the noise of the plane. As she said, it was very low and making a devil of a racket. But I have trained myself to separate sounds."

"That must be it," Haviland said. He turned back to Charity. "What happened after the Army hung up on you, kitten?"

"Why, I went to call David and Lois again, and David was just coming downstairs in his stocking feet and..."

"Stocking feet?"

"I hadn't undressed," said David, "except for pulling off my boots. I thought I might be needed during the night. Charity woke me."

"I was in the guestroom so I wouldn't disturb Lois if I was needed," David said. "I came downstairs without stopping to put on my boots. Charity was here, in this room. She said Diana was hurt. I went straight to the summerhouse."

"And you, Lois?" Haviland saked.

"I was awake, as I told you. I mean, the plane had awakened me. I heard Charity call to us and I heard David run downstairs. I followed as soon as I'd gotten a robe. David had already gone to the summerhouse, so, after Charity explained, I phoned Uncle Ned. I couldn't reach him. He's on a baby case in Bradford Hollow. No phone. While I was trying, David came in and said there was no hurry because we'd only need him in his capacity as-- as coroner."

"Then I called Hiram," David said.

"When you came up the path to the house the first time did you see anyone, Charity?" Haviland asked.

"No, Paul."

"And the second time...when you went to see why Diana hadn't joined you?"

"I didn't see anyone, Paul darling, but I guess I was pretty excited and maybe hysterical and..."

"Did you hear anyone? Anyone running or an automobile on the road?"

Charity shook her head.

"Well, that's that," said Haviland. "It was pretty neat timing.

Charity couldn't have been away from the Post over a minute."

"That's what I thought," said David, without looking up. "Very neat timing, indeed."

In the hush they heard the sputtering of Hiram Hargrove's old automobile, still far down the mountain road. Haviland stood up. "Would you come outside with me, Major?" he asked.

"Of course, Haviland." The blind man moved with assurance straight across the room to the terrace door. There he put his hand on Haviland's arm and they walked out onto the marble flagging.

Haviland said, "We're going to need you, sir."

"Need me?"

"You were Military Intelligence during the last war, weren't you?"

"Yes," said the major, his tone short.

"We're going to need all the help we can get. This is big-league stuff. Way over Hiram's head."

"Aren't you forgetting that I wouldn't be much use these days?" Wilmot fumbled in his pocket for his pipe.

"Hiram and I can be eyes for you," said Haviland bluntly. At the look on Wilmot's face he added, "That's what you meant, wasn't it?"

"Not entirely."

"What then?"

Wilmot struck a match and held it to the bowl of his pipe. The flame showed up the deep lines in his face. "Simply that I'm not taking a hand, that's all."

"But, damn it, Major..."

"That's flat, Haviland. I'm sorry. Incidentally, you're breaking a cardinal rule of police investigation. Why eliminate me as a suspect?"

"For God's sake, sir!" Haviland was impatient.

"If you don't think I could find my way around this garden, operate a .45 at close range, and get away in the confusion...well, you're not fully aware of the abilities of the blind."

"Nuts!" Haviland said. "Maybe I did it by remote control from my bed! Look here, sir..."

The major turned his black spectacles into the paling darkness. "Haviland, surely you understand? Lois and David are my best friends."

"Good God, man, you don't think Lois did it!"

"Of course, I don't."

"But David?"

"David's infatuation for Diana hasn't exactly been a secret," Wilmot said. "It's odd, Haviland, but there was something about Diana. Something that wasn't wholesome. I could sense it when she came into a room. There was a difference in voices. A kind of tension, a kind of excitement."

"Hiram won't catch on to that easily," Haviland said. "So you see you can help."

Wilmot shook his head. "I'm sorry."

"If David did murder Diana, you wouldn't want Lois to go on with him, would you?"

"Lois loves David, Haviland. That's enough for me. I'm not going to be one of the bloodhounds on his trail."

Hargrove's car had come to a halt in the yard, steaming like a locomotive. Hiram climbed out. He was a lanky New Englander with a drooping red mustache, vintage nineties. He wore a bearskin coat that hung down to his insteps. It reminded Haviland of something you might wear in a vaudeville turn. Incongruously he remembered a comedian who used to wear such a coat, lie down in the footlights, and munch sandwiches while he told jokes.

Hiram came toward them. "Got here as quick as I could. What's doin'?"

"I'm afraid it's murder, Hiram. Miss Phelps."

"Gee whittakers!" said Hiram. The only sign of emotion he showed was an accelerated chewing on the bulge of tobacco in his cheek.

"I've taken charge, Hiram," Haviland said, "because under Army regulations I'm in authority while there are observers on duty."

"It's lucky the major's here," said Hiram. "He's an old hand at this."

"The major isn't helping," said Haviland.

Hiram gave the blind man a shrewd look. "Like that, is it? Figger you might take the other side from us, Major?"

"Well, Hiram, I..."

"It doesn't surprise me none, Major. If I felt the way you do about Lois I reckon I'd stick around on her side of the fence." Then Hiram winked at Haviland. "But I ain't much of a detective. 'Twouldn't do no harm if you jest tagged along to see Lois's interests is properly protected."

"Well..." said Wilmot doubtfully.

"Where's the corpus?" Hiram asked.

"Down at the Post," Haviland said, and led the way.

They found Bill Barnum and Ray Allen sitting on a garden bench. Bill stood up. "For God's sake, Paul, you're not going to leave her down there all night!"

"Take it easy," Haviland said. "As soon as Hiram has looked the place over..."

"I suppose she's got a family that ought to be notified," Ray said. He glanced at Barnum. "What about it, Bill?"

"She never mentioned anyone," Bill said. He ran his fingers through wiry red hair. "It's been a long time since we-- we talked casually together." He looked away. "A hell of a way to die. Getting it in the back without ever..."

"You two better stick around after your watch is done," Haviland said. "Come on, Hiram."

At the door of the summmerhouse Haviland and the major stood aside to let Hiram pass. The sheriff just stared at the body on the floor. "Holy jumpin' gee whittakers!" he said. "Cripes! Whoever done it stuck the gun right in the middle of her back afore they let go. You can see the fur's all burned! Why'd she let 'em get so close?"

Haviland shrugged. "There was a plane flying over, Hiram. She was filling out a message form. She wouldn't hear anyone coming, I guess."

"Nasty hole," said Hiram. "Always use a rifle huntin' myself."

"Hiram," said Haviland dryly, "this is a murder case! You're supposed to find out who did it. Give this place a careful looking-over and let's move the body. We can't just let it stay here."

"Don't be in too much of a hurry, Haviland," Wilmot said. "The scene of a crime can often tell you a great deal."

"Ain't nothin' to see, Major," said Hiram. "She was facin' north. Someone let go with two shots. She fell forward. She was smokin' a cigarette and it burned down in her fingers till it scorched the flesh. So she must have died right off. They was someone else watchin' with her, on account of the cigarette she was smokin' had a cork tip and the ones in that ash tray ain't. A woman it was, on account of the paint marks on the stubs. They's been a flock of people in and out of this place since, and one of 'em was in stockin' feet. But they's nothing important, so let's heft her into the house."

"All right, Hiram," the major said.

"It was Charity who was watching with Miss Phelps, Hiram," Haviland said.

"Uh-huh," said Hiram. "Take her by the feet. The corpus, I mean."

Haviland took Diana's trim ankles in his hands and Hiram hoisted her under the arms. Those beads of sweat were on Haviland's forehead again. Nice work if you can get it...like hell! They had gone only a few feet, the major tapping along behind them, when Hiram said, "Set her down."

They set her down. Hiram stepped across the straw-covered flower bed, bent down, and picked up an old-style Army automatic which Haviland hadn't noticed in his earlier trips up the path.

"What is it?" the major asked.

"Kelcey's gun," said Hiram, without excitement.

"How do you know?" Wilmot's voice was sharp.

"I never fergit a gun, Major," Hiram said. "Kind of a hobby of mine. Kelcey come shootin' with me last fall. He don't care for huntin' but he likes trompin' through the woods. He's a fust-rate pistol shot, so he carried this with him jest for the hell of it. It's Kelcey's gun, all right."

"What about fingerprints?" Haviland said.

"Shucks, I wouldn't know what to do with 'em if they was any," said Hiram. "Besides, they wouldn't mean nothin'. David kep' his gun in the workshop 'longside the garage. Hung in a holster there on the wall. Everybody as's been in there this winter has likely handled it.

And I reckon the murderer wouldn't want to get catched, so he'd of wore gloves." He stowed the gun in his pocket. "Let's get this corpus inside."

The British staff captain came out of the officers' mess, where he'd had an early breakfast, and rejoined the colonel in the plotting-room. The colonel looked up.

"This may interest you," he said. "That freak call we had about someone bleeding to death? A girl was murdered at the O.P. in Fairview, Vermont."

"By jove, that is something."

"Great confusion, of course," the colonel said. "But, in relation to your question, the observers have continued to report with satisfactory accuracy."

When Haviland came downstairs from helping Hiram place Diana's body in one of the guestrooms, he found David Kelcey in the hall.

Kelcey's dark eyebrows were drawn together in a concentrated frown. "I wanted to talk to you for a minute, Paul."

"Okay," said Haviland, "talk!"

"You've asked Wilmot to help Hiram, haven't you?"

"Yes."

"Damn it all, Paul, this is a job for the cops, not every crackpot amateur sleuth in the neighborhood."

"Wilmot's a professional, of sorts," Haviland said.

David laughed mirthlessly. "I'm in a spot, Paul. Diana and I...well, you know about that. What you may not know is that Wilmot hates my guts. I cut him out with Lois years ago. Oh, he's always polite and smooth...all the merry little sunshine. But you're handing him a chance to stick a knife in my ribs. I think I have a right to at least an impartial investigation."

Haviland looked at David's angry face. "You're getting it," he said. "Wilmot's refused to help us, so that he can be free to help you and Lois."

"That louse!" David exploded. "Don't you see that's just his subtle way of telling you he thinks I'm guilty!"

"Well," said Haviland, "are you?"

Haviland went into the living-room, where Mrs. Watson was serving eggs, bacon, and coffee. Lois suggested he eat something, but Haviland wasn't hungry. "God," he thought, "it's a funny thing how a crisis changes your friends." David and Lois Kelcey had been, to his mind, a moderately happy couple. In fact, they had given him comfort from time to time. Haviland was twelve years older than Charity, and it bothered him. He had long-range visions of himself in a wheel chair while Charity, still young, would be wanting to have fun with someone else. There was about the same difference in the ages

of David and Lois. It had made Haviland feel good to see them
working things out...including Diana.

Now the Kelceys looked different...and felt different. Lois,
drawn and white, unable to keep her hands still in her lap, was a
stranger. David, with his insinuations about Charity, was definitely
an enemy.

Bill Barnum, who always made a party go, sat silent in a chair by
the fireplace, chain-smoking. Mrs. Watson had to tap him on the
shoulder to get his attention about sugar and cream for his coffee.
Ray Allen prowled around the room, picking up things and putting
them down.

Haviland thought that one of these hands that now held a cup or
a fork had planted an automatic against Diana's back and let her have
it. "You got to cut that out," he told himself. "Your friends don't
commit murder. Or do they?"

Outside, a car turned into the driveway with a screech of tires.

It was Dr. Graves. He came in the front door without knocking,
a stubby, irascible little man in his middle sixties. His sandy hair was
obviously thinner than it had been in his youth, he had more paunch,
and the lines at the corners of his mouth and eyes were undoubtedly
deeper. But he moved with the energy and speed of a boy of twenty.

"So someone finally caught up with that tramp," he said. "Where
is she?"

"In the back guestroom, Uncle Ned," said Lois.

The doctor gave her a sharp look. "You need a good, stiff drink,"
he said. "Get one." He trotted upstairs, carrying his black bag. They
heard him greet Hiram, and then their voices became an indistin-
guishable mumble as the bedroom door closed.

Once more they sat in silence. Haviland was puzzled by Charity.
Usually, in a room full of people, even though they couldn't talk
together, she would catch his eye from time to time and that "all's
well" feeling would pass between them. Charity was deliberately
avoiding that exchange now.

"Why the hell is everybody so edgy?" Ray Allen said suddenly.
"Diana's dead. It's a shock. But you all know damn well that none of
us..."

"Do we know that, Ray," asked Haviland.

Allen's eyes grew slowly wider, as if the idea had never occurred
to him.

Again that tight, anxious silence. It was broken by the doctor's
return from the floor above.

"I don't know who did it," he said, "but congratulations."

"Really, Uncle Ned!" Lois said.

"What's the use of beating around the bush?" the doctor wanted
to know. "That girl was poison. Told her so myself. 'Cut out your
cheap little blitzkriegs against other women's men,' I said, 'or you'll
wake up some morning with your throat neatly slit!' She laughed at
me. 'What's the fun in going after something you can have for the

asking?' she said." The doctor's angry eyes lit on Bill Barnum. "That meant you, I guess!"

Bill Barnum continued to study his cigarette, but a dark flush crept over his face.

The doctor had only begun. "And you, David. You'd better get down on your knees and thank God this happened before you made a fool of youself!"

"Uncle Ned!"

"Facts are facts, Lois! Everyone here has talked about it behind your back, and they're probably talking about it all over town now. And, David, I don't mind saying I've been close to the horsewhipping point."

"Has anyone ever told you, Graves, that you're an interfering, cackling old hen?" David asked. His voice shook.

"Truth hurts, eh?" said the doctor, untouched. "Well, let it hurt, by gad! If it teaches you to be a man and not a louse, so much the better."

"Easy, David!" Haviland said.

Kelcey had taken a step forward, his fists doubled. He checked himself now. "It would be just as well if you got out of here," he said to the doctor, "if you haven't more official business."

"Naturally, I'm going," said Graves. "Trying to save the life of an honest, God-fearing woman, who has just brought a child into the world. A worth-while job!"

He turned to Lois and dropped a hand on her shoulder. His voice lost its harshness. "It's not so long ago that I brought you into the world, Lois. I'm on your team, and don't you forget it for a minute." He picked up his bag and walked out of the room.

"Crusty old coot," said Hiram from the doorway. He came into the room and dropped down into a big wing chair by the fire. "There's ways and means of commencin'," he said. "Mebbe the best is to get right to the point." He tilted his head to look at Kelcey. "Why'd you do it, David?" he asked.

David just glared at him.

"It's your gun," Hiram said.

"I kept the gun," said David, spacing his words, "in my workshop, as you damn' well know. It's been there on a holster on the wall all winter, as you and everyone else here also damn' well know. Most of you have handled it at some time or other. What's more, Hiram, I have no bullets. Whoever used it tonight had to supply his own cartridge clip. That ought to be something to work on."

"Of course, I ain't no detective, but it ain't much," said Hiram, "when you boil it down. Sayin' you ain't got bullets don't make it fact, David.... Now, don't git sore! I'm jest doin' my duty, and there ain't no one I c'n treat special. In the second place, there's a lot of fellers had guns like that in the last war. There's over fifty Legionnaires right in these parts." He shifted his cud of tobacco from one cheek to the other. "How about you an' this Phelps girl,

David? Havin' an affair, was you?"

There was an awkward pause, and then Ray Allen said, "If I thought David had been double-crossing my sister, Hiram, I'd have knocked his brains out."

"Now, that's a right brotherly speech," said Hiram approvingly.

"What about the two shots I heard and the car driving down the hill?" the major said. "Doesn't that pretty well eliminate David? He was here within seconds of the time Charity called him."

Haviland wondered if David thought this was another complicated way of throwing suspicion on him.

"Hold yer horses, Major. You're takin' it fer granted the feller in the car was the murderer."

"Well, wasn't he?"

"Ain't sayin' yes, ain't sayin' no," said Hiram. "Somebody drove down the mountain 'bout the time of the murder. But nobody seen him! Mebbe 'twas somebody after a deer. You don't know them shots was the ones killed Miss Phelps. Mebbe they was more."

"For God's sake, Hiram, get on with the investigation," David said.

"All right, David; what d'you want me to do? Houck out a rubber hose an' git to work on you? You ain't none of you bein' real helpful. Mr. Barnum, fer instance, was quite a friend of Miss Phelps an' he ain't sayin' a word. You liked her, didn't you, Mr. Barnum?"

"No," said Bill flatly.

"Why, now, I kind of got the idea..."

"You asked me if I liked her," Bill said. "I didn't. But I was off my nut about her...for a while. Or is that too subtle for you, Hiram?"

"No-o," said Hiram. "It's like me and beef kidney. They make me sick, but I love 'em!"

"There's a difference," said Bill, unsmiling. "I doubt if the beef kidney has any real intent to do you harm, Hiram."

"Like how?" Hiram asked.

Bill's hand shook a little as he lit a cigarette. "Some people hunt deer or birds," he said. "Diana hunted men. The more contented they were the better the sport. She didn't want you, David. She used to laugh at you behind your back...mimic the way you talked to her." David kept his face turned resolutely toward the windows. "Oh, it was very funny, I assure you. That was when I had the inside track. But I was too easy. I didn't have a wife to lie to or get rid of! I didn't even have a girl I was interested in. So she got bored with me."

"So?" said Hiram.

"So that was that," Bill said. "I came to with a jolt. I started to see her the way other people must have seen her."

"Mebbe you didn't like what you saw."

"I didn't."

"Mebbe you was so tangled up you couldn't git yourself free," the sheriff said.

"Look, Hiram," said Bill earnestly, "I write stories for a living that nobody buys. I live in a one-room shack in the village. I had nothing in the world that Diana wanted. She put me on the toboggan. It wasn't fun on the ride down, but when I hit the bottom I felt better. She never gave me a second thought, and that was okay with me."

"She was a case for a psychiatrist," Ray Allen said, looking at David.

Hiram shook his head. "All the same, I got to find out who done this."

Major Wilmot took a step forward off the hearth. "You had quite a shock when you first saw the body, didn't you, Haviland?" he asked.

"I certainly did, Major. For one awful moment I thought it was Charity. They changed coats, you know."

"Exactly," said Wilmot.

"I don't get it," said Haviland.

"It was dark. With her back turned and wearing Charity's coat, Diana could easily have been mistaken for her."

"Thatcher, you're not serious!" Lois Kelcey said.

"I'm afraid I am," said the major. "And if it's a possible explanation, then we must not forget that Charity is in danger!"

"For God's sake, Major!" said Haviland. "There's such a thing as carrying your loyalties too far."

Charity was looking at the major, her eyes round. "I bet anything that was it."

"Know anyone that had a scunner on you, Mrs. Haviland?" Hiram asked.

"Oh, a great many people are my enemy because I am always butting into their business," Charity said. "Why, there must be dozens of people who would be simply delighted if I was not around to tell them things, so I think the major is right."

"Charity, you idiot!" Haviland said.

"But, Paul, it was very clever of the major, and _you_ thought Diana was me, too.

Haviland laughed, but it was feeble laughter.

"Whether it makes sense to you or not, Haviland," said the major gravely, "Charity should be careful not to be alone."

"Well, by Judas," said Hiram, "it'd make a difference. Mebbe I ought to have another look around." He got up from his chair and struggled into his bearskin once more....

This, Haviland decided, was cockeyed. When Hiram had gone he took Charity by the wrist and led her out of the room. "Borrow yourself a coat," he said. "We're going walking."

The sun was up now and the countryside was white with frost. Haviland glanced down to the summerhouse and saw that Mason and Caldwell were on the job. He slipped his arm through Charity's and they walked slowly up and down the path.

"What was the idea?" he asked.

"What idea, darling?"

"Of announcing that you are a sinister character whom everyone would like to see dead. We've been over and over the system in the drills. Everybody connected with the Post knew that you would go to the phone. No mistake was made and you know damn well you haven't got an enemy in the world."

"But, Paul, I..."

"You saw Diana! Somebody wasn't fooling."

The look in her eyes told him she hadn't forgotten. "Oh, Paul, it was horrible. But Diana certainly had it coming to her, and I simply can't bear to think of Lois going to jail and weaving baskets and doing laundry."

"Lois!"

"But, of course, darling, it has to be Lois-- don't you see?"

"No, I don't see."

"Well, it's perfectly simple, darling, because you can tell any time that Lois looks at David that he is her whole life, because she is simply radiant when she looks at him."

"So she blew a hole in Diana because she loves David."

"Of course."

"You can't go around making accusations without evidence, baby, because you'll get in a hell of a lot of trouble."

"But I'm not making accusations, Paul; and besides I have got evidence."

"You what?"

"You see, darling, when I found Diana I ran back into the house and called to David and Lois. Then I called up the Army people and asked them about the bleeding. Then David came downstairs and I told him, and he went out to the summerhouse. Then Lois came down... in a negligee."

"That, I suppose, is her regular shooting outfit," Haviland said.

"Paul, you're being mean, and if you don't want to hear..."

"I definitely want to hear, kitten."

"Well, wearing that negligee was as good as saying that she was in bed when I called, which maybe she was, but she hadn't actually got into bed, because I found that out when I went up to her room a few minutes later because I wanted to wash my hands after touching Diana. Darling, her bed hadn't been turned down at all, so she hadn't been sleeping in it. And there were the shoes."

"Shoes?" Haviland was no longer amused.

"Her walking shoes which were on the hearth in her room were all covered with wet mud, so I knew she had just been out."

"Did you mention it to Lois?"

"No," Charity said. "I just burned the shoes!"

"You did what?"

"I burned the shoes," said Charity, "because I just couldn't bear the thought of Lois working in a jute box."

"Jute mill," he corrected patiently. "Where did you burn the shoes?"

"I threw them in the furnace, so I am quite sure they are gone by now."

"Do you know what the penalty is for suppressing evidence?" he asked.

"I didn't suppress anything, Paul; I just burned the shoes and--and--"

"And what?" he asked grimly.

"And turned down the bed and kind of lay on it for a minute, so if anyone else went up they wouldn't know Lois hadn't slept in it."

Haviland stood looking down at Charity's eager, excited face. "You're a world beater," he said, and kissed her.

But the fact remained this <u>was</u> evidence. Lois had stated the plane had waked her. Of course, she might not have been in bed. Haviland remembered there was a chaise lounge in the room. "But what about the shoes, chum?" he asked himself.

"You're sure about the mud being really wet, angel?"

"Of course, I'm sure," Charity said, "because after I put them in the furnace I had to go back upstairs to wash my hands again, which was when I fixed the bed."

It made sense. Lois wouldn't be the first woman who had killed because someone was poaching on her territory. It would have been simple enough. David sleeping in another room. Lois knowing every detail of the observer system, so that whenever a plane passed over she could be sure Diana would be alone for a minute or so. She would have no trouble finding David's gun. And it explained why the murderer had risked walking up directly behind Diana and placing the barrel of the gun against her back. Lois never did any shooting, so she might have felt she couldn't take the chance of missing, even from a few feet.

"I think, baby, we ought to go to Hiram with this," Haviland said. "Not Wilmot," he thought, remembering the major's warning that he'd be working for Lois.

Charity planted herself in front of him on the path. "If you do, Paul, I will leave you by the afternoon train." Then she was clinging to him. "Oh, darling, darling, if it had been you instead of David I'd have...I'd have..."

"You'd have what, baby?" he said gently.

"I'd have fought just the way Lois did."

A sudden warmth flooded Haviland. He didn't want to make decisions. He just wanted to get ahead with his job at the plant and with his life with Charity. The immediate necessity to act was averted by the appearance of Hiram on the path above them....

Hiram looked thoughtfully at Charity. "Mebbe I ought to send you down to your own house," he said, "and set a deputy to watchin' you till we settle this."

"Oh, Paul," Charity said.

"Hiram, listen!" said Haviland. "Get rid of the idea that someone was after Charity. I tell you it's the bunk, coat or no coat."

"Whole thing makes my head spin!" Hiram said. "The facts fit that way, but I don't hardly know a soul in town that wouldn't let Mrs. Haviland stick a knife in 'em and thank her."

"That's very sweet, Hiram, but somebody..."

Haviland gave her a dirty look.

Hiram shook his head. "I ain't much use on a case where they ain't nothin' to see," he said. "Been tryin' to check up on that car the major was talkin' about. I figgered whoever drove it must be parked some'eres, and you can track down tire marks. The trouble is this feller didn't park nowhere 'cept in the middle of of the road. There ain't many places 'longside where you can pull up on this hill, and, such as they is, he didn't use none of 'em. I covered it five hundred yards each side of the major's house."

"You think now it may have been the murderer, Hiram?" Haviland's voice sounded false in his own ears. He was thinking of muddy shoes and an unused bed.

"I think so more'n I did," Hiram said. "Figger it for yourself, Mr. Haviland. If a feller was goin' to do a little illegal huntin', he'd find a place to put his car in off the road, jest in case somebody come along and saw. 'Specially when he knowed people'd be comin' up an' down the mountain to the Post. But this feller don't do that. He left his car near enough the major's house so the major could hear him start up and drive down the mountain. After checkin' it I know that means he left his car right in the middle of the road. Why? So he could make a quick getaway. He was bidin' his time, and when he'd done his work he beat it out o' there in one hell of a hurry."

Haviland was frowning. He would feel a lot better about things if a case could be built up against somebody besides Lois. An honest case, of course.

"There's a flaw in it, Hiram," he said. "If it was the murderer, he had to wait till there was a plane overhead...when the girls would be separated and their attention centered. There was no way he could tell when a plane would go over. Might not be one at all. So he would have to hang around for the two hours of their watch. Wouldn't that be risky, right in the middle of the road?"

"It might and it might not," said Hiram. "He might have a right up here. Might be one of the watchers that was jest leavin' or jest comin' on duty. He could say his car stalled or somethin', and they'd be no cause to wonder."

"That's possible."

"And he might have an even better excuse'n that," Hiram said. "He might be a member of the family."

"Kelcey again, eh?"

"Nope," said Hiram. "Wa'n't thinkin' of him. 'Cause't would be queer if he was seen goin' away from the house in the middle of the night. I was thinkin' of Mr. Allen."

"Ray?"

"He's Lois's brother, ain't he? Got the run of the place, ain't he? It ain't no secret the Phelps girl was on the point of bustin' up the

Kelceys. Allen probably told her to lay off or he'd give her what for. She didn't lay off."

"Wait a minute," Haviland said. "That's good reasoning, Hiram, except that Ray Allen picked Bill Barnum up in town and brought him here in time for the four-o'clock watch."

"And didn't Barnum say they was nearly late? 'Round ten of four Allen picked him up. This car the major heard pulled out twenty past three or thereabouts. Hell, he could have drove to Barnum's place in low gear in all that time. It adds up, Mr. Haviland. He knowed all about the gun...where it was an' all. Didn't he say if he thought Kelcey was double-crossin' his sister he'd beat his brains out? Showed he had feelin's on the subject." Hiram shrugged. "Of course, I ain't no detective," he said.

"And if you two have any sense you'll start talking about the weather," Charity said, "because here comes Ray."

Ray Allen came down the path buttoning his leather jacket. He was bareheaded and in need of a shave. There were dark hollows under his eyes.

"We've got trouble," Ray said. "The Taylors, who are supposed to relieve Caldwell and Mason, just phoned. Down with the flu, they say, but its ten to one Mabel Taylor has hysterics at the idea of spending two hours in the place where Diana was killed. On top of that, there's an alert just come over the radio which means we've got to keep manning the Post."

Haviland glanced up into the sky. "Those fellows that went over a while back were headed for business. Well, we'll piece out the watch somehow. Bill still here?"

Ray nodded. "We can manage," he said. "I guess he wouldn't mind another stretch if he had a cup of coffee to hold him together. I'll sub with Mason till he's freshened up, if you say."

"Swell," said Haviland. "By the way, Ray, did you spend the night up here or down in the village?"

"In the village," Allen said. "Why?"

"We were trying to dope out an explanation for the car the major heard. I thought if you'd stayed up here it might have been you going down to get Bill."

Ray shook his head. "Slept in my rooms at the Inn," he said. "Pounded my ear right through the alarm, which is why we were so nearly late." His eyes narrowed. "Wait a minute. You're really asking me for an alibi, aren't you?"

"Something like that, Ray."

Ray laughed. "Well, I turn out to be lucky. When I got down to the lobby I noticed my wristwatch had stopped. I woke up the night clerk and had him get the correct time from the telephone operator. He'll remember. It was ten minutes to four."

"I guess that's that," said Haviland. "Take over for Caldwell, will you?" And when Ray was out of hearing he said to Hiram, "That sounded straight enough, didn't it?"

"It proves," said Hiram, "that he was in the lobby of the Inn at ten to four, and that's all it does prove. It don't take him off the mountain at a quarter past three."

With his arm around Charity, Haviland watched Hiram walk up the path to the kitchen. It made things better to feel her there, warm and close.

"Look, kitten," Haviland said, "you haven't said anything about Lois to anyone else?"

"Of course, I haven't, Paul, because who can you trust not to go blabbing it to Hiram?"

"If you come across any more evidence, let it alone! If you have to talk, tell me."

"Yes, Paul."

He looked at her and shook his head. He wished he wasn't so dead certain she would plunge in over her depth if the opportunity presented itself....

Haviland didn't go into the house with Charity because just as they reached the door Dr. Graves came up the drive. Haviland thought he had gone back to his baby case in Bradford Hollow.

"Nothing I can do there at the moment," he told Haviland, taking him aside. "Had to make arrangements for having the body removed." The doctor cocked his head on one side. "Sounds like planes."

Haviland looked up into the empty sky. The throb of motors grew louder in his ears.

He went down the path to the summerhouse. Major Wilmot was there, along with Mason and Ray Allen. The blind man's head was raised, the sun glinting against his glasses.

"Hello, Haviland. Recognized your step," he said. "They're coming back from the south. Plenty of them. Twenty or thirty, I should judge. Bombers, fighters. See anything?"

Haviland picked up the glasses and focused them down the valley. Unless you're looking at just the right level it's hard to find planes against the horizon, particularly when the sun is bright. At last he saw them, like a flock of migrating birds.

"Ray! Hop to it, fella. Get in your call. I'll join you in a moment." Ray ran up the path. "Bombers at about ten thousand, fighter planes at fifteen."

"Can you identify them?" Wilmot asked.

"Not yet. Can't wait," said Haviland. He raced for the house. Ray was at the phone. He passed the receiver to Haviland.

"Army.... Go ahead, please."

"Army Flash," said Haviland. "Many-- All types-- Seen-- High-- 66B-- Southeast-- Fifteen miles-- Northwest."

"Check. Thank you," said the Army operator.

Haviland replaced the receiver on the hook. Mason came in through the door. "They're our planes coming back, Mr. Haviland. Looks like one of 'em is in trouble."

Haviland went out the door and down the path to the Post again. The armada of planes was very close now. He could see the U.S. Army insignia on the wings and fuselage. One big four-motor bomber had fallen behind and was flying dangerously close to the top of the hills. He could hear the irregular coughing of its motors. He found himself struggling with the insane desire to shout at the top of his lungs at the pilot. If he'd turn south, he could glide into the North Johnsbury airport.

Haviland turned and ran for the house again. He caught a glimpse of Charity, Lois, David, and all the rest of them on the terrace, watching. He signaled Ray to put through another flash call. As they waited for a connection, Major Wilmot came up the path, tapping with his stick.

"Perhaps I could handle the telephone end," he said. His lips twisted. "I'm no earthly good out there."

"Right, sir. Report that the planes sighted in our Flash Message have been identified as our own. One bomber apparently circling for a forced landing."

The colonel at Air Command pointed to the map table. It was ten o'clock. "Looks like the show's about over," he said. "Our interceptors and bombers seem to have driven off the enemy without damage to objectives."

"Casualties?" the British staff captain asked.

"Too soon for reports on that," the colonel said grimly, "but we've a report of a bomber in distress near Post 66B."

"That's your murder spot, isn't it?"

"Right. Reports coming in steadily though. I must compliment them on keeping their end going in spite of the mess they're in. They haven't slipped once."

Haviland watched the wounded bomber glide slowly downward. His breath was caught in his throat. He couldn't tell from the ground whether or not it was about to crash into the hillside. It went down over the crest of the hills and out of sight. He stood there, as if he expected to hear the sound of the crash that would take place miles away, if it did take place.

Then somebody had him by the arm and was shaking him. "Paul, for God's sake!"

It was Bill Barnum. His face was dead-white. It's Charity," he said. "Some kind of spasm. Poison, I think. Thank God, the doctor's here."

"Poison!" Haviland sprinted for the house.

Charity was stretched out on the couch in the living-room. It seemed to Haviland as he hurried to her that there were hundreds of people in the room just staring at her...doing nothing. Her tiny body was rigid except for a terrible spasmodic jerking. Her eyes were wide and panic-stricken. There was a little trickle of blood on her chin where she had bitten her lip. Haviland felt his heart turn into a cold, dead lump.

"Darling, darling!" he cried, going to his knees.

Her eyes turned to his face, but she couldn't speak. Then that dreadful yanking of her limbs. Haviland took her in his arms and held her close.

"Baby, what happened? What in God's name happened?"

"Well, do you want her to die?" demanded a harsh voice behind him.

Dr. Graves was there, his sleeves rolled up, holding what Haviland guessed was a stomach pump. "All of you...get out of here!" the doctor ordered. "Except Mrs. Watson. I'll need her help."

"I'm sticking," said Haviland.

"You're getting out," said the doctor.

Very gently Haviland let Charity down onto the couch. "I'll be right here...right outside the door," he whispered. "Chin up!" He stood up and followed the others blindly into the dining-room.

A hand touched his shoulder. It was Major Wilmot. "I was afraid of this, Haviland. How did it happen?"

"That's what I'm going to find out!" Haviland said. The blood was pounding in his ears. He walked up to Hiram. "What the hell kind of detective are you, Hiram, letting the murderer take a second crack right under your nose?"

"I never laid no claim to bein' a detective," Hiram said unhappily. "But could be the major was right about your wife, couldn't it? Looks like she was the one the murderer was after."

Haviland's rage grew. "You chump! That cockeyed theory put notions into someone's head. Someone trying to make it look right, so you'll turn away from the main trail. Damn it, isn't anyone going to tell me what happened?"

"Easy, son," Hiram said. "We don't exac'ly know. We was all on the terrace, watchin' them planes. All of a sudden Charity let out a yip. I took a look at her and figured she was havin' a fit, so I grab aholt of her to keep her from thrashin' round, and stuck a handkerchief in her mouth so's she wouldn't bite her tongue. Then the doc said not to be crazy...that it wa'n't no fit. 'Twas poison, he said."

"How did she get it?"

"We was all drinkin' some concoction of Kelcey's," Hiram said. His pale eyes drifted to David. "How about it, David?"

"In the first place," said David, "I didn't make it. I suggested an eggnog for everyone, and I got the rum and brandy from the liquor cabinet, but Mrs. Watson and Lois made it. I carried the tray in from the kitchen to the terrace and everyone selected their own glass."

"That's right, Dave," Hiram said. "Them glasses was set down any which way. We just picked 'em up without anyone tellin' us which was ours."

"Paul!" Bill Barnum interrupted in a hollow-sounding voice. "I handed Charity her drink. I was standing by the tray and she came up and..."

"Just any drink?" Haviland asked.

"There were half a dozen glasses on the tray, Paul. I..."

"The drink had to be poisoned, Haviland, after Charity had taken it from the tray," Major Wilmot said. "No one could be sure what glass she'd take beforehand. She must have put it down somewhere."

"Why, sure, Mr. Haviland; that's how it had to be," Hiram said.

"Have you searched these people?" Haviland demanded. "You have to carry poison in something."

"I reckon there's no use in that," Hiram sighed. "This feller wa'n't born yesterday, Mr. Haviland. They won't be nothin' to find. We got to start figgerin' this thing over again. We been tryin' to find someone who was out to git Miss Phelps. Now we know 'twas Mrs. Haviland was meant all along."

"That's utter rot and nonsense," Haviland said. "The reason this happened to Charity is because she knew who the murderer was! Only, it was tried too late. Because whether the doctor pulls her through or not I know the answer." He turned on Lois so savagely that she backed away. "So you made the drinks, Lois?"

"Why-- why, yes, Paul, Mrs. Watson and I made them."

"Then you or someone protecting you meant to murder my wife. Because she knew you'd shot Diana, Lois!"

"Paul!" Lois reached out instinctively to her husband.

"You're off your nut, Paul," Ray Allen said sharply. "If I didn't know how you're feeling about Charity, I'd..."

Haviland brushed him aside. His eyes never wavered from Lois. "So you didn't hear the shots that killed Diana, but the plane woke you up? That's your story, isn't it?"

"Yes, Paul. And it's the truth. For Heaven's sake..."

"Then would you mind explaining why your bed was never slept in? How your shoes were covered with mud at three-thirty in the morning?"

"So it was Charity!" Lois said. She glanced at her husband. "I thought David..." She looked back down at the fingers of her right hand, which were clutching David's arm. "What I told you and Hiram was the truth, Paul. I was asleep. The plane did wake me up. But you didn't ask me if I was in bed. I wasn't. I was on the chaise lounge in my room."

"And the shoes?"

"You didn't ask me if I'd been out," Lois said. The life left her voice. "I had been...for hours. I had been walking to try to get tired enough to sleep. I don't suppose I'd been back in the house for more than twenty minutes when ...when it happened."

"So you were just out walking at three in the morning!"

"I was just out walking," Lois said. She raised her eyes to his defiantly. "There seem to be no secrets about my life any longer. You all know how David felt about Diana. Well, I knew it, too. I knew that with Diana coming to the house, being out there in the garden for two hours, David would be thinking about her. That's a kind of torture you and Charity wouldn't understand, Paul.

"I couldn't sleep. I'd been trying to fight this thing out with myself, Paul. If it had been anyone but Diana...someone I thought could really make David happy...I'd have arranged for him to have his freedom. But I couldn't be sure that was the right thing to do. So after David had gone to sleep in the next room I went out for a walk. I thought if I got sufficiently tired I might sleep...might be able to forget for a little. So I took the long trail to the top of Glendon and back. That was about eleven. You know that must take at least three and a half or four hours. When I got back I was exhausted. Charity and Diana were at the Post. David was asleep where I'd left him. I went to my room, got out of my wet clothes, and into a negligee. Then I lay down on the chaise lounge."

In spite of himself Haviland believed her.

"Later," Lois said, "after Charity had called us and we found out what had happened I came up to my room to dress. The shoes were gone. My bed was turned down and made to look as if I'd slept in it." Her voice was suddenly unsteady. "I-- I thought David had done it. I thought he had decided I was the murderer and was protecting me. God help me, Paul, I got some happiness out of that! I thought if he-- if he was prepared to protect me then perhaps-- perhaps there was still some chance for us."

The door from the living-room opened and Dr. Graves stood there. "You can come in now if you want to, Haviland."

Charity was still lying on the couch but the rigidity was gone. Haviland sat down and took her cold hands in his. His eyes went to the doctor's face anxiously.

"A close thing," said the doctor, "but I think she'll do."

Charity opened her eyes. "I told him not to let you in," she whispered.

"Charity!"

"Because I look like somebody's old washing, darling."

"Dope!" He leaned over and kissed her. "Listen, baby; you realize somebody tried to knock you off? What did you do?"

She turned her face away and there were tears in her eyes. "I-- I didn't think she'd--"

"Darling, it wasn't Lois," he said. "I'm almost sure."

"Lois!" The doctor was indignant.

Charity's lips moved. "You...you?"

"I let her have it, kitten," Haviland said. "She explained about the shoes and the bed and I think it's all right."

Charity closed her eyes and gave his hand a feeble little squeeze.

"Listen, Charity. Somebody slipped poison into your drink. Can you remember how it happened?"

"I don't know, Paul darling."

"Bill says he handed you a glass off the tray."

"He-- he did. But I picked it out, Paul. He said would I have one with or without a cherry. I-- I pointed to one, and he gave it to me."

"And after that?"

Charity raised a hand to her eyes. Her voice trailed away. "I've b-been trying hard to remember, Paul. I was describing what was going on to Major Wilmot. I put my glass down on the table on the terrace. It could have been anyone."

"That will have to do," said Dr. Graves. "She couldn't lick her weight in butterflies right now. Mrs. Watson's fixing one of her guestrooms for her. Will you carry her up?"

Haviland lifted Charity in his arms.

Mrs. Watson met him in the upstairs hall. "Put her down on the bed and skeddadle," she said. "I'll tend to her."

Haviland went first into the room. When he had put Charity down he said, "I don't want her left alone for a minute, Mrs. Watson."

"My, my, my," said Mrs. Watson; "you talk like I was some kind of ignoramus. Would I likely let someone in here after what's happened? And that goes for that blundering galoot of a Hiram, too."

"We've got to find out who did this, Mrs. Watson. If I can count on you not to let anyone in here...not anyone..."

"You run along," said Mrs. Watson. "It's about time someone with brains took charge. For all I know you may be it. That Hiram! All he does is eat, eat, eat, and tramp around, and gossip!"

As Haviland returned to the hall Major Wilmot had just reached the top of the stairs. "Haviland? How is she?"

"Graves said she'll do. But I still can't buy your theory, Major," Haviland said. "But it doesn't make much difference. We're both after the same guy."

"That's true," said Wilmot. "Thanks for giving Lois a break."

"She sounded on the level. I had to. There are alibis that need checking with it. Bill and Ray's for instance. If Hiram will let me go down to the village, I may be able to do some leg work."

Wilmot frowned. "I hate to keep harping on it, Haviland, but Charity shouldn't be left alone."

"Mrs. Watson has promised not to leave her and not to let anyone into the room."

"Haviland!" David Kelcey was calling from the foot of the stairs. "Telephone for you from Air Command."

Haviland went to the hall phone. "Haviland, Chief Observer at Post 66B," said Haviland.

"Colonel Howard, here," said a cheerful voice. "Wanted to congratulate you on carrying out your duties under difficulties. First-rate job."

"Thank you, sir. There was one we missed, I'm afraid, but..."

"You reported everything that flew over your area," said the colonel. "Best record of the whole district. Hope your troubles there are being straightened out."

"Thank you, sir. I imagine the authorities will manage."

Haviland stood looking at the telephone for a long time after he'd hung up. There was one plane that had not been reported.

"The Chief Observer keeps a file of all actual messages sent."
Instructions for Observers.

Hiram was sitting in a chair by the fire in the library. He looked very much, to Haviland, like a man taking a catnap.

"I guess they ain't no reason why you shouldn't go down to the village," he said, when Haviland asked. "So long as you git back here by around one o'clock."

"Don't tell me something is going to happen at one o'clock," Haviland said.

"Well," said Hiram, "I got to git things cleaned up by then on account of I got to drive my mail route at half past. You can't hold up Uncle Sam's mail, y'know."

"For God's sake." Haviland went out, slamming the door on Uncle Sam.

On the terrace he encountered Major Wilmot again, pacing restlessly up and down.

"I got the green light from Hiram," he said. "I'm off."

"First rate," said Wilmot. "I'll see if Hiram and I can't sort this thing out somehow while you're gone."

"It'll have to be before one o'clock," said Haviland, still indignant. "Hiram's got to drive his mail route!" He started toward his car and then came back. "Say, Major. You heard the plane that flew over the Post at the time Diana was killed?"

"Yes, of course."

"I noticed you were able to distinguish the various types of motors during that flurry a while back. What about that one?"

The major raised a hand to slap himself on the forehead. "God, Haviland, what a fathead!" he said. "In all the excitement I'd forgotten. It wasn't a fighter or bomber, I'll swear to that. It was a small private plane. As a matter of fact, its motor had a rhythm like the ones at the local airport. Weren't they supposed to be grounded?"

"They were," said Haviland. "Strict orders from Air Command."

Haviland drove to the house in the village and picked up some things he guessed Charity would need. Then he went out to the North Johnsbury airport. The place was deserted except for the manager, a chap named Overton. Overton was fuming.

"First excitement in months, and I have to hold the fort!" he said. "Bomber made a forced landing on the golf course at Chatterton. My crew's gone over to help them out. I have to sit here and answer the phone."

"Tough luck," Haviland said.

"Nothing to do here any more," Overton said. "Everything grounded."

"Everything?" Haviland asked.

"Just one plane out of here in the last twenty-four hours," Overton said.

"What was that?"

"Middle of the night. Doctor's orders."

"Doctor?"

"Sure. Doc Graves. Had me rout out a pilot and send him off to Albany."

Haviland fought to keep his voice casual. "What time was that? A plane passed over in the night that we missed."

Overton got the time sheet from the drawer of his desk. "Took off at three-twelve A.M.," he said. "Say, that murder is a nasty business. Miss Phelps was in and out of here often. Pretty hot number."

"Too hot to handle," Haviland said. "What did the doctor want, do you know?"

"Oxygen tanks," Overton said. "Some white trash up in Bradford Hollow had a baby. Family name of Garrity. No dough. No nothing. But you know doc. If they can't afford a hospital, he'll see they get the best care, just the same."

"Would the plane have flown over our post?"

"Right over it. Matter of fact, the pilot told me when he came back he wondered if maybe his wasn't the plane that was going over when Miss Phelps was shot."

"I don't think there's a doubt of it," Haviland said. "When did he get back, and did he fly over our post again?"

"About an hour ago," said Overton, "and he skirted the other side of the mountains because there was a big flight of planes coming up the valley."

"There was," said Haviland. His face had taken on hard lines. "Did the doctor phone on for the plane?"

"Nope. He drove in here, hell-bent for leather. No phones in Bradford Hollow. Telephoned the Albany hospital from here."

"Did he wait for your pilot to take off?"

"Hell, no. The doc don't light long anywhere. Always on the go."

Haviland thanked the airport manager and drove away. He was beginning to get a picture of things...one he disliked.

He turned off on the road to Bradford Hollow. After a number of inquiries he located the Garrity place. It was a ramshackle gray frame building, its shingle roof patched with tar paper and its weather-beaten barn seeming to lean away from the prevailing northwest wind. The yard was cluttered with broken machinery and useless wagons. Under them a few scrawny chickens scratched for sustenance.

A tall scarecrow of a man came out of the house as Haviland pulled into the yard. His overall pants were torn, unmended. There was several days' growth of gray beard on a sunken face. "Oh, I thought you was the doctor," he said, as Haviland got out.

"Mr. Garrity?"

"Uh-huh."

"I was looking for the doctor myself. How is your wife doing?"

The man sighed. "The district nurse is tendin' her," he said. "Looks like them gas tanks jest did git here in time. Miss Kendall thinks she'll do all right now." Garrity wiped the back of his hand across his cheek, and Haviland was horrified to see tears in his eyes.

"Doctor was here most of the night, wasn't he?" Haviland asked.

"Did you ever see a feller buckle down an' roll up his sleeves an' fight, mister? That's the way he done with Carrie. In the middle of the night he says to me, 'Sam,' he says, 'we're gonna need oxygen,' he says. 'How much does it cost?' I ask him, on account of I ain't got hardly a cent of ready cash. 'It ain't gonna cost you a penny, Sam,' he says. 'The thing is to git it here,' he says. 'Have to send a plane to Albany for it.'"

"How long was the plane gone?" Haviland asked.

Garrity scuffled a worn shoe in the dirt. "You married, mister?"

"Yes, I am."

"Well, sir, if you was settin' by your wife, a-knowin' she was gonna die, and the only person who might save her left you alone and didn't come back for a while...I reckon maybe you'd think he'd cleared out forever. Seemed like a year afore he got back."

"But you don't know exactly how long it was?"

Garrity's bloodshot eyes narrowed. "What are you gittin' at, mister? If they's somethin' you wanna know about the doc, why don't you ast him yerself? I guess this is him a-comin' now."

The doctor's mud-splashed car bounced into the yard. Graves jumped out, his black bag in his hand. He didn't notice Haviland till he was on top of him. "What the blazes are you doing here, Haviland?"

"Looking for you," Haviland said. "I'd like to talk to you for a few minutes."

"You'll have to wait till I've seen Mrs. Garrity," he said.

"Okay," said Haviland. "I'll wait."

He sat down on the tail of a wagon and lit a cigarette. He wasn't going to enjoy this. The doctor was in the house about ten minutes before he reappeared. He walked up to Haviland.

"Well, son, what is it?"

Haviland inhaled on his cigarette. "I suppose," he said, "there's one problem in morality that will always go unsettled. That is whether or not it is ever justified to take a human life."

"What are you leading up to, son?" the doctor asked.

"Well Doctor, I know that you shot Diana Phelps," Haviland said.

The doctor said nothing. His iodine-stained fingers fiddled with the metal catch on his bag. "So you know that, eh?"

"It was the timing," Haviland said. "We know that a car was on the mountain just at the time the plane came over. Wilmot heard them. I've been wondering how anyone could take the chance of leaving his car parked in the middle of the road. But he could if he knew exactly when a plane was due. He thought the only person who would know that was the C.O. at Air Command. It turns out there was someone else. You, Doctor. That plane was the one from the airport, going for your oxygen tanks. You had time to get up there before the pilot took off. You knew he would fly over the Post. You knew the minute the plane appeared that Charity would go into the house and Diana would be left alone. You knew where David kept his gun, and you supplied yourself with bullets for it. You did the job, chucked the gun away, drove down the mountain, and came back here. You had a good alibi. Garrity had no sense of time."

"I ran a pretty serious risk leaving my car in the road even for a few minutes, didn't I?" Graves asked. "Mine's the one car everyone would recognize."

"Not much of a risk. There was no traffic at that time of the night. You would be down the mountain before Ray and Bill came up."

"I see."

"All this might be difficult to prove," said Haviland, " but for the fact you made a mistake in dealing with Charity."

"Good God," said the doctor in a startled voice, "you think I poisoned Charity?"

"What else can I think?" Haviland kept his eyes on the chickens scratching by the Garrity's porch. "The attack on her was an impromptu undertaking. I warned her. I warned her not to go looking for clues. But she simply can't keep her nose out of other people's business. I don't know what she found out. Maybe you'll tell me?"

"You're loony," said the doctor.

"Am I? Then perhaps you'll tell me who else in the crew had access to poison at exactly the right moment?" He nodded toward the black bag. "Who besides you, Doctor?"

"Anyone might," said the doctor. "And, if I did poison her, why did I work my fool head off to save her?"

"What else would you do, with Mrs. Watson standing at your elbow?"

"And why did I kill Diana?"

"Because of Lois," Haviland said. "I know you think of her as if she were your own daughter. Diana was raising hell with Lois's happiness. I think you decided Lois and David would never straighten themselves out as long as Diana lived."

"So I work out an elaborate time schedule and alibi, and blow her to bits with a blunderbuss!" The doctor laughed dryly. "Son, there are a million ways a doctor can commit a murder without getting caught. For instance, I gave Diana cold inoculations all winter. I could have slipped typhoid germs into the serum. Instead, you claim I fixed an elaborate thing with a plane, rushed up the mountain, running all kinds of chances of being seen, shot her in the back, making enough noise so that Wilmot could hear me more than two hundred yards away, dashed down the mountain, making more racket, and that I then poisoned your wife because she found out the awful truth, but go to the further trouble to save her so that I'll have to get rid of her all over again. Come off it, son; the strain's got you down."

"You wouldn't use those medical means of murder," Haviland said. "There are autopsies, you know. And, if some kind of medical hanky-panky was discovered, you'd be the only suspect!"

"That's swell, son," Graves said, "except that I'm the coroner. I'd perform the autopsy." He shook his head. "You know, I wonder I didn't think of it."

Haviland slid off the tailboard and stepped on his cigarette. "That's pretty clever stuff, Doctor. Maybe I'm being a sucker, but I want you to come back to the Kelceys' with me while I put this case to Hiram. I hope you'll come along without making a fuss."

"What could I do about it?" the doctor said angrily. "I'm thirty years older than you!"

Hiram listened. He sat in the big chair, tugging at the ends of his red mustache. "It's slick as a brown trout," he said, when Haviland had finished. "Only trouble is you c'n figger jest as slick three other ways."

"What three ways?" Haviland demanded.

"Well, outside of this here case you've lined up against the doc-- which I don't believe, on account of I've known the doc for forty years-- take the daisy your wife fixed up against Mrs. Kelcey. Lois might have been climbin' the mountain and she might have been polecat huntin'. And she made that drink for Mrs. Haviland. Then there's my own against Mr. Allen. Then David kind of hinted there might be a case against your wife, Mr. Haviland."

"Why, damn him!" said Haviland.

"Well, it could be," said Hiram. "We only got her word fer what happened. There was that plane she didn't report. Mebbe she didn't have time, what with fetchin' the gun and doin' a job on Miss Phelps."

"And I suppose she poisoned herself!"

"Why, now, Mr. Haviland, that wouldn't be so dumb if she was guilty, would it?"

"If she did," said Dr. Graves, "she came within a whisker of overdoing it."

"While you was gone," Hiram said, "the major and I set here, thinkin' what we know about this murder.

"Now, this here murderer had to know this place. Had to know 'bout this Observer Service. He had to be able to git bullets fer the gun, if Dave is tellin' the truth 'bout not havin' none. That'd be simple, on account of like I said, there's quite a few ownin' auto-matics. Doc, mebbe you got one of them automatics. Come to think of it, you was a medical officer, wasn't you?"

"I was," the doctor snapped.

"The trouble with you, Hiram Hargrove," said an acid voice from the doorway, "is talk, talk, talk. You don't do anything!"

Haviland was on his feet. "What are you doing here, Mrs. Watson? You promised not to leave Charity alone."

"Now, now, now, don't fret yourself," said Mrs. Watson. "She's all right, but she keeps asking for you, so I come down to fetch you. I left the major with her. No one'll bother her."

"God Almighty!" said Hiram. His lanky body seemed to catapult out of the the chair. He swept past Haviland and the doctor into the hall and took the stairs three at a time. Haviland, his heart pounding against his ribs, followed.

Hiram didn't stop for doorknobs. He smashed his shoulder against the paneling of the door and went sprawling into the room. Haviland, at his heels, brought up short at the doorway. Hiram's charge up the stairs had built a nameless panic in him. One thing he knew was that Charity was in danger. But what he saw was an anticlimax.

Charity looking incredibly improved, was propped against her pillows. Major Wilmot had turned from the window at the far end of the room, a half-smile on his face.

"Drop that, Mrs. Haviland!" Hiram said.

Then Haviland saw the tray across Charity's knees. Hiram snatched it away from her. He held it out to Dr. Graves, who pushed past Haviland into the room. "What about this stuff, Doc?"

"But, Hiram!" Charity said. "It's perfectly delicious chicken broth Mrs. Watson made for me, and why did you come charging in that way?"

"There's nothing the matter with this," said Dr. Graves.

Hiram let out his breath in a long sigh. "You sure are shot with luck, Mrs. Haviland!" He took a bandanna from his hip pocket and mopped his face. The other members of the party were crowding Haviland in the doorway-- the Kelceys, Ray Allen, Bill Barnum, Mason, Mrs. Watson.

"I hate to do it, but I guess I better 'fore I scare myself to death," Hiram said. "Darn it, Major Wilmot, I gotta arrest you for the murder of Diana Phelps."

There was a shocked silence until, with a cry, Lois Kelcey moved to Wilmot's side.

The major was smiling. "Hiram, you take my breath away!" he said.

"Think nothing of it, Major," said Dr. Graves. "They just finished strapping me into the electric chair...and then unstrapping me!"

"I ain't happy 'bout it," said Hiram, "but I'll jest have to go ahead the way I see it, and then you can sue me for false arrest, or have me tarred 'n' feathered, or whatever you like."

"You're being ridiculous, Hiram," Lois said. "I know you're anxious to settle this, but really! Why, you, yourself established the fact that the murderer escaped down the mountain in a car. Thatch can't drive!"

"Why, now, Lois," said Hiram gently, "if you'll stop t' think you'll remember 'twas the major, not me, who done the establishin'. Trouble is he kinda slipped up in the tellin'. Lay awake all night, he says. Heard the plane, the shots, and that car there a-leavin'. But he never mentioned hearin' it arrive. Kinda strange, don't you think? Then I found it could never have been parked nowheres 'cept in the middle of the road, right where nobody could git by it. The major must of forgot the mud could tell me a story, too. I ain't no detective, but I'm afeard there never was no automobile, Lois."

"What nonsense!" Lois said. "Can a blind man shoot a woman to death in the pitch-dark?"

"I guess," said Hiram, "it's always pitch-dark fer a blind man. We been tryin' to figger why the murderer walked right into the summerhouse and put the gun against Miss Phelps's back. Now, a blind man would have to do that, Lois, 'cause he couldn't be sure of hittin' anythin' unless he could feel the target right onto the end of his gun.

"He could travel your garden like the back of his hand. You folks had had a dozen drills for this here air show, so he knowed the first time a plane come over durin' that watch Miss Phelps'd be alone at the Post. All he had to do was git Dave's gun. Hell, he had bullets, I reckon, him bein' a major. Then he waited fer a plane. He wa'n't runnin' no risk. Suppose someone seen him in the garden? He lives next door. This here house is a kind of second home to him. He was part of this Warning Service. 'Course the gun would be hid in his overcoat pocket. If somebody did see him, he'd jest have to bide his time for another chance to git Miss Phelps. And, another thing, he wouldn't have been fooled by the gals changin' coats, 'cause he couldn't see the changin' been did."

"I simply refuse to believe it," Lois said. She had slipped her hand through Wilmot's arm.

"And I guess he could of got aholt of poison, all right," Hiram went on. "'Twas the fall of '39 when you tried t'commit suicide, wa'n't it, Major?"

Wilmot's white teeth bit into the stem of his pipe. "Who told you that tale, Hiram?"

"Why," said Hiram, "I carry the U.S. mail, don't I? Catch up with most of the talk 'round town, Major. Everybody said what a swell guy you was. Felt mighty sorry for you, they did. Said you got depressed when the war broke out in '39. Tried to poison yourself. Mason found you, phoned up here, and was lucky enough to catch the doc payin' a visit. He pulled you out of it."

"That's correct," said Dr. Graves.

"Mrs. Watson was tellin' me, only t'day, how Mrs. Kelcey nursed you; used to read t' you an' bring you special things t' eat while you was gettin' well."

"Lois was, and is, a saint," said the major.

"And I don't believe a single word of this trumped-up case!" Lois said. "Thatcher, tell them it isn't so."

The major smiled again. "You know, Hiram, I'm afraid you're guilty of a crime yourself."

"A million of 'em in my time, Major," said Hiram imperturbably. "Why, when I was goin' on four years old..."

"The crime I had in mind,"said the major,"is belittling your own talents. In spite of your protestations, you turn out to be a damn' good detective. And I can tell by the tone of your voice I won't be able to talk you out of it."

"'Fraid not, Major."

"Thatcher!"

"There's no use bucking it, Lois," Wilmot said. "Hiram had it taped right to the handle. I shot Diana. There never was any car going down the mountain."

"Well, I'll be a..." Dr. Graves muttered to himself.

"God knows I'd waited long enough for the chance this observation post gave me," Wilmot said. "I knew about David's gun. I'd handled it often. I still like to heft 'em. I used David's instead of my own, as a red herring. Like the car. I had bullets, as Hiram guessed." He drew a deep breath. "Mason is a sound sleeper. I slipped out of the house shortly after I heard Diana's car drive up the hill. I went to David's workshop, got the gun, and fitted my cartridge clip into it. Then I went down behind the hedge near the summerhouse. I was so close I could hear the sound of Diana's and Charity's voices. At last a plane came. I heard Charity run up the path. Then I walked into the summerhouse." The major's voice hardened. "I spoke to her. 'Oh, hello,' she said. I could tell she hadn't even turned around. She was always contemptuous of me. I was sorry she didn't turn. I wanted her to see the gun in my hand. I wanted her to feel one moment of terror. But I couldn't wait. So I put the gun against her back and fired... twice."

There was a sharp intake of Lois's breath. "But why, Thatcher? Why?"

The major's smile was twisted. "People with infirmities are apt to have somewhat different values. I don't have to tell you that when I first came to live in Fairview ten years ago I fell in love with you. You knew it then. I think perhaps if I'd asked you you might have married me. But I didn't ask you, because I knew there was a piece of shrapnel in my skull that might some day make me useless. Well, it happened. One morning I woke up in darkness. Oh, I was ready to face it. I had lost you, but you were near by, and you were kind, and it was as much as I could hope for. It was bad when you married David, but you stayed on here.

"For God's sake, don't be sorry for me," Wilmot said harshly. "I'm satisfied now, Lois. When this war started, two years ago, I hit bottom because all I'd lost, all I'd fought for, had been for nothing. Greed and violence and outlawry had the upper hand again."

Haviland's arm tightened around Charity.

"So I tried to poison myself," Wilmot said. "You pulled me out of the shadow, Doctor. I began to think there was some reason why I should go on." He patted Lois's hand on his arm.

"Lots of good chaps go off the trolley over women like Diana. David might have come to his senses without anyone's help. When he didn't I decided to take a hand. Diana represented to me all the things the whole civilized world is fighting: selfishness, ruthlessness, grabbing what doesn't belong to you. Worse than that, she represented a kind of propaganda, against decency. So...so there was still a blow I could strike for my kind of life, my kind of people. I had killed a good many innocent men on the battlefield, Lois. I confess I had no compunctions about adding one guilty person to that list."

The major turned his sightless black spectacles toward Charity. "Charity, my dear, you must believe I never meant to kill you. I saw no particular need to pay for Diana's murder if it could be avoided, but my one aim was to keep Hiram and Paul away from any scent that got warm. They made it simpler by inviting me to help in the investigation. When I heard that Paul had momentarily mistaken Diana's body for yours I saw the opportunity for another red herring." He shook his head.

"Unfortunately, as he said, Paul wouldn't buy it. I had to try to convince him. Because, if there had been a mistake, it argues the murderer had seen Charity's coat on Diana, and that let me out. So I took a shot at it. But the dose of poison I gave you, Charity, wasn't enough to make you more than very ill."

"How did you know?" Haviland demanded.

The major's head nodded at Dr. Graves. "You should remember, Ned. The stuff was in tablet form. When I used it on myself you told me that two wasn't enough for the job if I got immediate attention. And I knew you were here to look after Charity." He held out his blackthorn stick in the general direction of Hiram and slowly unscrewed the top. "It comes apart, you see. Since the day I knew I was hopelessly blind I've carried the means of finishing things."

"But the risk of being caught when you poisoned Charity's drink!" Haviland said.

"What risk?" Wilmot said. "We were all on the terrace. Charity was describing to me what was going on in the air. Everybody was watching that. I slipped two tablets into my own drink.

"Is there anything coming from the north?' I asked Charity. She put her glass down on the terrace table. I heard the clink of glass against metal. I heard the tapping of Charity's heels as she walked to the other end of the terrace. I knew from the sound exactly where to reach for the glass. I replaced it with mine-- the poisoned one. I didn't need eyes for that, Haviland." He shrugged. "There was one chance in a hundred somebody might see me and remember afterwards. I had to take it." He moved a step toward Hiram.

"If you're ready, Hiram, let's get started. I wouldn't want to face the added charge of tampering with the U.S. mails."

At last Haviland and Charity were alone. He sat on the edge of the bed and she snuggled in the crook of his arm.

"I wish he'd gotten away with it, Paul! I wish he had, because I think it was really a good deed and..."

"Darling, you can't go around knocking off unpleasant people at will."

"I don't see why not, and if I were a man and had anything to do with making the laws I'd see to it that..."

Haviland silenced her effectively by kissing her. "Fortunately," he said, "you are not a man. Very fortunately for me."

Murder
GOES TO
Market

by Mignon G. Eberhart

Born in Lincoln, Nebraska, in 1899, her first mystery novel, The Patient in Room 18, published in 1929, and still producing novels as of the mid-1980's, Mignon Good Eberhart rivals Hugh Pentecost in terms of longevity in the field. Her series detectives have been fewer: Nurse Sarah Keate and policeman Lance O'Leary in her first five books and occasional later encores; mystery writer Susan Dare in short stories of the thirties, several gathered in The Cases of Susan Dare (1934); Mr. Wickwire, the banker-sleuth of a series of fifties short stories in This Week and Ellery Queen's Mystery Magazine; and the nearly unique (if you don't count Jeeves) butler-detective known as Bland, featured in the following story and two other American novelettes, the excellent (and often reprinted) "Deadly Is the Diamond" (June 1942) and the very good and never reprinted collaboration with Grantland Rice, "Murder in the Garden" (May 1945), a boxing mystery that would have been in the present collection had the rights been available.

"Murder Goes to Market," published in the July 1943 issue, gives us a picture of wartime Washington and of the operations of an early supermarket. It was written at a time when a supermarket was still sufficiently unusual that it had to be described in detail, at least for the benefit of the male reader. Though the story was included in Five of My Best, a novelette collection published only in Great Britain, it here makes its first American reappearance.

MURDER GOES TO MARKET by Mignon G. Eberhart

It was on Monday night that I returned to Washington after a six-weeks' absence; on Wednesday morning I resumed the responsibilites of my small household-- comprising only Bland, the butler, his wife, and myself-- by going to the market, early. The small wicker market basket was on the hall table when I came downstairs. It looked like an ordinary, empty basket; in actual fact it represented a feud between me and Bland.

He was hovering in the hall that morning as I picked up the

basket, but pretended not to see me. The point was that both of us liked to do the marketing; and since I could and did take a mean advantage of my position as employer to do the job, there was nothing Bland could do but register passive resistance. And while he has a gift for that sort of thing in the way of a lifted eyebrow and a chilly blue eye, I am used to Bland and pretend not to see either.

It was a late-summer day, the air languid and humid. Later, I knew, in spite of lowered shades, the small house would be hot. It was a gem of a house, really; one of the charming old houses in Alexandria, which had been perfectly decorated and furnished, by its owner. That's Frieda Merly, from whom I leased it when I was sent to Washington to do some writing in connection with the war.

Another attraction was the existence of a huge and altogether amazing Supermarket within walking distance of the house. I happened to know the owner, Sam Boomer; white-haired, handsome, urbane, he could talk the price of potatoes with the air of a distinguished diplomat. He might not have been so cordially accepted in the inner circle, however, if he hadn't been a beau of Frieda Merly's. She was that type of rich, charming, and social widow which national capitals seem to develop.

Sam Boomer's Bel-Air Supermarket was not only an enchanting spot; it practically amounted to a neighborhood club. It was really astonishing, the stray items of information one was likely to pick up along with one's cabbages and sweetbreads during a morning's tour of the place. I don't say that Bland liked gossip. But both of us liked the market.

So Bland was very austere when I took up the basket that morning in late August. The opening and closing of the door was almost violently unassisted by him. Once out on the small, clean doorstep I felt the heat fall upon me like a blanket.

Washington is one of the most beautiful and gracious cities in the world, but I had forgotten, during my short absence, how hot it, and its suburbs, can be. Petunias bloomed from the window boxes of the lovely, narrow brick houses, with their beautiful old doors and bright brass knockers. Neat iron fences marked occasional green pocket handkerchiefs for lawns. The ivy here and there looked cool, and so did the Venetian blinds, slanted low over dark interiors. But nothing was cool.

I turned another corner and came upon the Supermarket. Or, more accurately, the Super-super-market. It was colossal, it was Gargantuan. I had learned to make my forays upon the place at the earliest possible hour before it was crowded. On this occasion the doors were just being opened for trade as I rounded the corner.

I was not the first customer. A girl all in white, with a long, blue-black bob that cupped her little head smoothly and made her face look rather white in spite of her crimson mouth, came from the other direction. She was running quickly and lightly, her white, neat pumps making staccato taps along the sidewalk. I caught a flash of blue eyes under soft black lashes. She was very pretty, and she looked frightened, which was odd, and I knew her.

She was Cynthy Farish. She gave me a flashing blue glance and didn't see me at all, but whirled into the store.

The door closed behind her just as I cried, "Cynthy!" She didn't hear me, and by the time I had followed her into the store she was going rapidly along one of the aisles. She was literally empty-handed, for she carried no handbag. But then the white dress she was wearing must have pockets, and anyway it was nothing to me how she carried money for the shopping she was obviously about to do.

Probably there is not a woman in America who is not thoroughly familiar with the Supermarket. Its plan is simplicity itself. Everything is made easy for the customer.

You enter a huge room which is railed off into aisles, along which the stocks of groceries, vegetables, fruits, and canned goods are arranged. At the starting point of your circuit you supply yourself with a cart which looks like a perambulator, and push it along ahead of you. You are at liberty to make your own choice, within the limits of the ration rules, to pause and take as much time as you wish to consider the relative merits of Camembert or Bel Paese, green beans or peas. Nobody hurries you. Nobody seems even to watch you. There are attendants, of course, if you want something raked down from the highest shelf along the wall.

But you can also venture a surreptitious pinch along the alligator pear bin, without being detected, or weigh in your hand every melon on display. That year there was a particularly good selection of melons, because Sam Boomer had made a specialty and hobby of melons. It was always something with him; the previous year it had been smoked turkey, and the year before that different kinds of bread. One could scarcely say "Good morning" to Sam Boomer without being obliged to listen to some fresh item about his current enthusiasm.

You put your selections in the perambulator, wheel it along ahead of you, and eventually emerge at a gate and a row of checkers. These sum up your purchases and send you on to the banks of cash registers, where clerks take your money and whisk you on through the gate. Here you may carry your loot away in a paper bag or in your market basket, or let a boy carry it for you. It is simplicity itself.

I selected my perambulator and dropped my bag inside it.

The attendants were as busy as bees about the chores that made the place ready for the day's onslaught of customers; it was all fresh and clean, and the air smelled deliciously of coffee, hot buns, and spice. I sniffed with pleasure and trundled over to the melons.

Shopping for fruit is a rite with me. I chose a long Crenshaw melon, mellow, heavy, and perfect. One that Bland himself would have approved.

And then I saw Cynthy. She was just entering the little brown door.

This was at the back of the great room, behind a long aisle stacked with rice and flour and sugar, and set into the wall, which was brightly lined with canned goods. It stood a litle ajar.

A moment or two may have passed before it occurred to me that there might be some special sort of delicacy stored beyond the little brown door. And if Cynthy Farish had opened it, I decided, why shouldn't I? So I dropped a carrot I'd been pretending to examine, went to the door, and had my hand on the door knob just as she came out, abruptly.

We met full tilt. There ensued one of those confused and ridiculous moments of grasping for balance and exclaiming; the melon she was carrying in her arm fell into my basket. I clutched the door casing, steadied us both, and cried, "Cynthy! Hello!"

It was only then, actually, that she saw me. She stood there momentarily frozen, pushing back her hair with one hand and looking at me with eyes that were direct and blue and-- again I had to use the word-- frightened. She didn't say anything, and I said involuntarily, "What's wrong, Cynthy?"

She caught her breath and spoke, then, quickly: "Nothing. That is I-- oh, I'm afraid I've dropped my melon." She scooped the melon out of my basket.

"But, Cynthy, I just got home! I want to see you."

"Yes, I know." Her blue eyes were almost desperate. "I'll telephone. I'll-- I've got to go now. I'm sorry." And to my astonishment she flashed around the aisle and disappeared toward the front of the store, leaving me worried and a little heartsick.

For the fear in her eyes was unmistakable. And I liked Cynthy Farish. I had known her and her mother for years. When the mother died and the annuity they lived on too disappeared, I had made Cynthy come to me. I would have liked her to live in my home permanently. Even Bland was austerely devoted to her. But Cynthy was not only independent; she had a clear integrity of character which I liked too much to try to conquer; she refused my offer, and when I saw she was determined to leave I helped her to find a job. For nearly a year she had been secretary-companion to Frieda Merly.

Frieda liked her, too, and saw that she went places and enjoyed Washington. Frieda always had protegees of one kind or another; indeed, Frieda's jeweled fingers were poked gracefully into more Washington pies than I could count.

I stood there for a moment or two, thinking of Cynthy, and then my curiosity returned. What was beyond that little brown door to interest her? My hand was on the knob. I pushed the door open a little more and went into the room beyond.

At first sight it was not at all an interesting room. It was lighted brightly by large, high windows which let in floods of sunlight, and it was stacked with neat rows of cases, arranged with aisles between, to utilize the floor space. I went further into the room, and saw on the stenciled cases the names of all sorts of well-known

brands of such things as canned tomatoes, ginger ale, and crocks of
Vermont maple sirup.

I couldn't help noting with a housewifely eye that the Supermarket was as clean behind the scenes as it was in the great salesroom.
But its very orderliness defeated me.   I didn't think Cynthy had
hurried into the stockroom to fasten her garter, and obviously she
hadn't tucked a packing case under her arm.   There'd been only the
melon in her hands when we met at the door.   I was a little shocked,
thinking how carelessly she must have selected it in her hasty
journey, the length of the big store.

I went still farther into the room, absorbed in discovery.   I
rounded a stack that held cases (cases!) of caviar, and went on,
scanning the rows until I reached the wall.   It was a housewife's
paradise in these days of rationed goods.   I made a dash for the
shelves and saw, beyond the next stack of packing cases, some little
earthenware jars that had a nostalgic look of familiarity.   They held
paté de fois gras with truffles, something that had assumed a
collector's value and price.   What a triumph to bring a jar home to
Bland!

I reached up gloatingly, and then, with the precious jar in my
hand, I looked down.   Down and around the end of the stack of
packing cases on my right.   I don't know why I looked down.   For the
thing that lay there looking at me really didn't see me.   Its eyes were
open and full of reflected light, but perfectly still and glassy.   Its
mouth was open, too.   Shockingly.

Then I was screaming, and I couldn't stop, because the man who
lay there was not only dead-- a knife was sticking out of his throat.
A plain, long knife with a black handle.   I shrank back against the
packing cases and could not look away from the dreadful thing at my
feet.

There was not really very much blood, I suppose because the
knife was still in the wound.   He was a man of about fifty; short and
stocky, with vigorous black hair, and thick features, and black
eyebrows.   A ray of sunlight fell across the ring on the hand nearest
me, an old-fashioned signet ring with the initials "A.B." scrawled
upon it, so worn that I could scarcely read them.   I stared at it, I
remember, taking a queer kind of refuge in deciphering those faint
and ornate initials.   He wore a gray seersucker suit and heavy black
oxfords.   And I told myself to stop screaming, just as the door burst
open and people ran into the room.

The first one to find us was an attendant in a white smock,
carrying, of all things, a basket of tomatoes.   He dropped the
tomatoes, turned green, and after one popeyed look sagged over
against the packing cases in a dead faint.

This was not a help.   Tomatoes were bumping and thudding
everywhere.   But almost immediately more white-smocked figures
rushed into the room and around the packing cases, and pandemonium
began.

It was, however, rather controlled. Attendants in a market of that size are schooled sternly in dealing with crises; not murder, naturally, but crises of the deep and fundamental kind that arise when two women simultaneously select the same watermelon. Gradually I became aware of a kind of Greek chorus from all of them:

"Call the manager!"

"Call Mr. Hibling!"

"Hurry--"

A clerk was running for the door, when it opened, and Sam Boomer himself came in, followed by policemen. Two of them.

"Mr. Boomer!"

"Mr. Boomer, there's an accident!"

"Now, then," said one of the policemen. "What's all this?"

Nine people told him; and everybody pointed.

There hadn't, of course, been time for anyone from the store to call the police. So someone else, obviously, had known of the murder and reported it. Cynthy? Was that why she had fled from the room? Was that, by any fantastic chance, why she had come there? I rejected the thought; I had to, but it lay there anyway, under the surface of my consciousness, while I listened and looked. Yet, if Cynthy had not reported the murder, then who had?

Suddenly no one was speaking. And both policemen were kneeling there beside the body and looking at it. One of them put his hand over the forever quiet heart.

Sam Boomer finally broke the silence. He knelt, too, tall and solid and neatly tailored in his thin gray suit, the sunlight making a silver cap of his white, thick hair. His usually rather rosy face was pale. He stared at the body and then at the policemen and said in a hushed voice, "My God, in my store! Who is he? 'A.B.' on his ring. Who do you suppose he is? That knife's from the cheese counter; I'll swear it's from the cheese counter." He looked up sharply towards the white-smocked clerks hovering around. "Get Hibling," he said.

"You don't know him, Mr. Boomer?" said one of the policemen.

Sam Boomer shook his head. "Where's his wallet? He must have a wallet. Or some papers in his pockets."

With that, really, the investigation began. Investigation into the murder of a stout, swarthy man in a seersucker suit, with a knife in his throat. For the first baffling development was that there was no wallet in his pocket and, so far as they could discover, no papers and no identifying cards. Nothing except that signet ring, so old and so long worn that it was deeply imbedded into the flesh of his thick finger. There were no fingerprints on the knife.

It was a long time before the police, once launched, let any of us leave. The customers then in the store were asked to remain while their names and addresses were taken, and they were questioned concerning anything they had seen that morning. It was, however, evident that the death had taken place some hours before the store had opened. I was still there when the medical examiner arrived.

"It's murder," said the doctor. "No man ever drove a knife into his own throat at that angle. He's been dead at least twelve hours; can't say more definitely. Any idea who he is?"

No one had. By that time fingerprint men were arriving and another man was taking pictures of the body from all angles. It was about then, I believe, that I was asked to remain, pending the arrival of a lieutenant of police who would want to question me. I was politely escorted up a little stairway to what proved to be Mr. Hibling's office. Sam Boomer went with me, and Mr. Hibling himself, who came in just after the arrival of the man with the camera.

The manager was a brisk, efficient-looking man in spectacles, and more agitated by his tardy arrival, it seemed to me, than by the news of the murder. He apologized to Sam Boomer, who brushed his apologies aside, but who nevertheless had a certain measuring look in his blue eyes which made me feel that Mr. Hibling's dereliction would not be forgotten.

"Go on downstairs, Hibling," said Sam Boomer, "and see to things. Anything the police say, goes. Say a soothing word or two to the customers. Don't let the clerks get out of hand. Put 'em to work."

"Yes, sir. Yes, Mr. Boomer. Yes, sir," said Mr. Hibling eagerly, and bobbed away.

Sam Boomer let his tall figure down into the swivel chair before Mr. Hibling's desk, twirling it around to face me, got out a white hankerchief and mopped his glistening forehead, and said, "Gosh!"

I leaned back in my own chair and took off my hat to fan myself with it. We eyed each other for a moment, and he said again, "Gosh. I can't believe it. How'd you happen to be there? Did anybody tell you? Here-- there ought to be a fan somewhere."

He twirled around again, found a fan on top of a steel filing cabinet, and turned it on; the little steady whir covered the sounds of the voices and heavy footsteps below. And I was brought squarely against what I had already realised was the problem of Cynthy Farish. With a swift sense of horror I saw that I could avoid it no longer.

The child had been running when I first saw her enter the store; she had gone swiftly and purposefully to the stockroom; she had fled from it with scarcely a word to me. And I didn't think that the time elapsing between our encounter at the stockroom door and the arrival of Sam Boomer with the police was enough to permit her to go to a telephone outside the store and report the murder.

No, someone else had reported it.

So what of Cynthy? True, she might not have seen the body. Because of the arrangement of the packing cases it would have been perfectly possible for anyone to enter the room and spend some time there, really, without chancing to go into the corner where the dead man lay.

But why had she gone into the room at all? And why was she so intent, so hurried, so frightened?

Boomer, of course, knew her. I hesitated, debating whether or not to tell him of her visit; and he said, sitting in the swivel chair and watching me, "This is going to be a nasty affair. But I don't think it'll hurt the store. It was you who found him just now, wasn't it? Somebody said--"

"Oh, yes," I said. "I found him."

"Tell me about it. What were you doing in the stockroom?"

Sam Boomer was nobody's fool; Frieda Merly, indeed, always spoke of his brilliance of mind, saying that with the right help he would go far. I rather surmised she meant with her help.

It was then I realized that if I told Boomer and the police of that visit, Cynthy Farish, with her youth and her sweetness, was going to be dragged into the sordid, long-drawn-out and horrible process of a police investigation into murder. I didn't for an instant think that she had had anything to do with the killing of the man who lay there in the stockroom. There was no real reason for her to become a suspect in a murder case. So I decided to trust my instinct.

This is not always a good plan. But I didn't have time to consider it further, for Sam Boomer was waiting for a reply.

"The stockroom," he reminded me, "is not open to the public. How did you get in?"

"It was open this morning," I said. "That is, the door was slightly open and I was curious. I thought there might be something-- well, special, back there. I was merely prowling."

"Oh, I see," he said. "You didn't see Jim Allen, did you?"

"Jim Allen?" I seemed to remember the name only vaguely.

He said, "Yes. He's in my office. A nice kid, twenty-four or so. He actually found the dead man. Found him this morning, early, before the store opened. Came to tell me. I rounded up a couple of policemen and came along."

So that was how they had known. "Oh," I said slowly. "Then I wasn't the first one to--"

"No," he cut in. "That was Jim. Feel better now?" he asked with a sudden smile.

"Yes," I said, and meant it.

He swerved around, got out shell-rimmed glasses, put them on his good-looking nose, and looked not a day older. I could see why Frieda Merly liked him. He reached for the telephone, and as he dialed, said, "Jim, of course, came straight to me. Very properly, I think. He didn't seem to want to take the responsibility for reporting the murder to the police." There was a little pause while he listened into the telephone. Then he added, "He was thinking of me, and the store. But this won't hurt it. Jim's all right....Oh-- hello, Rosita?"

Apparently someone said yes. He went on: "Rosita, Jim was right. The fellow's dead; seems to have been murdered....Yes, I thought Jim was having a brainstorm, too, but I guess he wasn't....No, I don't know who; the police are here now....Yes. Well, if the newspapers get hold of you, just keep quiet. Tell 'em you don't know anything. Williams will be back this afternoon. He'll take care of the newspaper end of it. And listen, Rosita-- keep Jim there. It'd be better, I think. He's impulsive, you know. But tell him the police will want to question him. That's all. 'By, dear."

He hung up, and twirled around again. "My niece," he said. "I imagine I'd better get downstairs again. If you'll excuse me--" He got up, and at the door said, "I wonder if you'd phone Frieda for me? Tell her I'm with the police and I'll call her as soon as I can. Thanks."

He disappeared, and I telephoned to Frieda. Having leased her house, she was living in an apartment in Washington. It was still early, but her voice was, as always, alert and musical. It changed, however, when I told her what had happened.

"Good heavens!" she cried, shocked. "Who was murdered?"

"I don't know. Nobody knows yet."

There was a pause. "But somebody must know!" she said finally. "Did Sam see him?"

"Oh, yes. His wallet was removed. Probably by the murderer."

"His--" Frieda stopped again. And then said quickly, "Oh, yes, his wallet. I see, I suppose that makes it difficult. What does he look like?"

"Dark," I said. "Middle-aged. I'd rather not talk about him, just now."

"Oh, of course, darling. What a shock it must have been. Is Sam still there?"

"Yes. He asked me to phone you. He'll call you later."

"Oh." There was another little pause before she said, "Nice of Sam. Are reporters on hand yet?"

"No. That is, I don't think so."

"Oh," said Frieda, and again seemed to be thinking hard.

I said, "By the way, is Cynthy there?"

"Cynthy?" said Frieda, a note of surprise in her voice. "Why, I believe so. I don't know. I haven't seen her this morning. I'm still in bed, having breakfast. Do you want me to come over?"

"No. I think they'll let me go after a few questions."

Again she seemed to wait, as if reluctant to hang up. Finally she said slowly, "You might let me know any-- well, developments. It must have been horrible finding him like that. And nobody knows who he is?"

"Nobody," I repeated, and hung up.

I called Bland. His voice was still full of hauteur; when I did the marketing he always stayed mad until well past lunch, and only warmed up after tea or cocktail time.

"Yes, madam," he said now frostily.

"Bland, I may be late for lunch."

A late meal affects Bland strongly. After a pause he observed bitterly that we were having a souffle.

"I'm sorry, but I have to see the police. It may take time."

"The souffle will be ruined, madam," began Bland icily, and then he did an audible double take. "Police?" he interrupted himself to say.

"Yes. I ran into what looks like a murder over here."

"Murder, madam!" And this time there was an effect of yoicks and tally-ho in his voice.

"Yes, but you are not to come," I said. "That's all, Bland." And I hung up, with the result that twenty minutes later, just as the Lieutenant of police began to question me, Bland arrived. Big, pompous, toeing out discreetly, eyes blank and blue, he stood behind my chair with such an effect of remote and impersonal duty that not even the most astute policeman could have guessed that in reality Bland was practically bursting out of his neat alpaca coat to hear all, see all, and know all.

Perhaps an hour later we were allowed to depart.

Bland carried my basket as we walked home. The interview with the police had not been bad at all. I had been fingerprinted, it is true, but so had everyone else. I had told them several times everything I knew, which was little enough. And that was all, except that I still hadn't said a word about Cynthy Farish.

While the Lieutenant was questioning me, reports were brought to him constantly about the inquiry going on in another part of the store; of the customers, all of whom were allowed to leave very soon, and of the staff. The results were definitely on the negative side.

No one knew, or admitted knowing, the identity of the murdered man, nor was there any way of knowing how he had got into the stockroom. In fact, nothing in the way of clues or evidence had developed up to the time I was permitted to leave.

Although none of the clerks confessed to remembering the murdered man, he might very well have walked through the store and into the stockroom unnoticed in the late afternoon rush. Or of course he might have entered, or been admitted, after hours.

There was a back door to the stockroom, as well as the entrance through the store, and the matter of keys was gone into rather thoroughly. I knew that, for I had heard them talking of it. Mr. Hibling had a key; but Mr. Hibling also had an alibi: He was in the dentist's chair from four o'clock until closing time, and in bed with a hot-water bottle and aspirin tablets until shortly before his arrival at the market that morning.

Sam Boomer had a key, and he, too, had an alibi. He had been in his office in Washington until five; Jim Allen, he'd told them (and I heard the stenographer read a transcript of his exact words to the lieutenant), was with him. He and Jim Allen had gone to the Mayflower for a drink, after which Jim had gone to take Rosita to a cocktail party somewhere and Sam Boomer had sat around the Mayflower bar talking to several people he knew.

"Who?" said the lieutenant.

The stenographer read four or five names. A plain-clothes man, who had turned up by then, stopped fanning himself with his white straw hat and said that he had already checked Boomer's story by telephone. "Seems to be right," he added gloomily. "All five men say they saw and talked to him after five, and one of them-- Claussen, works on a newspaper-- left him in time to keep a six-thirty appointment at the Carlton. That's five minutes' walk away."

"Did Boomer leave then?"

"About then," said the stenographer. "Here it is."

He read: "Mr. Boomer replied, 'I was waiting for Bill Williams, a friend of mine. He'd been in New York and thought he might get an afternoon train back to Washington. I was to meet him at the Mayflower bar, but he didn't turn up, so I went home-- to my house near Rock Creek Park-- about six-thirty. I'm not sure of the time. My niece, Miss Rosita Boomer, was out. Allen was with her. They came home about seven-thirty and we all had dinner together. I didn't go out again. I stayed home and read. Rosita was at home, too; so was Jim Allen. He lives in my house. Works for me.'" The stenographer paused.

The plain-clothes man sighed. "Maid at the Boomer house says he came in before seven. She doesn't know the exact time, but she saw him. There isn't time between six-thirty and seven, at the outside limit, for him to drive to Alexandria, commit a murder in his store, and drive home again. So it looks like an alibi. But I'll keep working on it, if you think he's drunk enough to murder a guy here, and leave him to be found."

"Hm-m," said the lieutenant thoughtfully. His eyes fastened absently on the toe of my white slipper, and then sharpened and became alert, as if he had forgotten my presence and Bland's and only then remembered. He turned to the stenographer again: "Did Jim Allen have a key?"

"A key," said the plain-clothes man. "And an alibi. Drinks with Boomer, cocktail party with Boomer's niece. Complete. You can check him off."

"We can't check anybody off," snapped the lieutenant, "till we know when the fellow was murdered."

Certainly, according to Hibling, there were no more keys, which, however, did not limit the suspects at all. In the first place, anyone knows how easy it is to have a duplicate key made, provided you can get hold of the original for an hour. Also, there was no particular evidence tending to prove that the back door had been used at all.

Indeed, it began to look more and more as if the murdered man, and his murderer, had quietly entered the store late the previous afternoon, along with some hundreds, probably, of other people, that they had entered the stockroom unobserved, and then, later, the murderer had calmly walked out.

The cashiers were questioned about people coming in and out of the store late the previous afternoon, for if the murdered man had been dead about twelve hours, the conclusion was, naturally, that he could have been murdered some time shortly before or after the store had closed; at five-thirty, that was. But none of them remembered anything.

It was just then, however, that I had rather a bad moment, for one of them said, as a kind of afterthought, that there were not many customers in the store in the morning at the time the murder was discovered, and that only one had left the store, for he had rung up only one charge-- for a Crenshaw melon-- just before the scream began in the stockroom.

The lieutenant had visibly pricked up his ears. "Do you remember the customer?" he asked.

"A young woman," said the cashier. "Pretty. Black hair and a white dress."

I held my breath, but the cashier proved to be a laconic man, not given to fine descriptions.

The lieutenant muttered rather fretfully that there were probably a thousand young women in Washington, black-haired, and wearing white dresses. And since, obviously, the murder had not been committed within the hour of my own grisly discovery he let the inquiry about Cynthy drop.

However, I knew that the investigation had barely begun. Eventually they would identify the dead man; eventually all the business of photographs and fingerprints and detailed and tireless inquiry would bring to light a few solid facts which, in turn, would lead to others. I had too much faith in the efficency of our modern police system not to be worried about Cynthy's part in this ghastly mystery.

That was, in general, how things stood when Bland and I walked home. Bland carrying the wicker basket with my melon in it. The heat made the old, worn bricks waver before my eyes, but Bland was unaffected by the heat or by the murder.

By more or less adroit and exceedingly detailed questioning, he made me go over the whole story of my discovery-- except that I didn't mention Cynthy even to him. He had, however, to admit himself baffled. "'A.B.' on his ring," he muttered, shaking his head. "Not very helpful. Do you mind telling me again, madam, exactly what you, and everyone else said and did? Before I arrived, that is," he added, with an effect of modesty.

I didn't mind, and told him again in great detail, but there was little to tell, and Bland looked discouraged. When we reached home, however, he had cheered up enough to make a long, cool drink and bring it to me as I lay in a deck chair on the tiny, enclosed lawn.

But he had scarcely padded away, when he padded back again. "Madam," he said, and pushed a silver waiter at me, on which reposed the melon I had bought and hardily clung to through murder, police investigation, and heat.

Except it wasn't.

My melon-- a long, large Crenshaw melon-- was whole and sound; the melon on the waiter, likewise a Crenshaw, had a large brown spot on it.

I cried, wounded by Bland's accusing look, "I didn't buy that melon! Bland, you know I wouldn't have bought a bad melon. Take it back at once."

Bland drew a long hissing, breath.   "Madam, may I venture to inquire," he said, venturing right ahead, "exactly why madam has secreted this-- object within the melon?"

With which, and with an air of great drama, he pulled out of the melon a long, thin piece of metal. It wasn't a poniard but it was like one. There was no handle; it was only a vicious, sharpened piece of steel, with one end horribly pointed.

It had thoroughly and neatly slit its way into the melon, which was easily long enough to conceal it. It was so small and thin that the slit it made in the outer rind of the melon was barely perceptible and easily overlooked, as we had overlooked it. It was, also, so firmly imbedded in the melon that Bland practically had to dig it out with his finger tips, even though he had cut into the melon with a knife.

"Where did it come from?"

"It was as you see, inside the melon."

"You brought the melon home," I said, remembering. "I didn't. It's your melon."

"Certainly. I'll turn it over to the police at once."

Police. And Cynthy hurrying out of the stockroom, bumping into me and my basket, dropping her melon, snatching it up again, and dashing away. Only, it was my melon she had mistakenly snatched up; not the melon she had dropped.

I sat up and reached for the poniardlike piece of steel. Bland drew it quickly away from me, his light blue eyes suddenly showing very bright and black pupils. "I beg your pardon," he said. "One must take a shive by the end. The square end."

"Square?" I said. And then: "Shive?"

Bland looked a little swollen around the chops. "I meant to say, madam," he said, "knife."

"You said shive."

"Why, I-- Perhaps I did, madam.   The term escaped me, inadvertently."

"Go on, Bland; come clean."

He contrived to look pained. "Very good, madam. I-- er-- as you may know, have not had an uneventful life." He took a long breath, fixed his blank blue eyes upon a goldfish in the pool. "At one time I was acquainted with a gentleman whose past was not only eventful, but dramatic. He told me a shive is a file, sharpened down into a dagger. A very efficacious dagger, as a matter of fact. This one, I would say, was sharpened to its present state in a cell block at one of our larger prisons."

"Bland! You mean it's a file that has been smuggled into a penitentiary and sharpened by a prisoner until he can use it to-- kill somebody? A guard or--"

"Possibly, madam; very possibly."

He looked broodingly at the dagger. I looked, too, naturally. This put another ingredient in our drama of the morning. A prison. And someone who had been in prison; someone whose tireless, deadly patient hands had ground down that file to be the lethal and horrible thing it now was.

Shock coursed through me as it suddenly occurred to me: Cynthy Farish almost certainly had inserted that dagger-- shive-- in the melon. It was an ideal receptacle and hiding place for the shining, deadly sliver of steel that Bland was holding. Cunningly, knowingly, she had concealed that awful weapon of death.

Or was it? For the dead man had been killed with another knife. A cheese knife.

Bland said, "Shall I telephone the police, madam?"

Police! This was evidence. They would make me explain the thing; they would go straight for Cynthy Farish.

"No, Bland. I want to think about it. I want to wait."

There was an instant of silence. Then Bland said very softly, "Madam, might I venture to inquire how you got this melon?"

"I-- " My hands made airy and futile gestures. "I just picked it up, Bland. I didn't know there was a knife in it. I mean a shive, of course. Such an interesting--"

"The exact nomenclature doesn't really matter, madam," said Bland. "Am I mistaken, or did you inform me of the fact that this was not the melon you chose? I believe you told me you wouldn't choose this one, because it had a brown spot."

"I must have done so, of course, without seeing the brown spot."

"Madam"-- Bland's voice was solemn-- "If you are trying to protect anyone it is a mistake. Murder is a dangerous business."

"Bland!" I sat up. "That will do!"

"Very well, madam."

"I'll have lunch now, please. Leave the knife here. On the table."

"Very good, madam. Very good." The sudden but suppressed fury in his voice was like a seething volcano. "I'll leave it here, madam. But perhaps madam had better know that to conceal evidence is to make oneself an accessory after the fact."

I was sure he was right. But I said, "Does it really, Bland?"

After that, lunch was a rather strained meal; and by five o'clock I still didn't know what to do. I had placed the shive in one of the two Victorian vases on the mantel in the little library, first making sure that Bland was not watching when I did it. But further than that I was at a loss. Clearly, my duty was to go to the police, and I simply couldn't do it. Not then, at least; not until I had talked to Cynthy.

At five o'clock Frieda Merly called up, ostensibly to remind me of the Simpsons' cocktail party, and really to say that according to the evening papers the identity of the murdered man had still not been established. She was brief and crisp, as she usually was; still, there was something worried in her voice. I hung up slowly, and rather horribly wondered whether she had been really surprised that morning when I telephoned her.

So I went to the cocktail party, and there I rather took the spotlight for a little from the visiting celebrity. But then Washington is full of celebrities; they are constantly underfoot, and a murder in a grocery store was a little unusual.

Ellie Wilde, an old school friend, asked me if there really were jars of paté, and such an acquisitive and earnest look came into her face when I said there were, that I took the first opportunity to detach myself from the others in the warm, scented garden and go into the house and find a telephone.

The butler directed me to a little, mirrored telephone-room, and after I'd got Bland on the telephone and told him to go straight out to the Supermarket and purchase the paté, he informed me loftily that he had already done so. This annoyed me naturally, no end, so I hung up, and it was then that I saw Cynthy.

Rather, I saw a slice of her; her profile and a smooth shiny pompadour-- she'd put up her black hair-- and part of a yellow dress. She was standing in the hall outside the little telephone room talking to someone beyond my range of vision.

The talk held plenty of feeling on both sides, for a man's voice said, "But I saw you, dammit! I saw you. Cynthy, what were you doing there?" And she said in clipped and cold accents, "Exactly what do you think I was doing?"

A kind of hollow groan came to my ears. The person out of sight said, "All right. All right. If you don't want to tell me you don't have to."

"Certainly I don't have to," said Cynthy.

There was a little silence, and I considered venturing into the hall. But just then the man said, with an effect of patience held hard, "Listen, Cynthy, I only asked you what you were doing in Boomer's study this morning. I started down the stairs just as you came out of it and I saw you go out the front door. I only asked you why you went there, and you turn on me like a tiger."

"I didn't," said Cynthy. "I didn't say anything. I-- " Suddenly her voice changed. "Oh, Jim, I do believe in you! Why won't you tell me the truth?" she cried, and instead of anger there was something in her voice that suggested tears.

Jim. Was this the Jim Allen whom Sam Boomer had mentioned? If so, it was he who had actually found the murdered man that morning, and told Sam Boomer instead of the police; who had been kept at home by Rosita Boomer, the niece.

He said, in a stunned way, "Why, Cynthy. What do you mean? You're not making sense. I don't under-- Why, Cynthy! You look as if you're going to cry!"

And at that point a door banged, and a new voice, a girl's voice, cried, "Oh, there you are Jimmy dear! I've been looking for you.... Oh, hello, Cynthy. I believe Mrs. Merly wants you."

I could see Cynthy move forward, looking so stately with her black hair high on her head, and yet very young. She said, "Hello, Rosita. Thanks. Where is Mrs. Merly?'

"On the terrace," the new voice said.

Cynthy said coolly, "Thanks." There were quick footsteps, and a door slammed.

Jim said, "For God's sake--"

"What's the matter, darling?" said the girl's voice.

Rosita, Cynthy had called her. So it must be Sam Boomer's niece. Rosita went on smoothly, "Jim dear, what's wrong? What were you talking to Cynthy Farish about?"

"I just asked her why she didn't stop and say hello this morning at the house."

"Cynthy! Was she at the house this morning?"

"Yes," he said. "But-- Did you say you were looking for me? Has Mr. Boomer come?"

"Yes, he was held up. The police talked to him again this morning, and then a reporter asked for a statement."

"Oh," said Jim. His voice was all at once extremely alert. It even struck me as being rather anxious. "Did he give them one?"

"He did. Williams got in on an afternoon train. He said to give a statement at once, and prepared it himself."

"Then that's all right," said Jim. "He's a good press agent. He knows his job."

There was a little silence. "Jim," said Rosita, "You really didn't know him-- the murdered man, I mean. Did you?"

"Good Lord, no. I told you that this morning when I got back to the house and told Mr. Boomer. You heard everything."

"Well, not quite everything," said Rosita. "I came downstairs just as you and Uncle were talking about it. I never heard how it was that you happened to-- to find him."

"It was just as I told Mr. Boomer. I'd gone to take a look around the market, as I usually do in the mornings before the staff gets there. I'd gone into the stockroom to look at some windows that the manager, Hibling, has been wanting bars for. Then I saw the body."

"How horrible," said Rosita.

He ignored that. "I started to phone to get the police. Then I thought I'd better tell Mr. Boomer first and let him handle it. So I locked up again and got to the house as soon as I could. That's all."

Then the girl said, "But, Jim, it was murder, wasn't it?"

Jim said briefly, "Yes, couldn't have been anything else. That knife--"

"What knife?" said the girl. "What kind of knife was it?"

"It came from the chese counter."

"Cheese!" The girl gave a kind of giggle.

"It's not funny," said Jim. "I tell you it was horrible. The police had me come over to the station and took my fingerprints."

"Oh. They suspect you?"

"Suspect-- My God, Rosita, I didn't kill him! I told you I never saw him before."

"I didn't say that you did, Jim darling. Come on; let's get a cocktail."

"I don't want a cocktail," said Jim.

"Nonsense. Come along."

"No. I've got to-- to telephone."

"I'll wait."

"Don't. It'll take a long time."

But I knew that it wouldn't take him long to locate the telephone, so I emerged. Quietly, really, but they both jerked around and stared as if I'd been a jack-in-the-box. Rosita was a very blond young woman, handsome in a somewhat buxom fashion.

Jim Allen was young, tall, red-headed, and very angry. As I started toward the terrace door trying to look nonchalant, he got his breath, strode to the door of the little telephone-room, and flung it open. He realized then, that I was not passing through the hall but must have been in the little room for some time, and thus had heard everything that had been said. He whirled toward me. "Who are you, anyway?" he demanded rudely.

And Rosita cried, "Why, it's-- Jim, she found the body! I mean, after you did. This morning."

I had reached the terrace door. "Sorry," I said. "But if you want to shout you can't expect people not to hear you."

The screen door made a sharp period. Behind it I heard Jim say, "You mean she was at the store?"

More people had arrived and the cocktail party was in full sway. I had reached the end of the terrace, when Frieda Merly saw me from a distance and came over at once.

"Well, you look very handsome," she said. "No one would think you'd fallen upon a murder this morning. What a terrible experience! But then you weren't the first to find him, were you? I'm told Jim Allen did that."

"Yes. Who is he, really, Frieda? I mean, beyond the fact that Sam Boomer employs him."

"Jim? Oh, he's another of Sam's proteges. A young lawyer who worked himself through school; he began, I think, as a page boy. Then, about five or six years ago-- just after Sam came to the capital-- Sam saw him somewhere and got interested in him, and loaned him money for law school. He always gave him work during vacations, and Jim graduated last spring. I think Sam had some idea of employing him permanently, but of course the war changed all that. I believe Jim expects to get in the air force and leave soon for training. Why?"

"I only wondered."

She eyed me. "You don't have an idea that Jim had anything to do with the murder of that man in Sam's market, do you?"

She took off her large, brimmed hat as she spoke; we had drawn away from the others and were standing under a tree, and the light drifting through the leaves fell strongly upon her fine-featured, nervously alert, rather lovely face. She held her broad-brimmed hat in one slim white hand and looked at me, and I felt again that Frieda was worried.

I said, replying to her question, "Heavens, no. Just because Jim Allen found him, that doesn't mean he murdered him. I was there, too, and I certainly didn't. I suppose you know Sam's niece, Rosita?"

"Yes, of course." She spoke abstractedly, her eyes roving uneasily over the groups of people. "She came to play hostess for him this summer. She's rather taken with young Allen. And he with her."

"I thought he liked Cynthy," I said tentatively.

"Cynthy?" She was still looking over her shoulder. "Oh, I don't think so. They've only known each other a few weeks. I remember they met at my house; Jim came in with Sam one night and I introduced them."

It was then that her eyes found their target and became fixed. Not only fixed but so intent that she seemed to be trying to hear with them. I turned to follow the direction of Frieda's gaze. And there across the green lawn, standing a little apart from the other clusters of people, were Sam Boomer, Cynthy, and another man whose back was turned toward us.

The three standing there, silhouetted against the laurels, were deeply intent upon their conversation. Sam Boomer was apparently questioning Cynthy, who replied; and then I saw Sam's eyes go to the man facing them, as if he had spoken. It wasn't Jim Allen. This man's hair was not red, but an indeterminate gray-brown; and he wore a suit of some thin, light material. There was nothing particularly identifiable about him.

Frieda murmured something that I didn't hear. I glanced at her, and when I looked back toward the three they were looking at Frieda.

No. It gave me an odd startled sensation to observe that they were looking very intently at me. Cynthy and Sam, that is. The other man's back was still turned.

Then abruptly Sam bowed to us across the width of close-cropped green lawn. He said something to the second man, who moved away as Sam and Cynthy came toward us. We watched their approach; Sam debonair and handsome, with his white hair and smile; the girl slim and pretty and unsmiling.

It was an opportunity to ask her about the melon; and I had to do it. It ought to be fairly easy to draw her away from Frieda and Sam, who were such close friends.

It was not, however, as easy as I had thought it would be. Frieda put her arm through mine, and when I made a motion or two to draw away, the light pressure of her arm became curiously tenacious.

"It does seem queer," said Frieda, "that no one knows who the man was. There should be a hundred ways of identifying him."

Sam shrugged. "Oh, they will, eventually. But with people

pouring in and out of Washington these days, it may take a long time. Nobody has reported this fellow missing. I understand the police have tried to check the hotels, but it would take weeks to do it that way. In any city, I suppose, it's possible for a man's identity to be lost, but now, in Washington, nothing could be easier."

"Do the police believe the murderer removed his wallet to make it hard to identify him?" asked Frieda, her voice light and pleasant, her eyes worried.

"Of course. At least it seems logical enough," said Sam.

"Then-- if they could identify him they would know who the murderer is?"

"Looks that way," said Sam. "Still, you never know. Maybe it was merely a ruse to hold up the police and give the murderer more time to escape. I'm no Sherlock, Frieda."

Cynthy, who had said nothing rather conspicuously, lifted her blue eyes to give Boomer a long look. And I resolutely disengaged my arm from Frieda. "Let's snare some of the food and drink, Cynthy," I said, and slid my arm through hers, much as Frieda had done to me.

Sam said, "See you and Jim tonight, Cynthy," as we moved away. And then quite distinctly, although in a lowered voice, he said to Frieda, "Don't worry. I'm all right."

I heard Frieda's reply; it was quite cool and self-possessed. She said, "I'm not worrying about you darling."

Cynthy heard, too; she couldn't have helped hearing, for there were no other groups near enough to submerge with talk our own little island of quiet, on the tranquil lawn.

Not as tranquil as it seemed, however. It was late; the sun had gone. The sky was a soft and opaque gray, and the lawn and the shrubs looked suddenly very green and very still.

"It's going to storm," I said to Cynthy.

"Yes."

It was only a word, polite and brief, but I could feel the child steeling herself against me. There was no question in my mind but that she knew why I had drawn her away from the others. That meant that she knew I had the wrong melon. And that meant-- well, what?

I glanced at her; she was walking slowly beside me, chin up and her lovely red mouth set. I cast about for an opening, didn't find any, and said rather desperately, "Cynthy, I saw you this morning."

There was a little pause. Clearly she wasn't going to be trapped into any quick and impulsive statement. Then she said, looking straight ahead, "Yes, of course. In the market."

I stopped, so she had to stop, too. "Cynthy, look at me."

She met my eyes then, but her own were blue and dark and unfathomable. I said, "Cynthy, that knife. That dagger. I've got to give it to the police. I wanted to tell you."

Her face was white and miserable, for she liked me and I knew it; but her eyes didn't waver and she wouldn't speak.

I said finally, "I don't want to. I don't want them to drag you into a murder investigation. It's an ugly thing, Cynthy dear. No matter how little you know of it, or how innocent you are-- and of course, I'm sure you're innocent-- I mean--" I was floundering and distressed.

She just got whiter and straighter, while her eyes kept staring into mine.

I put out my hand instinctively, as one does to draw a person back from danger. "Cynthy," I said, "Please tell me."

She said, after a moment, stiffly, "Tell you what?"

There was no use beating against the barrier she had put up. Somewhere near us a bird twittered in sharp alarm, as if it, too, had been suddenly made aware of storm portents. I said, "Listen, Cynthy. Think of what I've said. I want to help you. I don't believe you had anything to do with the murder. It's preposterous, even to think of it. But--"

Unexpectedly she put out her brown, slim hand and touched my arm. "Thank you," she said. "I've got to think. There's something-- I don't know what to do. I've got to decide something. May I telephone you? Tonight?"

Of course I said yes. I left her then. But as I walked slowly toward the long, beautiful house, I felt exactly as if I'd been run over by a power mower. It was strange that the short and altogether unsuccessful interview could leave me feeling so flat and exhausted. Or was it, already, the queer pressure in the air induced by the coming storm?

I was going home. I started to hunt for Ellie Wilde, who lived near me and I had suggested we walk home together, but I became involved with one group and another, and was finally dragged to meet a Chinese dignitary. I couldn't, of course, get away again without due, if brief, politenesses exchanged through a smiling member of his entourage who acted as interpreter.

By the time I was disengaged, the sky was faintly darker. I was about to start on alone when Ellie turned up. She was ready to go, and she had seen Sam and Frieda.

"They left a few minutes ago," she added. "Together. Do you suppose there's a marriage in the offing? It would be queer, after all these years, if Frieda were married again, and to Sam Boomer. Of course, he's rich, they say. But I always thought Frieda was-- well, ambitious. You know. She likes power and position and I don't think she'd marry again without getting it."

I murmured some remark, but I wasn't really interested. I was too busy trying to explain to myself my rather odd sense of exhilaration. The sky was gray and close, and the heat was terribly oppressive. Nothing certainly was any different, except that I had left the cocktail party behind and was out on a busy street, with a normal and natural world around me. Natural and without evil.

Suddenly and rather shatteringly I realized that the word "evil" was like a chink of light thrown upon a dark and nebulous experience. That was it; there had been evil at that cocktail party, unseen but threatening. It was not a nice thought. It was extremely fanciful and unreasonable. I heaped adjectives up in my mind and still felt exactly the same.

I said good-by to Ellie at her corner some distance from my own, and walked on alone through hushed and quiet streets. It was growing darker, quickly, on account of the storm, so it seemed later than it really was. When I reached home and saw that the lights had not been turned on, the blank windows surprised me. Bland was usually very prompt and watchful about lights.

The gate clanged behind me. I had my key, but I rang anyway, thinking the exercise of coming to open the door was good for Bland, who had lately been developing a decided thickness through the middle. He didn't come to the door, however, and after waiting a moment I let myself in.

It was very quiet in the house, too. Almost as if no one was there, which of course was absurd, for it was not the Blands' day out. But the tension of the storm, the forebodings of my thoughts about the cocktail party, my uneasiness about Cynthy-- everything made me nervous and irritable. I put my thumb squarely on the bell and kept it there.

And no one answered.

I put down my bag and hat and gloves and went quickly to the dining-room bell and rang that. Still no one answered. I went into the pantry, and it was dark. The kitchen was even darker, so the shapes of tables and cupboards and stove loomed up dimly and somehow threateningly. I made myself turn on the kitchen light, and the gleaming porcelain and glass and white paint leaped into visibility, all perfectly orderly and natural-- except it wasn't. What would have been natural would have been Mrs. Bland preparing dinner and puttering around in the pantry; the homely smell of cooking; and all the light and sounds of activity of seven o'clock in anybody's kitchen.

There was no Blands, and no note anywhere telling me where they'd gone.

By the time I got back to the front of the house again and turned on more lights, it was so dark that the windows reflected the lights and me in a rather unnerving and sentient way, as if they or someone out in the gathering night were watching me. Obviously the thing to do was get myself some kind of dinner; there must be food in the refrigerator. Settle myself with a book and wait for the Blands to return and explain themselves.

Yes, that was the thing to do. But first I would see that the doors and windows were locked.

Nerves, of course. I was getting a delayed shock from my ugly experience of the morning. But nevertheless--

I made the whole circuit of the house, upstairs and down. It didn't take long for it is a small house, and I hurried. I didn't go into the cellar; I didn't even open the cellar door, which Bland had apparently left unlocked, and resolved to speak to him sharply about it. Then I ran upstairs and saw no more windows. There was still no wind, no lightning, no rain. One thing was certain, I remember thinking as I came downstairs again: Nobody is in the house.

But I was going to call the police.

I was going to call the police, and I knew why. The house was empty. Nobody but me was in it. The doors were locked, the windows bolted. But there was fear in the house. And I was in danger.

All I could do was stare at emptiness and lights, and swallow hard, and listen. Listen with all my ears, listen with every nerve and every drop of blood in my body, so that I felt paralyzed and frozen. Don't be a dolt. Go to the telephone. Call the police, call the police, call the police!

I don't think I knew what I was going to tell them. It didn't matter. The thing that mattered was to move, to walk into the little library, to take up the telephone and-- what was the number for the police? Where was there a telephone book? In my bedroom, of course; on a shelf on the bedside table. But Bland had a book in the pantry, too.

Well, then, don't go upstairs. Walk through the dining-room and use the pantry telephone. That's quicker.

Besides, you'll be nearer the front door; nearer other people; nearer a way to escape.

Again I had very briefly that horrible feeling of nightmare helplessness. I struggled within its grip, knowing all the time that I must hurry. There was some reason, some strong and terribly urgent reason for me to call the police. No matter how much my mind questioned that impulse, all my instinct was for it. And somehow I managed to force myself into motion.

I went through the dining-room, where a mirror gave me a glancing reflection, and pushed open the pantry door, which squeaked loudly. I all but ran to the telephone, on the table by the window. A telephone book was there. I must hurry, I had to hurry. I--

Someone was breathing. Someone was in that empty house. Someone was standing in the doorway to the kitchen. Someone was watching me. I could see a reflection of that figure in the dark windowpane in front of me.

I turned around like a doll, stiff and without feeling. A policeman stood there, watching me quietly.

He was rather slender, with sharp features in a dark face, grayish dark hair, and extremely quiet and narrow dark eyes which did not move from me. It seemed extraordinary; it seemed miraculous, indeed. I had only looked up the number, and there he was, materialized out of space, in that silent and empty house.

My knees were shaking; my hand was shaking, too. I realized dimly that I was still holding the telephone, and I put it down clumsily in the cradle, so that it clattered and slid off and I had to retrieve it.

The quiet figure in the doorway said, "I'm afraid I startled you."

I tried to answer. I tried to tell him that something was wrong in the house, that I'd started to call the police, that I wanted him to-- Well, to do what? Look over the house. Find out what was wrong. Protect me from-- Well, from what?

I said none of those things. My hands were gripping the little table behind me, holding to it as if it were a raft on a dark and dreadful sea.

He said, "I'm sorry. I only came to get the melon."

I did speak then. I said numbly, "Melon." Just like that; neither question nor statement.

He said, "I am sorry. You are very frightened. There's nothing to be afraid of. What were you doing with the telephone?"

"I was going to call the police."

"The police? Why?"

I didn't answer. There was still something wrong in the house. A policeman was there talking to me, yet something in the house was wrong.

He said, "Were you going to tell them anything? Something you omitted telling them this morning? Were you going to tell them about the girl you met at the door of the stockroom? And the melon she dropped in your basket?"

So they knew.

Probably at the moment they were taking Cynthy to the station for questioning; I suddenly knew that I must say nothing.

He came a step nearer, and absurdly I pushed harder against the table behind me.

He said, "Don't be frightened. It's all right. We know about the girl and the melon. It's evidence. You don't need to tell us about it now. The girl admitted it. Forget the whole thing. Promise me."

"Promise--"

"Promise you'll forget it.... What frightened you so? Is there anything else you know besides the fact the girl was there?"

"No-- no, of course not. Only, she didn't do it."

"Didn't she? How do you know?"

"Why, I know her. She wouldn't--"

"Any other reason?"

"No. But--"

"Sure?"

"Yes, I'm sure. That is, I don't know who did murder the man, if that's what you mean."

"You don't know who murdered him?"

"No. Certainly not. I'd tell you if I did. I'd have told the police this morning."

"I see. That's all. I'll go along now. I'm taking the melon. I got it out of the refrigerator." He smiled then and said, "Good night," and turned around. As he did so there was something briefly familiar about him; then he disappeared into the kitchen.

I didn't move and I heard his footsteps, a soft click, and then the opening and quiet closing of the door that led from the kitchen to the step outside.

I knew he had gone but I couldn't move for a long moment or two. My thoughts were whirling around Cynthy, the melon, the police, murder, the empty house, but there was something in the center of it all; something that was a pivot, a small hub. Something I couldn't discover because the wheel was going too fast.

There'd been something; a small sound-- a click.

Why, that was it!

The click was the sound of the back door being unlocked. I had locked it. So that meant that the policeman had been in the house while I went over it, locking doors and windows. And that meant two things: first, that he'd hidden somewhere in the house-- in the tiny vegetable pantry, or in the cellar, or in some closet-- and, second, that while I was upstairs closing the windows, he could easily have left without seeing me, or being seen. Yet he hadn't done so. Why?

The conclusion was only too clear: He'd wanted to question me, in order to find out how much I knew of the murder. And he'd wanted to keep me from going to the police about Cynthy.

Why should a policeman act like that?

And then suddenly I knew the answer. But the answer was no longer important in itself, because it meant just one thing:

Cynthy was in danger. Terrible danger.

I was as sure of it as if someone had told me. As, in effect, someone had.

There was a distant roll of thunder, soft and sure of itself, as if it were aware of the power it could unleash whenever it chose. I went to the kitchen and looked in the refrigerator. The melon was gone. But the policeman hadn't known that Bland had taken the dagger from the melon and that I had hidden it in the vase in the library.

I went into the library and, standing on tip toe, tilted the vase and explored within it, cautiously. But the dagger-- shive, as Bland had called it-- wasn't there.

Well, it didn't matter. Cynthy was the important thing.

I called Frieda's house, and was told by the maid that Miss Cynthy was gone and so was Madam. The maid knew only that Cynthy had gone out to dinner, and that Madam was not expected back till late.

I remember going to the hall closet and getting out a raincoat and tying a red scarf around my head, peasant fashion. Sam Boomer had said he would see Jim Allen and Cynthy that night, so it was possible that Jim had taken her to the Boomer house for dinner. It was worth a try, anyway, and there was no time to waste. After I had Cynthy in a safe place I could think and reason.

As I hurried through the hall I gave another thought to the

Blands. Their absence fitted right into the pattern of ugly surmise that was forming in my mind. Lightning flashed across my eyes as I opened the door, and the gate and the trees loomed up eerily for an instant, looking yellow and strange. The trees were moving now, swaying and gathering motion mysteriously; yet I could feel the wind and there was as yet no rain. I ran back toward the garage, and as I fumbled for the door I discovered it had been left open.

My car was there, although Bland's smart coupé was gone. I slid into the seat and turned on the ignition and dashlight, so that I could see the gasoline gauge. There wasn't much gasoline, and I'd already used up my ration for that period. But I had to take the chance. I backed out, scraping a fender.

It was working up to a wild night. After I left the dimmed lights of Alexandria and took the road past the airport, with the terrible and fantastic bulk of the Pentagon Building away ahead of me, mine seemed to be almost the only car on the road. Lightning was clearer now and nearer, more nerve-shattering in its sudden brightness, particularly since my lights were dimmed.

I took the first bridge over the Potomac; the river was like ink except where it reflected bright flashes of lightning. I passed the Lincoln Memorial, and it suddenly occurred to me that I didn't know the exact address of Sam Boomer's house, only that it was near Rock Creek Park.

Winding curves of roadway and trees brought me eventually into a business street. I stopped at a drugstore and called Frieda's house again. The maid promptly gave me Sam Boomer's address.

"Is Miss Farish with Mrs. Merly?" I'd known all the way from Alexandria that I ought to have asked that question when I first telephoned Frieda's house.

"Mrs. Merly--" began the maid, and apparently fainted away, maybe died, for all I know. For there was a sudden and terrific crackle along the telephone wire, and the whole street outside lit up. The line buzzed a while and then went dead.

It was a long time before I found Boomer's house. There is a section near Rock Creek Park that is a maze of irregular turns and twists and unexpected small "Places" which now and then prove to be dead ends. Twice I got into someone's driveway and had to back out again.

And then almost unexpectedly, I found the address I was looking for. It was a large, substantial brick house, set well back of some thick shrubs. There was a small light turned on above a bronze number, so I knew I was right. I went past it, stopped, and turned off my engine and lights. Now for it.

I crawled out of the car, cowered under a brilliant flash of lightning, and then crossed the sidewalk into the shelter of a thick, high hedge.

Suddenly and disconcertingly I caught the quick shadow of another movement farther down the walk. Rather as if the hedge had momentarily bulged out toward the sidewalk and then flattened again. I crouched against the foliage beside me, stared into the darkness ahead, and listened. But another flash of lightning revealed only a straight line of hedge and white sidewalk, and a car standing at the entrance of a driveway some sixty feet ahead. Before I had seen anything, it was no longer there. Then the lightning was gone.

I was left wondering again, rather desperately, exactly what to do. Walk up to that house, all at once so forbidding in the gloom beyond the hedge, and demand Cynthy? And then what?

I took another step forward and, as if at a signal, the curtain rolled up, to the accompaniment of a lingering roll of thunder. Rather it shot up.

The big house beyond the hedge had been dark behind its carefully drawn blackout curtains.

Now, as the front door was flung open, a path of light shot startlingly across the porch. Two figures came hurrying out of the house, a woman and then a man. I crouched back close to the hedge as they came rapidly down the walk toward the street.

As the first figure reached the break in the hedge, the door was flung open again and closed with another bang. Footsteps came running down the steps and along the sidewalk, and a voice called huriedly, "Go back. He wants you. Quick! Something's happened. I'll see to--" It was a man's voice, but so hurried and blurred that I couldn't identify it. And just then a hot gust of wind shook the trees and shrubbery wildly, drowning all other sounds.

When it began to die away, footsteps again were pounding along the walk leading to the Boomer house. Then there was silence.

It was a curious silence, because only one person had gone back to the house; I was sure of that. Therefore two people must be standing on the other side of the hedge not far from me. Yet they neither moved nor spoke-- No, I was wrong.

For the frantic sigh and murmur of the trees above us stopped altogether, as if the conductor of that stormy orchestra had made a motion with his baton. And I could hear voices, a man's and a woman's, muffled but jerky and vehement, as if in anger.

There was something terrifying about that muted quarrel, there in the deathly lull of the storm. It was impossible to distinguish words, but there was no mistaking the passionate urgency of the argument.

And then the man's voice came clear: "I tell you you've got to go. She's waiting. It's the best for you and for everybody."

The conversation stopped then, and the curtain swept up on a second act. For a vivid flash of lightning came, and I saw two figures running toward the car that was parked in Boomer's driveway. The man I did not know: the girl was Cynthy.

The man had Cynthy by the arm, urging her in the direction of the waiting car. I had the impression that she was reluctant. Then everything was blotted out as the darkness swallowed up the blue-white glare of lightning. There was a long, long crash of thunder. I put my hands to my ears and held my breath. I didn't know that I had shut my eyes too, until whiteness beat upon my closed eyelids again. I opened them to another flash of lightning, and this time I saw a queer thing.

Cynthy was getting into that car. But she was alone; the man who had been with her was gone. And though she was moving hurriedly, there was no longer any suggestion of unwillingness on her part.

I saw only that; then it was dark again.

I knew then that I was really terrified. Not as I had been before, in my queerly empty house, afraid of the unknown, but wildly terrified of a menace I now knew to be real.

Scarcely knowing what I was doing, I started toward the car, running along the sidewalk in a blackness so dense that only the touch of the hedge brushing my arm and shoulder guided me. The engine of the car ahead started; I heard it just as I stumbled upon something very soft and still. I lost my balance and fell to my knees on the sidewalk. My flailing hands touched something horribly inert and quiet.

It was the body of a man.

I saw it only dimly, not clearly enough to discover who it was. He was lying close within the black line of shadow made by the hedge.

I didn't know what had happened, but one thing was clear. He had been attacked, obviously, during that long roll of thunder; it had been a swift and merciless attack, devilishly spaced, so that it occurred during the darkness between the lightning flashes. Did Cynthy know?

I was just stumbling to my feet, when a man threw open the door to the Boomer house and came hurtling down the steps and along the walk. He stopped almost at my shoulder to stare at the moving lights of the car, which was already turning into the street, and began to swear. I knew who it was.

I told him, "Cynthy's in that car."

There was an instant's silence as a faint glow of lightning revealed us to each other. Jim Allen clutched my shoulder so tightly it hurt. "Cynthy is in that car? Who's with her?"

"I don't know. But there's a man here beside the hedge. He's dead."

He bent quickly and groped about. Then the car began to move down the street, and at the sound he shot up again. He started to run after the car, and I ran after him.

"Wait-- wait! I've got a car."

He slid to a stop. "Car? Where?"

"It's back this way. Hurry."

We left that dark huddle in the shadow of the hedge as if it had never been a man. It now seems inhuman; it wasn't then. I only thought of Cynthy. We had to find her.

When we reached my car, Jim Allen got into the driver's seat with a decision that gave me no chance to argue about it. Then I began to see that I could very easily have jumped from the frying pan into the fire. Obviously, he was pursuing Cynthy, and I had leaped to the conclusion that his motive was the same as mine. Yet it might be something quite different.

We reached the corner, turned, and saw no car anywhere along the street. We reached another cross street in what seemed a split second, and hesitated there while Jim Allen peered one way and then another and then swerved. "Here we go," he said. "Into the park it is."

We turned into a narrow, steeply sloped road. At that moment the storm broke.

There followed something out of a nightmare. If we could have talked, even, there might have been some sort of order and direction to the thing, but the sudden lashing of rain, the constant crackle of lightning and frantic rolling of thunder, the slippery, glistening road visible only in wavering patches through the streaming rain, made talk impossible. What we did say had to be shouted; we were lost in a world of bedlam, both straining our eyes and every nerve to see ahead.

Suddenly Jim stopped the car. "It's no good," he shouted. "It's like looking for a needle in a haystack. We could have missed them at twenty different curves. Three, anyway." He turned, and in the glow from the dashlight I could see his face. "What are you doing in this?" he demanded. "You're the woman who found Benkham, aren't you? And you were at the party this afternoon. Why are you after Cynthy?"

"I'm one of Cynthy's friends." I told him my name.

He recognized it instantly. "Oh, of course. Cynthy has talked of you. I'm sorry."

It was only then that something struck me as queer about what he had said. Something out of the picture, something sharply new. "Benkham!"

Jim Allen was getting into gear again and leaning forward to peer through the rain. I said it again, "Benkham! Is that the name of the murdered man?"

We shot forward. "Yes."

I shouted, "But no one knew him! You knew his name. Who is he? How do you know?"

He didn't bother to answer. He swerved around the curve. "I'll get the police! I've got to find Cynthy. If she's gone voluntarily-- But she knows. She knows something. I've got to find her.

It didn't answer my spoken questions, but it answered a big unspoken question. If he was willing to get the police to help him find Cynthy he didn't intend to murder her.

It was just then that he said slowly and with a kind of horror,

"What the hell!" For at exactly that moment the gasoline gave out.

Jim tried over and over to start the engine, and got nowhere. Finally he said despairingly, "Lost in Rock Creek Park. No gas, and Cynthy-- oh, my God." He gave another push on the starter, then reached for the door.

"What are you going to do?" I asked.

"Walk back to a phone and call the police. Nothing else to do. I was a fool to try to follow her in the first place." He opened the door.

"I'm going, too."

"You can't."

"I can't stay here. Don't try to stop me. I'll follow you. You may as well let me come along."

I got out, and the rain drenched me through in a couple of seconds. I gasped at the coldness and fury of the onslaught. Jim Allen was drenched, too; I caught a glimpse of his face, glistening from the rain, and his red hair already dark and wet. He seemed to decide that he didn't care what I did, gave a shrug, and started along the road. I went with him. Rain and darkness and wind and more rain. I hoped he knew where he was going; I didn't. The lightning and thunder had worked away toward the north, but the rain seemed never-ending.

All at once Jim said, "Why are you after Cynthy? What's your part in this?"

"Cynthy never killed that man, and I think she's in danger."

"She didn't kill him. But she's mixed up in it, and she's worried and scared."

It was queer walking there in the rain, with the tumult of the storm dying away, speaking what we knew of the truth.

"You said his name was Benkham?"

"Yes. Alfred Benkham. Williams knew him."

"But who was Benkham?"

"I don't know." We trudged on in silence. At last he said, "I don't know why, but I think you're all right. I mean-- well, you're on Cynthy's side. There's something going on, and I don't understand it. But his name was Alfred Benkham, all right. Williams knew it, and said so to Frieda Merly. She was there for dinner tonight. So was Cynthy. So was I. Williams came in later. I kept trying to get Cynthy alone; I'd got to thinking, and I had to talk to her. It was a short dinner. Boomer was a little tight, and Mrs. Merly didn't like it. She's been boosting him, you know. The idea is to marry him if things go well and he gets launched into his political career."

"Political career! Boomer?"

"Of course. He's ambitious; wants to run for office in his native state. She has advised him from the beginning. She's ambitious, too. He's got the money and Mrs. Merly's got the brains and political acumen. But she gets furious if he drinks a spot too much. He's a swell guy and only gets a little exuberant, but she likes him better suave and dignified. So it was an unpleasant and a short dinner. Rosita got Boomer upstairs, and I got hold of Cynthy and started to take her away to talk; but just as we got out of the house, Boomer sent for me. I went back, but Rosita said he hadn't sent for me at all. By the time I got out of the house again, there you were, and Cynthy--" He gave another groan and said, "Can't you walk any faster?"

"But that's not all," I said. "Why did Williams tell Frieda Merly the name of the murdered man? How did you know he was talking about the murdered man?"

"Oh, he said so. They spoke of the murder, in the library just after Boomer went upstairs. She wanted to know if the murder could affect Boomer's career, and she asked Williams because he's Boomer's press agent, you know. That and general adviser. Boomer depends on him for everything. Doesn't say a word or move a finger unless Williams approves."

"What did Williams say?"

"He said the murder of a man like Alfred Benkham couldn't hurt anybody's political career. She picked him up, of course. Her face got very queer and sharp, and she said, 'Alfred Benkham! So that was his name!' It was just then that I had a chance to grab Cynthy and get her out of the house, and I did."

"Did Frieda know Benkham?"

"Did--? Why, what makes you think so?"

"The way you quoted her. You said, she said, 'So that was his name!' As if she knew it."

"Oh. Well, yes; that's the way she said it. But all I was thinking about was Cynthy."

"Didn't you ask Williams how he happened to know the man's name?"

"No." Again he seemed to brood heavily, while our steps squashed steadily and wetly along the road. Finally he said, "No, I didn't. Williams somehow always does get the low-down on things. If any of us would know who the murdered man was, it would be Williams. I mean he'd find out." He added thoughtfully, "Unless, of course, he already knew him."

"Whoever murdered that man knew him!"

He frowned down at me. "But Williams couldn't have. He was out of town."

"Are you sure?"

"Reasonably. Anyway, it could easily be established by the police. Why, it was Boomer's alibi that he was waiting to meet Williams at the Mayflower, and that Williams didn't turn up. They check all those things."

"How about Boomer?"

"I'm his alibi; he's mine, too, I guess. I left him in the Mayflower bar last night, as I said, waiting for Williams. I went back to the Boomer place, picked up Rosita, and we went on to the Drake

cocktail party. Boomer came home a little later, when Williams
didn't turn up. The maid let him in. She told Rosita he was a little
tight even then. He went to his room, where he keeps a liquor
cabinet, and that was the last she saw of him. But it's an alibi, in its
way. And Hibling, the manager of the store, seems to have an alibi.
Yet whoever murdered Benkham had to enter the store before closing
hours, or else had to have a key."

"Had Williams a key?"

"Not that I know of; but it would have been easy enough to get
one. I think the murder must have been done after the closing hour.
It would have been too dangerous to try whilst there were people
around."

"That means whoever did it had to have a key.   If Cynthy
doesn't have one--"

"I'm sure she hasn't. Besides, Cynthy wouldn't murder anybody!"

"Why are you so worried about Cynthy?"

"Because-- well, the fact is, she knows something. I don't know
what. She was at the house this morning. I was on the stairs as she
went out, and she wouldn't even stop and speak to me. Then this
afternoon--"

"Yes, yes, I know. I heard you. You've forgotten. What you
don't know is--" I paused for another brief self-reassurance about
Jim Allen; decided again that I could trust him, and hurriedly told
him all. Or almost all. I told him about meeting Cynthy in the store;
I told him why I had not mentioned her presence to the police; and I
told him about the melon with the dagger in it.

He gave a sharp exclamation when I came to that, and when I
went on to tell of what finally happened to the melon I brought home,
he said, "For God's sake! Well, go on! What then?"

"That is all," I said, "except that Cynthy is in terrible danger.
Because of the knife--"

"Shive," he interrupted. "It was mine."

I stopped literally in my tracks. "Yours!"

"Yes. And I"-- He stopped, too. He reached out and clutched
my arm, and then abruptly put his hand over my mouth. Which was
just as well, for I looked then, and saw what he saw.

We had rounded a black blotch of trees and shrubbery. Behind it
was a thin path of light streaming from the lights of an automobile
which had been run up over the curb and onto the wet grass.

Directly in the path of the light a man, big and bulky, was
stooping over something that lay like a log on the grass. I thought it
was Cynthy, but it wasn't Cynthy, for all at once I saw her, too. She
was sitting on a rock, at the very edge of the path of light, taking off
her stockings.

We stood there as if paralyzed. She calmly removed one stocking
and then the other, and thrust her slim white feet back into sodden
pumps. She got up and went to the man stooping over, she gave him
the stockings. He bent still farther and seemed to be very busy,

while Cynthy, her hair wet and plastered away from her face, watched.

"My God!" said Jim Allen huskily. "He's tying something. He's-- Who is he? I never saw him-- Cynthy!"

He called that out loud and plunged toward the girl, who turned wildly to meet him as if she couldn't believe he was there. And the big man in the middle of the light finished whatever he was doing and straightened up and looked, too, toward Jim.

It was Bland.

He stood between me and the figure on the grass. But of course I knew who it must be.

I have never understood Bland, but I am fairly well conditioned to him, so that his activities gave me little or no surprise. This, however, was one of the times when the conditioning broke down. He didn't see me at first, for Jim was standing, with Cynthy, in the glow of the headlights and Bland just stood watching in majestic and somehow triumphant silence. I struggled on up the slippery little slope; then emerged into the lights, too.

Bland saw me and gave a fishlike gasp. "Madam," he said. "Dear me."

He moved chivalrously but unnecessarily to block my view of the thing at his feet, just as Cynthy remembered his presence.

"This is Jim," she cried, turning her face toward Bland. "This is the man-- Jim Allen."

So she'd told Bland about him.

Bland said, "Good evening, sir. May I suggest that you take Madam and Miss Cynthy in that car to the Boomer house? If you'll kindly get in touch with the police then, and send them here, I'll join you at the house shortly. Thank you," he concluded with the finality and decision of a great conqueror. And wafted us toward the car.

As Jim backed hurriedly into the road, Bland was seen taking stately refuge under a pine tree. "They'll be here right away," shouted Jim back.

I held onto Cynthy around the curves, but she was crying softly and I couldn't talk to her.

We were unexpectedly close to the Boomer house; it couldn't have been more than three or four minutes before we turned into the street before it. But the house was different; it was a blaze of lights, and there were cars out in front, police cars. Three policemen fell upon us just as an ambulance swept around the corner and stopped behind our car. It had come for the man who still lay there on the sidewalk.

There were policemen everywhere. They moved us along, and presently we were inside an old-fashioned library with worn brown leather furniture. Frieda Merly was standing beside the massive table, her small head uplifted, her fine features set and determined.

It was Frieda who dominated the scene that followed. Frieda, that is, until Bland arrived. Jim must have sent police to him instantly, for very soon he appeared, genie-like, in the doorway, and quietly became, as only Bland can do,the scene's most vital figure.

But it was Frieda, at first. She saw Jim and me and Cynthy. Her small head went a little higher, and then she smiled defiantly. "Oh, there you are, Cynthy," she said. "I'm glad."

Cynthy went to stand beside her.

Jim said, "It's all over, Mrs. Merly."

Frieda said quietly, "Thank you, Jim. I think I understand." She turned to the police lieutenant, who had apparently been questioning her. "It's all right, then," she said. "This is the child I was worried about. As you see, she is safe."

The lieutenant nodded. "Now then, Mrs. Merly, if you'll tell me the whole story--"

"Certainly," said Frieda. She looked very pale and put her small, jeweled hand upon Cynthy's. "You knew," she said. "Didn't you?"

"I heard the name tonight," said Cynthy. "Alfred Benkham.. I remembered he had called to see you yesterday; the maid said 'Mr. Alfred Benkham.' I happened to see him leave. So this morning when I was sent to the market to get the dagger that belonged to Jim--" She closed her eyes as if to shut out the picture, and then met Frieda Merly's searching gaze. "I saw him. I recognized him. I'd been told that there was danger to Jim; I'd been told that Jim had been at the market early, that he'd come back here with a story of a murdered man, that police had to be called, and that a dagger that belonged to Jim and could be traced to him was in the storeroom."

"What else were you told, child?" asked Frieda gently.

"I was told that Jim was in danger from the police; that he'd got himself in a jam-- I wasn't told what-- but if I-- liked Jim I could help by removing the dagger before the police arrived. I was told not to tell <u>anyone</u> that I knew of the dagger. It was all said very quickly and very convincingly. I was told to get the dagger, to have faith in Jim, to keep quiet. Explanations would came later; the main thing was to hurry. Jim had showed it to me."

Jim said quietly, "Everybody knew it; it was a kind of curiosity. I had a client, during a short time when I had a job in a law office, a client who had been in and out of penitentiaries most of his life. He was really innocent of the current charge and I got him off. In gratitude he gave me the shive."

"Made in one of the cell blocks of--" I named the prison Bland had named. It was almost my only contribution to the moment; but it elicited a somewhat speculative glance from the police lieutenant.

Jim nodded. He said, "I didn't know it was missing till this evening, when you told me."

I said, "Cynthy, who was Alfred Benkham? Why was he murdered?"

Frieda broke in: "Yes, Lieutenant. You wanted to know, too. When I telephoned for the police a few minutes ago I did so, first, because this child"-- she pressed Cynthy's hand again-- "had disappeared. I didn't know where she'd gone. I only knew she'd left the house before I could stop her. I had been talking to Williams; he told me it was Benkham. It gave me a-- kind of shock. I came here, to this room, to be alone for a moment in order to think and arrange my course of action.... After a little I realized the house was quiet, terribly quiet. Then I looked, and Cynthy was gone, and I was afraid. So I called the police. But I also did it because I-- well, sooner or later I knew I'd have to tell the police the whole story."

She took a long breath. I've got to be on the right side of this, Lieutenant. I hated the publicity, but the truth, or part of it, had to come out sooner or later. I won't be in a pretty position, either way, but I've got to be at least on the side of the law--"

"Go on, Mrs. Merly," said the lieutenant. "Who was Alfred Benkham?"

She took another long breath; the jewels in her ears gleamed and flashed under the light. She said steadily, "He was a shyster lawyer. Many years ago he defended Sam on a charge of using the mails to defraud; it was some get-rich-quick scheme. The point was, he cleared Sam, but he knew Sam was actually guilty. Benkham not only knew it, but he managed to get and keep the evidence that would ruin Sam." She paused, and said to Cynthy, "It's all in an envelope in my bedroom desk. The upper left-hand drawer."

"Oh," said Jim. "You paid for the evidence Benkham had?"

A little flush crept up into Freida's charming, well-bred face. "I needn't spare myself anything," she said. "I-- bought Benkham, or thought I did, because I wanted to keep him quiet, yes. Sam's future was going to be my future. However--" She swallowed and went on, "I also thought it an excellent idea for me to have that particular-- source of control in my own hands. It sounds-- however, that was what I did. Our arrangement was fairly practical."

I liked Freida more at that moment than I had ever liked her before. It was not her courage in admitting the truth; it was the quality in her that made her see it, which is a quite different and rarer thing.

Cynthy put her arm around Freida's slender waist. Freida looked at her and said quietly, as if only she and Cynthy were in the room, "What happened? Just now, I mean."

Cynthy replied as quietly, "Williams came after Jim and me when we left the house. He stopped us and told Jim that Mr. Boomer wanted him at once; he said it was urgent. Then, as soon as Jim was gone, he told me that the police had learned of my presence at the market. He said they were going to question me, and that the thing for me to do was to go with Rosita to a little town in Virginia. He said she'd meet me at the train and she'd bring some clothes for me; he said I had to go and stay away until the thing blew over.

"I didn't know what to believe or what to do. I started toward the car, and then I don't know what happened. He let go my arm and seemed to hang back. I decided to go on and get in the car, and drive away alone if I could. But before I could find the starter, someone opened the door and told me to move over. He said he'd take me to meet Rosita, and we started out."

"And that was-- ?" began Frieda stiffly.

Bland, in the doorway, said, "That was Sam Boomer. He murdered Benkham. He murdered Williams." His light blue eyes shifted to me. "Let me get you a chair, madam."

He did so, and I sat down. "He also," said Bland, "was about to murder Miss Cynthy. This time I believe it was to appear to be suicide or accident."

Cynthy was looking very white. She said slowly, "When Mr. Boomer phoned me early this morning he didn't tell me there was a murdered man in the stockroom; he just said Jim would be in trouble if the dagger was found. He said he would go and get it himself, or send Jim back, but that he had to call the police at once, and if I hurried I could get there and away before the police came. I didn't suspect Mr. Boomer even when I saw the murdered man. He had sounded so natural when he talked to me, and it was so like him to help Jim. He-- he was always so friendly and charming."

"It was what he was building his career upon," said Frieda.

"But then," said Cynthy, "I didn't know what to do. I recognized Benkham and I knew it was murder. I knew Jim always went to the market early in the mornings, and that he had a key. And Boomer had said he wanted to help Jim. And I knew Mrs. Merly knew Benkham. If I went to the police-- I didn't know what to do! So I did what Sam Boomer had told me to do. Then in the afternoon Williams came to the party, and he and Mr. Boomer told me I hadn't brought the shive. I knew of course what had happened to it, and I told them. As soon as I had done it I was afraid. I don't know why-- there was just something about the way they took the news."

She looked at me. "I was going to come to you," she said. "I was going to tell you everything I knew. But I wanted to talk to Jim first, and to Mrs. Merly." She stopped, and Frieda said, "Thank you, child," and smiled faintly.

It was like Cynthy, of course; caught by her loyalties, plunged into a horribly perplexing situation, fighting through as best she could alone. All of it complicated by the shock and horror of the morning.

Bland said suddenly to Frieda, "And you believed, madam, that Miss Cynthy was in danger?"

Frieda gave him a long look before replying. Then she said, "Not until after Wiliams had told me it was Benkham; and then I felt it only because Cynthy was gone and I knew something was wrong, and I knew-- I knew Sam had already murdered once." She shivered, and said, as if it told the story, "The house was so terribly quiet."

The lieutenant said, "Mrs. Merly, have you any idea what Williams thought he would gain by sending Miss Farish out of town?"

She thought for a moment, and said, "It would have been merely a temporary expedient, of course, but it was an expedient. It would

keep Cynthy away from the police for a few days, and it might serve
until Williams had time to make a better plan for ensuring Cynthy's
silence. Also, he knew Sam. He knew that Sam's blind panic had
already led him into murdering Benkham, and into the fatal mistake
of sending Cynthy for the dagger. Sam must have realized later that
Cynthy would get to thinking Jim was innocent, and that she'd better
tell the police the story. Once he realized that, he might have lost
his head again and tried to get rid of Cynthy. So Williams, to avoid
another murder, tried to send Cynthy away, until he could evolve a
better plan."

The lieutenant said suddenly, "And your own theory about the
murder, Mrs. Merly?"

She looked at him wearily. "It's quite obvious, isn't it? Benkham
got all he could out of me; then he went to Sam. Williams was gone.
If he'd been here he'd have kept Sam on an even keel. But Sam
alone...." She shrugged. "He lost his head completely."

The lieutenant said, "You don't believe, then, that murder was
premeditated?"

Frieda frowned. "I don't know. Knowing Sam, I'm inclined to
think that he did not admit to himself that he had determined to
murder Benkham; perhaps he hadn't determined to do so. But I think
it was in his mind, nevertheless, as a recourse if Benkham held his
ground. That's why he took the shive, obviously; not only because it
was a lethal weapon, but because it belonged to Jim. And it would
have been easy for a man as important as Sam to frame an unknown
assistant like Jim, a man with no close connections but himself."

With a little choked cry, Cynthy reached for Jim. He drew her
down on the big sofa and sat close to her, with her trembling hands
caught in his two big ones.

The lieutenant said quietly, "But he sent for the shive the next
morning. He told Miss Farish to keep quiet about it, to protect
Allen."

"Yes," said Frieda painfully, "but-- don't you see?-- it wasn't
really to protect Jim, but to protect himself from Jim. I don't like to
say this, because, after all, I meant to marry Sam, but I do know that
he could be friendly, charming, even go out of his way to help a
person, as long as that person did not interfere with his own aims.
But he was a pusher. He'd come up the hard way, and he had never
really matured; he'd never learned, the way most people do, the line
where ambition stops and love of your fellow men becomes the most
important thing in life. It's a hard thing to say, but Sam, with all
his-- yes, his lovable traits, simply had no moral sense." She turned
to Jim. "I'm sorry. I had no idea how far he'd really go."

Jim said gruffly, "If he'd wanted to throw the blame on me, why
didn't he leave the melon in the stockroom? It would have been found
without his interfering. He could even have called the attention of
the police to it. It would have been easy to pin a knife like that on
me."

The lieutenant said, "I can answer that. From the point of view of the police, a knife, no matter how sinister, hidden in a melon, is not incriminating evidence. It's a crazy idea to stick a knife in a melon, but we couldn't put anyone in jail for it. Besides, we knew you hadn't committed the murder. Your alibis had been thoroughly checked; there was no evidence pointing that way. You couldn't have done it--"

"That's just why Sam couldn't let you find the knife," Frieda cut in excitedly. "Because, if you found the knife, Jim would know where it came from! Jim kept it on his desk, in Boomer's own house. Lots of people had seen it there. He had to get it back to Jim's desk before it was missed."

Jim said, "If he forgot the shive, why didn't he return it to the store during the night?"

The lieutenant said rather dryly, "Perhaps the concrete and imminent fact of police investigation threw him into a panic."

Frieda nodded. "Yes. That would be like Sam; he wasn't very clever about murder, was he?" she said in a queerly weary tone.

The lieutenant replied, "No, he wasn't clever. No murderer is really very smart; if he were he wouldn't murder. No murderer is infallible, either, or he wouldn't be caught. It's their mistakes that make discovery and conviction possible."

Frieda said, "He made his first mistake in the way he hid the knife. A Crenshaw melon is an ideal place for inserting a sharp weapon of that shape. The very hiding place an impulsive man like Sam would choose, without considering how he could get it out. I believe what happened was this: He may have left an end sticking out of the melon, but when, in the course of his talk with Benkham, he realized the-- murder must be done, he discovered the end had slipped inside the melon, out of reach. Either the other knife was at hand, or he may have left the room on some pretext and gone for it. Afterward, he left the place in a panic, forgetting the melon."

I asked, "But why would the knife ever have been found? After all, a melon has a right to be in a grocery store."

Jim said, "Not in the stockroom of our store. No perishable goods were ever placed there. Anyone noticing the melon would have examined it and found the slit where the knife went in. Boomer knew that."

"Yes, he saw that, too late," said Frieda, very white but somehow gallant. "But Sam's biggest mistake was sending Cynthy for it. He knew she would do it, because she loved Jim; I see that now. He didn't stop to think that her very love would make her believe in Jim's innocence and confide in him sooner or later. Sam simply acted, and then waited for Williams to put the whole thing in his hands. That's all," she said. "Except that he and Williams had different views about--" She stopped.

About Cynthy, of course. When Sam realized his mistake, he must have decided to save his own pink, well-cared-for skin at any cost-- even Cynthy's life.

Eventually they pieced it all together, the lieutenant and Jim and Frieda. And Bland. But first they asked me why I had felt that Cynthy was in danger. My first inkling came, of course, I told them, when I recognized Williams, dressed as the policeman, when he turned to leave my pantry. I'd seen him talking to Boomer and Cynthy from just that angle scarcely more than an hour before, though he'd carefully kept his face hidden from me. He'd hurried away from the cocktail party and rented a policeman's uniform, and gone straight to my house. He wanted to get hold of the melon and shive, of course, but the uniform was a a perfect disguise in which to confront me and question me as to how the situation stood.

It might have worked, too, if I hadn't caught that particular view of Williams. I realized then that he might have been sent by Boomer to recover the shive. That didn't necessarily mean that either of them had murdered Benkham; it did mean that they knew something about it, and they knew that Cynthy knew and had been sent to recover the knife.

That was what was important; for no matter why Cynthy had been sent, she was in danger, <u>for she knew who had told her to get the dagger.</u>

I felt proud of my detection of Williams's identity and wasn't quite prepared for the look of shame on Bland's face when I concluded. He coughed delicately. "Madam," he said, "you have forgotten to tell them the clue."

The lieutenant snatched on the word with joy. "Clue?" he said.

I said it, too: "Clue, Bland?"

"Yes, of course, madam. The initals on the ring. You described them most minutely to me."

"Yes. A.B. But--"

"And then, madam, Mr. Boomer came into the stockroom, looked at the body, and said, if I remember accurately what you told me, 'Who is he? A.B. on his ring. Wonder who he is.'"

"Yes. I--"

"But, madam, you told me that the initials were very worn and difficult to read, yet Mr. Boomer was not wearing his glasses."

"Why, Bland!" I cried. "That's true. You asked me hundreds of questions. But to think you remembered that one little detail."

Bland interrupted, loftily, "Thank you, madam, I had occasion to confirm my impression this evening. I-- er-- had a chat with the cook here just before I took refuge in Williams's car, which he left in the driveway. She said that Mr. Boomer could scarcely see his hand before him without spectacles. So--" Bland coughed lightly. "It appeared to suggest his implication in the crime; he must have known that ring, and what initials were on it, for he couldn't have deciphered the initials without glasses.

"Furthermore, while his alibi was apparently substantiated for the time between five o'clock and about six-thirty, there was no real alibi for him for the hours between six-thirty and seven-thirty. The housemaid let him into the house but was not sure of the time, only that it was about six-thirty and certainly not later than seven. But it developed when I had a few-- er-- quiet words concerning household routine, that she was busy laying the table for dinner and pressing a dress for Miss Boomer, and would not have seen or heard Mr. Boomer leave the house. As I suggested he did, very quietly, at once. She would not have been likely to note his return, later, either. An hour gave him all the time he needed, to meet Benkham at his store, which would have seemed a natural rendezvous to the unhappy victim, yet would seem an unlikely place for murder, since suspicion would so obviously point to the owner."

The silence in the room seemed to catch him in full flight. He stopped; all of us were staring at him, but no one spoke for a moment. Then the lieutenant voiced what I believe we were all thinking. "Exactly what is your story?" he said.

Bland blinked; his glacial blue eyes were perfectly blank. "Oh, quite simple, sir. Not much, really. I simply sifted in my mind the evidence I had learned from madam, but I had no clues until this evening, when a policeman came to tell me and my wife that we were wanted at the police station in Washington. He said he would stay at the house in order to send you, madam"-- he nodded austerely at me-- "when you returned. I took my own car and set out, but on the way I realized that he was not a policeman at all, so I left Mrs. Bland at a movie in order to ensure her-- er-- safety and returned to the house. I was in time to see the policeman leave with the melon in his hands; and it was no trick to follow him. He came straight to the Boomer place, where I judge, he changed clothes again quickly.

"I didn't know just what course to follow, however. The cook, who let me in under the impression that I had an appointment for an interview concerning a job, was told by the housemaid that I had no such appointment. I believe she spoke to Miss Rosita. At any rate, I was obliged to tell them I had come to the wrong house and leave. In order to make sure that Williams and Boomer did not escape without my knowing it, I got into the back seat of Williams's car. The rest of it you know."

"But we don't know," said Jim rather savagely. "Did Boomer try to murder--?"

"It's all right, dear," said Cynthy quickly.

Bland said, looking at the ceiling, "There was a steep bank and a ravine, a few feet beyond the spot where he stopped the car. He had dropped the heavy spanner-- with which he must have killed Williams, under cover of the storm-- in the back of the car as he got in. Barely missing me," Bland added, with a look of haughty disapproval in his face. "However, he provided me with a weapon. When he stopped the car, in order to arrange what I imagine he thought would look like an accident, it was a simple matter to-- er-- eliminate him."

Jim hadn't looked at Bland during the whole speech, for he hadn't taken his eyes from Cynthy. But all at once, ignoring the other people in the room, he put both arms tight around her and drew her close to him. She said, into his shoulder, "I didn't know. I didn't know what had happened to Williams. I didn't know what Boomer-- not until the last minute or two. Then I was-- I wanted you." Her voice wavered upward.

At that Jim gave a frenzied look around, and suddenly put Cynthy on the sofa and came over and wrung Bland's hand in an inarticulate way. The lieutenant coughed this time. And as he did so Rosita, in hat and coat, walked into the room.

"I got tired of waiting for Cynthy," she said simply. "Williams told me to take her to the place in Virginia and stay there. He said it was important and he'd explain later. But I came back. I've been listening. I went upstairs, and this was in Uncle-- in his room. Under the mattress. It was pretty silly of him not to destroy it but-- anyway, here it is. I only wanted to say I had nothing to do with all this, so you can't hold me." At which she put a black leather wallet on the table.

It was Benkham's wallet. It had various identifying cards in it and a few bills. It also had a check signed by Frieda Merly.

That, really, was all. The lieutenant said, in a worried way, "Of course, I'll have to check on all of this. I'll have statements drawn up."

"You'll want the shive, I presume," said Bland, in exactly the manner he gives a departing guest a hand with his topcoat.

"Oh, yes. The shive--"

"It's in a vase on the library mantel," began Bland.

I interrupted. "No, it isn't. That's where I put it, but it's gone."

"I beg your pardon, madam," said Bland, looking slightly ashamed of my obtuseness. "It is in the other vase. I thought it an excellent hiding place. I merely shifted it."

There was a silence. Cynthy seemed to move a little closer to Jim.

Then the lieutenant said suddenly, to Bland, "Look here, how did you know Williams was a fake policeman?"

Bland's eyebrows lifted coldly, but there was a dreamy look in the blue eyes below them. "I have had occasion in the past to observe policemen and their methods somewhat closely. Not for myself, I might say, but for--"

He left that point unelucidated and glided suavely on: "Therefore on the way to the station it suddenly struck me that Williams, presumably a Washington policeman, was wearing a New Orleans badge. I daresay it was on the costume he rented and he did not look closely; they are somewhat alike. The San Francisco badge, now, and the New York badge--" He stopped delicately again and said, "But I'm sure you aren't interested in these little technicalities. It's merely a hobby."

I think it was then that Cynthy got up from the sofa and went to Bland and kissed him.

He neither blushed nor froze with disapproval; he liked it. "Thank you, Miss Cynthy," he said, with what was practically a beam. "And may I be the first to wish you well."

the
disappearing
hermit

by
PHOEBE
ATWOOD
TAYLOR

Phoebe Atwood Taylor (1909-1976) created one of the most popular detectives of the thirties and forties in Asey Mayo, known variously as the "Codfish Sherlock" or the "Hayseed Sleuth." Communicating in the deceptively slow New England dialect of Pa Kettle or the Fred Allen radio program's Titus Moody, he was both a mechanical and a ratiocinative genius. In the course of the series, he went from general handyman to executive of the Porter Motor Company. As had Agatha Christie when she created Hercule Poirot, Taylor started her famous character out a little too elderly when he made his first appearance in The Cape Cod Mystery (1931). As the years went by, she allowed him to grow subtly younger. Taylor's stories are fast-paced, light-hearted, sometimes farcical. Under the pseudonym Alice Tilton, she created the even wackier (and to some tastes even better) series about Shakespeare-lookalike Leonidas Witherall. Though humorous mysteries tend to age less well than others-- see, for example, the present obscurity of the once very popular Craig Rice-- Taylor's works continue to attract new readers. They were reissued in hardcover by Norton in the sixties and seventies, and more recently some have been reprinted in paper by Foul Play Press, an imprint of Countryman Press.

Asey Mayo appeared in eight novelettes, six of them included in a pair of collections, Three Plots for Asey Mayo (1942) and The Asey Mayo Trio (1946). The final two, both of which appear in this book, have never been reprinted since their original appearance in American. "The Disappearing Hermit" (April 1946), set in Boston, is one of the few Mayo stories to venture away from Cape Cod.

THE DISAPPEARING HERMIT by Phoebe Atwood Taylor

Asey Mayo pointed up at the clock of Boston's Customhouse tower and tartly informed his housekeeper cousin Jennie, sitting beside him in the parked Porter roadster, that he was giving her just five minutes more.
"If you haven't located that address by five-thirty, we're going

straight home to Cape Cod!"

"But it's here somewhere!" Jennie leaned forward, her flower-decked hat slightly askew, and pawed at the contents of the open glove compartment like a terrier going after a rat. "I just can't put my finger on it! And we've got to see Laura! We must!"

"Five minutes," Asey repeated firmly. "Because inside of six, that cop yonder's goin' to give us a ticket for overparkin'. Honest," he added, "what have we got to see this stray relation for, anyway? I never heard of the old girl till she all of a sudden popped into your mind this afternoon. What's your hurry?"

"If I could just remember the name of that street!" Jennie sighed. "It's on the tip of my tongue, but I can't say it. Don't start up the car, Asey! We got to see her!"

"Look, this old Cousin Maria Whoosis--"

"Laura, not Maria," Jennie corrected him. "Laura King."

"Whatever her name is, I don't know her, an' I don't feel any burnin' necessity for payin' her a visit," Asey returned. "I can't think why you're so suddenly dead-bent to-- There, your time's up! We're headin' home!"

Jennie reached past him and turned off the ignition.

"Now, Asey Mayo," she said briskly, "you listen to me! We can't sit idly by and let a relation that's just got left ten thousand dollars of her father's insurance get taken in by some slick city man that's lived in the same boardinghouse with her all this time, and never noticed her till she come into money! Furthermore, when Laura's Aunt Nellie heard yesterday that I was comin' to Boston with you for a day's shopping while you went to the Porter directors' meeting, she phoned and begged me to look into things, and I promised we would. And we're going to!"

Asey leaned his elbows on the wheel and grinned at her. "So this visit to old Laura wasn't a sudden impulse at all, but another one of your deep-laid plots, huh? An', as usual, you thought I'd fall for it if you sprung it on me as a surprise?"

Jennie ignored his questions. "'Course," she said, "maybe every-thing's all right. Maybe this Perry person loves her. Maybe he even means to marry her. Maybe that ten thousand dollars hasn't a thing to do with it all! But if, by some mere chance, it has-- well"-- she shrugged her shoulders-- "I guess any shady business would stop pretty quick if Laura's cousin, who dropped by and seemed to be taking an interest, turned out to be none other than Asey Mayo, the famous detective, the famous Codfish Sherlock, the famous--"

"No," Asey said gently. "Soft soap isn't goin' to induce me to butt into-- Oho! Here comes that cop, fingerin' his tickets! Now, don't sass him, Jennie! Don't try to alibi us by tellin' about old Cousin Laura, an' her lost address, an' all your dire forebodin's about her love life, an'--"

"Asey!" Jennie grabbed his arm and shook it excitedly. "If he doesn't give us a ticket, will you go to Laura's? Will you? Promise?"

"Just keep mum an'--" Asey broke off.

Jennie had already begun to talk to the approaching cop. "Officer," she said, in her folksiest tones. "I was just goin' to ask your help! We're out-of-towners from the Cape, an' first we misplaced our cousin's address, an' now we're all mixed up with these crooked streets! Can you tell us where Dyer Street is, please, an' how to get there?"

Five minutes later, Asey was guiding the long, black Porter roadster through the maze of Boston's downtown traffic in the general direction of Beacon Hill.

"Honest, now, come clean!" he said. "You invented that address to sidetrack the cop, didn't you?"

"Why, I never! It's real! I told you the street name was on my tongue-tip, and when you said 'dire forebodin's', it come to me-- Dyer Street! Seventeen Dyer! Now stop fussin'. I've saved you a ticket!...Left turn here." She consulted the paper on which she'd jotted down the cop's directions. "Then right, then left once more, and that'll be Dyer. He said it wouldn't take two minutes to get there."

But Dyer Street was still eluding them half an hour later, even though several pedestrians whom they accosted helpfully assured them it was just around the corner, somewhere, and they couldn't possibly miss it.

"Stop grumblin', and pull over to the curb," Jennie said, "and let me ask someone else. There's a woman steppin' out of that alley-- see her, in the fur coat? She looks as if she'd know her way around.... Yoo-hoo! Where's Seventeen Dyer, please?"

"Seventeen?" The plump woman in the mink coat sounded tremulous. "Seventeen Dyer?"

"That's right," Jennie said. "D'you know the place?"

"Ooh! Ooh!" The plump woman squealed, turned, and scuttled off down the street.

"Well, for goodness' sakes!" Jennie said. "These city folks! What d'you s'pose was the matter with her?"

"Maybe she's a Cabot," Asey suggested dryly, "an' found out we wasn't Lowells, or someone it was proper for her to speak to. Maybe the new roadster fooled her into thinkin' we was higher class-- Try that man comin' out the alley now."

The elderly man nodded in response to Jennie's question, and smiled pleasantly. "Dyer? Ah, yes, indeed! I'd be delighted to tell you all about Dyer Street."

Slinging a green flannel book bag over the shoulder of his dark topcoat, he proceeded to deliver a short lecture on the cowpath origin of Boston's narrow and crooked streets. Dyer, he informed them, was particularly interesting. Both its name and its direction had changed often in the course of the centuries. Lafayette had once dined on it, and Washington was said to have slept there. "Although I, personally, am inclined to doubt that statement. At the present time, it is primarily notorious for the exceedingly eccentric--"

"I'm sure it's a very famous an' historic place," Asey interrupted politely, "but-- uh-- just where is it? Specifically, where's Number Seventeen?"

"It was my impression," the man said icily, "that you desired information, not directions! That is Dyer Street!" With a stiff gesture toward the alley from which he had just emerged, he marched away up the street.

Asey got out of the car. "Come on, let's find Number Seventeen an' get this crazy visit over with!"

As he reached the entrance to the narrow cobblestone alley, a quartet of gas street lights flickered on, to reveal that Dyer Street was only two houses deep.

Asey paused and surveyed them.

The first was a grubby old two-story brick building whose sidewalk was littered with empty ash cans and still hummocked with mounds of dirty snow from the last April storm. The farther house was a well-kept four-story brownstone, with an iron fence surrounding its neat little front yard.

"Wait up!" Asey said as Jennie started toward the latter. "That brownstone's number seven. There isn't any Seventeen Dyer! I knew you dreamed it up!"

The very distinct "7" on the brownstone's outside gate light caused Jennie to hesitate for a moment. Then she pointed to the faded numerals just visible on the weatherbeaten wooden door of the brick house. "See, Smarty? Seventeen! This is it!"

"Quaint old Boston," Asey said. "Number the first house seventeen, an' the next one seven. Looks like Dyer Street's every whit as interestin' as that fellow said. Okay, so this's seventeen, but it's no boardin'house! Or, if it is, no relation of ours, even an old thirty-eighth cousin, would ever hang out in it! Why, use your eyes! No one's lived in that rat hole since Lafayette ate his baked beans an' brown bread--"

"It's Seventeen Dyer," Jennie said with finality. "This is it!"

"But look here, be reasonable! It's empt--"

"The door's ajar." Jennie picked her way across the snow patches. "And there's a light on."

"Jennie, don't go bustin' into that old--"

While Asey tried to think of a more pungent phrase than "rat hole," Jennie shoved the front door open.

"My goodness!" she said blankly. "My goodness, gracious! Asey, come look inside here! Why-- why--" Her voice trailed off.

Asey found himself blinking, even after his eyes had adjusted themselves to the glare of the naked electric-light bulb dangling on a wire from the ceiling of what must once have been a wide, gracious, paneled hall.

He shook his head and waited for Jennie to sum up the scene. As the silence grew, he realized that a minor miracle had taken place.

For once, Jennie was speechless.

"Asey, look at the stuff!" she said at last in an awed whisper. "Look at the junk! Look-- pianos! I never saw so many pianos! And on top of each other! Look-- those piles of mattresses! Look-- that heap of harps! Asey, I never saw anything like this! Look at it!"

"Uh-uh," Asey said. "I'm lookin'."

"Look! Look at those crates! What d'you s'pose is in 'em? And the tea chests! And the barrels! And look at those ash cans! And the stoves-- why, you couldn't hardly pick your way through all this mess to get up the stairs, or even into another room! Look, it's piled clear to the ceilin'! Asey, look!"

"Uh-huh."

"Those cherubs!" Jennie went on. "Look at that mound of plaster cherubs! And all those old-fashioned iceboxes....Asey, what's the matter with you? Whyn't you say something?" She swung around and looked at him. "What's wrong? What're you staring at?"

It took her several moments to find the gap in the mountains of pianos and crates and boxes through which Asey was gazing so intently. But finally she, too, saw the bloodstained face of the man who was wedged between crates and the barrels that all but blocked the entrance to the room on their right.

By standing on tiptoe and craning her neck, Jennie could see just enough to realize the man was dead. And he was still erect only because there wasn't any empty space in which he could fall.

"Well." Jennie paused and gulped, and, when she spoke again, her voice was half an octave higher. "Well, I s'pose we should be thankful it isn't poor Cousin Laura!"

"S'pose," Asey returned, "that we stop pretendin' that Seventeen Dyer's the right address! I certainly hope you see what happens when you go buttin' into affairs that're none of your business!"

"Cousin Laura is our business!" Jennie said stubbornly. "And Seventeen Dyer is the right address!...What killed him, Asey, and who d'you s'pose he is? Asey, do you s'pose it's him?"

"Who?"

"Why, the Perry person who wanted to marry Laura, of course! I told you all about-- Asey, where are you goin'?"

"To fetch the cops," Asey said wearily. "Havin' stamped ourselves on people's memories as the ones huntin' for Seventeen Dyer, we got to do our civic duty. Come along."

He took her arm and started to draw her out of the doorway, but she pulled back. "But, Asey, you got to find out who he is, and what killed him-- He was killed, wasn't he?"

"He never got like this without some outside lethal assistance," Asey returned. "Now, will you come along?"

The small flower bed on her head jiggled vigorously as Jennie shook her head. "I won't! Not till you've wiggled through this clutter and found out if he's the Perry person. And if you don't, I'm going to!"

From the stubborn set of her jaw, Asey knew that she would, too, without the slightest concern for the inevitable results. Eying the free space available for any maneuverings of her ample figure, he calculated roughly that she might take as much as a step and a half before dislodging enough of the assorted junk piles to bury them both.

"All right," he said. "I'll take what the reporters call a cursory look, an' then we're gettin' out of this rat hole, but quick!"

From where he had been standing by the door, Asey figured that it would take plenty of wriggling and edging to make his way to the body of the man beyond. Actually, as he moved along, he found his progress extraordinarily easy. While someone of Jennie's girth might have to inhale deeply and move with caution, there was no trick to it for anyone his size, or smaller. Automatically he filed in his mind for future reference that this hodgepodge was well planned.

The bloodstained face of the man wedged in between the crates and barrels was, on closer inspection, grim enough to make Asey wince. Without doubt, he thought, the fellow must have had some premonition of the fate which was overtaking him, and started to turn and cry out. His expression, his position, indicated that he had not been taken entirely by surprise.

For several minutes, Asey stared at the man, at his powerful shoulders, his well-cut dark gray suit, at his iron-gray hair, and his sharp profile. There was something magnetic about that profile. His eyes kept coming back to it.

At last, Asey made the tremendous mental effort of trying to visualize the face as it must have looked an hour or so before, without those bloodstains.

Almost at once a name came to his lips. "No!" he said to himself. "It can't be!"

Then he bent over and read the name engraved across a small gold football dangling from the man's watch chain.

He sighed as he straightened up. If he and Jennie managed to get back to Cape Cod within a week or two, they could count themselves very fortunate, indeed. Because this job was going to smear itself-- and everything and everybody involved with it-- over the headlines for days to come!

"Stabbed, wasn't he?" Jennie's voice sounded strangely hollow and far away, as she called out to him across the heaped-up barrels.

"No, he wasn't." Why, Asey wondered bitterly as he slowly made his way back to the door, couldn't fate have picked some nondescript individual, some tramp, some nonentity, to wedge between the crates in this gruesome manner? Why did it have to be a political figure like John Michael Sumner, whose death, even from the most natural and normal causes, would have raised a loud furor?

"Shot?" Jennie demanded. "He doesn't look shot!"

"He wasn't. Somebody bashed him."

"You mean he was hit? But all that blood! He must've been cut, somehow!"

"That came from scratches," Asey told her. "What killed him was a heavy blow over the back of his head, an' whatever was used as a weapon had three nails stickin' in the end of it. My guess is that it was a slat from one of those crates. Or maybe it was a loose barrel stave. Anyway, I think someone caught him from behind as he was goin' into that room to the right."

"Tch, tch!" Jennie clucked her tongue sympathetically. "Felled with a blow, as you might say."

"Wa-el," Asey said, "they felled him, though he couldn't fall."

"When did it happen?" Jennie asked eagerly.

Asey shrugged. "Oh, maybe about the time you were askin' that cop the way to your dear old Cousin Laura's. Maybe while you were jumpin' over the snow patches on the sidewalk outside. Or any time in between."

"That gives us two suspects, doesn't it?" Jennie said reflectively. "That fat lady in the mink coat--"

"Jennie, don't be crazy!"

"Why, there's nothing crazy about suspecting her!" Jennie said. "If you'd just killed a man at Seventeen Dyer, and practically the first people you saw afterwards yelled at you and asked what you knew about Seventeen Dyer, why, I guess you'd run away squealing with fright! And as for that old professory character, why, he'd gladly have chatted all night about Dyer Street. But when you mentioned Seventeen, he beat it! Yes, you got two good suspects, Asey. Only thing is--"

"Only thing is, you're talking through your hat!"

"Only thing is," Jennie went on, "if you think it could've happened so recent, just those few minutes ago-- Yes, I guess you better search this place right away, Asey. I'd say there's a real good chance that a murderer might be here, right now!"

Asey drew a long breath. "Listen-- we're not pokin' our noses any further into this mess! This isn't any sand-lot-league killin' you've butted into! That man yonder is--"

He broke off abruptly as the electric-light bulb dangling from the ceiling suddenly went off, leaving them in total darkness.

Just as suddenly, it returned, and then went out for perhaps twenty seconds before it flashed back on again.

"That wasn't bulb trouble," Asey thought. "Nor current failure." Someone was playing with the main switch!

Simultaneously, Jennie's fingers dug into his arm. "I hear someone! Footsteps!"

Asey heard them, too-- quick, anxious footsteps that seemed to be marching somewhere in the rear of the house, apparently inside of the thick wall. Second-guessing, and recalling how oddly Jennie's voice had sounded only a few feet away, Asey decided that the piles of assorted junk were playing tricks with the acoustics and that someone was in all probability coming up the cellar stairs. After all, main switches were in the cellar.

Asey shoved Jennie down behind a barricade of crates and mattresses, and then crouched down, himself.

"Maybe," Jennie said witheringly, "that might just <u>possibly</u> be the murderer."

"Probably," Asey retorted, "it's only your poor old Cousin Laura! Now <u>hush!</u>"

As they waited, he craned his neck to read the printing on a label, dirty and fly-specked, that was tacked on the crate beside him. "Bayard," it said. "17 Dyer Street."

A slow grin spread over Asey's face, and he stifled his inclination to call the name to Jennie's attention. This was not the time for startling disclosures and fuller explanations. Not with those footsteps drawing nearer!

Now they had lost most of their muted thumping sound, and the little half-beat accompaniment was turning very definitely into the tap-tap of high heels.

So it was a woman!

He waited until a white hand stretched out past him for the front door handle, and then he jumped up and grabbed it.

An ear-splitting scream   stopped in mid-air as the woman overcame her initial fright, recovered herself, and promply tried to struggle out of his grasp. "Let me go!"

Asey had a brief photographic impression of a dark-haired girl, perhaps in her middle twenties, dressed in a dark-red suit and a white blouse. There was no time for him to notice in more detail either her face or her features, for he was too busy ducking away from the five scarlet-tipped fingernails slashing forcefully and accurately at his eyes. He sensed rather than saw that she was carrying something in her left hand.

"Watch out!   She's got a crate slat!" he heard Jennie's shrill warning. "<u>Nails</u> in the end of it-- watch out!"

With the introduction of that crate slat and nail angle, whatever Chesterfieldian notions he had about not treating a lady too roughly vanished at once into thin air. Asey proceeded to put some steam into his wrestling match.

Even so, he was grateful for Jennie's spirited assistance in a flanking attack.

After the girl was finally thrust on the floor, with her hands pinned behind her back with the belt of Jennie's dress, and her ankles hobbled with Jennie's scarf, she continued to struggle.

"Well!" Jennie was panting, and her hat was a hanging garden over one ear. "Well, for goodness sakes, isn't she the scrapper! But I guess you've solved this one quick and without much fuss. Yes, sir, you got her red-handed. Who d'you s'pose she is?"

"Be consistent," Asey said.   "If Seventeen Dyer's the right address, who else could she be but Cousin Laura King?"

Jennie sniffed. "Think you're terrible funny, don't you? Just the same, Number Seventeen <u>was</u> what Nellie told me-- Better see if she's wriggled her wrists free, Asey. She's being awful quiet all of a sudden!"

"How," the girl said in a strained voice, "did you know?"

"I didn't know," Jennie said. "I just guessed when your face lit up that you'd wriggled free. You'd been so--"

"I'm not talking about my wrists!" the girl interrupted impatiently. "I mean my name-- how did you know who I am?"

It was fortunate, Asey thought, that his back happened to hit against a pile of three solidly crated upright pianos. Anything lighter would unquestionably have given way under his sudden start of astonishment.

Then he relaxed. "Old Cousin Laura, huh?" he said with a chuckle. "I hand it to you, young woman, you're quick to pick things up!"

The girl stared up at them. "You haven't your yachting cap and the usual rotogravure trappings, but you are Asey Mayo, aren't you? Well, Cousin Asey, take off these improvised handcuffs and help me up. Believe it or not, I was on my way to get hold of you!"

"So?" Asey leaned against the pianos. "Funny, I just thought you were runnin' out to catch a streetcar. Carryin' that slat, of course, to hail the motorman with. No, young woman, that line won't work. Old Cousin Laura is--" He paused and turned to Jennie. "How old is she?" he asked curiously. "Sixty-five or so?"

"She's twenty-four," the girl said briskly, as Jennie hesitated. "Twenty-five on August third. Now, help me up."

"Come to think of it," Jennie said in thoughtful tones, "I don't know as Nellie actually told me exactly how old Laura is, but she's old."

"What happened," the girl said, "is that Aunt Nellie referred to me as an old-maid schoolteacher, didn't she?...I thought so! But just you remember that she was the mother of four at twenty, and looks on anyone single at twenty-four as an Old Maid, in capitals. Really, did you come to see me?"

Asey and Jennie looked down at her without answering.

"Of course, Auntie sent you!" she went on. "I should have realized she'd get excited at the coincidence of my getting engaged to Reed Perry the week after that insurance money!...Now, do untie me. If you're still dubious, look at my watch. You broke the crystal, but my name's engraved on the back."

Jennie's eyes were the size of saucers, as she passed the small gold watch to Asey a moment later. "Look! It does say Laura King!"

"Furthermore," the girl added, "I can tell you anything you want to know about the family!"

"Okay," Asey said. "How are we related to you?" That, he thought, would throw her!

But it didn't. "Great-great-grandfather Reuben King had six sons," she informed him. "Noah, the youngest, married your grandfather's half-sister, Maria."

"Wa-el," Asey drawled, "you couldn't invent that genealogy on the spur of the moment!...So you're Cousin Laura. Er-- what were you doin' in here? This certainly isn't your boardin'house!"

"Oh, no; I live in the brownstone next door. I--"

"But that's Number Seven!" Jennie broke in. "Seventeen's what your aunt told me!"

"I'm sure she did," Laura agreed. "She always addresses my mail to Number Seventeen. I don't know why. A year ago I gave up trying to make her change....Asey, I don't know where to begin to tell you things-- and so many of 'em are going to sound insane! Listen. As I came up the street-- around half past five or so-- I noticed that the front door here was open. Acting entirely on impulse, I came in. My only motive, if you can call it a motive, was curiosity in its simplest form. And-- there he was! And there on the floor at my feet was that awful slat!"

"Why in time," Asey said, "did you pick it up?"

Laura shook her head. "I was too shocked and bewildered to know what I was doing, I guess. And then I heard a strange thumping noise in the rear of the house, and even though I was frightened to death, I made my way back there. I decided the noise came from the cellar, so I went down there, and-- biff!"

"Biff what?" Jennie asked.

"Biff, something hit me, that's all! I don't know who, or what. When I came to, I was lying on that dank, smelly floor. It was pitch-dark, and I was awfully confused and I kept bumping into piles of things. I was trying to find a light, you see. At last I located a switch box by groping around the wall, and I jerked that handle a couple of times, hoping something would light up. It didn't, so I kept pawing around till I found a light cord."

That, Asey thought, cleared up the mystery of the brief black-out. And not much else!

"Then I picked up the slat, and came back upstairs," Laura went on. "When you jumped at me, I assumed you were the same person who'd biffed me before. It frankly never occurred to me you might be my famous cousin, the Codfish Sherlock! My one idea was to break away and get to a phone. Believe it or not, as I said, I intended to get hold of you and beg you to come and rescue me from this mess. Uh-- aren't you really ever going to untie me and let me up?"

Unlike Jennie, she hadn't bothered with any eager, excited questions as to Sumner's identity, so she must have recognized him, Asey concluded. Did she perhaps know him? She must, he guessed, as he leaned thoughtfully back against the pianos while Jennie untied her bonds. Since Laura had taken it for granted that she'd need expert rescuing, she must have checked herself off as a legitimate suspect. And, in his experience, the average legitimate suspect was not inclined to be a complete stranger to the corpse.

"Now"-- Laura got to her feet-- "let's hurry over to my rooms before anyone comes, or the police barge in. There are some-- well, complications I've got to smooth out."

"An' where are you aimin' to take that thing?" Asey inquired, as she picked up the crate slat.

"I'm certainly not going to leave it here, not with all my fingerprints on it!" Laura returned. "Before the police find this, you're going to find the murderer for me!"

"That all?" Asey commented dryly.

"It's your business, isn't it?" Laura smiled at him. "Where did my pocketbook fall when you jumped me? Oh, I see it!"

"What," Asey said, "are you aimin' to do, exactly? Because we can't just rush off casual-like an' leave him here, you know."

"Oh, Asey, hush!" Jennie said. "Stop frettin' so! And for goodness sakes, tell me about that poor fellow-- Is he Laura's beau, the Perry man?"

Laura said hurriedly, "Oh, no, no!" and Asey found himself wondering whether it was his imagination, or whether the girl's lips had tightened at the mention of Perry's name. "No! And now, please, I don't want to stay in this place any longer!"

"I've had enough of it myself," Jennie said. "Come on, Asey!"

But Asey didn't follow the two women out.

He knew he ought to hotfoot it to the cops, taking Laura with him. He also knew that the minute he did, his troubles would really begin. To these city cops, Jennie's explanation of visiting a Cousin Laura would have sounded fishy enough when no Cousin Laura was forthcoming. Now that Cousin Laura had been found, with the lethal weapon in her well-manicured hand, their visit would probably be magnified-- by the newspapers, at least-- into a rendezvous with a murderess.

In short, Asey thought, his first impression that it would be best for him to know as little as possible about Sumner's murder was rapidly resolving itself into a feeling that the more he knew, the better for himself and Jennie.

And Cousin Laura was obviously the person who could tell more!

"I guess," he murmured "that civic duty's goin' to suffer a little temporary setback. Huh, I wonder-- Do I want to leave this rat hole without stagin' a rat hunt? Laura's biffer could still be hidin' here! Now, I wonder!"

Common sense told him that he could grope around the heaps and mounds and piles of junk till doomsday while someone with a knowledge of the layout kept a jump ahead or a step behind him.

Asey grinned suddenly. Turning, he picked his way quickly through the crates, mounted the stairs to a window on the landing, and, with his pocketknife, sliced off a strip of the grimy cardboard covering the glass. Then he returned to the front door and put out the light. No one who entered Number Seventeen, or who tried to leave it, could make much headway without lights of some sort. By taking an occasional look at that landing window, he could easily keep tabs on the place.

"Comin'!" he called out, in response to Laura's demand to hurry. He caught up with the pair on the steps of the neat brownstone next door.

"Hey, where's that slat?" he asked, as Laura took her key from her pocketbook and used both hands to open the door.

"If you didn't notice what we did with it," she retorted, "no one else will!"

"My goodness what a big place!" Jennie commented, as Laura swung open the inner vestibule door, with its long oval insets of flower-patterned frosted glass.

While she continued to murmur about the size of the house, Asey glanced around the wide hall, which seemed to him a welter of overgrown rubber plants and white marble statues. Through portieres of green tasseled rope, he caught a glimpse of a long living-room, of dark-green wallpaper, of gilt chairs, and tables covered with bric-a-brac.

"Don't let our decor throw you," Laura said, "and do let's hurry upstairs before Superwoman stalks out--"

"Who?" Jennie interrupted.

Laura giggled. "That's what we call our oversized landlady, Miss Maxwell. She's simply overpowering. And every time the front door moves, she stalks out to see what's going on. Her only weakness is-- Oh, oh, good evening, Miss Maxwell."

At Laura's sudden shift to what Jennie would have called "company" tones, Asey turned to look at the tall, broad-shouldered woman who'd just appeared from the rear of the house. The aptness of her nickname was immediately apparent, and Asey hazarded a mental guess that she topped him by four inches and overweighed him by fifty pounds. Her severely tailored gray suit was topped off with a white silk shirt and a black necktie, and her iron-gray hair was cut like a man's.

"May I present--? Why, Miss Maxwell," Laura went on brightly, "don't tell me you don't recognize my guests! Oh, I see. You've lost your glasses again!"

"Left 'em at Jordan's." Miss Maxwell's voice, Asey thought, was pretty Superwoman, too. It boomed so that he expected the rubber plants to shake. "I was there matching the silk for Mr. Sumner's new draperies."

At the mention of Sumner's name, Asey surveyed the rugged Miss Maxwell with renewed interest. The huge, brown diamonds gleaming on her left hand he checked off as in keeping with her size but not her job. Conversely, he noted that her heavy-duty, flat-heeled brogues were smaller than either Laura's pumps or Jennie's sensible oxfords.

"My cousin, Asey Mayo," Laura said, "and my cousin, Jennie Mayo."

"Ah, Mr. Mayo!" Asey found his hand being mangled in her hearty handshake. "How I've looked forward to meeting you! Of course, I've always followed all your cases, but after Laura and her sister moved in here, I've taken particular interest in your work. Feel you're one of the family. Now"-- she rested her elbow on the wide black-walnut newell post, effectively blocking the stairs-- "there are a number of questions I wish you'd clear up for me. How, in the Tinsbury affair--?"

By combining forces, Jennie and Laura managed to get Asey out of her clutches ten minutes later.

"My face," Laura said as she closed the door of her room behind them, and tossed her pocketbook down on a mahogany desk, "my face is red. But a good murder is the breath of life to our landlady. That was what I was trying to tell you when she pounced. Murder trophies are her hobby. Her sitting-room's lined with the most ghastly things, like murderer's neckties, and bits of hangman's nooses, and locks of Lizzie Borden's hair."

"If she gets another chance to buttonhole Asey," Jennie said, with a sniff, "I dare say she'll most likely snip off a few locks of his! Goodness, what a woman!...What a nice, big room, Laura. And d'you have the one beyond, too? It's so homey, compared to that gloomy room downstairs!"

"This was literally the only spot Sister and I could find when our old apartment building got condemned," Laura said, as she smoothed out the couch pillows and tossed the contents of an ash tray into the fireplace. "Mercifully, we bullied Superwoman into letting us use our own things."

"Tell me about this sister." Jennie sat down in the chintz-covered armchair and took off her hat. "Nellie never said a word to me about any sister!"

"Aunt Nellie doesn't count Didi," Laura said, "because she's the child of Father's second wife, whom Auntie cordially hated. If she mentioned her at all, she probably called her 'the Baby.' She's twenty-one. We've never dared break the news to Auntie that she sings what they call intimate songs in a night club for a living. She just calls herself 'Didi'-- the family name isn't bandied out. Anyway, we have these two rooms, and Reed Perry has two pleasant rooms on the front, larger than these, but--"

As Laura chatted on at length and in detail about room dimensions and southern exposures, Asey decided that the girl was extraordinarily interested in architectural problems for someone who'd been so anxious to wrench them away from Number Seventeen in order to tell them all about a murder and its complications. But he understood the sea-change that had taken place. Now that the first shock and excitement had begun to wear away, the girl was running true to murder-suspect form, and stalling as hard as she could.

He let her run on about the room's wonderful morning sun, while he took a quick glance across at Number Seventeen's staircase window, which was still dark. Then he settled down on the upholstered window seat.

"I'm sure you know who that man is next door," he said casually to Laura when she finally paused for breath.

He could see the girl's hands grip the arm of her chair, as if she were bracing herself. "Yes," she said. "Yes, that's Complication Number One. You see, this is John Michael Sumner's own house!"

"So that's who he is!" Jennie said. "Sumner-- he's the one you were always warning me never to vote for, isn't he, Asey? But how can this be his house? You mean that he boards here?"

"No, it's his. He owns it and lives on the upper floors," Laura said. "Miss Maxwell has the first floor and basement in return for running the menage. He doesn't need to rent rooms, of course, but he was born here and has a sentimental attachment to the place and wasn't happy rattling around by himself. His new secretary, Walter English, lives in a tiny little room in the rear--"

"An' when," Asey interrupted, "are we goin' to stop this cosy palaverin' about rooms, an' how big an' sunny they are, an' who lives in which one, an' get down to brass tacks? An' don't tell me," he added, "that you don't know what I mean!"

"But I don't," Laura said.

"No? Then listen!" Asey said. "First off, you tell us that idle curiosity led you into that house next door, where you found a murdered man, an' where you got bopped on the head while tryin' to locate a strange noise. Now, it seems you live in the murdered man's house. You know him well enough so when you say his name, it's like a kid spittin' out nasty-tastin' medicine. You keep his picture in that whoppin' silver frame on your desk, even though when you first come in here, you tossed your pocketbook at it careful, hoping it would cover up his face!"

"I didn't," Laura said. "That is Sumner's picture, but it doesn't belong to me. It's Didi's."

"Ah!" Asey said. "So it's your sister you're tryin' to keep out of this!"

"I'm not trying to keep anyone out of anything!" Laura retorted. "Didi has nothing to do with this, nor have I!"

"Then I wonder," Asey said gently, "why you shoved the morning paper under the couch with your foot when you come in here?"

"Why, because it was untidy-looking, that's all!"

Asey's voice was so gentle it was almost a purr: "I noticed the page the newspaper was open to. You see, while I was waitin' for Jennie to get through buyin' that silly new hat of hers I read every single last word of that paper, down to the classified ads. I even plowed through the gossip columns."

"The-- Oh. Oh, then you saw about--" Laura stopped short.

"Uh-huh," Asey said. "I saw it. 'What pretty young blond singer known only by her first name got fought over at the Bell Club last night by what well-known political figure and what unknown knight with glasses? Our spies report she didn't want to go home with Sister.' Or words to that general effect. Now, Laura, let's have the truth. You didn't go slippin' into Number Seventeen out of sheer curiosity. You went in there after your sister."

"No!"

"But," Asey said softly, "you came out of there with her pocketbook under your arm, didn't you?"

"No! No, I didn't! I--" Laura leaned back in her chair and sighed. "It's no use, I guess. How did you know that was Didi's bag?"

"Wa-el," Asey drawled, "I noticed that the bag on the desk is dark green, an' then I noticed that there's a red one that matches your suit over there on the far table. 'N'en I wondered why you weren't carryin' the one that matched the outfit. 'N'en I wondered if the green one was yours. I guessed it might be your sister's. You really told me."

"You notice a lot, don't you, Cousin?" Laura said dryly. "All right; you've made your point!"

"Meanin' you're goin' to tell the truth? All of it?" Asey inquired.

"It's certainly going to be simpler than to suffer through any more nerve-racking evasions while you're practically splitting me like an atom!" Laura said. "What actually happened is that I glanced out of the window after I came home from school, and I was dumbfounded to see Didi slipping into Number Seventeen. I really had noticed on my way up the street that the front door was ajar, and I remembered Didi's threat to go into that place if ever she saw her chance. And partly because I didn't consider her marching in alone such a bright idea, and-- well, to be honest-- partly because I had a yen to see the place myself, I went rushing over there after her, and then--"

"Wait, now," Jennie interrupted. "Why ever would either of you want to go inside that awful rat hole, for goodness sakes?"

"Why, to get a glimpse of the hermit, of course," Laura answered matter-of-factly.

"The what?" Jennie stared at her. "How's that again?"

"The hermit. You know-- the man who lives there. The hermit."

"Now, Laura," Jennie said, in the tones of one who has been tried beyond endurance, "there aren't hermits in Boston, or Beacon Hill, and I know it!"

"She's right, Jennie," Asey said. "I spotted the name on one of those crates, when we crouched down in the hall, just before Laura come on the scene. I meant to tell you then, but there wasn't time. The mornin' paper had a piece about him-- I'll show you."

"I never thought to say anything about him," Laura said apologetically, as Asey fished the paper out from under the couch. "You never asked about that junk over there, or commented on it, so I took it for granted you knew!"

"Listen," Asey said. "I'll read it:

"'Spring is here. The Swan Boats are back in the Public Garden, first Robins are lighting all over the place, and, to make the season's opening completely official, Boston's most eccentric character, the Hermit of Dyer Street, has been sighted by an eagle-eyed resident of

Beacon Hill. Clad in his usual chic ensemble of seven suits, one on top of the other, topped off by his usual three scarves and his famous ear-lapped bicycle cap, with his gray beard falling into a gentle tangle around his ankles, Christian Bayard--'"

"Tch, tch, tch!" Jennie clucked her tongue. "I still can't believe anything like this'd ever happen in Boston! Go on, Asey, is there more?"

"'Christian Bayard,'" Asey continued reading, "'the Millionaire Recluse, the Triple-plated Troglodyte, popped out of his highly cluttered household long enough to sniff at yesterday's balmy breezes. Upon being apprised of the Squire's Annual Spring Outing from the Old Homestead, your reporter rushed to the scene. After repeated poundings and dulcet yoohoos, the front door was swung open almost a good three-quarters of an inch.

"'We can now inform the hermit's public that the famous pile of pianos has blessed-evented during the long winter months of hibernation. There are now four midget pianos on top of the twelve uprights, and, before the door was ungraciously slammed on our upper incisors, we spotted a brand-new item-- six or eight hundred bird cages.

"'Well, anyway, no matter what the weather may be next week, spring has come, and the Hermit of Dyer Street is apparently all oiled and greased to meet it....P.S. No, no, of course we didn't see him, but we heard him growl.'"

"Goodness sakes!" Jennie said. "I suppose if it's in the paper, it's true."

Asey said, "Remember, Jennie, that man with the book bag started to tell us that Dyer Street was mostly famous now for the eccentric-- an' just then I stopped him an' asked directions? He was goin' to mention the hermit, then.... Laura, do you mean that in spite of livin' next door, you've never seen the fellow?"

"No, none of us ever has. I've saved a lot of clippings about him, by the way," she added. "Perhaps you'd like to look at 'em?"

"I would," Jennie said. "Honest, I can't understand why you didn't speak right out and tell us about him at first, Laura, so we could go right straight to the police! Because that crazy hermit bashed Sumner and biffed you! He's the murderer!"

"But--" Laura paused as she drew a batch of newspaper clippings from a desk pigeonhole and gave them to Jennie. "Oh, this is going to sound absurd to you, I suppose, and it would be so-- well, so convenient to think he was the murderer! For a moment, I thought he was. But I don't, now! I don't even think the hermit's crazy!"

"He certainly doesn't sound to me like what I'd call a normal man!" Jennie commented acidly.

"He isn't. Not John Doe normal. He dresses in all those layers of clothes, and he's hoarded those quantities of junk, and he's bearded and frowsty and all, but I always felt," Laura said, "that he was more eccentric than crazy. I don't think he killed Sumner."

"What makes you so sure it couldn't have been him?" Asey, who had expected her to fasten the affair on the hermit with the casual finality of someone hanging a star on a Christmas tree, looked at her curiously.

"When I went rushing in there, I stood in the hall-- feeling utterly thwarted and overpowered by all that junk, and knowing I never could weave my way through it-- and I called Didi at the top of my lungs." Laura lighted a cigarette. "Her pocketbook was on the floor, just about where you two were crouching, later. I called and called her, but there wasn't any answer. I called Bayard's name over and over. Then I saw Sumner's face, and I screamed. I screamed for Didi, for the hermit, for help. I screamed till I choked and lost my voice. It was then I heard that noise and went down the cellar-- that part was true. Only, I was shaking like a leaf, and not wanting to go, and so terrified something had happened to Didi. But, Asey," she said earnestly, "it wasn't a man who biffed me! It was a woman; I know it was!"

"How could you tell?" Asey asked.

Laura made a gesture of despair. "I haven't any proof! I didn't actually hear any swish of skirts, or smell any exotic perfume. It's simply intuition-- Don't laugh, Asey! If it'd been the hermit down there, he surely wouldn't have made any noise knocking things over. He'd know his way around the place! And it wasn't Didi, either-- the perfume she's wearing these days simply hits you in the face a mile away! But it was a woman!"

"Look at these clippings, Asey!" Jennie said. "They claim Bayard took to a hermit's life through grief, after his beautiful wife died abroad, and they say he's never left that house in years and years. Now, if he never leaves, why he must be there--"

"But I'm positive he's not!" Laura interrupted. "That front door was never open before in all the time I've lived here."

"Then," Jennie said, "he just killed Sumner, and beat it out!"

"But he never knew Sumner, and Sumner never knew him!" Laura protested."The hermit hasn't any reason, any motive, for killing him!"

"Not knowin' someone intimate over a long period of time," Asey said, "hasn't ever proved much of a bar to murder. But I keep wonderin'-- You say Sumner was born here an' lived here always, an' apparently Bayard's lived next door a good, long while. P'raps they did know each other, Laura."

"Sumner never mentioned knowing him! Of course, he talked about the hermit-- we all did! But--" Laura paused a moment. "Well, I suppose you're right. Sumner could have known him, and not have told us!"

"Sure, Sumner knew him," Jennie said flatly. "He just never mentioned it!...Asey, what I don't understand about these articles is why the writers tried to make him so _funny_!"

"Probably," Asey suggested, "they kept him on file for a dull day, along with sea serpent rumors, an' such. When news was scarce they wrote a funny hermit story."

"But he isn't funny!" Jennie insisted. "Not to me, anyway. Why'd they bother kidding about the pianos and the rest of the junk? Whyn't they find out why he got 'em, and so many of 'em? If I was a reporter, I'd've looked into practical things, too. Like food. Now, how'd your old hermit get food, Laura, if he never left the house?"

"It was delivered," Laura said. "Miss Maxwell told us she was terribly upset about him when rationing was first announced during the war, but she stopped worrying when cases and cases of tinned food was delivered at the back door. Enough to last a family ten years."

"Ever hear if his gettin' violent, or fightin' anyone?" Asey asked.

"I've read of him tossing things at reporters who bothered him, and at people who stood outside and catcalled-- After all, anyone would do the same!" Laura said. "But he never attacked anyone that I know of."

"I still think he isn't funny!" Jennie tossed the clippings back on the desk.

"None of this business is funny," Laura said. "Sumner's being killed is awful enough, but Didi's going over there is pretty frightful after that horrid mess last night!...Oh, Asey, aren't the police and the papers going to leap on this with a glad cry! Think of what they've got-- Big Mike Sumner murdered in the hermit's house, with a blond night-club singer involved!"

"What d'you think became of her?" Jennie asked eagerly.

"I rather think she must have spotted Sumner as soon as she went in, and rushed out again before I got over there to Seventeen," Laura said. "I can easily understand her dropping her bag and forgetting it. I'd have dropped mine, if I'd had one with me!"

"You think she's likely to go back in there for it?" Asey inquired.

Laura shook her head. "I'm sure she wouldn't be foolish enough to stick her neck out that far. Probably, when she caught her breath and thought the situation over, she-- well, remember, Didi's been singing for a living since she was sixteen. She's neither soft nor stupid. When and if she's confronted with that bag, she'll swear that it was snatched from her this afternoon, that she reported it to the insurance company-- and she'll probably produce witnesses. That," she added with a frown, "is the sort of thing that hit me and worried me at once. It's going to be what Didi lies herself into while trying to wriggle herself out-- if you follow!-- that's going to get her into real trouble!"

"You don't think anything's happened to her, do you?" Jennie demanded. "Where d'you s'pose she's at, now?"

"I know she had a rehearsal from six to eight," Laura said, "and I'm very sure she's at it. Yes, we'll find her at the Bell Club, all right, and she'll stalwartly deny ever having been near Number Seventeen. But that mess last night--"

"What about that, anyways?" Asey asked, as he casually leaned

back on the window seat and glanced again at Seventeen's still-dark
staircase window.

Laura sighed. "I'm remembering with regret all that loose talk
of mine about smoothing out complications," she said. "Wasn't I a
naive child, 'way back there half an hour ago? Well, Asey, Sumner
paid a lot of attention to me when I first moved in here. I nipped him
in the bud as nicely as I could, in order to maintain this much of a
roof over our heads. Didi was on tour with a road company of Conga
Girl. And when she came back here to stay--"

"I bet Sumner went for her!" Jennie broke in. "I've read those
hints about him and his goings-on in the papers. They always made
him out an awful ladies' man!"

"That's one way to phrase it," Laura remarked dryly. "I don't like
the situation that's arisen. Neither does Reed. We hate it."

"That's your beau, Reed Perry?" Jennie asked.

"Yes, his picture's on the table beyond you-- I meant to have
pointed it out before. Didi makes fun of him and says he's a dull,
solid citizen with glasses, and his clothes are stodgy. But Reed's a
dear. And, in passing, he's a successful lawyer, and Aunt Nellie
needn't have the slightest qualms about Father's insurance money."

"In passin'"-- Asey strolled over and looked at the leather-
framed photograph-- "where is he at the moment?"

"I can't imagine!" Laura said. "He ought to be home by now, and
taking me out to dinner. Anyway, Didi's as stubborn as any King who
ever lived, and Reed and I knew that trying to reason with her about
Sumner would only make matters worse. Besides, there wasn't very
much we could say. Sumner wanted to marry her."

"So?" Asey strolled back to the window seat.

"It surprised us plenty, too," Laura said. "And I really think she'd
have married him, in spite of the difference in their ages, if Sumner
didn't have streaks of drinking like a whale. That brings us to last
night. That was the problem then. Reed and I just happened to drop
in at the Bell Club-- we go there only once in a blue moon-- so we
went back to pick up Didi when she was through. Sumner was there,
very drunk, and he had a fight with Reed. At that point, he'd have
fought with his cane, or a doorman, or a trolley car, or a pack of
tigers. Anything. Anyone. In fact, if he'd been anyone else but Big
Mike Sumner, he'd have been trundled off in a patrol wagon about two
hours before. Didi was furious with Reed and me. She said we hadn't
any need to butt in, and she could have handled him, all right. Maybe
she could have except-- Oh, I want to skip this part!"

"Truth comin' a mite hard?" Asey drew the curtain back and
glanced out on Dyer Street.

"Makes me feel like such a tattler," Laura said simply. "Didi
probably might have managed him, except that he was madder at her
than he was at us. To plunge in, the trouble was Sumner's new
secretary, Walter English. Until Walt came, about a month ago, Didi
was perfectly happy playing around with Mike. She adored having a

lot of money spent on her, and she did Mike's vanity a world of good. Reed and I told ourselves they broke even. But Walt--"

"Didi fell for him?" Asey suggested.

"No," Laura said, "no, not exactly.   But Mike thought so. Actually, I think she just finds him different-- and he's young and amusing and full of bounce.   The complete opposite of Mike.   But last night Mike was drunk enough to make a real issue of Walt-- he's only kidded about him before.   He started to strike Didi, and then Reed stepped in-- it was all pretty heated and childish."

"I wonder," Asey said, "could you think of any reason for her meetin' Sumner at Number Seventeen this afternoon?"

"Whatever makes you think anyone would chose that spot for a rendezvous, with the rest of the world available?   No!" Laura shook her head.   "The way Didi was feeling about Mike this morning, she'd have flown out through the roof rather than meet him in the hall.   She was mad with him, and mad with Reed and me, and I was provoked with her, and mad with Sumner, and sore with Reed for letting himself get into that brawl-- Oh, things were unquestionably going to be very, very tense around here for a few days; I knew that! And then--"

She paused as Asey suddenly rose from the window seat and started to tiptoe across the room, but continued talking as he gestured for her to go on.

"And then Superwoman's sore with Didi because she thinks Didi's trying to snare Mike for his money--"

Asey, having crossed the room, quickly jerked open the the heavy walnut door.

Miss Maxwell standing there on the threshold, didn't appear a whit embarrassed at having been found with her ear to the keyhole.

"I knocked half a dozen times," she said easily.   "I was quite sure I hadn't heard you go out, so I leaned down to listen for the sound of voices....Laura, Reed asked me to give you a message when he left just now--"

"When he left?" Laura interrupted in amazement.   "When he left where?   When?"

"Here, just a moment ago.   I told him the Mayos were visiting you, but he said he hadn't the time to stop and meet them.   He was in a frightful hurry.   Only had twelve minutes to get to the station and catch his train--"

"Train?" Laura sounded bewildered.

"This business trip came up most unexpectedly."   Miss Maxwell took obvious pleasure in being able to produce the explanation.   "Said to tell you he didn't know exactly when he'd be back."   She paused and looked curiously at Laura.   "Nothing's wrong, I hope?"

Asey, who had walked back over to the window seat, answered for her: "No, nothing's wrong, thanks.   We were just sort of-- of waitin' for Reed to show up and have dinner with us.   Jennie"-- his voice suddenly took on a brisker tone-- "you know what?   I left my brief case in the car, an' I think I better hop out an' get it, quick!"

"But, Asey--"

Jennie's attempt to protest that he had no brief case with him died on her lips as Asey slipped past Superwoman's bulky figure and ran down the green-carpeted stairs.

Less than a minute later, he had opened the door of Number Seventeen with such gentleness that the man who was busily going through Mike Sumner's coat pockets never suspected his presence.

Asey stood there, staring quietly at the man, and letting his eyes get accustomed to the glare of the hall's unshaded light. Then, after glancing briefly up in the direction of the slit he'd cut in the staircase window covering, he grinned and spoke.

"Is this train trip," he asked conversationally, "really necessary, Mr. Perry?"

As Reed swung round, clumsily dislodging a bird cage with his elbow, Asey decided that the fellow's photograph had pictured him with unflattering accuracy. While he was tall and dark and well-enough built, he was unquestionably stolid. He had the nearsighted person's trick of seeming to peer through his glasses, too, and his clothes very nearly deserved the cracks that Didi had reportedly made about them.

And right now he was wearing a dazed expression, rather as if he'd been struck smartly over the head with a sledge hammer.

"Or are you maybe huntin' for the club car?" Asey drawled. "Because I was told that you'd rushed off to catch a train. Now, I happened to see you hurryin' up Dyer an' into Number Seventeen a while ago-- in fact, I even erroneously suspected you of doin' some keyhole listenin'. I saw you scurry out of Number Seven. I saw the light go on in here. So, Mr. Perry, s'pose you start makin' some explanations! I am--"

"I know," Reed smiled, a pleasant, friendly smile that lighted up his whole face and erased in a flash the stolidness. "You're just the same, aren't you, Asey?" he continued. "Last time you demanded explanations from me-- let's see. It was the Fourth of July, twenty-four years ago. I had three lobsters in my hand, and your storage trap had just been robbed."

"So?" While Reed sounded convincing, Asey had no recollection of any previous meeting with him.

"My memory's better than yours," Reed said. "I was a bellhop at the Shore Inn that summer. I explained the lobsters to your satisfaction, and I can explain this, too. You recognize Sumner, of course?"

Asey nodded.

"When Superwoman excitedly broke the news of your being here," Reed went on, "I wondered if you knew about this. But I couldn't dope out how you could possibly know. Asey, I--"

"I do remember!" Asey said with satisfaction. "Freckles an' a broken front tooth, an' you'd bought the lobsters, an' proved it....Go on. I feel better now I've pulled that out of the past an' caught up with you!"

"Asey," Reed said seriously, "I don't know what you may have read about Mike. Some papers always give him credit; some give him the works. He picked me up at a newsboys' club when I was a kid, helped me through college and law school, gave me a start as his secretary. He never batted an eye when I told him I didn't want to go into politics with him, but helped me set up my own office. He's the best friend I ever had. Yes, he had his shortcomings. But as far as I'm concerned, he's the finest man I ever knew!"

"In my line of business," Asey said, "we sort of tend to be suspicious of that kind of post-mortem talk. We call it--"

"Flag-waving, probably," Reed interrupted impatiently. "I know. But it's the truth, and you've got it for the record....Now, d'you know about this being the hermit's house?...You do? Well, listen-- because I think you're going to find this information very interesting. Asey, Mike Sumner's managed Bayard's affairs for years and years. He got a note from Bayard this morning telling him to come here, alone, at five-thirty this afternoon. He--"

"Hold it!" Asey broke in. "You're sure about this note?"

"Sure? Wasn't I over in Mike's office when he opened his mail? I'd dropped in to see him, because Mike was drinking last night, and--" Reed paused, and smiled again. "I see you already know about the fracas at the Bell Club. It's written on your face. Well, also for your record, Mike was completely blank on anything that happened to him after nine last night. I had to read him the gossip columns before he'd believe that he and I had actually mixed it up.... Anyway, I didn't like the tone of Bayard's note. Particularly that 'alone' part. The whole business was queer. I spent half an hour trying to persuade Mike that he shouldn't come here by himself-- oh, I'd told him long ago I thought the old boy was cracking up!"

"So," Asey said, "you knew Bayard, too?"

"When I was Mike's secretary, I did most of Bayard's estate work, and I still do some. I've really seen more of him than Mike has. I knew Bayard was slipping," Reed said earnestly. "The last time I brought some papers here for him to sign, he suddenly announced out of a clear sky that Mike Sumner was persecuting him brutally!"

"Just how?" Asey inquired.

"Seems that people were throwing stones at his house every night," Reed answered, "and Bayard said that Mike sent 'em. His eyes began to burn-- I frankly didn't like the look of them, or the way he kept muttering that he'd get even with Mike! A minute later he appeared to have forgotten all about his persecution, and was telling me to thank Mike for sending him some books. I reminded Mike of that episode this morning, but he just laughed and said Bayard was harmless. But I couldn't get that note out of my mind, Asey. It kept bothering me. I intended to drop in here around five-thirty, but I got all tied up in a labor case. And when I walked along the street a while ago, and saw the front door open here--"

Open? Asey clearly remembered having closed that door when he'd left, after first carefully setting the latch so that he could get in again!

"I knew something was wrong," Reed continued. "I felt it. I came in and put on the light, and called for Bayard-- and then I saw Mike."

Asey's mind was racing back, fitting things together.

That hall light had gone on once. Only once. Just after he'd seen Reed hurry away from Number Seven, and while Superwoman was still delivering Reed's message to Laura.

Except for the very brief interval when he'd crossed the room to look at Reed's photograph, Asey had watched that staircase window like a hawk. And those few seconds weren't enough for Reed to have entered Number Seventeen, put on the light, called Bayard, found Sumner's body, and turned the light off again.

In a nutshell, it began to look very much as if Reed were making all this up as he went along!

"I couldn't think clearly," Reed went on. "I could only stand here berating myself for not coming earlier. Then I suddenly thought of Laura-- I was going to have dinner with her-- and I hurried over next door--"

"Did you put the light out then?" Asey asked casually.

"No, I left it on," Reed said without hesitation. "I called Superwoman and gave her that fake message for Laura. I knew she'd insist on coming here if she knew what had happened to Mike, and I didn't want her to mix herself up with any of this. Then I hurried back here."

Now Asey knew that Reed was lying. Because the hall light hadn't been on all that time! "An' why," he asked, "did you come back, anyway?"

"To see if that note from Bayard was still in Mike's pocket, of course!" Reed sounded surprised that Asey should question his action. "That letter's the key to the whole business, and I'm sure Mike had it with him! He folded it and put it in his inner coat pocket this morning. But the letter isn't there-- it's not on him anywhere! Don't you get it, Asey? Bayard wrote that note as bait, to get Mike here alone. When Mike came, Bayard killed him, then took the note and beat it!"

"Beat it," Asey said gently, "where?"

"How should I know? But he's certainly not here! That front door was never left open an inch in all the years I've known him! But if we can only find that note, then the police will have everything they need!" He paused. "What makes you look so dubious? There surely can't be any explanation other than Bayard's killing him and running away!"

"I'm wonderin'," Asey said. "How easy would it be for him to run anywhere? Between his clothes-- I assume he's wearin' his usual outfit of all those layers of suits-- an' his long, wavin' beard, I'd say he couldn't get to the end of the next block without bein' spotted an' mobbed an' followed like a parade. Furthermore, where could he run to? Accordin' to the papers, he hasn't been out of here in years!"

Reed peered at Asey through his glasses. "I never thought that part out," he admitted. "But look-- if he was crafty enough to plan Mike's murder, he could plan his own get-away! He could have shaved off his beard, and peeled down to one suit. Asey, that's still another angle I never considered! Without his trappings, who'd recogize him? I couldn't!"

"Did he say in his note why he wanted to see Sumner?" Asey asked.

"Yes, about his will. He's always changing that damn' will. Every few months he reads in the papers about someone who sounds to him like a nice, deserving heir. At one point during the war," Reed added, with a grin, "he left everything to Winston Churchill. Then he had a change of heart and gave it to Eisenhower."

"How'd Sumner get in here?" Asey wanted to know. "Did he have a door key?"

"Mike had one, yes. But he probably rang-- three longs and three shorts. Bayard knew that was either Mike or me."

"I see." Leaning back against a pile of pianos, Asey looked thoughtfully up at the networks of cobwebs and long fringes of dust that hung from the hall ceiling. "What was the reason for this hermit business of Bayard's anyway?"

"Little by little, I've pried it out of Mike," Reed said. "In May, nineteen-ten, Bayard's wife died very suddenly in Paris, on her annual shopping trip. The cable telling him about her came in the middle of the night. Mike said he was awakened by a blood-curdling shriek, and then Bayard was pounding on the front door of Numer Seven screaming for Mike to help him. Mike said the wife was young, rich, and beautiful, and that Bayard adored the ground she walked on. Her death knocked him out. Floored him. From then on, he just couldn't cope with things."

"Judgin' from the number of things in this hall alone," Asey remarked, "he must've done a little copin'!"

"This junk, you mean? The doctor told Mike it had to do with Bayard's sense of insecurity-- having had one wife and having lost her, something in his mind wouldn't permit him to be caught with just one of anything again. He wanted dozens and hundreds, as a sort of cushion against being bereft another time, so to speak."

"I see," Asey said. "So Mike had always been a friend of his?"

"No, the Bayards had lived here only a short while before she died," Reed said. "Mike and Bayard were in college at the same time, but they hardly knew each other. Bayard just turned, that night, to the nearest person, and he was such a pitiful figure that Mike said to leave everything to him. And Bayard did. Mike's virtually taken care of him ever since, and managed the Bayard estate, too-- No small job, I might add."

And not a poorly paid job, either, Asey thought to himself. Mike's good deed had paid off well.

"Tell me," he said casually, "why did he keep his relationship to Bayard so secret?"

"Mike was running for office even way back then," Reed answered. "He said he didn't think he'd do himself any good by letting people know he was helping Bayard. You see, Asey, the minute his wife died, Bayard began to let himself slip. Didn't bother about his personal appearance or his clothes. There was a lot of talk about him. And Mike-- well, Mike was always an astute politician. He knew better than to let his name be linked with anyone that queer! And as Mike progressed politically, Bayard grew queerer-- You see what I mean?"

"Uh-huh I think I do," Asey said. "Mike wasn't goin' to give some bright reporter the chance to bust out on the day before elections with the startlin' tidin's that the crazy hermit of Dyer Street was one of Mike's closest associates. Somethin' like that?"

Reed frowned. "Yes, but Mike's motives weren't entirely selfish, either," he said. "There was the problem of Bayard's wife's family. As Bayard grew to be more and more of a recluse, Mike was afraid they might try to have him committed to an asylum, and Bayard wasn't irrational in those days, Asey! Only wrapped in grief, and wanting to be left alone. That's why Mike first engineered those stories about him, to establish the fact of his being eccentric, but-- well, funny. Harmless."

"I see!" Asey said. "I begin to get it! I must tell Jennie she's a perspicacious woman, too! So the hermit was made a funny character by Mike Sumner, so that the hermit's inlaws would keep their hands off the Bayard estate, so that Mike Sumner could continue managin' it! Uh-huh, I see."

Reed protested at his irony. "You're altogether unfair to Mike! He didn't help Bayard solely for what he could get out of the estate! When he took Bayard in and calmed him down that night long ago, he wasn't thinking in terms of future rewards! Mike was sorry for the man!"

"Big Mike Sumner, the People's Friend," Asey slyly quoted an old campaign poster. "'He Has a Heart of Gold.'...Who else knew about Bayard's note besides you?" he asked. "Anyone?"

"The three girls in Mike's office," Reed answered, "and Walt English, Mike's current secretary. They all saw it....Asey, just what was used to kill him?"

Asey bent down suddenly and started to poke under the piano crates. "Slat," he said. "With nails in the end."

"A slat with-- Asey, that's what Bayard always kept by the front door!" Reed's voice rose with excitement. "That's what he always armed himself with whenever the doorbell rang! Let me see it-- Where is it?"

"Been moved." Asey knelt down and tried to work his hand into a space between a crate and a tea chest. "I'm not quite sure where to, but knowin' my cousin Jennie, I'd wager it's lurkin' behind the lilac bush in the front yard next door. Jennie always hides things behind lilac bushes, if she hasn't a window box of geraniums handy. Or petunias."

"What are you grubbing for?" Reed peered down curiously over his shoulders. "Those pieces of glass?"

"The glass is incidental," Asey said. "Those are just bits of Laura's watch crystal that she broke. My real objective is the lipstick she lost here this afternoon. She--"

"Laura? Laura's watch? Her lipstick? You mean-- you mean Laura was here? This afternoon?" Reed seemed almost to be talking to himself.

"Uh-huh, she was here around five-thirty," Asey said. "I thought I spotted that lipstick, but it's only a piece of broken Christmas tree ornament--"

He broke off as Reed's hand gripped his shoulder.

"Get up!" Reed said. "Get up! Listen! I've lied to you, Asey! I was here earlier but it was just after five-thirty! I've known about this since then! Now, let me have her lipstick-- I know you've got it in your hand! Give it to me, and then you can go call the cops!"

"Come now; cool off!" Asey said soothingly as he got to his feet. "I knew you'd lied about when you came here, because I was sittin' next door watchin' for a light to go on. But what I aimed to extract from you was the truth, an' not a lot more lies to shield Laura!"

"I'm not shielding her!" Reed was almost shouting. "She's not even going to have her name mentioned in connection with this mess! I came here, and I found Mike dead, and I left-- no matter why! You can't prove I didn't kill him! I've plenty of reasons to kill Mike!"

"So?" Asey said. "Name three, quick!"

"I-- I-- the--" Reed cleared his throat. "Well, the Bayard estate, for one! Mike found out I was gypping the Bayard estate. There you are! That's enough of a motive!"

"I don't know as it's enough," Asey said, "but it's more the kind of thing I was hopin' you'd bring up. Because that's what Mike Sumner really had done, wasn't it? He'd gypped the hermit's estate! An' wasn't that just exactly why Bayard wanted to see him? Hadn't Bayard begun to suspect something was wrong about his money an' his affairs?"

Reed's eyes met Asey's for a fraction of a second. Then he turned away.

"I won't let you say that about Mike! And, anyway, nobody can prove a thing! I've seen to that! It'll never come to light that Bayard killed Mike for any other reason than that he was crazy! The estate-- and Mike's handling of it-- will never figure, see? But if you want a temporary scapegoat until you've caught Bayard, I'm it! Not Laura! And that's all I've got to say!"

"Okay," Asey said cheerfully. "I've got what I was lookin' for, a real, genuine motive for the hermit's killin' Mike Sumner. Looks like I've made some progress since the time Laura assured me they were strangers! An' I've also learned why you were lyin'. After findin' Mike's body, you rushed off an' destroyed any evidence that might've proved Mike was gyppin' Bayard. So--"

"Oh, stop ruminating, and give me that lipstick of Laura's!" Reed interrupted irritably. "Let's get to the cops and get this over with!"

Asey smiled. "I sort of hate to break it to you that the lipstick business was just a bluff," he said. "You can't really shield her very much, you know. I found her in here, myself. I know Mike pursued her, an' I know what she thought of him-- it's in her voice every time she says his name. I know Didi was in here this af--"

"Oh, gosh, not Didi, too!" Reed broke in. "And after that mess last night-- Why, mayhem was the very least she threatened Mike with then, and at the top of her lungs, too! If Didi gets involved Laura'll rise to her defense without any thought of herself."

"Wa-el," Asey said, "if you really want to, you go right on tryin' to protect Laura an' Mike's memory an' anything else you've a mind to protect, but--"

"I shouldn't have burned those papers!" Reed said. "I shouldn't have touched them. It's only going to make matters worse-- I can see that now! I made an awful mistake! I shouldn't have done it!"

"Nope," Asey agreed. "It was a lost cause. You only--"

He stopped short, swung around, and stared at the wall to his right. Something had begun to hammer dully inside the plaster!

"The cellar!" Reed said. "No, I know it sounds as if it's inside that wall, but all this junk plays tricks with sounds. That's from the cellar. The hermit's still here, after all. Come on!" Darting ahead of Asey, he weaved his way toward the cellar door. "Hurry!" He called back. "Hurry-- the sounds stopped!"

"Hold it a second," Asey said. "Is there a cellar door or a back entrance?....Yes? You know where, so you skip out the front way, and hop around and cover it. I'll go downstairs. Between us, we should flush him out."

After squirming past Reed, Asey jerked open the cellar door, groped for the light switch, and snapped it on. Then he edged his way down the stairs, packed high with tins of food.

While the cellar clutter was worse than the mess in the upstairs hall, the single path was wider and more easily navigated, and went directly to a comparatively open space by the furnace and coal bin. An even broader path, which looked to Asey like a six-lane highway after what he'd been wriggling through, led from the heater to an open door a few yards beyond. Asey stumbled through the foot-deep accumulation of ashes and clinkers, and found himself at the threshold of Number Seventeen's brick-paved alley.

It was empty.

Its side, which faced him, was a high board fence topped with five-strand barbed wire. To his right loomed the hermit's junk-cluttered back yard, enclosed by a modern and efficient wire fence that was surmounted by more barbed wire, and its entrance blocked with a heavily padlocked gate. To his left the alley ran up an incline to Dyer Street.

Whether the hermit or someone else had been responsible for that hammering sound, Asey thought, his only sensible exit was to Dyer Street. And certainly Reed had hustled out in plenty of time to grab their quarry there. Reed couldn't have missed.

But Dyer Street, like the alley, was empty.

"For Pete's sakes!" Asey muttered. Then he raised his voice: "Reed! Hey, Reed!"

There was no answer. Asey turned up his coat collar, leaned back against the entrance to the alley, and waited. Obviously, Reed must have seen someone and given chase. In a few minutes he'd return.

A quarter of an hour later, Asey started slowly over toward the brownstone, after closing Number Seventeen's front door, which Reed had left open. There weren't any two ways about it, he thought, he'd have to phone the police without any further dallying. They could question Didi and Laura, and track down the hermit. And Reed.

"An' stop wonder'n' if that fellow seen a good chance to blow!" he said aloud. "After all, he could've ducked out of the hermit's hall whenever he wanted! He was between me and the door most of the time-- Oh, drat that piece of clinker!"

The sharp, splinterlike particle, which had slipped into his shoe during his rush to the hermit's alley door, was cutting into his foot, and he bent down to untie the lace and rid himself of the nuisance.

It was after the shoe was retied, and while he was stamping off the film of cellar ashes, that he first became aware of the footprints on the bricks-- ashy footprints that paralleled his own from Number Seventeen's alley, and led along the sidewalk toward Number Seven. And, he rapidly found out, straight to Number Seven's front steps!

"Now," he murmured to himself, "let's see! Someone in the hermit's cellar, prowlin' around for goodness knows what reason, accidentally topples over a pile of tins. That's the thuddin' sound we hear. He knows we're upstairs, knows we heard, an' he beats it. He--"

The front vestibule door swung suddenly open, and a broom, wielded with considerable force, all but swept him back down on the sidewalk.

Miss Maxwell's apologies were profound. "I'd no idea you were there, Mr. Mayo!" she said in horrified tones. "Walt English just came tramping in and left these footmarks all over everything-- He's so careless and so untidy! I was thinking that I hadn't heard you come in. Nothing happened to your brief case, I hope?"

Asey, who had forgotten his mythical errand to the car, impro-vised quickly: "It's locked in the baggage hatch, all safe. Trouble now is a flat tire. Will you tell my cousin I may be some time?"

"I'm so sorry!" she said. "I'd hoped to ask you about the Horton case and that Godden murder, and so many others! And before you leave you simply must see my trophy wall! Murder is my hobby, you know!"

"In a sense," Asey returned, "it's mine."

He set off briskly down Dyer Street. Within five minutes he had crept back to the alley entrance of Number Seventeen and was flattened against the wall, waiting, and telling himself he was a lame-brained fool!

Because if Reed, as Sumner's former secretary, knew of the tie-up between the hermit and Sumner, of course this Walt English, the present secretary, knew it, too! Reed had said he knew about the hermit's note and Sumner's five-thirty date.

Some possible motive for his killing Sumner? He could think of a hatful, Asey reflected, running the gamut from love to revenge and money. After all, English's attraction for Didi had been the real provocation for that fight in the Bell Club. While Sumner had apparently controlled his jealousy during his sober moments, last night's public and drunken airing of it might have had any number of repercussions today. Say that Big Mike salved his vanity by firing English. Say that English retaliated with a threat to expose Mike's handling of the Bayard estate.

Starting from any of those sparks, the blowup could have occurred there at the hermit's. English, knowing that the hermit kept a slat by the front door, could have cleverly utilized the hermit's weapon-- which, Asey had noticed as he stood on the brownstone's steps, was now under the lilac bush, as he'd guessed it would be.

But why hadn't Reed grabbed him before English returned to the brownstone? And where in thunder was Reed now?

The sound of footsteps on Dyer Street's cobblestones put an end to his conjecturing. Asey peeked out as someone started hesitantly up the street, only to turn and walk away again at once.

Had that been a book bag over the man's shoulder?

Asey shook his head. Of course not! And what if it had been? Thousands of Boston men carried those green flannel bags!

More footsteps heralded a group of teenage boys who rushed past the alley entrance without noticing Asey. Clustering Number Seventeen's front door, they catcalled and whistled and yelled obscenities at the hermit until Superwoman appeared on the top step of the brownstone and indignantly threatened to call the police. Whereupon they catcalled at her until the pastime palled, and then they suddenly rushed up Dyer Street, kicked open a door in the high board fence marking the end of the street and disappeared.

Asey, who'd never suspected the presence of the door, realized, as he followed the sound of the boy's whoops, that it must lead into a back alley at right angles to Dyer Street. Since the gang was now whooping somewhere behind him, it stood to reason that that alley must turn and run parallel with Dyer Street, behind its two back yards. Probably it was a service alley for the back yards of the adjoining block.

Suddenly he heard the sounds for which he'd hopefully been waiting-- the faint slam of Number Seven's vestibule door and the clop-clop of someone coming down the steps. Now if fate would only arrange to have Walt English return to whatever he'd been doing in the hermit's cellar before he'd toppled over those tin cans and beat it!

"Dear God," Asey thought, "don't let that just turn out to be Superwoman goin' to the store for a chocolate cone!"

He waited tensely, but no one came. Peering out, he found Dyer Street empty!

"So?" Asey said. "Well, I know where you went!"

Running along to the board fence, he opened the wooden door and slipped through. The short alley at right angles to Dyer Street was empty, except for ash cans and garbage pails and piles of rubbish. The branch alley-- which ran parallel to Dyer Street, as he'd guessed-- was also empty!

"Nobody went past me, nobody's here," Asey muttered. "For Pete's sakes, did he fly off on Superwoman's broomstick? I'm sure a man came out of that brownstone an' down those steps! I'm bettin' money it's English. I'm bettin' he came here, an' I'm bettin' he is here, somewheres!"

The dull clank of an ash-can cover made him turn his head in the direction of the sound. There was a second clank, and Asey saw the figure of a man gliding out from the shadows beyond the first puddle of gaslight.

Automatically, as he started to follow the swiftly moving figure, Asey marked the spot from which the man had appeared-- in front of a four-tiered clothes reel, and next to a picket fence with a gap in the middle.

Somewhere in that area was the ash can whose lid had been involved in all those clankings. But what English had so surreptitiously rid himself of mattered less at this moment than what English intended to do next. Because, Asey told himself, this had to be Walt English! After all, no honest Boston burgher would be sneaking around dark alleys, using strange trash cans to dispose--

Asey stopped so short that he nearly lost his balance. For directly behind Number Seventeen's cluttered back yard, English abruptly turned to the left, swung into the back yard opposite, and disappeared inside the building beyond.

Two seconds later Asey was reading the large sign on the yard's fence.

"BELL CLUB," it said. "SERVICE ENTRANCE ONLY."

Asey's first reaction was to reflect sadly on his own gullibility. He'd really believed that Laura's amended version of the afternoon's doings was the whole truth.

Now it seemed that she'd merely omitted to explain that her

sister Didi, after leaving the hermit's with such mysterious haste, had only to leap through that fence door at the end of Dyer Street, scamper around an alley, and be smack back at her old Bell Club!

"How," Asey murmured, "without ever sayin' so, did she lead me to believe this joint was miles an' miles away?"

He concluded that Laura hadn't brought up the nearness of the club because she'd known all along it was Didi who biffed her in the cellar, and was trying desperately hard to pretend otherwise.

He strolled through the gate into the back yard and stood for a moment on the threshold of the night club's kitchen.

"Hey, you!" A little rat-faced man in a green, double-breasted suit marched over to him. "You can't come in here!"

Asey smiled at him and stepped inside the kitchen.

"Hey, you--"

"Mike Sumner sent me," Asey said. "Where's Didi?"

The rat-faced man's manner underwent a sudden change, and he took Asey's arm in a chummy fashion. "She's on," he said. "I'll show you her dressing-room. This way."

Beyond the swing doors at the end of the kitchen passage, the decor of the Bell Club began to assert itself with a clang. Asey felt practically deafened by the bulging red plastic bells that covered the silver-painted walls.

Rat-face pointed toward an open door at the end of the hall. "In there," he said, and left.

Before Asey even got inside the room he began to grin. In clear view on the floor, surrounded by a dozen outlandish furry animals with pink velvet eyes and purple ears, was a pair of green leather pumps. They matched the green bag Laura had taken from the hermit's, and they had been shined until they glowed.

No one, Asey knew, would ever find on them a trace of the hermit's dusty front hall floor! No ash film, either, or clinker scratches, or alley mud! He didn't need to pick them up to know that the soles had been taken care of, too!

Now he began to understand what Laura'd meant when she said Didi would probably be able to produce witnesses to prove her handbag had been snatched. Anyone who'd cleaned those shoes and planted them out in the open like that could produce witnesses for anything!

Asey paused in the doorway of the cell-like little room and looked interestedly at its occupant, a tow-headed, tousle-haired young man sitting with back toward him on a hassock.

Then he unashamedly blinked. For, as the young man hummed unconcernedly to himself, he pulled packets of money from the pockets of his jacket and put them on the glass top of the dressing table. Maybe they weren't twenties all the way through, Asey thought, but even if only the top bills were twenties, several thousand dollars was being casually tossed around.

"Hi," Asey said. "You're Walt English, aren't you?"

"Hi." The young man turned around and smiled. He had a round, boyish face, and wide blue eyes. "Yes, I'm English."

"Do you follow up this act by snatchin' rabbits out of a tall silk hat?" Asey inquired dryly, as the piles of bills continued to mount. "Or d'you saw a lady in half, maybe?"

"My impulse," English said presently, "is to saw the lady in half, since you ask." He turned his back to Asey again.

"Whose dough?" Asey asked. "Mike Sumner's, or yours, or Didi's?"

"It was planted on me," English told him. "I'm giving it back to Didi, who planted it, and if I have to saw her in half, she's going to give it back to Mike. In short, it's his."

"Oh." Asey found himself fascinated by the fellow's disarming candor. "An' how did Didi happen to steal it from him?"

"That," English returned, "you'll have to ask her. That's not my department. I'm just starting the ball rolling. Just a step in the right direction, to coin a phrase."

"An' what," Asey said, "were you doin' down in the hermit's cellar a little while ago?"

"Fixing the furnace," English answered.

"Why would you be fixin' the hermit's furnace?"

"Because it's growing cold and the poor old duffer's arthritis has been bothering the hell out of him lately," English said, "and because it's my turn. Mike did him yesterday."

"So?" Asey looked at him quizzically. "An' what made you rush out so sudden?"

"Look Sherlock Mayo; what makes?....Oh, of course I recognize you! Your picture's always in the paper."

Asey persisted. "Why'd you rush out-- to catch a train?"

"No, to see an acquaintance who was passing by."

"I think I'd have liked a train better," Asey said. "What did you throw away in that ash can in the alley?"

"One pair of gold cuff links," English said promptly, "and one gold wrist watch with a gold link strap."

"Just bored with 'em?"

"No," English said, "I threw them away so that I could tell Didi I'd thrown 'em away, and where."

"Isn't that the hard way to drum up amusin' conversation?" Asey inquired.

"It's not my intention to amuse Didi," English returned. "On the contrary. I want her to get a very clear picture of what I think of her damned presents! If she doesn't get the idea, at least Laura should understand what I think of her precious sister!"

"Maybe I got it wrong." Asey leaned against the doorjamb and told himself sternly not to turn and look at Didi, now standing behind him, and practically asphyxiating him with the heaviest perfume he'd ever encountered. "But in the family-- I'm a cousin, you know-- they said you were pretty interested in Didi."

English drew a long breath, and for a second Asey thought his bantering aplomb was going to crack.

"What you laughingly refer to as my interest in Didi," English said, "has several phases. First, I looked on the little brat as a wedge. You see, Laura only goes for boys with glasses and serious purposes. I'm the type she pats on the head, like a nice doggie. So I decided that the one way to force her into taking me seriously was for me to tackle the job she and Reed didn't dare touch-- to get Didi down to earth and away from Mike. So I tried. You could sum that up as my missionary interlude."

"An' do I gather from the gold trinkets that the interlude backfired on you?" Asey could already sense Didi's seething rage.

"I tried to be the helpful playmate steering her into the paths of righteousness-- and she cooed, and said I was just like Van Johnson! And all the time she'd been playing Mike for a sucker which is a highly dangerous business. That money"-- he pointed to the packets of bills on the dressing table-- "is the last phase-- pfft! She swiped that money from Mike's tin boxes and put it in my room. Thought she had me so gaga about her that I'd let her hide it there, and not tell anyone. Well, that I won't take! Laura may not believe me when I tell her, but I'm going to. Mike already knows....And now that you know all, Didi my chick, come out from behind Mayo-- I've smelled you there for hours!"

As he swung around and looked at the girl, Asey conceded to himself that she was better looking than Laura, except for her mouth. Even as much lipstick as she was wearing couldn't conceal its hard, sullen pout.

Ignoring Asey completely, she looked pityingly at English, and began to bite her lower lip. "Oh, Walt, you've hurt me so! Such horrible lies-- and I trusted you so!"

"You'll like this," English said conversationally to Asey. "It's her screen test, and she really does it well. Only when she stops emoting, you'll notice that her eyes aren't even red....About Mike's tin boxes"-- he raised his voice to compete with Didi's mounting sobs-- "they're Mike's system of testing the honesty of employees and friends and associates. Sort of a character index. He divides the world into those who don't swipe any, and how much the others swipe. Poor Reed's been in a tough spot; he's walked a hairline, knowing about Didi's little thieveries, knowing that Mike knew, and not wanting to tell Laura! But until today, Didi never went in for such volume. She--"

"Duck!" Asey said, as Didi leaned over suddenly, picked up a chromium wastebasket, and hurled it at English's head.

English ducked. The basket crashed past his head into the dressing table mirror and sent it smashing to the floor in a thousand pieces.

The shattering havoc seemed to have an equally shattering effect on Didi, who started to shiver and then broke into a paroxysm of sobbing.

English stared at her and shook his head. "That seems genuine!" he said.

"Say, what's the idea?" Rat-face interrupted indignantly, as he appeared in the doorway beside Asey. "What's the matter with you guys? She's got two more shows, and lookit her!"

Asey, who had been observing Didi as she lay sobbing hysterically on the small chaise lounge, knew he'd be wasting his time trying to question her now. And he strongly suspected that after she'd pulled herself together Didi would deny everything anyway, from having entered the hermit's to having stolen Mike's money.

"Listen," he said to Rat-face; "do you want her to finish her shows?....All right, then you calm her down! Mike said to tell you she's not to leave here until I come for her; an' if she's through before I get back, you're to bring her straight home, yourself. Got that?... Come on, English!"

Out in the Bell Club's back yard, English paused. "Look, Mayo, I'm a little tired of proceeding under sealed orders. What's happened?"

"Altogether too much to cram into any nutshell now," Asey said. "Can you think of any reason why Didi would go into the hermit's?"

"Sure. She's always had the idea that he hid clumps of money around, and she yearned to get inside and hunt for it. Treasure-trove stuff," English said, with a laugh. "In fact it's a stock joke of hers that Mike gets all his money from the hermit's hoard-- they kid a lot about it."

"An' you think she might've believed enough of the joke to have followed Mike in there, or to go in if she happened to see the door open?"

English nodded. "Yes, Mike warned me not to let her see me slip in while I was tending the furnace. He knew if she found out about his life with Bayard, she'd have it all over town in half an hour.... But will you tell me what's going on? Is it something to do with the hermit? Have those two stinkers--? Hey, where are you starting off to?"

"To see," Asey said, as he set off down the alley at top speed, "who's puttin' on lights up in the hermit's second story!"

With English racing along behind him, he sped through the alleys, around through the fence door, and up Dyer Street into Number Seventeen. At the top of the front-hall stairs he looked up. Then he stopped short, took off his hat, and gently fanned himself with it.

"For goodness sakes!" Jennie said indignantly, as she edged her way down through the stair clutter. "Where've you been, Asey Mayo? I've waited and waited-- What're you so red in the face for? Been running?"

"For your sake," Asey returned. "I think it's lucky I'm too winded to say very much. So what are you doin' in here? Was that you who put on the upstairs lights?"

"Why, of course!" Jennie said. "You wouldn't expect me to go
into that place in the dark, would you?   And look what I found on a
desk in the hermit's bedroom-- that's the only spot that isn't cram-
full, just like the hall here," she added parenthetically. "I roamed all
over while I was at it. Look, Asey; I was right all the time about
those two!"

Asey stared at the two large photographs which she thrust under
his nose.

"See?" she said with triumph. "The man with the book bag, and
the fat lady in the mink coat! They're the hermit's cousins-- it says
so right on 'em. 'Cousin Christian from Cousin Thurman' and 'Cousin
Christian from Cousin Pearl.' So they were here, just as I said at
first; remember?...Now, who's this nice-looking boy with you?"

Asey introduced English and passed the photographs to him.
"Happen to know anything about this pair?"

"I started to mention them just before you set off on your world
dash record," English said.   "I was trying to say, if anything was
wrong here, or with the hermit, those two stinkers were at the
bottom of it. What's happened to Bayard, anyway?"

"Not Bayard." Asey pointed across the hall. "Mike."

"I see," English said, after a long pause. "I see! No wonder you
stared at me that way when I japed about fixing the furnace! Oh, this
is bad!   Listen-- Thurman Otis and Pearl Featherstone are Bayard's
wife's cousins. Their greatest desire in life is to slam Bayard into an
asylum and get themselves appointed his guardians, so they can get at
his money. It's largely his wife's fortune, you see, and they cherish a
bizarre notion that it should have gone back into their family instead
of to Bayard.   And the pair loathes Mike because he's always
thwarted 'em. He's loaned them hunks of money at times--"

"Bayard's money?" Asey interrupted. "Why? How would that
thwart them?"

"Mike made them sign notes for it," English said. "Then, if they
decided to play rough, he could show a court they were less
interested in Bayard's well-being than in washing out their debts to
him and getting their hot hands on his estate. See?"

Apparently, Asey thought, it hadn't occurred to English that
Mike's motives in keeping off the cousins weren't entirely altrustic!

"Mike," English continued, "felt that his job was to keep them
reasonably quiet and pacified, and off Bayard's neck. Fortunately,
Thurman and Pearl are insanely jealous of each other's assets and
income, and they fight like cats and dogs. It's never dawned on 'em
to gang up on Bayard."

"Neither of those two looked a bit poor to me, or as if they
neeeded money!" Jennie said.

"Needs vary so," English said. "They've each got an income that
would keep a family of ten in comfort. But Pearl plays bridge from
morning till night for staggering stakes, and Thurman buys expensive
first editions and precious jade. They're constantly broke. For the

last week they've been hounding Mike. Only this afternoon I brushed
them out of the office--"

"Hold it," Asey broke in. "Could they have known about the
hermit's note asking Mike to come here at five-thirty?"

English frowned. "I don't see how-- unless they overheard the
girls in the office talking about it. Look; you asked why I rushed out
of the cellar, and I said to see someone passing by-- That was true!
I thought I saw Pearl peeking in the alley door! It startled me so, I
knocked over a lot of tins, and tripped on 'em. When I finally
untangled myself and got out, she'd gone. So I hurried home to see if
Mike had left word as to where I could find him. I thought he should
know she was here worrying Bayard."

"Have either of 'em come here often before?" Asey asked.

"That's the point! Mike said he'd told 'em long ago if they ever
bothered Bayard, or talked to reporters about him, they'd damned
well never be lent a cent. That's why I wanted so to get Mike. I felt
Pearl must be in a desperate jam to come here. But Superwoman said
he'd left no message where he'd be. And, at that point, I found those
bills in my bureau and went bouncing off after Didi-- You know the
rest!"

"I wish I did!" Jennie said acidly. "But what I want to know is--
where's Laura? What did you want her for, Asey?"

"I didn't want her! What're you talkin' about?"

"Why," Jennie said, "she went to the phone to answer a call, and
she never come back upstairs again. I thought of course you wanted
her! I got so tired of waiting, that's why I came over here. Where is
she, d'you s'pose?"

Asey shrugged wearily. "Who knows? Where's Reed? For that
matter, where's the hermit?...English, why would he trouble to write
a note to come here if Mike was in an' out fixin' the furnace, an' he
had any number of chances to talk with him?"

"To quote you, who knows?" English returned. "Sometimes the
old boy's like that. Does things I consider rather odd, but Mike's
never bothered by--"

He broke off as the front door of Seventeen swung open.

Reed Perry marched in. Behind him was Thurman Otis, grasping
his green flannel book bag. Pearl Featherstone, in her mink coat,
followed him, and Laura brought up the rear of the procession.

"There!" Reed said with an explosive sigh of relief. "I'm sorry to
have seemed to disappear, Asey, but when I ran out, I saw Otis
legging it down the street-- Incidentally, he's a cousin and she's a
cousin--"

"We know about 'em, in a rough way," Asey said. "Go on."

"Well, I chased him and lost him. He's written books about the
narrow, crooked streets of Boston, and he knows every last damned
side alley around here! Then, when I came back up the street here, I
spotted Pearl. But she ducked into a cab and beat it back to her
hotel. I had to phone Laura to help me get her, because she planted

herself in the ladies' room of the Winfield, and I couldn't drag her out of there! So Laura managed that. Then I got Otis at his apartment. I really had a time bringing them here."

"I am at a loss to understand," Pearl began in the chilliest and most dowagerlike tones, "why--"

"I fail," Otis chimed in quickly, in his scholarly precise voice, "to see why--"

Asey ignored them. "Were they actually in here earlier?" he asked Reed. "Did you find that out?"

"They claim they weren't together-- I believe that, for they're usually at swords' points-- and each claims just to have rung the front doorbell and gone away," Reed said. "But you know just as well as I that the door was open earlier! And I'm sure you and I didn't hear any bell later?"

"I am at a complete loss--"

"I fail utterly to see--"

"If you'll crane your necks and look yonder"-- Asey drowned out their protests-- "you'll both gain insight. Mike Sumner was killed here around five-thirty. I saw you both in the vicinity then, an' you both been back here later. Now, if you're both innocent of any connection with this affair, I'm sure you'll be happy to straighten things out."

"I'm sure," Otis said nervously, "that I wish to co-operate in every way! I was only bringing some books and a bit of jade for Cousin Christian to examine! I was sure if he just saw them, he'd unquestionably wish to help me acquire them for my collections!"

Mrs. Featherstone announced with great dignity that she was sure everyone would understand that she was merely paying a call on Cousin Christian. That was absolutely all, she added, as Reed made an exclamation of disbelief, except that she'd rather hoped Cousin Christian might render her some slight assistance concerning certain financial matters.

"Bridge debts again!" Otis said acidly.

"For one as heavily overdrawn as you, such an insinuation is infamous!" Mrs. Featherstone retorted. "You--"

"S'pose," Asey interrupted, "that we continue this over at Number Seven. It's roomier, an'-- Wow!"

Reed's elbow had caught on the broken wire of a bird cage and dislodged it from a pile. For the next two minutes that hall seemed to rain bird cages.

"Everyone okay?" Asey asked when the shower ceased. "Wa-el, pick your way out careful-- don't let anything else fall! Help escort 'em over, Jennie. I'll be along in a jiffy."

He paused by the stairs after they filed out, and pensively surveyed the cluttered hall. It had looked like the Grand Central Station with all of them packed in the narrow path, yet they'd all been here that afternoon. And Didi, too.

The sudden pealing of a telephone bell shocked him. Then he

smiled to himself. If the hermit had a furnace and electricity, why not a phone, too? After all, he'd had to order food somehow!

As the ringing continued, he tried to locate the instrument, but it was hidden from sight somewhere in the clutter. Then, at the sound of someone moving upstairs, Asey felt his hair rise on the back of his scalp.

Down the front hall stairs came the hermit, a small, frail old man with a gray beard. While he wasn't as padded as the papers had suggested, he certainly was wearing two sweaters, and he had several mufflers around his throat. He was limping painfully, and the hand resting on the stair rail was gnarled and mishapen-- too crippled, Asey decided, to do much biffing with a slat!

Halfway down the stairs, Bayard paused and took a phone receiver from somewhere within one of the tall heaps of crates.

"Hello," he said in a flat voice. "What?...Wrong number!" He replaced the receiver.

"Mr. Bayard!" Asey cleared his throat and wished he could dispel his nervous feeling that the man was going to disappear into thin air at any instant. "I'm Asey Mayo-- please wait. I want to talk with you about Mike Sumner."

Bayard stared down at him. Then, after a long interval, he said, "Porter cars."

Asey blinked. "Yes, I've always worked for that company ever since old Cap'n Porter founded it." And how in thunder had Bayard made that connection?

"You demonstrated my first auto at the old dirt track." Bayard came laboriously down the stairs within a foot of Asey, and thrust a forefinger almost in Asey's face. "What do you want here?"

"To ask about Mike." Asey drew a long breath. Apparently the hermit hadn't seen Sumner's body. "Did you ever feel he wasn't entirely honest about the handlin' of your money?"

After another long silence, Bayard nodded. "I don't miss or care about the small sums I've felt unaccounted for. But"-- a sudden angry note entered his voice, and his small eyes gleamed-- "I won't change my will the way he wishes! I will not!"

That, Asey thought, was an angle Reed couldn't cover up for Mike! "I see. Where you been all evenin', Mr. Bayard?"

"In the attic. I fell asleep up there. I never care whether it's day or night. I eat when I feel like it and sleep when I feel like it. Mike phoned and said if he wasn't here in a few minutes, he'd be much, much later. He asked me to get some old papers in the attic for him. It was warm up there, and I got sleepy--" His flat voice trailed off.

"When did Mike call an' say that?"

"Oh, a while ago. I don't know."

It began to dawn on Asey that time in the sense of hours and minutes meant nothing to the man. "Would you care"-- he picked his words carefully-- "to come to Mike's house for a short time? You

won't have to see people. Reed an' English'll look after you.   You
know them, of course."
     "They are nice boys. Very kind. Mike said they would look after
me if anything happened to him."
     Asey found himself gulping. "Then-- then you can see Mike's
body?"
     "Yes. I am very used to this hall," Bayard said. "I know
everything in it very well."
     If he felt any emotion over Mike, he certainly didn't show it!
     "Could you tell me what's been moved or touched or is differ-
ent?" Asey asked quickly.
     "My slat is gone from beside the door."   Not realizing that
Bayard had even glanced in that direction, Asey blinked again.
"Someone has moved that case." Bayard pointed to where Asey had
grubbed around while Reed was there. "The bird cages have fallen.
Will the police have to come here?...Yes? Then," he said, in tones of
one making a momentous decision, "I will stay at Mike's until they
have gone." He limped past Asey to the front door, grasped the knob
firmly, and jerked the door open.
     Watching him, Asey revised his previous opinion about those
hands being too crippled to grip a slat! "Maybe you better put on a
coat?" he asked.
     "Certainly not!"   Bayard's eyes gleamed angrily at the sugges-
tion. "And don't take my arm! I don't require assistance!"
     "Okay." In silence, they walked over to Number Seven.
     As he was opening the vestibule door, Asey glanced down at the
lilac bush and discovered that the slat was no longer there....
     Reed and English took charge of Bayard and led him upstairs.
     "Gracious, Asey!" Jennie said as the trio disappeared in the upper
hall. "Was he there all the time?...Where? Did he see anything?
What d'you think of him?"
     "He's got a fine memory for the past, none for the present, an
eye like a hawk; he's not as frail as he looks; he's no one's fool," Asey
told her with a grin; "an' he says he was up in the attic all the time,
asleep."
     "Bosh!" Jennie said. "Of course, I didn't poke into all those fifty
million mattresses and bundles of rags up there, but I looked, and I
never saw him! He's lying--"
     Miss Maxwell strode up to where they stood by the newell post.
"Think of it!" she said excitedly. "A murder next door!"
     Apparently, Asey thought, the nearness of the crime moved her
more than the identity of the vicitm!
     "Just like the Smyth case-- Oh, Reed look out!" she added, as he
ran down the stairs. "Your sleeve nearly caught that Sevres figurine
on the table!...You rememeber the Smyth case? Six years ago, ex-
Senator Smyth was killed by an old hermit--"
     "Seven years ago," Reed said. "September, nineteen-thirty-eight.
Would you be a dear and get--"

"This old man--" Miss Maxwell ignored his interruptions.

"Old <u>woman</u>!" Reed corrected her. "Yes, it was! I was in the Providence railroad station on September twenty-first, and I remember reading the headlines about Smyth....Look: would you get Bayard some coffee and a sandwich? He can't remember when he ate last....Asey, his hands are worse than I've ever seen them. I don't think he could have held a slat--"

"Will you promise to get me a trophy from him?" Superwoman's brown diamonds flashed as she made excited gestures with her hands. "One of his scarves? Will you, Reed?"

"I'll try. Get him some food, like a good girl!"

Asey wondered as she strode down the hall, why she had changed from flat-heeled brogues to high-heeled pumps. "Say, Reed," he said suddenly, "is she any relation of Mike's?"

"No, just his housekeeper. Been here for years. She gets a huge salary, but she earns every-- Where are you going?"

Asey smiled. "To look into the cousins, an' other miscellaneous odds an' ends. You an' Jennie hold the fort!"

Two hours later, he returned.

It occurred to him as he stood on the threshold of the living-room that the group sitting there among the rubber plants and bric-a-brac had something of the stiffly rigid quality of an old-fashioned family daguerreotype. Otis, with his book bag, was perched primly on a gilt chair next to Pearl, who hadn't removed either her gloves or her mink coat. Reed and Laura were sitting bolt upright on a green plush couch. Didi, presumably delivered by Rat-face, sat on a fringed footstool. Jennie and Superwoman, looking at an album of snapshots, might well have been viewing stereopticon slides.

"Hermit okay?" he asked.

"Walt's got him listening to the radio in the dining-room," Reed said. "He's fascinated. Wants fifty radios at once."

"So? Jennie, Miss Maxwell-- the rest of you, too, if you want to come--"

He led them back to Miss Maxwell's sitting-room and opened the door. The light was on, and Superwoman pointed at the two men standing there. "Who are they?" she asked. "How'd they get in?"

"Friends of mine," Asey said. "Meet Lieutenant Murphy an' Sergeant Trask. I had 'em drop in the back way. Now, I want to show all of you Miss Maxwell's trophy wall. It's got three brand-new items on it!"

"I don't understand!" Superwoman said. "What items?"

"First"-- Asey paused as English and Bayard edged into the room-- "this slat with three nails. I didn't think it'd be very far away-- time was scarce-- but it took some time to locate it in the gutter outside this window! Then there's this envelope." He unpinned it from the wall, opened it, and poured a few pieces and slivers of glass out onto a table. "Now, that's one of the major clues, if you happen to notice, or could make anything out of it! I thought first it was Laura's broken watch crystal, but, on closer inspection, it turned out to be a glasses lens--"

"Miss Maxwell's!" Jennie broke in.   "She said she'd lost her glasses at Jordan's!"

"No, not hers," Asey said. "Reed's. He dropped 'em an' stepped on 'em there in the hermit's hall, after bashin' Mike with the slat. But he didn't pick up all the pieces. Maybe he's so nearsighted without his glasses, he missed 'em; maybe they were out of his reach. But mostly I think he skipped 'em because he was interrupted. First by Didi, who popped in, spotted Mike, an' popped out. Then by Laura, who stayed-- thus forcin' him to hide in the cellar. After accidentally makin' a noise bumpin' into some tins, an' biffin' Laura to keep her from discoverin' him, he let the rest of the pieces go. He had another idea about 'em."

"Reed biffed me?" Laura said in a dazed voice. "But I thought it was a woman!"

"Your subconscious was workin' overtime. You thought it was Didi," Asey said. "You got me broodin' about Superwoman an' Pearl before I come to realize, you'd never seen anyone, an' it could be a man!"

"How--?" Reed's mouth worked, but the words wouldn't come.

"How'd I find out they were your glasses?" Asey smiled.   "You told the world, peerin' and bumpin' around! You bumped a bird cage when you an' I were at Bayard's, later you knocked 'em all down. You nearly smashed that figurine here. In short, you're wearin' glasses, but not your real ones! Just plain-glass jobs you picked up in a drugstore, or a Five an' Ten."

Jennie said she didn't understand any of it.

"After breakin' his real ones an' leavin' these bits behind, he thought quick, see? He knew these could be put together an' traced, an' that the cops probably would investigate everyone's prescriptions here. So he rushed to his eye man's just before the place closed-- not to Mike's office to burn papers, as he told me. He'd attended to that before," Asey said. "While the eye man was gettin' some lens wipers Reed asked for, Reed sneaked his own prescription from the desk file. Then he threw away his spare pair. So that these bits couldn't be traced to him, see? Luckily, he forgot to destroy a glasses case. We got the eye man's name from that, an' Murphy dug up all the details. Then there's this third item." He unpinned from the wall a piece of paper on which a date was written. "This proved he was lyin' like mad about everything."

"Why?" Jennie demanded.

"September twenty-first, nineteen thirty-eight," Asey said, "is when he claimed he was in Providence when the Smyth case broke. He wasn't puttin' himself there for any reason except to prove how accurate an' truthful he was-- dates always make you sound so honest! But I remembered that date. I was personally rowin' a boat through the square by the Providence station, rescuin' people. That was the day of the Big Hurricane. Seemed to me you'd've remembered that if you'd been there!"

"But why did he kill Mike?" English asked.

"Oh, there's one more thing I should've put on the wall.... Murphy, where's the bills we brought from the Bell Club?....Reed's been stealin' from Mike's tin cash box for a long time. I'm guessin' he's told Mike lots of people were responsible that really weren't, like Didi. Tonight Reed planted his biggest haul on you, English-- an' you suspected Didi because he'd confided to you she stole. Actually, she never did. An' he's been stealin' from Bayard's estate, too. Bayard thought as I did, that Mike was takin' a cut, but it was Reed all the time."

"And Mike finally found out?" English said.

"I think that's what brought all this to a head today. Reed took advantage of the hermit's note very cleverly," Asey said. "He phoned Bayard just before five-thirty, an' said he was Mike, an' if he didn't come right off, he'd be very late, an' please to get some papers in the attic. Bayard waited a few minutes, then obediently went up in the attic. He was there when Mike came.

"That gave Reed the opportunity to kill him with Bayard's slat, thus makin' him Suspect Number One, as Reed carefully pointed out to me. By stealin' the note from Mike's pocket later, he added more suspicion to Bayard. He must have forgot that note on his first visit-- what with breakin' his glasses an' all.

"Oh, it was a nice plan! He'd get rid of Mike before Mike told on him; he'd get the hermit accused of the murder-- an' Murphy an' I think we'll find a fake will leavin' Bayard's estate to Reed. I'm sure he tried to get it left to him,telling Bayard Mike wanted it that way! So, that's that!...Jennie, I want to see you a minute in the hall."

"What is it?" Jennie demanded as he took her arm.

"Come along home before they start askin' questions! Get your hat-- better still leave it! That infernal flower bed led us into this! I'll get you another. Come on!"

"Asey, did you see how Walt English looked at Laura, and how she looked at him? He's her boy; I thought so when I first saw him! Mark my words, they'll-- Oh, won't Nellie be pleased to hear she and I were right about that insurance money all the time. We said if a man lived in the same boardin'house with a girl, and never proposed till she come into money, it ought to be looked into, and you were just the one to do it! And you were!"

Asey chuckled as they set off down Dyer Street. "Ah," he said, "but you knew who the villain was , all along!"

Crime on the Pegasus

Complete
AMERICAN MYSTERY NOVEL

by H. W. RODEN

ILLUSTRATED BY
KENNETH THOMPSON

The body was missing, completely vanished
from the racing luxury train. Seventeen people
hoped he was dead; only two were sure...
and one was the murderer

Henry Wisdom Roden (1895-1963) had a long and varied business career, primarily in the food industry, holding sales and executive positions with such firms as Johnson and Johnson, American Home Products, G. Washington Coffee, Crown Zellerbach, and Chef Boy-Ar-Dee. He was also a U.S. Navy aviator during World War I, a flying instructor after the war, and a member or officer of numerous business and charitable organizations. Somehow amid all that activity, he managed, during a brief creative period in the mid-forties, to produce four novels about private eye Sid Ames as well as the non-series novelette that follows. Two biographical sources list "Crime on the Pegasus" among Roden's novels, suggesting an expanded book publication was anticipated, but Allen J. Hubin's authoritative Crime Fiction, 1749-1980: A Comprehensive Bibliography (Garland, 1984) lists no such volume.

As demonstrated in such works as Agatha Christie's classic Murder on the Orient Express and Lawrence G. Blochman's Bombay Mail, trains are a perfect setting for both detective novels and thrillers. Adding to the reader's enjoyment today is nostalgia for a mode of transportation that still exists (barely) but will never be quite the same again. Roden's exciting account of a danger-packed but luxurious cross-country railroad journey proves these points once more.

CRIME ON THE PEGASUS by H. W. Roden

Its silver sides gleaming in the sunlight, the Pegasus, pride of the National Western Railroad, wound its sinuous way through the yards as it commenced its forty-hour run between Chicago and Los Angeles.

In Compartment G of Car K-7 a tall young man with wavy brown hair and friendly gray eyes was stowing away the last of his luggage, when he was startled by the sound of his room's buzzer. He quickly turned to the already open door, to find a girl standing there.

She was tall and slender and lovely. Her ash-blond hair curled at her shoulders, framing a sensitive face in which startlingly blue eyes smiled a warm greeting. He remembered her thus from their last meeting in Paris.

"Pam," he said softly. "Pamela Gordon."

"Les, what luck!" she responded, giving both of her hands into his firm grip. "I was certain it was you. It has been a long time."

"Five years, I guess it is, since we did that trick with AP together...Berlin, Paris, London. I'll never forget them. But you didn't go on to London, did you Pam?"

She settled herself comfortably on the couch before answering. "No," she said slowly; "I caught the last boat sailing from Cherbourg for New York before the big push. You and some of the others of the old newspaper crowd got across the channel." Her voice trailed off at the memory. Then she repeated, "It has been a long time, Les...and I've been proud of all you've done with it."

"There hasn't been much that any individual could do, Pam," he answered, his face puckered in an unaccustomed frown. "What little I could contribute ended in Leyte, where the Nips decided they wanted a road-block worse than I. Then there was a long spell in the Naval Hospital at San Diego."

"Was it there that you wrote Midway?"

"Yes," he smiled again. "I always said that one day I was going to write the great American drama. I had to take my crack at it, I suppose."

"It's a fine play and you have every reason to be proud of it," the girl said solemnly. "But now that it's such a smash hit I suppose you're headed for Hollywood." She said it as if she hoped it were not true.

"Yes, Super Opus Selections has bought Midway and I'm to work on the script."

"So S.O.S. got you." For some unaccountable reason there was no enthusiasm in her voice. Then she added with what seemed unnecessary bitterness, "Let me take it from there. Five hundred a week for thirteen weeks. An option on your services for another thirteen weeks at seven hundred and fifty-- if they want you."

"That's true. But how did you know? I mean about the option."

"Honey," the girl answered sympathetically, "I'm in my seventh one of those things. You sign a contract. You're all set. Thirteen weeks seem like forever. You start taking on expenses. Permanent ones. Then you get into the eighth week, and you start to wonder. Will they take up your option? You commence being sweet to people; only, you can't be sweet, for being sour-- you're that worried and irritable. You pull all the wires you know; and chew your nails off up to the elbows; you reserve a nice niche at Forest Lawn. Then the fatal day comes. If you're lucky you get a new contract. Then you take on new expenses again. Somehow they become permanent, too. They usually run about a hundred and fifty a week more than your new contract calls for." She let her voice trail off. Then she added, somewhat irrelevantly, "I've had a hard day. Buy a gal a drink, will you?"

Lester pushed the bell button, and the chimes sounded loud and clear at the end of the car. Nothing else happened. La Grange went by in a blur. "That brings us to you," he said quietly.

For a long minute the girl gazed out the window at the flat greens and browns of eastern Illinois. Then, turning to Lester, she asked, "Remember the last time you took a trip West?"

"Of course. I couldn't overlook the contrast with this luxury of having my own room. On my last trip I shared a tourist car with forty-seven other leathernecks."

"That's what I mean, Les." She said it quietly. "We were going to talk about you. Remember?"

"Yes. Let's talk about me." Again there was that note of bitterness so at variance with the normal ebullience of the girl. "I've joined the world's newest profession. I'm a wet nurse, a stooge, a stool pigeon-- in short, a studio publicity representative."

"From what you just said about options you've been at it for two years. That means you've been successful. Which studio are you with?"

"Why, none other than your new and my old alma mammy, S.O.S., the pride of Culver City. And what do I do, my love? I play pat-a-cake with those two sterling actors of the stage, radio and screen-- those peerless exponents of wit, humor, and corn-- those factional wits--" She threw the line away.

"I'm sorry, Pam," he smiled contritely. "I'm a little behind in my movie going."

"Why, who else but-- Durand and Martin!" She mentioned the names of two former burlesque artists who had recently catapulted into fame and fortune via the radio and screen.

"I know exactly what you mean," he said. "There was one night at Bougainville when they showed a Durand and Martin picture. Anything should have looked good to me under the circumstances. It was horrible. Another time I was dining in a restaurant in Chicago. It was a good restaurant-- until they came in and took over. In my carefully considered opinion Durand and Martin are a couple of vulgar, odious, and completely objectionable heels. You have my complete sympathy."

"That will help me over the rough spots, Les," the girl responded, giving the bell button a vigorous push. "You see, my job is to keep Fats Durand and Slim Martin before the public eye. I see that their vicious insults are all interpreted as good, clean fun. I explain to outraged hosts that they are only boys at heart. I keep photographers from immortalizing their most tasteless antics on film. And finally-- if you need any more-- I try to make the public forget what Durand and Martin have long since forgot, that one of them once ran a hamburger stand in some hillbilly Tennessee village and the other was a gas-station attendant."

For a little while neither of them spoke. Then the girl said, almost petulantly, "That was Aurora we just went through. I always like a drink at Aurora. Where do you suppose that porter is?"

Lester pushed the button again. The ding-dong of the chime reverberated up and down the empty corridor. Finally the buzzer sounded, and the porter put his head through the doorway. There was a harried expression on his face and perspiration glistened on his dark brow.

"Do you suppose you could go to the club car and get us some drinks?" Lester smiled at him.

"Yas, suh; yas, suh," the porter replied hurriedly and with no more than halfhearted assurance. "Just as soon as I can get to it. Right now I got to take care of Mist' Durand and Mist' Martin. They're in the car ahead, you know, and I'm helping their boys." The door closed gently and very firmly.

"Well, my dear," smiled Pam, turning to Lester and showing lovely, even, white teeth, "you are now roughly three thousand miles from Hollywood and Vine and you have just encountered that phenomenon known as the Hollywood caste system. The manifestation enlarges in direct ratio as the mileage decreases. And was it I who stepped off the curb to talk about publicity people? Wait until you see where Hollywood fits writers into the scheme of things." She nodded bright blond curls at him, then added hopefully, "You can always get off at La Salle, you know."

"You make it sound something less than enticing," Lester said, falling into the girl's mood.

Immediately she was contrite. "I'm sorry, Les," she said. "I suppose it's that darned option. It comes due next week, and I always get this way just before option time. But Hymie Rappaport thinks of everything. Actually, we've got the best lot out there. If anyone will do justice to Midway you can be reasonably certain that S.O.S. will do the trick."

"Let's forget S.O.S. and Midway and your two comics," Lester responded. "How about a spot of dinner? We can catch a cocktail in the club car on the way."

"Sorry, Les," the girl replied. "Some other time. My workday doesn't stop when the five o'clock whistle blows. As amah to the two great men I must parade them on the platform at Peoria for the fans-- dear little autograph fans." She repressed a violent shudder.

"Isn't there anyone else with them?" Lester asked.

"Are you being naive, Les?" Pam replied as she stood up. "The great of Hollywood always travel in a caravan. There are, in addition to the two valets and maid who attend this priceless pair of panjandrums and their respective helpmates, exactly eleven members of this entourage. To name them briefly: the Messrs. Durand and Martin, with their current wives, Mollie, a former showgirl, and Eudora, erstwhile singer in a band, respectively. In addition, we have their two sisters with their husbands, known as Mr. and Mrs. Simeon and Mr. and Mrs. Carlyle, and carried on the pay roll for tax purposes as secretaries. If any one of the four of them can add up two and two I'm a graduate of McGill, McGee.

"Then there's Garret Fabian. He's their manager in the books, but actually he writes their material, coaches them, makes their deals, collects their money, and invests it for them, keeping a neat twenty percent for himself. And he hates one of them-- Slim-- with as deep and abiding a hatred as you're liable to witness either side of the Rockies."

"They hardly seem the sort to make lasting friendships," Lester put in dryly.

"With Garret it is something special," Pam continued. "He used to be a pretty regular person. Then about a year and a half ago he fell in love with a pretty singer with a second-rate band playing the cheap clubs around Santa Monica. Her name was Eudora Duncan. It looked like a sure middle-aisle trip for Garret and Eudora. Then Slim Martin discovered what was going on. He didn't like the idea of his manager getting soft. Might not be so cagey in his business arrangements. So he looked up the girl. Then he got to playing around with her. When that didn't break it up between Eudora and Fabian, Slim decided to do something about it. He married the girl himself."

"Just a pal," Lester said in a low voice.

"A real one," Pam responded. "If Slim had loved the girl Garret could have taken it. But even Eudora had no illusions about that by the second day of the honeymoon. Now he treats her like a door mat and takes a sadistic pleasure in parading that fact before Fabian."

"Why doesn't Fabian take a sock at Martin and then walk off the job?" Les wanted to know.

Pamela shrugged. "Those two boys gross a hundred and eighty thousand apiece each and every year. Twenty per cent of that is a lot of moola, and with our silly tax setup he keeps about as much of his as they do of what they earn. And of course they hate him for that."

"Seems like a lot of people hate each other in this outfit," Lester interjected.

"You're right," the girl answered thoughtfully. "Small, selfish, cruel people like Durand and Martin can generate a lot of animosity in those around them....But to get back to my counting-- there's me. And that about does it."

"You're short one," Lester said, ticking them off on his fingers. "You've named ten of the eleven. Is the eleventh something special?"

He did not know why he asked the question just that way. Nor could he account for the fact that Pamela suddenly and unaccountably reddened as she started for the door. It seemed for a moment as if she were not going to answer him at all. Then she said quietly, "Yes, very special. He is Durand and Martin's agent. His name is Sherwood Schyler. As he handles other stars as well as the two comedians, his presence on this trip might be called incidental. It was to have been a honeymoon. His-- and mine. Somehow we never got around to the marriage." She opened the door and stepped into the corridor.

Lester hurried to her side and, placing a hand on her shoulder, said gently, "I'm sorry, Pam. I didn't know."

She managed a small smile, then, tossing a "See you later" over her shoulder, she strode forward toward the car ahead, her tall, impressive figure straight and her head held high.

Lester watched her until she disappeared around the turn in the corridor. The low moan of the train's whistle could be heard far up ahead, its tones swirling and twisting over the tops of the flying cars to reach his ears. A freight train clattered by going east. Outside it had commenced to get dark.

At eight o'clock Lester decided to take a short walk through the train before going back to the dining car. As he passed through Car K-8, the one directly ahead of his own, he unwittingly was made aware of a disturbing incident. As he drew abreast of Room E he heard from within a brief, shrill scream, followed almost immediately by a blow and the sound of a body falling against the closed door.

Then came the unmistakable high-pitched voice of Slim Martin shouting, "Give me any more of that stuff, you little tramp, and I'll kick you back in the gutter where I found you." Finally, the sound of broken sobs came from behind the door, and Lester, feeling uncomfortable and embarrassed, passed on through the corridor.

Before he reached the most forward car the train came slowly to a stop, and Lester dropped off the station platform of what he learned was the little city of Burlington. A porter informed him that there would be a ten-minute stop to service the train. It was here that he again saw Pam. He swung along beside her, and after a few steps together in silence he asked, "How about letting me buy you that drink we never caught up with this afternoon?"

She agreed readily enough, and the constraint apparent at their last parting seemed to have left her. As they sat in the club car sipping their drinks, a tall, handsome young man approached them. His carefully set hair was blond and he wore a small matching mustache. He was dressed in a pair of slacks and a sports coat of a different pattern. The lines of the coat had been so tailored as to give him a rather grotesque appearance of overdeveloped shoulders. Notwithstanding, he was an arresting figure and stood before them with somewhat arrogant yet complete self-assurance.

As Lester rose to acknowledge the introduction Pam said, "Sherry, this is Mr. Clifford. Mr. Schyler, Les."

Les put out his hand, then flushed as the man, merely nodding, ignored it. In a lazy drawl Schyler said, "I waited for you, Pam. But I see you found something better to do. It's time for dinner. I'm very hungry."

It was Pam's turn to flush, the color suffusing her face. To

Lester's surprise, however, she arose and accompanied the young man toward the diner, tossing over her shoulder a casual "By, now." Schyler continued to ignore him.

In a savage mood, Lester finished another drink, then strode back to the dining car. But he was too late to be seated immediately. The steward indicated that no seats were vacant and that he would have to wait a few minutes. As he stood at the entrance to the car, its door opened and two men came through the narrow corridor. One of them was large and gross and rumbled constantly in a low drawl. The other was small and slight and spoke in a high, nasal voice. They were arguing unrestrainedly. They were also a little drunk.

The small one's whine came to Lester over the train noises: "Now, Fats, twenty-five gees you owe me from gin rummy on this trip alone. And a lot more from before this. What I want and what I mean to get is less talk and more dough."

"Stow it, Slim," the huge one bumbled heatedly. "Before this trip is over you'll be owing me jack. Why, we've got two whole nights left to play yet." Ignoring the smaller man's rejoinder, Durand signaled the steward. "All right, Captain," he droned out his companion's words, "we're ready for a table. Make it four; the wives will be right along."

The dining-car man was almost obsequious in his apologies. "I'm sorry, Mr. Durand," he mouthed his excuses. "There isn't a table for four available at the moment. It will be only a matter of a very few minutes, though, sir, and I'll take care of you and Mr. Martin."

"Take care of us now," thundered the fat man. "If you haven't got a table, root some of those people that work for me out of one. Tell 'em I want to eat. Tell 'em I'm hungry."

Fortunately, four people left the diner by the opposite door before the confused steward had to do anything about evacuating some members of the comedian's troupe. Durand and Martin headed for the vacant table without so much as a by-your-leave to Lester. Their wives came in shortly and sat down with them.

Lester continued to stand in the little rotunda at the end of the car waiting his turn for a seat. The panorama which was spreading itself before him slightly sickened him, and had it not been for the lateness of the hour he would have returned to his own car and waited until the diner had emptied before attempting to have his dinner.

The steward continued to fawn upon the great men, while the waiters paraded by their table an unnecessary number of times to better view the stars. For their part, Durand and Martin, now the cynosure of all eyes in the car, at once became the famous Hollywood comedians, and they worked at it every minute. Each word they uttered was for the benefit of the entire car, and the response was terrific.

Lester finally obtained a table, and after a hurriedly eaten dinner, he left the dining car, intending to return to his own room in Car K-7. Passing through the lounge, he once again encountered

Pam, apparently alone, an empty seat beside her. He hesitated for a moment, but her quick smile and cheery invitation caused him to drop into the empty seat.

"I'll buy you a drink this time," she said, with a wry smile. "I owe it to you."

They ordered brandies. When the waiter brought them she continued, "My swain mentioned something about a game of cards and went forward to his car to get them. That was a quarter of an hour ago, so it looks as if I'm stood up."

"Lucky me," Lester responded. "What car is privileged to house the handsome Mr. Schyler?"

"K-8, I believe the number is. All of our people are in it except me. I'm in compartment C in Car K-7 with you."

"Was that deliberate, or did they run out of rooms in K-8?"

"The latter. As a mater of fact, between the servants and Garret Fabian, all of the bedrooms are taken; Sherry, the Simeons, and the Carlyles occupy three of the compartments, and of course the Durands and the Martins have the two drawing-rooms. Opening into the Durands' is a compartment which is kept empty during the entire trip."

"For heaven's sake why?" Lester cut in.

"Strict orders from the two great men. The porter isn't allowed at any time to even so much as make up a berth. It is their sanctum sanctorum-- and all on account of gin rummy."

"Gin rummy?"

"Yes. Two greater addicts have never come out of the Westwood Hills-- and that is saying something. They play it morning, noon, and evening. You'll find them there hard at it most, if not all, of both nights until we get to Los Angeles. And quarreling and arguing over who is cheating whom. They had quite a row on that subject earlier tonight."

"I caught a part of that," Les replied. Then he continued, "And do they-- cheat each other, I mean?"

"Probably. They would think it cute. And they play for high stakes. Ten cents a point and all the trick ways to pile the score up fast. Slim usually wins. And they fight about it a lot. When they get tired of that subject they get into which one carries the other in the act. That's always good for several hours."

"Which one really has what it takes to make people pay money to see them?" Les asked.

"I honestly don't know. It's a double act. Durand gets off the lines. He has the gas and the funny business. He's big and fat and reasonably comical-looking. Martin is the straight man. He's small and a perfect dead-pan type. He feeds the lines, and his timing is uncanny. Without it I doubt if they would go over nearly so well. So it's probably a pretty even split. Of course, each thinks the other smells and that alone he'd be terrific."

"When I said earlier that you had my sympathy I didn't realize what a masterful piece of understatement it was," Les said, shaking his head. "I hadn't seen your bosses in action."

"They are not my bosses," Pam hastened to correct him. "Thank heaven for that. Good old S.O.S., as bad as it is, gives me my orders. When this trip is over and they complete the picture we're about to begin they go back on the air as a package show, and I'm through with them. At least until they do another picture-- God forbid!"

Finishing her drink, Pamela announced that she was tired, and shortly arose and left the car. After she had gone, Lester picked up a magazine and idly commenced to turn its pages. In a little while he found a story which intrigued his interest and soon lost himself in it. He did not realize that he was almost alone in the car until the porter started dimming the lights. His wrist watch showed it to be only a few minutes before twelve. He started forward to his own room.

The corridor lights of K-7 had been dimmed, all the doors to the rooms were closed, and the occupants presumably abed and asleep. He paused before the door to compartment C, undecided for a moment whether he should disturb Pam at such an hour. Then, in the hope that she had not retired and might be willing to talk with him a while he rapped lightly. There was no immediate answer, and he rapped again. When there was still no response he gently turned the handle of the door. It was not locked and swung inward under his hand. The room was empty. The ceiling lights were out, but the glow of the soft reading lamps revealed a berth that was turned down and awaiting its occupant. But Pam was not in the room.

Closing the door to the compartment, Lester found himself more wide awake and restless now than before. He decided on a walk through the train. He worked his way forward through car after car, until further passage was barred by a locked door to the baggage car. He encountered no passengers at all and only two sleepy-eyed porters busily shining shoes. They each glanced, but incuriously, at him. The Pegasus was bedded down for the night.

Some of his pent-up energy dissipated by his long hike, he retraced his steps back toward his own car. He had just opened the vestibule door, preparatory to entering the forward end of Car K-8, when he heard the door at the opposite end of the car click shut. There was no mistaking the sound. He would have thought nothing of this, but when he made the turn into the corridor he saw a man emerge from one of the rooms in the middle of the car, close the door, then hasten along the corridor, only to disappear into one of the rooms at the far end. Even in the subdued light Lester could not fail to recognize the unmatched sport ensemble and exaggerated shoulders of Sherwood Schyler.

The man's actions and movements had been furtive and surreptitious. Had this not somehow aroused Lester's suspicions he might have passed Compartment C without noticing that the door was slightly ajar. But as he came abreast of it the train rounded a sharp curve, and the swaying of the car caused the compartment door to swing wide open. To his own amazement, Lester found himself gazing into the startled face of comedian Slim Martin.

Martin was sitting on the room's couch, his head resting in the right-angle formed by the seat's cushioned back and the steel side of the car. A folding table stood before him, and at its opposite side there was an empty chair. His hands were clasped in front of him on the table and a pack of playing cards was spread out on the table's flat surface. Martin continued to stare at Lester with that surprised look on his face.

Suddenly, Lester knew why. He would have known why even if he had not seen the handle of the knife protruding from the the man's left breast. Slim Martin was dead.

Shouldering the door open to its full width, Lester stepped inside the room. He approached the dead man, but he touched neither him nor any object in the compartment. Spread out on the table before the empty chair were ten playing cards lying face up. Glancing at them, Lester recognized that they represented the perfect gin rummy hand, all of the cards being matched in suits and sequences. Across the table under Martin's clasped hands were ten ill-sorted cards, each of high point value and not one meld in the hand. The two exposed hands represented good fortune for someone; bad luck to Martin.

Lester knew that he could not long delay notifying the train conductor of the grisly happening in Compartment C of Car K-8. Yet he slowly and methodically searched the room for some key to the mystery of Martin's death. He even tried the door between it and the drawing-room to the rear, which he knew to be occupied by the Durands. It was locked. When he was certain that he had overlooked no possible clue to the riddle, he closed the door and started in search of the conductor.

Passing Pam's room in his own car, Les stepped to the door and pushed the buzzer. He heard sound within the room, but there was no immediate response. Trying the door, he found it locked. Again he pushed the buzzer button, and this time he could hear faint stirrings inside. Pam's voice asked through the door, "Who is it?"

"Open up please, Pam," he responded. "It's Les. Something important has happened."

Without delay the door swung open, and Pam stood before him dressed as she had been when he had last seen her. "I've been reading," she said. "Guess I fell asleep." Her eyes showed no signs of sleepiness.

"How long have you been here, Pam?"

"Here? Why, all evening; since I left you in the club car. I haven't been out of the room."

Les did not pursue the matter. He told her what he had discovered in the car ahead. She appeared shocked and upset by the news. When she recovered her composure she said, "Les, have you any idea what sort of explosion this will create? As soon as it hits the wires it will crowd everything else right off the front page. And

I'm the gal who will have to send out the story. It's like writing my own obituary."

"What do you mean by that?"

"Just that Martin and Durand were S.O.S.'s most valuable property. I was the studio's representative on this junket."

"But you weren't supposed to--?"

"I was supposed to deliver them back in Hollywood alive and all together....Oh, Les, are you certain?"

"Very certain, Pam," he answered. "He is sitting there with an ordinary knife such as you can buy at any sporting-goods store sticking in his heart. He is staring at the door, but he isn't seeing it. He rolls a little with the motion of the train, but he is dead. I made very sure of that."

Pam shuddered. "Who could have done it?" she asked.

"From what I've heard, any one of seventeen people," he answered shortly. "No, make it eighteen. I've begun to thoroughly dislike the man myself."

Lester found the Pullman and train conductors and again told his story. With mixed skepticism and alarm they both started for Car K-8. Pam and Lester followed. The train conductor kept repeating over and over, "I've been on this line thirty-nine years and nothing like this has ever happened to me before."

Les finally attempted to bring the man to earth with, "Well, it's happened to you now. You're in charge. The authorities will hold you responsible for what goes on here."

"Do you know who did it?" The Pullman conductor, whose name was Leininger, spoke up.

"Of course not. I merely meant that your partner here has to take over. He's in charge of the train."

They had arrived before Compartment C. The door to the room remained closed, as Les had left it. The train conductor threw it open. On his face was an expression plainly indicating his expectation that they were about to walk into a scene of bloodshed and carnage. He looked as if he might be sick at any moment.

Suddenly the expression on his face altered. He still looked stunned, but somehow different. The other three pressed forward to peer around him into the room. What they saw astonished them quite as profoundly as it had the conductor.

The table stood as it had earlier, between the couch and the empty chair. There were no playing cards on its flat, dull surface. And there was no Slim Martin sitting on the couch dead or alive. The room was empty.

The white-haired train conductor was the first to recover his wits. "Young man," he said, turning to Lester, "if this is some trick you are trying to play I'll see that you are put in jail."

"Maybe it's some publicity stunt, Frank," the Pullman conductor said. "Somebody said this young woman is in movie publicity."

"Perhaps it's one of Durand and Martin's wacky ideas of a joke,"

Pam put in hopefully.

"It wasn't a trick, a publicity stunt, or joke," Les interrupted wearily. "You don't land with the marines at Saipan and Leyte without knowing a dead man when you see one. I tell you, Martin sat there on that couch with a knife in his heart and as dead as he'll ever be."

"Then where is he at?" bellowed the conductor in exasperation.

"I don't know. But fifteen minutes ago his body was in this room."

"If he was stabbed, where's the blood?" asked the Pullman man reasonably.

They examined the upholstery and the rug. There was no damp spot.

"I don't know that, either," Les answered bitterly. "I didn't examine the knife too closely, for I didn't want to ruin any fingerprints on the hilt. But I did notice that there was only a small amount of blood around the wound. It would stay that way unless the knife was removed."

"Are you still certain, Les?" Pam asked hopefully. "You don't know how diabolically clever those two can be. If they thought they could scare somebody, this is precisely the type of hoax they would pull."

"It was Martin, Pam," Les answered simply. "He was here and he was dead."

"Well, I can't turn the whole train upside down on your say-so, young man," the conductor interjected, obviously relieved. "We will have to wait until morning and see if Mr. Martin shows up."

"You can at least determine if he is in his drawing-room," Les answered shortly. "Understand," he added, "all this is no skin off my knuckles. But we are newspaper people and we know how these things work. If there has been a murder-- and I assure you there has-- you do nothing for the rest of the night, and every newspaper in the country will make a monkey out of you and your road."

That did it. The trainman mumbled to the Pullman conductor, "What room are Mr. and Mrs. Martin in?" got the answer and strode to the door. The others trouped after him. His hand hesitated on its way to the buzzer button, but, making up his mind, he pressed it vigorously.

After a while they could hear someone stirring around the room. Another pause, and then the door opened, at first part way, then fully. Mrs. Martin stood on the threshold, a negligee thrown over her nightgown. Her eyes were red. "What's all this?" she asked in a husky voice.

The conductor responded with surprising dignity, "Mrs. Martin, is your husband in the room with you?"

Mrs. Martin answered angrily, "Of course he's not with me. He's only my husband. You wouldn't expect him to spend any time in our room, would you?"

"Eudora, it's important," Pamela interjected. "Slim is missing. Something may have happened to him. The conductor is making a search. You must help if you can."

Mrs. Martin was still far from convinced. "Look in that room he and Fats play cards in all night? He's probably there."

"He isn't there," the conductor said flatly.

"Are there any blondes on the train? Try a few of those rooms," the woman retorted angrily. "You'll find him in one of them." She started to close the door.

Les thrust his foot between it and the jamb and then pushed it open again. "Mrs. Martin," he said quietly, "I have reason to believe your husband is dead. That he was murdered by someone on this train. It might be well if you would co-operate with those of us who--"

He broke off. The woman was staring at him as if transfixed. She had turned a ghastly white. Almost as a reflex action she cried, "He didn't do it." Then her hand flew to her mouth as if to prevent whatever else might have slipped out. She clutched at the door, then fainted onto the berth beside her.

They left Pam with her and went on to awaken the Durands in the next room. Both took the disturbance easier than had Mrs. Martin, but they either could not, or would not, give any hint as to the whereabouts of the missing partner. Fats Durand was inclined to scoff at the entire matter and to suggest by indirection the same solution as had more bluntly been suggested by Mrs. Martin. After some discussion, during which Lester managed to search the room, they departed. Durand maintained to the last that he had left Slim playing solitaire in the next-door compartment when he retired.

Having got so far the conductor decided to complete the job. One by one he routed out all the occupants of the car.

Starting with Bedroom J, he worked from the rear forward. First the two valets, Arthur and George, were interviewed. They returned to their bunks with little actual consciousness of what the inquiry was all about. It was then that Pam rejoined the search party, saying that Eudora Martin was now quietly sleeping. At the door of Compartment H, Sherwood Schyler protested the intrusion on his privacy and resented their entry into his room. He seemed disinclined to take Martin's disappearance seriously. Lester wondered if Schyler habitually slept with his pajamas over his tweed trousers. He certainly had them on that way now.

The Simeons and Carlyles, in Compartments G and F, respectively, awoke as if coming out of hibernation, stared stupidly at them, answered their questions stupidly, then asked if they might go back to bed. The conductor searched their rooms, then dismissed them.

Garret Fabian strove to ignore the search party as nearly as possible when they reached him in Bedroom B. When acquainted with the reason for the disturbance he said vehemently, "This is the best news I've heard in weeks. I hope he has fallen off the train and broken his neck." With which rejoinder he closed his door on their faces.

In the one remaining room in the car slept the two maids, Cleo and Pearl. No amount of buzzing served to awaken them, so the conductor was forced to unlock their room with his passkey. Even with the lights on and a couple of people looking under the lower berth for a corpse, Pearl and Cleo slept peacefully on, completely oblivious of the commotion going on around them.

"That finishes the car," the conductor said. "I don't dare go any farther tonight. I can't dig everybody on this train out of bed at this hour looking for a man I don't even know is missing."

They all went off to get what rest they could. Pam locked herself into Comparment C, and Lester returned to his own room and waited.

After perhaps fifteen minutes there came to his ears the slight sound of a room's door being opened. He moved swiftly and applied his eyes to the space between his own partly open door and its frame. He was just in time to see Pam moving silently along the corridor headed in the direction of Car K-8.

After he was certain she was no longer in the car, he followed after her, moving cautiously along the corridor and out onto the vestibule platform. He swiftly opened the door into the car ahead, closing it as quickly after him. Should Pam still be in the corridor she would undoubtedly hear the upsurge of noise in the brief second that the door stood open. Les made the turn and had moved several feet into the long passageway. The car was in darkness. The corrridor lights had been extinguished. Only the faintest of glows at each end of the aisle indicated that the cars on either side of K-8 were still lighted.

He moved cautiously. Suddenly he stumbled. His foot had struck some object on the floor, blocking his further passage. Something soft and yielding. Swiftly he knelt down, his fingers groping for the obstacle and encountering soft, warm flesh. A human body lay there on the corridor floor. "Pam," he cried softly. "Oh, Pam!" Without knowing why, he was certain it was she.

He slipped one arm under her head and gently raised it. With his other hand he sought and found his automatic lighter and flicked it into action. By its feeble flame he saw that it was Pam and that she was unconscious but breathing. They were directly before Room C, the compartment in which he had found Martin an hour or so earlier. The door was closed.

Opening it, he carried Pam into the room and laid her on the couch. Then he lit the light once more and returned to the corridor. Quickly he went forward to the end of the car searching for a fuse or switch box. He found the electrical locker, its door ajar. Opening it farther, he discovered that the master switch had been pulled. Someone had deliberately turned out all the lights of the car.

He pushed the switch back into position again. At once the

corridor was filled with the soft, warm radiance of the indirect lights set flush in the ceiling.

Les hurriedly returned to Compartment C. The lights were on in there too now, having evidently been extinguished with the turning off of the master circuit. Pam lay as he had left her, her eyes closed. He had not noticed before how pale she was. He hurriedly poured some water from the carafe onto a towel and placed it over her eyes and forehead. He felt her pulse and found it strong.

Presently she opened her eyes. There was fright amounting to panic in them. Then she recognized him, and the expression passed.

"I'm all right now, Les," she said. There was little vigor in her voice. "What happened?"

"I don't know, Pam," he answered. "I heard you go out, and thought you were taking chances coming to this car alone, so I followed you. I found you on the floor."

"I decided to be a smarty-pants," she said, some of the old zest returning to her voice, "and find out what this was all about. I wasn't quite convinced that you weren't the innocent victim of one of the boys' more gruesome capers."

"Convinced now?" Les asked softly.

For answer she took his hand and guided his fingers along the back of her scalp, where he felt a formidable raised area. That it was painful was evident from her wince as his fingers probed. "I'm convinced," she said simply. Then she said, "Les, I want you to know the truth about why I came back here. It wasn't true that I stayed in my room after dinner."

"I know."

She looked at him quickly, then away again. "When I told you so," she went on, "remember I did not know anything had happened. It seemed best at the time that I fib about it. You see, my pride was involved."

"Do you want to tell me this, Pam?"

"Yes. I want you to know where I stand." She paused a moment as if collecting her thoughts. "Sherry and I were going to play gin rummy after dinner. He excused himself to go to his room in the next car for the cards. He never came back. He has been quite indifferent for some time lately, and this was the last straw with me. After waiting for a very long time I determined to go to his room in K-8. He was not there. I decided to wait for him. I was more determined than ever to have it out. But he outstayed me, at that. It finally got so late that I went back to my own room."

"That must have been when I heard the door closing as I came back from my walk," Les interrupted. Then he added, "Schyler returned to his room five seconds after you had left."

"What do you mean?" she said, obviously puzzled.

"Never mind, now. Go on, Pam."

"Well, later when the conductor was turning out everyone in the car, I noticed that Sherry tried to give us all the impression that he had been asleep, but that actually he had his clothes on under his pajamas."

"Yes, I noticed that, too," Les said quietly.

"And I got to wondering where Mr. Schyler had been all evening. Then it dawned on me that possibly he had been visiting the attractive Mrs. Martin. Oh, purely to console her, of course. But I recalled that he had been consoling Eudora pretty consistently throughout this trip."

"Eudora seems to transfer her affections rather rapidly," Les retorted.

"If Eudora had been endowed with the virtue of fidelity do you suppose she would have tossed Garret over for Slim?"

"No, I suppose not."

"I'm not unlike any other female, Les, when my affections are being trifled with. So when everything quieted down tonight I determined to go back and beard Mr. Schyler in his den and demand his vote on whether he meant to do right by our Nell or not."

"Then why did you pass his room and come up to the end of the car?"

"I wanted one more quick peek inside this room. I wanted to see for myself if there was anything at all to prove the truth of what you had seen. I meant to take a quick look here, then call on Sherry for the showdown."

"But you didn't make it."

"I didn't make it." She closed her eyes again as if the memory of her experience was still strong in her mind. "No, I didn't make it, Les. I turned the handle of the door before I realized that the lights were out. The whole car was in darkness. Then I heard movement. Someone was coming swiftly along the corridor toward me."

"Could you tell if it was a man or a woman?" Les interrupted.

"No, I was so frightened I couldn't move-- couldn't even yell. Then whoever or whatever it was stood suddenly beside me; a huge sky-rocket exploded in my head, and the next thing I knew I was lying here and you were looking at me as if you were seeing a ghost. If I haven't remembered to thank you, Les--"

"Forget it," he interrupted her. "It was just my good luck. It still scares me to think what might have happened to you if I hadn't opened that door. You interrupted the killer in something he wanted to do. Then, when he had disposed of you, I came along and opened the door. He heard the outside noises and knew someone else was in the car. He didn't dare take a chance on trying to slug a second person, so he abandoned whatever it was he was after and--"

Les's voice trailed off and a startled expression came over his countenance.

Pam suddenly sat erect. "What is it, Les?"

Les stared at her, his eyes wide with the impact of his discovery. "Don't you see, Pam?" he said slowly. "Whoever it was was still in the car when I entered. He knew I was here, from the outside noises which came in when I opened the door. If he had left the car, then I, in turn, would have heard the noises when he opened the door."

"That means he stayed in this car," Pam answered evenly. "It means--"

"That the man or woman who killed Slim Martin, and who, I'm convinced, slugged you, is somewhere in this car."

Both Les and Pam, the latter now fully recovered, set to work searching the room. They took it slowly, methodically and thoroughly. But they found nothing-- that is, nothing but a single playing card which had slipped down behind the seat cushion. It was the ten of spades.

Finally Lester persuaded Pam that further search was useless. They turned out the lights in the compartment and returned to their car.

Just before Pam closed the door to her own room Les said, "I'm sorry, Pam."

"About what?" she answered.

"About how things have turned out for you."

She almost closed the door then. But she opened it again and said softly, "You needn't be, Les." This time she did close it. He heard it lock.

Next morning Lester and Pam sat in the latter's compartment discussing the case. The buzzer sounded, and before either could respond, the door opened and a man stepped into the room. He was tall and dark and thin.

"I'm John Blake, assistant division superintendent of the road," he said. "Our conductor has told us about the disappearance of Mr. Martin, and I'm going on with the train. I'd like to hear what happened."

Lester told Blake the story precisely as he had related it to the conductor, including Pam's misadventure.

"It sounds reasonable the way you tell it," Blake said after he was through. "I don't mind telling you, though, Mr. Clifford," he continued, "that Rolph-- that's the man I relieved-- had come to the conclusion that it was all some kind of a joke."

"That was his attitude," Lester replied. "Perhaps that was why he didn't get farther in his investigation."

"I'll admit he seemed plenty relieved to pass the buck on to me and step out of it."

"What do your officials say about it?"

"We didn't have time to go very high. Rolph told his story to me in Denver and I called in my superior. He decided that we didn't have sufficient evidence that a crime had been committed to call in the law. We are carrying important people, government mail, Army and Navy officers who have to make plane connections taking them West. Instead, he ordered me to go on with the train and do the best I could, while he got in touch with our general offices at Chicago."

"Seems sensible," Lester replied. "What do you propose to do?"

"Keep my eyes open. Find out what I can."

"Do you mind a suggestion?"

"Shoot."

"I'm a newspaper man," Les said, "trained to note and observe detail. Perhaps I can help you. Miss Gordon, here, was in charge of this party for S.O.S. Studio. They are big and powerful, and as their representative she has a stake in this affair. Let the two of us work with you. I think between us we might do some good."

The man pondered the idea for a moment. Then he said slowly, "I'm not a detective. This is all Greek to me. The road is checking with the police in every town we stopped at to see if anyone even remotely resembling Mr. Martin got off there. Section hands are patrolling every mile of the track between those stops in case he might have fallen off. Rolph went over each car of the train." He paused briefly; then added, "What have I got to lose? It's a deal."

Compartment C in Car K-8 being the only vacant room on the train, Blake commandeered it to assure some privacy for his interviews. In taking it over he was forced, however, to dispossess a disconsolate Fats Durand, who sat despondently alone before the folding table playing solitaire.

He left willingly enough, going into his adjoining drawing-room. Before doing so he asked, "Any news?"

On being told there was none he said sadly, "I miss the little guy. I hope he turns up."

Blake asked Pam to accompany him while he notified the members of the Durand-Martin party that he wished to talk to each of them. They had scarcely left the room when the connecting door between the compartment and Drawing-room D opened and Durand stood in the doorway. Lester observed him closely for the first time. He was a large man weighing probably two hundred and fifty pounds. His clothes, although of expensive cut, were baggy and badly worn. Shaggy hair topped coarse features in which his eyes were watchful.

"Who are you, chum?" He spoke slowly.

Lester did not arise. "My name's Clifford," he said. "Lester Clifford."

"What are you, a snoop?"

"Snoop?" Les was puzzled. "Oh, you mean a detective. No. What gave you that idea?"

"Oh, I don't know," the big man drawled. "There's something screwy going on on this rattler. I thought maybe they called you in at Denver."

"No, again," Lester answered. "I got on the train at Chicago. In fact, I was on the Century out of New York with you."

Durand chewed on that for a while. "You a mobster? One of Cirolli's boys?"

"Keep guessing. Or maybe I'd better tell you. I'm an ex-newspaperman turned playwright. I'm on my way out to the Coast to do a script for S.O.S."

"Oh, oh," Durand remarked. He seemed to lose interest. Pam and Blake could be heard coming along the corridor. "Keep your nose clean," he said. Then he disappeared into the drawing-room, closing the door behind him.

Les arose, walked over, and slipped the bolt on the connecting door's lock. Blake, coming into the room at the time, saw him do it, but did not say anything. Les shot Pam a glance in which there was a tacit warning not to disclose too much.

In a few moments a hostile and indignant Schyler joined them. His eyes demanded an explanation for the presence of Pam and Lester, but Blake came straight to the point.

"Mr. Schyler," he said, "I'd like to ask you a few questions."

"On what authority?"

Lester thought Schyler's voice cold and austere but he failed to detect any note of anxiety in it.

Blake answered without heat, but with considerable force, "I'm in charge of this train. Although subject to the civil authority of the land we pass through, I am, nevertheless, in command here. I can ask questions and you can answer them and we can go on our way. Or I can stop the train and turn the matter over to some local authority. Barring a jurisdictional dispute and lengthy examination, we might not be held up for more than a week or two. My decision will depend on how you and the others co-operate. With reasonable help, maybe we can clear this mystery up between here and Los Angeles and reduce to a minimum any personal inconvenience to you passengers."

For a moment Schyler fingered his small blond mustache, his handsome face a study of indecision. It was Pam who decided him. "With your predelictions, Sherry," she said, "you would be most uncomfortable spending two weeks in one of those little Colorado or Utah towns."

Without looking at her, he nodded his head at Blake. "Go on with your questions."

"Where did you spend your time from dinner until the conductor talked with you in your room about one o'clock?"

Without hesitation Schyler answered, "Miss Gordon and I talked a while in the club car. I walked up to my room in this car to get the cards, but felt tired so decided to go to bed, instead. I knew Miss Gordon would understand."

Lester wondered if this was Schyler's idea of an appropriate apology to Pam for his failure to return. If so, it wasn't getting him far. The girl gazed straight at him without the slightest change in expression.

"Then what?" the assistant superintendent asked, almost casually.

"I retired, naturally." Schyler's voice was bland, assured.

"And you were in your room continuously until Mr. Rolph, the conductor, called you?"

"Certainly."

"Mr. Schyler," Blake answered in a voice seemingly resigned to the inevitable, "you are lying. When you didn't come back to join Miss Gordon she went in search of you. You weren't in your room. You weren't in it until some time between twelve and twelve-thirty Central Time, for she waited there for you. At about twelve-twenty-five Mr. Clifford saw you come out of a room in the center of Car K-8 and go to your own room"-- here Blake consulted the rough chart he had made of the two cars-- "which is Room H. Where were you all this time?"

Schyler shrugged. "There must be some mistake," was all he said.

"There is no mistake." Blake's voice had authority in it as he continued. "Rolph reported that when he interviewed you you tried to give the appearance of having been asleep, but that you were wearing your clothes underneath your pajamas."

"He was mistaken."

"I noticed that too, Sherry," Pam interjected quietly.

"And I," put in Lester.

Schyler looked levelly, first at Pam, then at Lester, then back to Pam again. His lips curled slightly as he answered, "You are all mistaken."

"You could have been in Compartment C, where Mr. Martin was seen last, or couldn't you?" the railroad man asked.

"I could have-- but I was not," Schyler retorted evenly. "Not that it matters, however. No one seems to have seen Slim last night except this fellow Clifford here. And how do we know he isn't lying?"

"We don't," Blake answered shortly. "Right now we're talking about you. And we do know you are lying. Where were you from ten o'clock until half past twelve?"

"In my room."

Suddenly Pam spoke up, her voice furious. "Stop acting like an idiot, Sherry," she snapped, the blond curls tossing on her shoulders. "Gallantry neither comes naturally to you nor becomes you. You've handled actors so long you've started acting like a ham, yourself. You want us to think you are protecting someone. The beautiful Eudora, no doubt."

Schyler smiled. "My dear," he said, "you surprise me. I had no idea you were capable of such violent-- and flattering-- jealousy." He stood up.

"If that ends your questioning," he said, "I'll leave you and your two amateur sleuths to your detecting." He walked out of the room.

Blake interviewed Mr. and Mrs. Simeon, and Mr. and Mrs. Carlyle, the two valets, and the pair of maids next, and in that order. The questioning took a long time, for Blake, as he had done with Schyler, wrote down in slow and laborious longhand every word that was spoken.

Though bored with the pedestrian pace of the proceedings, Lester nevertheless admired this sagacity displayed by the man.

Should it become necesssary to turn the matter over to the police authorities, Blake would be in a favorable position if he could produce a complete transcript of the statements made.

While necessary, these eight interviews produced precious little information of a helpful character. The maid Cleo did, however, supply one jot of information which might or might not have been of some significance. After slow and patient prodding Blake was beginning to get impatient at the monosyllabic responses from the dull-witted girl. "How do you ordinarily sleep?" he snapped.

"In bed," answered the girl. It wasn't intended to be funny.

"Of course you sleep in bed. But do you always sleep soundly? Dead to the world?"

"Oh, no, sir."

"Well, how do you account for the fact that no amount of pounding on your door could wake you or your friend last night? The conductor had to unlock it from the outside. Even with two or three people searching your room, you still slept on. Explain that."

The girl looked puzzled. "Don't know, sir," she said. "I usually sleep light. Pearl she sleeps hard. I sleep light."

"Well, you didn't sleep light last night," Blake said sharply.

"No, sir," answered the girl. "I usually get up at six. It was eight-thirty before I opened my eyes this morning." Her face twisted in the contortions of unaccustomed thought. "Maybe it was on account of that wine."

"Oh, so you had some wine last night?" Lester injected. "Where did you have it-- in the club car?"

"No, sir," the girl answered ingenuously. "The-- the-- gentleman in the next room gave it to us. Pearl and me were going to bed about ten o'clock. We were both in our nightgowns when there came a loud rap on the wall. Scared us to death."

"Then what happened," Blake urged her on.

"This gentleman, Mr.-- Mr.-- Fabian, he hollers through the wall, 'You girls gone to bed?' I tell him we have, and he says that's too bad because he wanted us to have a good-night drink with him. When Pearl hears that she's all for getting dressed, because Pearl likes her little nip."

"So you got dressed and joined Mr. Fabian for a nightcap?" Blake asked.

"No, sir; I wouldn't do it. But we told the gentleman he could come around to the door and hand it in to us and we'd be obliged."

"And did he?"

"Oh, yes, sir. He handed in to us two paper cups, each full of purple wine. It was right nice, too. We each drank our cup, and then we put the lights out and went to sleep."

When Cleo had left the room Blake said, "Maybe we ought to talk with Mr. Fabian next."

"I'll send him in to you. I won't sit in on this interview. I have an idea." Pam started for the door.

"If the porter of the car tries to stop you, tell him I said it was all right," Blake remarked dryly before she closed the door. Once again Lester had reason to admire the man's astuteness.

A few minutes later Garret Fabian entered the compartment. As he did so the speeding train began to slacken its run. Blake glanced hurriedly out the window, then at his watch. "Got to pick up wires here," he said. "Be back soon."

Fabian scowled at Lester.

"My name is Clifford," Les said. "I found Slim Martin. I am trying to help Mr. Blake determine what might have happened."

The man's eyes were as hard and unyielding as agates. Yet there was no animosity in his voice when he spoke. "Mr. Clifford," he said, "what has become of Slim Martin is a matter of colossal indifference to me. It suits my ideas of propriety and justice that he has returned from whence he sprang. Don't disappoint me by telling me there is a chance he may yet turn up alive."

The train, which had rolled to a standstill, now started to move again. A steam engine had been added to the Diesel for extra power against some heavy mountain grade ahead. Lester could hear it puffing away as it tugged at its heavy load of steel.

Les answered slowly, "I can assure you, Fabian, that Martin will not turn up alive. He's dead. I saw him."

Only the eyes changed expression in Fabian's countenance. The train rolled into a long tunnel. Lester clicked on the room's lights. He wondered where Blake was and why he didn't come back. He started writing on the big yellow sheet what had been said.

"Why do you tell me this?" Fabian asked.

Les looked at him a moment before replying. "Because I know your story," he said finally. "Of all the people on this train you had the soundest motive to kill him. Either you did or you didn't. If you did, you already know he's dead. If you didn't, maybe the knowledge will do you some good. Maybe you'll stop going around with that tortured look on your face."

They were still in the tunnel. In the dim light Lester couldn't be certain, but he thought that the dark, saturnine countenance softened momentarily. Then Fabian spoke. "I've thought of killing him many times," he said. "I even wished that I had. If anyone ever needed killing he did. I envy whoever did it. But it wasn't I."

Almost at that moment two simultaneous incidents occurred to alter the mood. The train passed slowly out of the tunnel, and Blake came back to the compartment. The mask of starkness slipped once again over Fabian's face.

The conductor sat down and read the notes Lester handed to him. He placed them on the table without comment. "Where on the train did you spend last evening?" He addressed himself to Fabian.

"Mostly in my room. I had dinner alone. Afterwards I smoked a cigar in the club car."

"Talk with anyone?"

"I don't know. I may have briefly. I'm not very gregarious."
Blake looked uncertain, but Lester noticed that he spelled the
word properly in his notes.
"Then what?" he asked.
"I went to my room. Read a while. Oh, yes, if it's of any
interest, I had a bottle of wine in my bag. A rather nice domestic
cabernet I'm fond of. I drank a glass or two before turning in."
"Alone?" Blake asked it softly-- casually.
The black eyes flicked quickly to those of the railroad man, then
to Lester's, and as swiftly away. Perhaps they read something. At
any rate, Fabian answered-- not too readily, "Alone? Yes. But as a
matter of fact I felt a little sorry for those two servant girls sharing
the room next to mine. No one had spoken to them in my presence
since the trip started. I called in and asked if they would like some
wine. They agreed, so I passed it in through the door."
"I understood you weren't very-- gregarious," Blake responded
quietly. Fabian did not reply. "Then what?" the superintendent went
on.
For the space of a minute it appeared as if the dark man was
going to ignore the question. Then, as if suddenly making up his mind
about something, he turned and spoke directly to Lester.
"You will understand what I'm talking about," he began, "and
perhaps it will save some time. Last night I was troubled in my mind,
as I have been for months. I determined I was going to have one more
talk with Eudora, in the hope that it might not be too late to patch up
our lives. There's Reno for her, and I could break my contract with
Durand and Martin. I determined to sever that relationship, in any
event. I lay on my bunk and figured things out. I've saved my money,
and while the twenty per cent I own of Durand and Martin is a small
gold mine, still I could support my wife happily and well on what I've
got. Besides, I'm a good manager and could pick up other acts.
"Finally I decided the thing to do," he continued, "was to get
Eudora out of her room-- their room-- and to mine, where we might
talk quietly and undisturbed. I knew Slim would be at his eternal card
game most, if not all, of the night. I waited until the train had
quieted down and the porter had turned out most of the lights and
departed. Then I slipped down to Drawing-room E, and was about to
knock, when I heard voices inside the room. A woman's and a man's.
The man was not Slim Martin. I've coached that high nasal twang too
many years not to recognize it. It was someone else. You may
imagine my feelings. I returned to my room."
The man was torturing himself, Lester thought. He didn't even
seem to know that they were in the room.
"After a while, as I lay there, there was some commotion, and I
was told that Martin had disappeared from the train. My room was
searched. I don't remember what I said, but I'm sure I gave the
intruders, whoever they were, short shrift. I lay awake for another
hour, and then I began to realize that this might make a difference.

If I could only talk with Eudora, I felt certain we could work out our problems. I started for her room again. It wasn't until I was half way there that I felt there was something strange, something unusual about the car. It was very dark. Then I realized that the lights were out."

"Go on." Blake spoke softly. He had even stopped writing, he was following Fabian's story so intently.

"I was unaccountably frightened. I suppose it was my over-wrought nerves. I wanted to get back to the security of my own room. I abandoned my intention of paying a call, and started to retreat. Then the strangest thing of all happened."

"What was that?" Lester asked breathlessly, remembering his own experience.

"I sensed rather than heard the cautious opening of a door into the corridor. Opening softly, as if someone were trying to peer into the darkened aisle. Then I knew someone was approaching me along the carpeted corridor, approaching stealthily and with evil purpose. I'm not a coward, but I tell you I was scared. I stood perfectly still."

"Where were you located in the car at the time?" Blake asked, his pencil once more at work on the yellow paper.

"I'm not certain. But I'd guess at about the center of the car. In front of Room F or E. Whatever it was, it was coming right for me-- and it was laboring. Breathing hard as if it were bearing a heavy load. I stood petrified-- rooted to the spot right in the middle of the passageway. I couldn't have moved if my life had depended on it. Maybe it did, at that. For I stood stock-still until the thing touched me."

"You mean the man bumped right into you?" Lester asked.

"No. Not actually. But the thing he was carrying-- it touched me. Touched my chest. Then all forward motion ceased. For he knew someone else was there. We both stood still. Still as death itself. It was horrible."

"Why didn't you yell?" Blake asked.

"I couldn't. Or maybe I was about to when the vestibule door at the rear end of the corridor opened. You know the sound it lets into the car. It was the most wonderful sound I have ever heard. It meant someone else was coming. I could have yelled then with joy or relief. But as quickly as it had come, the thing standing before me suddenly faded away-- retreated-- disappeared in the direction from which it had approached."

"What did you do then?"

Fabian's thin straight lips smiled for the first time. "I ran like a frightened schoolboy for my room and locked myself in it until morning," he answered.

"Was it a man or a woman who bumped into you in the passageway?" Blake asked.

"I thought it was a man. I still think so, in fact. But it could have been a woman. There is just no way I can be sure."

"Could the thing that he-- or she-- was carrying have been a body?"

"It might have. Again, I don't know. Whatever it was, it was inanimate, lifeless."

Lester scarcely heard these last few questions and answers. For some time now he had been watching the thin line between the doorjamb and the door into the corridor slowly widen into a sizable gap. He was reasonably certain that the door had been closed, that Blake had closed it when he had returned to the compartment. Now, however, he was certain it was ajar.

He stretched a long leg forward, then laterally, and hooked the toe of his shoe in the door itself. With this purchase, he accelerated the door's opening movement. An unwinking eye in the arc of a round, almost comical face stared directly at him through the crack.

He pushed hard with his toe, and door flew open. Fats Durand stood outside.

"How long you Joes going to use my room for your third degree?" he asked blandly. "I'd like a little privacy to moon in by myself. Mollie and me ain't exactly what you'd call en rapport this morning. How about holding your line-up somewhere else?"

How long Durand had been there or how much of Fabian's story he had heard Lester could not know. Nor could he tell if Blake was aware that Durand had at least been attempting to eavesdrop.

"We'll need your room for some time yet, Mr. Durand," was all the conductor said. Then he added, as if in an afterthought, "And we'd like to talk with you in a little while."

The fat man slowly turned and went away. Shortly afterward he was followed by Fabian.

Pam picked that moment to return. She placed a small pharmacist's bottle on the table. It had a prescription label, on which were written the word, "Nembutal," and the usual instructions for taking. The bottle contained a half-dozen apparently one-grain capsules of the drug.

"I found it in the medicine chest in Fabian's bedroom," Pam said simply.

"Two of those in a glass of wine," Lester remarked, "and anyone not used to them would sleep through an earthquake."

"I don't know much about these things," the conductor said, "but I'll take your word for it." He seemed to dismiss the matter. Then he asked Pam to fetch Mollie Durand.

Mollie, a former show girl, was a striking brunette of Amazonian proportions and a casual, almost indifferent manner. Early in the interview she let it be unmistakably known that, as far as she was concerned, anything that might have happened to Slim was in the interests of the people and she hoped for the same for her own husband.

"Mrs. Durand," Blake asked, "you and Mr. Durand occupied the adjoining drawing-room to this compartment. Did you hear or see anything out of the ordinary? Anything which we should know?"

Mollie Durand smiled the dazzling smile that had put her on the end of the row in many Broadway musical shows. "Mr. Blake," she replied good-naturedly, "the way this gulley-jumper locomotes at night I'm strictly concerned with staying anchored to my berth. They could have played a second-act finale in the next room last night and I wouldn't have heard a note."

"Were you awake when Mr. Durand came in?"

"I wouldn't know," Mollie answered. "He was in and out of the room during the early hours. To get cigarettes, the cards, his slippers, and all. From eleven o'clock or so I was more or less asleep, depending on how playful the engineman felt at the moment."

"Did you hear him go to bed, Mollie?" Pamela asked. "Think about it a minute. It may be important."

"I honestly don't know, Pam," the woman answered. "The first thing I remember distinctly about the night was when there was a lot of pounding on our door, and some jerks came trooping in saying they were looking for Slim. Then they were gone, and Fats gave me a sleeping pill so I could get back to sleep, and in five minutes I was plowing the deep. Never opened my eyes again until morning."

"Did your husband take a sleeping pill to get himself back to sleep, too?" Lester asked.

"Yeah. I guess so. He said we'd both better take one; then he went into the whoosis there to get some drinking water out of the whatsis."

That was all they got out of Mollie Durand.

Eudora Martin was asked to come in, following Mollie's departure. Just as Mollie had proved friendly and disarmingly frank with them, so did Eudora prove to be inimical and suspicious. If she were worried about her husband's disappearance it was not obvious. But it was clear that she was apprehensive about something. Blake and Clifford tried to draw her out, in turn. It was Pamela who got out of her the only information that added anything to their total knowledge of the affair.

"Eudora," Pam asked, "when you were told last night that Slim might have been killed you said, 'He didn't do it.' What did you mean?"

"Did I say that? I have no idea."

"You not only have an idea, but you know perfectly well why you said it," Pam answered sharply. "Perhaps I can refresh your memory. Sherry Schyler was seen leaving one of the rooms in the center section of this car two minutes before your husband's body was found in Compartment C. He could have been coming from your drawing-room, which is E, only two doors away. It was one or the other."

"Very well," the woman said at once, "I didn't want to hurt your feelings, Pamela, but you've asked for it. I was pretty sick of spending night after night alone with Slim playing cards. I left a note in Sherry Schyler's room asking him to come visit me. He was in my room from ten-forty-five until twenty minutes past twelve. We talked about our future. You might as well know it all. I had decided to divorce Slim, and Sherry was going to get me some engagements. He thinks my face and my figure good enough to land me jobs with some top bands."

"He didn't ask if you could sing, did he?" Pam asked dryly. Then she continued, "And after these few minor preliminaries were disposed of, you and Sherry didn't plan to-- to-- get married, did you?"

Eudora Martin looked directly at Pamela Gordon for the space of five seconds before a slow, triumphant, and unlovely smile appeared on her undoubtedly pretty face. "As a matter of fact, we did," she replied. "We talked it all out last night. We agreed we would be married just as soon as I could get rid of Slim."

Suddenly it dawned on Eudora what she had said. Her gray-blue eyes were suddenly frightened and she placed her hand on her mouth in a gesture of alarm. "But he couldn't have done it," she protested vehemently. "He was with me every minute of the time until just before the conductor came to my room. He couldn't have done it."

"You say he was with you all the time from a quarter to eleven until twelve-twenty," Blake put in. "Think, now-- was there not one minute when the man left the room?"

"Yes. I mean, no. He was there all the time."

All three of her listeners knew that she was lying. Eudora Martin was far too shallow to be able to dissemble successfully.

"He did leave the room at least once, didn't he, Mrs. Martin?" Blake followed up the advantage.

"Yes, he did," she answered defiantly. "But only once. And then for just a matter of a few minutes. I was out of cigarettes. He went to his room to get some for me."

"He did not go to his room," Pam said quietly. "I was waiting there for him."

"Then he must have gone to the club car," Eudora said hastily.

"That can be checked," Blake answered, making a note.

A few minutes later a distraught and nervous Eudora Martin retired to her room. Not once during the interview had she asked if there was any news of her husband.

When she had gone, Pamela lit a cigarette, inhaled deeply, and then let the smoke curl slowly and lazily out her nostrils. "Thank you, Eudora," she said softly to no one in particular. "That does it nicely, cleanly, painlessly, permanently, and irrevocably."

Blake wrote more furiously than ever on his yellow sheets, and Lester looked out the window. But he did manage briefly to squeeze the soft, strong hand lying beside his on the couch.

At Monticello, Utah, where the Pegasus paused briefly at about four o'clock in the afternoon, the superintendent received a telegraphic report from the head of the railway's police force. No trace of Martin had been found at any place along the line, even after a careful search of every inch of the track and a thorough check in all the towns at which the train had stopped.

He also received orders from his superiors. Blake was told to continue his search for Martin aboard the train, carry on with his investigation, and proceed with the train on into Los Angeles. None of the passengers involved were to leave the train, at any station. At Pasedena, railroad and Los Angeles police would board the Pegasus and take over.

As Blake showed Lester the wire, he smiled wryly and said, "Well, I guess that keeps the tin star on my chest for a while. I hoped I'd have word that Martin had been found, and we would at least have that worry over with."

Pamela also received a wire at Monticello. It was from her studio, was 600 words in length, and read as if it had been dictated by someone in a frenzy. Boiled down to its essence, it said, "How could you do this to us?"

"Know anybody who needs a nice, ready-to-wear publicity gal, Les?" Pam asked. "When we get to L.A. in the morning I'm going to be about as popular as a crack in a glass eye."

The final meeting of the day came at sundown, just after the speeding train had crossed over the border into eastern Nevada. Stops in this picturesque and remote country were few and far between, and Blake, although grumbling a bit about it, had been able to pursue his inquisition without interruption from his other duties.

"Tell Durand we're ready for him," he said to Lester, and in a matter of seconds the big man was seated in the metal chair across the table from the three questioners. Out came the inevitable deck of cards, and fat, pudgy hands began to arrange a Canfield layout.

"Well, Hawkshaws," Durand asked in a slow, lazy drawl, "how goes the dragnet? Catch any fish?" Then, without waiting for a reply, he went on, "No, I guess not. I'd have heard about it if you had. You guys sort of voted me out of the meeting this morning, so I been sitting there with my drawing-room door open ever since. When you'd finished with each victim I'd catch him as he passed my door, invite him in for a little sympathy. Wonderful how people uncork when you sympathize a little bit with them. Guess I pretty near got the whole story you fellows did. Maybe more."

His voice trailed off as he turned an ace, then gave his attention to his game as he followed it with a run in the same suit.

"No, Mr. Durand," Blake said, "we haven't found your partner. Every inch of the right-of-way covered last night has been gone over. A check has been made at all the towns where we stopped. The train has been thoroughly searched. There is no trace whatsoever of him. From all appearances, Mr. Martin might as well have vanished into thin air."

"The poor little guy," Fats mourned sadly. "You know, I can't help missing him. Oh, we squabbled a lot and maybe said things to each other at times we didn't really mean. But we were pretty close, at that." He laid the cards down for a moment and looked at each of them-- Pam, Lester, Blake in turn. "For eight years we been together. We never missed a show, a broadcast, or a take. It's going to seem awful strange if he doesn't show up. Strange and sort of sad." He picked up the cards again and started flicking them over. "Maybe he will, though," he concluded. "Maybe he'll turn up, huh?"

Blake said that he hoped so. But that the longer the time elapsed with no trace of him, the more remote he felt were the chances. "I'm curious to know, Mr. Durand," he continued, "why were you so interested in what Fabian had to say to us this morning."

A good run of cards delayed the man's answer for a moment. Then he replied with a laconic, "Meaning what, chum?"

"While Mr. Fabian was in here I noticed the handle of the door separating this compartment and your drawing-room turn slowly once or twice. You were on the other side intending to open it just enough perhaps to permit you to overhear what was being said in here. You did not know, of course, that Mr. Clifford had locked it some time earlier. I figured that your next move would be to come around to the corridor door and try to get it open. You did, and were there exactly four minutes by my watch when Mr. Clifford discovered you."

Durand was seemingly so engrossed in a new game of solitaire which he had laid out before him that there was some doubt in Lester's mind that he had even heard Blake.

"Chum," he finally drawled, "you keep going around saying things like that to innocent people, like me, for instance, and somebody is going to let you have it one of these days. Besides, I wouldn't believe too much of what that guy Fabian tells you about certain things. Seems Slim took his girl away from him a year or so ago, and the guy has been mostly off his nut since. He's a good manager, though. We pay him too much, but he's good."

Blake wrote a few words before he next looked up and asked. "At what time did you leave this room to go to bed last night?"

"Don't know exactly. Think it was about twelve o'clock. Slim wanted to play all night; I wanted to go to bed. We argued about that a while."

"Quarrel?" Blake cut in.

"Well, maybe you'd call it that. We was always arguing. This one was no different from the rest. After a while I just walked out on him. Went through the connecting door here into my room and went to bed."

"Where did you leave Martin and what was he doing when you left him?"

"Right where you're sitting and just what I'm doing," the big man replied. "That is to say, he was sitting on the couch there and he was playing solitaire."

"Did you stay there? I mean, in bed?" Blake asked.

"Nope."

Three pairs of eyes focused on him. He went on blandly shuffling and redealing the interminable hands of Canfield. Finally Les asked, "You mean you went out again?"

"Nope, I don't mean that, either. I mean, I didn't stay in bed. Some clown comes pounding on the door some time after one, and I had to get up and let him search my room. That's when I heard about Slim. I thought it was some sort of joke. Slim can be sort of comical at times."

"Then you went back to bed?"

"Right. Even gave the little woman a sleeping pill and took one myself, to be sure we'd get some shut-eye. Did the job, too."

"When I talked with you earlier today, Mr. Durand," Les spoke up, "you asked me if I was one of 'Cirolli's boys.' What did you mean by that?"

"You ain't heard about Cirolli?" Durand drawled unbelievingly. "Say, bud, what racket you in, anyway?...Oh, yeah, you told me-- a scribbler....Well, Cirolli is a nice, pink-faced, bald-headed, fat little guy who looks like he wouldn't kill a fly. And he wouldn't either, providing the fly kicked in with part of his sugar. In this business you pay so much a week to Cirolli for protection. Because if the little gu-nomie ain't around to protect you, somebody's liable to get up right in your studio audience right in the middle of a broadcast and yell, 'Brother, you stink'-- or you may get tear-gas bombs let loose in the theaters your pictures are showing at. Oh, according to Cirolli, there are just lots and lots of places where an artist like me and Slim needs protection."

"Why did you think I might be one of the mob?" Les asked, interested in spite of himself.

"Well, you see," the fat man declared, throwing his cards on the table in disgust at his unsuccessful attempts to beat the game, "when we was in New York, Slim insisted we go to see Mr. Cirolli and tell him we didn't want his protection any longer. Slim figured we could save five hundred bucks a week. Cirolli was quite put out about it. I thought maybe he sent you along to put the heat on."

Pamela had dinner with Lester in his compartment. They talked mostly about the mysterious disappearance of Slim Martin and what might have happened to him.

"Could he still be on the train?" Pam asked.

"Do you mean dead-- or alive?"

"Either. Would it be possible for him to affect some disguise which would make the crew overlook him?"

"It's possible, of course," Lester answered slowly, "if he were alive. But he isn't. Besides, I understand that the two conductors and the train secretary interviewed every person on the train and found utterly no trace of Martin."

"That means that somehow he must have gotten off the train--" Pamela commenced, when Lester interrupted sharply with, "No! It means that his body must have been taken off the train, because he was dead as he ever will be when I saw him last night. He was sitting on that couch where we sat most of the day; there was a knife in his heart and he was dead, I tell you-- dead!"

"Take it easy, junior," Pam said, rising and placing a hand affectionately on Lester's shoulder. "It's been a long twenty-four hours and all our nerves are pretty well shot. What we need is a night's sleep, then perhaps tomorrow--" She let the sentence die. Tomorrow's prospect was not a pleasant one for Pam.

Les glanced quickly at her. "Thanks for the morale boost, Pam," he said. "I realize, of course, that I'm the only one of us who really knows that Slim is dead. You and Blake fear that he is, but you cling to the hope that he may still be alive; that somehow or other in some inexplicable way that this may all yet turn out to be a joke. But you see, I know better. Therefore, it's up to me to find out who killed him and what has become of his body. I think I'm beginning to get some ideas."

"I'm beginning to get ideas, too, Les," Pam said slowly. "I've just got one that should have hit me at nine o'clock this morning. The arrested-development member of the Gordon clan, they call me. Anyway, I'm going to check up on it right now."

"Tell me what it is. Perhaps I can help."

For a moment she hesitated. Then, as if suddenly making up her mind about something, she started for the door. "Sorry, Les. I want to look this one over by myself. The old pride again, I guess. If there's nothing to it, no harm done. If I'm right, I'll tell you all about it. That's a promise."

"How long will you be at it?" Les asked, a worried look in his eyes. "Remember, you promised me you wouldn't take any more chances like last night."

"There is no danger attached to this one," she answered from the corridor. "I may have to maneuver a couple of people out of a room before I can check out what I'm after. Give me a half-hour. That should do it easily."

Soon after she had gone, Blake joined him, and together they went over the case again and again, reading from the voluminous notes which the railroad man had made during the day's investigation. The soft lights of the room, the drone of Blake's voice, the mysterious train noises, all combined to produce a somnolent effect on Lester. Part of his mind was somewhere in the car ahead with Pamela, guiding her, watching over her.

An unexpected and unscheduled stop shot Blake out of his chair as if from a gun. He was back in a few minutes, and the train got under way again. "Mail car broke a coupling," was all he said, except to add, "It's fixed now." Then he went back to discussing the case.

Lester liked the man, admired him for his astute handling of the interviews earlier in the day. But he wished that he would leave now. There was Pam to be looked after. She had said she would be gone only a half-hour. That was when? Surely she had-- Lester looked at his watch again. The setting of the hands back one hour for the next time belt had confused him. He had lost track of the time. Pam had been gone, not a half-hour, but much nearer an hour and a half. It was nearly one o'clock Pacific Time.

"Good Lord!" he cried. "I'd no idea it was so late!"

Blake, taking this to mean Lester wished to retire, said good night and departed.

At once Les went to Pam's room. The berth was made down, but there was no trace of the girl. The porter of the car, who had been ordered by Pullman Conductor Leininger to stay on duty all night, had not seen her. Next, Lester went through the rear vestibule into the club car, thinking she might be there in conversation with some member of the studio crowd.

There was a surprising number of people in the club car for so late an hour, but Pam was not among them.

Garret Fabian was sitting alone reading. Across the aisle from him sat Sherwood Schyler deep in conversation with the Simeons. As Les approached them the latter ceased talking, then all three exchanged questioning glances.

"Any word from my missing brother-in-law?" Simeon asked.

"None," Lester answered shortly. "My concern right now is for Miss Gordon. Have any of you seen her?"

They shook their heads. Then Schyler volunteered the information that Eudora Martin had suffered a nervous collapse and that Mollie Durand had agreed to stay the night with her in the Martin drawing-room. Presumably was there now, comforting Eudora.

When Les finally reached Car K-8 it was bedded down for the night.

One door of the ten private rooms which made up the accommodations of Car K-8 remained open-- that of Compartment C. In it was Fats Durand, the inevitable solitaire game spread before him. Lester stepped into the doorway of the room.

Durand, his heavy jowls covered with the blue-black stubble of a new beard, looked up from placing a card on one of the little packs before him. "Come on in, chum," he said in the slow drawl he affected when observing the amenities. "Sit down. Maybe you would like to play a little gin." His voice ended on a hopeful note.

Les dropped into the chair opposite Durand, but shook his head. Durand looked disappointed, but went on with his own game.

"I'm looking for Miss Gordon," Les said. "You haven't seen her, have you, Durand?"

"Pam? No. That is, not lately," Durand answered. "Not since a couple of hours ago. She came and got Mollie and persuaded her to spend the night with Eudora. Seems that my partner's wife was having an attack of the vapors. So bighearted Pam gets hardhearted Mollie all worked up over it."

"You said Mrs. Durand is now in Mrs. Martin's room?"

"That's the general idea."

"Could Pam be with them?"

"No, chum. When Pam finished her good deed for the night she left."

Lester sat quietly for a few minutes. He tried to think exactly what it was that Pam had said when she left him: "I may have to maneuver a couple of people out of a room." Had that been it? He believed it was. Then the pattern fit. Mollie Durand was spending the night with Eudora Martin. Could Eudora's nervous spells have been induced by Pamela, who in turn, "maneuvered" Mollie into sleeping in another room?

"Anyone in the drawing-room?" Les asked Durand suddenly.

Durand looked up, surprised. "Nope. It's as empty as a movie director's head."

"Mind if I look?"

"Nope."

Les flung open the connecting door and stepped into the room. The ceiling lights were out, but the reading light was on over the one lower berth that was made down ready for its occupant. The room was empty of any person.

He returned to the compartment just as Blake passed the door. Les joined him, and together they went back again to K-7 and Lester's compartment. In a few quick words Blake was made acquainted with the situation.

"But there must be some explanation as to where the young lady has gone," he insisted. "People don't just vanish on a train."

"They do on this train," Lester replied without humor.

"What do you want me to do?"

"There is only one thing to do-- search the train."

Blake emitted a groan.

"It's got to be done," Les pleaded. "Don't you realize there is a killer running loose on this train. He has struck once. We've got to prevent his acting again-- if he hasn't already done so. We've got to find Pam."

In the end Blake capitulated. All porters and other members of the train crew were interrogated, many more rooms than Blake had intended were opened and searched. It all netted exactly what the other searches had revealed-- absolutely nothing.

It was almost four o'clock when the three tired and discouraged men finished their weary trip through the 18-car train and realized that nothing more lay behind the observation car. Blake and the Pullman man, Leininger, flung themselves into the leather chairs and confessed defeat.

"There is nothing more we can do until morning," said Blake. "In two and a half hours-- at six-thirty-- we'll be in Pasadena, and then, thank heaven, people who know about these things will take over. There is nothing more I can do, Clifford."

Despite his anxiety, the fear gnawing at his heart, Lester acknowledged the reasonableness of Blake's position. He thanked him and said he would go to his room. Blake could reach him there if anything turned up.

But Lester did not go to his room. He stopped before Compartment C.

The door was open, and Fats Durand still sat on the couch before the flat-topped metal table.

He sat in his shirt sleeves, his coat and vest flung carelessly on the couch beside him. He had removed his tie and unloosened his sweat-stained collar, revealing a hairy chest gleaming with perspiration. His abnormal paunch balanced precariously and almost obscenely on the edge of the couch. He looked up.

"Oh, it's you again, chum," he said in that same flat, almost mournful drawl. "Seems like you keep getting around this way every few minutes. Find Pam?"

Les ignored the question but sank into the chair opposite the comedian. He was tired-- desperately tired-- and discouraged, but his eyes were bright and his mind was sharp.

The porter followed him into the room. "You gem'man goin' to set up all night?" he asked, half asleep himself.

"Yeah, probably," Durand answered, without glancing at him. "Got any objections?"

"No, suh-- no, suh," the Negro replied. "Only if you gem'man don't mind I'd like to go back to the crew car and catch a couple of hours' sleep myself."

"Go ahead, George," Durand answered.

The porter was about to leave, when he was obviously struck by another thought. "Don' you want a pillow, Mist' Durand?" he asked. "Can get you one in a minute out o' that upper."

For the first time Durand gave his attention to the man. "No, I don't want any pillow," he shouted. "Now get out of here."

The porter, frightened by this unexpected outburst, started back out of the room.

Lester said, very quietly, "I'd like a pillow, please, porter."

Durand turned his beady eyes away from the porter and under half-closed lids gazed at Lester.

The Negro put his hand in his pocket. A puzzled look spread over his face. "Lawd-a-mercy," he said, frowning, "I must be losin' my mind. My berth wrench is gone again. Tha's two berth wrenches I'se misplaced since this trip commenced. Can't open that upper, yonder, mister, without my berth wrench."

The man retreated in confusion. A few seconds later they heard him leave the car.

Durand went back to his solitaire. Lester watched silently as he played game after game.

"Durand, you haven't won one game of Canfield tonight, have you?" Les asked, trying to keep from his voice the discovery he had made.

"Can't say I have, chum," the man replied, leaning his great belly against the edge of the table. "Can't say I have."

"No, and you won't win one," Les went on in a flat unemotional voice. "Haven't you noticed that you can get your hearts, clubs, and diamonds out, but that you always come a cropper in spades? I've been watching you play that game off and on all day and not once have I seen you run your spades out. Nor will you. Because the deck you are using has no ten of spades in it."

It was some time before Durand replied. Before he did so he swept all the cards into a pile and hurriedly flicked through it. Then he said, "You're right, at that, chum. I've been wasting my time." There was a long pause. A pause in which Lester counted slowly up to ten. Then started counting again, and was at seven, when Durand said, "But how do you know?"

"I knew, Durand, because I've got the ten," Lester answered. "It's been in my pocket ever since I found it stuffed down behind that seat cushion when I found Slim Martin's body. There was a pack of cards spread out on the table in such a way that it formed two gin hands. The hand in front of Martin was a dud-- a nullo. When I went to get the conductor someone moved Martin's body-- and picked up the cards. Picked them all up but the ten of spades, which he didn't know was missing. I guess now it's pretty simple to figure out who picked up those cards. I should have known all along. It was you, Durand."

The big man placed his hands slowly and carefully on top of the table. The agile fingers roved like the tentacles of an octopus. "That's an interesting deduction, Clifford," he said.

"I should have known earlier, Durand," Les said. "We all should. You are the only one in this group who would have thought of that Rabelaisian touch of the two gin hands. You owed Martin a gambling debt of a good many thousands of dollars. I heard him demand payment. You refused, and quarreled about it. And another thing, the two of you have been fighting recently about which one carried the other one in the act. Each thought the other was dead weight and himself alone the star. It all adds up.

"Last night you quarreled for the last time. Things came out that neither of you could ever retract. You were sitting over here in this chair I'm occupying. Martin was on the couch, wedged into a corner. It was a very easy thing for you to whip out that knife, lean over, and plunge it into his heart. He probably was sitting there thinking he'd like to do the same thing to you. Maybe that's why he looked so surprised in death."

"He did, at that, didn't he?" the big man whispered softly. The hands had stopped moving now. "Go on, chum-- you talk like a snowbird, but I got nothing to do until morning."

Lester lighted a cigarette. "I knew it must have been you," he went on. "But what had you done with the body? That's what stumped me. And it was so obvious that any one of us should have known at once. The porter had to hit me over the head when he was in here a few minutes ago before I got wise. I know now where Slim Martin is, Durand-- where he has been since he disappeared in that fifteen minutes last night. <u>He is closed up in the upper berth above your head.</u>"

Now once again the fingers of the huge hands began to move restlessly, to rove over one another, to beat an endless tattoo on the table-top. In no other way did Durand display any agitation.

"Yes," he said finally, the eyes still sunk in their pouches. "It's like you say, Clifford. I killed Slim for the reasons you've stated and some others you won't think of. I had it all planned out ahead of time-- just what I would do with him. But your butting in-- your finding him on the couch there-- started a chain of things to upset my plans."

The fingers were roving the table, picking up and discarding little objects. "I meant to throw him off the train. Let him be found a mangled corpse-- a suicide or the result of an accidental fall. It would have been easy. But I had to wait until the train quieted down and there was no danger of my being interrupted. In these air-conditioned trains you can't raise the windows. That meant I had to carry him to the vestibule, where I could open an outside door and toss him out."

"But I came along; you heard me in the compartment and knew someone had discovered the crime. Right."

"Yes. You gave me a bad ten minutes. But it worked out all right. Earlier I had stolen the porter's wrench, the one which unlocks the upper berth and lets it swing down on its counterbalance. So I hurriedly changed my plans. After you had left the room I came back in through the connecting door, opened the upper berth, and stuffed Slim's body in it."

"And that is the only berth on this train that hasn't either been opened or slept in in the last twenty-four hours," Lester said, in astonishment. "You knew you had a certain amount of protection in the fact that orders had been given never to make up this room for sleep. It was so obvious that we overlooked it. It wasn't until the porter offered to get us pillows from it and you reacted too violently over such a trivial thing that I realized this was the one berth we hadn't looked into."

"Don't fool yourself, Clifford," the big man said, all the drawl now gone from his voice, "that any of this will do you any good. I've been too smart a gee for you right along and I stay smart-- see? But maybe you'd like to know the rest of the story. Why I never did get rid of Slim."

"I know most of it," Les answered, fighting down the great weariness that was engulfing him. "After we'd searched the car and things had quieted down, you figured you could still get Slim off your hands. You gave your wife a sleeping pill so she wouldn't know you were going out of the room again. Of course, you never took the one you pretended to take, yourself, but merely palmed it and dropped it down the drain."

"A lousy script writer," Durand said wonderingly, "and he does this to me."

"After she was asleep," Les continued, oblivious of the interruption, "you slipped out, pulled the switch in the electrical locker, got Slim out of the upper berth, and started down the aisle with him in your arms. But something you didn't know was that there was someone else standing there in the dark directly in your path."

"Was that you, chum? That's been bothering me all day."

"No. It was Fabian."

"Fabian? I couldn't know." The fat man took up the burden of the story quickly, almost eagerly. His restless hands continued to move as he talked. "If I'd known, maybe things would have been different. At any rate, my luck was one of a kind then-- bad. Someone else had to come into the car just at that time, so I beat it back here and laid Slim on the couch. Then I ducked through the drawing-room and out into the corridor again to see what's up. Only I couldn't see, because it was too dark. But I could tell it was a woman by the faint perfume that was in the aisle, and I could feel her standing before the door to the compartment.

"With Slim inside, I couldn't let her go in. I still had the berth wrench so I let her have it. When she hit the floor I stepped over her into the compartment, stowed Slim away again back in the upper. Then I went into the drawing-room to bed. I really went to beddy-by this time, too. I didn't know how badly I'd hurt the girl, but I knew there'd be a stink raised and I didn't dare try again to dump Slim."

"It was Pam you struck, Durand," Les said. "And you'll pay for the blow, regardless of what happens about Martin."

"Pam, eh?" the actor said, then added callously, "I always thought she stuck her nose too much in other people's affairs."

"It was Pam you hit, Fats," Les repeated. "And for that, before I turn you in I'm going to come across that table and beat your round, comical face into jelly. When the officers get you at Pasadena they won't care how tough it was for me to take you. How tough it was-- on you."

The big man's eyes were roving very nearly as swiftly as his fingers. From lowered lids they darted to Les, then almost wildly about the room. It was nearly light outside as the train sped at ninety miles an hour across the flat desolate country. Sage and cactus appeared as a vague, shadowy monotone outside the car's windows.

The big man leaned forward on his elbows. Suddenly the darting beady eyes were still and they gazed steadily into Lester's. "There ain't going to be any cops take me at Pasadena, Clifford," he said. "And you ain't going to get rough. There's a little matter maybe you've forgot about. Fats has got-- the girl."

For a stunned moment Les sat immobile, his worst fears realized. A cold, still fury embraced him. "Where is she?" he demanded.

"Nice and comfy-- where I've got her."

"Where is she?" Les repeated.

"Listen, Clifford," Fats Durand thundered. "I've got the girl, see? You'll be a good boy, do exactly as I say from here out or you'll never see her again. Now get moving. We-- you and me-- are dropping off the train at San Bernardino. I've got a hideaway up in the mountains back of Arrowhead. It'll take some time for them to find us there-- if ever."

Suddenly, as if a light had been turned on in his mind, Lester knew where Pam was. Knew where she had been all the time. It was, again, something the porter had said which brought this revelation to him. That attendant said he had lost <u>two</u> berth wrenches in the past twenty-four hours. Durand had taken one of them, and now Lester knew that Pamela had taken the other.

In retrospect, now that it might be too late, it was easy to follow the pattern. Ahead of all of them Pam had worked out where Slim Martin's body might be hidden. It was obvious that her idea was that Slim had been placed in the upper berth in Mollie and Fats Durand's <u>drawing-room</u>; for hadn't she persuaded Mollie to sleep with Eudora Martin so that she might investigate the empty room? Then she must have slipped the second wrench from the pocket of the sleeping porter and tackled the job alone. Somehow Durand's attention had been attracted in the adjoining room, his suspicions aroused, and he had found her lowering the heavy frame which supports the upper berth.

Durand's roving fingers suddenly darted to his coat beside him, and when they emerged they gripped a long-bladed, wicked-looking hunting knife whose point was quickly pressed against Lester's chest. It was undoubtedly the same knife which had protruded from Slim Martin's body when he had first found him.

"Don't get any ideas, Clifford," the fat man said meaningly, dropping once more into the drawl. "You and me are moving-- together."

In one violent movement Lester's knees and fists came simultaneously upward, dealing the metal table between himself and Durand such a violent blow that it was wrenched bodily from its moorings and catapulted onto the huge man on the couch. The edge of the table struck him under the chin with such tremendous force that he slowly crumpled into an inert mass, sliding first to the couch and then onto the floor. The knife dropped from his nerveless fingers.

Hesitating but for a second, Les frantically searched through Durand's clothing for the missing berth wrench. He found it in a pocket of the discarded coat. In another second he had flung open the door into the adjoining drawing-room.

As it turned out, however, he didn't need the wrench. There was a gap of an inch of two around the body and frame of the upper berth where, in closing, it had stopped at the moment of exact balance before it had snapped shut and locked.

And this, of course, had saved Pam's life. For when he pulled the berth down to its horizontal position Lester found a frightened, but otherwise unharmed, Pamela wedged between the stored matresses and pillows and thoroughly gagged and trussed with strips of pillow-case.

Not until he had lifted her gently down and torn away the bindings did he trust himself to speak. And then it was only a soft, "Pam-- oh, Pam," that he dared essay as she lay in his arms.

"I wondered if you'd ever find me, Les," she said, choking back the sobs. The wide blue eyes were still full of fright. "It was horrible, shut up in here--"

"Then don't think about it, Pam," Les said tenderly. "It's all over now."

A sudden movement behind them caused them to turn in unison. A battered Fats Durand stood in the doorway clinging to the frame for support. A wild light gleamed in his half-closed eyes, and small drops of saliva appeared at the corners of his thick lips. In his right hand he held the knife again.

"Yeah, it's all over," he said. He moved close to Pamela, placing the point of the weapon against her side.

"Listen, you two," he continued, "and keep your ears wide open. No back talk. No arguing. Just listen-- then move. My number's probably up now anyway, see? But I'm going to have my one chance of getting into the mountains. To get it I won't hesitate at anything. Anything, understand? You, Clifford, walk straight to the rear end of the train, opening the doors between the cars for us. We'll be right behind you. The girl, then me. The knife will be between me and the girl. Don't try anything. Don't hesitate. Don't talk to anybody. When we get there I'll tell you what's next. Now march."

Something in the man's manner, the mad, resolute purpose evident in his tone caused Pam to say, "Do as he says, Les."

In single file they entered the corridor of K-8 and in single file they marched through ten other cars to the observation lounge. In neither sleeping cars, club car, nor diners did they encounter one living soul. Only in one of the diners was there any movement, and here but the faint stirrings of an early-rising chef as he started the morning fire in his kitchen. Throughout the long, dreadful march Les tried desperately to think of some ruse, some device through which he could get at Durand, knife or no knife, without endangering Pam. But nothing seemed possible. The outlook appeared hopeless.

As they entered the last car of the train, the engineer was signaling the approach of the grade that would take them through the pass in the San Bernardino Mountains.

Blake and the conductor, Leininger, sat alone in the center of the car where Les had left them-- a half-hour, an hour, a day, a week ago. Time had ceased to have meaning to him. They both started to their feet as they saw Pam, but Les through frantic facial expressions signaled them both to remain where they were. The strange procession proceeded to a spot before them, where Durand called a halt.

"Durand killed Martin," Les said. "Slim is in the upper in that empty compartment. He also had Pam locked up, until I found her. Do as he says. He has a knife in her back."

The fat man almost swaggered.

"The guy is right," he boasted to the two seated men. "Do exactly as I tell you, and everything will be all right. Try to stop me, and I'm in too deep to care now what I do." His accompanying gesture was eloquent. "In ten minutes' time we'll be in the pass. I can make my way from there to a cabin I've got hidden in the mountains. I've used it as a hideaway before. Nobody knows it's there."

"You can't get away with it, Durand," Blake interrupted savagely. "Every man, woman, and child in the country knows your face from movies and your voice from the radio. You can't hide a week."

"I can try," Durand shot back at him. "And you'll help me, Blake. Right now. Here is what you are to do. Soon we'll reach a spot where the track levels off. Get up and stand where you can grab that signal cord. When I tell you to, give whatever signal will stop the train. I go over the back railing-- and the girl goes with me. Get that. The girl goes along to guarantee that after we're on the ground you then give the right signal for the train to proceed on its way. I want to see it disappear out of sight right on schedule."

"Then you'll turn Miss Gordon loose?" Les asked tensely.

"That depends, Clifford, on a lot of things," Durand replied. "But the chances are I'll take her along into the mountains. She's not a bad-looking dame. Maybe I'll need company. But don't forget she's a hostage. That'll slow up the hunt for me."

"It will only make us hunt you more relentlessly."

Durand shrugged. "What happens to me happens to the girl," he growled. "Get ready, Blake. When I give the signal--"

He left the sentence unfinished. Blake, his face white and set, reached for the cord. Les, his hands clenched tightly at his side, tried desperately with his eyes to give Pam some reassurance and encouragement, while she, horror written on her countenance, started for the rear door with the stiff, jerky movements of a sleepwalker.

Seeing her move thus, Les dropped dispiritedly into one of the car's heavy chairs, seemingly resigned to the inevitable.

Durand smirked at him as he gave his last curt order to Blake: "All right, yank that cord." Then he started after the girl.

But he never quite made it, for suddenly Lester's right leg moved in a swift, vicious arc, and his shoe struck Durand's right elbow a bone-crushing blow which caused the knife he held to spin through the air and then hang crazily downward from a piece of the ceiling decoration.

Durand, in a panic of pain and fright, started in a run for the rear of the car. Blake, who had never quite pulled the signal cord, started for Durand. He was only the slightest of split seconds after Lester, who had leaped up and moved in the same direction.

Pam chose this moment, as she had every right to do after the ordeal she had been through, to collapse quietly on the floor. Her recumbent form did, however, impede Les and Blake in their attempt to capture Durand, who darted, with surprising agility in one so huge, for the smooth glass oval that was the car's rear surface.

Set in the exact center of this crystal parabola was a small glass door with lucite frame and hinges, one which could be used for emergency exit, but would not obstruct the view. Durand made this in two great leaps, flung it open, and somehow wedged his big form through the narrow opening.

Those inside the car gazed spellbound in a sort of horrific fascination as, with one backward glance, he hurtled over the low guardrail. For some minutes the train had been proceeding downgrade, accelerating in speed with every turn of its wheels. It must have been traveling sixty-five miles an hour when Durand catapulted from its rear platform and struck the hard roadbed. His body bounced high in the air, rolled heavily in a cloud of dust and gravel, then lay still.

Les was glad that it was but a small black dot in the distance, lying between the two parallel rails which seemed to reach back to that infinity where they are said to meet, when Pam opened her eyes again.

He was also glad when she placed the blond curls on his shoulder, held her face very close to his, and again closed her eyes. It was a fact, although he didn't care, that Blake and the Pullman conductor were still gazing out the rear window when he kissed her.

The Pegasus, like the creature for which it was named, spread its wings and soared on into the valley.

DEADLY
FESTIVAL

Phoebe Atwood Taylor

The second of the previously unreprinted Asey Mayo novelettes finds the "Codfish Sherlock" back in his more familiar Cape Cod locale. This story is the penultimate Mayo tale, with only the novel Diplomatic Corpse (1951) to follow before his creator, who lived until 1976, brought her mystery-writing career to a puzzlingly premature close.

DEADLY FESTIVAL by Phoebe Atwood Taylor

With the visor of his yachting cap pulled down over his eyes, Asey Mayo sprawled across the seat of his Porter roadster parked behind the Skaket Town Hall, and congratulated himself on his successful imitation of a tired man sleeping soundly. For twenty peaceful minutes neither his cousin Jennie nor any of the other women milling around in the hall's auditorium, where preparations for that afternoon's Grange Fair were reaching fever pitch, had yelled at him to lug more bundles or move trestle tables again.

But he forgot about his act when a rattle-trap beach wagon parked so close to the roadster that a cornstalk protruding from its load actually brushed the yachting cap off his head.

Retrieving it from the seat, Asey sat up and stared with annoyance at the beach wagon's driver, a fat young man in faded denim pants and a flapping blue shirt, who had jumped out and was talking to passengers Asey couldn't see behind the heaped-up sheaves of cornstalks.

"This project is one of Jack Straw's brain waves," he was explaining in a high-pitched voice. "He thought it would be wonderful advertising for the Jackstraw Players to decorate a corner of the harvest festival, because cornstalks and a scarecrow are our official trade-mark. We'll rate a flock of pictures in the local press, at least. Of course, as set designer and scene builder, I'm stuck with all the dirty work. I was up at dawn despoiling strange cornfields, and now I've got to set this up....Mind getting out, darlings? I can't drag this stuff past you. Yes, it's your old Grampa Hamlin who always catches the work details around the Jackstraw Players."

Although he had pulled his cap visor over the top of his eyes, Asey covertly peeked at the couple as they got out of the back seat.

He immediately recognized the tall man in immaculate white flannels and the slim, very blond woman in yellow from the posters plastered over every fence post he'd passed this morning. These two were Edith Hamilton and Kenneth McClay, "The Stage's Favorite Couple," and, for that week only, they were starring at the local barn theater.

"You know we'd love to help, Cass, old boy." McClay's rich baritone reminded Asey of a church bell. "But we'd just be in your way. Don't know the first thing about sets....I say, why not wake up that fellow and hire him to take this stuff in? You-- you in the Porter! Want to make a dollar?"

Without raising his head, Asey tranquilly said, "No, thanks," and enjoyed the surprised expression on McClay's face.

"The industrious Cape Cod native you read about," the fat boy said, "is exclusively in fiction. You two go loll in the cool pines while Grampa Hamlin sets up his decor. Just a slave boy-- that's what I am! Just a drudge."

He continued to rattle on flippantly to himself, but once his passengers were out of earshot, he launched into such an acrid commentary on them that Asey strained his ears to listen over the noise of the sheaves being unloaded.

"You two pouch-eyed, pin-brained, rusty-jointed hams! You've fooled the rest, but Grampa Hamlin knows you're going to pay Dilly back for swiping your show-- Oh, damn that straw man!" He jammed a straw head back on the scarecrow and wired it into place.

For a young man who was easily fifty pounds overweight, he worked with amazing speed and deftness, Asey decided as he watched. Even after his fifteenth trip up the steep back stairs to the auditorium, he was still muttering away to himself without displaying any signs of breathlessness or fatigue.

"And now the work's done, the gentry can come back....Edith!" Hamlin raised his voice. "Ken! Ready, darlings!"

When the pair returned, he regaled them with a flip description of the fair hall. "I should have made you clamber up and gaze at the natives' idea of art--" He broke off, looked over at Asey, and bowed formally. "Next time, Cap'n Clamshell," he said tartly, "I'll charge you a small admission fee for my show!"

As the beach wagon rattled away, Asey's housekeeper cousin Jennie called from the hall's back door. "Now that crazy Hamlin's through with his corner," she announced, "we can lock up and go. And I must say nobody can complain we don't do our duty by our relations! If I ever get appendicitis the morning of our fair, I hope cousin Eva'll take hold and run the last-minute business for me as good as I've run this for her! Not to mention your lugging all those things upstairs, and you all tired out from that terrible plane trip....Hear anything new about the weather?"

"Same thing. Probably occasional showers in perhaps some areas. You mean you're really through, and ready to leave?"

Jennie nodded. "Start the car. I only got to lock up. Mrs.

Jenks's due to carry on from twelve-thirty."

But after waiting ten minutes, Asey turned off the Porter's engine and wearily climbed the stairs to see what was causing the delay.

He stood for a moment in the doorway and gazed through a welter of crepe paper decorations into the large hall, whose floor space seemed overflowing with trestle tables, each disguised with a frilled paper skirt of a different pastel color. Those tables which bordered the walls were laden with assortments of aprons, quilts, fancywork, dolls, candy, pies, bric-a-brac and antiques, and those in the center of the room displayed fruits and flowers and vegetables.

The stage to his left was roped off into two sections named Baby Show and Atomic Fortuneteller, and the little narrow gallery at the far end of the hall was devoted to Mystery Chances, Fishpool Grabs, and Auction Items.

An air of tense preparedness hung over the place.

"I'm sorry," Jennie said contritely as she caught sight of him. "Just as I was locking the front door, those dahlias came, and then Mary Longworth's chauffeur brought these gladioluses, and I couldn't leave 'em to wilt. Mary Longworth always expects first prize for her glads. They're awful jealous over here about their prizes. Last year some folks claimed their entries got spirited away, and that's why I had to be careful about locking up. Look at the corner Cass Hamlin decorated-- isn't it wonderful?"

Asey conceded that Hamlin's chunk of imitation cornfield was good.

"How's that straw man held up?" he added curiously as he strolled over toward the blue-overalled scarecrow with its battered gray felt hat.

"Hamlin hooked it onto a crossbar stand arrangement." Jennie was too occupied with the gladioluses to be aware of Asey's sudden muttered exclamation. "Came from the Jackstraw Players-- they got dozens of scarecrows decorating the inside of their barn theater....There, I'm done! Mrs. Jenks'll be here any minute, and the judges're due at one."

She walked over and joined Asey in front of the cornstalks. "The official opening's at two. Honest, did you ever see a more lifelike scarecrow? Why, if it wasn't for that straw face with the features painted on, I'd say--"

Her voice trailed off as she pointed with horror at the figure. "Asey, this isn't a scarecrow; it's a person! It's a woman! Asey Mayo, look at those bloodstains on her shirt!...Asey, it's a body!"

A second later she was repeating her statements in the form of breathless, anguished questions: "It is a woman, isn't it? And she's dead-- she's been stabbed, hasn't she? Oh, Asey, how could Cass Hamlin have done this, how could he ever have dared, with me and the other women right here?"

"He didn't. At least, what he lugged up from his beach wagon was a real, honest-to-goodness scarecrow. I was watchin' him."

"It couldn't have been real!" Jennie said. "He only fooled you into thinking so, same as he fooled us women! We were too busy to pay close attention to him-- and, after all, when you see a scarecrow, you think scarecrow; you don't think dead body! Of course Hamlin brought it-- who else could have? Now, take off that straw mask and find out who the poor creature is!"

"Look." Asey pointed to the last tier of bound sheaves set against the wall. "See the blue denim leg stickin' out behind the last clump on the right? That's the real scarecrow that Hamlin brought in."

He edged through the cornstalks to the wall, bent over, and lifted up the figure. "I know this is Hamlin's-- here's the slapdash wiring job I seen him do on the neck. This's the one he set up, the one you women saw. Somebody jerked it off, chucked it back here, and stuck the body on the stand in its place....Jennie, when'd you lock the front door?"

"When I carried in the flowers. All the exhibits and everything was supposed to be here by noon, and I pinned up a note saying so. I decided Mrs. Jenks-- goodness knows where she is! --could cope with the late comers....Oh, stop staring at that dummy and find out who this poor woman is! Take off that mask!"

"I want to see first if it's like the dummy's--"

"Those masks are all alike!" Jennie interrupted. "Just straw doilies from the Five-and-Ten. Hamlin said so. They paint a face on, and then bend 'em around to fit the scarecrow's head, and pin the ends in back. Oh, the poor--"

With a quick gesture, she reached past him and removed the battered felt hat, and screamed as the woman's wealth of blond hair fell down over the mask.

"Oh, Asey, how awful! I know her just from the hair. She's that beautiful blond girl from the Jackstraw Players!"

To the accompaniment of Jennie's heartrending sobs, Asey removed the painted face and found himself looking at one of the most singularly lovely girls he'd ever seen.

"It is Dilly Currier!" Jennie said. "She's the one who made such a hit at the opening last night. They say she stopped the show-- stole the play right away from that Hamilton and McClay couple. At the Beauty Shop this morning they even claimed she's already had offers from Hollywood. I never saw her near to before. She's not--"

"Not what?" Asey said as she hesitated.

Jennie appeared embarrassed. "I was just thinking what Mother used to say about some people being beautiful not from the inside, but from the outside. Only, it seems like a terrible time for me to think a thing like that-- Oh, Asey, do something!"

"There's a phone downstairs, isn't there? S'pose you go call Doc Cummings-- he being Medical Examiner for this section-- and tell him what happened. Ask him to call the state cops before he comes here."

As she hurried away, Asey surveyed the figure on the stand. The arms, stiffly extended along the crossbar piece, were held in place by four metal clips, which fitted around the bar and bit hold of the shirt.

Acting on sudden impulse, he pushed the long shirt sleeve and cuff away from the red-nailed finger tips and up the right wrist, turned over the small, jeweled platinum wrist watch, and read the inscription engraved on the back. Then turning back the collar of the shirt, he looked at the name printed in indelible ink under the label.

With a shrug, he walked over and sat down on a wooden stool behind the nearest table. If Jennie identified the girl as Dilly Currier, she was unquestionably Dilly Currier. But her watch bore the name of Bette Wood, and her shirt was Jack Straw's.

Asey stared at the assorted antiques in front of him without noticing any more than a huge, old-fashioned red coffee mill with side wheels. He was sure that what he'd seen Hamlin lug in was the genuine scarecrow, but he had to admit the possibility of Hamlin's secreting the body in one of the sheaves he had also carried in.

Only, the timing wouldn't work out! What Jennie first saw was the real scarecrow, and Hamlin had had no time to make the switch from real scarecrow to body. Jennie had been upstairs until he drove away. She hadn't locked up until after her return. As long as the front door was open, the hall probably was empty.

"But nobody certainly could've <u>counted</u> on its bein' empty, which is the important thing!" he murmured. "Even after she locked up, the place still wasn't empty then! She had to go downstairs to the sink in the kitchen to get water an' more vases. Say she was gone five minutes--"

While that gave someone both an empty hall and the necessary time in which to put the body where the scarecrow had been, nobody could possibly have guessed that Jennie might ever absent herself at all, let alone the actual duration of her absence.

"An' Hamlin had left fifteen mintues before. Now, those bloodstains on her shirt aren't smudged any. I wonder!"

Asey got up from the stool and began to peer down at the worn wooden floor. But he found no trace of bloodstains anywhere.

"Okay!" he said wearily. "Let's start in fresh. She was probably stabbed somewheres outside an' then brought here. She probably was killed over in the corner where she is now. She was here, alive, an' whoever stabbed her was here, too. Both of 'em must have come in before Jennie locked up. But if Jennie'd seen 'em, she'd have told me. So she didn't see 'em. So they must have been hidin'-- Oh, that's crazy!"

He looked up and considered the narrow gallery above his head. Since he and Jennie arrived, around ten o'clock, scores had milled in and out of the hall, and scores had gone up and deposited their offerings for the Mystery Chances and the Fishpool Grabs and the Auction Items which were located up there. Two people could easily have remained hidden in the gallery.

But the person responsible for the stabbing had to get out of the hall afterward. And the front door was locked. And he hadn't seen anyone emerge from the back door by the parking space. And the windows were two tall stories from the ground.

"I finally located Doc Cummings. He's on his way," Jennie announced as she returned. "And I've decided everything must have happened while I was filling vases downstairs. I suppose someone was hiding up here-- only, how'd they get out later without my knowing, unless they had a spare key?"

"Spare keys could be one answer, an' so--" Asey broke off as the handle of the door in front of them was suddenly rattled.

Jennie fumbled in her apron pocket for the key, but when she unlocked the door and swung it open, no one was there.

"I thought surely that would be Mrs. Jenks. Goodness knows why she's so late! But I suppose"-- she locked the door again-- "it was just kids."

"Listen!" Asey took her arm and drew her back under the gallery. "Listen! I think maybe we got the answer!" He pointed to the window nearest them.

Her eyes widened as she became aware of the sound which had caught Asey's attention, and then her jaw dropped as she saw a man's head appearing at the open window.

A second later, Hamlin was scrambling down from the wide window ledge into the hall, and heading for the imitation cornfield in the corner.

"What I forgot," Asey said in a low whisper to Jennie, "was the fire escape on that west side. You lose sight of it entirely, with all those vines. Now, don't mention that body!" He raised his voice: "Lookin' for something special, Mr. Hamlin?"

"Oh, there you are!" Hamlin sounded completely at ease, as if it were his invariable custom to enter a hall by such unorthodox means. "I hoped you'd still be here but the front door was locked when I tried it just a minute ago, and as I cut back to the parking space to see if your car was there, I noticed the fire escape. Sheer wanton impulse made me grab it and--"

"What's happened to you, Mr. Hamlin?" Jennie interrupted in shocked tones. "Your face's bleeding, and your shirt's all torn--"

"Accident," he said lightly. "I suddenly realized, as I was driving along, that the native with the blue dungarees and yachting cap, that tall, lean, salty, keen-eyed character in the Atomic Porter roadster, was none other than the Codfish Sherlock, the Hayseed Sleuth, the very boy I want-- Crash! Jack Straw'll never forgive me for what that phone pole's done to our beach wagon-- and I suppose Mr. Mayo won't ever forgive that Cap'n Clamshell crack....I was trying to figure something out, and you were the answer all the time, if I'd only had wit enough to recognize you!"

"You mean you never knew Asey when you saw him?" Jennie was

incredulous.

"I've seen him in newsreels and gravures as the famous Cape Cod detective, and director of the Porter motor works, but he's never been here in the flesh since I came to the Cape in June....Mr. Mayo, how does someone go about hiring you and seeking your aid?" Hamlin asked seriously.

"What d'you want my aid about?"

Hamlin said earnestly, "What do you do when you're convinced, without any tangible proof, that people are out to do someone dirt? Specifically, the people are Edith Hamilton and Kenneth McClay, the stage stars you saw with me, and the someone is this simply terrific kid in our company, Dilly Currier."

"Oh?" Never, Asey thought, had anyone tossed out a blander and more deliberate bit of implication. "An' why?"

"Because Dilly walked off with Lover Beyond at our theater last night. That's the play Edie and Ken have been starring in for two solid years. If you've read the morning papers you know how simply sensational Dilly was-- and Edie and Ken are so mad they're going to have Dilly's scalp!"

"Why, they aren't either!" Jennie said unexpectedly. "Over at the Beauty Shop this morning they said Hamilton and McClay made the most wonderful curtain speeches about how marvelous the Currier girl was."

"Oh, they're smart!" Hamlin said. "They slavered over her. I didn't catch on till this morning, driving 'em from town. They were saying how wonderful Dilly was-- much too good to be long for our little group-- and I caught sight of them in the rear vision mirror. They were looking at each other, and it was a murderous look. I suddenly knew. If I hadn't had that corner to set up here I'd have driven straight to Jack Straw-- he's the producer-manager of our theater-- and dumped the problem in his lap. No sense trying to warn Dilly herself after the way those two buttered her up. She'd only laugh in my face."

"Don't you honestly think," Asey said, "that you're sort of lettin' yourself get wafted away by your imagination?"

"No!" Hamlin shook his head. "My hunches pay off! Listen-- the instant we drove away from here, Edie and Ken started to fidget around in the back seat and look at their watches and say they had an important lunch date-- which they never mentioned before! And I heard Edie muttering something to Ken about 'That Dilly!' They made me stop and let 'em out so they could cut over through the fields to the Black Whale Inn, where they're staying. I knew they were cooking up trouble for Dilly. I just knew it! I sat there in front of that yellow house with the cupola, where they got out, kicking myself for letting 'em go!"

Asey deliberately edged a lace-edged pot-holder off the fancy-work table so that he could pick it up and give himself time to digest the full significance of Hamlin's words. For the yellow house with the cupola was a two-minute walk from the Town Hall. Hamilton and McClay could have left the beach wagon there and been inside the hall, by way of either the fire escape or the open front door, before Jennie had finished talking with him at the back door. Hamlin, Asey decided as he gently replaced the holder, was a smooth operator. First, he blandly implicated the two stars; then he furnished them with a powerful, justifiable motive; and now he'd even accurately plotted out their timing

"An' just what," he drawled, "d'you think that pair meant to do to Dilly Currier?"

"When I pumped 'em, they muttered vaguely about lunching at the inn with 'some man.'" Hamlin agilely ducked   direct answer. "They just gargled when I asked who-- hadn't even the ingenuity to invent a name. Anyway, I started back to the theater.   Then I remembered who you were and swerved off the road in my excitement. I hot-footed back here--"

"Well, welcome home, Asey!" The short, stocky figure of Dr. Cummings appeared at the rear door. "Didn't expect you back till next week. European trip successful? Solve Porter Motors' problems? Man, you look tired!...Hi, Cass. Jennie, you look exhausted, too!"

"And why not?" Jennie demanded as the two men shook hands. "With Asey only getting off the London plane this morning, and me not sitting down since goodness knows when! While I was under the drier at the Beauty Shop this morning, they brought me a cable saying Asey'd landed in New York today, and then came the message about Cousin Eva's having appendicitis and wanting me to help here! And while I'm being combed out, Asey drove up! His plane'd had to land in Boston, so he hitched a ride home. Then we rushed here and worked like dogs....Of course we look tired!"

Cummings grinned at her vehemence. "I'd have been here sooner, but, like a fool, I stopped to direct a lost tourist. Great, hulking oaf of a fellow, couldn't tell north from south!...Oh, the state cops said to carry on till they could send men down. Now, where's the body?"

Hamlin's head went back as if someone had thrown an uppercut to his jaw. Then he looked accusingly at Asey. "It's Dilly-- I know it's Dilly! I told you something was going to happen to her. Where is she?"

When Asey silently pointed to the figure, Hamlin seemed for a moment to turn to stone. Then he darted over to the corner.

A split second later, he disappeared through the back door.

"Get him!" Jennie said. "Don't let that rascal run away!"

Cummings raised his eyebrows and looked questioningly at Asey. "Don't tell me you're entertaining any base suspicions about Cass Hamlin! Not Cass!"

"He fixed that corner in the first place!" Jennie retorted. "Then he sneaked back through the window, and just brazened it out when he found us here....Why'd you let him go after the way he's acted,

Asey? And I mean acted!"

"Cass can design sets and build scenery," Cummings said, "but he's the only one in that Jackstraw outfit who can't act, and doesn't. I know. I've treated 'em all. What's the story here?"

Briefly, Asey summed up what had happened.

"Hm," Cummings said. "I see Jennie's point about Cass. But, as you say, he hardly could have made the switch from scarecrow to body unless he did it with mirrors. Cass likes to clown and jape, but it's all armor. He's sensitive. I learned that when I prodded him about his weight....Yes, I think I'd be inclined to believe he did have a hunch. He's the type. And particularly a hunch about Dilly. He hasn't thought of much else except her, all summer."

"What!" Jennie stared at him. "But at the Beauty Shop they said it was Jack Straw who was so crazy about her!"

"Oh, Jack, too, and every male in the county. This girl was a ball of fire." Cummings walked around the figure. "Yes, stabbed in the heart-- determined sort of job. Nice sharp knife. Dagger, I'd guess. You found it?"

"Where"-- Asey nodded toward the laden tables-- "would you suggest startin' to hunt for it-- in the Fishpool Grabs? What's your opinion, Doc? Was she stabbed right there on the stand?"

Cummings nodded. "I think she was alive when she was put there. But I can't think she'd let herself be put on this stand arrangement without some good reason, and I can't believe she just stood here meekly waiting for someone to kill her, either. No, she never suspected whoever was with her....Who're all those people filing in there?"

"It's the judges," Jennie said, as half a dozen men entered and gathered in a little knot around the stage. "It must've been one-thirty they were supposed to come, not one. And there's Mary Longworth with 'em-- I forgot she was some sort of judge, too! Oh, Miss Long--"

Asey's hand clapped firmly over her mouth and stifled the rest of her words.

"If they don't know this isn't a real scarecrow," he said, "let's not enlighten 'em. Save a lot of fuss an' bother if we put the real scarecrow back on the stand, an' take the body over to our place, Doc. Right? As Medical Examiner, you can always move a body for further examination if you want....Jennie, go stave off that female with the fancy hair-do!"

"It's Mary Longworth." Jennie made no effort to intercept the approaching woman in the smart blue linen suit. "And she's no female in that tone of voice! She's very nice, and her hair-do's the very newest. I was with her when she got it this morning! And she's only heading for the Antique Table, like she always does!"

"I'm afraid she's heading over here," Cummings said as he held the stand steady for Asey, "but it's all right. Mary's not the hysterical type, and she ought to know about this, anyway. The

Jackstraw Players are her current hobby. She's their founder and sponsor and guardian angel--"

"I could scream!" Mary Longworth's face was strong and tanned, and she was older than Asey had guessed from a distance. In her middle thirties, he mentally amended. "I could scream! They've put my precious heirloom coffee mill on the Antique Table instead of among the Auction Items where it'll bring them ten times as much-- Good Lord, that's Dilly!"

"It was Dilly," Cummings corrected her, as Asey finished putting the real scarecrow back on the stand. "Now, don't scream! We're trying to avoid a lot of hue and cry by this transfer, and there's no time for explanations-- or introductions, either, though I'm sure you'll recognize Mayo, the Codfish Sherlock. Jennie'll tell you everything while he carries Dilly down to my car for me."

"But who did it?" Mary Longworth's voice was barely under control.

"I hope you can help me find that out," Asey said. "There's a lot I want to know. Will you wait here till I get the Doc started off with this? I won't be a moment."

But as he turned away from watching the doctor's sedan speed down the driveway, he happened to glance at the pine woods.

What he saw there suddenly sent Asey pounding toward them on a dead run.

He kept telling himself, as he raced along, that it wasn't another human scarecrow swaying there by the biggest pine, that he hadn't seen it topple and then pick itself up again. It couldn't be another!

But it was.

Asey stopped a few feet short of the reeling figure, and drew a long breath.

More blue overalls, another checked shirt, and battered gray felt hat. And hands covered with white cotton work gloves whose fingers were stuck out stiffly, and whose wrists were tied high on the shirt sleeves. Hands that kept stabbing out and clawing at the air. Another staring face-- But this one was real, and contorted with sobs.

The figure pitched forward, fell at his feet.

Asey knelt down beside her and jerked off the hat. The girl was dark as Dilly Currier had been blond, and even prettier, Asey decided. Her eyes were closed, but after a moment she opened them and looked up at him. Then she extended the cotton gloved hands toward him and shook them feebly.

"Oh," Asey said, "I get it. You want the gloves taken off?"

She nodded, and Asey realized from the way in which she flexed her fingers after the gloves were removed that the wires which caused the glove fingers to stick out so stiffly had also trapped her own fingers.

"Thanks!" she gasped. "I was nearly crazy! I felt so helpless!"

"What's the idea of the costume, anyway?" Asey inquired.

"To think of Jack Straw wiring those gloves on my hands and pinning on that mask and then leaving me here-- By the way, where is that mask?' She frowned. "Anyway, I nearly suffocated. After a while you just can't breathe through that straw mat! And it's so sweltering hot today! I hope you tell Jack that by the time you finally found me, I'd collapsed but utterly! What became of him?"

Asey shook his head. "I couldn't say. I'm just an innocent passer-by, myself."

"Jack Straw didn't send you to find me?" The girl sat up straight. "What time is it?"

"Around quarter of two."

"Of two?" She stared at Asey, her blue eyes wide with bewilderment. "But it was twelve-thirty when Jack left me-- Oh, something's frightfully wrong! I can't possibly have been stumbling around groggily for an hour and fifteen minutes! Do you see anything wrong with my head, like a lump or something? I thought I just dreamed that part about falling and hitting my head!" She ran her hand experimentally through her curls. "There is a lump-- on top of my head! Look!"

Asey glanced at it. "Did you really fall," he asked, "or were you hit?"

"Of course I fell!" she answered without hesitation. "But I wish I could remember how it happened or understood where the time went! You see, Jack got me all ready, and then he went off to the hall to see how we could best sneak into the fair."

"What was the general underlyin' idea?" Asey tried to sound nonchalant.

"Oh, Jack had arranged for the Jackstraw Players to decorate a corner of this Grange Fair with a sort of splotch of cornfield containing a scarecrow. And then he decided this morning that it would be simply terrific to dress me up and put me there in place of the scarecrow, just about the time the judges were picking the Prize Turnips and the Biggest Clam and all. There'd be photographers there, of couse, and Jack thought a live scarecrow should cause a small riot. And a scarecrow's our trade-mark. Get it? Or does it sound too silly to you?"

"No, it sounds pretty good to me!" Asey told her honestly. "A mighty fine explanation, an' one that wouldn't have occurred to me in a hundred years if I was asked to figure out the reason why a live person should substitute for a scarecrow."

"It only occurred to Jack because one of our company used to pose among the dummies in store windows," she remarked. "People love that sort of thing, you know. They stare for hours, trying to pick out the real girl. Dilly--" She stooped and drew her breath in sharply. Then she continued, "Dilly was frightfully good at it, too."

"Oh? You mean the girl that stole the show last night?"

"Yes. Our brilliant new star." Something hard and metallic entered the girl's voice. "I must get along." She swayed a little as she got to her feet, and Asey suggested gently that she rest a few minutes longer.

"That was quite a crack you took," he added. "Can't you really figure out how it happened?"

"It's so hard to remember anything when you couldn't see!" She sat down again on the pine needles. "I couldn't use my hands enough to work that mask off!...But it's gone now, isn't it? I don't understand....And those funny faces-- Were those from concussion or something, d'you think?"

"What funny faces?" Asey demanded.

"The ones that kept staring down at me," she said simply. "Distorted faces. Dream faces. Edie Hamilton's, and Ken McClay's-- Ken's face was looming out of a white suit, and Edie's out of a yellow dress. That proves it was all concussion, of course, because I've never seen either of them dressed that way!"

With some effort Asey kept from saying that the two were dressed that way when they arrived with Hamlin at the Town Hall!

"And then that big, dark man!" she went on. "I can't imagine where I ever dreamed him up! Oh, those faces are going to haunt me for a long time!"

Asey suspected that they were going to haunt him for a long time, too. For the girl's accurate recollection of McClay's white suit and Edith Hamilton's yellow dress served to whisk those funny faces right out of the hallucination class. That, in turn, meant that someone must have removed her mask during her period of unconsciousness. Only, where was the mask now?

Asey said, "Uh-- I gather you act in this Jackstraw group, like the Currier girl?"

"No! I mean," she explained, after a quick glance at his face, "I don't act like Dilly! One Dilly Currier is all any company can take!"

"But you act, don't you?" he persisted.

"No." She turned her face away from him, and Asey wondered if it mirrored the deep bitterness in her voice. "I was hired to act. I came here expecting to act. But my role seems to have turned out to be the care and feeding of the apprentices of the cast. I meet busses, too, and soothe guest stars-- Look; who are you, anyway? You look familiar, but I can't place you!"

"I'm just a native son. Say, is this Currier girl as good as they claim?"

"If you were a green apprentice two months ago and a star today, you're certainly not bad, are you?" She pulled up a shirt sleeve and looked at her wrist. "Oh, I forgot Dilly grabbed my watch this morning-- but you said it was two-ish, didn't you?"

Asey nodded, and mentally identified this girl as Bette Wood, the owner of the platinum watch on Dilly's wrist.

"Tell me," he said, "is it true what my cousin said about the Currier girl bein' offered a wonderful movie contract?"

She shrugged. "How would I know?"

"Since you're both in the same company," Asey drawled, "I just took it for granted you might!"

"You can take it for granted"-- that metallic note was back-- "that we in the company'll be the last to know what her future offers and plans are. When the Hollywood agents began phoning this morning, she casually tore up her contract with us and told Jack Straw to jump in the lake! We don't count any more. We've contributed our bit to her career! Oh, to think how ecstatic Dilly was, back in June, when she was a waitress at the Black Whale Inn, and Mary Longworth finally gave in to her pleas and let her join us as an apprentice!"

"Sounds," Asey said, "like she's bounced up the ladder of success in something less'n two short hops an' a jump!"

"Dilly never bothered with that old-fashioned ladder nonsense-- she's been bowling along a superhighway! You can get where you're going in nothing flat if you just whoop along through red lights and pedestrians! She used everything on Edie and Ken last night except brass knuckles, but she made it!"

"You mean she got her Hollywood contract?"

"I told you, I wouldn't know! But if she isn't signed up by now," Bette said grimly, "it's because she dropped dead! Lord knows I can't say a kind word for Edie and Ken, but don't I feel for them! They worked for two solid years to wangle the starring roles in the film version of Lover Beyond, and now they're sunk! Whatever part Dilly may be signed for, she'll be the star. She'll grab again and Edie and Ken know it. They know it'll be 'Dilly Currier, Supported By,' and not 'Hamilton and McClay In.' It's the beginning of the end for them!"

And that, Asey reflected, was a far more plausible motive for their murdering Dilly than mere jealousy!

"So you think she'll get top billin'?"

"I know she'll get top billing! And top salary! Edie and Ken'll take it both ways. Oh, how I felt for'em last night! I'd have understood if they'd torn Dilly to pieces with their bare hands! They had thrown at 'em in one swoop everything I've been talking about in little doses all summer-- only, it was tragedy for them because they have so much more at stake!"

"I'm slow catchin' on," Asey said softly. "I've just got it! You were hired to be the star, an' she got your job!"

"My job, and-- and Jack!" She suddenly burst into tears, and then as suddenly brushed her sleeve across her eyes and faced him. "You want to know who knocked me out, Mr. Mayo-- yes, I've remembered who you are! Well, I couldn't see anyone with the mask on, and I didn't hear anyone, but if you go to the Town Hall and find that the Jackstraw exhibit has a live scarecrow, and if the live scarecrow's our photogenic blond star who simply adores posing for publicity shots-- well, you can add it up and guess it was Dilly's handiwork! A brisk little knockout wouldn't cause her any little qualms if she thought she could grab off a few pictures by it!"

"Oh? Then she knew all about Jack's plan to ring in a live scarecrow at the fair?"

Bette hesitated. "He insisted we keep it a secret so it would be a real surprise, but Dilly must have guessed, or overheard! It's all clear enough. She followed us, lurked in the pines while Jack got me ready, and sneaked out and hit me after he left for the hall....Of course!"

"How d'you think she worked it out from there?" Asey knew Dilly could never have ensconced herself as the scarecrow without someone else's help.

"That's easy! She rushed after Jack and told him some tale about my suddenly feeling ill or something-- she's a genius at improvising. I suppose if she intended all along to hog this act, she had a spare mask with her and was all set to walk on. I'm sure that's what happened!"

Bette's version, Asey thought, certainly gave Jack every chance to be the person who'd sneaked into the hall with Dilly, and killed her. And Bette's remark about the torn-up contract posed the question of how violently Jack might have reacted to the prospect of seeing his new star, whom he'd launched, go shooting out of his sight before he could cash in on her success. And then there was Jennie's Beauty Shop gossip, which tagged Jack as the main contender for Dilly's affections. You could make something out of all that, Asey told himself, if you wanted to. And if you didn't bother asking why Jack had a dagger handy to kill the girl whose presence he had no reason to expect.

Asey was poking the leaves, thoughtfully, with his foot, when an unexpected edge of straw caught his eyes. Bette's mask!

"Are you sure it was on tight?" he asked. "It didn't just slip off?"

"With that hat on?" she snorted.

He looked thoughtfully at Bette, suddenly recalled Cummings's comments to the effect that Hamlin was the only one of the Jackstraw group who didn't constantly act, and wondered how much stock he should take in her recital. After all, Dilly had grabbed both her job and her boy-friend, and people had been killed for less!

Suppose she'd told the truth-- but not all of it. Suppose that Bette herself had told Dilly about the live-scarecrow stunt and banking on her love for publicity, suggested that Dilly secretly take her place. She could have sold the idea as a great joke on Jack. Suppose Bette had deliberately sent Jack off on some pretext, then summoned Dilly from the pines, and accompanied her to the hall! After the murder Bette could have run back, struggled into her scarecrow trappings-- except for the mask, which was too hard to put on-- whacked her head against a tree-- what an alibi she had in her helplessness inside those trappings!

"Dilly probably told Jack I'd gone home," Bette put an end to his suppositions. "That's why he didn't come back. Look; you've been sweet to take such an interest in this affair! I mean, I can see that when you found me, you probably felt you'd landed on a nice, juicy murder, or something. But I was only knocked out!"

"That's an angle," Asey said slowly, "that I hadn't exactly considered! You weren't killed. Only knocked out!"

"Well, it's all over and I'm all right, so let's forget it, shall we?" she said brightly. "Let's just never mention this to anyone! Dilly'll probably be leaving after Lover Beyond ends on Saturday, and I don't want any fuss and trouble. We've had enough fuss and trouble at the theater with that horrid accident. If this episode gets talked about, those men will only start poking around again and pestering us all to death."

"Which men?" Asey asked. "An' what horrid accident? I've been away all summer."

"Oh, it was ghastly! The morning following our opening night in June, the body of a town man was found on the edge of our parking lot," she said. "Apparently he'd been hit and killed by a car racing up the drive, and then dragged off to the bushes. His sons are the local traffic cops, and they're convinced some one of us hit him-- as if we had time on opening night to race around in cars! About every two weeks they come pestering us with more questions. They mean to find out who killed their father if it takes a lifetime! A thing like my getting knocked out would only start them up again."

"But why should they suspect any of you?" Asey demanded.

"Well, we did race around the lot when we first came. The roads were empty, and we had so much to do in such a hurry. I suppose we did look like a bunch of reckless drivers," Bette admitted. "Actually, we always thought it was someone rushing to make the first act who got panicky when he saw the body. So will you just please forget this scarecrow business? Oh, look! It's going to rain. Before it starts, I've got to hunt up my pocketbook!"

"Where is it?"

Bette shook her head. "Wherever it was when Jack left me. And I'll be sunk without that bag. It's got practically all my valuable worldly goods in it. If you don't want your private possessions bandied about our theater, you have to keep 'em in your pocketbook in your hot hand! Our apprentices are the most lawless lot of bobby-soxers. I must find the thing, because, in two seconds, it's going to pour!"

"Not for ten minutes or so," Asey said, squinting at the overcast sky. "What's your bag look like? I'll help you hunt."

"It's an over-arm job, a pouch with a shoulder-strap. Red leather, with a little brass scarecrow figure on the side. Back at the start of the season Mary Longworth gave one to each of the girls in the company....She's the angel of the Jackstraw Players, you know....They've turned out to be practically our duffel bags, and we couldn't live without 'em. Even Dilly, who's as casual about other people's belongings as anyone I know, always keeps hers glued to her shoulder--" She broke off at the sound of someone approaching through the pines.

"S'pose that might be Jack?" Asey guessed.

"If it is, won't he find out that I can pull an act on him, too!"

Asey stared at the tall broad-shouldered young man coming along the path, and decided he looked more like the fullback on a college football team than the head of a summer theater. After a closer glimpse of the sleepy, slightly sullen face, he decided that what the fellow really resembled was a fretful baby who'd been waked up in the middle of a nap.

Expectantly, he turned to Bette, wondering why she didn't begin her proposed act. But she was pointing a shaking forefinger at the newcomer. "It's the big dark man! I never dreamed him at all-- he's real! It was his face peering down at me-- and look! He's got my pocketbook!...What are you doing with my pocketbook? Give it back to me! Give it-- Oh, don't let him run away with it! Get him!"

As the fellow swung around on his heel, Asey jumped. For a second, he clutched a handful of coat sleeve. Then his hand was empty, and the man was out of sight!

It occurred to Asey, as he set out in pursuit, that if he'd considered Hamlin quick on his feet, then the only adjective for this lad was jet-propelled! Asey raced along, skidding over the slippery pine needles on the path and following the sound of the footsteps crashing ahead until they were drowned out by the first rumbles of thunder.

Asey stoppd short. He certainly wouldn't gain anything by pounding blindly on.

Straining his ears to catch some noise of crackling twigs or rustling bushes during the brief intervals when the thunder momentarily let up, he waited. Suddenly King-size tiptoed into sight on the path ahead. He was backtracking, staring back over his shoulder so intently that he never spotted Asey until the latter lunged for him.

A moment later Asey picked himself up from the bushes and ruefully surveyed the red leather bag which was dangling from the broken shoulder-strap whose end he held in his hand. That and a couple of bruises were all he had to show for his second round with King-size, who by now was probably two counties away.

He gave the strap a disgusted flip, when the brass side clasp suddenly gave way.

The ensuing cascade of papers and miscellaneous small objects from the red bag left him open-mouthed. Papers, bills, lipstick, compact, loose change, combs, peanuts, hairpins, keys, candy bars, mascara, sunglasses, perfume, a bankbook, a tube of suntan cream...Asey stared as things continued to fall down among the pine needles, until a stronger gust of wind started to blow the papers around and forced him to begin picking them up. Pouncing on a post card, he automatically looked at the name and address, and an exclamation of honest surprise came to his lips. He grabbed up a bill, and a letter, and then the bankbook.

They all belonged to Dilly. This was her bag, not Bette's!

Asey scrambled around as the wind increased, stuffing things back into the red pouch, and berating himself for letting King-size get out of his clutches.

"All right!" he muttered as he prodded among the pine needles for a key. "Bette always said Dilly kept her pocketbook glued on her shoulder. So she must've been wearing it when she went into the hall. But she never wore it out! So who took it? Whoever killed her....For something in it?"

Bette's comment about the use of the red bags as general safe-deposit boxes indicated that Dilly's murderer might very well have expected to find whatever object he was after in her bag! But why had he let it be snatched from him if he'd killed Dilly for something in it? Conversely, if he'd already removed what he wanted, why was he marching around with the bag in his hand?

"An' if he just happened to pick it up in passin', whyn't he give it back to Bette when she said it was hers, instead of rushin' off with it? An' who is he? Bette didn't know him!"

But her instant recognition of him as the big, dark man whose face peered down at her seemed indisputable. She actually had seen those faces, however distorted they may have appeared to her.

"But why should all three of 'em gape down at her, an' then flit away without apparently liftin' a finger to help her any?"

Heavy drops of rain were falling as Asey turned and started for the path leading back to the Town Hall. Bette'd probably taken refuge there from the storm, he guessed, and he still had Mary Longworth to see.

With his mind focused less on the path and its branches than on Dilly's bag, Asey tramped through the downpour. A few minutes later, soaked to the skin, he found himself standing at the edge of an unfamiliar clearing, with the spire of the Town Hall silhouetted against the black sky to his left.

Directly ahead, the ground sloped sharply away to a broad meadow yellow with goldenrod. Beyond that, the main buildings and the guesthouses of the Black Whale Inn gleamed white in their setting of green lawns and bright flower beds.

A shattering bolt of lightning tore into the earth at his right, and Asey instinctively looked in that direction. He recognized the vast barn and buildings beyond the narrow inlet of the bay as the old Ross estate, a former showplace which had been literally falling to pieces when he last saw it. Now it looked rebuilt and refurbished.

The truth dawned on Asey as he spotted the billboard-size signs and the floodlights: The old Ross estate was the Jackstraw Players' outfit, and the barn was their theater!

"Whyn't someone think to tell me the place was right over there!" he said in exasperation. "Why, Dilly Currier or anybody else from that crew could've run over to the Town Hall any time. Cuttin' across the fields on foot is a quarter the distance goin' by car."

As he contemplated the triangle formed by the hall, the Inn, and the theater, Mary Longworth strode across the path right in front of him. Although the rain had reduced her smart linen suit to the shapelessness of wet linen dish towels, she was futiley attempting to protect her fancy hair-do by holding an open newspaper above her head. When Asey spoke to her, she jumped in surprise.

"How you frightened me! I waited and waited for you to come back, but I simply had to leave. I told Jennie you'd find me at home. Ross's is my house, you know. Where've you been? D'you know where Cass went? What've you found out?"

"I haven't seen Hamlin, an' about all I've gleaned is that Dilly was probably playin' live scarecrow to cash in on the publicity, an' was probably killed for something in her pocketbook."

"In her pocketbook?" Mary stared at him unbelievingly. "In her bag? Oh, nonsense! Dilly hadn't any jewelry or any money-- she was perpetually broke. I can't understand how you'd think that-- but then I can't understand any of this! Bette Wood trailed into the fair with some weird story of live scarecrows and a big, dark man. She was utterly shaken when she heard about Dilly. Your Cousin's calming her down in the kichen. Why didn't you tell Bette?"

"I've always found," Asey said, "that folks are so much more fluent-like, if they don't know why they're being asked questions. On the other hand, if they're tryin' to hide things, it gives 'em a nice chance to cross themselves up. Look; there's some things I'd like to know about Dilly, but I don't want to keep you standin' here soakin' in this rain."

"I doubt," she said with a wry smile, "if either of us can get any wetter. You look drowned, and I feel so. I forgot my umbrella when I left the hall, I was in such a fury at that idiotic Mrs. Jenks! I practically had to use force to make her move that old coffee mill I donated from the Antique Table to the Auction stuff, where it'll bring in twice as much-- and she retaliated by giving my gladioluses Second Prize, at which I boiled over! What d'you want to know about Dilly?"

"Anything you think is important. Has she any family? Any enemies?"

"She has no family." Mary paused. "I suppose there's no sense being less than frank, is there? Letting her join our company was my fault, probably the worse mistake I ever made, and I knew it twenty-four hours after I succumbed to her teasings-- she could be most charmingly persuasive. And, to give the girl her due, she really was terrific!"

"Why was she such a mistake, then?"

"Her one idea was to get to Hollywood. Within a week she'd wound Jack Straw around her little finger and grabbed Bette's job. That was when I should have put my foot down, hard. I didn't. I thought she'd be a flop. Instead"-- Mary pushed a sopping strand of hair away from her forehead-- "she was better than Bette ever could be. She learned like a streak-- picked something more from each week's guest stars. Last night she put it all together and loused Edie and Ken out of their play-- and made Hollywood!...Don't look now, but I think the rain's stopping."

"I s'pose"-- Asey sounded unusually pensive-- "you feel she was a mistake because she got Bette so jealous, an' Hamlin all worked up, an' Jack Straw in a stew?"

She smiled. "That's a smart trap you're baiting, but I shan't be lured into making any comment which might even remotely sound like an accusation against anyone in my company. If anyone's been jealous of Dilly, and worked up about her, it's myself. I've entertained more murderous thoughts about that girl than you can imagine!"

"So?" Asey said with a grin. "Why?"

"I founded the Jackstraw Players three years ago. I'm its sponsor. I pay the bills and make up its deficit. Behind the scenes, I'm the boss-girl. But the day after Dilly came I found myself taking a back seat-- and I haven't liked it! So if you and the police want a whipping boy, whip _me_! Don't badger Bette or any of those kids. They've been badgered enough since that ghastly hit-and-run accident at our place in June!"

Asey, looking at the set of her firm jaw, decided to postpone his questions until her attitude of a lioness defending her cubs had somewhat moderated.

"Jennie's convinced," Mary went on, "that Cass used some trickery in setting up the dummy scarecrow, but she's wrong. I know Cass! And I'm sure he never meant to implant any sinister ideas in your mind about Edie and Ken, either. Cass is over-imaginative, but he's honest!"

"At least, he was honest about smashin' up the beach wagon," Asey remarked. "I've just spotted it at the fork of the Shore Lane an' the theater driveway-- See it, against the phone pole?"

"He's so careless! That's his third crack-up!" She bit her lip. "Well, you can see there was nothing sinister in Edie and Ken's short-cutting back to the Inn! This is the _place_ to short-cut!"

"Uh-huh. It is" Only, Asey thought, they hadn't cut through here at all. Bette had seen them away back in the pine grove.

"Yoo-hoo! Asey!" Jennie came bustling down the path behind them, bone-dry under her tentlike black umbrella. "Where've you _been_ all this time?...Why, Mary Longworth, what a sight you are! Asey; stop your old questions and let her get home and into some dry clothes. She's sopping!"

"It's not his fault," Mary said. "I forgot my umbrella. Besides, the rain's stopped."

"Why don't you run along an' get dried out?" Asey suggested. "I've ben seized with a sudden desire to chat with Hamilton an' McClay, an' I can drop over an' see you later. Okay?"

The instant Mary left, he turned quickly to Jennie. "Tell me," he said; "who runs the Black Whale Inn nowadays?"

"That Jenks woman!" Her sniff of contempt was close to being a sneer. "The one who didn't come to the hall at twelve-thirty when she was supposed to. The shirker! And I must say it-- the barefaced liar! Announcing calm as you please that I left a message telling her not to bother coming! And I never did! I had to grit my teeth to keep from saying right out that if she'd only been on her job, there wouldn't have been any murder at all-- would there?"

"Wa-el," Asey began, "I hardly--"

"Why, nobody'd have had the chance to kill the girl if that Jenks had done her duty. Cousin Eva'd planned for somebody always to be there in charge-- her husband said so when he phoned this morning. He said Eva'd meant to go home at twelve-thirty, and that I could go then, too, because Mrs. Jenks was taking over. Why, her name was posted right on that typewritten list Eva'd pinned up!"

"Where?"

"Out on the bulletin board at the front door of the hall. 'Jenks,' it said. 'Twelve-thirty.' Right there in black and white for all the world to see!...Asey, some fine day I'm going to tell that Jenks what I think of her! Swishing around in those fool dirndls all the time, and being so quaint and old Cape Coddy for the tourist trade, and wearing that sunbonnet-- where are you going?"

"I'm goin' to put my finger on the one tangible thing," Asey informed her, "that I've heard so far."

"And what's tangible," Jennie said, with rising inflection, "about a message I never left? What's--? Wait! Wait for me!"

Ten minutes later in the lounge of the Black Whale Inn, in an atmosphere so redolent of the past that Asey felt overwhelmed with whales' teeth and spinning wheels and warming pans, he studied the slip of paper which Mrs. Jenks had just given him.

"Jennie looked so upset when I remarked about her message," she said, "I fished it out of the trash basket when I came home. I sensed there'd been some mistake, but there's the message!"

Asey read it aloud: "'Jennie says not to bother coming at twelve-thirty.' Huh. When did this come?"

"I found it here on the desk around noon. One of the guests had answered the phone and taken the message for me."

"An' I don't s'pose you could tell which guest," Asey said, "since they didn't sign any name on it?"

"Oh, I couldn't mistake that distinguished hand! Of course, I know Miss Edith Hamilton's writing!" With a swish of her full skirts, Mrs. Jenks walked across the hooked rug and sat down opposite Jennie. "Really," she continued proudly, "you'd never guess she was world-famous, and one of our most celebrated actresses! She's so human and so democratic! Think of her bothering to take a phone message for me!"

"I'd like to see Miss Hamilton," Asey said. "Is she in one of the guest cottages, or here in the house?"

"Oh, she can't be disturbed!" Mrs. Jenks sounded shocked. "We have to respect her privacy, you know! We can't impose on her--"

"I want to question Miss Hamilton," Asey broke in crisply, "about an accident involvin' Dilly Currier. But if you'd prefer havin' the state cops mill around your inn, instead--"

She swished to her feet with alacrity. "An accident to Dilly? Oh, how unfortunate! I noticed that Cass had smashed up the beach wagon again. Was she in it? Out this side door, Mr. Mayo. Miss Hamilton is in the cottage we call Aunt Phrone's."

"Just show me. You needn't bother to come," Asey said.

"I do hope it's nothing serious." She hovered anxiously between him and the doorway. "Miss Hamilton and Mr. McClay are so proud to have discovered her talent. But, of course, I take some credit for bringing Dilly to Mary Longworth's attention when she was one of my waitresses."

Asey, who had been edging gently around her to the door, suddenly stopped. "D'you happen to know if Miss Hamilton an' McClay had a lunch date with anybody today?"

"Well, just before they left for town with Cass, they ordered a terrace table for three at one o'clock."

"Who was lunchin' with 'em?"

"I really couldn't say, but I do know their guest never came!...Aunt Phrone's is the second cottage on your left, Mr. Mayo. Are you sure," she added, as she stepped out on the terrace, "you don't wish me to introduce you to Miss Hamilton and her husband?"

"Thanks," Asey said. "We've met."

After Mrs. Jenks had swished away, he turned to Jennie, who had trailed along behind. "Want to do something for me? Call Doc Cummings an' see how things are, an' then call Mary Longworth an' ask if Jack Straw's at the theater, or where I can find him. I don't s'pose you can prevent Mrs. Swish from 'overhearing' every word you say, so be careful. Wait for me in the lounge....Oh, and take care of this pocketbook of Dilly's, will you?"

"That all you want?" Jennie asked with irony.

"Wa-el, if a king-sized, baby-faced fellow drops in," Asey said, "you might throw a half nelson on him for me!"

He walked briskly along the terrace ignoring the second cottage on his left, and marched on across the lawn to the edge of a little locust grove. Instead of calling formally at the front door of Aunt Phrone's, he decided that he'd tackle the rear entrance and sort of sneak up on--

"Ahoy, Cap'n."

Asey swung round to find Cass Hamlin sitting a yard away with his back propped against a tree.

"A man could rust and fall apart," Cass observed, "while he sat here wondering what was keeping you from Edie and Ken. The inn cook tells me they actually did expect someone for lunch, but the waitress said nobody came. You can play it either way. I prefer to think they were faking."

"Look here," said Asey; "why'd you rush out of the Town Hall like that?"

"I panicked," Cass answered simply.

"Expect me to believe that?"

"I loved that girl, Mayo. I couldn't have stayed there without going to pieces. Everything hit me at once-- Dilly, and what had happened to her, and what I'd been telling you. Everything boomeranged. I didn't know what I was doing for half and hour; then I pulled myself together and came over here and waited."

"Why?" Asey said. "Why here?"

"I expected you'd come right after Edie and Ken. When you didn't, I decided to stay and keep an eye on them myself. In books"-- Cass was maintaining his flippant tone with difficulty-- "there's usually some character who sits and watches suspects, and broods usefully the while. I've been brooding over that fire escape I used so blithely, for example. That's how they got in and out of the hall, isn't it?"

"Out, I think. You seen Jack Straw?"

"No. I phoned him from the inn a while ago, but nobody's seen him, or knows where he went. Look, Mayo; you've probably found out that Dilly turned him down, too. Sure, sure, she turned me down! And you probably heard about the contract row that Jack and Dilly had this morning. But Edie and Ken are the only ones who could have killed her."

"Not Bette?"

"Bette?" Cass sounded incredulous. "Because Dilly got her job, you mean? Oh, just skip that! Bette didn't care. The theater never meant to her what it meant to Dilly. Bette's just having fun till she marries and settles down, probably with Jack. She didn't have to be a success or else starve, like Dilly. She didn't land here with exactly twelve cents to her name!"

"Did Dilly?" For a fleeting moment Asey had a mental picture of a bankbook falling onto pine needles from Dilly's bag. A Boston bankbook. He hadn't stopped to look at the balance, but it wasn't a canceled book. No perforations. Dilly must have had a bit more than twelve cents.

"She had just twelve cents left," Cass said with feeling, "when she came here to the inn. Her one idea in coming was to bust into summer theater, somehow. She had to succeed! But if Bette wants anything she writes her father, and he stops cutting coupons long enough to send it....What're you grinning at?"

"You," Asey told him. "D'you really believe in your heart that it doesn't hurt to lose your job if your father's got means? Or that a capital of twelve cents proves you love the theater an' got to succeed in it? Honest, now, do you?'

"Dilly said--"

"Uh-huh, I guessed Dilly sold you those goods." Asey glanced sideways at Cass. "Wa-el, considerin' you're a mite biased, I'll just have to ask Mary Long--"

"Don't kid youself you'll get any unbiased reports from Mary!" Cass jumped head first into the trap. "She's never liked Dilly, and rued the day she let her join us. Always muttering what a mistake she made, and how Dilly wheedled her when she was so upset, the day after that hit-and-run accident we had. Actually, of course, Mary knows that if she'd kept Bette as lead, Bette's precious father would probably have crashed through and helped with the deficit. Mary's moneybags always come first."

He stopped short and looked reproachfully at Asey. "No fair, Cap'n Codfish! You deliberately played on my feelings for Dilly to make me spit out a lot of thoughtless venom. I'll have to watch my step."

"You can begin," Asey said, "by comin' with me. I want your co-operation in interviewin' Hamilton an' McClay."

The sound of voices rose from Aunt Phrone's cottage as they crossed the lawn.

"They're rehearsing," Cass said. "I heard snatches of dialogue over where I was sitting, when the wind was right. Ken can't remember lines overnight, you know."

"Take it, Ken!" Edith Hamilton was saying sharply as Asey and Cass paused on the doorstep. "From 'proud and happy.'"

"Proud and happy-- stuff, stuff, stuff-- to talent. I've got that, Edie! It's just that other bit about veterans and richer traditions, or something."

"That's not Lover Beyond," Cass said blankly. "I know every line--"

But Asey had already pushed open the door and was striding into the minute living-room.

His first reaction was that he must have entered the wrong cottage, for the Stage's Favorite Couple looked considerably different with their hair down-- and off, he mentally added, as he spotted McClay's toupe sitting on a table in front of him. Edith Hamilton, in a soiled green bathrobe and a pair of green harlequin glasses, whose wide bows were mended with adhesive tape, was hardly recognizable as the well-dressed and self-assured individual who'd stepped out of the beach wagon by the Town Hall. McClay, stripped down to yellow shorts, sat on a stool and chewed a pencil like a tired, elderly schoolboy. The air was thick with cigarette smoke, and the floor around the wicker couch where Edie sat was littered with papers.

"I'm sorry to bother you like this," Asey said smoothly before either of them could speak, "but on behalf of the state police, I'm investigatin' a serious accident that happened to one of the Jackstraw Company. Now, when you two cut across the fields back to the inn a while ago before lunch, you found Bette Wood lyin' unconscious in the pine grove, didn't you?"

McClay looked wistfully at his toupe, as if he yearned to put it on and run, but Edie assumed an expression of deep anguish, rose from the couch, and extended her arms in a dramatic gesture.

"But she was only sleeping!" she said in her throaty voice. "She was sound asleep! We never dreamed that she might be unconscious. We'd taken a wrong path and were hurrying back here when we saw her. We tiptoed over and looked at her, and then just tiptoed away again. Oh, if we'd ever dreamed there'd been any sort of accident, you can be sure that the thought of the resulting publicity would never have deterred us from getting help for the poor child at once. Never! But how frightful for her. Is she at all seriously hurt?"

"She's recovered." The literal translation of all that, Asey thought to himself, was that Hamilton and McClay very well knew that Bette was unconscious when they peered down at her, but they weren't the ones to stick their selfish necks out into any hint of unpleasantness or trouble. And you couldn't prove it, or disprove it, either. "Now," he went on, "about Dilly Currier--"

"I cannot tell you," McClay said promptly, as if her name were a cue, "how proud and happy we both are to have had the privilege of discovering Dilly Currier's great talent. As veterans of an older and if I may say so, richer tradition of the theater, I-- we--"

While he floundered, Asey picked up the paper which had been lying in front of McClay on the table. "We feel," he read, recognizing Edie's sprawling handwriting from Mrs. Jenks phone message, "'that at the height of our long, full careers, it is only fitting that we introduce to the world this new, brilliant, and so unique, star.' And stuff, stuff, stuff! Uh-huh. I can read the rest of what you think about Dilly Currier right from this paper. Now, tell me all about this lunch date of yours. Who'd you expect as a guest?"

"Really," Edie said haughtily, "I quite fail to see why we have any need to answer."

"You missed the name, darling," Cass interrupted. "He's Mayo, of the detecting Mayos. So speak right up and tell him."

"But Cass, darling, we just don't know! Last night we had a phone call, very late, from some man who wanted to see us at once, but he wasn't a reporter or anyone we knew, so we ignored him. But this morning he kept calling, and finally he said it was in connection with Dilly, and he had something of the greatest importance to tell us about her. And of great interest. So--"

"So, hoping wildly that it might be an item of value to you," Cass said, "you at once asked him to lunch. Yes, indeed! Nothing like a wee bit of blackmail to dangle over the head of a new protege and keep her toeing the line."

"Cass, how dreadfully unkind!" Edie sounded as if she were going to cry. "With Dilly's best interest foremost in our minds, naturally we wanted to take advantage of all the angles useful for her publicity."

"What," Asey said, "was the name of this man?"

"I keep telling you, I don't know. I couldn't understand it. He had the most frightful diction. He spelled it out, but all I could make of it was Logo-something!"

"I thought more Coco-something when I talked with him," McClay put in defensively.

Asey shook his head at Cass as the latter started to speak. "Okay. One more thing, Miss Hamilton. D'you remember taking a phone message for Mrs. Jenks?"

"Oh, distinctly! Something about her not coming somewhere."

"What time did the message come?"

"My dear man, I haven't the vaguest idea about time."

"Was it a woman's voice," Asey asked.

"Oh, yes! Definitely! Or was it?" Edie frowned. "Oh, I really don't recall."

"Okay. Now, you're not to leave here tor any reason unless you go over to the theater. It's for your own safety." Asey added that lie solely to forestall any complaints. "Good-by."

Outside the cottage, Cass glared at him. "Why did you drop them in mid-air like that? You're not going to let 'em get away with this, are you?"

"If they know more, I bet Edie's written 'em lines to fit. Don't worry. If anything tangible turns up, I'll jump on 'em hard enough. Doggone, I been hopin' maybe I could hook King-size up with 'em somehow-- like his bein' their lunch date!"

"Hook who?"

"King-size. Tall, dark fellow," Asey said. "Oversized job with a baby face."

"Hey!" Cass said. "Hey! That's the one who was bothering Dilly last night after the show!"

Asey grabbed his arm. "Go on!"

"There's nothing much to go on about," Cass said. "This big, dark lad was pushing his way through the crowd around the dressing-rooms towards Dilly, and she asked me to keep him away from her. I just think he was pestering her--"

"Asey!" The screen door slammed behind Dr. Cummings as he hurried out to the terrace. "I had no idea where you were till Jennie phoned a few minutes ago," he said irritably. "How d'you expect things to get organized? The state cops came-- I sent one over to the fair, thinking you'd be there, and one's waiting at my place. Where've you been? What're you doing?"

"Tryin'," Asey said, "to find out about a big, dark man. Don't you think Dilly knew him, Cass?"

"She didn't call him by name, and that hulking brute of a St. Bernard certainly didn't bear any family resemblance to her."

"Oh, that fellow!" Cummings said with a snort. "That great, hulking oaf!"

"An' what do you know about him, Doc?"

"I told you I was delayed getting to the hall because I stopped to direct a tourist. It was that hulking oaf."

"But what makes you think it was the same fellow Cass was talkin' about?" Asey persisted.

"Why not? Can't be an indefinite number of big, dark brutes of St. Bernards around," Cummings retorted. "The fellow couldn't tell north from south, and he was trying to find his way over here to the inn. Had a lunch date, he said. You'd think he was trying to find the South Seas--" He broke off. "What's biting her?" He pointed to Jennie, who was running toward them from the inn.

"What's the matter?" Asey said quickly. "What's wrong?"

"I don't know what's wrong, that's what's the matter! I had a terrible time getting the theater, and finally Mary Longworth answered and said 'Hello'-- and then there was nothing! I've waited and waited, and the operator says there's nothing wrong with the line, so something must've happened to Mary."

"Where's your car? Out front?" Asey said to Cummings. "Come along!"

Jennie and Cass piled into the sedan with them and they sped wildly to the Jackstraw Theater.

"Phone's in the box office," Cass said as he and Asey jumped out and raced inside. "You look there. I'll go backstage."

Their footsteps rang hollowly through the empty, musty-smelling barn theater as they joined Jennie and the doctor in the lobby five minutes later.

"She's not here!" Cass said. "I don't understand it. What number did you call? Two-ten or three-ten?"

"Goodness, I called the first number in the book," Jennie said. "I don't know which one. Why's everything so deserted here? Isn't Wednesday the matinee?"

"Thursday," Cass said. "And the kids went off on a sailing picnic. Let's try the house, Mayo. She must have answered one of the house phones."

Finally they found Mary lying in the hall on the second floor of the old Ross place.

"She's dead!" Jennie's voice rose to a scream.

Mary raised her head, looked at her dourly, and experimentally felt her jaw. "Not dead; just wishing I were. That big ox gave me a clip on the jaw that knocked me down and took my breath away. It was the same fellow who was bothering Dilly last night, Cass. But I'm all right. Go see what's he's done to Jack!"

"Where are they?"

"Chasing each other around like comic strip characters! Hurry-- find them!"

Some fifteen minutes later, down by the shore of the inlet, Asey spotted the inert figure of King-size stretched out on the beach. Beside him sat a slight, scholarly-looking young man with horn-rimmed glasses.

"Congratulations, Mr. Straw!" Asey said with honest respect. "How'd you manage?"

"Unfair practices. I caught him with a rock. You're Mayo, aren't you? Did Mary call you? I've been wondering if you were the man to go to if it turned out I'd killed him. He's been like this for some time."

"Give me your belt," Asey said briskly as he removed his own. "I know King-size. It's refreshing to have him out cold, but I'll feel better when he's also bound up snug. What happened?"

"Actually, I don't know. I came into the house"-- he nodded in the direction of Ross's-- "and heard noises, and found him knocking Mary around....Is she all right? Unhurt?...Good!" Jack got to his feet. "Look; I wonder if you could wait here and cope with this fellow till the police come? I've absolutely got to locate a girl, one of our company, right away."

"If it's Bette," Asey said, "she's all right, too."

"Thank God!" Jack sat down again. "You know, I left her hours ago in the woods, all decked out as a scarecrow."

"Uh-huh. I know. What happened to you after you left her?"

"I ran into him." Jack pointed to King-size. "He didn't recognize me, but I recognized him as the lad who was pestering Dilly Currier after the show last night. He asked me the way to the Black Whale Inn, and I told him, and then he asked me where the Jackstraw Theater was. I said if he had any more ideas about trying to annoy Dilly, he could forget 'em-- and that's all!"

"All what?" Asey inquired.

"Just all! I came to in a truck full of cranberries."

Asey looked at him quizzically. "I think, Mr. Straw, that cranberries is maybe carryin' local color a bit too far."

"I said cranberries," Jack told him firmly, "and I mean cranberries! I couldn't get out. The rear doors were bolted, and there wasn't any opening to the driver's seat, and he didn't hear all my banging. Finally we stopped at a cranberry storage place up the Cape, and I got out."

"Whereabouts?"

"East or West Quisset-- I never stopped to find out which," Jack said. "I just rushed over to the main road and thumbed my way back here as fast as I could. Oh, I've been sick with worry about Bette! First I looked around in the pines where I'd left her, and all I found was her handbag. Then I rushed over here-- and into this mess!"

"I kind of wonder," Asey drawled, "why you didn't phone for someone to locate her."

Jack blinked. "It never entered my head to phone!"

"Funny," Asey said. "I think I'd have called the theater the first chance I got, an' asked 'em to send out a posse after the girl. On the other hand, I don't think I could dream up a yarn like your cranberry-truck job if I beat my brains out. Takes dramatic ability to figure out a sequence where nobody could possibly prove whether you was lyin' or tellin' the truth."

"What are you driving at, Mayo?"

"Wa-el, you may be interested to know that at some time durin' your cranberry outin', Dilly Currier was--"

"I'm not interested," Jack interrupted coldly, "in anything concerning Dilly. She's chosen to leave our company."

"But I think," Asey said, "you'll be interested in her murder in spite of yourself. I think you better do some quick guessin' as to which Quisset town you stopped at, an' I think you better remember lots of details about the cars you thumbed your way back here in. I think you'd better write it down for me. Soon!"

"Dilly was-- murdered?" Jack continued to stare at him openmouthed, as Cummings and Jennie and Cass and Mary came streaming down the path.

"So you got him!" Jennie said. "Asey, we found out what he was doing-- ransacking Dilly's room! Mary heard him, and dropped the phone to see what all the racket above her was, and he hit her when she walked in on him. Tell him, Mary!"

"You've told him what matters," she said. "He was clearly after something of Dilly's-- the other rooms weren't touched. With the name cards on the doors, he had no trouble locating hers."

"See, he was after more papers!" Jennie said excitedly.

"What do you mean, more papers?" Asey asked.

"Why, he must have been the one who took all the papers out of her pocketbook, Asey! The personal ones, I mean!"

"An' what leads you to those conclusions?"

"Why, I looked through the bag, of course," she retorted. "While I was trying to get Mary on the phone, over at the inn, I just thumbed through things. There's plenty of papers-- bills, and receipts, and post cards, and fan letters. But nothing you'd ever call personal. Which was a funny thing, since the girls use those bags as safes-- better'n locking doors and forgetting keys, they argue. I just figured, then, that somebody'd taken out the personal things. And if this fellow ransacked her bag, I guess you can figure he ransacked her room, too."

"Only a woman," Asey said, "can figure anything from another woman's handbag. I handled every last item in Dilly's bag, but I didn't even try to assess 'em....Huh. Let's see!"

Kneeling down beside King-size, he systematically rifled the pockets of the tan gabardine suit-- and came up with one thin leather wallet!

"Is that all?" Jennie asked disappointedly. "I suppose he's hidden the papers. Is his name in the wallet?"

"Uh-huh," Asey said. "He's Bobo Currier."

Cass let out a yell. "Hey! Logo-something. Coco-something-- Remember what Edie and Ken said? Bobo Currier! Why didn't Dilly ever mention having a brother?"

"Maybe because he's her husband," Asey said. "Here's the

marriage license."

Jennie sighed with relief. "There!" she said. "Now that's all settled. Her husband killed her for some papers, and all you got to do is find out where he's hidden 'em."

"I'd watch Bobo!" Cummings said suddenly. "I think he's coming to."

With a quick motion, Asey grabbed the doctor's stethoscope from the pocket of his coat. He dug it in the small of Bobo's back as the latter sat up.

"That's a gun, Currier!" he said. "What was it you wanted from Dilly?"

"None of your business! Who beaned me? The little guy with the glasses? I'll get him--"

"Okay, Doc," Asey said. "Phone the state cop at your place to come arrest Currier for his wife's murder!"

Bobo's reaction stunned them all. "Gee! You mean Dilly's dead?" he asked in a pleased voice. "Gee! That settles everything! I don't need a divorce, and I get my dough back, and I can marry Isobel."

"Not when you're in jail for killin' Dilly," Asey said.

"I didn't kill her! I didn't even see her except at the show last night, and then she wouldn't let me talk to her."

Asey looked at him sharply. "What were you goin' to tell Edith Hamilton an' McClay about her?"

"Gee, nobody let me get anywhere near Dilly," Bobo said in aggrieved tones, "and I thought if I could tell those two about everything, and ask 'em to talk to her for me, maybe she'd give me the divorce, and give me back my dough so I could marry Isobel."

"Who the hell is Isobel?" Cummings demanded.

"The girl I want to marry! I told her all about how Dilly and I met at that bar that afternoon and got married that night, and how she called me her wonderful hunk of man and all, and how when I came back out of the service we were going to have a little white house with green blinds and all, and how I sent all my dough to her. Then, when I came back, she wasn't there and I couldn't find her, or my dough!"

"Let's get this straight," Asey said. "You married her, went overseas, sent her money, an' came back to find her gone. Do you mean you haven't seen her since you came home?"

"Not since that night we got married. I went next day," Bobo said. "When I came back to the rooming house, they just said she'd gone. I never found any trace of her till I saw her picture on that poster yesterday, from the bus I was on."

"You know what?" Cummings said to Asey. "I have the most extraordinary feeling he's telling the truth! Er-- what've you done since you got out of the Army, Bobo, besides hunting Dilly and courting Isobel?"

"I go to schools," Bobo said simply. "The first ones were too

hard, but the one I'm starting next month, everybody gets passed. It's
for doormen."

"I'm inclined to agree with you, Doc," Asey said. "It's got to be
the truth!...Bobo, why'd you knock out Jack Straw?"

"This little guy with the glasses? Gee, I was so tired of people
saying I couldn't see Dilly! I was sorry afterwards," he added
contritely. "There was a truck there by the field, so I put him in it so
somebody'd find him and take care of him."

"I see. An' then you found a girl knocked out?"

"Gee, yes! I thought I should ought to get somebody to look after
her, but then I was afraid after the little guy that somebody might
claim I hit her too, see?"

"Uh-huh. Did you open up that red bag you found?"

"Gee, no. I only picked it up just before I seen you and the girl.
I'd have given it back when she said it was hers, only she recognized
me and told you I stole it."

"Why'd you clip her?" Asey nodded toward Mary. "Just because
she got in your way?"

"Gee, I was so sore! I couldn't find the Whale place, or Dilly, or
my dough in her room. I'm sorry-- but I never hit her hard! Will I get
my dough back?"

"If you promise to do exactly as you're told, we'll see what can
be done," Asey said.

Back at the Ross house, Cummings followed Asey into one of the
first-floor sitting-rooms, and threw himself onto a chintz-covered
couch. "That stupid oaf!" he said. "If he couldn't locate the inn
when he was practically standing on it-- oh, you can eliminate him
from your calculations. Asey, I never saw such a mess!"

"You should talk from your comfortable side-lines seat!" Asey
picked up Dilly's bag from the table, where Jennie had apparently left
it, and unbuckled the side clasp. "Listen to my side of it!"

Cummings frowned at the conclusion of Asey's recital. "Edie and
Ken stand to gain most from her death," he said. "Unquestionably.
But I'll wager it was Jack she goaded the most."

Asey nodded. "From the way he froze when I mentioned her
name, I guessed that contract-tearin' scene was a rip-roarin' blowup,
with Dilly crackin' high, wide, an' handsome."

"Probably she slashed him and his outfit to the core," Cummings
said, "and Jack takes both very, very seriously! Hm. Mary's always
fussed about Dilly, but last year fussed just as much about the girl
who played lead. Mary doesn't spare her claws. And if this had
happened in June, I'd think more about Bette. After Dilly supplanted
her, Bette had a couple of nervous kick-ups which she and I tactfully
called 'nervous indigestion.' She took it hard-- Asey, that business
about Bette in the woods confuses me a lot. How d'you figure that?"

"I've decided it was a sort of double-take. Someone kills Dilly,
grabs her bag, rushes out the fire escape, an' runs plumb into Bette in

the pines, dressed up like a scarecrow, lookin' just like Dilly! You'd already killed her-- an here she is again. Get it?"

Cummings whistled softly. "And how! It would've taken the hair off my head, if it'd been me. So whoever killed Dilly biffed Bette out of sheer panic, probably with a rock, and took off the mask to see who it was-- then jammed that hat back on without bothering to fuss with the mask."

Asey nodded. "Hey, this is funny, Doc! I've just pawed through Dilly's bag twice-- an' no bankbook. It's gone!"

"Bobo's work-- No!" Cummings promptly corrected himself. "No, he hasn't been in here! I remember Jennie slung the bag down while we were hunting for Mary when we first came....Good God, Asey! Cass was the only other person here!"

"Huh!" Asey said. "Wa-el, maybe it did seem like a good idea to swipe it. Nobody could know that I knew every last thing in the bag, an' nobody could ever reckon on Jennie's just 'thumbing' through everything. Jennie'll know the balance in that bankbook down to the last penny!"

Asey stood up. "Doc, call the cop over from your place, an' keep Bobo from mayhem."

"And where are you going?" Cummings demanded.

"To find out the balance from Jennie," Asey said. "Then I'm goin' to the hall an' check up on a few odds an' ends-- before I come back here."

As the Town Hall clock finished striking eight, the auctioneer on the stage banged his gavel until the noise and bustle of the fair subsided. Simultaneously, Asey propelled Jennie through the entrance, where they'd been waiting, and brought her to a halt on the outskirts of the crowd.

"This is the craziest thing I've ever heard of," she said crossly. "How do you know it'll be auctioned off first?"

"Because I arranged it. Pay attention, now!"

The hubbub arose again as Mary Longworth's old-fashioned red coffee mill with the side wheels was displayed to the crowd, and then the bidding for it began.

"Mary said this evening she didn't think she could part with that mill, after all," Jennie remarked. "She said she might bid it back. Hear that? She's already bidding!"

"You do what I said-- on the second 'Going!'"

"Seventeen-fifty from Miss Longworth!" the auctioneer's voice called hoarsely. "Going! Going--"

"One hundred dollars for Asey Mayo!" Jennie said at the top of her lungs. "There," she said conversationally. "Now what?"

"That's all," Asey said wearily. "Now, come on!"

"But why'd you make me bid for that old mill? We got one at home! And that's the craziest price....What on earth's the matter with Mary? Why is she--? Why, she can't walk out that window!"

"If she does, an' lives, the cops are waitin' for her."

"Asey! You mean that Mary--? Oh, I don't understand any of this, about the coffee mill or anything else."

"The mill's where Mary hid her dagger....Come out of this hubbub into the hall. She was awful stuck for time, Jennie. She sneaked in with Dilly an' killed her. She heard you talkin' to me at the back door, an' heard me start the car, an' thought we were goin', see? Then when she heard you comin' back with those flowers, she shoved the dagger into that coffee mill."

"But there's no dagger in that! I pulled out the drawer and looked in, and so did everybody else who went by."

"Uh-huh. But nobody bothered to lift off that heavy dome top," Asey said, "an' look inside the grinder!"

"If you knew it was inside all the time, why all this crazy business of bidding?"

"Because if I'd tried to confront her with the dagger, she'd only have denied it was hers," Asey said, "But her tryin' to buy the mill to get the dagger back is somethin' else again. An' when you made that bid for me, she knew the game was up. Remember, she mentioned that coffee mill the instant she came into the hall? She wanted to know right off if I suspected anything about it, or her. When she saw I didn't, she pretended it belonged in the Auction stuff, an' not on the Antique Table. That was quick thinkin'! She couldn't just buy the mill back right then, an' she didn't want anyone else to buy it, an' she saw the best chance was to keep it in the Auction things, an' bid it in later."

Jennie stared at him. "How'd you ever guess about her?'

"She was the only one of the crowd who knew you were takin' Cousin Eva's place an' who'd have started the message that kept Mrs. Jenks out of the way, with 'Jennie says'!...Think back. She was gettin' her fancy hair-do in the Beauty Shop when you got the call about comin' here because Eva had appendicitis!"

"Why, I forgot she was there, Asey!"

"So'd I, till I met her durin' the rain, when she was tryin' to keep her hair-do dry. I was sure of her after we found out about the message, but I couldn't figure why she did it. Even after you doped out that Dilly's personal papers were missin' from her bag, I still couldn't get it. But when the bankbook disappeared, I started to catch on."

"Which is more," Jennie said with a sniff, "than I do!"

"Wa-el, in June there was a hit-an'-run accident-- you know all about that? Mary was responsible. An' Dilly was in the car with her when it happened. In a panicky moment, Mary moved the body into the bushes, an' lied when it was found. But Dilly knew. That's how she started her career-- she got her apprentice job the next day. That's why she climbed so fast-- she blackmailed Mary. That's why she had such a tidy balance in her bankbook. Not from Bobo's allotments or from what she earned. She squeezed it out of Mary!"

"Oh, why didn't I think when I looked at those deposits!" Jennie said. "They always said at the Beauty Shop that the Jackstraw people weren't paid but a pittance! So Mary sneaked the book out of the bag when it was on the sitting-room table. I suppose she forgot it when she took out the papers. There were some, weren't there?"

"Yes. Dilly wrote down a very highly colored account of the accident," Asey said, "an' kept it with her. Probably she threatened to give it to those whose father was run over if Mary didn't keep on crashin' through. Now I'm guessin' at this part, but I think that after her triumph last night, Dilly really put the screws on Mary so she could set off to Hollywood in style. An' I think Mary decided not to take any more. Just stealin' those papers wouldn't help, because Dilly'd only write another account. Only way to put a stop to the squeeze was to kill the girl. So she did, with as smart schemin' as I ever run into. An' she got the papers, too."

"How do you know what's in them?" Jennie asked curiously.

"I had one tough job findin' 'em a few hours ago," Asey said. "The Doc nearly had apoplexy keepin' all of you out of my way till I fished the papers and the bankbook out from under Dilly's mattress. Mary stuck 'em there till she had a chance to burn 'em up-- but she never got the chance. When she heard Bobo ransacking Dilly's room, she rushed up to keep him from findin' the papers-- and got knocked out for her pains."

"But how'd she get Dilly to play scarecrow?"

"Lured her with talk about publicity pictures. She must have had the same idea Jack did--" He broke off as Mrs. Jenks came swishing up to them.

"There's been the most awful accident!" she said. "Mary Longworth fell out of a window, and she's fatally hurt, but the committee's asked us to carry on for the good of the fair. Wouldn't you like to take a chance and figure the number of beans in this jar? The prize is a copy of the play Lover Beyond, autographed personally by Edith Hamilton and Kenneth McClay!"

"Thanks," Asey said, "but I think I done enough figurin' at this fair! Come on, Jennie; let's finally go home!"

The HOODED HAWK

BY HERBERT BREAN

ILLUSTRATION BY GEOFFERY BIGGS

Ken knelt down and began making
calculations with his tape measure

Herbert Brean (1907-1973) was not a notably prolific mystery novelist, producing seven novels, beginning with the memorable Wilders Walk Away, and a handful of shorter pieces between 1948 and 1966. His major career was in journalism-- at various times he worked for United Press, the Detroit Times, and Life magazine-- and his most successful book was How to Stop Smoking (1951). But his mysteries, many in the locked-room, impossible-crime vein of John Dickson Carr and Clayton Rawson, were excellent enough to gain him a term as President of Mystery Writers of America. "The Hooded Hawk" (November 1949) is notable for the scrupulous fair play clueing that marked Brean's novels as well as for its rarely employed background of the car business. (Brean's appropriate birthplace was Detroit.) It's amazing to remember (or discover) how scarce new American cars were in the years immediately after World War II and the lengths to which some were willing to go to jump the waiting list.

THE HOODED HAWK by Herbert Brean

All day a warm, cloying air mass had hung over that part of Ohio. By late afternoon there was a hint of storm, and the crowds that packed the Hawk agency in Sheffield to see the new 1950 Hawk automobiles had left early, fearful of being trapped by a sudden rain. But the storm held off. Darkness fell. Then, at just ten o'clock, it broke with sudden fury, a roaring swirl of rain and wind and lightning.

On the outskirts of Sheffield, a Hawk convertible drew up before a neat Cape Cod bungalow. A young man leaped out, ran around, made a shelter of his raincoat, and escorted a dark-haired, slim-legged girl up the flagstone walk. They arrived at the front door laughing and breathless, and were greeted by a blond woman whose face was so evenly, so perfectly featured that some people, meeting her for the first time, mistakenly thought they had seen her in minor movie roles.

"Hi, Helen!" said Ken Wilson, as he helped the girl with him take off her jacket. "You tending door tonight?"

Helen Craig laughed the laugh she reserved for the witticisms of

attractive young men. "I guess I am, temporarily....Hello, Jane."
This in the disdainful tone Mrs. Craig used for younger women.

"Sorry we're so late. All my fault, of course," said Ken. "Are
you dry, honey?"

Jane Robbins smiled. "All but my legs. Those big feet of yours
splashed me good....Hi, Helen. Where're the O'Haras?"

"Your hostess is fixing cheese things and beer. Your host is
trying to turn his furnace into an air conditioner. They'll be along in
a minute." Helen Craig's hand went to her perfectly coifed head in
mechanical motion. "Gordon's in the living-room. Come on in. Isn't
it warm?"

But having started Jane Robbins toward the living-room, Helen
Craig turned back and spoke in a low voice to Ken Wilson, hanging
the wet coats in the closet: "Is Carney at the agency?"

Ken looked surprised. "Of course not. Should he be?"

Carney Craig was the owner of the Hawk automobile agency in
Sheffield and Ken was his sales manager. Helen Craig was Carney's
wife. Carney was fat, fiftyish, and, outwardly at least, placidly
good-humored. His wife was still in her early thirties, very youthful
in face and figure and waspish in temperament-- at least, where
Carney was concerned. Her present anxiety, therefore, was surprising.

"I guess-- Oh, I don't know what's the matter with me. Of
course, you must have left the agency an hour ago."

"Well, as a matter of fact..." Ken took a package of cigarettes
from his pocket and looked at her speculatively. "Smoke? I left
there an hour ago. And Carney had been gone some time then. He
said he had to drive over to Lawrenceville. It happens I went back to
the agency since, though."

"Why?"

"Oh-- it wasn't important."

"But it couldn't wait until morning?"

She essayed one of her coquettish smiles, but suddenly she
ground out the cigarette he had given her and turned away. From the
living-room beyond came the murmur of conversation between Jane
and Gordon Birmingham.

"What's the matter, Helen?" asked Ken sharply.

"Oh, I don't know-- I don't know at all." He was shocked to
discover that she was close to tears. "It must be this weather. I've
felt it all day. I'm glad it's storming. Maybe it'll clear the air! But I
wish Carney would get here. I knew he was going to Lawrenceville,
but he should be back by now.

He took her by the arm. "Nerves," he said. "That's all. Come in
the living-room."

She flung his arm away. "It isn't nerves! It's just-- Oh, Ken,
why would someone who didn't like him call Carney up at three in the
morning?"

She was holding him by the arm, talking in a low, tense voice as if she didn't want anyone to hear her.

"Tell me, Ken, what's <u>wrong</u>?"

"Why, nothing," he said.   "The premiere came off just as we planned. The new building is working out fine. Business is good. We wrote fourteen orders today, and we'll do better tomorrow; the threat of rain drove them away."

"It isn't that!" She made an impatient gesture; the madonna-like face seemed haloed by fear. "Ken, this happened a week ago. A week ago last night, it was. I always sleep well. But suddenly I woke up-- I don't know why. I hadn't heard anything, as far as I know! It was after three." Her voice sank to almost a whisper.

From the kitchen, Eileen O'Hara called, "I'm coming, good people!"

"Our twin beds are side by side. Carney was not in his. I called his name. Then I heard his voice, far away. He was talking on the phone downstairs.

"We have an extension in the bedroom. I picked the phone up. I heard someone say, 'How'd you like the company to know what you've been up to?' There was a long silence.   Then another voice said, 'We're still in business. We'll discuss that tomorrow night.' One hung up. Then the other hung up. I heard the two clicks.

"I turned out my light and waited for Carney to come back to bed, but he didn't. I lay there, wondering what it meant. I suppose I finally dozed off, because a long time after I heard him sigh as he climbed in and pulled the covers up. It woke me up, and I began to wonder if I had really heard it. Because--"

"Because why?" he asked, to be polite. Not because he needed her to tell him. He could understand a lot of people asking Carney Craig if he wanted the Hawk Motorcar Company to know what he'd been doing.

But Helen Craig was white and trembling. All because of a conversation she had overheard. He smiled reassuringly.

The smile didn't work. "You didn't hear that voice," she shuddered. "It was terrible! I'm not even sure it was Carney talking. He sounded so different-- horrible-- if it was Carney."

"It was undoubtedly some dope complaining about his car or something."

"Maybe you're right. It-- Oh, I don't know why it suddenly started bothering me tonight. But somehow it sounded so terrible-- so deadly at the time."

He gave her a friendly push and she smiled at him, wanly, but still the old, self-conscious Helen Craig smile, and he followed her into the living-room.

It hadn't occurred to her that if the call had come from some crank complaining about his Hawk or about Carney Craig's service, the telephone would have rung in the bedroom and awakened her. Obviously, this was a call that Carney had made. Had it been Carney making the threat, or someone else?

So what? And tomorrow he wouldn't be working for Carney Craig.

"Hi, Gordon," he said to the slight, well-tailored man who had been sitting with Jane.

Gordon Birmingham said, "Hi, kid; how many'd you sell?"

Ken grinned. "Only fourteen, Gordon. But we'll do better tomorrow."

Birmingham chuckled, a middle-aged man whom golf kept slim and a pleasant sense of humor kept youthful.

"You better," he said. "Brother, how nice it is to get back to the good old days of the postwar, when you could sell everything you could make, and the only headache was getting steel." He sighed elaborately and everyone laughed.

Gordon Birmingham was the biggest success story Sheffield had ever produced. The son of a poor widow, he had gone to Detroit, a scant 200 miles away, and had risen through the years to become production chief of the Hawk Motorcar Company. Now back home on one of his infrequent vacation trips, he was the house guest of the Craigs.

Eileen O'Hara, a tiny girl in a tinier apron, came in bearing a huge tray of hors d'oeuvres. A moment later, bearing a second tray with bottles, Eddie O'Hara came in, grinning happily, a tall, heavy-set redhead. He was the Craig agency's service boss.

He distributed glasses to everyone, and then sank into a chair and said, "Hey, Ken, what delayed you?"

"'Business' is what he told me," said Jane Robbins. She had blue eyes and blue-black hair and a profile whose perfection did not stop at her firm little chin. "Where were you really, darling? I mean, I know it was another woman, but which one this time?"

Ken took her hand, sipped his beer, and then lay back in the deep chair. It was nothing that should get around town, he reflected. But all these people would know about it sooner or later. Carney especially. Where was Carney?

"Well," he said, "after I closed up the place, I went home to change before picking up Jane and coming over here. I was just putting on a clean shirt when Lu Trowbridge called me."

"Lu Trowbridge!" said Eddie.

"Who's that?" asked Gordon Birmingham.

"The sheriff. You must remember him, Gordon."

The telephone rang.

"There he is now," grinned Eddie O'Hara, and he went to the phone in the hall.

"What?" they heard him say. Then, "Yes, sure. Sure, Lu." He hung up.

When he came back in the room, he wore a strange expression. "It was Lu Trowbridge," he said. He looked from one to another, as though he could not believe what he was saying. "He wants you down to the agency right away, Ken. Something's happened. There's--

Someone is dead."

His indirect stumbling conjured more fear than any simple statement could have. Helen Craig's eyes widened. She suddenly screamed, "It's Carney!"

Ken leaped to his feet. "Eddie! Is it?"

But Eddie O'Hara shook his head. "No, it's Frank Fliel. Trowbridge just found him outside our agency. His head's all smashed in."

"Oh, no!" cried Jane. "It can't be. Poor Vera Fliel-- with all those children!"

"Fliel," said Birmingham. "Isn't he that nasty little son-of-a-gun you had a few words with this afternoon, Ken?"

"Yes. And I'd have had a few more with him if I had seen him tonight. He tried to plaster the agency with a big sign saying the Hawk is no good. That's what delayed me."

Birmingham's face hardened. "Good riddance, I'd say."

Eddie O'Hara said, "We'll go down with you, Ken."

Helen Craig said, "Where in the world is Carney?" Her voice fluttered with fear.

Frank Fliel had been a small, thin man, with graying hair and a hatchet face. He had never amounted to much in Sheffield, until the war. Fliel enlisted early, and then suddenly he was a national hero. There had been many newspaper stories date-lined Guadalcanal and Kwajalein, lauding his almost neurotic courage and his incredible sharpshooting skill with any kind of gun. Badly wounded at last, after being repeatedly decorated, he had returned, bemedaled and honored, and had since tried to support his wife, his taste for whisky, and his growing brood of children on a scraggly chicken farm well beyond the city limits.

He had ordered a Hawk panel truck, which he had never received because Carney Craig had seen to it that what few panel trucks came through from Detroit went to whoever happened to be offering the highest price at the time. This was in keeping with the Craig sales policies, and Fliel finally had angrily taken back his deposit on the order.

Death had dealt terribly with Fliel's face. It had always worn a sly expression suggesting a slightly dissolute fox. But the heavy tire iron that had been sunk into his brain had first been smashed against his jaw, leaving it set in an expression of demoniac leer. The rain had made his clothing sodden and was still sending bloody rivulets down his cheek.

Ken said, "How did you-- how did you happen to find him?" and saw that the sheriff was looking at him speculatively.

Behind the sheriff a deputy was painstakingly measuring distances from Fliel's head and feet to the smooth stucco wall of the new agency building.

"You told them about the sign, Ken?" asked the sheriff, gesturing toward Birmingham and Eddie O'Hara.

"I was just about to when you called."

"Someone started to put a big sign up on the agency here tonight," said Lu Trowbridge. He was a big, bulky man with iron-gray hair and deeply creased felt hat. "The sign sort of insulted Hawk automobiles-- and Hawk dealers. I happened to be driving by on patrol and scared the guy off. I saw him running across the fields in the dark. It looked like Frank Fliel. Now I'm sure it was.

"I got to wondering whether he might not come back-- Frank was a persistent cuss, you know. He proved that on Guadalcanal. So, next time around, I drove up into the driveway. My headlights hit that window and it reflected their light back on the lawn, right on Fliel's body lying there in the dark. Otherwise I'd never have seen it."

"I guess there's no doubt that he was murdered," said Birmingham.

The sheriff sniffed. "That's for sure, if you study the angle he was hit from. Someone came up from behind and hit to kill. But let's go inside. I'd like to see if he got in or anything was disturbed."

"I have a key," said Ken. "And just for the record I'd like to account for my movements tonight. Fliel certainly gave me reason to want to do something to him. But--"

"Sure, sure," said the sheriff absently. "Let's go in." And when they were inside the salesroom he said, "Everything looks okay in here. You fellows stay here. I'll just smooch around a little."

He returned in a couple of minutes and they went back outside.

"Nothin's disturbed in there at all," he frowned. He pulled a big, curved-stem pipe from his pocket, packed it, lighted it thoughtfully, and said, "I'm going to wait here for that state policeman. Ken, why don't you give me that account of your movements now."

Ken leaned against the cool stucco wall of the building agency, out of the steady drizzle of rain. "I'll begin at the beginning," he said.

There had been so much to do that afternoon that he had not even left the agency for a sandwich until close to 4 p.m. That had been the hour set by the Hawk company for every one of its dealers all over the country to unveil the new cars; a widely publicized "premiere" suitably dramatized by a radio program and tantalizing advertisements.

When Ken returned from his brief lunch, Helen Craig, Birmingham, Carney Craig, Eddie O'Hara, and the several salesmen were standing in the big salesroom. The new Hawks stood like white-sheeted ghosts around the floor, and, outside, dozens of curious townspeople pressed noses against the salesroom's big plate-glass window.

"You had me worried," Craig called in his best good-humored manner. "Can't be late today, you know, Ken. Turn up the radio, somebody. It's nearly four."

Ken had put his fingers on the bolt of the front door. Behind him the others stood one to a car, ready to strip off the wrappings. The courthouse clock hoarsely boomed 4 p.m.

"Let's go," called Carney Craig.

Even above the rattle of the bolt and the first surge inside, he heard the murmur of appreciation as the white gowns slipped from the new cars' gleaming flanks. The Hawk had been widely heralded as the most advanced line yet in postwar engineering and styling, and the first glimpse at least had not disappointed the crowd. But as they pushed past Ken, it seemed that many turned to look at him as though to say, "Sure, they're beautiful-- but I wish you weren't selling them, chiseler."

He shrugged the feeling off and pushed toward his desk through the crowd. If all went well...

Landseer, Hawk's newest and fastest-moving rival in the low-price field, was planning to establish a dealership in Sheffield, and, some time before, Ken had quietly started negotiations to try to get it. At the thought of what that could mean to him and to Jane Robbins, he smiled. Then he'd show the town what sort of automobile dealer he really was!

"What about this coupe?" a man demanded. "When can I get one."

"We're taking orders on the basis of delivery within a month. It might be less. Production is just getting under way."

"A month! How many heaters and fog lights and radios do you have to order with it?" The man's mouth twisted into a bitter smile.

The grim look returned to Ken's chin as he pushed on. The crowd was especially thick around the pearl-gray convertible. He passed a familiar blue-serge-clad back, and heard Carney Craig say, "We got them to you as fast as we could, Woodie. I know that Ken did everything he could to--"

"Maybe there's things you don't know, Carney," said the other man.

Ken acted as though he hadn't heard. Working his way around the new four-door sedan, he encountered Helen Craig arm in arm with Birmingham. "And less than eight months ago all we had was hammer models," Birmingham was saying.

"Hammer models? What are they?" she asked wonderingly.

"It's the first full-size model of a new car in metal," Birmingham explained. "It's hammered out of a steel sheet over a full-size wooden mock-up. Usually, it's a year at least between--"

Ken had finally reached his desk. His phone was ringing. Katie, who was secretary to Carney Craig and was also the agency's switchboard operator, said, "Detroit's been trying to reach you. A Mr. McDonald."

Ken's heart stopped. McDonald was the Landseer regional sales manager.

There was a series of distant clicks. Then, "Hello, hello?" said a quick, irritated voice. "That you, Wilson?"

"Yes." Ken glanced around nervously. With customers and one of his own salesmen standing near by, this was a bad time to be discussing business with Hawk's chief rival.

"I suppose you fellows are pretty busy right now," McDonald said, "so I'll be brief. I'll be in Sheffield tomorrow to sign the papers for your Landseer agency. We've decided you're the man we want, Wilson, and we're mighty glad to have you with us...Hello? Are you there?"

He couldn't talk. He forgot about the people around his desk, about where he was, about everything except that it had come. He was free of Carney Craig, free to show the town what--

"Wilson!" the man on the phone barked. "Did you hear me?"

"Yes, I heard you, Mr. McDonald. You'll be here tomorrow."

"Right. We can iron out the financing then. You still want to put in ten thousand, right?...Okay. We can arrange-- Well no need to go into that now. I'll call you after I get in tomorrow. Good-by, Wilson. We know you'll do a fine job for Landseer."

"What'll that panel truck deliver for, mister?" said an overalled farmer. He looked at Ken oddly, and Ken suspected himself of smiling into empty space for some seconds.

"Panel truck? Oh, that panel truck." He took the man by the arm. "Let me just take you over and explain about that panel truck." He had never been happier in his life.

"That truck will deliver in Sheffield, with all taxes paid, license, heater, and grille guard, as you see it here, for twenty-one ninety-three," he said. "Beautiful, isn't it?"

"And an extra three hundred bucks for you, eh, Wilson?" said someone.

Ken wheeled. Frank Fliel stood behind him. Next to him was his wife, Vera. She looked anxiously at him.

"Soon's I get the dough together," Fliel went out, "I'll be in to take delivery on my truck-- the one I ordered three years ago."

He smiled at the people whose heads turned at the loud talk. "I'm going to have a new Hawk truck someday, too. I haven't been able to get it so far because I don't have no trade-in-- sold my car when I went into the Marines-- and I ain't got the money for Wilson's commission yet. So of course my name stays far down the list. Hey, Wilson?"

In the circle of people who had turned to listen, someone snickered. Ken felt his face go red and then white.

"Not that I really want a Hawk so bad," went on Fliel. "They really are a lousy car. I saw one just the other day-- last week it was-- parked in the lane behind my farm. You know, I got pretty good eyesight. Right away I saw something wrong with this car. And you know what it was?"

He paused for full effect. "Darned if the wheels aren't off center." He laughed loudly. The crowd snickered. "I mean it. I could tell by the fenders. The wheels were cockeyed, almost rubbing the fenders. Guess maybe they were rushing too many through the production line that day. But that's Hawk for you.

"I been waiting three years for a car," Fliel continued, "that's because I'm not a friend of Wilson's. Why should I be? A foot soldier never got acquainted with the air corps guys, believe me! We were out fighting!"

Ken pushed a customer out of his way, feeling rage well up inside of him.

Fliel also moved forward. His pale wife was a drag on his arm, but not enough. "We were out _fighting_," he repeated. "And I'm still man enough to tell any chiseling skunk--"

Vera Fliel cried, "Frank!" Ken's right arm, carrying his full weight with it, moved up-- and two blue-clad arms seized it in a grip of iron.

"Easy, son," said Carney Craig. "Fliel's drunk and you know it."

Ken tried to push Craig's big bulk away, but Carney had strength as well as bulk. And he was talking in a loud voice intended for the whole salesroom.

"Listen, Fliel; you can't come in here and abuse my men like that! We've never been able to get all the Hawks everyone wants since the war. You know that. Everyone knows it! Why"-- he put his arm on Ken's shoulder affectionately-- "the idea that Ken Wilson would accept a bribe is just too silly to anyone who knows him! He--"

Ken pushed savagely at the fat man and started again for Fliel.

This time he was stopped by a girl. "How about showing a girl the new cars, honey?" said Jane Robbins casually.

Carney Craig moved around her and grabbed Fliel's arm. "Get going, Frank," he ordered. "A little coffee'll fix him up, Mrs. Fliel. Have him come in and see me tomorrow morning and we'll see what we can do for him. That goes for anyone who wants to place an order," he added for the benefit of the others listening.

Jane took Ken's arm. "Well, what are we waiting for?" she asked brightly.

Ken permitted her to lead him to the chair behind his desk while she perched herself on the desk corner.

"Looks like the U.S. cavalry got here in the nick of time," she observed.

Ken looked up sardonically.

"I was the U.S. cavalry," she added explanatorily. "Don't you think so? Or don't you think so? And what _do_ you think, by the way?"

"Oh, shut up," he said. "Golly, it's going to be awful, being married to you."

Jane Robbins laughed. "That's what all my other husbands said. Tell me, if I'm not getting too inquisitive, what took place just now before I walked into Craig Sales and Service, New and Used Hawk Automobiles, We Repair All Makes?"

"Fliel was making a speech."

"About?"

"About the sales manager of Craig Sales and Service, New and Used Hawk Automobiles, We Repair All Makes."

The amusement in her face died. She leaned over to pick an imaginary speck from his lapel. "Oh, darling, I'm sorry."

"Don't be," he said. "I'm glad now I didn't hit him. It would have just advertised the whole rotten situation to all the town. And, what's worse, it might have gotten back to-- Hey!" He grabbed her arms. "The news!"

"What news?"

"Miss Robbins, allow me to present the owner of the Landseer Automobile Agency franchise in Sheffield."

"Oh, no," she said softly. "Oh, darling, I'm-- I'm so happy I think I'm going to cry."

"Don't," he said, and chucked her under the chin. "Everyone would know then that you are really happy, women being the contrary things they are. Then they might guess. And I'm keeping this a secret until the papers are signed tomorrow."

"Of course."

She blinked fast and smiled and squeezed his arm, as they both became aware that this tableau was being observed by some of the customers. "You can go back to work and sell Hawks-- while you can. Do you still think you'll close at nine tonight?"

"On the button. I should pick you up at nine-thirty."

"Good. It'll be a nice party, I think. Although any party I can get you to these days is a good party."

For the next two hours he worked his way around the sales floor several times, seeing that his salesmen were on the job, pausing to greet an old customer or two or to record the name of a new prospect.

As he worked, an idea slowly grew in his mind: Why not resign now? He had worked for months, helping get the new building ready for the premiere, but now everything was done. It was not an illogical time to leave, he thought, and by resigning before his own agency became public knowledge, he would separate the two in the public mind.

It was the dinner hour; the crowd had thinned out. Impulsively, he turned down the long corridor leading to Carney's office, passing the desk and switchboard where Katie sat during the daytime. He walked in without bothering to knock, and instantly regretted it.

It was like walking in on the climactic scene of a play. Helen Craig's shapely back was to him, arms akimbo, in the traditional attitude of determination, and the words she was addressing to her husband were in keeping.

"You can darned well give me the combination to that safe right now, cheap skate," Helen Craig declaimed doggedly, "or else you can take out insurance on my rings so I can keep them at home."

Black fury eclipsed Carney's big moon face. He deliberately poured himself a glass of water from the carafe on his desk, like a man trying to keep his temper, and his hands shook so much he made a clatter with the glass.

"If you think I'm going to give you the combination to the safe with all my business papers in it you're a fool! Why, even Birmingham told you that this afternoon when you brought it up. Why should I pay for insurance when--?"

He caught sight of Ken. "Well! What do you want?"

"Sorry. I wanted to see you about something. I guess it will keep." He started to close the door.

"Just a minute," Helen Craig called. She turned to her husband. "I'll leave it up to him. See what he says. Look, Ken. What do you think of a husband who makes his wife keep her jewels in his office safe rather than pay insurance, and then won't even give her the combination so that she get them when she wants to wear them?"

Carney Craig threw the glass at his wife. It was the measure of his rage, for its contents drenched the furniture and carpet. But the glass missed her and dropped unbroken to the carpet.

"Some day, Helen," said Carney Craig softly, "I'm going to kill you." His face contained lines Ken had never seen in it before.

He closed the door before she could again draw him into it and, turning, almost bumped into Eddie O'Hara. He caught Eddie by the arm. "Don't go in now. Carney's having wife trouble."

"Wife trouble isn't anything to what he's going to have," said Eddie wrathfully. "You know what he's done to me? He's ordered those cheap two-dollars-a-set rings for me to install in motors instead of regular Hawk rings, because he can save a buck a set on them. I'm going to tell that tight--"

Ken grabbed him. "Not now, Eddie. I'm telling you, it will do no good. Listen." He led the other away from the door, explaining the Craigs' quarrel. "Go on home," he ended. "You have guests coming tonight. Go home and put the beer on ice."

Eddie grinned sheepishly and went back to the garage.

It had been close to eight o'clock, when the threat of a storm had thinned out the crowd, that Ken noticed the man in black.

He was studying the business coupe with pursed lips, a tall, cadaverous figure in funereal black who carried a furled umbrella. Ken got the impression that he was waiting to be approached.

"Any information you'd like to have?" he asked cordially.

"Yes," said the man abruptly. "When can I get one?"

"We're taking orders on the basis of delivery in a month," said Ken. "It might be even sooner, of course, although we've already got a sizable waiting list."

The tall, thin man waved an impatient hand. "No, no. I need a car now. And I'm willing to pay for it."

Ken smiled understandingly. "Of course. Lots of people are."

Again the impatient gesture. "You misunderstand me. I'm willing to pay for one. I'd give a hundred dollars over the delivered price for a car like that if I could get it in less than a week. And if I could drive this one off the floor, I might go as high as two hundred."

"Sorry," said Ken stiffly. "That would be very unfair to our customers who signed up months ago. We don't do business that way."

A gleam appeared in the man's deep-set eyes. "Maybe I've been misinformed," he said. "Isn't your name Wilson?"

Ken flushed. "It is. And if you want a car, I'll be glad to put your name on the list. But you'll wait your turn like everyone else."

"Everyone?" said the man softly. "That isn't the way I heard it." He turned away.

The thunder was louder and more frequent now; lightning flashed and snapped steadily above the low, scudding clouds. When the closing hour finally came Ken was last to leave.

He had been putting on a clean shirt in his room, when the phone rang.

"Ken, this is Lu Trowbridge. Can you come down to the agency?"

"What's the matter, Lu?"

"Well, nothing to sound so alarmed about. But I can show you better than I can explain. You better step on it if you don't want to get caught in the storm that's blowing up."

He had stepped on it, and he saw what had caused Lu's call before his convertible braked to a stop in front of the modernistic sales agency.

"Guess somebody doesn't like you people so good," Lu said amiably.

Standing against the big plate-glass window of the showroom was a huge section of wallboard, hung with festoons of lemons. Someone had printed on it, in red-paint letters:

THE HAWK IS A LEMON AND ITS DEALERS ARE THIEVES

Ken, stung, pushed open the car door.

"I spotted it when I went by on the road patrol just now," said the sheriff casually. "Suppose he figured no one would see it until tomorrow morning, when the whole town would go by on its way to work."

"'He'?" Ken stopped. "You know who it was?"

"Well, I heard you had a little trouble with someone this afternoon. And when I turned in here, my headlights caught someone running fast across the field there behind the garage. Of course, I only got a glimpse of the guy, but--" The sheriff's slow, rumbling voice died.

"Frank Fliel!" said Ken.

"Mind, that ain't a positive identification, Ken." The sheriff raised a hamlike hand. "I didn't see his face, and it was dark. But if it wasn't Frank-- here, let me help you with that."

"Thanks, I've got it."

He smeared red paint all over his hands, awkwardly dragging the big sign around to the parking space in the rear. He turned, wiping his hands on a rag. "I'm obliged to you for calling me, Lu," he said. "That would have been rough."

"Rough is right," the sheriff agreed mildly. "Fliel's a mean little cuss, isn't he? Well, I have to get back on patrol. Zandt's sick tonight. Be seeing you."

Watching the sheriff's car pull away made Ken feel curiously cheerful. During the postwar car shortage Lu Trowbridge had been one of the many Sheffield residents who had waited long, long months for a new car-- while Carney Craig quietly sold most of the Hawks that the company allotted his agency to out-of-town customers whom he could charge a premium price.

Carney had arranged these things personally, either over Ken's head or without his knowledge, and had thus escaped all censure. As sales manager, Ken had borne the brunt of the blame. Just how heavy a burden that was he was only beginning to learn, now that it was again a buyer's market in which the salesman once more had to compete for customers. Many a former customer-- and some personal friends-- had let him know in various ways what they thought of the Craig Agency sales policies. There was no doubt as to who they thought had been behind those policies.

But apparently Lu Trowbridge still felt friendly toward him.

Maybe, as Jane had always maintained, more people recognized Carney for the smiling hypocrite that he was than Ken thought.

But it's not very likely, he told himself bitterly, and then decided he ought to drive around by himself for a few minutes to cool off. He went for a short ride off Cemetery Street. Driving toward Jane's to pick her up and take her to the O'Haras', he managed to whistle in the face of the rumbling thunder.

After all, he was just about through with Carney Craig.

The drizzle had stopped before Ken finished his story, leaving the night damp and chilly. The sheriff relit his pipe and said thoughtfully, "You went for a ride out Cemetery Street, eh?"

"Now, listen, Lu--" Eddie O'Hara began.

"No," Ken cut in sharply. "I know what Lu's thinking. I might have driven back here and caught Fliel trying to put up his sign again or something. Just for the record, I didn't. But Lu has to go into all the angles, Eddie."

"I wasn't thinking anything like that," the sheriff protested. "I don't figure you killed Frank Fliel. You're just not the type. I think whoever killed him was awfully mad or awfully frightened. You don't hammer a guy to death like that without having some strong feeling about it....Well, you fellows go along. You'll be around here in the morning, Ken?"

"Sure."

"The state cop will want to talk to you. But you haven't got anything to worry about."

It was a subdued party that gathered again in the O'Hara living-room over coffee and sandwiches. When they finished eating, Ken turned to Birmingham and said, "Gordon, what do you people in Detroit think of the Landseer?"

Gordon Birmingham chewed reflectively on his cigar. "Frankly," he said, "since it's all in the family here, we think they've got a pretty good automobile."

"But it's nowhere near as good as the Hawk," Eileen O'Hara chided.

Birmingham smiled. "Of course. And I'm not kidding. It's not as good a car as the new Hawk. We're still ahead of them. But they've got new automobiles coming. If what I hear is true, the fifty-ones are really terrific."

"Fifty-ones," gasped Jane. "This is only 1949, after all. Do they work that far ahead?"

Birmingham chuckled. "Everyone works that far ahead. I saw roughs on our 1952 body styles just before I left. They can change a lot between now and then. In fact, they will. But, whatever happens, they'll be the best automobile in their class."

The women went into the kitchen with the plates and Eddie O'Hara went with them for more beer. Birmingham said, "You like the Landseer, Ken?"

Ken flushed a little. "Why should I?"

"Possibly because you are going to be their dealer here."

In spite of himself, Ken's jaw dropped. He started to say, "Why, Gordon," and then laughed. "All right," he said. "I was going to announce it tomorrow anyway, after the papers are signed. But how did you know?"

"Easy," Birmingham chuckled. "We know Sheffield is one of about forty towns they've had their eye on as possible expansion spots. I was just thinking today who they might get here. Then I put myself in Sam McDonald's place and it wasn't hard to dope out. He obviously needs a young, able, experienced, local boy whom everyone likes. When I asked myself who fitted that description--"

Ken said, "I'm not so sure of your last qualification. Maybe things aren't quite as rosy with the Hawk Agency and its sales manager as you think. You got a sample of it today when Fliel shot off his mouth."

Birmingham's face darkened. "I know what's really going on at the agency, Ken. I mean, I know what a skinflint Carney Craig is. Doesn't the whole town know?"

"Carney's not only a skinflint," said Ken, speaking so low as not to be overheard, "but he's a darn clever bird. I'm the guy who has taken most of the raps. And Carney was so smooth about it that I didn't know what he was doing to me until comparatively recently."

"Have there been other incidents? I mean, insults and putting up signs?"

"None quite so obvious, if that's what you mean. But there are plenty of people who got short-changed like Fliel did, by Carney simply refusing to deliver cars to them if he could get more money elsewhere. Of course, they didn't necessarily blame Carney." His tone was bitter. "But, believe me, they have come to hate the name of Hawk."

Gordon Birmingham crushed out his cigar with an angry deliberation.

"You and I know," Ken went on, "that not more than one or two per cent of the entire Hawk dealership chiseled like that-- nor did any other group of dealers. But there are plenty of people in Sheffield who'd like to have seen that sign decorating the agency."

Birmingham leaped to his feet. "That swine is ruining our business," he snapped.

His sudden emotion surprised Ken. He said, "Hell's bells, Gordon, it takes more than one selfish dealer to ruin a company as big as Hawk."

Birmingham gave him a curious look. "And now you're going to give him more competition with Landseer, eh?" he said. "I should think you might have preferred to hang on a while and take over the Hawk franchise from Carney."

"What makes you think he'd want to give it up?"

"What makes you think he can hang on to it forever?" returned Birmingham savagely. "Do you think the company doesn't know what's going on here? The sales department has had plenty of complaints-- plenty! I've tried to talk to him..." His voice dwindled. "And it's a good agency, too. I wish I owned it."

"You!" Ken was genuinely startled.

"Sure, me," Birmingham smiled. "There are plenty of Hawk executives who are tired of the pressure of production and competition and would like to retire to a nice little town like this one and run an agency that's a sure $20,000 to $25,000 a year profit. But you know the unwritten law. No one connected with the company can own an agency."

"I know. And there are good reasons for that rule. If--"

The women returned. "It's midnight, ducky," said Helen Craig to Birmingham, running an affectionate hand over his hair. "Let's go home. Carney certainly is not going to meet us here now."

They all left together.

Ken lit a cigarette, a thing he seldom did before breakfast, and stared out the window of his bedroom.

McDonald, the Landseer man, would be in town today. By

nightfall the contract would be signed. Ken was a little shocked to discover that he was too tired to feel any great elation. He angrily crushed out the bitter-tasting cigarette and went downstairs quietly, so as not to wake his mother, and left the sleeping house. As he drove past the courthouse its familiar dial registered 7:45.

When he pulled into the driveway behind Craig Sales and Service, Lu Trowbridge walked out of the garage.

"Been here all night?" Ken called.

Inside the garage, steel clanged on steel. "No. We just got here a little while ago. O'Hara let me in," said the sheriff.

A second man emerged from the garage, a tall, lean man whose sun-bronzed face made his blue eyes look off-white. He wore the uniform of a state policeman. "This here's Ken Wilson, Quinlan," the sheriff said. "Ken, meet Trooper Vic Quinlan."

They shook hands. "What do you make of it, Quinlan?"

Quinlan's handshake was perfunctory. He looked appraisingly at Ken. "Could we talk in your car a minute?"

"Sure."

"I'll go see if Carney's free yet," said Trowbridge.

They settled back in the Hawk's wide front seat. Quinlan said, "The sheriff has given me an account of your movements last night. Let's see if I have it right. You were last to leave here. You went home and were dressing when he summoned you back. Afterward you went for a short ride-- out Cemetery Street, wasn't it?-- then picked up a Miss Jane Robbins and went to a party at Mr. O'Hara's."

"That's right." He was glad to observe that his voice and the hand holding his cigarette were perfectly steady.

"Mr. O'Hara accounts for your time from then on," Quinlan observed.

"But it's that ride out Cemetery Street that worries you, eh? You figure I might have come back, seen Fliel--"

"I didn't say anything like that," Quinlan cut in quickly. "But the fact is that the coroner examined the body early this morning and he puts the time of death at somewhere between nine and ten-thirty-- or centering around nine-forty-five. According to the time chart I've tried to compile, that's just about the time of your solitary ride. Right?"

"Just about."

"Do you know anything inside Mr. Craig's office that might have attracted Fliel last night?"

"No. Was he in there? Lu and I went all over the building and found no trace of a break-in."

"He wasn't in there, as far as I know. But he must have stared in, through the office windows, for a while. His fingerprints are all over the window ledge outside, clearly defined in red paint."

"I see. Well, you might ask Mr. Craig."

"I will as soon as he's free. He seems to be tied up with a very important visitor. Fliel didn't have any reason to like either you or

Craig particularly-- right?"

"I almost had a fight with him yesterday, if that's what you're driving at," Ken said. "For three years Frank had his name on our order list for a panel truck. He thought it was time he got delivery. He was sore about it."

"But you didn't think it was time he got delivery?"

"Well-- yes."

"Well, then, why didn't he get it?"

Ken's jaw set stubbornly. "You had better talk to Mr. Craig about that."

"I will. Right now I'm talking to you about it."

Ken said nothing, but it was with a feeling of relief that he heard the sheriff's feet crunch the driveway gravel.

"The stranger's still in there, Quinlan," said Lu Trowbridge. "I knocked on the door, and Carney opened it only a crack and begged me-- he begged me-- to let them talk for just another three minutes. Then he said he'd be free. I've never seen Carney look like that before; he looked scared stiff."

"He's been dodging us for half an hour," said Quinlan coldly. "We've waited long enough. Let's make the visitor wait a while."

"I doubt if Carney will be able to tell you very much," said Ken. "He was out of town last night."

Quinlan gave him a curious look. "Is that so?" he asked.

As they walked toward the salesroom the sheriff said, "Ken, do you know a tall, thin guy, all dressed in black, with an umbrella? He's in talking to Carney."

"I don't know who he is, but he was in looking at the new line last night. They probably have some business deal on."

"Funny time of day for a business deal," said Quinlan.

"Not for Carney Craig it isn't," said the sheriff. "He's famous for being an early bird."

The salesroom was stuffy with the smell of yesterday's crowds. While the others clumped down the hall toward Craig's office, Ken took off his coat, opened doors and windows, and started a minute inspection of the new cars. The four-door sedan had a long scratch along one fender, and the convertible's cigarette lighter was missing.

Katie came in, called "Good morning" to him, and went to her switchboard. Almost immediately the phone rang; someone wanted the sheriff. Lu Trowbridge listened a few moments, said "Okay," and hung up. "Ken?"

"Yes?"

"You know Vera Fliel, don't you?"

"Jane knows her better than I do. They were in the same sorority at State. Why?"

"I understand she and Frank had a loud fight at the Happy Hour bar yesterday, after they left here. I sent Zandt out to their farm this morning to talk to her. He just called-- says Mrs. Fliel told him she left Frank in town about seven-thirty last night because he was getting mean and ornery. She drove to the farm alone. I was just wondering--"

"Jane knows more about how they get along than I do," said Ken. "But I think they often fight like that."

Once more the phone rang under his hand. Ken said, "Hello, darling." The sheriff, having waited to see that it was not for him, went outside.

Carney Craig walked across the sales floor with angry purpose.

"Ken, I'm worried," Jane's voice said in the phone. "About Fliel, I mean. I know it's silly-- but--"

"Put that phone down," snapped Carney. "Did you tell those cops I was out of town last night?"

"You won't be in any trouble, will you, Ken, just because of that silly fight?" Jane asked.

"Go 'way, Carney," Ken snapped. And then into the phone he said, "No, not at all, Jane. Incidentally, I wish you'd have a talk with Vera Fliel. Why don't you go out there this morning and see what she says about last night."

"Damn it, Wilson--"

"You sound sort of strange," said Jane, "as though--"

"Carney, give me that phone!"

But Craig had grabbed it from him and crashed the phone into its cradle. "Come into my office!"

He turned curtly on his heel, a world of contempt expressed in his certainty that Ken would follow. Ken stood still, in such a white-hot fury that he did not know what to do; he did not want to follow that fat back waddling down the hall, but he had no idea of letting the matter drop.

He waited, a long-breathing minute until his feelings were under some semblance of control. Then he followed Carney Craig down the hall, past a curious Katie, and into the office.

"Listen, you fat, chiseling--"

Carney put back his head and opened his mouth in a laugh that was long and loud but mirthless. "I don't know what's getting into this place," he said bitterly. "O'Hara was in here just a minute ago mad as a wet hen because I saved a little money on piston rings. Now the police accuse me of all sorts of things just because I went to bed early like any sensible man. They tell me that you said I sneaked out of town."

"I didn't say 'sneaked'! You told me yourself you had to drive over to Lawrenceville last night. Why shouldn't I have told them? It's an alibi for you, isn't it?"

"Maybe. And I did go to Lawrenceville. But that didn't take long. I was dead tired and wanted to get some sleep, so I went home to bed instead of meeting Helen at O'Hara's. The sheriff says he called me at home after he found that sign Fliel put up, and got no answer. Well, maybe so. I was so tired I could have slept through anything. But one thing, Ken-- I'll thank you to stay out of my affairs. Just run your end of the business and don't try to--"

Carney paused, and Ken became aware of a curious change in his manner.

"--don't try to make anyone pay you bonuses," Carney went on, "or accept accessories they didn't ask for. I've told you this time and again, but this is the last time! If I get one more complaint I'm going to-- Oh, hello, Mr. Norton."

Ken had sensed the meaning of the change before he even turned. A man had quietly entered the room behind him, a tall, funereal-looking man dressed, except for his shirt, entirely in black.

"That will be all, Wilson," said Craig.

"You lousy hypocrite," Ken snapped. "You money-grabbing liar! You know I've never got a cent more than my salary and commissions out of this place. You know who shuffled the delivery lists and--" He moved toward Craig as he spoke.

"Please, please," said the man Carney had called Norton. "Mr. Craig and I have business to discuss."

Ken brushed angrily past him.

People began thronging the salesroom shortly after nine o'clock. This was Saturday; many were farmers.

"Mr. Wilson, it's gonna be more crowded than yesterday," said the agency porter. "It'll be hot, too."

"You're right, Billy. Guess I'll put on my coat, though, and look like a gentleman until it warms up....Hey, where is it?"

He had left it on the chair behind his desk. Now the coat was gone.

McDonald called about 11 o'clock. He had just arrived at the Stratford House, he said, and wanted to freshen up a little; could Ken come over around 12? They could talk over any details that remained unsettled and sign the contract.

By now, the salesroom was stifling; big globules of sweat crawled slowly down his forehead as he listened to the Landseer representative's precise voice. But, for the first time since yesterday afternoon, Ken again began to feel excited about what lay in store for him.

Just a few more hours, maybe only two, and he would have the exquisite pleasure of telling Carney Craig to take his job and go to the devil with it.

"Mr. Wilson," said Billy, the porter, "I can't find that coat nowhere. You sure you had it when you come in?"

"I'm sure, Billy. But never mind. It will turn up. And if it doesn't I had my wallet in my trousers pocket anyway."

A woman wanted to know whether it was possible to get the business coupe in robin's-egg blue. A man who had brought his wife along placed an order after being assured that gasolines of the proper octane were available for the new motor. Ken took two other orders-- he was doing a good day's work on his last day, he reflected-- and it was almost noon when he looked up into the thin, brown face of Trooper Quinlan. Next to Quinlan stood Lu Trowbridge.

"Mr. Wilson, I wonder if you'd mind coming down to the sheriff's office and answering a few questions about the death of Frank Fliel."

"The sheriff's office? Why should I go there? Someone might get the idea I was arrested." He laughed uneasily. The clock read 11:56. He had to get down to the Stratford House and McDonald.

"Arrest is a word I don't like to use," said Quinlan. "But for your own sake I think it might be better to talk in some less public place."

"What is this?" said Ken. "I didn't have anything to do with killing Fliel! And I have an appointment downtown right now."

"All right, Mr. Wilson," returned Quinlan steadily. "If that's how you want it. I noticed some reddish stains on the jacket of your suit this morning. The sheriff said it was the one you had on last night. So I took the liberty-- I admit I had no legal right-- of borrowing it long enough to take a scraping of the stain and test it."

Ken sighed with relief. "For a minute you scared me," he said. "I have an important business appointment, and I was afraid I might have to miss it. I can go home and get another coat if you want to keep that one. Because, Quinlan, when you get the results of the test, you'll learn the red spots are paint. Lu could have told you. I got paint all over myself moving that sign last night."

"I know you did," said Quinlan. "Some of the spots are paint. But some of them are blood."

Everything in the world seemed to stop. "You're-- you're crazy," Ken breathed. "I just had that suit cleaned. I put it on fresh yesterday for the premiere. There couldn't be blood on it."

"But there is," said Quinlan quietly. "I ran the preliminary test myself. Now the coroner is typing it to see if it corresponds to Fliels's blood."

Outside, the hoarse gong of the courthouse clock began tolling noon. This was the moment at which he was supposed to meet McDonald!

How could he explain to this ominous polite cop what the next hour meant to him?

He was on his feet, although he didn't know how he got there. All the sneers and insults he had to accept, the bitter indignation at the position into which Carney Craig had forced him, in the last twenty-four months, boiled up suddenly.

"Look, Wilson," said Quinlan.

With a sudden movement he pushed Quinlan aside. He started running toward Carney Craig's office.

Quinlan yelled, "Hey!" and lurched after him.

Ken ran down the long hall and pushed the door open with a bang. Carney Craig stood beside his desk.

Ken smiled bitterly. "You lousy heel," he said.

Carney's usually ruddy face was livid, but his lips were white.

His hands were pressed to his big stomach; his mouth was opened wide and it seemed as if he could not close it. From his eyes shone pure terror.

Ken moved across the thick carpet for the long, savage right hook that had become the most important thing in the world.

But Carney Craig, with a sudden, loud cry, arched his back, threw up his head, and fell over backward, while Ken was still two paces from him. As he went down, his head struck a chair.

Ken paused, incredulously.

A uniformed figure moved between him and Craig. Quinlan studied that contorted face only a moment. "He's dead," he said softly. "That was quick. What did you do to him, Wilson?"

"Do to him?" It was impossible. He hadn't touched Carney. "I didn't do anything to him."

"He's lying, Officer," a voice said. Ken turned. He saw the man Carney had called Norton standing behind him.

"I was just outside the other door which leads to the service garage," Norton went on. "I heard this fellow burst in and curse Mr. Craig. Then I heard a blow--"

"That was no blow!" cried Ken angrily. "He fell over by himself; what you heard was his head hitting a chair."

"I know what I heard, young man."

"What were you doing just outside the other door?" said Quinlan.

"Mr. Craig and I had been in conference most of the morning. As we were talking just now, he had to get some papers to show me some figures. He said they were in his safe, and, since he preferred to have its whereabouts kept secret, he asked if I would mind stepping out of the room a moment. Of course I said I would. I was waiting just outside that other door when I heard Wilson burst in through this door."

"Your name?"

"Norton. Abner Norton. I am vice-president in charge of sales for the Hawk Motorcar Company."

"Oh!" Ken was stunned. "So you are Holy Abner."

Norton ignored this. "Well, Officer, what are you waiting for?"

"Where's the safe, Ken?" asked Lu Trowbridge.

"How should I know? Carney and I weren't bosom friends, you know!"

"Apparently not," said Quinlan dryly. He bent over the body a long moment. When he looked up, it was with a curious light in his eyes. "You claim Wilson slugged him, eh, Norton?"

"Well, considering what I heard--"

"But you didn't see any blows struck?"

"We-e-ell, no, I didn't."

"It's lucky you said that," said Quinlan, getting back to his feet. "As a matter of fact, it looks as if no blows were struck. I'd guess that, as Wilson says, his head hit the chair when he fell."

"But what made him fall?" asked Lu Trowbridge wonderingly.

"Poison," said Quinlan curtly. "He must have been dying when Wilson busted in here." He bent down and smelled the glass and carafe on Craig's desk. "And this is where it came from. It's cyanide-- potassium cyanide, rather than sodium, I'd say. Somebody put it in his water jug."

"That must have been done since last night," said Ken. "Because when I was in here about six-thirty he drank some water from the carafe."

Quinlan looked around at the curious faces framed in the doorway. "Clear them out, Sheriff. I want to question everyone separately. I'll start with Wilson. Keep Mr. Norton around. And that repairman, O'Hara. Also, Mr. Craig had a secretary, didn't he?"

"Had a secretary?"

Helen Craig had pushed past the people in the doorway. She was followed by Birmingham.

"Has something happened to Katie?" she asked. The desk screened her husband's body from her.

She was in shorts and flame-colored sweater, and Birmingham was in golfing slacks. She said, "Where's Carney?"

Birmingham turned to Ken: "What happened?"

Helen Craig screamed. She had seen beyond the desk. "No! Oh, no!" She threw herself on her husband's body.

"Get her out of here, Sheriff," said Quinlan. "Get them all out of here."

Assisted by Birmingham, the sheriff gently wrested Helen Craig from her husband and carried her out. Only Quinlan remained in the room with Ken.

"Do you know whether cyanide is kept on the premises?" he asked.

"Sure. Eddie uses it all the time."

"What for?"

"Eddie's always experimenting-- mechanically, I mean. He occasionally does some plating, and, of course, cyanide is a plating bath component. But he chiefly uses it as a rust inhibitor."

"A what?"

"You keep steel parts that might rust in a cyanide bath until you're ready to use them. That way they don't rust."

"Who could have got at it?"

"Anybody. Eddie keeps it in a can on his workbench, plainly labeled."

"I see. Were you in here earlier this morning?"

"Yes, for a little while. Long enough to have a fight, as you might have heard. Carney was sore because I mentioned to you that he was out of town last night."

"I suppose you might have doctored the water jug then?"

"Under Craig's nose? Well, maybe. Just for the record, I didn't."

"I'm glad you put it that way," said Quinlan. "I really didn't think you had. But if what you say about his drinking from it last night is true, the poison must have been put in it some time since then-- this morning, presumably. Who else was in here today?"

"His secretary, Katie, could tell you better than I."

Quinlan's eyes narrowed. "I forgot about her. I suppose she always filled his water carafe?"

"Every morning. Katie is very efficient. But-- that's ridiculous. You might as well suspect Lu Trowbridge."

"I suspect everyone."

Ken thought of Sam McDonald, pacing one of the Stratford House's neat, chinz-curtained rooms.

"As I mentioned before, I've got a whale of an important business engagement. Can I leave now, if you are through with the questions?"

Quinlan smiled sardonically. "I'm afraid not right now."

"But--"

"Don't worry, Wilson. We'll get the guilty man soon enough."

"As a matter of fact," said Ken, "that may be impossible."

"Why?"

"Because maybe Carney and Fliel killed each other."

Quinlan began to look annoyed. "Maybe you think it's a good time to be funny!"

"Look, Quinlan; supposing Fliel decided to kill Carney because we haven't sold him a car. He breaks in here last night and poisons Carney's water jug. But, just after he got out, Carney sees him. Maybe Carney had come back to do a little work-- he was a hard-working guy, you know, down here early and late. Carney sees what Fliel was up to with the sign-- he was going to disgrace the new Hawk. In a fit of rage he kills Fliel. But Fliel, in a sense, has already killed Carney, or at least arranged his death. This morning Carney comes in early as usual, presently gets thirsty and-- bingo! Fliel kills him, from beyond the grave."

Quinlan shook his head. "I won't buy that until I've exhausted every other possibility. Or found Fliel's fingerprints on the carafe and Craig's on the tire iron. The thing that interests me right now is that two men were killed here, by different methods, but within only fourteen hours of each other. And within just a few feet of each other, oddly enough. Do you realize that Fliel lay just outside that wall, not more than ten feet from where Craig's body is?"

Lu Trowbridge stuck his head in the door. "Doc's here, Quinlan."

"Send him in, and keep Wilson out there with the others."

The others, Ken found, had been herded into the parts department. Eddie O'Hara was leaning moodily against a metal rack of generator parts. Someone had brought Helen Craig the skirt that went with her shorts, and now she sat on a carton, staring at nothing. Birmingham stood near her, looking out the window. Katie dabbed at her eyes with her handkerchief. Norton looked coldly at Ken as he came in and then continued studying a parts price list on the wall.

Just outside the window the sheriff's car was drawn up, Deputy

Zandt at the wheel. Next to him sat Vera Fliel.

"What is she doing here?" Ken asked the sheriff.

Lu Trowbridge removed the toothpick from his mouth. "Doc found some scratches on Frank's face. When he got Frank's face sort of back together, that is. So we asked Vera to come down and try to tell us whether they had that fight in the bar yesterday."

Ken nodded, sat down on the counter, and lit a cigarette. Its fragrance was a warm comfort as he thought over the events of the last sixteen hours. Curiously, he presently found himself mentally reversing some of the things he had learned, and when he did that a pattern began to emerge. The voices Helen Craig had heard in the phone, for example.

Katie stood before him, blinking back fresh tears. "Oh, Mr. Wilson, isn't it terrible? Poor Mr. Craig--"

"Yes. Katie, tell me. Who went into that office this morning?" He spoke in a low voice.

She caught his urgency and answered in the same way. "Mr. Norton was already in with Mr. Craig when I got there at eight," she said. "Then, besides you and Eddie, there was the sheriff and that state policeman, and a Mr. Chelsea."

"Who was he?"

"I'd never seen him before, but he said that yesterday when you and Mr. Fliel had that trouble, Mr. Craig told everyone they could see him today about placing orders."

"Oh, yes." Carney wouldn't have wasted much time with him! "No one else?"

"No one else."

"Katie, think back. Did you fill Mr. Craig's water bottle this morning?"

"Of course. I do every morning."

"I see. Notice anything special about it?"

"It was empty, that's all."

"Isn't it always?"

"Not often. Mr. Craig doesn't drink-- didn't drink much water. Guess he used it mostly for a chaser with the shot of whisky he always had before leaving."

She was probably right, Ken thought. He, himself, had had an occasional drink with Carney at quitting time; the chaser had always come from the carafe.

There was an ash tray near Helen Craig. Ken walked over to it to snuff out his cigarette. He looked at her.

"To think," she said woodenly, "that I insulted him when I drove him down here this morning. He made me get up early to drive him down. Gordon and I wanted the car later for golf. I was mad. He had misplaced his keys to the office and I-- I refused to get him mine for a moment. But it was only a moment, Ken--" She grasped his hand. "You understand, don't you? I didn't mean--"

"Really, Helen!" said Birmingham. His pleasant features were twisted into a scowl.

"Poor dear," said Katie pityingly.

All of the others had gone into Carney's office, one at a time, to be questioned by Quinlan and had not returned. Quinlan himself appeared, gestured to the sheriff, and they retired to the other end of the room and engaged in a low conversation, during which Trowbridge seemed to be arguing spiritedly. Presently they returned to Ken.

"Wilson, was Craig in any financial trouble?" asked the state trooper.

"Not that I know of. Carney never showed me the books-- I was just a salaried employee. As a matter of fact, his finances have always been something of a mystery."

"Like where he got the dough to buy this agency," said Lu Trowbridge.

"Sure. But Carney always had all the money he needed. Why, we even paid cash for our cars lots of times, instead of financing them the way most agencies do."

Quinlan looked troubled. He frowned, and then carefully took a green slip of paper from his wallet. "How do you explain this?" he said.

Ken took the paper. It was a cashier's check, made out to bearer, for $30,000, and dated nine days before.

"The bank says Craig had it drawn."

"I can't explain it," said Ken wonderingly. "Even without knowing much about the agency's financial standing, I know we couldn't have owed anything like this. And I don't know what in the world Carney would be buying for that much money. He had paid off the contractors on our new building."

Lu Trowbridge grunted. "The whole business ain't worth that much."

"No, you're wrong," said Ken. It's worth at least twice that-- and probably more. Maybe a hundred thousand dollars. Where did the check come from?"

"I found it folded up under the ink stand on his desk."

"That's odd," said Ken thoughtfuly. "Carney wasn't careless about money. And that check, technically at least, was as good as cash."

"Sure," said Quinlan. "To me it suggested that he expected to use it in a business deal momentarily-- with someone he expected to see today.

"You won't be held, Wilson-- for the present," he said. "The sheriff vouches for you, for one thing. But don't leave Sheffield for a while."

"Okay."

Quinlan turned his back elaborately and said to the sheriff, "I've let all the others go. As of now, there's no reason to hold anyone. I asked Norton to stay here overnight, however. He was sore. Seems to be quite a big shot."

"Why'd you call him 'Holy' Abner, Ken?" asked the sheriff.

"I guess he's the most famous salesman in the auto business," said Ken. "He's famous because he's successful, and he's successful because he believes in what he sells. To Norton the Hawk is a religion. When he gives the dealers one of his pep talks-- well, it's like a sermon."

"I see."

Ken said, "I'll be around if you want me."

He left the agency as quickly as he could and drove coatless to the Stratford House.

Sam McDonald was a surprisingly young man, short and peppery-looking, with a fringe of rust-colored hair around a balding head. He had been dictating letters to a public stenographer whom he dismissed as Ken came in. He said, "Hello, Wilson; I'm Sam McDonald," in the easy, quick way of a man accustomed to meeting many people. Having said that, he stopped and looked Ken over.

Ken said, "Hi," and stopped too. McDonald said, "I received a very good report on you from our man over in Lawrenceville."

"That's good. I'm sorry about the time. I'm not usually three hours late for business appointments."

"I gather something unusual occurred."

Ken smiled wryly, "I expect you heard what has occurred. Carney Craig has been murdered. The police have been talking to me-- among others."

"You mean you are under suspicion?" said McDonald.

"Not exactly. If I were, I don't think I'd be walking around like this. But--"

"The cops don't know what to make of it, eh?"

"Apparently."

McDonald seemed deep in thought. "I'll tell you, Wilson, frankly, I had already heard something about what has happened around the Hawk agency. And I'd be dishonest with you if I didn't tell you that it has altered my thinking just a little bit. I mean by that--" He turned and faced Ken, squaring his shoulders. "I mean by that, frankly, that I'm not as sure as I was that you are the man for us. I understand that there was bad blood between you and Craig-- that, in fact, there was considerable speculation around town whether it was you or he who was responsible for some of the deals the Craig agency made when cars were in short supply. If it turned out that Craig was killed over some feud over car dealings-- well, I'd rather get a sales representative here whose hands were clean. However if the whole thing is cleared up--"

"Well?"

"The deal is still on," said McDonald heartily. "But for the present it's off, so I'm catching the late train back to Detroit tonight. I can come back again, of course, when things are-- well-- arranged."

Ken said, "I see."

He had parked in front of the Stratford House in such a hurry he had forgotten to put a nickel in the parking meter, but luckily there was no ticket tied to the convertible's steering wheel. He climbed in, shook a cigarette out of his pack, and lighted it.

When he had inhaled and exhaled the first cloud of smoke, he leaned back against the seat and started thinking the facts over, one by one. It was getting dark and colder when he finally headed for Jane's house.

Jane said, "You didn't have any lunch! I'll get you something."

"I don't want to eat. I want to talk."

"I want you to. I want to talk myself. Eileen O'Hara called me a while ago about Carney being poisoned. What has happened, Ken? What does it mean? And what did Vera Fliel mean? I went over to their farm this morning and-- Oh, you've had nothing to eat."

"I can wait."

"No, you wait a second. I've got things to tell you and things to ask you."

She was back in the small, cozy living-room in a moment with milk and a plate containing cold chicken slices, salad, and buttered rolls. She poured a glass of milk, and said, "You talk first-- I want to hear about Carney."

"No, you. My mouth's too full. What's going on at the Fliels'?"

"Well, Vee Fliel isn't as much cut up as you might think. I gather Frank beat her oftener even than everyone suspected. But-- do you remember Fliel saying something about seeing a Hawk in that old lover's lane behind his place?"

"Yes. He said the wheels were off center or something."

"Well, it might have been true. At least, Vee says Frank came into the house one night about a week ago, saying he had seen these two cars."

"Two?"

"Apparently there were two of them. Both black sedans with cream wheels, parked next to each other. He'd been out shooting squirrels, Vera said. He noticed the wheels of one of them was off center. Or so he said."

"If he said so, they were. Whatever else you can say about Frank he had eyes like a cat. He'd won every sharp-shooter medal in the Marines, you know."

"But, Ken-- could the cars' wheels really be off center?"

He laughed. "No-- never. Except in one case, maybe. But you know Carney drove a black sedan with cream wheels. Where did Frank see this car?"

"Vera said in that grove of pine trees that's behind their place. And I went over there, after I left her, and played detective."

"What did you find?"

"The tracks of two cars."

"Hawks?"

"Cars, darling. I can't tell one from another just by the tracks. But the marks were clear-- this was under big trees, that protected them from the rain."

"Look!" He took out a pencil and began to draw on a magazine. "Hawk gets all its tires from L.L. and T. Rubber Company, and this year they are supplying us with a new tire that has a pattern like this. Recognize it?"

"No."

"Also the engineers changed the wheel tread a little. That's the distance between each pair of wheels, front and back. Now Hawk's front-wheel tread is wider than the rear. Did you happen to notice--?"

"Ken Wilson! Do you think anyone would notice a thing like that?"

"Okay, okay. You did fine without measuring."

She gave him a long look. "You sound like a man trying to play Sherlock Holmes."

"Maybe that's what I'm doing."

"Ken! The best thing you can do is steer clear of all of it. After all, you've got your franchise--"

"No, you're wrong. I haven't. That's why I am trying to play detective. I'm already mixed up in this thing enough so Sam McDonald doesn't want any part of me until he's satisfied I am not involved in any of the various scandals being noised abroad about the Hawk agency. Another is because as soon as Quinlan runs out of suspects, I am going to become the prime one. And the third reason is that I think I am the only person who knows who the killer is."

"But, honey! I don't see what motive there could possibly be." She stopped, and a dawning light appeared in her eyes. "Maybe I do. Both of them, in their way, were injuring Hawk. I mean, Frank was putting up that sign and Carney had made lots of enemies for the company."

"No," he said. "That's wrong. It's a good theory, but it's wrong. I don't know everything, but I can tell you this: They were both killed by the same person but by different means and for different reasons. Frank was killed because he was just an unfortunate fool. He picked last night to play a dirty, contemptible trick, so he happened to be around when the killer was making his preparations to kill Carney, which was his only real objective. But, as Fliel's fingerprints on the window sill showed, he saw the killer doing what he wanted to . And he was dumb enough to let himself be seen. So he was killed-- suddenly and on the spur of the moment."

He put down his plate and got up. "I've got work to do, and not too much time. See you sugar."

Outside it was pitch-dark now. He'd stop off at his house and get his crepe rubber shoes and a flashlight. A tape measure, too, he thought, as the motor spun into life under his toe.

"Just a minute," said a husky voice.

For a moment, he thought of the voice Helen had told of hearing on the telephone. A hand took his arm. Automatically he thrust it aside and grabbed at the coat, which was all he could see.

"Hey," said Jane Robbins. "Why so rough? I decided to go along. You'll need someone to show you those tracks out near Fliel's."

"Okay, okay," he sighed resignedly.

But it was to the agency that he drove first, after making a brief stop at his home. The long, modern building was utterly dark, and when he had opened the door with his key he stood for a second, orienting himself and smelling the exciting, new-car scent.

He inhaled it deeply, realizing with a pang how much all this meant to him-- the beauty of the new cars with their sleek fenders, their throaty motor purr, the stimulus of competition for sales, back again for the first time since the war began....At his desk he found his own water carafe, which was a duplicate of Carney's.

Leading an unusually silent and breathless Jane, he carried the carafe down the pitch-dark hall and into Carney's office. There, he closed the Venetian blinds and turned on the light.

"Now what?" she said. He did not answer, but began a close, board by board inspection of the walls. But he circled the room without finding what he sought.

He sat down at the desk and stared at the two carafes. The cigarette smoldered and died. Presently he held the carafe he carried in up to the lamp and tried to look in it. Then he looked into the one that had held Carney's death potion.

"What do you see?" said Jane.

Ken didn't answer. He ran an exploratory finger around inside of the neck of the carafe, and pulled something out. Then he pulled out a second something.

"What in the world is that?" asked Jane.

"Two little sections of scotch tape," said Ken. "Quinlan didn't find them, because they couldn't very readily be seen. And being stuck to the inside, they didn't come off when he poured out the poisoned water."

"But why were they there?"

"Because they held a lethal charge of cyanide in place. In lumps, or maybe--"

"Maybe what?"

"Druggist capsules. Two big capsules, filled with cyanide, and stuck to the inside of the carafe with scotch tape. Get it?"

"No."

"Easy. As soon as the water jug was filled with water, the capsule would dissolve, releasing the cyanide into the water. Or, as I said, maybe it was just a hunk of cyanide. It's crystalline, you know, something like salt. And it dissolves practically instantly. As soon as the jug was filled with water, the water was poisoned."

Unconsciously his voice had dropped; now they became aware of the silence in the room and the grim preparations which it must have witnessed not many hours before. Jane shivered.

Ken then turned his attention to the desk. The drawers were unlocked, so he did not bother to ransack them. Besides, Helen Craig had argued about a safe.

He yanked the carpet aside to examine the floor boards, and even moved the desk. It must be here-- unless, of course, Carney had kept things like that in some secret place at home or in a safe-deposit box. And if Carney did, then he, Ken Wilson, was washed out.

Jane said, "Look, darling," and, seeing the expression on his face, stopped.

His fingers trembled as he lit another cigarette. It had to be here!

His eyes rested suddenly on the oil painting. He leaped to it and began running his hands over the ornate gold frame. It swung outward on hinges even before he found the catch, and revealed a little square of glossy black steel inset in a paneling, which bore a single heavy steel dial and a handle.

Impulsively his hand went out to the handle and tried it.

The door swung open on oiled hinges. And even as it did, he realized he should have expected this, as well as the way the concealed picture had been unlatched. "He had to get out some papers to show me some figures," Norton had said. Carney had gone to the safe and had just opened it when the poison struck. He had staggered away, and the picture had swung back into place, closing the safe's door, but naturally not locking it.

He put a hand inside. There were long, flat jewel boxes, some checkbooks tied together, and several manila envelopes. One of them, unsealed, contained a thick sheaf of thousand-dollar bills; another, sealed with wax, bore a legend: "To Be Opened in Event of My Death."

His fingers tried the heavy blobs of wax, and then he thought better of it. He put that envelope back. If he was right, he knew what was in it. If he was wrong, it didn't matter. He examined the contents of the rest. They contained insurance policies and other important but conventional papers. He closed the safe door and restored the picture to its proper position. He said, "That does it, Jane. Let's go for a ride."

As the car flashed past the Fliel farm they caught a glimpse of Vera Fliel silhouetted in the window against a kerosene lamp. A little farther along Ken pulled into a side road, stopped, and switched off the lights. He helped Jane out, and they began walking in almost complete darkness, letting their feet find the road. He located the lane he wanted almost by instinct.

The darker mass of a pine grove loomed against the dark of the sky and they paused a moment to listen. Nothing broke the silence except the sleepy chirp of an insect. As they walked on, he occasionally flashed his light on the loamy road before him, but saw no tire tracks.

"At least, no other car came in and messed up whatever you saw," he said.

Under the trees, he turned the flashlight on permanently and started a careful examination of the lane. Almost at once, he found it; the tracks of new tires whose crisp, geometric tread had bitten deep into soft soil. Those tracks were overlaid in places by a second set whose tracks were different and less clearly defined.

The tracks showed the cars had driven in, stopped, backed up to turn around, and then driven out again. There were scuffed footprints at one point, but he could make little of them.

Fixing his flashlight in the fork of a bush so that it illuminated an area where the tire tracks were especially clear, Ken knelt down and began making careful calculations with his tape measure. He got to his feet after a few minutes, whistling softly. The tread of the first car's rear wheels was 57 inches, that of the front wheel was 55½.

And only a new Hawk's wheels had those measurements.

He was strangely silent driving back to town. "This was the payoff," he thought. What would happen in the next hour would either solve the murders or make Ken Wilson the laughingstock of Sheffield and perhaps land him in jail.

At the town's one all-night drugstore he paused briefly to buy some druggist's capsules and make a series of telephone calls-- to the Craig home, the county jail, Eddie O'Hara, Mrs. Fliel, and Katie, and finally Sam McDonald, who, catching a train in less than an hour, was at first completely uninterested in Ken's proposal. Then they drove to the agency, went in, and Ken turned on the lights. He visited Eddie O'Hara's workbench in the garage, and then busied himself at Carney's desk with his own water carafe, some Scotch tape and some whitish lumps of chemical which he handled with extraordinary care. Carney Craig's carafe he put out of sight in a closet.

As Jane saw what he was doing, she breathed, "You're mad!" and her blue eyes were dark with apprehension.

"Maybe I am. But I'm either going to make myself or break myself," he said simply. "We solve these murders and win back the Landseer franchise-- or else!"

Quinlan and the sheriff were first to arrive. The state policeman grunted a greeting and took a chair, near the door. "I hope this is as good as you promised over the phone," said Lu Trowbridge.

They were followed almost immediately by Birmingham, Helen Craig and Norton. Vera Fliel arrived at the same time and came in with the newcomers. Eddie O'Hara and McDonald walked in next, and McDonald and Norton stared at each other in surprise. Katie was last to arrive.

Ken said, "Will you please all find seats?" He rubbed his hands like a master of ceremonies. "I've asked you here because all of you, in various ways, are concerned with the murder of Carney Craig. I propose to hold a brief demonstration"-- he gestured toward the water carafe on the desk-- "and lay a few facts before you which should indicate who killed Carney."

"This carafe," he went on, "is an exact duplicate of the one that was on Carney's desk this morning. The original I have preserved for the police, for use at the trial. But I warn all of you-- this is an exact duplicate in every respect." He took out its stopper and held the carafe upside down. "As you can see it appears to be empty, just as Carney's did when Katie filled it this morning."

He put the carafe on the desk and leaned forward like a lecturer.

"The solution of this crime depended on correctly putting together just a few basic facts," he said. "I say 'crime'-- singular-- because the murder of Fliel was purely secondary. It begins with a phone call Mrs. Craig overheard about a week ago. She recognized neither voice, although one must have been her husband's, and someone said something threatening about 'How'd you like the company to know what you've been up to?' Since Carney Craig had been chiseling his customers a long time, this presumably was said by an indignant customer. But it occurred to me that it might possibly have been Carney speaking. To whom?

"Next comes Fliel's own revelation of seeing two Hawks parked one night a week ago behind his farmhouse. One answered the description of Carney's personal car. The other, Fliel's keen eyes told him, had wheels that seemed a little off center. While there are several Hawks around town with a paint job like Carney's, this suggested that this might be the meeting referred to in the phone conversation. And the off-center wheels make it really interesting. For the benefit of those of you who are not in the auto business, I'll point out that when a new car is being planned and tested, it is customary procedure to start with the chassis. An engineer wanting to test-drive such a chassis himself over a period of time, will not infrequently have a standard, current-model body put on the new hand-built chassis and drive it around the country in comparative disguise-- unless someone as sharp-eyed as Frank Fliel notices the small, telltale deviation between body and wheels. This suggested someone connected with the Hawk, since no one else could have such a car.

"Now we come to Fliel's murder. As the fingerprints on the window showed, he had been looking into this office. The killer, in here for a purpose I will presently explain, spotted him, quietly ran out through the garage, siezed a tire iron, and slugged him as he put up his sign.

"Now, Lu Trowbridge said he saw Frank run away. Yet when I handled the sign a few minutes later, I got blood on my coat-- as Trooper Quinlan's test subsequently showed-- although at the time I thought it was paint. Therefore, Fliel was dead when Lu Trowbridge discovered the sign. It was spattered with his blood. Lu didn't see

Fliel's body, because of the darkness. But-- and this is the important point-- it was the killer that the sheriff saw running away. He mistook him for Fliel because they were both of the same build.

"Now for a little re-enactment," he said. "Katie will you be good enough to fill this carafe with water just exactly as you did this morning?"

They all watched her as she walked out of the room, then listened to the bubbling from the water cooler in the hall.

The instant she put the carafe back on the desk, Ken poured a glass of water from it. For an almost imperceptible second, he paused to sniff the glass's contents before he drank from it. He stood smiling at them for a minute.

Then he poured a second glass. "Anyone want a drink?" he asked.

Quinlan jumped up. "Let me see that!" he said, and seized the glass from Ken and sniffed it.

He looked up thunderstruck. "Cyanide! That water's poisoned like the other. But how in the world--? You didn't have anything palmed."

"No. Nothing up the sleeve, Quinlan. But something in the carafe. A couple of druggist's capsules, to be exact, taped to the inside. Each capsule contained enough cyanide to kill a horse. It took the capsules a minute or two to dissolve in the water that Katie put in, so I could drink it safely. After that, the carafe contained a lethal dose. The killer was rigging the carafe in just that way last night when Fliel had the misfortune to see him. And having   been seen, the murderer had to silence Fliel forever."

Lu Trowbridge came forward. "Let me see that," he began.

But someone else stepped in front of him. "Damned ingenious," said Gordon Birmingham, and took the glass from Quinlan. He raised it to his lips and had drained half of it before Quilan could knock it away.

"But why-- why?" cried Katie some time later.

"That was the subtlest point of all," said Ken, "but also the most logical. It begins with the threat over the telephone-- 'How'd you like the company to know what you've been up to?' If you assume, as I did, that it might be Carney who said that, then it was the person with whom he was arranging a meeting on the following night who was 'up to' something. But every other clue indicated that the person with whom he had that clandestine meeting was Gordon Birmingham. Gordon was one of the very few who could have a test model Hawk. He was also the only person involved who was of slight, slender build like Fliel.

"So Carney was threatening Gordon with a disclosure of some sort. But what? I thought of how no one ever knew where Carney got the money to obtain his Hawk franchise. And how it's an unwritten law of the motor business that no one connected with an auto company can own an agency. And how one of the voices Helen

Craig overheard also said, 'We're still in business.' That sounded like a partnership. And how, as Gordon himself told me, an agency was a very attractive thing even to a Hawk executive.

"If you draw the obvious conclusion, it explains a great deal. Gordon was well-to-do-- he could have supplied the money Carney needed to go into business. If he was a silent partner, he could have been quarreling with Carney about how the agency was being run. Incidentally, I found a bundle of money in the safe which presumably represents the illegal profits Carney took out of the agency with his chiseling deals.

"Finally, Gordon was one of the few people involved whom Carney could have threatened to expose to the Hawk Company-- exposure of the partnership, that is. Now, the cashier's check showed Carney was prepared to buy something big. How many things are worth that much in a town of this size? But a partnership in this business was one, if you were trying to beat the other guy down.

"There was still another clue, however. Last night, when Gordon and I discussed how Carney was running the agency, Gordon blurted out the truth, as a man under the stress of emotion. He said something about Carney 'ruining our business.' I thought at the time he meant the Hawk Company's business. But another explanation presently occurred to me. For a long time Carney's tactics have been running this agency into the ground. Gordon, being in the home office, was in a position to know about it. He was also in a position to get pretty mad about it.

"They must have quarreled about it for a long time, and the secret meeting at Fliel's farm, well away from where they might be seen-- since they were supposed to have no mutual business inter- est-- was arranged to settle this. Carney figured he could buy Gordon out, at a low price, under threat of exposure. But Gordon had other ideas, and when he realized how Carney was thinking during the secret meeting, he decided that he would have to put it into effect."

"He decided the easy way out was to kill Carney," said Lu Trowbridge.

"Yes. And perhaps he had reasons. What I mean is-- Well, I've observed that Helen Craig didn't exactly look on Gordon with disfavor. If Carney was put out of the way, Gordon not only got rid of a dangerous threat, but might well have married Helen Craig. As he, himself, said, it's an attractive business and all he would have had to do is prove his claim on half of it to keep it all in the family."

"Young man," said Abner Norton, "Hawk will, of course, reassign the franchise here. From what I've seen of you and heard just now, I'm inclined to think--"

"Nothing doing, Norton," cried Sam McDonald. "I saw him first! Wilson, I can promise you a Landseer dealership that will make you more money in the next five years than you'll make with Hawk in a hundred."

Lu Trowbridge chuckled. "Mister, when this town learns what

this boy has done and how Carney Craig made him the scapegoat for all his crookedness, you can be darn' sure he'll be successful in any agency he starts."

Ken smiled. Suddenly he felt tired and spent. "Thanks," he said. "Thanks to both of you. That will take a little thinking over....Come on, Jane. Let's get going. I want a chance to discuss things with my own silent partner."

"Silent, indeed!" returned Jane with spirit.

But she took his arm affectionately.

Murder
AMONG Ladies

BY KELLEY ROOS

The husband-and-wife detective team has a distinguished history, dating at least as far back as Agatha Christie's Tuppence and Tommy Beresford in the twenties and Dashiell Hammett's Nick and Nora Charles in The Thin Man (1934) and a subsequent series of films. Perhaps the most famous such team were Frances and Richard Lockridge's Mr. and Mrs. North, who appeared in a long series of novels as well as radio and television series. Comprising one of the best and brightest crime-solving married couples were Jeff and Haila Troy, who debuted (not yet married) in Kelley Roos' Made Up to Kill (1940) and continued throughout the forties, making a brief comeback in One False Move (1966). Three of their numerous American appearances were gathered in Triple Threat (1949) and several others were reprinted in Ellery Queen's Mystery Magazine. The story that follows, set in Washington, D.C., appeared in June 1950 and has not reappeared since.

Like the Lockridges, the Troys' chroniclers were a married couple, William Roos (1911-   ) and the late Audrey Kelley Roos (1912-1982). Besides the Troy books and many non-series mystery novels, they wrote the successful play Speaking of Murder (1957) and an Edgar-winning teleplay of John Dickson Carr's The Burning Court (1960). On his own, William Roos is the author of plays and musical comedy librettos. In a letter written in December 1984, Roos reported that the Kelley Roos byline will appear once more on a juvenile mystery, written in collaboration with the team's son Stephen Roos, to be published by Delacorte in fall 1985.

MURDER AMONG LADIES by Kelley Roos

The spring sun was shining down upon the capital of the United States of America as though its trip around the world to be here with us was more than worth it. The District of Columbia birds seemed to be singing a filibuster to keep this glorious day from ever ending. The people on the streets weren't walking; they were strutting. Even the men carrying the brief cases that contained the worries of the world looked like boys again. Our cab driver was whistling a tune that strongly recommended love in April. Then I looked out the window and saw the cherry trees. They were in full bloom. I couldn't stand it.

"Jeff," I sang, "darling, I love you, love you, love you!"

I turned to my husband, and the scowl on his face was a horrendous thing. Suddenly the sun ducked behind a cloud, the birds shut their traps, the cherry blossoms wilted. Maybe nobody else noticed this, but I did. Jeff's gloom had turned the lovely day into awful night.

"Correction," I said. "I do not love you."

"That's right," Jeff said. "You must hate me. That's the only explanation for what you're doing to me. Listen, Haila; Aunt Ellie is your aunt, not mine. Why do I have to go along with you?"

"Because Aunt Ellie wants Mady Simpson to meet you. She said so in her letter."

"I told you not to read that letter! Why did you have to let people know where we are?"

"I'm sorry I sent that postcard," I said.

But I wasn't really sorry. I was proud of Jeff. He had been chosen by a very famous magazine to photograph Washington, D.C., in the spring. He was putting the Washington story on film. It was an important assignment, a big break for Jeff, and I had spread the good news among all my friends and relatives.

I was surprised, though, when Aunt Ellie promptly answered my post card with a six-page airmail letter. After five pages of family gossip and a recipe or two, she had brought up the subject of Mady Simpson. Of all things! Here we were in Washington right when Mady Simpson was coming! Well, we must look her up. This was the first time Mady had ever gone farther away from home than the corner drugstore, and we must keep an eye on her. Furthermore, Mady was a "real good sport with a grand sense of humor." I had to admit it didn't sound good.

The cab stopped in front of the Waverly Hotel. I took Jeff by the arm, pulled him out of the taxi and into the hotel lobby. I held onto his wrist while I used a house phone to call Miss Mady Simpson.

A soft, pleasant voice said, "Hello?"

"Miss Simpson," I said, "I'm Mrs. Jeff Troy. I used to be Haila Rogers. My Aunt Ellie-- that's Mrs. Lambert in Spokane-- suggested that my husband and I look you up."

"Oh, yes," Miss Simpson said. That was all she said.

"Well," I went on, "we're in the lobby and--"

"You're in the lobby? Now?"

"Yes, and we thought if you weren't busy, Miss Simpson--"

There was a long uncomfortable pause. Then Miss Simpson said, "My room number is 808." She hung up.

I put down my phone and said, "Jeff, she doesn't want to see us any more than we do her."

"Well, let's skip it," he said cheerfully. "We've tried."

"She's expecting us, Jeff."

Jeff sighed. "Let's go," he said. "But remember, we're not staying."

The second time I knocked on the door of room 808 a voice called, "Come in." We stepped into the living-room of a suite, and the voice said, "Hello. I'm Mady Simpson."

She pulled the bedroom door shut behind her and came toward us. I looked at her, too surprised to speak. But Jeff was equal to the occasion, more than equal. He was saying, "Well, hello! Welcome to Washington, Mady!"

Mady was in her early twenties and Mady was beautiful. Her hair was dark and curling, her complexion creamy, her figure-- well, if there were any more at home like her, Spokane was quite a town. And she was smiling at us; she was glad to see us. Something had changed her mind since I had talked to her on the house phone.

She said, "This is wonderful of you! Won't you sit down?"

I said dutifully, "We can only stay a minute."

Jeff said, "Don't be silly, Haila; sit down. Take your coat off."

"Yes," Mady said, "please do, Mrs. Troy."

"That's Haila," Jeff said. "And you call me Jeff, Mady. Well! It certainly was nice of Aunt Ellie to tell us about you, Mady! How is the old girl?"

"She's fine," Mady said. "I've heard her speak of you two, but she didn't say anything about your being in Washington, when I told her I was coming."

"Did you come by train?" Jeff asked.

"Yes"

"Well, Aunt Ellie got Haila's card after you started and she wrote us airmail....How long are you going to be in Washington, Mady? Is this a vacation? Or have you been elected to something?"

Mady laughed. "In a way, I've been elected to something. It's an advertising campaign." She extended one foot toward us and said, "Did you ever see a shoe like that, Haila?"

"No, I have not," Jeff said.

"She asked me," I said. "It's a beautiful shoe, Mady. But what is it? It doesn't look like leather-- or suede."

"That's just it! It's something new. It's Wamptex."

"I get it," Jeff said. "Wampum plus textile. Wamptex."

"Yes," Mady said. She changed her voice into a parody of a radio announcer: "Wamptex...stronger than leather...softer than silk! It looks good on you, and you, and you! It looks good on everybody!"

"I'll buy it," Jeff said.

"It's a new plastic material," Mady said, "and it's wonderful, really. Well, the advertising agency dreamed up a scheme to introduce the stuff. They chose six of us at random....You know-- pointing blindfolded at names in telephone books of different cities and rural places, until they got six women who would accept a free trip to Washington."

I said, "What if they got a woman or two who never wore shoes? That would've been embarrassing."

"They kept on checking and pointing at names," Mady said, "until they got the right women. Six ladies of different ages and who represented different types...a grandmother, a young wife...you know. Well, all we have to do is wear our Wamptex shoes and have our pictures taken in them as we go gadding about seeing the sights of the capital."

"And you have to look foot-happy," Jeff said. "So when the ads come out your pictures sell Wamptex."

"Yes," Mady said smiling, "and we are foot-happy, too. We all saw a movie last night, and Mrs. Wilkins-- she's the grandma in our group-- she said it was the first time she ever sat through a movie without taking off her shoes."

"I bet," I said, "the advertising boys love Grandma Wilkins for saying that!"

"What's your program for this afternoon, Mady?" Jeff asked. "Maybe Haila and I will go sight-seeing, too. Then, afterward the three of us can have dinner together."

"Dinner together?" Mady said. "Oh, I don't think--"

"Sure, Mady," Jeff said, and he grinned at me. "We'll go some place where there's dancing. Of course, Haila won't be able to dance in those old-fashioned shoes of hers, but she won't mind watching you and me."

"I'm sorry," Mady said, "but I must stay with the group."

I said, "Jeff will take all the ladies dining and dancing. He'd love to, Mady! I have some post cards to get off this evening. So I'll just go sight-seeing with you. Where are you going today, Mady? What's your first sight to see?"

"The Washington Monument," Mady said. She stood up quickly. "I'm awfully sorry, but I'll have to dress now. Why don't you meet us at the Monument? In half an hour, say."

"Fine," I said. "That'll give Jeff time to make himself look a little more presentable."

The second bedroom door on the other side of the room opened and a woman of about forty stepped into view. I looked at her feet. She was wearing a pair of Wamptex shoes. Hers were not as high-heeled nor as dashing as Mady's; they were more sensible, but they were still smart. Wamptex shoes looked good on her.

Mady was saying, "Miss Worden, this is Mr. and Mrs. Troy. Grace-- Haila and Jeff."

"How do you do, Haila and Jeff?" Miss Worden said.

There was a pleasantness, a warmth about her that made me think her at once the nicest woman I'd ever met. Her plain, sweet face exuded generosity and selflessness. If you had your pick of neighbors, you'd choose Miss Worden. And there was a bond of friendship between her and Mady that was, somehow, immediately apparent. I wasn't surprised when Jeff asked, "Have you two known each other for a long time?"

"Oh, no," Miss Worden said. "Just since I got on the train at Denver."

"Do you live in Denver?" I asked.

Miss Worden shook her head. "Kingville, Colorado. A tiny little place north of Denver. You could go through it without even knowing it. But everybody in Kingville would know! Strangers there are a curiosity." She turned to Mady: "My dear, we mustn't be late. It's nearly time."

Mady laughed. "We have plenty of time." To us she said, "This is Grace's first vacation in years and she's not going to miss a thing. Grace is a nurse. She's been taking care of an elderly couple for the last three years."

Miss Worden nodded, smiling. "The Colbys. But a daughter-in-law came to stay with them while I'm away, so I needn't worry."

I stood up. "We mustn't keep you from the Washington Monument. And if Mady still has to dress--"

"The Washington Monument?" Miss Worden said. "Why, we visited that yesterday."

"Oh, yes," Mady said, and a pink flush crept up her creamy face. "Yes, I-- I forgot about that."

Jeff shook his head in awe. "If you can forget the Washington Monument," he said, "you sure must lose a lot of umbrellas."

Mady laughed. "I didn't really forget. I mean-- Where are we going, Grace?"

"To the Smithsonian Institution. Then we're to have the rest of the afternoon to ourselves, for shopping or anything we like. We're all to meet again for a dinner and a concert...Mady, you aren't going to change, are you? You look fine."

"I guess I'm all right. We'd better be getting down to the lobby."

As the four of us stepped out of the elevator, a young man came hurrying across the lobby toward us. He was a good-looking kid, about twenty-five, blond with an attractive rugged ranginess. Mady introduced him. Mr. Ray Caldwell said a polite hello to Jeff and me, but he no more than glanced at us. It was too much of a struggle for him to take his eyes off Mady Simpson.

She said, "Mr. Caldwell, the Troys are related to a friend of my father. She asked them to look me up."

"How nice for the Troys," Caldwell said dreamily.

Conversation seemed destined to languish, when a voice bursting with personality boomed in my ears: "Well, Miss Simpson! Well, Miss Worden! Aren't we looking lovely this afternoon!"

This middle-aged cheerleader in a three-hundred-dollar suit and a twenty-dollar necktie, was Mr. Larry Bryant. He was with the advertising agency that handled the Wamptex account. Ray Caldwell was his assistant, and that must have been quite a strain for Caldwell. Just meeting Larry Bryant was nerve-wracking. Inside of thirty seconds he had pumped our hands, invited us to have a drink with him, any time, any place, given Jeff the name of his tailor, cracked four jokes, got one laugh-- not counting his own appreciation of his wit.

Miss Worden got a word in. "This was all Mr. Bryant's idea," she said. "The whole advertising stunt."

He put his arm around her. "My press agent!" he said. "Isn't she terrific?"

"It's a good idea," Jeff said.

"Only good?" Bryant said. "Brother, guys who only get good ideas in this racket aren't long for this racket!"

"Who's your photographer on this job?" Jeff asked.

"Barney Kendall."

"He's one of the best," Jeff said. "I'd like to see him at work."

"You a photographer?" Bryant asked. When Jeff nodded, he said. "Well tag along! Barney won't mind!" Suddenly he raised his voice from its usual shout to a bellow: "Well, here are the rest of my lovely ladies!"

Four women joined our group. There was the grandmother, Mrs. Ida Wilkins, of Providence, R.I. There was a society-matron type, a Mrs. Lillian Allenby, of Evanston, Ill. There was a young-wife type, a Mrs. Francine Shelley, of Savannah, Ga. And, finally, there was the trim, efficient-looking, business-type girl, Miss Roberta McCall, of Harrisburg, Pa. Each of them was wearing her Wamptex shoes, and looking beautifully shod.

Mr. Bryant made the dramatic announcement that he could not accompany the ladies that afternoon. He had to stay at the hotel and wait for a phone call from the New York office. He made a speech, turning the group over to his able assistant, Mr. Ray Caldwell, then disappeared in a cloud of personality.

In a few minutes Jeff and I were in a cab following the other two cabs that were transporting the Wamptex party to the Smithsonian Institution.

Jeff said, "Haila, I forgive you for sending the post card to Aunt Ellie."

"So I noticed," I said tartly. "Jeff, Mady didn't want to see us when I phoned. And then she tried to send us to the Washington Monument, where she definitely would not be. Why doesn't she want us around?"

"You're imagining things, Haila."

"She liked us, all right, but she tried to get rid of us. I wish Aunt Ellie had told me more about her."

"Maybe she's a spy," Jeff said darkly.

"I'm worried about her. She's a nice kid, and if she's in any kind of trouble--"

"Haila, don't be silly!"

We got trapped by a Constitution Avenue traffic light, and then by the time our cab had pulled up in front of the National History

Building of the Smithsonian Institution, the ladies and Ray Caldwell were out of their cabs and out of sight. Jeff and I walked into the building.

There were very few people in the museum today; the cherry blossoms were apparently too much competition for the Smithsonian. We saw practically no one, and none of the Wamptex ladies, until we reached the extinct monsters department. There we found Mrs. Allenby, the Evanston matron, looking disapprovingly at the giant dinosaur of them all. She seemed to thinking that it was ridiculous for anything to let itself get so bulky, simply a matter of diet.

We walked along and went around a square fence of screens that probably shielded an exhibit in the making; then we stopped dead. We were looking at something almost as ancient as the old dinosaur. We were looking at a boy kissing a girl. It was a nice kiss, and both parties to it were being extremely enthusiastic about it. One of the parties was Ray Caldwell, the other was Mady Simpson.

Then Mady opened her eyes and saw us. She stepped away from Ray, the color flaming into her face. Ray, if possible, was even more embarrassed than she.

"Well, Haila," Jeff said sternly, "your Aunt Ellie is right. Mady Simpson does need chaperoning....Young man, what is the meaning of this?"

Ray's poise was on the way back. Smiling, he said, "It was all Mady's fault. She was too beautiful."

"Jeff," Mady said, "how long was it after you met Haila that you kissed her?"

"Haila and I never met," Jeff said, "It wasn't all that formal. She attacked me on top of a Fifth Avenue bus."

"So you Troys," Mady said, "were love at first sight, too."

Our double date was broken up by the photographer, Barney Kendall. He had just taken a picture of Roberta McCall, her Wamptex shoes and a rare Peruvian mummy. Now he wanted a shot of Mady, her shoes, and a meteorite. I watched until Jeff and Barney got too technical about the simple act of snapping a camera, then I drifted away to see a sight or two myself.

The varied interests of the women had separated them and scattered them throughout the huge building. I found the young wife from the South, Francine Shelley, enviously eyeing a collection of rare gems. I saw Grace Worden on the second-floor balcony, shaking her head in wonder at the historical collection of pianos. The Rhode Island grandma, Mrs. Wilkins, was entranced by the whales. She told me proudly that her grandfathers had both been whaling captains.

Somehow Ray Caldwell finally got his herd of ladies started across the Mall to the ancient turreted Arts and Industries Building of the Smithsonian. The women were enthralled by the transportation exhibit: the stagecoach, the old street-car, the early automobiles and airplanes. They were touched by the shell-torn original Star-Spangled Banner. When we got to the Costume Hall and the collection of

White House dresses, their cries of delight almost raised the roof.

I was standing beside Mady when she turned questioningly around. "Grace?" she called. "Where's Grace Worden? I want to hear her ooh and ah over these!"

But Grace wasn't with us. Nobody remembered having seen her since we left the other building.

I said, "The last time I saw her was at the piano collection."

Mady said, "I'm going back to get her."

"Haila and I will get her, Mady," Jeff said. "Barney wants to take a picture of you and Dolly Madison."

When we got outside we found that the day had begun to darken; a storm was gathering. A great, black cloud was billowing over the Washington Monument, surging across the Mall. Over on Constitution Avenue a police siren whined, as though in protest against the ruination of a lovely day.

In the Natural History Building we decided first to see if Grace Worden was still being enchanted by those strange and wonderful pianos on the balcony. But we never got beyond the landing. As we climbed the staircase, two men ran past us up the stairs.

When we reached the balcony landing, a crowd of people, all strangely quiet, had gathered there. They were standing in a circle about something I couldn't see. I stood on tiptoe, and saw a man kneeling beside the prostrate form of a woman. Then I saw the woman's face, and I knew that Grace Worden was dead and that she had died horribly.

I turned away, leaned against Jeff. He was talking to a man who said, "She was lying right at the head of the stairs when I found her. I thought she'd fainted." I heard another voice, quietly official, say, "She was strangled."

And then Jeff was saying softly to me, "Come away, Haila."

I knocked once on the door of Room 808. Mady Simpson called out, "Who is it?" and I knew from her voice that I was going to be the one to tell her about Grace Worden.

Only a little more than an hour had passed since Jeff and I had found Miss Worden dead, savagely murdered. Jeff had stayed with the detectives; I had been allowed to run my tragic errand.

I called back to Mady, "It's Haila Troy."

"Come in, Haila. The door's open."

I walked into the living-room, and Mady smiled at me from the bedroom doorway. She was vigorously drying her hair. She said, "Be with you in a moment, Haila. I got drenched." Then she stepped back out of sight.

I moved across the living-room to the window to steady myself.

The window had been closed against the storm, but too late. The draperies hung limply on each side of it like wet shrouds. A pool of water lay on the floor beneath them. It was still raining, so hard that I could barely see the glow of the Capitol dome. The rain slashed violently against the windows. Then, as suddenly as if Nature had pulled a lever, the rain stopped. It was so dramatic that, in my present state of mind, it frightened me. I moved away from the window.

I forced myself to sit quietly on the divan, while I waited to tell Mady her friend had been murdered. When she came into the room she was smiling. She said, "I'm sorry I took so long--"

She stopped abruptly. "Haila," she said, "what is it? Is it-- Grace?"

There was a gay rat-a-tat on the door. As it swung open, a bubble of laughter floated into the room, and a Southern accent followed it. "Anybody home?" Francine Shelley cried. Then she saw us. "Mady, darling! I found the most adorable little dress in the most adorable little shop! I must tell you!"

The young housewife from Savannah twinkled across the room toward us. Her face was aglow with delight. The dampness had tightened her little blond curls into golden ringlets. She looked like a Christmas doll.

"Oh, Mady," she babbled on, "I wish you'd gone shopping with me."

"Francine," Mady said, without looking at her. "Francine, wait....What is it, Haila? Tell me."

"It's Grace Worden," I said.

"You couldn't find her?"

"We found her," I said. "Mady, she's dead. Murdered."

Mady stared at me dumbly. It was Francine who spoke. "Murdered!" she said inanely. "You mean somebody killed her, somebody--"

"Francine!" I said.

The sharpness of my tone got through to her. She looked at Mady's white face; then, quietly, she turned and crossed to the door, closing it after her.

Mady moved to a chair and sank down upon it. "But why would she have been murdered?" she whispered. "Why would anyone want to kill Grace?"

"The police have started working on that already," I said. "They'll be asking you questions, Mady. You seem to have known her better than anyone in the group."

She nodded. Then after a moment she said, "I've known her such a short time, but somehow-- in these few days Grace has come to mean more to me than than some friends I've known all my life. Oh, Haila, I can't believe--"

The scream wrenched both of us to our feet. Together, we ran out into the corridor. A door down the hall, next to Mady's suite, was standing open. I led the way to it.

Francine Shelley stood frozen in the center of the living-room, her back to us. She turned when she heard us and, speechlessly, raised one arm and pointed toward the kitchenette. The door was standing ajar. I kicked it wide open, and the odor of gas swarmed into my nostrils. Even before I saw the little gray-haired woman, I heard her moan. She was lying on the floor, her head below the two-burner stove. She was struggling to lift herself up on one elbow.

I stepped across her and snapped off the two jets. I lunged to the window above the sink, pushed back the fluffy cretonne curtains, and then I saw why Ida Wilkins was still alive: The window behind the curtains was open.

I turned back to Mrs. Wilkins. Mady was beside her, helping her to her feet. Together we got her out into the living-room and onto the divan. I went to the phone.

"Operator," I said, "there's been an accident. Send a doctor to Mrs. Ida Wilkins' room at once. And then-- then you'd better call the police."

Detective Lieutenant Allan Morowitz was a slow-moving, heavy man in his fifties. He was a policeman, not a career man. He wanted this case solved quickly, but he didn't care especially whether or not it was solved by him. When he learned that my husband was the Jeff Troy who had helped out the New York City Homicide boys a few times, he was glad to see him.

The three of us sat with Ida Wilkins in her living-room. The hotel doctor had come and gone, leaving the elderly woman feeling well enough to talk. Her suite-mate, Francine Shelley, was in worse shape than she. The doctor had given Francine a sedative, and she had gone to bed.

Mrs. Wilkins took the cold compress from her head and thrust it away. She smiled grimly and made a brave little joke. "My nut's too tough to crack," she said. And she added proudly, "I didn't even bleed."

"Atta girl," Morowitz said. "Now, Mrs. Wilkins, tell us just what happened. What time did you get back to the hotel?"

"Just before five. I met Mady Simpson as I came into the lobby. We were both wet to the skin, so I made Mady promise that as soon as she changed she'd come here and have a cup of hot tea. I came in and--"

Jeff said, "You left the door unlocked?"

"Yes, so Mady could get in if I was still changing. I thought before I changed, though, I'd put the kettle on. That's what I was doing when I heard a noise behind me. Before I could turn around something hit me on the head. The next thing I knew, somebody was screaming, and then Mrs. Troy and Mady were helping me up off the floor."

"It was a lucky thing for you," Morowitz said, "that you had opened that kitchen window."

Mrs. Wilkins shook her head. "I didn't open it," she said. "It must have been open all along."

I said, "It was those cretonne curtains that saved your life. The killer didn't realize the window behind them was open."

"Mrs. Wilkins," Morowitz said, "you have no idea who it was who knocked you out?"

"It was too quick. Just a step behind me and then bang--! Why would anyone do that to me?" The little lady was indignant. "I've lived sixty-three years without anyone trying to kill me! I have four sons, two daughters, and eleven grandchildren! When they hear about this the fur will fly! It's a good thing for the murderer my husband isn't alive!"

Jeff sat down beside her. "Mrs. Wilkins," he said, "do you know what this means? It means you must have seen something, or heard something, at the Smithsonian this afternoon when Grace Worden was killed. That's why the murderer has to get you out of the way."

"You mean-- he may try again?"

Morowitz said, "We won't let anyone get near you; don't worry. But maybe you can solve this case for us in ten minutes, if you can remember what it is the killer knows you saw."

Mrs. Wilkins shook her head. "I don't even know how to go about remembering."

"Tell us what you did at the Smithsonian. From the second you got out of the cab."

"Well, we all went in together. We all stopped to look at the paintings....Let me see. Most of the ladies went on, but Roberta McCall and I stayed a while. I was with Roberta until we went upstairs and got separated. You know how you do in a museum."

"Yeah," the policeman said wryly. "In a museum you wander. All the ladies wandered. At one time or another every single one of you must have been out of sight of everyone else. It's hopeless to figure out who was where, and with whom, and when. Any one of your party could have killed Grace Worden."

Mrs. Wilkins gasped, "You don't think one of us did it! Why, I've never seen a nicer crowd of ladies!"

"Well," Morowitz admitted, "someone could have followed Mrs. Worden here to Washington, or been here waiting for her. Someone we don't know about. But we can't ignore you ladies as suspects."

"But we've never seen each other before in our lives!"

"I know, I know," Morowitz said unhappily, "and that fact doesn't make things easier for us. If only you could remember what it was you saw."

"But I can't," Mrs. Wilkins said helplessly. "I don't think I ever will!"

"Maybe," Jeff said, "it was something you heard. Try to think."

The old lady closed her eyes in concentration, but it was no use, she soon said. She was tired, so tired. Jeff helped Mrs. Wilkins to her feet, escorted her to her bedroom. I offered to help her get into bed, but she would have none of that. She said, as I closed her door, that all she needed was a little nap.

Morowitz was slumped down on the divan. He said, "This may

sound ridiculous, but we've got to consider it: Maybe Mrs. Wilkins staged that attempt on her life to throw us off."

I said, "You mean that she killed Grace Worden? That little old lady? Then knocked herself out?"

"You can knock yourself out," Morowitz said, "if you got the nerve."

Jeff smiled. "But where is the blunt instrument? She couldn't have hidden it after she was unconscious. And the doctor says she was really knocked out--"

The door of the bedroom was wrenched open. Ida Wilkins stood teetering in the doorway. Her face was ash-colored as she held out a piece of paper toward Morowitz. "This was on my bed-- on my pillow."

We were all beside her, then. Morowitz took the single sheet of hotel stationery from her. Across his elbow I read the message. It was written with an ink-pot pen in letters that looked as though they had been printed by someone's wrong hand. Morowitz read the words aloud, in his harsh, flat voice:

"You are the second of the six."

It was a long moment before anyone spoke. Then it was Ida Wilkins who whispered, "We're all to be killed, aren't we? All-- all six of us ladies."

"We've been wrong," Jeff said. His voice was tight. "Mrs. Wilkins didn't see anything or hear anything. The killer didn't want her out of the way to protect himself."

"No," Morowitz said. "She was the second-- on his list of six."

"But that's insane," Mrs. Wilkins breathed. "Insane!"

"He meant for you to see that note-- before," Jeff said. "He wanted you to suffer before he killed you. Yes, he's insane, but he's a maniac with a motive, a motive to kill all six of you women."

"Unless," Morowitz said grimly, "the murderer is one of you women."

"Six would still die," Jeff said. "Five would be murdered, the sixth would be a suicide."

"But why?" Mrs. Wilkins said hoarsely. "Why would anyone want to kill us ladies? We've never seen each other before! We have nothing in common-- nothing except this trip to Washington!"

"You have something in common," Morowitz said. "The reason for someone wanting you all dead. The thing that made someone dream up the scheme of getting you all here, in one place, where he could..." Morowitz jerked around to face Jeff. "Who is it?" he said. "Who engineered this thing?"

"Bryant," said Jeff. "Larry Bryant."

"He's here? At this hotel?"

"Yes."

The policeman had started for the telephone when Jeff's voice stopped him: "But Larry Bryant bragged about his idea, his baby. So he was lying. It wasn't his idea. If it had been..."

Morowitz turned and looked at Jeff. I saw the same look of horrified realization on both their faces.

Jeff said, "It may be too late now. It's been three hours since Grace Worden was killed."

Morowitz was barking into the telephone: "Operator, get me Larry Bryant's room!" The phone in Bryant's room was answered immediately. "Bryant?" Morowitz snapped. A look of relief flooded his face; then just as quickly, it was gone. "What?" he said. "This is Morowitz-- Homicide Squad."

He listened for a moment, then said, "I'll be right there." His face was gray when he turned back to us.

Jeff said, "That wasn't Bryant."

"No, it was a bellhop. He just found Bryant."

"Dead," Jeff said. "Murdered."

"Yes, dead. Bludgeoned to death with a brass lamp. And he died because he knew whose idea it was to bring these women to Washington. He was murdered because he could have told us the name of the killer."

Young Ray Caldwell sat on his bed in Room 917 with his head bowed into his hands. In the past few minutes he had heard from Morowitz and Jeff that Grace Worden had been murdered, that Ida Wilkins's life had nearly ended, that his boss had been beaten to death, that more death was scheduled to arrive. He seemed stunned and bewildered.

He had left the ladies, he said, when the group disbanded, and started walking back to the hotel. He had been caught by the cloudburst, and spent some time in store doorways, futilely trying to catch a cab. When the rain stopped he had come back to the hotel, blithely dressed for dinner, still unaware of what had happened.

His shock, naturally, centered on the death of Larry Bryant. Why had he been killed? he asked. Jeff told him, and then said, "Ray, you can help us, and we need help fast. If you can tell us who sold Larry his advertising stunt, you'll be naming the murderer."

"But," Ray said, "I always thought it was Larry's own idea. He was proud of it."

Jeff shook his head. "Someone sold the idea to Larry. They must have told him he could take all the credit for it. And they must have been pretty sure he would do just that, and never mention their name."

"They weren't taking much of a chance," Ray said. "Larry was on the skids, on his way out. He needed an idea, or else. And this idea-- well, it saved his job for him."

"The whole setup was brought to him, of course," Jeff said. "The names of the women, everything."

"Yes," Ray said thoughtfully. "Yes, looking back now, that's it. Lining up the women would be the kind of thing that I, as his assistant, would ordinarily do. Larry wouldn't have touched any of

the details. So somebody did it for him. Look; could it-- could it
have been one of the women themselves? She might have sold him
the idea, let him take all the credit for a thousand bucks, say, and a
free trip to Washington as one of the Wamptex models."

Morowitz said, "It makes sense, Caldwell. It could be one of the
ladies. But it could be someone else-- someone in your agency, for
instance."

"No," Ray said. "Well, maybe-- but that person would have to be
in Washington, and nobody else from the agency is here except Larry
and--"

He stopped, and stared at the detective. "I could have given
Larry the idea," he said softly.

Morowitz nodded. "There's the ladies themselves and you.
Nobody else."

"No, wait!" Ray cried; then he sank back. "No, skip it."

Jeff said, "I know what you're thinking, but it wasn't Barney
Kendall. I was with him every second at the Smithsonian, watching
him take pictures. He's the only one, I guess, who does have an alibi.
He's out of this."

"Maybe," I said, "Ray was always with Mady Simpson."

Ray shook his head. "No, I wasn't. I haven't an alibi, and I can't
prove I didn't sell this idea to Larry. But I never saw these women
before. They never saw me. How could I have any reason to kill
them?"

"Sonny," Morowitz said, "that's what you're all saying-- or will
say. All of you, including the murderer."

"Ray," Jeff said, "we came up here hoping you might be able to
tell us who gave this idea to Larry Bryant. You might have seen or
heard something."

"No," Ray said tonelessly. "You can bet that Larry made sure no
one discovered this idea was not his own."

The telephone rang, and Morowitz answered it himself. To Jeff
he said, "They've rounded up all the ladies. They're waiting for us in
Ida Wilkins' suite."

In the corridor outside Room 810 the detective stopped to speak
to two of his colleagues. At the end of the hall three more policemen
stood. The hotel seemed to be crawling with the forces of law and
order. I followed Jeff into the gathering of ladies.

They sat there, the five of them, from five widely separated
points on the map of the United States, and each of them was
affected after her own fashion by the tragic turn of events. Ida
Wilkins was calm now, with a forced serenity designed to be a
comfort to the others. The giddiness had gone out of Francine
Shelley's face; she was blatantly, unashamedly afraid. Mady Simpson
was trying not to look frightened, and almost succeeding. Roberta
McCall, the young business woman from Pennsylvania, appeared
completely incredulous that death could so have disrupted the smooth

holiday plans. The Evanston clubwoman's long, patricianly handsome face indicated that she thoroughly resented the fact that she had become a part of this spectacular tragedy; yes, Mrs. Lillian Allenby was obviously more incensed than frightened.

Then Morowitz was in the center of the room, speaking quietly.

"Girls," he said, "if we can find the reason for someone wanting to-- to end your lives, I think we'll find who that somebody is. He or she is insane, of course, though, looking at him, you probably wouldn't think so. Personally, I doubt if he could get away with another murder. I believe I have things organized so that couldn't happen. But it takes only a second to fire a bullet or use a knife. So we've got to find him before he strikes again."

Francine rose to her feet, shouting hysterical accusations of inefficiency at the police. Quickly, Mrs. Wilkins went to her. She pulled her down on the couch beside her, quieted her; then, after a moment, said, "Go on , Mr. Morowitz."

"Well-- how shall we go about this? You ladies have been together now for almost two days. Some of you longer than that; you traveled here together. You've talked to each other. Have any of you found that you have anything in common with any of the others?"

None of the ladies said a word. They were like a class whose teacher had asked a question too difficult to answer.

Jeff said, "It might be a person you all know. It might be a place or--"

"A place!" Roberta McCall said suddenly.

She was sitting very straight on the edge of her chair, taking a minute to organize her thoughts. She was cool, unruffled, and I could see why her employer in Harrisburg, Pa., was fortunate in having her as his secretary. She had seemed retiring, unobtrusive. But now that there was business to be done, she was a confident and forceful person.

"It was yesterday," she said, "on our way to the Washington Monument. I rode in the cab with Grace Worden and Mrs. Wilkins. We were chatting, getting acquainted, and Mrs. Wilkins said that she hadn't always lived in Rhode Island. After her husband died she had lived in Santa Fe with a son several years."

"Yes!" Ida Wilkins said. "Yes, I remember now!"

"Grace Worden," Roberta went on, "said that she had spent some time in Santa Fe. It turned out that you two were there at the same time."

"That's right," Mrs. Wilkins said. "We had a nice talk about Santa Fe, Grace and I. And we thought how funny it was that there we were in Santa Fe and never bumped into each other, but that we should meet like this in Washington several years later."

"Did you discover any mutual friends in Santa Fe?" Jeff asked.

"No, we didn't. We didn't talk long, though."

"What was Grace Worden doing in Santa Fe?"

"Why, I don't believe she said. I can't remember." She looked to

Roberta for help.

"No, Grace didn't say," Roberta said. "We arrived at the Monument right after Grace and Mrs. Wilkins began talking about Santa Fe."

"Mady," Jeff said, "you were with Grace more than anyone else. Did she--?"

"No," Mady said. "She never mentioned Santa Fe to me."

"Her family?" Morowitz asked.

"Grace hadn't any family, so far as I know," Mady said. "But there are the Colbys. She'd been taking care of them for a long time. They probably know a lot about her."

"They live in Kingville, Colorado-- right?" Morowitz asked. Mady nodded.

Morowitz said, "I hope they have a phone."

He went to the corridor door, summoned one of his assistants, and conferred with him briefly. Then he came back.

"Santa Fe, seven years ago," he said. "It might not mean a thing, but we've got to run it down. Was anyone else there, then? Think!"

Francie said, almost tearfully, "Seven years ago I was still in college down in Florida."

"Seven years ago," Mady said, "I was thirteen years old."

"That makes it absurd," Roberta McCall said. "A thirteen-year-old child, a schoolgirl, a grandmother--"

"You're absolutely right, Roberta!" Mrs. Lillian Allenby, the matron from Evanston, sounded as though she were seconding a motion in her home-town club. "We could have had nothing in common! Nothing!"

There was a sudden banging at the door, voices were raised in an angry chorus in the hall outside. The door burst open. A bull of a young man with flaming red hair dragged two of Morowitz's men into the room after him.

"Mrs. Shelley!" the young man shouted. "Francine!"

Morowitz took over. He quieted the young giant down, had his men unhand him. He asked the redhead who he was.

"I'm E.M. Zack," he said. He looked around the room at the women.

Morowitz said, "What do you want with Francine Shelley?"

"I've come to take her out of here!" He was looking now at Francine, who was in a state of bewilderment. "You're Francine!"

"Mrs. Shelley," Morowitz said, "do you know this man?"

"I never laid eyes on him in my life!"

"Of course you never did, Francine," E.M. Zack said, "but I'm an old friend of your husband's. Harrison and I went to college together."

"I never heard him mention any E.M. Zack!"

"Maybe not, Francine. Harrison used to call me Easy-- E. Z., you know."

"Well!" Francine cried. All the fear and worry went out of her face; it sparkled again. "So you're Easy!"

"Yes, sir! And when old Harrison called me here in Washington and told me somebody was trying to murder his wife-- Well, you're coming home with me, Francine. Harrison is on his way up here by plane to get you. He'll pick you up at my house."

"Why, Easy!" Francine said. "This is nice of you!"

"Mrs. Shelley," Morowitz shouted, "what is all this!"

"Why, it's like Easy said. When I phoned my husband, he phoned Easy."

"And when did you phone your husband?"

"Why, the second I found out I was going to be murdered!"

"When was that?"

"When I heard you and Mr. Troy saying we were all supposed to get killed. After Mrs. Wilkins found the note to her. In spite of the pill the doctor gave me, I couldn't sleep, and I was listening, and I called my husband."

E.M. Zack said sternly, "Francine, you get your things."

"Mrs. Shelley," Morowitz said flatly, "is not leaving here."

"Now, listen here," Zack said; "I promised old Harrison--"

"The police," Morowitz said, "can take better care of her than you can. But that isn't the only reason we are keeping this woman here." The detective turned his back on the redheaded young man and spoke to the five ladies before him. Gently, he said, "One of you might be the murderer, you know."

They sat there shocked into quiet.

Looking at the five of them, I knew how utterly impossible that thought must seem. It couldn't have been the frivolous Southern belle, Francine; nor Mady Simpson, who was so young and gay. It couldn't have been a society dowager who probably worked endlessly for worthy causes in Evanston, Ill. It couldn't have been a prim, proper secretary nor a sweet, gray-haired grandma....Yet Grace Worden was dead, Larry Bryant was dead, and others were meant to die. It was a fact: One of these ladies could be a murderer.

They sat staring silently at one another, and I sensed the slow, growing fear that crept through them-- the fear of one another. It was a cold, insidious thing, and it filled the room.

Francine was sobbing quietly now. "I want to go home," she repeated over and over. "I want to go home."

Morowitz said flatly, "You have no choice, none of you. You're here to stay until this thing is settled. But I'm sure that each of you-- except possibly one of you-- wants to co-operate and help us find the person who wants you dead."

One by one the women nodded their heads in assent, and Francine, in a small, trembling voice, said to Zack, "You go home. Explain to Harrison when he comes."

Without a word the redheaded young man turned and walked from the room.

Morowitz was speaking again: "I know how your families are

suffering over this, but I'm going to ask you to try to keep them out of Washington. There's nothing they can do that isn't being done. Frankly, they'll only make things tougher for us, maybe make it drag on longer. You can talk to your folks back home on the telephone as much as you like." The policeman smiled grimly. "But be careful what you say. We'll be listening in."

He stopped as his young assistant came back into the room. "Well, Handley? Did you get that call through?"

Handley nodded. "I talked to a Henry Colby in Kingville. Grace Worden was taking care of him and his wife. She'd been with them three years, but they couldn't tell me much about her. She hadn't any family-- at least, none she ever spoke to them about."

"She was all alone," Mady said, "ever since she was a young girl. She told me that."

"Go on, Handley," Morowitz said.

"Well, before she worked for the Colbys, she spent several years taking care of an invalid lady in California. When she died Grace Worden went to the Colbys."

"What about the time she spent in Santa Fe?" Jeff asked. "What do you know about that?"

"Not much. That involved a nursing job, too. It seems she and a patient, an old man that time, took a trip to Santa Fe. They were spending the winter in Arizona, and visiting Santa Fe for a couple of weeks."

"Who was the patient," Jeff asked. "Is he still living?"

"The Colbys aren't sure. They think Miss Worden's job ended with him because he went abroad to live." Handley glanced at his notebook. "His name was Cooper, Daniel Cooper--"

The gasp was so loud, so sharp, that everybody in the room heard it. We all turned; we were all looking at Lillian Allenby. She was no longer the poised and dignified clubwoman. Her eyes were bulging, her face had gone gray.

Morowitz was walking toward her. "What is it Mrs. Allenby? What are you trying to say?"

She swallowed convulsively before she managed to speak. "Daniel Cooper-- he may be a relative of mine, a distant relative. It may be the same man."

Morowitz tried to keep the excitement out of his voice: "But you aren't sure, Mrs. Allenby, you don't know?"

"Yes, it must be he. I know that he spent several winters in the Southwest. I know that later he went to France. Yes, he could have been in Santa Fe several years ago. I know that after his wife died he had a professional nurse to care for him. Yes, the Daniel Cooper who was in Santa Fe with Grace Worden must be related to me."

The detective gave up trying to be calm, businesslike. He almost shouted. "That's the third link to Santa Fe! Ida Wilkins lived there seven years ago. Grace Worden visited there. You're related to the man Grace Worden took care of there. You went to see Daniel

Cooper when he was in Santa Fe."

"No," Lillian Allenby said. "No, Mr. Morowitz, I did not visit him there. If I had ever been in Santa Fe, seven years ago or any other time, I should have told you so."

"All right; you weren't there. But he must have told you about something that happened there. Something that Grace Worden knew about, that Mrs. Wilkins once knew but has apparently forgotten. It's something you know, too, and that's why your life is in danger. Think, Mrs. Allenby. What did Daniel Cooper ever tell you about his visit to Santa Fe?"

She shook her head. "I know nothing at all about his visit there."

"But there's some connection," Morowitz said desperately. "Try, Mrs. Allenby, try to help us!"

"There is no connection," she said firmly. "I didn't know until right now that Daniel Cooper had ever been in Santa Fe. I didn't know that Grace Worden had been his nurse. Actually, I have never even met Daniel Cooper."

"But you corresponded, you were in touch, somehow?"

"No," Mrs. Allenby said. "In fact after Christopher died--"

"Christopher?" Morowitz said.

"Mr. Allenby, my husband. Actually, it was he who was related to Daniel Cooper; he was a nephew. Since Christopher passed on I have heard very little about Daniel Cooper. I knew that he had gone to live in the south of France, that he had shut himself off entirely from America. He was always eccentric. Christopher would never tell me how he made his money, but it was in some unsavory manner. Speculation of some kind. Christopher was never close to his uncle and, of course, neither was I."

Mrs. Allenby had recovered her poise. She glared at the detective.

"I consider all this ridiculous," she said. "Oh, I admit I was frightened for a moment, but it was foolish of me. If you went at it hard enough you would probably find a dozen places where two or three of us have been at the same time." Acidly, she added, "And I do not mean places where distant relatives have visited, but where we ourselves have been."

Roberta McCall said, "I agree with Mrs. Allenby. How many of us, I wonder, were at the New York World's Fair the summer it opened. I, for one, was there."

"I was, too," Mrs. Allenby said.

"And so was I," Ida Wilkins said.

"All right," Morowitz said wearily. "You're making a point. You're proving how impossible it's going to be for us to find the killer and save your lives."

He sighed and looked at his watch. "It's time you ladies had some food. There'll be a policeman or two stationed in the hall outside each of your rooms. Be nice to him. He's working for you."

The ladies rose and went their ways. Ida Wilkins and Francine

went into their bedrooms, and Jeff and I, Morowitz and Handley were
the only ones left in the living-room.

"Troy," Morowitz said, "what do you think?"

"I don't think we ought to give up on Santa Fe. World Fairs don't
count. Big cities like New York and Chicago don't count. But a place
like Santa Fe--"

"That counts, huh? Well, it better count quick. Lord knows how
soon one of these women will do something silly and get herself
knocked off. I'm going back to headquarters, get some more men
assigned to this case. C'mon, Handley."

After the two men had gone I said, "Jeff, I'd like to go see Mady.
She's all alone in that big suite now that Grace--"

"Let's go see Mady," Jeff said.

We found Mady Simpson sitting desolately in her living-room.
Before we had time to do more than close the door behind us the
phone rang. It frightened Mady; she leaped to her feet at the sound.

"Hello?" she said. Then she glanced at us, and in a moment I
understood her embarrassment. "Oh, hello, Ray," she said. "Yes, I'm
all right. It-- it's nice of you to call." She was being formal, even a
little cool. "No, I don't believe there's anything, thank you....Haila
and Jeff Troy are here and....Yes....Yes, good-by, Ray."

Jeff said, "He's a good guy, that Ray. I like him."

"Yes," Mady said. "He's nice."

"You were careful just now not to let him think you thought so."

"Look," Mady said; "about Ray and me this afternoon. I-- I don't
know what made me do that. I'm not a girl who kisses boys I've
known only two days! It must have been the excitement of being in
Washington and having such a wonderful time and--"

"And it's spring," I said.

"Yes. That could be it. It's spring."

"Or," Jeff said, "it could be just Ray Caldwell."

"Oh, I do like him," Mady said. "He's attractive and-- fun to be
with, but I hardly know him!...Please, let's change the subject. I'm
embarrassed."

Jeff obliged, but not very tactfully. He said, "Mady, tell me.
Does your family know about Grace? Have you phoned them?"

"Not yet."

"You'd better call, Mady. They'll hear about it on the radio or
from the newspapers."

Mady was reluctant. "There's only my father, and he never
listens to the radio. He won't know about it until tomorrow when he
gets his paper."

"Someone will tell him tonight, Mady, and he'll be frantic," I
said.

"All right. I'll call him pretty soon." Her mouth tightened
grimly. "I can just hear what he'll say. He didn't want me to take
this trip. He'll say he told me so."

"Why didn't he want you to come to Washington?" Jeff asked.

"It isn't Washington; it's any place. He hates to let me out of his sight. When I was in high school he wouldn't even let me go to football games that were away from home. He wouldn't let me go away to college; I had to take a secretarial course right at home. If this trip hadn't been free I couldn't have come, and even then it took days of pleading to let me....Oh, I know. You're thinking that my father had to bring me up all by himself and he's just trying to be a good parent. But it's more than that. He's strict because he likes to boss people! And he's always right!"

She got to her feet and walked away from us. "I'm sorry," she said.

"Mady," Jeff said, "do you have any special boy-friend back home?"

"No," she said. "Boys don't like my father-- and the feeling's mutual."

There was a brisk rat-a-tat on the door. Mady looked almost wildly at Jeff. He went to the door and opened it.

A bellhop walked into the room. "Package for Miss Simpson," he said.

"It can't be," Mady said. "I'm not expecting anything."

"Sure, it is," the boy said. "The desk clerk made a note of it." He read from the package: Mady Simpson, 808. To be delivered between eight and eight-thirty P.M."

"But it couldn't be--" Mady started.

Jeff gave the bellhop a quarter and the boy went away.

"Mady," Jeff said, "it's probably just a small gift from your new admirer. Stop worrying."

She laughed, self-consciously. "All right; I'll open it."

She snapped the string that bound the package, pulled away the wrapping, and revealed a small, square cardboard box tied with a white ribbon. She put the box on the table, undid the bow, and lifted the lid.

She looked down into the box and her forehead wrinkled in a puzzled frown. Then, suddenly, the bewilderment was gone and her face was filled with fear.

"Mady!" Jeff said. "Mady, what is it?"

With one hand she shoved the open box across the table toward Jeff. Arranged on white cotton were four small objects: a ten-cent-store spray of artificial forget-me-nots, a pocket mirror with a small crack at one corner, a lipstick, and a lovely old cameo brooch that was the real thing, the kind that grandmothers leave to their first granddaughter. That was all. There was no card, no word of writing in the box.

I said, "Mady, what do they mean?"

She laughed, and the laugh was forced and uncertain. "It's silly, isn't it? It-- it's some kind of joke."

Jeff looked slowly from the box to Mady. "It frightened you, though. Why?"

"No," she protested, "I wasn't frightened. Only surprised. I don't know what I expected-- but nothing so strange as this."

"You haven't any idea who sent it to you?"

She shook her head.

"And you don't know what they mean? Look at those things, Mady. A cameo, a mirror, forget-me-nots, a lipstick. Does the combination mean anything to you?"

"No. Nothing at all."

Jeff looked at her for a moment. Then he said slowly, "We'll have to get these to Morowitz right away."

"Morowitz?" she said. "The police? But this hasn't anything to do with the murders, Jeff! It can't have!"

"But that thought occurred to you, didn't it, Mady? That's what frightened you so when you opened the box. Instead of a note, like Ida Wilkins got, the killer sent you this. Is that what you thought?"

"No!" she cried. "Oh, I've told you already I was just surprised! These things-- what could they mean?"

"I don't believe anyone could ever figure that one out but you," Jeff said. "Try, Mady. Open the lipstick. See if it's your shade."

She opened the gold-colored tube. She said, "It's my shade."

"Then the person who sent it probably knows you. And it might mean, too, that's it's a woman. I doubt if I could match Haila's lipstick."

"You think," Mady said slowly, "that one of the women in our group sent me these things. You think she meant it as a warning and--" She stopped suddenly and buried her face in her hands. "No, you're wrong, I tell you! It doesn't mean anything! Nothing's going to happen to me, nothing."

I put my arms around her and she sobbed, like the child that she was, onto my shoulder.

When I awoke the next morning Jeff was standing, already dressed, at the window of our hotel room. He didn't look any happier than I felt.

It had been long after midnight when Jeff had insisted that I return to our hotel and get some rest. The night, for me, had seemed endless; for the ladies who had been invited to Washington by a murderer it must have been incredibly horrible. The police had pounded at them relentlessly, hour after hour, trying to find a clue that would save their lives.

Mady Simpson, because she had received an inexplicable gift from an anonymous giver, had been the center of their concern. At last she had collapsed under the strain and a police nurse had put her to bed, stayed beside her. It was after that that Jeff had sent me home while he stayed on with Morowitz.

I pushed myself up on one elbow. "Jeff," I said.

He turned to me. "Good morning." He came over and sat down

on the edge of my bed.

"Darling," I said, "are they-- are they all right?"

He nodded.   "Up until five minutes ago when I talked to Morowitz they were all right."

"Jeff, what about the package Mady got?   Did you find out anything new?"

"Nothing that helps. Morowitz and I talked to the desk clerk who accepted the package.   He didn't get back to the hotel until four o'clock this morning."

"And he can't remember who gave it to him?"

"No. He thought it was unreasonable of us to even hope he would. He figures he gets mixed up with about five hundred people a day. But he remembers the package, and that he made a note on it. He thinks it was handed to him about noon yesterday."

"Noon! That was before any of this started!"

"Yes," Jeff said, "but does that mean anything?   It doesn't to me." He rose and roamed the room. "And what do those four idiotic objects mean?   That brooch-- it could be an antique, an heirloom. And the mirror-- that's second-hand. I mean, it wasn't just bought, like the forget-me-nots and the lipstick probably were."

"There's no chance of tracing where the flowers and lipstick were bought?"

"No.   The police are trying but there are a lot of stores in Washington. It's pretty hopeless." Jeff picked up his coat. "I'm going back to the hotel now."

"Wait for me," I said. "I want to be with Mady when she wakes."

The corridor outside Mady's room and the Wilkins-Shelley suite was empty. The police guards, I thought, were probably stationed in the ladies' living-rooms.   But then, all the bedrooms had hall entrances.

I knocked quickly on the door of Mady's room.   There was no answer. I tested the knob; the door was locked.

Jeff said, "Relax, Haila. Morowitz said he was going to get them all together this morning. Let's try Ida Wilkins' room."

The meeting wasn't being held in 810, either.

I said, "Do you know where Mrs. Allenby and Roberta McCall are?"

Jeff said, "Ten-twelve." He nodded toward a fire door at the end of the corridor. "Let's use the stairs. It's quicker."

"Now who's nervous?"

"We're all nervous."

I followed Jeff down the corridor. He opened the fire door, took one step through it, then stopped.   Silently, he backed out again, pushed the door back into its frame.

"Jeff," I whispered, "what is it? What did you see?"

"A pair of Wamptex shoes," he whispered back.   "A pair of Wamptex shoes tiptoeing down the stairs this way."

"Who was in them?"

"I don't know who."

He held his finger to his lips. Slowly he pulled the door open, not wide enough so we could see anything, but enough so we could hear the click of heels. The lady was across our landing now and going on down. As she descended she became less and less cautious. Now she was hurrying, and either she didn't care if anyone heard her or she was confident that no one would.

We stepped out onto the landing. We waited until the footsteps seemed two full flights beneath us, then we started down, quietly, in pursuit.

It was a long journey, seven flights of stairs. When we reached the second-floor landing we heard the slam of a door below us. We ran then, down the last two flights. Jeff eased open the exit door. We looked down an alley and saw Lillian Allenby moving rapidly along it toward the street. As we watched, she turned to the right and out of sight.

We ran to the street; we turned right. Mrs. Allenby was standing at the corner of Louisiana and New Jersey Avenues, waiting for a light. Then she was across New Jersey and we followed her. She seemed to know exactly where she was going, and she was wasting no time in getting there. She hotfooted it into Constitution Avenue; at Pennsylvania she crossed over to the left side of Constitution and kept going along the Mall.

"Jeff," I said, "she may be headed for the Smithsonian."

"She could be, yes."

But we were wrong. Mrs. Allenby marched into Mr. Andrew Mellon's thoughtful gift to his country, the National Gallery of Art. The moment she had disappeared behind its doors we broke into a run. When we saw her again she was climbing the last few steps to the second floor. We hurried up after her. She was in the incredibly beautiful rotunda with the soaring dark-green marble columns. We watched her as she quickly circled the statue of Mercury in the center of the rotunda. Then, abruptly, she headed back for the stairs. Jeff and I just had time to step behind a column, so she didn't see us.

Jeff said, "She was looking for someone."

"That's the impression I got."

We reached the foot of the steps as Mrs. Allenby was hustling out through the front doors to the street. She crossed Constitution Avenue at Seventh Street. Then she was climbing the tremendous terrace of stairs at the Archives Building.

Now we took a chance, and it didn't work. We knew that we couldn't wait until Mrs. Allenby was safe inside the building; she would have won too great a lead on us. So we started up the steps. We were on a landing, a fourth of the way to the top, when Mrs. Allenby reached the doorway. She turned, then, and she saw us.

Even from that distance I could see her large features twitch with surprise. The surprise immediately turned to extreme annoyance. She started down the steps, and by the time she had reached us she was steaming indignation.

"Well!" she said. "May I ask why you two are spying on me?"

"Haila and I are lousy spies," Jeff said. "You foiled us. Now we'll never know why you sneaked away from the hotel."

"Sneaked!" Mrs. Allenby's indignation was volcanic. "Sneaked! I don't know the meaning of the word!"

"I'm not blaming you," Jeff said. "There's something you intended to do this morning that you didn't want the police to know about, so you had to-- to tiptoe away."

"Young man," roared Mrs. Allenby, "I have nothing to hide! I can tell the world my intentions this morning!"

"Lower your voice," Jeff suggested, "and just tell us."

"Next Tuesday I am to deliver the main speech at my club in Evanston. My topic is to be: Washington, D.C., As I Saw It. Now I intend to see Washington, and no idiotic policeman is going to stop me!"

"Oh," I said, "you're sight-seeing."

Jeff said, "But how fast can a sight be seen? You spent a minute and a half at the National Gallery."

"I spent all of yesterday morning there, while the other ladies were resting after their trips. I have a special interest in the art galleries here. My late husband was an artist. If he had lived, by now Christopher Allenby's portraits might very well be famous."

"But," Jeff said, "about the ninety seconds you just used up at the National Gallery. I don't understand that."

"I was just checking on something, a bit of research. I wanted to know the exact number of columns in that rotunda. It's facts that make a speech interesting. There are sixteen columns in the circle and two in each of the four hallways leading to the circle, making a total of twenty-four. The ladies of my club expect a great deal of me. If I do say so myself, my speech last fall, Paris, As I Saw It, was very well received."

"But, Mrs. Allenby," Jeff said, "you can't go running around like this. It's dangerous for you."

"Mr. Troy, I am in no danger. I won't presume to speak for the other ladies, but nobody wants to kill me. Of that I'm positive. I have not lived that sort of life which would--"

"Mrs. Allenby," Jeff said, "I'm sure your life is as blameless as Mrs. Wilkins', but someone tried to kill her."

"I know nothing of Mrs. Wilkins' past. But I do know that for me to sit cooped up in that hotel is ridiculous! I accepted this offer by the Wamptex people because I wanted to see Washington, and nothing is going to stop me."

I had seen the prowl car slide slowly up beside us. Now it stopped. The policeman on the right got out.

He said, "Mrs. Lillian Allenby?"

Puzzled, she said, "Why, yes."

"I thought so. You fit the description. We got orders to take you back to the Waverly Hotel."

"But I'm not ready to go back to the hotel. I'm not nearly ready!"

"Sorry, lady." The policeman looked at Jeff and me, then back at Mrs. Allenby. "Do you know these people?"

"I'm Jeff Troy," Jeff said, "and this is my wife."

"Oh, yeah. You're working with Morowitz on this....Ready, Mrs. Allenby? We'll drive you to the hotel."

"I refuse to enter that vehicle! I will not permit myself to be arrested!"

"This is not an arrest," the cop said. "At the most it's protective custody."

"Keep your eye on her," Jeff said, smiling. "She's an escape artist."

Mrs. Allenby snorted. "My slipping away from the hotel is an example of the inefficiency of the Washington police! No wonder you never caught John Wilkes Booth!"

Jeff asked, "How did you get away from Morowitz and his boys?"

"It was ridiculously simple! All the police were in my living-room with us ladies. No one was in the corridor. I simply said that I had a headache and needed an aspirin. I went into my bedroom, put on my hat, powdered my nose, and walked out of the bedroom door that opens onto the corridor." Mrs. Allenby was pleased with herself. "I fooled Morowitz completely!"

"He was seeing that a killer didn't come into your suite," Jeff said. "He wasn't expecting one of his victims-to-be to try to get out of it."

"Mr. Troy, kindly do not use the word 'victim' in my presence. I explained to you that I am not to be a victim. And, furthermore, I plan to get to Mount Vernon this afternoon. Nothing shall stop me."

"Please, Mrs. Allenby," the policeman said. "Please let us ride you back to the hotel."

"Well!" Mrs. Allenby said. "Well, if you're going to be so nice about it, I accept your invitation. You Troys will have to walk back, and it serves you right! Spies!"

She seated herself beside the driver of the coupe; the other cop squeezed in beside her. Somehow, as she sat there, Mrs. Allenby made the two policemen look as if they were under arrest. The car started off for the Waverly Hotel.

Jeff looked at his watch. "Haila, we've got to beat it back to our hotel. I did come to Washington on assignment, you'll remember, and my pictures are due tomorrow. If I airmail them now, they'll get there tonight. Come on!"

When we stopped at the desk for our key, the clerk told us that for the past hour Spokane had been trying to call Mr. and Mrs. Troy. It had seemed urgent. We went directly to our room and I called Aunt Ellie. In an incredibly short time she was on the wire.

"Haila, dear!" she screamed. "Haila, can you hear me?"

"Yes, Aunt Ellie," I said, holding the phone at arm's length.

"Haila, I'm going to get right to the point! Has anybody else been murdered yet?"

"Not that I know of, Aunt Ellie. How did you--?"

"I talked to Mady's father this morning. Mady phoned him. He's terribly worried, naturally. But I told him nothing could possibly happen to Mady."

"Why are you so sure, Aunt Ellie?"

"Because you and Jeff are taking care of her, of course."

"Oh," I said.

"Haila, dear, you won't let anything happen to Mady, will you? I promised Mr. Simpson that you wouldn't--"

The operator cut into our conversation. She said, "Sorry; this is a police call....Go ahead, Hotel Waverly."

"Troy?" Morowitz's voice said.

"This is Haila, but Jeff's here."

"Tell him to come over to the Waverly, will you? Another note has popped up, another death warning."

Five minutes later Jeff and I were in the corridor outside the Wilkins-Shelley suite. The detective handed Jeff the piece of paper. This one, like the other, was written on Hotel Waverly stationery, and the writing, as before, was in rude, characterless block letters. There were just four words: "Now it's your turn."

"Cozy," Jeff said. "Whose turn is it now? Which of the ladies got this one?"

"We don't know," Morowitz said.

"You don't know! How was it delivered?"

"We don't even know that. I thought it would be good for the ladies' morale if they all got out of a hotel room for a while. I took them downstairs for lunch in the Foutain Room. It was a good idea," Morowitz said belligerently, "until this note was found."

"Who found it?"

"A waiter. We were all leaving the dining-room when he caught us at the door. He'd found the note on the floor. We figure it was delivered in the dining-room. One of the ladies could have slipped it into another's coat pocket. Or dozens of other people could have managed it as they passed our table. But whoever got the note never knew it. When she got up it must have dropped to the floor. It was kicked around for a couple of minutes before the waiter picked it up."

Jeff jerked his head toward the door of Room 810. "Did you get anywhere on a common motive in your session this morning?"

"No," Morowitz growled.

"You can't make Santa Fe mean anything?"

"Troy, I can't make anything mean anything."

"Are all the women in there?"

"Yes, and I've got three of my boys in there with them. I've got

the whole floor blocked; no outsider can get near this suite. I don't
see how another murder can happen, but...Troy, I want that killer!
There's no better way to make sure there isn't another victim.
Listen; I'm a great, big, ugly cop. The girls tighten up when I'm
around. You'd think I'm against them, not for them. See what you
can do for a while."

"Sure," Jeff said; "I'll try."

"I'm wanted back at headquarters. I'll be back as soon as I can."

There was an awful stillness in the living-room. The murderer's
failure to deliver his note properly had multiplied his intended cruelty
by five. Now five women, not one woman, were suffering the fear of
imminent death.

Perhaps not five. If one of the ladies was the murderer....But as
I stood in the doorway of the room it was impossible for me to accept
that theory. To me these were still five women who had lived
reasonably happy, normal, useful lives. I still could not believe that
inside one of them burned the maniacal revenge that must possess the
killer.

Before Jeff and I had stepped away from the door, there was a
knock. One of the guards unlocked the door, and admitted young Ray
Caldwell.

None of the ladies greeted Ray. He spoke quietly, haltingly:
"I've just talked to our New York office...the president of our agency
is flying down..." Then he seemed to realize that what had been a
comfort to him on the telephone was none at all to them. Ray
dropped into a chair, fumbled in his pockets for a cigarette. "You
don't mind if I stick around, do you?"

"Of course, stick around!" Francine Shelley's Southern accent
could not dilute the harshness of her voice. "Stick around, by all
means! The more the merrier!"

"Now, now, Francine," Ida Wilkins said.

"Stop it-- stop being so calm! You don't feel that way-- you're
just as frightened as I am."

"Francine," Mrs. Wilkins said, "all of us are frightened, but we
have to be calm. And I think we're doing a very good job of it, all of
us."

"I think," Mrs. Allenby said, "that we're behaving just as well as
any group of men under these circumstances. The superstition that
women are weaker than men is just a lot of masculine nonsense."

Roberta McCall said, "I agree with you, Mrs. Allenby, and--"

"Call me Lillian," Mrs. Allenby said.

"Thank you, Lillian. I was just going to say that my boss would
change his tune about how jittery women are if he could see us now.
And I'll tell him that, too, when I get back to Harrisburg-- if I ever
do get back."

"Roberta, don't waver!" Lillian snapped. "Don't spoil your point!"

"Even our baby has been just fine," Mrs. Wilkins said. "Mady has been the best of all."

"Oh, no," Mady said. "No, last night I had to be put to bed."

"You were physically exhausted," Mrs. Wilkins said, "that was all. Why, when you and Mrs. Troy found me there on the kitchen floor, you were as cool as a trained nurse. You put wet towels on my head, you made me comfortable-- you were splendid!"

Mady said, "Oh, no, I wasn't splendid! I was running around like a scared rabbit. All I can remember doing is drying my hands on the kitchenette curtains. Yes, right on those pretty curtains! A girl who isn't hysterical wouldn't do a thing like that! You were the calm one."

"No, I wasn't then and, despite what Francine says, I'm not calm now. When you're as old as I am you learn to hide your feelings. Then, too, when you're as old as I am you don't mind dying so much....Oh, dear, please forgive me for saying that." Quickly Mrs. Wilkins went on, "You know, I'd like a nice cup of tea! We could all do with a cup of tea!"

"Yes," Francine said, "there's nothing like a cup of tea while you're waiting to be..."

"Francine-- dear," Mrs. Wilkins said.

As she started to rise, Mady put a hand on her arm. "I'll make the tea," she said.

"Why, thank you, Mady, that would be lovely of you."

"Mady!" Ray Caldwell blurted in a loud voice. "May I help you?"

"Why-- yes, if you want to."

Ray followed Mady into the kitchenette. One of the policemen moved so that he could see into the little room. The ladies were quiet now. Mrs. Allenby rose and paced briskly back and forth before the windows; she seemed to be exercising. I saw Roberta McCall wearily put her hand over her eyes, then quickly jerk it away as if ashamed of such weakness. Francine Shelley abruptly went to the telephone. She asked the operator to page her husband in the lobby.

She was babbling to him pathetically, when Jeff moved away from my side. I saw him walk toward the policeman outside the kitchenette. He drew him away from his post, spoke softly to him. The two of them turned, watching the kitchen doorway. I watched it, too.

Francine suddenly started wailing tearfully into the phone. The three other women in the room rose and went to her. I stayed where I was and saw the kitchenette door slowly close.

Jeff tiptoed over and put his ear to it, listening. Then he shook his head at me; he had heard nothing. He opened the door. Ray and Mady were standing beside the window. They jerked around to face us.

Jeff closed the door behind us. He said, "I hate to interrupt again. This is the first chance you've had to be alone together since Haila and I broke up your love scene at the Smithsonian....At least, Ray's in love. Anyone within miles of him can see it. It's harder to tell about Mady, though she seems willing."

"All right," Mady said defiantly. "I am in love with Ray. I have been from the very first minute we met-- at the Washington, D.C., Union Station. I--"

"Mady," Jeff said reprovingly, "I believe you when you say it was love at first sight with you two. Only, your first sight wasn't just the other day in Union Station. It was probably as long as five years ago. Maybe at the high-school prom."

"Jeff!" Mady said. "How can you--? I don't understand!"

"You two were going to get married. Was it to be last night?"

Ray laughed. "You couldn't be more wrong."

Jeff said, "A cameo...a new lipstick...a mirror...forget-me-nots. Something old, something new..."

"Oh," I said. "The mirror-- that was borrowed! And forget-me-nots are blue!"

"That's right," Jeff said. "For the bride: something old, new, borrowed, blue. When I saw you two walk into this kitchen together I thought how these murders had ruined a beautiful romance. I thought that some day, except for this, you two might even have got married. And while I was hearing your wedding bells in my mind, I got the meaning of your four gifts, Mady. Did Grace Worden send them to you?"

Mady was silent. She looked at Ray.

He said, "We've got to admit it, Mady. Jeff knows he's right."

Mady said, "Yes. Grace sent them to me. She knew about us; I told her. She knew we were going over to Maryland last night to get married. And she arranged to have that package delivered just before I was supposed to leave. That cameo-- that was her real wedding present to me. The rest of the things were just-- Grace being sweet."

"Mady," I said, "that's why you weren't glad to see us. You were furious with Aunt Ellie for sending us to see you. It's because your father is against your marrying Ray, and you thought we might be spying on you."

"That's right. My father is against my marrying anyone, but most of all Ray."

"Are you school sweethearts?" I saked.

"No. Ray worked for almost a year in an advertising agency in Spokane. Then he went to Los Angeles, then to New York. He wrote me in care of a friend, he phoned me at a friend's house. Of course, father never knew that Ray was even in New York, let alone with the agency running the Wamptex stunt. After Ray left Spokane his name was never mentioned in our house."

"But this wasn't a coincidence," I said. "You knew Ray would be in Washington."

"Certainly. We were going to be married last night. I was never going back to Spokane. I was going to New York with Ray. And if father didn't want to forgive me, he'd never see me again."

"But you'll still be married!" I said. "Things will work out that way--"

"Haila, wait," Jeff said.

"Now," Ray said. "Now here it is."

"Sorry, kid," Jeff said, "but here it is. Even after the murders you two kept your plan to elope a secret. Mady wouldn't tell us what the four gifts meant. Why was that?"

"You say it, Jeff," Ray said. "I'm afraid I'll strangle on it."

"You put Mady's name on the list, Ray."

"Yes....Now say the rest of it, Jeff."

"And maybe you put all the names on the list. Maybe the scheme to get all these murder victims to Washington was your idea."

"But you don't believe that, Jeff!" Mady pleaded. "The police might believe it, but you don't, do you?"

"Ray," Jeff said, "tell me how it happened."

"Larry Bryant handed the whole campaign to me, just as I told you. And I thought it was Larry's idea. One of the six women on the original list couldn't make the trip at the last minute. Larry told me to find a substitute. Of course, I thought of Mady. At first we thought it would just be a way for us to see each other. Then--"

"It was I," Mady said, "who thought we should get married."

"Jeff," Ray said, "do the police have to know about this?"

"They should have known about it right away. If you've told us the truth, it means that Mady isn't on the killer's list; she isn't in any danger. Think of the time the police have wasted thinking of Mady as a victim."

"And she isn't to be!" I said. "That's what's important! Mady isn't in any danger!"

"If I'm telling the truth," Ray said quietly. "But I can't prove anything. Maybe I want Mady murdered, not married to me. It might have been my scheme, the whole thing. I haven't been able to figure out how to prove that it wasn't."

"But he wanted to tell the police," Mady said. "I made him promise to wait-- a little while. Jeff, help us!"

"I'd like to, Mady," Jeff said. "I'm going to try, but--"

"But the police have to know about it now," Ray said.

"Right now," Jeff said.

In the living-room Jeff spoke briefly to one of the policemen. Then we started out to find Morowitz. In the cab, Jeff lapsed into a silence that was of the tomb. I let him alone.

Then an idea hit me that I couldn't keep quiet about. "Jeff," I said, "the woman who couldn't make the trip, the person Mady is substituting for-- she might give us the answer to this whole thing."

"She might," Jeff said. "Ray will have her name, her address--"

His voice snapped off. He was looking out of the curb side of the cab as it slowed down in front of police headquarters. Down from the entrance of the building ran a man. He raced toward the line of police cars parked ahead of us. His face was grim.

Jeff was out of the cab. "Morowitz!" He yelled.

The police detective shouted back, "Come on! My car--"

Jeff threw some money at our driver. We were in the police car and it had started. Morowitz said, "I don't know how it could have happened, but it did."

"Who?" Jeff asked.

"The girl," Morowitz said. "Mady Simpson."

"No!" I said. "She can't be dead."

"There's a chance she'll live. She was poisoned."

"Poisoned!" Jeff said. "But how? Your men were there, watching--"

"Troy, did you ever see a batch of nervous dames attack a tea tray? There's confusion, and in the confusion the poison was slipped into Mady's cup."

"But Mady Simpson wasn't on the list," Jeff said. "She wasn't meant to die; she wasn't one of them."

The detective turned sharply. "What?"

"Listen," Jeff said.

He told Morowitz about Ray and Mady Simpson, how Ray had substituted her for a woman who, at the last minute, could not make the trip. The policeman heard him out and said nothing. I knew what he was thinking. He was thinking that Ray Caldwell had tricked Mady into believing he put her name on the list because he loved her, that Ray had selected each of the six women, lured them to Washington to murder them. I knew it was wrong, that it couldn't be, and yet...

We were back in the living-room of Suite 810. There were more policemen now than before; there was one less young lady than before. I knew instantly where Mady Simpson was. Every eye was fixed on the closed door of the bedroom. They were waiting-- Ray and Ida Wlkins, Roberta McCall and Francine and Mrs. Allenby, waiting to see if Mady Simpson would live or die.

I saw Morowitz touch Ray Caldwell's shoulder. The boy lifted his stricken face, and the policeman made a motion toward the other bedroom. Ray got to his feet and followed Morowitz.

"Jeff," I said, "you told me Mady wasn't in danger-- she wasn't even on the killer's list." I found myself talking so loudly that the four ladies turned and gaped curiously at me. I didn't care; I went right on: "You believed Ray's story then. Do you still believe it, Jeff?"

"Yes."

"Then, why? Why was she poisoned?"

"I think it was for the same reason that Larry Bryant was killed. She knew something that would reveal the murderer. She didn't realize, herself, what it was, or she would have told us."

"But what could she have known? Where could it have happened?"

"At the Smithsonian, maybe. Haila, you were there, I was there. All four of you ladies were there. One of us, or all of us together, might be able to figure out what it was that Mady knew. We've got to try-- all of us."

They nodded their heads, Francine and Mrs. Wilkins, Lillian Allenby and Roberta McCall. One of these was the murderer, and she, too, was nodding, pretending she wanted to trap the killer.

Jeff was saying, "Maybe it was nothing at the Smithsonian. And it certainly is nothing connected with Larry Bryant's death; Mady was never near his room. She might have seen something when Mrs. Wilkins was attacked. Haila, you and Mady took care of her, then. What could Mady have seen or heard?"

"Nothing. Nothing that I didn't see or hear, too."

"Think, Haila. Try to remember. Think of every second-- from the moment you heard Francine Shelley scream."

I closed my eyes. I forced my mind back over each slightest detail, each move that I had made, that I had seen Mady Simpson make.

I shook my head. "There's nothing, Jeff. I was first in the kitchen. I pushed by Francine and ran into it. I remember hearing Mrs. Wilkins moan, seeing her move trying to get up off the floor. I turned off the two gas jets, and I pushed back the curtains and saw that the window was already open. Mady was helping Mrs. Wilkins by that time."

I stopped, and it was something I, myself, had said that stopped me. But I didn't know what it was, nor why. I tried again to remember those moments in the tiny kitchen, to relive every one of them. I could smell the odor of gas as I snapped off the jets. I could feel the crisp ruffled curtains as I thrust them back. I could see again the glow of the Capitol dome through the open window. Then I had it...."Jeff," I said, "I remember now. I know."

Jeff was leaning toward me, waiting. The eyes of the plain-clothes men were riveted on me. The four ladies bent their heads in my direction. One of them, a murderess, was waiting for me to speak.

I said, "Do you remember, Jeff, just a few hours ago-- here in this room-- when the ladies were talking about being calm? Mady said she was so flustered she dried her hands on the kitchen curtains....Jeff, that's why she was poisoned: because she touched those curtains and she knew, just as I did, that they were dry. They shouldn't have been dry, Jeff."

"Because of the rain?" Jeff said. "It was coming in that direction?"

"Yes. I was in Mady's room just before that, and the window there had been left open. Those curtains were soaked, dripping. Mrs. Wilkins' kitchen window looks out on the Capitol, too; her curtains should have been wet. But--"

"But they weren't," Jeff said. He jerked around to face Ida

Wilkins. "It was still raining when you got back to the hotel?"

"Yes. Yes, it didn't stop until I was taking off my hat and coat here in the living-room. Then it stopped so suddenly that I noticed it."

"Mrs. Wilkins," Jeff said, and his voice quickened, "you said before that you didn't open that kitchen window. You're sure of that-- sure?"

"Yes, I'm sure," Ida Wilkins said. "I never touched it."

"Then," Jeff said softly, "it was still closed when you were attacked. It wasn't opened until after you were knocked out and the gas turned on. Only one person could have opened that window-- the killer."

"Yes," Mrs. Wilkins said, "but-- but what does that mean?"

Each of the women had the same look of perplexity on her face that Ida Wilkins wore-- even the killer, herself.

He said, "Don't you see what it means, Mrs. Wilkins? The killer opened the window and pulled shut the curtains. She wanted us to believe that she had overlooked the open window, that that was why you didn't die. She didn't want us to know that she was saving your life."

Roberta McCall said hoarsely, "She didn't want Mrs. Wilkins to die?"

"Right," Jeff said; "it was all a phony. The attempt on her life, the note she got, the note that was found in the dining-room today. Everything phony. The whole idea of the chain-killing was staged. Only one person was meant to be murdered: Grace Worden."

"But Larry Bryant was killed," Ida Wilkins whispered, "and Mady--"

"That was because they could have eventually named the killer."

"Then the rest of us," Ida said, "are safe. We aren't going to die." She shuddered, then went on. "She is insane, though, to make us all suffer this way. It's a mad woman who--"

"No," Jeff said. "It was a clever, careful, methodical woman who created this advertising scheme and sold it to Larry Bryant. It was a scheme to put one person, Grace Worden, within her reach. She must have meant her death to seem accidental, for there to be no investigation at all. But she failed; it was murder, and the police were called....So one of you has a connection with Grace Worden, and a motive for her murder. It's so strong, so clear, that if we had looked for it after Grace Worden had died we would have found her murderer at once. That was why one of you invented this mass murder. You wanted us to look for the link that chained all of you together. We never would have found it, of course, because there wasn't any. But you were safe as long as we kept searching for it."

"But none of us even knew Grace before," Roberta McCall said. "Why would we want her dead? What would be the motive?"

"It has to be big, and obvious-- or the killer never would have gone to such frantic lengths as the mass-murder scheme to cover it.

It's something that we could verify quickly, in a matter of hours, maybe. A radiogram to the south of France might do it. When Grace Worden was in Santa Fe, she was taking care of an old man named Daniel Cooper. A rich old man--"

Lillian Allenby rose slowly to her feet. Slowly, she sidled toward the windows, eight floors above the street. Then Jeff moved, and Lillian Allenby screamed as she lunged toward the window. She stumbled and, still screaming, pitched headlong to the floor, where two policemen caught her.

At ten o'clock the next day Jeff and I were saying good morning to Mady Simpson. She was sitting up in bed, looking slightly pale and very, very lovely. The young man who sat on the foot of her bed thought so, too. Ray Caldwell could hardly take his eyes off Mady to greet us.

"I'm going to get up at noon," Mady said. "The doctor said I could. Fortunately, I didn't take too much tea."

"Mady," I said, "have you talked to your father again?"

"This morning. And listen! Ray talked to him, too!"

"Yeah," Ray said, "and he was so glad Mady was all right he was even civil to me."

Mady said, "Jeff, about Mrs. Allenby--"

"She confessed, Mady, and it was a pretty awful thing to hear. I could see her counting all of old Daniel Cooper's money that was almost hers."

"Daniel Cooper," Mady said. "Oh, he was the gentleman Grace Worden was nursing in Santa Fe."

Jeff nodded. "When his name came up," he said, "Lillian had to admit that she was distantly related to him. She didn't admit, of course, that she was his only relative. She also let Haila and me know that she was in Paris last summer, but she didn't tell us that the whole greedy purpose of her trip was to look up old Daniel. He hadn't even known that she existed. He was surprised to know that his only living relative, Christopher Allenby, with whom he had quarreled years ago, had married Lillian. In his lonely senility he was touched by her visit; it was easy for her to get him in a will-making mood. But he threw a shock at her. One half of his fortune would go to Lillian; the other half to a nurse who had been wonderful to him years before."

"Grace Worden," Mady said.

"Yes, and Lillian couldn't bear the thought of sharing any of that money. Right there she went into the act that ended in Grace's death. She promised Daniel that she would locate Grace for him, and she did. But she didn't let the old man know that, of course, nor Grace. She began to plan how she would kill Grace."

"But why," Ray said, "didn't she just go to Kingville, where Grace was, and--"

"She couldn't. She couldn't get in and out of that tiny place

without being noticed. Besides, Grace's death had to seem accidental; it must not be a murder that the police could probe for a motive.
The motive was too obvious. So Lillian knew that she had to get
Grace to a big city, where there are tall buildings to fall from and
where fatal traffic accidents can happen. Then, after she had racked
her brains for months, along came Larry Bryant, who had been
racking his brains for an idea to exploit Wamptex shoes."

"Then she'd known Larry Bryant before," Ray asked.

"Slightly. Her husband had been an artist. Not the genius she
wanted us to believe but a commercial artist who did advertising
stuff. It was through him she knew Larry, still saw him occasionally
when he went to the Chicago office. Well, she dreamed up the
Washington idea for Wamptex and Larry. She knew he'd jump at the
chance of taking complete credit for it. All she asked was to be one
of the Wamptex models."

"So she did hand Larry the whole idea," Ray said. "The ladies
and all."

Jeff nodded. "Five of them she picked at random; the sixth was
Grace Worden. And, like old Cooper, Grace didn't know that Lillian
ever existed. So she could get real palsy with Grace, and she did--
until that certain moment at the Smithsonian.

"She found Grace alone on the landing with the stair well
dropping down to the ground floor. That was the place for an
accident. But Grace moved her head at the wrong time, and she saw
Lillian coming at her and the murder in her eyes. Before she could
scream, Lillian strangled her....Now Grace was dead but the plan was
ruined. It was murder, not accidental death. And the motive for her
murder, and the killer, would come out as soon as the police went to
work. So Lillian did the one thing that might save her: She
camouflaged her motive by making it look as though all the women
had been brought here to die.

"Of course, that necessitated killing Bryant, the one person who
knew that the whole exploitation scheme was hers. She got herself
some sleeping pills and called on Larry before he even knew that
Grace was dead. But she couldn't use the stuff, because Larry wasn't
drinking. So she waited until his back was turned and hit him with a
brass lamp. Then she started on the chain-killing scheme.

"She wrote a warning note and went hunting Ida Wilkins. She'd
meant to bang her over the head-- not too hard-- and hoped we
would think Ida had been left for dead. But when she found Ida in the
kitchen, she had a better idea-- gas. With Ida knocked out and the
gas turned on, we would know that the murderer meant business; we
would assume that Ida was supposed to have seen the note before the
attack, but hadn't found it. Actually, Lillian planted the note on the
pillow after she had taken care of Ida in the kitchen."

"And that," I said, "turned out to be her big mistake."

"Why, Haila?" Mady asked.

"She'd heard Ida and Grace at dinner, still talking about Santa

Fe. She thought that the police would use that coincidence as a possible linking of all the ladies, which they did. And she knew it would be a dead end, which it was. What she didn't know was that Grace had gone to Santa Fe with Daniel Cooper, the one name that had to be kept out of all this. When this fact came out-- the one fact that could hang her-- she was forced to admit her relationship with Cooper. Then, to get the police off that track, to make them forget about Santa Fe, she sent a death note to a woman who had no possible connection with Santa Fe-- Francine Shelley."

"Francine? The note in the dining-room was meant for her?"

"Yes," Jeff said, "and Lillian had a tough time delivering that one. Haila and I caught her the first time she tried, sneaking down the fire stairs to Francine's room. She knew we'd caught her, only we didn't know that. She made us think she was sneaking out to do some sight-seeing. And the second time she tried in the dining-room, Francine dropped the note, never even knowing that she'd had it. Then, before Lillian had a chance to correct her mistake, Mady tipped off the fact that she could solve the whole case."

"I could," Mady said. "How?"

"You knew that the kitchen window had been closed all during the storm."

"Yes!" Mady said. "You know, I was thinking about that when the poison hit me. Those curtains-- they shouldn't have been dry. It meant something--"

"It meant that the killer opened the window," Jeff said, "because she didn't want to kill Ida Wilkins. Only Grace was meant to die."

"Mady," Ray said, "if I had been Lillian I wouldn't have poisoned you. I never would have thought you were smart enough to figure all that out."

"Oh, I'm smart," Mady said. "I know that when windows are left open rain comes in them and curtains get wet. And speaking of windows-- there's something I've wanted to do all morning."

Mady got out of bed and did what she wanted to do. She picked up her Wamptex shoes and threw them out of the window. A moment later I heard a scream, a familiar scream.

I said, "Mady you've hit Francine Shelley on the head with a pair of Wamptex shoes."

"That's all right," Jeff said. "They look good on everybody."

Broadcasting figures at least twice among the unusual backgrounds employed by Hugh Pentecost in his American novelettes. "Murder on the Fred Allen Show" (July 1944), written with Virginia Faulkner, marks one of the first times a real-life personality made an extended "guest" appearance in a mystery story. (S.S. Van Dine's The Gracie Allen Murder Case was published in 1938, but there Gracie appeared as a "civilian" character, not as her show-biz self.) Even better than the Fred Allen radio mystery is the story that follows, from the nerve-shattering days of live television drama, the demise of which may be regretted by some television critics but not (we suspect) by actors.

The Web was an actual mystery anthology series that appeared on CBS, and Pentecost adapted this story for a segment of the program. It was scheduled to appear in June 1951, the same month American published the story.

DEATH IN STUDIO 2 by Hugh Pentecost

The atmosphere in the darkened control booth of the television studio was one of calm efficiency in the midst of organized confusion. The play was the thing now; the actors coming to the climax of the show; stop watches ticking toward the exact second when it must end, smoothly and without a slip. The show was called The Web.

I sat in the back row of the booth, along with the producer and his girl assistant, watching the monitor-- a replica of an ordinary television screen-- centered over the glass panel of the booth. In that monitor I could see the same picture which was being seen on a million home television sets.

People sitting at home, watching the unfolding of a mystery drama, were absorbed by the story. So was I, but for a more personal reason. I was watching one man who was, in a way of speaking, fighting for his life. Here, in Studio Two, the tensions were far greater than anything the script writer had been able to put down on paper.

The control booth is the nerve center of the show. Directly in front of me the switcher, the director, and the associate director sat side by side, their eyes fixed on another monitor panel showing four different screens, each screen duplicating what one of the four cameras on the floor was taking. Each of these men wore headphones and intercom microphones-- a way of communicating with cameramen and technicians on the floor.

The audio engineer sat to their left, delicately manipulating the dials on a complicated panel in front of him. His job is to blend voices, sound effects, and music, so that all are distinct and clear.

In the well, the lowest level of the control booth, were the shaders-- two men sitting before two more monitors, controlling the quality of the picture being seen by the public at home, keeping it sharp and unblurred.

All of these people in the booth were responsible for getting the maximum effect from the work of the cameramen, dolly pushers, boom men, and assistant technicians who were moving about amongst hundreds of yards of cable and wire on the studio floor under the hot blaze of lights from the vaultlike ceiling.

"Take One!" the director said.

The switcher pressed a button. The Number One camera was in action, taking a tight two-shot of Michael Kerry and an actress named Jan Harder in the living-room set.

There had been some concern about Mike Kerry, felt by the crew and cast, on this particular show. It was his first try at television; in fact, it was his first public appearance since he had retired at the height of a brilliant moving-picture career some four years ago. He had been terrific up to now-- the old Mike Kerry, with all the charm and vitality that had made him a public idol in the late '30's and early '40's.

"Ready on Two," the director said.

The associate director's voice was quiet as he spoke into the intercom microphone: "Camera Two-- ready to take the walk down the hall. Don't forget, Lefty-- frame that door shot on the vase."

I could feel my palms sweating. I knew things about Mike Kerry that no one else in the studio knew, because I was one of the two people who knew the real story of Mike's retirement. Fifteen years ago they had called him a second Jimmy Cagney. I'd had a hand in that. In those days I was handling talent on the Coast, and Mike was one of my clients. But pretty soon no one compared him to anyone. He was Michael Kerry, one of the six big box-office draws in pictures. Suddenly, in '47, Mike retired. He was forty-two years old, at the very top of his career. At that age most of the big male stars are just starting really to cash in. Mike quit cold. He had to.

A violinist can't play the violin without fingers; a track star can't break records if he loses a leg; an actor can't function if his memory freezes so that it's impossible for him to remember lines. That's what happened to Mike. It came out of the blue one day when he was called to the studio for some retakes. In a simple scene he froze up at a certain place and had to stop. They tried the scene, I hear, thirty or forty times and he simply couldn't get by the block. Finally, they printed his lines on a blackboard and he stumbled through them.

He took a rest, then, before his next picture. When he came back the memory block was still there. Somehow he finished the picture, using his blackboard technique. After that he quit. People said it would be just for a long holiday; I, his business manager and closest friend, thought it was worse than that. Mike disappeared. I knew he was alive, because he continued to draw on his personal bank account. But I never heard from him, never saw him, until about three months ago.

I had left Hollywood, myself, and had come back to New York to try my hand at my real love-- producing plays. One day I ran into Mike on a side street off Broadway. I was walking along with Valerie Crane, one of our good actresses, and a woman I'd have given an arm for if she'd asked me. Mike seemed embarrassed. But he agreed to call me later, and he kept his word. We had a talk. He told me he'd spent more than three years, first with doctors, then by himself, trying to beat his memory problem.

"Only you can understand it, Nick," he said. "I'm not broke; there's no reason for anyone to feel sorry for me. But I'm an actor. It's all I know. It's all I like. If I can't act I might as well not live."

Yet he wasn't discouraged. He said he'd heard of some sort of memory course that he thought might cure him. Then, one day, Valerie mentioned casually that she'd seen Mike again. Even now I don't know if he called her or if she called him. I do know that she'd taken a terrific header for him. She was helping him, holding the book for him while he tried to memorize; she even gave up a good part in a play of mine to keep on helping him.

"He's got so much fighting heart, Nick," she told me, "such a will to work this out. I think he can."

To my surprise a little more than a week ago Mike had phoned me. He told me he had an offer to do a television show.

"I think I can get through it, Nick," he said. "If I could, I'd just about have this thing licked. The point is, can I accept without telling the producer the truth about myself? Can I let him take the risk without warning him?"

"If you're satisfied you can make it," I told him, "keep your mouth shut and take the job."

"I want you to promise one thing," he said. "Don't tell Valerie. I don't want her to suffer through it in case-- in case I fail."

That was what I was doing in the back of the control booth that night. I felt Mike needed a friend there. I'd come in the late afternoon, eaten with him during the break for dinner, seen him go smoothly through the dress rehearsal; and now Mike was about three minutes from beating a problem that had kept him heartsick and lonely for four long years. I was so proud of him I could feel a choking lump in my throat.

Mike's voice filled the control booth, sharp and clear. They were coming to the quarrel scene, the climax of the story. The chief character is a middle-aged husband, played by Mike, married to a young wife who wants his money. There is a conspiracy between the wife and a young doctor to convince the husband he is going insane. In the scene just finishing, the wife has come home carrying a bag of groceries, which she takes into an imaginary kitchen. A quarrel starts, which results in a running verbal fight down the hallway to the front door. The wife leaves.

The husband comes back into the living-room and throws himself down on the couch. Then the wife reappears, carrying an identical bag of groceries. She is sweetness and light, acting as though she hasn't been there before. The husband, convinced he has suffered some kind of mental aberration, goes to the phone and calls the doctor, telling him he'll submit to an examination by a lunacy commission.

"Take Two!" the director said.

The switcher pressed his button. The Number Two camera took up the hallway scene, following slowly behind Mike and Jan Harder as their quarrel mounted to a crescendo. This Jan Harder, a vivid blonde, had the fire to match Mike's staccato harshness.

"Get in tighter, Lefty," the A.D.-- the associate director-- told the cameraman.

I couldn't see the actual set from the booth. It was obscured by a projecting flat. So I was watching the scene in the monitor above the glass panel. Mike and Jan Harder were almost at the door. Her voice was raised to an hysterical pitch as she went into her exit line. Suddenly the camera lost the actors, and the monitor showed nothing but an expanse of blank wall.

"Lefty! Lefty, you're off the actors," the A.D. said sharply. The director was swearing, softly and steadily, to himself.

Seconds later the camera picked up Mike at the door, but Jan Harder had already disappeared off the set.

"Steady, Lefty," the A.D. said. "Get ready to pull back as he starts up the hall."

Mike came forward, walking toward the retreating camera. Of course, he was unaware that there had been a slip-up in the shot on the door.

"Ready to take One," the director said. Then: "Take One."

The switcher pressed his button, and the Number One camera took over, showing Mike as he moved slowly to the couch and threw himself face down on it. The organ played a sharp discordant sting.

"All right, Jan; come on," the director said. He was talking to himself; there is no way for the actors to hear. "Come on! Come on!"

The booth was instantly electrically charged. I leaned forward gripping the rail in front of me. Why was Jan Harder delaying her entrance? If she didn't make it snappy she'd throw Mike badly.

"Where the devil is she? Jan, come on!" the director shouted. Then he got hold of himself and spoke into the intercom microphone to the floor manager: "Sam! Can you see her? Cue Her!"

At that moment I felt a sudden faint draft of air, and thin, cold fingers closed over my wrist. "Nick! What's wrong?"

I turned, and in the gloom saw Valerie Crane standing by me. There wasn't any time to ask her what she was doing there.

"The leading lady's blown it!" I said. "Mike's out there holding the bag."

I heard Valerie's sharp gasp.

The switcher turned toward the producer: "What'll I do? Cut us off the air?"

"Keep the cameras on Kerry," the producer said. His voice was tense but quiet. "He may pull us out of it. Get Harry to play a little mood music underneath."

"Harry!" It was the A.D.'s voice. "Improvise. Stall under Kerry. You two've got to carry the ball."

The organist, a dead cigar between his teeth, headphones over his ears, lifted his fingers to the keyboard of the organ. A quavering, minor chord sifted into the control booth. We could see Mike in the monitor. He was getting up from the couch. His lips moved, but no sound came from them. His eyes shifted, empty and frightened, toward the entrance where Jan should be and was not.

"Mike!" I heard Valerie whisper. "Mike! They can't do this to you!"

"He's gone!" the switcher muttered.

"Keep on him," the producer said.

Then Mike began to talk, in a low , husky voice. That voice, the vague frightened look, were still in character for the bedeviled husband of the script "She must have been here-- the package she brought in-- in the kitchen--" His feet took him toward the far door of the set.

"Pete!" the director called out. "Get Number Three on him-- dolly in after him. He's doing us a miracle."

"Fifty-eight seconds," the producer murmured.

"Take Three!" the director ordered.

A button clicked in front of the switcher. There was a new angle on Mike, almost a close-up, as he looked out what was supposed to be the kitchen door.

"All he has to do is walk off and let us die," the switcher said bitterly.

But Mike didn't walk off. He turned. He came slowly back toward the living-room set. A choking sob escaped Valerie.

"Take One!" the director said.

Another angle and Mike began to talk again. In the story as written, the wife should have come back, pretending the first visit and quarrel had never taken place. The husband, convinced he's gone off his rocker, calls the doctor. To save the show, Mike had to convey the same thing without Jan there to do her part.

Mike's voice, rough and shaken, filled the booth: "No groceries in the kitchen-- but I saw them! I saw her bring them in! I saw the brown-paper bag!" The camera had moved in on him now, tight and close. He was working his face, forcing a slight twitch at the corner of his mouth. "I saw her here, as clear as day, and yet--" He pressed his hands against his temples. "I _am_ going mad! It's true-- what they've been telling me all along. I'm dangerous to her! I'm dangerous to myself!"

"Thirty-five seconds!" the producer said.

Mike moved toward the phone. I realized that now he would work the dial, make the last speech as written in the script. He was going to get them out of it.

Then it was over. The actor who did the commercial was into his routine. Valerie buried her face against my shoulder.

"Let's go find him," I whispered in her ear.

We slipped out the rear door of the booth while the commercial was still in progress, edging past the producer and his girl assistant. The hallway outside was dimly lit, stacked with unused scenery from other studios. About twenty yards down it from us was the entrance to the main studio floor.

Valerie, still shaken, was dabbing at her eyes with a handkerchief, when Mike came into the corridor from the studio. He stood there, looking lost and despairing.

Valerie forgot about her eyes or straightening her lovely red hair. She flew to him, and I hurried after her. She threw her arms around him and pressed her cheek against his.

"Val!" I heard him say, like a man in a dream. Over her shoulder he saw me, and there was tragedy in his blue eyes. Ordinarily, you'd guess Mike was ten or twelve years younger than he really is. Now he looked much older than his forty-six years, old and beaten. "How did you get here?" he asked Val

"Never mind that now. You were wonderful, Mike-- Oh, darling!"

He turned his face away so that I wouldn't see it. "Don't, Val!" he said. "I muffed it. I don't know how. I drew a complete blank. I--"

"It wasn't you, Mike," I told him. "It was Jan Harder. She just didn't make her entrance."

"It must have been my fault," he said. "The same old thing. A complete blank. I probably didn't cue her."

"No, Mike; you were perfect!" Val cried.

Neither of us had a chance to say more. The studio door was flung open, and the cast and crew came surging out into the hall. They crowded aroung Mike, pounding him, punching him, shaking his hand. He looked utterly bewildered.

Then I heard the producer's voice on the talk-back: "Mike Kerry! I want him here in the booth. Where is he?"

Val's eyes were shining. "Come on, darling," she said.

We climbed the three concrete steps to the control booth and went in. Tod Franklin, the producer, his young face topped by prematurely gray hair, put his arm around Mike. "That was just about the greatest piece of trouping I ever saw, Mike. You saved our hides."

A telephone shrilled, and the perspiring A.D. took it off the hook. "What happened?" He turned to Franklin and mouthed, "The agency." Into the phone he shouted, "I'll tell you what happened! That blankety-blank dame never made her entrance. Kerry ad-libbed the last three minutes....You were worried! Look, brother; we're all fifty years older here!"

A voice came through the talk-back from the floor: "Tod! Tod Franklin!"

Franklin reached over the A.D.'s shoulder and pressed the button that would clear his voice to the floor below. "Here, Sam, What is it?"

"Jan Harder," the voice said. "She seems to--"

Franklin cut off the voice by pressing the button again. "She should drop dead!" he said, and released the button.

"Tod!" The voice from the floor wavered. "That's what happened. Back of the hallway set. Someone ran a knife through her!"

There was a paralyzed moment. I heard Mike's voice, odd and strained, say the one word. "Jan!"

Then the control booth and studio turned into joint madhouses. The booth emptied of everyone except Mike, Valerie, and me. People spilled out onto the studio floor and pushed down the fake corridor to the door through which Jan Harder had made her last exit. The talk-back mike was open, and through it came a jumble of voices. A woman screamed.

Soon I saw Tod Franklin separate himself from the crowd and start toward the booth. At almost the same moment Guy Lindsey, the handsome young actor who had played the doctor in the script, also started for the booth, running past Franklin in his hurry.

Suddenly, Lindsey was in the booth. He brushed past Valerie and me and stood in front of Mike, who was still sitting in one of the chairs. Before any of us realized what was coming he took Mike's coat lapels in his left hand and swung a short vicious punch to Mike's chin with his right. Mike went toppling over backward.

Valerie and I both grabbed Lindsey, while Mike struggled to his feet.

"Guy! Cut it out! What the devil is going on here?" It was Tod Franklin. He came forward and took Lindsey's other arm. "Haven't we got enough trouble without this?"

I could feel Lindsey relax. He gave Franklin a kind of blank look, and turned to go out. I wasn't taking any chances. I went out into the hallway with him, still hanging on to his arm.

"What's the matter with you, you crazy jerk?" I said.

Lindsey glared at me out of red-rimmed eyes. "He killed her!" he said.

"Who killed her? What are you talking about?"

"Kerry! She was afraid of him. She knew something would happen. She knew--"

"Stop talking like a lunatic!" I said. "Mike couldn't have killed her. He was acting in the show. He was never off the set. He didn't even know her before this last week."

"Didn't know her!" A sound came up out of Lindsey's throat that was meant to be a laugh. Then he wrenched free of me and started on the run down the hall.

I went back into the booth. Franklin was on the telephone, and I gathered he was talking to the police. I rejoined Mike and Valerie. Mike was feeling his chin, tenderly.

"You all right?" I asked him.

"Sure," he said. "I wasn't expecting anything, that's all." Mike isn't the rugged type; he's medium height, wiry, and very quick in his movements. But in his movie career he'd learned boxing and fencing. Given an even chance he could probably have taken young Lindsey apart without any difficulty.

Mike glanced across at Val. "Look," he said, "you'd better go home while you can."

"Don't be silly, Mike," she said. "I'm sticking."

"You weren't here when this happened," Mike said. "I didn't ask you to come here, Val. If I'd wanted you I would have asked you. Now please go on home."

I saw her mouth start to tremble. She looked like a child who'd been undeservedly slapped. I could feel my own anger rising. There was no reason for him to be so tough with her.

"Whatever you want, Mike," Val said, fighting to keep her voice steady. She got up and walked out of the booth.

Mike slumped down into a chair.

"Everybody in the whole place is nuts," I said. "Why did you have to talk to her that way, Mike? Don't you know she's head over heels in love with you? She just wanted to stand by."

"Do you?" he asked. "Stand by, I mean."

"You know better than to ask that," I said.

"Thanks, Nick." He sat there for a moment, looking down at his square competent hands. "I know how Val feels," he said. "But don't you see, Nick, I can't have it that way? I'm a man who can't function, who can't work at his trade, I can't ask any woman--"

"You don't have to ask. She's offering her love."

"I can't let her," he said. "If tonight had come off-- if I'd licked the thing-- Well, it didn't come off, so that's that."

"What do you mean it didn't come off? The whole place has been telling you how terrific you were."

He raised his tired eyes to me. "Jan _is_ dead?'

Death in Studio 2

"I guess there's no doubt of it," I said.

"Don't you see, Nick? It's ironic, but if she <u>had</u> made her entrance I'd have been lost. I drew that blank again. If she had come on and spoken her lines I'd have been gone. I know that. I know that I failed."

I could see that this feeling of defeat was foremost in his mind. The mob of people at the end of the studio, standing around a dead woman; the full implication of what it was presently going to mean-- police, publicity-- hadn't really penetrated. I tried to bring him back to reality.

"Mike, did you know this Harder girl before you did this show?"

"Know her? Yes, I knew her."

"Where? When?"

"Does it matter, Nick? It was a long time ago."

"It matters," I said, "because that crackpot Lindsey is broadcasting the notion that you killed her. He says she was afraid of you. I gather he thought you'd threatened her."

"No," he said. "No, I didn't threaten her."

"If Lindsey shoots off his mouth to the police, they're going to ask you," I said. "What was your connection with the girl?"

He looked up again, and his lips moved in a humorless, one-sided smile. "Once," he said, "I asked her to marry me."

That one was a jolt. I had been close as a brother to Mike for fifteen years. I thought I knew him better than any other person in the world. In all his Hollywood glamor period he'd never been in love; I could have sworn to that. He'd been Hollywood's most eligible bachelor for a long time, but he'd always played the field, never picking out any one woman for special consideration. I had never heard of the Harder girl until I came to rehearsal this afternoon. There was, of course, the four-year gap in our relationship.

"When was this, Mike? After you left the Coast?"

"You were in England, doing a picture, when I-- had my crack-up," he said. "That's why you don't remember."

It was true. I'd been away for four months, taking my first fling at producing, when Mike had come a cropper over those retakes.

"Jan had a bit in that picture," he said. "She was a radio actress. Somebody saw her and gave her a chance. I-- What is love, Nick? How does it come about? Chemistry? Biology? I don't know the answer. Jan wasn't really my type; she was too vivid, too brash, sometimes even vulgar. But I fell for her. When the picture was over I asked her to marry me." He drew a deep breath. "She laughed at me. I realized she thought of me as an old man! That she'd just been working me for what I could do for her in Hollywood. I was ashamed. Ashamed I'd been so blind. My pride was hurt. It was the next day I was called back for those retakes."

"That's when the blackouts started?"

He nodded. "The psychiatrist I went to had an explanation. The lapse of memory invariably came in emotional scenes. He said my experience with Jan, when for the first time I'd opened up my heart to someone, only to be rejected, had left me temporarily afraid of all emotional outbursts, even sham ones. It was nice to know why, but it didn't do any good."

"When you found she was cast in this show, why did you go on with it?" I asked him.

"Maybe I just wanted to be a hero," he said dryly. "No, Nick; the real reason was that I knew if I could get through this show, with Jan in the cast, I'd have licked my problem forever. I almost made it, too."

"You did make it!"

He shook his head. "Whatever it looked like," he said, "I know."

That was the last chance I had to talk to Mike privately. The police acted with impressive speed. Two prowl-car cops were there almost before Franklin stopped talking to headquarters. The twenty-five or thirty people involved in the show were asked to line up in the studio.

Mike and I were still in the booth when the cops began to write down names and addresses. The first name they took was Valerie's. She'd been stopped on her way out, but made no effort to rejoin us. Mike saw her in the studio and went down to her at once. As we approached the crowd, everyone was watching Mike, almost pulling back from him. It was clear that Guy Lindsey had been spreading himself.

Mike walked straight up to Valerie and put his hand on her arm. "Val, dear, I didn't mean to be tough. I just wanted you to avoid all this."

"It's all right, Mike."

"It isn't all right," he said. "I didn't ask you to come to the show or tell you anything about it, because I didn't want you in on any failures. I never want you in on any failures, Val."

"It's all right, Mike." This time she meant it. You could see it in her eyes.

"When I saw you, after it was all over, running down the hall toward me," Mike said, "I--"

I moved away from them, figuring this was getting into a private area. People were milling about aimlessly. A porter was sweeping up some trash into a long-handled dustpan, as though it was easier to keep up routine than stand around and wait. Then I collided with Miss Abigail Pitcher. She was Tod Franklin's production assistant. I'd met her at supper. She was about twenty-four, I should think. Horn-rimmed glasses partly obscured violet eyes that were the best features of a rather plain face. Her figure wasn't bad, but it wasn't shown off to advantage in the severely tailored suit she wore. She had a pencil and paper and was making some kind of list. Production assistants spend their lives making lists.

"Isn't this awful, Mr. Styles?" she said.

"Not good," I said.

"They say it was a carving knife-- bought in a shop near here on Forty-second Street."

The studios were located in the office-building part of Grand Central Station.

"The thing is," Miss Pitcher said, "how could anybody have got into the space behind that door and got out again without being seen? It's walled off. There's no way to get in there or out except through the hall set."

"Well, it looks as though somebody wasn't where he should have been," I said.

"Sam Dakin-- our floor manager-- has been checking. Nobody seems to have been out of place."

"The police will figure it out," I said.

"I suppose so." She glanced down at her list and then up at me. "I imagine Mr. Kerry's pretty upset."

"Aren't we all?" I said.

"I mean-- knowing Miss Harder for so long, and all."

"You've been listening to ghost stories," I said.

She flushed, and looked down at the list again. "We've got permission to send out for coffee and sandwiches. Can I order something for you and Mr. Kerry and Miss Crane?"

"Coffee sounds fine," I said.

I watched her trot off to another group of people and I felt anger beginning to stir in me. With Lindsey shooting off his mouth, this could turn out to be a really nasty business for Mike. No doubt, Jan Harder had done plenty of talking to her friends about her conquest of the famous Mike Kerry and her turndown of his offer of marriage.

The press would have a field day with it, even though Mike ran no real danger of being connected with the murder. The girl had been killed after she had made her exit and before the show ended, and all that time Mike had been acting before the cameras. All they'd have to do to be sure was to run off the kinescope, the moving-picture record of the show. It was the prospect of the publicity hoopla that made me angry.

I started trying to figure out how I could protect Mike from the photographers and reporters I knew would be waiting for him when we got out there. Just about then it became clear we weren't going to get out for a long time.

The police arrived in force: the Homicide lieutenant, a neatly dressed, dark-faced man named Mason, who looked like a business executive; an assistant district attorney named Hershman; the technical crew from Homicide; the medical examiner and the men with the basket; police photographers, and a plain-clothes sergeant named Heller, who seemed to be Mason's right hand. They spent a good half-hour in the corner where Jan Harder had died.

We waited.

Mike and Val and I found chairs near the organ and we sat there, separated from the others. You could almost feel the suspicion emanating from the rest of the group.

"It seems we have a small touch of leprosy," Mike said.

"Lindsey," I said.

"I feel sorry for him," Mike said.

"Why should you? He's making nothing but trouble for you with his irresponsible talk."

Mike looked down at his hands. "He and Jan were going to be married next week," he said. "Jan told me."

Because of Val, I kept my mouth shut. But, brother! You could see what they'd make of that: The rejected suitor, enraged by his discovery that the girl is going to marry someone else, goes berserk. I wondered how much more there was about these relationships I didn't know.

Then Heller, the plain-clothes sergeant, told us to join the others across the studio. It was quite a gathering. In the booth there had been ten people, including Valerie and myself; on the studio floor had been four cameramen, two dolly pushers, two boom men, Sam Dakin, the floor manager, a prop man, and Harry, the organist; on the bridge, an iron catwalk near the ceiling, the electrician and two men who operated the sound-effects table. Then there were the surviving members of the cast: Mike, Lindsey, a character-woman named Barbara Motley, and an old man named Walter Clark who had played a bit. Twenty-eight people in all.

Mason had come over to where we were herded together. He had a deep, pleasant voice when he spoke.

"Every one of you," he said quietly, "was within a hundred feet of the place where Jan Harder was stabbed to death. Not one of you has volunteered any kind of eyewitness statement. It's going to be a long, tedious business unless all of you who were friends of hers, or had any contact with her, come forward and tell us what you know."

"I've been trying to tell someone what I know for the last hour!" Lindsey exploded.

"What do you know, Mr. Lindsey?"

"I know who killed her!" Lindsey said. He pointed a dramatic finger at Mike. "She's been terrified of him the whole week of rehearsals. She knew he'd do something to hurt her. Anything he could!"

"Including murder?" Mason asked.

"She's dead, isn't she?" Lindsey said. "She's dead, and Kerry killed her."

"You saw something-- you have evidence?"

"No. I was sitting over there in the doctor's office set with Miss Motley and Mr. Clark-- this is the set next to the barroom set. We couldn't see the hallway set. But--"

"Then you're just guessing?"

"I'm not guessing! I keep telling you, Jan knew he might try

something. We've been watching him all week-- waiting. I never
dreamed it would happen on the show, in front of the cameras."
    Mason turned slowly to Mike: "Well, Mr. Kerry?"
    Mike raised his eyes. "I'm sorry," he said in a low voice. "I'm
afraid I wasn't listening."

    Across the hall from the studio was the office of the special-
effects department. It was deserted at this time of night, and Mason
had taken it over for his own use. Immediately after Mike's
unfortunate response, Lindsey was whisked off to this office to make
a formal statement.
    Again we waited. It was the better part of an hour before
Sergeant Heller reappeared and asked Mike, Valerie, and me to come
with him to the office. Mason was there, sitting behind a flat-topped
desk, and Hershman, the assistant D.A., was installed at one end of
it. Tod Franklin, looking incredibly tired, and Dakin, the floor
manager, were standing behind Mason. Dakin was a thin, dark-haired
chain smoker, whose bright eyes kept darting from face to face.
    Mason was doodling on some papers stacked in front of him on
the desk. "As a rule," he said, "we interrogate our witnesses
separately and privately. The whole setup here, however, is so
complicated I've asked Mr. Franklin and Mr. Dakin to stand by so I
can check with them on details." He looked at me: "You are Nicholas
Styles, a theatrical producer?"
    I told him I was.
    "You were a guest here tonight?"
    "Yes."
    "And you've been a business associate of Mr. Kerry's for years?"
    "Yes."
    He turned to Valerie: "Miss Valerie Crane." He glanced again at
the stack of papers. "An actress but not connected with the show
tonight. Also a friend of Mr. Kerry's?"
    "Yes," Val said.
    "I'll tell you why you're here, Miss Crane-- and you, Mr. Styles.
Mr. Kerry is something of a public figure. I don't want any stories
leaking out that we have treated him unfairly, or put words into his
mouth. I want you both to bear witness to that. But I don't want any
advice or interference. If I get any, out you go. Is that clear?...All
right. You sit here, Mr. Kerry. Mr. Styles, you and Miss Crane can
sit down over there by the wall."
    There was something ominous about Mason's calm. Mike took
the chair he'd indicated. He saw that the lieutenant was smoking,
and reached for his own silver case. It was empty. Mason pushed his
pack across the desk. At the same time he moved a long narrow
cardboard box into a prominent position. It caught Mike's eye as he
reached for the cigarettes, but I couldn't detect any particular
reaction.
    "Ever see that box before, Mr. Kerry?" Mason asked.

"I don't know," Mike said. "I've seen one like it. It's for a--" He stopped.

"Yes, Mr. Kerry?"

Mike looked straight at him. "It's for a knife," he said. "A carving knife. There was a sale of them a few days ago in Wolfart's Novelty Shop on Forty-second Street. I happened to notice."

"You happened to notice?"

"Yes. There was a window display. There were seventeen of them."

Mason's eyebrows shot up. "You remember the exact number?"

"Yes."

"That's rather an extraordinary thing to remember."

"I suppose it is," Mike said.

Mason picked up one of the papers on his desk. "I'm going to try to save us some time, Mr. Kerry. This is a floor plan of the sets for tonight's show. On the right-hand side of the studio were the sets for the advertising commercial, the living-room set, and the fake hallway with the door at the end through which Miss Harder made her exit. Outside that door was a cul-de-sac, a small closet-like space, shut off on all sides. Mr. Franklin has explained that ordinarily there is a way to get around behind the sets, but in building for this show they were crowded. Miss Harder had only to go off stage, and then almost immediately enter again. So there was no other way out of the space where she waited. Correct?"

Mike nodded.

"To the left of the door was a console table with some objects on it-- a lamp, a silver plate, a man's hat. Correct?"

Mike didn't answer at once. He was frowning at the plan.

"Well, Mr. Kerry?"

"Yes-- yes, I think that's correct," he said.

"Okay. Now, the wide wall of the commercial set, here, cut off the hallway set from people in the booth. They could see what went on there only in the monitors. On the other side, the flat of the doctor's office set hid that hallway. The cameraman and the man with the microphone boom were the only ones who were working the set-- except, of course, yourself and Miss Harder. It was an awkward shot for the camera; it had to be moved in through the living-room set in order to clear the end wall of the hallway set. It was even more awkward for the boom man; his boom was hoisted over the top of the left wall of the set. He had his position chalk-marked on the floor. He couldn't actually see you or Miss Harder. Clear?"

Mike nodded.

Mason picked up another paper. "And this, Mr. Kerry, is a list of all the people connected with the show tonight. The ten people in the booth could check on each other, so it seems clear that not one of them could have left the booth, gone down into that cul-de-sac, and murdered Miss Harder without being noticed. Everyone on the floor had a job; no one could have left his post without someone's having to take over for him. That didn't happen.

"There were two who had sort of roving assignments-- Mr. Dakin, here, the floor manager, and the prop man. The prop man was outside the door opening to the supposed kitchen to take the bag of groceries from Miss Harder. He was there. He took them. He couldn't get back to the cul-de-sac in time to kill her. He'd have been seen, because the action moved to the hallway. Mr. Dakin was outside the window of the living-room set. He had to signal the audio engineer when you started to use the dial phone, so that the sound of the dialing could be clearly heard over the air. The audio engineer says he was there and did signal."

"That's right," Mike said. "I saw him."

Mason looked up at Mike. "Do you see where this is leading, Mr. Kerry?"

"You'e trying to show me that no one could have hidden in that cul-de-sac," Mike said.

"Quite right, Mr. Kerry. And, if that is so, there was only one person in the studio who was close enough to Jan Harder to touch her. Only one person, Mr. Kerry."

"What about the men on the bridge?" I blurted out. "The electrician? The sound men?"

"Checked, Mr. Styles," Mason said. "No one left his post."

"I was the only person close enough to Jan to touch her," Mike said. He spoke in the voice of a man who is studying a complicated alignment on the chess-board. "But of course the kinescope will show that I didn't touch her-- let alone stab her."

"The kinescope won't show that, Mr. Kerry," Mason said. "Lefty Sanders, the Number Two cameraman, missed his shot on you at the door for ten or twelve seconds. There is that much time for which there will be no photographic record."

"That is something!" Mike said, still undisturbed. He looked past Mason to Tod Franklin: "How did Lefty come to lose his picture?"

Franklin shrugged. "It was a tough shot. He was following you down the hall on his pedestal camera. He just missed it, that's all. It's one of those things."

Mike looked at Mason and smiled. "I couldn't have counted on that, you know."

"Maybe you didn't care," Mason said.

Mike's smile broadened. "That seems to be the first piece of guesswork you've attempted, Lieutenant. It has a sour ring to it."

"Has it?" Mason motioned to Sergeant Heller at the door. "Bring in Max Wolfart," he said.

Mr. Max Wolfart was a small, fat, highly excited gentleman who couldn't take his eyes off Mike once he was in the room. He seemed both impressed and confused by meeting a famous screen personality face to face.

"I want you to repeat the statement you gave to Sergeant Heller earlier, Mr. Wolfart," Mason said. "I want to hear it myself, in your own words."

Wolfart began to talk, rapidly and with gestures. He was the proprietor of a novelty shop on Forty-second Street. He had spent a relaxed evening at home with his wife, watching their new television set. He had actually seen the mystery show, The Web, starring Mike. This, he said, was a coincidence.

"Coincidence?" Mason asked.

"Yeah," Mr. Wolfart said. "It's a funny thing about Michael Kerry." He glanced uneasily at Mike. "It started about a month ago. One of the clerks said to me, 'Say, isn't that Michael Kerry, the old movie star?' Sure enough, it was him, looking in at my display window. We pretended not to watch, but we did. I was hoping he'd come in, because my wife is a great autograph collector. I thought it would please her if I got Mr. Kerry's for her."

"Did he come in?" Mason asked.

Wolfart shook his head. "He stood there a minute, maybe two. It was funny-- peculiar, because his lips were moving, like he was talking to himself."

I looked at Mike. He had lowered his eyes from Wolfart's face and was staring down at the toes of his shoes.

"Go ahead, Mr. Wolfart," Mason said.

"Suddenly Mr. Kerry turned and walked away," Wolfart said. "We figured that was that. But about three minutes later he's back. He has a notebook in his hand, and a pencil, and it's like he was checking off stuff in the window against what was written in the notebook."

The storekeeper looked at Mike, as if he hoped for an explanation. Mike didn't move or speak.

"What do you think he was doing?" Mason asked.

"I couldn't figure it," Wolfart said. "One of my clerks said maybe he was planning to rob the joint. A joke, of course."

"Go ahead."

"Well, the next two, three days he comes back and goes through the same routine. He stands in front of the window for a minute or two, goes away, and then comes back with the notebook and pencil. After that we don't see him for ten days. Then we change the window display....We carry everything, Lieutenant. Glassware, hardware, cutlery, kitchenware, games, cards, bar supplies, clocks, watches--"

"Okay," Mason said. "So you changed your window display."

"And the next day he came back, and for three days he goes through his hanky-panky with the notebook. Then we don't see him again till last Monday-- that's four days ago."

"You changed the window display again, then?"

"Yeah. He came that Monday, went through his routine. And that's the last I saw of him till just now."

Mason picked up the cardboard box. "This came from your store, Mr. Wolfart. Could you say who bought it?"

"Are you kidding, Lieutenant? Hundreds of thousands of people go along Forty-second Street. A lot of them come in my shop; we see 'em once and never again. We're not like a neighborhood store. We don't have regular customers."

"Did Mr. Kerry buy this knife from you?"

"I'm pretty sure not. We get so we don't look at people-- but him we'd have looked at." Wolfart showed his teeth hopefully at Mike. "I was still anxious for that autograph."

"Suppose he came in wearing-- say-- dark glasses? Or had his hat pulled down low over his face? Would you have noticed, particularly?"

"Well--"

"You can't swear that he didn't buy the knife?"

"No-o. I got clerks. I couldn't swear."

"I want all your clerks here, Mr. Wolfart," Mason said. "I want your whole staff to check everyone here in this studio, on the chance they'll recognize someone who bought a knife like that....That's all for now."

Heller took the perspiring Mr. Wolfart away with him.

"So you just happened to notice that there were seventeen knives in the window, Kerry," Mason said.

Mike sighed. "It's a long story," he said.

"I've got all the time in the world, Mr. Kerry."

A nerve twitched in Mike's cheek. "About four years ago I retired from the screen, Lieutenant, because I developed a peculiar occupational hazard of actors: I couldn't remember lines. I've spent a lot of time since, trying to get rid of what I believe is called a 'block.' Nothing seemed to work.

"A few months ago I came across a system of memorizing things by associating them with visible objects. It may sound absurd to you, but-- the housewife, trying to remember a shopping list, puts the bacon in her purse, the sugar in the coal scuttle, the bananas in the heel of her shoe. The theory is that the reason we forget things is because they remind us of distasteful memories or experiences. Deliberately associating what we want to remember with tangible objects helps to eliminate the painful recollections that make us forget. Do you follow me, Lieutenant?"

"I think so."

"That's when I began looking in the windows of stores," Mike said. "I'd look over the display for a minute or two, trying to memorize what I saw. Then I'd go away, write down everything I remembered in a notebook, and come back to check on how good I was. I found I had a phenomenal memory when it came to observed detail. I began to have hope. I tried associating lines in a script with physical objects. Miss Crane helped me." He glanced at Val. "When I got the call to come on this show I thought I could risk it."

"As I understand it," Mason said, "you weren't called for this show. You made the overtures to Mr. Franklin yourself."

For the first time I thought Mike seemed startled. "Of course I was called-- by Network Casting. I found a message at my hotel to report to Tod Franklin's office. I went there, and he hired me."

"What about it, Mr. Franklin?" Mason asked.

Tod Franklin looked unhappy. "I'm sorry, Mike," he said, "but you know it wasn't that way."

"Of course it was that way!" Mike said sharply. "What are you trying to say?"

"How do you go about hiring a cast for your shows, Franklin?" Mason cut in.

"I call Network Casting and give them two or three choices for each part. They get whoever is available for me."

"And you hadn't asked for Mr. Kerry?"

"No," Franklin said. "I wouldn't have thought of him. Ours is a low-budget show. I couldn't afford his salary."

"Now, wait a minute!" Mike said. "I--"

"Let me ask the questions," Mason said. "What happened, Mr. Franklin?"

"He came to my office," Franklin said. "He did say something about a call, but you know how actors are. I thought it was just a little pride-saving. He said salary wasn't important. Television was a new medium to him. He wanted to try it. Naturally, I jumped at the chance to hire him at my figure."

"I tell you," Mike said, "I was called."

"Can you prove it?" Mason said. "You see, we've checked Franklin's story with Network Casting. They say they never called you."

Mike's hands closed tight on the arms of his chair. "What's going on here?" he demanded.

"What's going on, Mr. Kerry, is that you're stalling," Mason said grimly. "You knew Jan Harder in Hollywood. You were in love with her. She turned you down when you asked her to marry you."

"Yes. But--"

"You had a crack-up as a result of it. A crack-up so severe it cost you your career. Then, just recently, you heard Jan Harder was getting married. You wrangled your way on this show. You were determined to keep someone else from having her if you couldn't have her yourself."

Mike laughed outright, but I could see perspiration glistening on his forehead. "How corny can you get, Lieutenant?"

"You had the motive. You arranged the opportunity. With your sick mind, you stared at those knives in Wolfart's window. You bought one. You carried it here to the studio in its original box. You were so careless of the outcome that you threw the box away where we found it. You didn't expect to get away with killing her. But when the camera slipped up-- when you realized no one had actually seen you-- you decided to try to brazen it out. Isn't that the whole of it, Mr. Kerry?"

Mike leaned back in his chair. He pressed the tips of his fingers against his eyes for a moment. Then he lowered his hands and looked at Mason. "If you tell me there are fingerprints on the knife, I'll know I'm dreaming," he said. "Because I never touched the knife."

"The knife has a plastic handle that won't take prints," Mason said.

Mike's mouth moved in that humorless one-sided smile. "Don't let it get you down, Lieutenant," he said. "How many nails do you need to fasten the lid on the coffin?"

I know I felt as though the walls of that office were closing in on us, like some kind of nightmare trap. If Dakin's check in the studio was right, and Mike was the only person close enough to Jan Harder to stab her, then the rest of us were pretty deadly confirmation. The motive sounded thin, but not if four years of loneliness and despair had eaten away at Mike's emotional balance. Why had he lied about being called for the show? It was so easy to prove or disprove. Had it been that important to protect his pride? While Wolfart's evidence didn't prove he had bought a knife, it would certainly indicate his preoccupation with the window which had displayed it.

I tried to push the whole idea away from me, but it was like smothering, immovable weight. The staunchest people in the world do crack. The very things that had made Mike a great actor-- temperament, volatility, the capacity for emotion-- things that would make him an easier victim to stresses and strains than the average person. Had four years left only the outer shell of the man I had known and loved? He looked the same, he sounded the same, but was he the same?

One thing I knew: Guilty or innocent, I would stand by Mike. If he had killed Jan Harder he was desperately ill, and in greater need of friendship than he had ever been.

I moved over and stood beside him. "I don't think you have to answer any more questions, Mike," I said. "Mason is charging you with a crime, and you have a right to legal representation."

He reached out and touched my hand. His fingers were like ice. But when he spoke to Mason his voice was clear and steady.

"Are you charging me with murder, Lieutenant?" he asked.

Mason's answer was a change of pace. "What would you do if you were in my position?"

"It would be different from whatever you will do," Mike said.

"Why?"

"Because I know quite a few things you don't know."

"What?" Mason asked, leaning forward.

"To begin with, I know I didn't kill Jan," Mike said.

"Oh." Mason settled back in his chair.

"I know I didn't buy a knife-- that I've never been inside Wolfart's store. I know that I did get a call that was supposed to be from Network Casting. I know, if Lefty Sanders hadn't muffed his

picture on the door, the kinescope would have proved my innocence.
And I know, despite all the checking you have done, you've missed
something."

"How do you figure that?" Hershman, the assistant D.A. asked,
from the end of the table.

"Because I didn't kill Jan," Mike said doggedly. "That means
someone was waiting for her in the cul-de-sac. That means somebody
was out of place."

"Why would anyone fake a call from casting?" Mason asked.

"Don't you see, Lieutenant?" Mike's voice was urgent. "I'm being
set up as a patsy, a fall guy, by someone who knew all about my past
relationship with Jan, someone who knew I'd bite at an offer to do a
television show, someone who knew Tod Franklin would hire me if he
got the chance. That someone has set me up to take the rap. It's not
coincidence. It must have been carefully planned."

"Are you suggesting that this same person arranged for the
cameraman to miss his shot at a critical moment?" Mason asked.

"Yes," Mike said.

"How?"

"The cameraman could have done it deliberately, of course. But
he couldn't have stabbed Jan. He wasn't anywhere near her. He
could be an ally of the murderer's, but I admit that seems far-
fetched. So there must have been some way someone could have
made sure he'd miss."

Mason turned to Tod Franklin: "Is there a way?"

Franklin moistened his lips. "It's possible. I don't know how
Lefty had his shot set up. He may have made chalk marks on the
floor to be certain of his position. They could have been rubbed out
or moved."

Mason gestured to Sergeant Heller. "Get Lefty Sanders in here."
Then he looked back at Mike: "Okay, Mr. Kerry; so you have a theory
that you're a fall guy for someone; that someone must have it in for
you. Had you ever known any of the other people on the show
before-- cast or crew?"

"No." A shadow crossed Mike's face. "Certainly not that I
remember. And that makes it a little more frightening, for my
money, Lieutenant. This person doesn't care anything at all for me--
whether I live or die."

It was only a matter of seconds before Heller appeared with
Lefty Sanders, the cameraman, in tow. Lefty was a fair-haired, nice-
looking kid. He was coatless, as he had been when working the show,
and his intercom microphone and earphones were still draped around
his neck. In him I could see symptoms of the tension under which we
were all laboring: His eyes were red-rimmed and tired, and his smile
was forced. Before Mason could speak to him he walked straight up
to Mike.

"I wish I could tell you how sorry I am I muffed things there at
the door, Mr. Kerry," he said. "If I hadn't blown the shot, you'd be in

the clear."

"I'm sure it wasn't your fault, Lefty," Mike said.

"I still don't get it," Lefty said.

Mason cleared his throat. "That's why you're here, Sanders," he said. "To tell us what was supposed to happen and what did happen."

"Mine is a pedestal camera," Lefty said. "The dollies are the bigger cameras, and there's a guy to push 'em. The pedestal jobs are operated entirely by the cameramen. Sometimes when you have a complicated shot things go wrong."

"Tell us," Mason said.

"It was the quarrel scene," Lefty said. "The Number One camera took the first part of the scene in the living-room set. I was set up near the mouth of the hallway. When Mr. Kerry and Miss Harder started down the hall the show was switched to me. I had to follow them, pushing the camera, and at the same time keeping them in frame. That's sort of a view-finder in the back of the camera-- same shape as the TV screen. What you see there is what you're sending out over the air."

"So you're looking in this finder all the time?"

"Right," Lefty said. "I was taking the shot a little bit from one side. Just when they got to the door I had to arc left and come in on them close-- a tight two-shot. It was tough, and I built up to it all through rehearsal. I thought I had it cold. I guess I didn't."

"What do you mean-- you built up to it?"

"It worried me. But I figured it out with the A.D.-- the associate director. I framed my picture on the vase that was standing on the end of the console table by the door. With the vase in the left side of my frame I should have been square on the actors and the door."

"The vase!" Mike said. It was practically a shout. We all looked at him, but he didn't say anything more.

"So you didn't get the vase in your frame," Mason said, "and you missed the shot?"

"Oh, I got the vase all right," Lefty said. "But something went wrong just the same. That's why I was off the actors so long. The vase was in my picture, and I figured for a moment the actors were out of position."

"The vase wasn't there!" Mike said.

"I'm sorry, Mr. Kerry. It was there, all right."

"It wasn't there!" Mike was on his feet. His face seemed to come alive. "I know it wasn't there, and I can tell you how I know."

"Oh, Mike," Val said, and clapped her hand over her mouth. She looked excited, too.

Lefty Sanders shook his head.

"How do you know, Mr. Kerry?" Mason asked.

"I've been sitting here for hours, thinking that my system of associating lines with objects failed me. You see, I drew a blank there at the door, Lieutenant-- before I dreamed anything had happened to Jan. In the excitement afterward I just thought I'd blown up. But the reason I drew a blank was because the vase wasn't there! The vase was the object with which I was associating my next set of lines."

Lefty Sanders continued to shake his head. "I'm sorry, Mr. Kerry. You'll see, when the kinescope is developed, that the vase was in the left side of my frame."

"It couldn't have been!" Mike said. "I looked for it instinctively. When it wasn't there I got lost."

"It was there," Tod Franklin said wearily. "I remember hearing the A.D. remind Lefty to be sure and frame his shot on it. I remember seeing it in the monitor just before Lefty got on the wall by mistake. I'll show you in the kinescope. There's no doubt of that."

"But I tell you--" Mike's voice rose in a kind of desperation. Then, swiftly, he moved close to the desk and pointed down at Dakin's plan. "The table was here by the door. The vase was supposed to be here, at this end. Right, Lefty?"

"Sure," Lefty said.

"When you arced left and picked it up you'd be straight on the door, wouldn't you?"

"That's right."

"Now, Listen, Lefty: Suppose the vase had been moved to the other end of the table? You'd have kept arcing left until you found it. But you wouldn't be on the door then. You'd be on the wall behind the table!"

"Yeah-- if that's what happened," Lefty said slowly.

"It has to be what happened!" Mike said. "Because when I looked for the vase it wasn't where it was supposed to be-- at this end of the table-- and I went into a panic and drew a blank."

We all crowded around the table, staring at the plan. If Mike could make this point, he would have driven a wedge into Mason's case.

"Who could have moved the vase?" Mason asked.

Lefty said, "Almost anybody. It's the prop man's job to see that it's in place."

"Get him here," Mason said to Heller.

"It was all right in dress rehearsal," Lefty said. "You agree it was all right then, don't you, Mr. Kerry?"

"Sure," Mike said. "Everything was as smooth as silk in the dress."

"You say a lot of people had the chance to move it after that?" Mason asked Lefty.

"Yes. There's a half-hour break between the dress and air time. Everybody's wandering around."

"But wouldn't the prop man check?"

"Yes. But he'd have a lot of things to check, and that might have come first. It's an unwritten rule that nobody touches or moves anything on a set, but there's no one to enforce it."

"Wouldn't you check yourself?"

Lefty shook his head. "That wasn't the only shot I had in the show, Lieutenant. When it went right in the dress I figured there was nothing to worry about."

The prop man came in. He was an old-timer who seemed to know his job thoroughly. He said he had checked the vase before the dress rehearsal. He knew Lefty was using it to frame his shot on the door, so he'd made a chalk circle on the table-top. The vase was centered on top of it.

"I asked Lefty after the dress if it was okay," the prop man said. "He told me it was perfect, so naturally I didn't touch it."

"Don't you see," Mike said to Mason, "it's just as I said? There is someone who knew all about me-- every detail of my past, as well as every detail of tonight's show, down to so small a point as how Lefty was planning that shot on the door. What do I have to do to convince you, Lieutenant?"

Mason didn't answer. He was reading back over the notes he'd been taking. "We photographed and listed every item of that hallway set," he said carefully. "I went over it with you, Mr. Kerry. I asked you about the console table and the objects on it-- a lamp, a silver plate, a man's hat."

Mason raised his eyes. "No vase," he said. "No vase when we got here and photographed and listed." He suddenly brought his fist down on the desk as though his patience had snapped. "No vase!"

It was gone. It had been nearly two feet tall, made of green pottery. It wasn't something you could hide. But it couldn't be found in the studio. Franklin thought some of the stagehands might have started to strike the set the moment the show was over-- before Jan was discovered. Someone might have taken the vase back to the property department....It wasn't there.

All during the search Mike was acting as happy as a kid at the circus.

Finally I warned him: "You're a long way from being out of the woods, Mike. You could have moved the vase as well as anyone else. If Mason thinks you did, his case may be even tighter."

"Hang Mason and his case!" Mike said. "Don't you see, Nick? My system didn't fail! I made it!"

It was all he cared about, and I could understand it. He had won a victory, after all, in his long, bitter attempt at a comeback.

It was along about then I began to develop a real respect for Lieutenant Mason. At first I had seen him as man intent on wrapping up a case against someone, Mike in particular, and getting home to bed. Despite the fact that he was exhausted as the rest of us, he seemed to find new energy to start almost from scratch again.

We had migrated into the studio while the search for the missing vase was on.

He sent Abbie Pitcher, the producer's assistant, to the booth for the "As broadcast" scripts. These were the copies belonging to the director, associate director, switcher, and audio engineer. In the margins were written the personal notations of the men involved: cues for camera movement, sound, music. On the director's and A.D.'s scripts were timings every half-page, noted by them during rehearsals, and making it possible for them to know during the show whether they were running fast or slow. From these time notations Mason narrowed things down. He got Franklin, Abbie Pitcher, the director, and the A.D. around him.

"If someone was hiding in that cul-de-sac," Mason said, "he could have been there all along-- but only if he had nothing to do with the show. Is that right?"

"No," Franklin said. "At the beginning of the quarrel scene Jan made an entrance from there. She had time, while we were playing in the doctor's office set, to get the groceries from the prop man, go off, and wait. She came in, went into the quarrel, backed slowly down the hall with Kerry in front of her-- and out. The person who hid there must have gone in during the quarrel scene in the living-room."

"Split-second stuff," the director murmured.

"I don't see why," Mason said. "The someone in the cul-de-sac could have been someone she didn't suspect. She wouldn't have made an outcry or done anything about it. You were on the air!"

"But no one could have stayed there that long without being missed," Franklin insisted.

"Okay. You keep telling me it couldn't have been anyone from the outside. Why?"

"The entrance to Studio Two is through the reception-room. The receptionist would have stopped anyone who came from the outside hall."

"There are back ways in," Mason said. "The station-- the whole building-- is a labyrinth of hallways, stairways, elevators."

"Well--" Franklin hesitated. "You'd have to know it, though."

"Suppose you could get by the receptionist. There'd be nothing to stop you walking into the studio."

"There's a red light outside," Abbie Pitcher said, "warning you that there's a show on the air."

"Is there a guard there?"

"No."

"A red light wouldn't stop a killer," Mason said. He turned suddenly to Valerie: "Miss Crane, you got here late. How did you get past the receptionist?"

"I wasn't really late," Valerie said. She smiled at Mike. "Mr. Kerry had reasons for not telling me he was doing this show. But he forgot that, of course, they would advertise him. I didn't tell him I knew, but I came here a few minutes before air time. I wanted to be here in case-- well, in case he didn't make it."

"You came into the studio?" Mason asked.

"No. I waited in the reception-room," Valerie said. "There's a

monitor out there. I watched the show, along with a lot of others.
When I saw something was going wrong I-- I just came into the
hallway and ran for the control booth."

"The receptionist didn't stop you?"

"He was watching the show," Val said.

"And you knew where to go?"

"I'm an actress," Val said. "I've worked in these studios quite
often."

Mason glanced down. "How did you hurt your hand, Miss Crane?"
he asked casually.

Suspicious eyes turned to Val. She'd been carrying a long white
chiffon handkerchief which I'd noticed she'd been twisting round and
round in her fingers all evening. I'd thought it was simply a nervous
fiddling. Now I saw the handkerchief was wrapped around her right
hand and there was a dark blotch of dried blood on it.

Val gave Mason a level look. "When I ran down the hall," she said,
"I bumped into some scenery that was stacked there. I didn't notice
till later that I must have scratched it on a nail or something."

"You've had enough fantastic ideas for one evening, Mason,"
Mike said. His voice was hard. "So she cut her hand on a nail. She
didn't know this show, so she couldn't have planned anything in
advance."

Valerie looked at Mike, and her eyes were wide. "I'm afraid that
isn't true, Mike."

"Of course it's true. How could you know?"

"I'd seen a script as long ago as last Monday," Valerie said. She
turned a little helplessly to Abbie Pitcher.

Tod Franklin's assistant stared straight ahead of her through the
horn-rimmed glasses she wore. "Miss Crane called me last Monday
and said she wanted to see a copy of the script for tonight's show,"
Miss Pitcher said. "I knew who she was. I left one for her at the
office and she picked it up."

"Why did you want a script, Miss Crane?" Mason asked.

"I wanted to see what Mike was up against," Valerie said.

Mike had moved so that he was standing close to Val. "She
couldn't know how the set was laid out," he said. "They don't provide
maps along with the script!"

"She didn't have to have a map!" It was Guy Lindsey. "How
dense can you be, Lieutenant?"

"That'll do, Lindsey," Mason said.

"It won't do!" Lindsey shouted. "Can't you see they were in on it
together? He told her what the layout was. He told her exactly what
time to slip down the hall and hide. He moved your vase-- not to
cover himself but to make sure there'd be no chance of Miss Crane
being seen when Jan opened that door to go out. Have you had that
storekeeper check on whether she bought a knife?"

I have said that Mike was fast on his feet. He was greased
lightning now. He took one step forward, feinted a left, and landed a

right uppercut squarely on Lindsey's jaw. The young actor went down, flat as a beached flounder. Heller, Mason, and a couple of the crew grabbed Mike, but he seemed to have lost interest. He turned on Mason, his blue eyes winter-cold: "Is it your intention to let a hysterical ham run you, Mason? What you need is some tangible evidence, not curtain speeches!"

After that we waited through some rather bad moments. Mr. Max Wolfart was brought out to peer at Val. Finally he shook his head.

"I don't remember ever seeing her in my place," he said. "I couldn't swear she hadn't been there, though. Like I said, there are so many people in and out."

Four frightened clerks of Wolfart's, who had been routed out of their beds, were asked to do some staring. They all repeated Wolfart's story about Mike and his window-gazing. They all said they were sure he hadn't bought anything in the store; they would have remembered. They couldn't identify Valerie. It wasn't as conclusive a clearing as I could have wished; but at least it didn't help Mason to drive any more nails into Mike's coffin.

Shortly thereafter, Heller came over and said Mason wanted to see me alone. The little office across the hall was heavy with smoke, and I had a sensation that Lieutenant Mason and Hershman, the assistant D.A., had been having some kind of argument.

"I've been checking on you, Mr. Styles," Mason said. "You're evidently a responsible citizen. Got any ideas about this?"

"I think Mike is right," I said. "I think he's being used as a decoy by the real killer. I know he and Valerie Crane had nothing to do with the murder."

"Because you love them both," Mason said, "and because you're sure no one you love could be guilty of murder. Well, I'll tell you something, Mr. Styles. It's always someone whom somebody loves!" He leaned forward, and his air was suddenly confidential. "I could take every one of you here down to the pen and hold you as material witnesses," he said. "Hershman and I have been discussing the possibility. He's for wearing you down till somebody cracks. I'm for letting you get some rest, so that perhaps you'll think a little more clearly-- recall things you haven't been able to remember in the excitement."

I wondered. Was he setting himself up as the kindly one so that we'd all lower our guards?

"You are the one person here tonight who seems perfectly alibied. Franklin vouched for the fact that you never left the booth. You'd have had to push him aside to get out, he says."

"That conveniently alibis him, too, doesn't it?" I said.

"I'm tired of smart cracks, Styles," he said. "I'm tired-- period. I'm going to release Miss Crane and Mr. Kerry in your custody. I'm going to hold you responsible for their reappearance here tomorrow morning at nine o'clock."

"It's a mistake," Hershman said.

"Where can Kerry go?" Mason said impatiently. "He can't walk a block in any town in this country without being recognized. Besides, he's no use to me now. He's so hopped up over discovering he can remember his silly lines, he doesn't seem to realize he's in a jam. Maybe, by tomorrow, he'll get his feet on the ground. Try and explain to him, Styles, that he's in trouble. Real trouble!"

"I'll do my best," I said. "And I'll have him and Miss Crane here at nine."

Everyone was ordered to go out through the reception-room. Mason apparently still had the missing vase on his mind, because each of us was subjected to a casual inspection to make sure we weren't walking off with it.

We were so anxious to get away from the studio that we forgot about the reporters and photographers who had been kicking their heels for hours in the reception-room. Now they swarmed out of every darkened corridor, crowding around Mike and Val. Mason had to get a couple of uniformed cops to escort us to a taxi. Valerie lived only a few blocks away in the Murray Hill section of Park Avenue, but we'd have been snowed under if we'd tried it on foot.

Valerie sat between us in the back seat of the cab, and I saw that Mike had slipped his arm through hers.

"How's your hand?" he asked her.

"It's nothing," she said. "I truly did scratch it on a nail, Mike."

He laughed. "Did you think I had visions of you testing the point of the carving knife on your own flesh?"

"Mason may think that," she said.

"Mason's no dope," I said.

"Neither is the bucko who planned this thing," Mike said. "Except for the fact that there are no fingerprints, and that they can't prove I was ever in Wolfart's store, I'd be spending tonight in jail. I may make it yet, if Mason can dig up one or two more convincing angles."

"They don't convict innocent people, Mike," Valerie said.

Mike drew a deep breath. "Let's hope so.... Do you realize, Val, I can really dream of going back to work?"

She looked up at him. "Darling, I haven't had a real chance to tell you how good you were-- and how glad I am."

"I haven't had a chance to tell you a number of things," he said, giving her that crooked smile of his. "You were there ready to pick up the pieces. I should have known I couldn't fool you." Then his face clouded. "Who do you suppose made that call to my hotel-- pretending to be Network Casting office? It was all carefully planned."

"Who hated Jan Harder that much?" I said.

"Any one who knew her," Valerie said. "She was greedy, chiseling--"

"Hey! Take it easy," Mike said.

"It was someone who knew your story, Mike," Val said.

"It's a nasty thought," he said dryly, "but I daresay Jan told everyone she knew. We'll never get at it that way. There has to be something more direct, simpler, positively incriminating."

"Such as?" I said. I was just making conversation.

He looked across Valerie at me. "Such as a green pottery vase," he said. "How did it disappear? And why did it have to?"

We dropped Valerie, and I persuaded Mike to spend what was left of the night at my apartment. It was nearly two-thirty.

Mike seemed glad not to be alone. He said he was hungry, and there was some cold steak, cheese, and a loaf of Italian bread at my place. We didn't talk much. We were too tired. But Mike did say one thing which I kept thinking about as I got ready for bed:

"The producer, the director, and the producer's staff have the script for a show well in advance, Nick. The production department, the people who build the sets, the scene designer-- they know the details of the show long before anyone else, even before the actors are hired. The actors are next to see the script, but we rehearse in hotel ballrooms, store basements, wherever we can-- for all but the last day of the show. Then we come to the studio set. Only then do the cameramen and the crew know what they're going to have to do. So, in terms of time for planning, the production department comes first, the cast second, and the crew third." Then he shook his head. "Except that any interested person could get a look at the setup through the production department if he had an in."

Those were the sheep I counted when I went to bed: producer, director, scene designer, set builder, property people, actors, technicians, cameramen, organist and electricians, sound men and dolly pushers. I didn't have to count them long. I went to sleep quickly, but it wasn't restful sleep. I dreamed about some sort of police line-up being held in the studio, with the lights blazing down from the ceiling, and the cast, the crew, the whole staff parading back and forth in front of me. It always ended up with Mike in the middle of the stage, improvising one of those charming little curtain speeches actors make when the applause has been sufficient. I kept straining to hear the words of the speech, but they faded off, and left him gesturing like a silent movie actor, smiling and nodding.

About the third time I went through this routine I woke up, and lay there tossing and trying to get comfortable. There was nothing for it but to get a sleeping tablet from the bathroom. I had to switch on the hall light to see where I was going. As I went by I glanced in at the day bed in the living-room where Mike was supposed to be sleeping. Mike wasn't there!

"Mike!" I called out.

He didn't answer. I turned on the living-room lights. He wasn't there, or in the kitchenette. He wasn't in the bathroom. Then I noticed that his clothes were gone!

On the table, at the head of the bed, was an ash tray, and from it rose a thin curl of blue smoke. I went over to it. There was a cigarette there, which had been snubbed out carelessly. There was about a half-inch of ash where it had been burning. Then I saw the note, on the table:

"Nick:

"Don't worry. I'm not jumping bail! Couldn't sleep. Where the heck is that vase, and why?

"Mike."

I figured from the cigarette he couldn't have been gone more than five minutes.

The fool, I thought! Suppose he went back to that studio and started snooping around, and one of Mason's men found him there? An attempt to tamper with evidence would be the charge. It occurred to me he might have called Valerie. People in love do crazy things. I rang her number, and after a while she answered, sleepily. She came wide awake when I told her Mike had gone.

"I've got a hunch he went back there to figure things out on the scene," I said. "I'm going after him."

"I can be there as soon as you can," she said. "I'll meet you at the information booth on the Upper Level."

She didn't give me time to argue. She hung up.

Ten or twelve minutes later I came in the Lexington Avenue side of Grand Central and started across the echoing floor of the empty station toward the information booth. At the same time I saw Valerie running down the flight of steps at the Vanderbilt Avenue end.

She was breathless when she reached me. "He may not have come here at all," she said. "He may just have gone for a walk."

"I'd have thought so if he hadn't mentioned the vase," I said, and showed her the note. "Maybe he went back to his hotel."

"I tried that," Valerie said. "His room didn't answer."

"So we go up to the studio and take a look," I said.

"Mason's bound to have left someone in the reception-room to keep people out," she said. "Mike would have known that. He won't have used the elevators--"

"Then?"

"This way," she said.

I remembered she'd worked there. She took me to an inside stairway near a bank of elevators. We climbed to the fourth floor, one level above the studio. Then she steered me through an iron door to one of the catwalks that bisect the glass-enclosed ends of the station. Looking down I could see a couple of people, like pygmies, navigating the station floor. Once across the catwalk we were in corridors of offices again. They were dimly lit, the frosted glass doors of the offices dark.

"There's a fire stair over here that will bring us down at the opposite side of the hallway from the reception-room. Mason may not have left that guarded."

"Let's pray," I said. "If they catch Mike alone, it will be bad. Bad enough if they catch us all together."

We moved quietly, then, literally tiptoeing down the concrete fire stairs. When we gained the hall below, Val made a silencing gesture with a finger to her lips, moved softly to the turn in the hall, and looked around. Then she beckoned to me.

I found we were in the hallway outside the studio, the hallway stacked with scenery where Val had cut her hand. She went ahead of me to the studio door. It was fastened back, open. There was a stage light-- a bare, glaring bulb on a stand-- burning in the middle of empty, silent space. Then we nearly jumped out of our skins as a tinny counterfeit of Mike's voice came to us:

"What are you two dopes doing here?"

Valerie recovered first. She was used to the studio mechanisms. Mike was in the control booth, and he'd spoken to us through the talk-back microphone.

"I'll get him," I said to Val. "You wait here. If the cop in the reception-room heard him, he'll come on the run. Turn on the charm, Val."

I hurried down the studio to the inside door of the control booth.

When I went in Mike was standing by the phone. "Blasted thing seems to be disconnected," he said, casually.

"I suppose you were calling Mason to tell him you're here!" I said.

"Right on the nose, Nick. I think I've figured this thing out-- I mean, the why of it."

"The why of what?"

"Why the vase is missing," he said. "You see--"

He didn't finish. Valerie's voice, calling Mike's name in panic, came through the talk-back. There was a short, sharp scream. Then the whole place was plunged into black silence.

Mike brushed past me, and I realized he was reaching for the button on the talk-back. "Val! Val, what is it? Are you all right?"

No answer.

"The cop in the reception-room must have heard her!" I said. "He'll come running."

"Not if someone shut the studio door. It's soundproofed. And if it wasn't shut, we'd see a light from the hall."

"What's it all about?" I said. "Why should someone--?"

"Not just someone!" Mike's voice was harsh. "The murderer. He had to come back for the vase and destroy it, or it will hang him."

"But, Mike, I don't get it!" I said.

"This isn't any time for dialogue," he said. "We've got to get down there to Val!"

I tried without success to swallow past the dry place in my

throat. Mike's hand was on my arm.

"Go out the rear door into the hallway," he said, in a normal, conversational tone. "Get that cop out of the reception-room."

"Whoever is in the studio will hear you," I whispered.

"Not unless I press the button on the talk-back," he said.

"What about you?"

"I'm going down into the studio," Mike said.

"But you can't see a thing!" I said.

"I don't need to see. Get moving, Nick."

I barked my shin on a chair getting to the rear door of the booth. I pushed against it, but nothing happened. I put my shoulder against it and shoved.

"I can't get it open," I said.

Mike joined me and we both gave it the works. It moved, maybe a quarter of an inch, and that was that.

"Something wedged under it from the outside," Mike said. "Come on! We've got to hustle or he'll be gone."

There wasn't a speck of light from anywhere. You couldn't see a thing. I heard Mike draw a deep breath.

"Now we'll see how good I am at remembering detail," he said. "Put your hand on my shoulder, Nick." He moved forward. "Two steps down here. Watch it."

I thought I knew what had happened. The murderer must have been right on our heels-- Val's and mine. He'd peeped through the glass panel in the rear door of the booth and seen Mike there. He'd wedged something under the door so we'd have no way out except into the studio. Then he'd plunged the place into darkness. He knew exactly where he was going and what he had to do, but we'd have to stumble through sets, over cables spread on the floor, past cameras and audio booms. We could shout our heads off for help and, with the hall door closed, no one would hear us in this soundproofed studio. Meanwhile, the murderer could get what he was after, slip out into the hall, and take off the way Val and I had come. It was brilliant spur-of-the-moment tactics.

But he had left one factor out of his reckoning: Mike! Mike who had spent four grim and dismal years sharpening the blunt instrument of his memory; who had used as an exercise the constant recalling of physical detail. I began to see, as we moved down to the control booth door that opened into the studio, that Mike was like a blind man, walking about in a familiar room. Instinctively, he had memorized the layout of the studio.

"The door," he said. "Once we're out there he can hear us."

Mike whispered now: "Organ and bench to the right." He stepped out, almost rapidly. Then he stopped. "We're in the center alley. Pick your feet up, so you don't trip over wires."

I could feel curled cable under my feet. We moved more slowly now, but we kept moving.

"Easy," Mike said. "The commercial set's to our right. There's a pedestal camera and a microphone boom parked in front of it."

Just as he spoke we heard a sudden clatter from the far end of the studio. Our man was still there. It sounded as though he might have knocked some objects off a table. My fingers hooked tightly into Mike's shoulder.

"Living-room set coming up," Mike whispered. "We bear a little right, now. The couch should be about here." We halted. I could feel him reach out with his hands. He touched something and held on for a second or two. "Bull's-eye," he muttered. "Listen, Nick. We cross this set and come to the hallway set. It's about fifteen yards, I should think. The main door to the outside hall is to our right. When I give you the signal, plow straight at it. Get the door open and start yelling for that cop! Got it?"

"I hope!"

"Here we go. The easy chair should be-- here! Hey, I'm not bad at this."

I began counting the steps we took-- twelve, thirteen, four-teen-- eighteen, nineteen, twenty. Off to the left there was a scraping, fumbling sound. We were quite close to it. Mike stopped. He turned and put his hands on my shoulders. Without a word he pivoted me to the right. I realized he was facing me directly at the door. "Now," he whispered. "Walk straight ahead. It's about ten good, full paces. Go!"

I took off. I knew the minute I got the door open there'd be some light. Mike would be able to see who was behind us in the studio. I stepped out big, the way he had said. My foot snagged on something soft, yet bulky, on the floor and I fell flat on my face, unable to stifle a cry of surprise. I remember thinking Mike had been right-- down to the last ten feet.

Then there was light. The bright beam of a torch from somewhere overhead. It swung around until it caught Mike full in its circle. For an instant I saw what it was I'd tripped over. It wasn't something Mike had forgotten; he couldn't have known that Valerie would be lying there unconscious.

Mike turned blinking eyes upward. The light was coming from the electrician's bridge at the top of an iron stairway. The light went out.

"Now. Hurry!" a man's voice shouted.

Simultaneously, there was a sickening impact of body against body. The man on the iron stair had hurled himself straight down on top of Mike. There was the noise of a violent struggle in the dark. I tried to grope my way toward them. But Mike's hoarse shout stopped me:

"Nick! Block the door! Don't let the other one out!"

The other one! Of course. The clatter we'd heard had come from the far side of the studio. The man on the iron stairs couldn't have made it. My ear picked up running footsteps headed my way. I backtracked toward where I thought the door must be and, by some miracle, I found it. At the same moment someone charged into me, running full speed. It nearly knocked out the last of my breath, but as I clawed out, our feet got tangled and we fell heavily to the floor. Luckily, I was on top. My left hand felt a smooth, cold cheek, a pointed jaw, I swung my right fist with everything I had left. The body under me went limp.

Somehow I struggled up and found the door once more. I pushed it out-- into the light, I shouted:

"Police! Help!"

Then I staggered back toward the studio to help Mike. But he didn't need it. I saw him rising slowly over the sprawled, still figure of a man whose face I couldn't see. I turned to look down at my own antagonist, and found myself staring, wide-eyed, at the shapely legs of Miss Abigail Pitcher.

There was a brief case lying beside her. Mike came unsteadily over and picked up the case. He opened it and turned it upside down. Out of it fell a collection of pencils, some copies of the show script, and the broken pieces of a green pottery vase.

"That does it, baby," Mike said.

"Who's the man?" I asked, moving toward Mike's assailant.

"Something of a surprise," Mike said. "The great lover! Mr. Guy Lindsey!"

Then the cop appeared in the doorway with drawn gun.

Mason looked like a man who'd had ten hours sleep. He seemed irritatingly fresh, compared with the rest of us who were gathered in the special-effects office across the hall from the studio. Mike's mouth was swollen, and there was a cut under his left eye. Valerie was nursing an egg on the top of her head. I felt as though I must resemble a package of freshly ground hamburger. I hadn't realized at the time, but Abigail Pitcher's fingernails had raked my face.

Miss Pitcher sat, frozen and immobile, opposite Mason. Her glasses had been broken in the scramble and her eyes were staring and enormous. Lindsey sat across from her, his face buried in his hands.

"I couldn't stop thinking about that vase," Mike told Mason. "It had to be moved so Lefty Sanders would miss his picture on the door. If someone moved it they'd have to leave fingerprints on it-- fingerprints that shouldn't be there. There'd been no chance to wipe them off afterward. Then I remembered--"

"For a man whose memory bothers him, you do okay," Mason murmured.

"I remembered, when everyone rushed down to see what had happened, hearing something break."

"Good lord!" I said. "I saw a porter sweeping it up! It didn't click at the time-- didn't mean anything."

"You were looking for the whole vase," Mike said to Mason. "Actually it had been smashed to bits and dumped in a corner along with the trash. But the murderer still couldn't risk it. I was sure of that.   You'd find   it   sooner   or   later,   and   might   still   raise   an incriminating print on one of the fragments."

"A sound theory," Mason said.

"But that's all it was-- a theory." Mike smiled. "You weren't in a mood to listen to ideas from me, so I came back to try to prove it for myself. I guess it's a good thing I did, or Lindsey and Miss Pitcher would have got away with it."

Lindsey raised his battered face. "I had nothing to do with it," he said. "I really thought Kerry was guilty. I didn't know the truth till an hour ago. I swear that."

"And then you decided to become an accessory after the fact," Mason said. "That wasn't a very wise move."

"I know-- I know."

Before anyone could stop her Abigail Pitcher was out of her chair and had dropped to her knees beside Lindsey. "Darling, darling-- you're not involved!" she cried. "You didn't know why I wanted you to come back here. Don't let them make you say you did."

"Abbie," Lindsey said, in a dazed way. "Abbie!"

The girl turned her wide, blurred eyes on Mason. "You kept saying it had to be someone who knew the show! Well, I know it better than anyone. I time the rehearsals, check the costumes and props, take care of all the mimeographing. But once the show goes on the air, I'm through. I'm supposed to be in the booth, but I don't really have a job unless Mr. Franklin wants me to run an errand. Nobody noticed when I slipped out-- or when I came back. I was the one person nobody would notice, because if I was seen leaving it would be natural. I knew how Lefty had planned the shot. I actually suggested it to the A.D. He didn't remember, of course-- nobody remembers anything I say!" She was breathing as though she'd been running hard. "Jan Harder had been on this show before. I hated her."

"Why?" Mason asked.

"It doesn't matter," Abbie said. "Mr. Kerry thought he had a secret, but Jan Harder had told the story over and over of how she'd turned him down. I figured I could use him. I knew Mr. Franklin would hire him if he had the chance, so I put in the call for him, pretending it came from Network Casting. I come through Forty-second Street every day and I'd seen him staring in Wolfart's window. I bought the knife. I took off my glasses-- no one remembers me without them."

That wasn't quite true. I had a feeling I'd remember her, as she was now, for the rest of my life.

"Lefty had to miss that shot on the door for two reasons. It would keep the kinescope from clearing Mr. Kerry-- and there was always the risk that I might be seen when the door was opened."

"Wasn't there a chance Mr. Kerry would see you, too?" Mason asked.

"Yes. But at the worst, it would be his word against mine. And with everything else pointing at him--"

"Take your time, Miss Pitcher."

She swallowed. "I left the booth about three minutes before the hallway scene. I walked onto the set, moved the vase, and slipped into the cul-de-sac. I had the knife in its box, in my handbag. When Jan backed out of the door I--"

"Abbie!" Lindsey said brokenly.

"As soon as the Number Two camera was off the scene I had to get back to the booth fast. I was worried about fingerprints, but I thought I could get rid of them later. When everyone rushed down there, after Sam Dakin discovered her, I managed to knock the vase off the table and break it. I saw the porter sweep it up and throw it in a pile of trash in the corner. That's when Mr. Styles saw it, too."

Yes. And she had calmly engaged me in a conversation about coffee and sandwiches to distract my attention.

Mason turned to Sergeant Heller: "Didn't you go through that pile of trash when you were searching for the vase?"

"You're darn' tootin' we went through it," Heller said. "The vase wasn't there-- nor any pieces of it."

"What about this porter? Wasn't he questioned?"

Heller shook his head. "There wasn't any porter here, Lieutenant. He wasn't on the list of people involved."

"The sergeant's right," Abbie said. "The porter isn't part of the crew here. He works the whole floor-- two other studios, the master control, the kinescope room. He came in here when we went off the air, and started to clean up, automatically. He's an old man, not too bright. He just wandered off. Either he didn't realize what was going on, or he wanted to get away. You never asked for him because he wasn't listed as part of this show or the crew and cast. Remember you got the list of people from me!"

"Why didn't we find the broken pieces in the trash pile?" Mason asked.

"I didn't dare leave them there," Abbie said. "If anything came up about the vase you might find them. While everyone was milling around I slipped over to the corner and put the pieces in my brief case. I couldn't take it out with me when I heard you give orders to have people checked when they left. So I planned to come back later. It seemed safer to leave my case here behind the set. Even if you found it, it was ten to one you wouldn't look through it for a two-foot vase! If I could get rid of those pieces the only evidence against me would be gone. Even if you suspected me, you couldn't prove I'd made the call to Mr. Kerry; Wolfart's clerks swore they'd never seen me. Without fingerprints, without motive, you couldn't connect me."

She moved her head from side to side, as though she were in pain. "I lost my nerve at the last moment. I asked Guy to come back with me-- to stand guard while I got my brief case. He didn't know what it was all about. He--"

"It won't do, Miss Pitcher," Mason said. "He wedged the door of the control booth shut. He attacked Miss Crane and Mr. Kerry; he might have killed either of them. He was in this up to his neck. Why? Why did Jan Harder have to die?"

"He didn't know. He just did what I asked him!" Abbie wailed.

Lindey's voice broke in: "He's right, Abbie. It won't do." He looked at Mason. "I wish I could take all the blame," he said, "because it's all my fault. You see, I was going to marry Jan, but I hated her. The story will come out, so here it is. Three weeks ago I signed a long-term Hollywood contract at a fancy salary. It was my big break. Mr. Kerry will tell you about Jan. She used people. She bled them till they were dry. She failed in Hollywood herself, but she saw a way, through me, to get out there and have herself another chance. We were to be married as a matter of convenience to her."

"But how could she force you into that?" Mike asked.

"Everyone makes a mistake once or twice in his life," Lindsey said, "and Hollywood contracts have a morality clause. Jan had pictures of me. A wild crowd-- narcotics parties. I was to do it on Jan's terms or else. So I planned to do it her way."

"I couldn't let it happen to him," Abbie said. "I met Guy when we were both working in a summer theater two years ago. I love him. I always will love him. I couldn't let her do it to him-- I couldn't let her have him. No matter what!"

"Abbie," Lindsey said.

She reached up and touched his cheek with her fingers. "Darling, I'm so sorry," she said softly. "So very sorry. I only wanted things to be right for you-- for us. I shouldn't have asked you to come back here with me. I should have carried through alone."

"It's all right, Abbie," he said. "If I'd known I would have come without your asking." He gestured over the top of her head at Mike. "I'm sorry I poured it on you, Mr. Kerry. I really thought it was you in the beginning. I never imagined--" He looked down at Abbie and was silent.

The city was stirring in the gray light of dawn as Mike, Valerie, Lieutenant Mason, and I came out of the all-night counter place where we'd gone for coffee. We stopped outside on the pavement, preparing to separate. Mason held out his hand to Mike.

"Could I say 'Congratulations'? You were in a pretty tough spot, Mr. Kerry. I don't like amateurs who try to play detective-- but thanks. If those two had got away with the broken vase--"

"I played in luck," Mike said.

"Poor little Abbie," Val said. "To look at her you'd never have guessed what was smoldering there."

"If we could see into people, Miss Crane," Mason said, "we could prevent crimes instead of solving them after the fact." He gave Mike a sheepish look. "My wife," he said. "She's-- well, kind of movie crazy. Would you consider--?"

"Autograph?" Mike grinned at him. "Sure thing."

We watched Mason go off, and then started walking toward the corner for a taxi.

Mike slipped his arm through Valerie's. "That Lindsey was a heel," he said. "He wasn't worth what Abbie tried to do-- wrong as it was."

"You can't always fall in love with the right person," Val said.

"Sometimes you can't let yourself," Mike said. "You can't saddle them with your problems." We walked on a little way, Valerie looking straight ahead of her.

"I did get through that show tonight," Mike said. "I would have got through it perfectly if Abbie hadn't messed things up. It looks as if I might work again-- might be myself again."

"Mike!" Val said.

He turned to her with that special smile. "In which case I could be had, Miss Crane. If you wanted me, I could almost certainly be had!"

The shadow of murder invades
a silent house as a relentless
killer strikes again

ONE VICTIM TOO MANY

by Kelley Roos

DAVE LOGAN sat in the top row of the bleachers of the Ridgefield, Ohio, High School football field. He glanced at his watch
impatiently. If they didn't get this daring daylight robbery moving
in a hurry, it would be too dark. He spoke into the microphone;
his voice filled the air.

"Ross," he called. "Ross Anders."

Down on the thirty-yard line a stalky, vigorous figure turned
away from the sheriff and waved up to Dave.

131

The Kelley Roos team may have employed more unusual back-drops for murder than any other American contributor save Hugh Pentecost. Among their settings: a show boat, a dance studio, a charm school, an antique car museum, a university library rare book room, and a tourist cavern. In the story that follows, the setting is pure Americana: a small-town centennial celebration. It first appeared in September 1953.

ONE VICTIM TOO MANY by Kelley Roos

Dave Logan sat in the top row of the bleachers of the Ridgefield, Ohio, High School football field. He glanced at his watch impatient-ly. If they didn't get this daring daylight robbery moving in a hurry, it would be too dark. He spoke into the microphone; his voice filled the air

"Ross," he called. "Ross Ånders."

Down on the thirty-yard line a stalky, vigorous figure turned away from the sheriff and waved to Dave.

"Ross," Dave said, "what's the delay?"

Ross Anders cupped his hands into a megaphone and shouted, "One of the bandits lost his gun, Dave. We'll be ready in a minute."

Dave sighed and shook his head. This pageant, depicting the highlights in Ridgefield's hundred years of existence, was about the twentieth such pageant he had produced. He had helped towns and cities all over the country celebrate their centennials, sesquicenten-nials, all kinds of centennials. He was beginning to lose patience with bandits who lost their guns, founding fathers who forgot their wigs, Indians who put their feet through their war drums, pioneer women who wore lipstick and mascara.

Dave was tired. He shouldn't have let Ed Merrill Sr., head of the Merrill Producing Company, talk him into doing this one more assignment before his vacation. Ed could have postponed his road trip drumming up new business and taken over the Ridgefield pageant himself....But, Dave thought, if he hadn't come to Ridgefield he would never have met a local citizen named Sarah Cummings. Sarah was one of the most unfriendly natives he had ever encountered. Maybe not unfriendly, exactly; maybe just aloof. How could anyone so beautiful be so aloof?

"Come on," he growled into the mike. "Let's get this holdup on the road."

Ross signaled to him they were ready.

"All right," Dave said. "Listen, everybody; this is the biggest scene in the pageant. That's why we're running through it again. Now, be on your toes. This is your last rehearsal. Let's go!"

Now it was 1912 in Ridgefield, Ohio, population only 1,200. It was nearly five o'clock of a Saturday morning. In the office of the Drake Stockyards, a mile outside of town, two young men were counting and stacking the money that they would pay that day to farmers for their cattle. Then young Tom Drake, son of the owner, rose from his desk and turned to his cousin, Luther Dunning. He told him that he was going to take a little walk to clear his head. Luther nodded, and Tom went out of the office, walked up the dusty, deserted road out of sight.

Then over the loud-speaker came a voice saying it was now half an hour later. Suddenly Luther lifted his head, listening. Three masked men on horseback came galloping up to the door. They dismounted, stormed the office. Luther Dunning was wrenching a gun from his desk drawer when the bandits fired. Luther fell to the floor, badly wounded, helpless. The bandits scooped the bills and coins into a sack.

Tom Drake came running up to the building. Luther's shouted warning to him was too late. As Tom crossed the threshold three bullets cut him down. The bandits stepped across his lifeless body, ran to their rearing horses. They raced away...and a curtain of steam rose from the pipes stretched across the football field, blotting out the scene.

When the steam curtain drifted off, the stockyard office was gone. The scene was now a nearby country road, and down it came thundering the three bandits, firing over their shoulders. Then, at a signal from their leader, they reined their horses, leaped from them to wait in ambush in a thicket of bush. A dazzling red Hupmobile touring car roared into sight. The driver was crouched low over the steering wheel. Beside him was Sheriff Arch Steuben, his guns blazing. He saw the ambush just in time. The car skidded to a stop and the sheriff was behind it, shooting it out with the desperadoes. One of them fell dead, another slumped to the ground. The third tried to run for it. Sheriff Arch Steuben took careful aim, fired, and did not miss.

The sheriff rose from examining the third of the bodies. He nodded grimly to his companion. Below in the valley the church clock chimed five, the death knell of the notorious Kiley brothers, who never again would terrorize this countryside. The sheriff slowly removed his hat...and the curtain of steam rose again.

The next scene would be the laying of the cornerstone for the Ridgefield College for Women, but that was all the rehearsal for tonight.

Dave spoke into the mike: "That was fine. Try and do as well tomorrow."

He started down the aisle to the field to congratulate Ross Anders. It was having assistants like Ross that kept supervising directors like himself out of madhouses. Ross had written a whale of a script; his research on the history of this town had been brilliant. And this was one of his best jobs of direction. There was no doubt that the pageant part of Ridgefield's Centennial would be a success. Now, if only the parade, the beauty contest, the crowning of the Centennial Queen, the fireworks, the Centennial Costume Ball, if everything else went as well, they were in.

Dave saw the angry old gentleman shouting at Ross and he groaned. He cursed himself for breaking the rule that no one but the cast and crew be allowed at rehearsals. But old Arch Steuben had been so anxious to see the scene that had made him a hero that Dave had finally okayed his presence. Daniel McKevin, Rear Admiral, retired, and Luther Dunning, Centennial Committee Chairman, were trying to placate the ex-sheriff, but he would have none of it.

"That young whippersnapper takin' my part," Arch was sputtering. "Why, he don't even know how to handle a gun! And, another thing-- that ain't the way it happened at all!"

"All right," Ross said wearily; "there's one like you in every town."

"Take it easy, Ross," Dave said. "What was wrong Mr. Steuben?"

"Them Kiley boys didn't ambush me. I got every single one of them while they was goin' fast as they could go. Shot each one of them right off their horse! You ask Ed Feeley that drove that Hup! He was one of my deputies. The two of us was gettin' an early start for West Virginia to extradite a chicken thief. Bret Lindsey, it was. Luther, you remember Bret, a great one for stealing chickens..."

Ross groaned in impatience; Dave shook his head at him.

"Well," Arch went happily on, "we was going to Kirby Hill when we seen the Kileys cuttin' across the fields for the highway. We didn't know where they'd been or where they was goin'. All we knew it was our chance to get them at last. Well, we lay low till they was a bit ahead of us so they couldn't turn back. Then we set out after them, Ed drivin', me shootin'. I shot all three of them right out of their saddles. There was no ambush."

"I know," Ross said. "But we couldn't stage it that way. We didn't have the space."

"Of course not," Luther Dunning said. "Arch, you have to take some dramatic license in these scenes."

"Arch," the admiral said, his eyes smiling maliciously in his rugged sea-dog's face, "Arch, don't you object to the church clock striking five like that?"

"Course not! What you gettin' at?"

"I didn't think you'd object. It gives you a fine, heroic moment, standing there listening to those bells."

"That's the way it happened!"

"No, Arch," said the admiral stubbonly, "the stockyard robbery didn't even take place until after five o'clock."

The ex-sheriff snorted. "How would you know about it, anyways? You weren't even there. I recollect two things happened that morning: The Kiley boys got killed and young Dan McKevin ran away."

Luther Dunning turned to the admiral: "He's right, Dan. You ran away to join the Navy then."

McKevin's face reddened. He obviously wasn't used to being contradicted. "And that's how I happen to know the time," he said, his voice frosty. "I swore Tom Drake to secrecy that I was going to hop the morning freight train when it stopped for water at the tower. Tom met me there to say good-by. We hid in the bushes waiting for the freight. And, Arch those bells struck five just before I sneaked onto the train. I missed the newspaper accounts of the robbery, and I didn't even hear about Tom's death for a long time, but I've often thought that if that train had been late, Tom wouldn't have got back to the office until after the robbery was over. He might be alive today. That's how I know--"

"You don't know nothin'!" Arch Steuben thundered.

"Now, Arch," Luther Dunning said smoothly, "you're wasting Dave and Ross's time. They've got a lot to do."

"They got plenty of time to distort the historical facts."

"Come with me, Arch." Luther Dunning led the irate old man away. "You'll be late for the fireworks."

"Oh, Ross, could I see you a moment?" It was Margot Durante, the staff member in charge of costumes. "It's important, Ross."

"Sure, Margot."

Dave watched Ross and Margot cross the field, then he turned back to the admiral: "You like the pageant, sir?"

"Fine, fine."

"Did Mr. Dunning like it?"

The admiral chuckled. "Luther said it was so real he could feel that bullet in his shoulder again."

"I was afraid it might upset him."

"You mean his cousin being killed in the robbery? That was over forty years ago, Dave, a long, long time. No, I think you've done a wonderful job, you and Ross. I'm glad the committee picked your outfit. I imagine you've got everything as historically accurate as you possibly could. Except, of course," he chuckled again, "about those bells."

"But you don't think that matters, do you, sir?"

"Not a bit. As I told Ross, it's a fine effect. I shouldn't have riled the sheriff, either. He's told the story his way so often he probably believes it himself."

Dave nodded diplomatically; then he said, "Got your speech ready for tomorrow, Admiral?"

"Yes, but I'll never forgive you for that."

Dave laughed, pleased with himself. Admiral Daniel McKevin had been a hero in the Pacific and he was Ridgefield's first citizen now. Recently he had returned to his hometown, the first time since he had run away as a boy of fifteen. Dave had cajoled him into leading the parade and making a speech. It would be a highlight in Ridgefield's Centennial.

Dave left the admiral and went looking for Ross Anders. There were a couple of things he wanted to take up with Ross. The high-school boy at the steam control was too slow, making the curtain late; the microphone that picked up the Kileys' horses' hoofs was out of kilter. Down at the other end of the field Dave saw Ross and Margot. The place was nearly empty now. The town's young people had hurried into the dressing rooms to get out of their costumes. It was darkening fast; the fireworks in the park would soon begin.

Dave stopped short. He couldn't see Margot's face, just the shine of her bright blond hair, but he could hear her voice. It was snapping with angry finality; she was evidently scolding Ross about something. Dave retreated; he'd spare himself the headache of this staff squabble. He needed some food, and if he was quick about it, and persuasively charming enough about it, it could be the most impor-tant meal of his twenty-nine years.

He was quick enough. When he got there Sarah Cummings was just locking the door of the gift-shop lending library where she worked. She smiled at him with her lips, but her wide gray eyes were somber, unwelcoming.

"Hello, Dave," she said.

"Let's you and I have something to eat together, Sarah."

She shook her head. "Sorry, I've--"

"You're hungry," Dave said. "On Mondays, Wednesdays, and Fridays you always eat at nine o'clock."

"Yes, but tonight I--"

"This offer won't be repeated. Tomorrow night I'll be on a train going far away. If we don't have dinner tonight I won't feel I know you well enough to write you every day and send flowers on Sundays. Let's eat, Sarah. You may have the dollar-eighty dinner."

"I'd love to, Dave, but--"

"Say that again."

"I'd love to, really, I would."

"That's the first time you've sounded as if you meant it."

"Dave, I've got to hurry. And if I shouldn't see you again--"

"Yes?"

"I've enjoyed working with you and the gang on the pageant."

"Oh, that. Well, you were our most valuable volunteer. Shall I write you in care of the shop?"

"No, I won't be--" She hesitated.

"You won't be here?"

"Dave, I've got to hurry."

She turned and walked rapidly away. He had the impression that she was running from him. Or, he wondered, was it that she was running to something? He watched her cross the village green that was a reminder in the town that its settlers had come from old New England. She turned the corner of the simple white church and was gone.

There was a low boom and a rocket exploded in the sky, sending its dazzling shower down to the tall trees beyond the church. Dave heard the children scream their wonder and delight. The little dopes making all that noise over a sky-rocket. He'd skip the fireworks. He was afraid he might go around knocking cute little heads together.

The hour-long program of fireworks was reaching its grand finale when Dave had given up wandering aimlessly around the deserted town and gone back to the football field. He wanted to check the public-address system. The mikes that weren't behaving were strung along Elm Street, which ran between the north end of the stadium and the park. He could use the fireworks to test for sound.

He turned on the light in the enclosed press box high above the center of the field. He sat down at the portable control panel and switched on mike five. Nothing at all happened. He fiddled with some wires, tightened some connections. The booming of the fireworks, the vocal appreciation of the crowd grew louder in the stadium. He had managed to fix it; the audience here tomorrow would be able to hear the ominous hoof thunder of the Kiley boys' approaching horses. He was about to flick off the switch when he heard a voice, a voice he knew despite its present harshness and cruelty.

"...You'll pay me," Ross Anders was saying; "you'll pay me anything I ask. And tomorrow. I've waited long enough now. You'll do it because there's nothing else you can do-- because of what I can do to you, what I can prove about you. And I do have proof, you know that..."

A set of rockets exploded, drowning out the voice. Dave sat staring at the microphone before him, stunned at what he had heard. But it was a moment before the full implication of Ross's words hit him, before he realized that Ross Anders was a blackmailer, that right now he was closing the vise on his victim.

The din of rockets and cheering crowds died down, and now he could hear Ross speaking again, but the words were an indistinct blur. He turned up the volume; it didn't help. Then he snapped off the switch and was out of the press box, moving diagonally across the bleacher seats toward the north-gate exit.

He was out of breath when he reached the gate. It was closed, the corrugated iron door was down. He turned back toward the west entrance, through which he had come. At last he was outside the stadium, rounding the curve of its north end. He crossed the parking space and was on the corner of Elm Street. If Ross and his companion were standing down there in the shadow of the big trees he couldn't see them. He moved along past the row of frame houses. There was nobody. He kept going. There was one more mike in front of the town library.

He had cleared the far side of the library when he saw the figure, far back from the street, crouched in the shadow of the wall. Her back was toward him, but he could see that it was a girl. Then she rose abruptly and he saw her profile. She was running now across the rear lawn of the library toward Ridge Avenue beyond.

He shouted, "Sarah!"

The roar of the fireworks drowned out his voice. Sarah had turned the corner of the building without looking back. He started after her along the wall, and he came to a stumbling halt. Beside a basement window, his right arm twisted unnaturally along its sill, lay Ross Anders. Dave dropped to his knees beside him, and in the center of the crimson splotch on the white sports shirt he saw a small black circle. Ross Anders had been shot to death.

The deafening, blinding finale of the fireworks was in progress. It would be over in a minute and its audience homebound, some of them passing by here. Dave decided that he would stay where he was. By now, Sarah would have got to a phone-- no, by now she would have reached the police station, just half a block down Ridge Avenue. The police should be on their way. It would take them only a minute to get here, actually no more than sixty seconds.

He heard the final, grateful applause of the audience in the park. He saw the first of the crowd drift though the trees on their way to the street. He walked quickly to the end of the building. From here, through the edges of the shrubbery of the library lawn, he could see the police station. There was no one coming down its steps, no one hurrying across the street toward Ross Anders' body. Then, as he watched, half of the big front door of the station swung open. A young policeman in his shirt sleeves stepped out. He sat down on the steps, lit a cigarette.

Sarah Cummings had not gone to the police. She had not reported finding Ross Anders' body, she was not reporting his murder. She had fled on past the police station.

Behind Dave, a woman screamed and a man shouted. The crowd formed quickly, and it was all that the policeman who came sprinting from the park's entrance could do to get through the mob. Then there were other policemen, and the semicircle of Ridgefield's curious, shocked citizens was being urged back and away from the body of the murdered young man.

Chief of Police Winters was looking across the desk at Dave. His eyes, behind the steel-rimmed glasses, were narrowed in appraisal, an appraisal so acute that Dave wondered if Winters could have sensed that he had not told all he knew about the murder of Ross Anders. His decision about Sarah had been unpremeditated. When the moment had come for him to tell about Sarah's flight he had instinctively not mentioned it. Now he knew that he wouldn't. At least, not until he had seen Sarah, and had given her a chance to explain.

Winters said, "You're sure it was Anders' voice you heard over the public-address system?"

"Yes," Dave said. "It was Ross."

"Then that gives us a motive for his murder. Anders had discovered a secret about someone. He was trying blackmail. His victim wouldn't-- or couldn't-- pay. He shot Anders. You didn't hear the voice of the other person, at all?"

"No. The fireworks--"

"Yes." Winters rose, encircled his desk. "How long has Anders been in town here?"

"About five weeks. He came a week before the rest of us to write the script for the pageant."

"Did he get to know anyone in town especially well?"

"I don't think so. Ross didn't make friends very easily."

"He knew the people working for the Merrill Company well, though," Winters said thoughtfully. "How many are there on your staff?"

"There was Ross. There's Margot Durante and Alice Knapp and Eddie Merrill."

"Eddie Merrill-- his father owns the company?"

"Yes."

"I've seen him. A nice-looking boy. Margot Durante-- she's the blonde in charge of the costumes?" Dave nodded. Winters said, "Alice Knapp-- I haven't met her."

"She was Ross's assistant. She helped him stage the pageant."

"How old?" Winters was trying to place her. "What's she look like?"

"Twenty-two or three, maybe. Reddish hair, tall."

"Oh, yes. That busy girl, always in a hurry."

"Alice works hard. She's ambitious."

"I'll want to talk to all of them. You're staying over at Arch Steuben's guesthouse, aren't you?"

"That's right."

Arch Steuben's place was near the center of town. It was one of the oldest houses in Ridgefield. It stood, a little shabby but still proud, among the stores and shops of a growing business section of a growing metropolis. Arch Steuben's father had been born in it and died in it; Arch swore vehemently that he would do the same. When the ex-sheriff had been forced into retirement ten years ago, it had been financially necessary for him to turn his home into a tourists' house. A grandniece of the old widower did most of the work for him.

A uniformed policeman walked down off the high, narrow porch to meet Winters and Dave, "I phoned you," he said to the chief, "but you had left."

"Something important?"

"You told us to go through Anders' room-- well, somebody got there first."

"Searched it?"

"From top to bottom. The place has been turned upside down. Someone was in a big hurry to find something."

The screen door slammed, and Arch Steuben was stamping down the porch steps. "I seen him go into Anders' room, I seen him."

"Well, why didn't you--?"

"Now, wait a minute, Winters. I didn't know anything then. I didn't even know Anders was killed. I thought it was Anders going into his own room."

"Do you know now who it really was?" Winters asked.

"No, I only caught a glimpse of his back from the hall stairs. Only thing I'm sure of is it was a man."

"What time was this, Arch?"

"Few minutes before ten. About five minutes to ten."

"That was after Anders was killed," Winters said. He turned to Dave: "Then it was his murderer. The proof that Anders was using to blackmail him-- that's what he was looking for."

"I guess so," Dave said. "It makes sense." And he felt a partial easing of the worry tormenting him. Whatever had motivated Sarah Cummings' wild flight from the murder scene, it had not been a need to search Anders' room.

Winters said, "Arch, you got any roomers here besides the Merrill Company people?"

"No, they filled me up."

The policeman said, "I've rounded them up for you, Chief. They're in the living room."

As the four men went up the porch steps, Arch Steuben said, "Winters, don't you think you ought to deputize me? I can be of help to you."

"Maybe later, Arch." Winters turned to Dave: "Tell the others I'll be with them in a minute. I want to see Ross Anders' room first."

Dave went into the living room. Eddie Merrill looked up from stamping out a cigarette. His handsome young face was without its usual wide, friendly grin. Margot Durante and Alice Knapp had been talking quietly together at a window, their backs to Eddie. Now they broke off their conference and moved away from each other. Margot was grim, and Dave saw a hardness that he had never realized the high-humored blonde was capable of showing. Alice was jumpy; it was as if she thought that time was being wasted, that by now this unpleasantness should have been eliminated, that, were she in charge, it would have been.

But, Dave thought, there was one thing that they all, himself included, had in common, and the realization of it shocked him. Not one of them was feeling any grief or loss because Ross Anders had been murdered.

Alice said, "So Ross was trying a little blackmail."

Dave said, "How did you know that?"

"We could hear the police talking out front just now. That's it, isn't it, Dave? And instead of getting money, he got himself killed?"

"Yes, that's it."

Eddie said, "Are the police sure about that, Dave?"

"It's a fact, Eddie." Dave repeated what he had heard over the public-address system. "And when they find out who it was that Ross was blackmailing, they'll have the murderer."

"Dave!" Margot's voice was urgent. "Dave, did you mention me to the police?"

"I don't know what you mean, Margot."

"Ross and I had a fight tonight-- just before he was killed. You must have heard us, Dave. I saw you walking away."

"I hadn't thought of it since, Margot."

"Oh." She moved indecisively toward a chair, then swung back to face Dave. "I think I should tell you what the fight was about. I guess I should tell the cops, too. They'll probably hear about it. I don't want them to think it was anything-- anything important. It was just that I was fed up with this job. I'm not the costume-mistress type. I told Ross I was leaving, and he didn't like it. He went on and on about my ingratitude to him. He got me this job, he gave me a raise. Okay, so I was grateful to him. But, after all, it wasn't as if he had saved me from starvation."

Dave smiled. "I believe that."

It was hard to tell exactly how old Margot Durante was, but girls with her warm attractiveness didn't often starve to death. It would be another five years or so before Margot's lush prettiness would be overblown. It was a surprise to Dave that she had stayed on this job as long as she had. He always thought that Margot was looking toward something more exciting, more glamorous. Or perhaps it was just the reverse-- something more secure.

Chief of Police Winters was standing in the doorway. He said, "We think we've got the fingerprints of the person who ransacked Anders' room. So that calls for printing the four of you."

"But you'll find all our prints in that room," Alice Knapp said. Her usually brisk, businesslike voice took on a note of shrillness. "We've all been in his room, we've had conferences there, we--"

"But not all of you have been opening his dresser drawers, going through his desk and his trunk. Just one person did that."

"But why must that person be one of us? And why have you decided that?"

"I haven't decided anything, Miss Knapp, but I want your prints."

"Mine, too?" Alice persisted. "Why? Mr. Steuben told you it was a man in Ross's room."

"Yes," Winters said patiently. "I still want everyone's prints, Miss Knapp."

It was a half-hour later that Dave managed to slip away from the others without raising any questions. He walked quickly through the quiet town, thinking about Sarah Cummings. He realized, with a growing anxiety, how little he knew about her.

She had come only recently to Ridgefield. She worked in a gift-shop lending library, and she lived alone in a small apartment. He had never heard her say anything about a family. She didn't seem to have any close friends. He wondered now if she had worked so hard on the pageant because she had been lonely. The staff had accepted her as one of them. She had almost always joined them at the town's diner for a late snack after the evening's rehearsal. She had always been charming and humorous, but her talk had never been about herself. Perhaps that had been because she was a completely selfless person. Or perhaps there had been another reason for her personal reserve.

Dave turned into the block of new two-story buildings that had smart shops on their ground floors and apartments above them. He walked up a flight of stairs between an interior decorator's studio and a hobby shop, and went down the corridor to the door at its end. There was no answer to his first ring, nor to his second. He tried once more and was about to turn away when an uncertain voice called out, "Who is it?"

"Dave Logan. May I see you a moment?"

"It's so late, Dave."

"It's important, Sarah."

The door was opened reluctantly. Sarah's face seemed pale to him, her eyes wider. He wanted to take her in his arms and tell her that everything was all right, that there was no trouble she could be in that he wouldn't somehow fix.

She said, "It's something about Ross, of course."

Dave nodded. She closed the door, motioned him to a chair. She sat on the edge of the studio couch.

"What is it, Dave?"

He hesitated a moment, rejecting an impulse to try to trap her. He said, "I saw you tonight, Sarah, there with Ross. And I saw you run. I thought you were running to report the murder."

He waited. She was looking directly into his eyes, but she didn't speak.

He went on; "You didn't go to the police. Why, Sarah? Where did you go?"

"I was going to them. I-- I never got there--"

"Why? What happened?"

"I was so frightened, Dave, finding Ross like that, knowing he was dead. I-- I just ran-- as fast as I could go. And I stumbled and fell headfirst through a hedge. It knocked the wind out of me, I-- I blacked out. Then, when I got back on my feet, I saw the crowd around where-- where Ross was, and the police.   There wasn't anything for me to do then. I came right home."

"So that's how it was."

"Yes." She looked up at Dave in quick surprise. "What else could it have been?"

"I was afraid you didn't want the police to know about Ross until-- until you had time to do something. I don't know what."

"Dave," she said, her voice lowering in fright, "you didn't think that I might have killed him?"

"No, I never thought that, Sarah, do you need help?   Is there something wrong?"

"No, there's nothing.   I'm still shaken from finding Ross, and from my tumble. That's all."

"Sarah, did you know Ross before?   Did you ever meet him--?"

She shook her head.   "I never saw him in my life before he came here to Ridgefield."   She looked at Dave, her gaze clear and direct. "You believe that, don't you, Dave?"

"Yes," he said, "I believe it, Sarah."

Later down in the street, after walking around the block more times than he knew, he still believed her, everything that she had told him. But he knew, too, that there was something frightening Sarah, something more than that she had found a new and casual acquaintance dead and that she had taken a shattering spill running for the police.

He walked past the diner, the only restaurant that was still open at midnight, then turned back to it. He went through the counter and booth section of the place into a dining room that had been tucked on as a left wing. At the moment three persons were missing from the large, round table in the far corner-- Ross Anders, Sarah, and himself.   Eddie, Merrill, Alice Knapp, and Margot were there, as usual at this time of night. Luther Dunning, as usual, also was with them.

In his position as head of the Centennial Committee, Dunning had quickly got to know all of the staff. But he had gone farther than that. He had taken to dropping into the diner each night to talk over with them the problems of the Centennial, and to turn these midnight snack sessions into his parties.

He could easily afford it.   He was now sole owner of the Drake Stockyards and its affiliate packing company. As the town had grown to its present twenty-thousand population and its present prosperity, Dunning's personal fortunes had expanded with it. For years, now, he and his handsome, dignified wife had been the royal family of Ridgefield.

Tonight the laughter and jokes were missing from the round table. It was a somber, nervous group that Dave joined.

Luther Dunning said, "Dave, I've talked to Winters. He doesn't see any reason why the program tomorrow shouldn't go on as planned."

"We'll get it on," Dave said. "As planned."

"It's not just for the Ridgefield people, you know. There'll be crowds coming from miles around."

"Don't worry," Dave said. "We'll manage it. Alice could keep the pageant moving by herself, but I'll be there to help....Alice, I've got Ross's script in my room."

"I won't need it, Dave. I've got a duplicate."

"Eddie, the floats for the parade are all set up, aren't they?"

"Yes, and they're great."

"Did you see that Queen got to bed early? So she'll be sparkling for her Coronation?"

"The Queen will be sparkling," Eddie promised.

"You see, Luther, everything's under control," Dave said.

"Fine....Margot, can I give you a ride home? Anybody want a lift?"

Luther Dunning's offer was declined in favor of another round of coffee. On his way out they saw him stop at the cashier's desk and ask for the bill. In a few minutes a waitress was bringing new coffee. She was followed across the room by a man whose mission had stamped an ominous look on his face.

The Chief of Police sat down beside Dave. He waited until the waitress had left. Then he spoke quietly, his eyes never directing his words to anyone in particular:

"The prints we found in Anders' room weren't of any help. As you said, all of you had been in that room. But whoever searched it must have left in a hurry. He forgot something. He left the key in the lock. The prints on the key itself were smudged, but there were some clear ones on the mailing tag. There's a woman's print on it."

"Not mine," Margot said.

"No, not yours, Miss Durante. And not yours, Miss Knapp."

"Of course not," Alice said.

"We don't know yet whose the woman's print is. But we have identified the men's. There was a partially smudged one of Anders and a very clear one of Eddie Merrill's."

They were all waiting, looking silently at Eddie. His face was white. Then, as suddenly, he was grinning, and Dave thought, looking like a college kid about to explain his latest misadventure to the Dean of Men.

"Sure," he said, "my prints would be on that key. I should have told you that before."

"Tell me now," Winter said.

"At the start of the rehearsal tonight Ross asked me to get his script for him; he'd forgotten it. He gave me the key to his room." Winters was about to speak, but Eddie went on, nipping the interruption: "And I forgot the key. I was in a hurry. I guess I did leave it in the lock. That's how whoever it was was able to get into Ross's room. Brilliant me, I left the key in the lock for him."

"So," Winter said, "it wasn't you who searched the room."

"No, I walked in, picked up the script, walked out."

"About what time?"

"Oh-- seven-thirty."

"That's your story, is it?"

"That," Eddie said, "is what happened."

"Well," Winters said, and there was no way of knowing what he was thinking, "well, don't let me keep you folks up. Good night."

After he had gone, Dave said, "Eddie, let's you and me take a walk."

"Don't you believe me, Dave?"

"Do you think Winters believed you?"

"I don't know....Yes, he must have. It's the truth."

"Let's take a walk," Dave said. "Excuse us, girls."

Outside, moving down the street of the darkened, silent town, Dave said, "Listen, Eddie--"

"Yes, Uncle Dave?" His voice was thick with sarcasm.

"No, not that, Eddie. This is different."

This was very different; this involved murder. In the past Dave's reluctant and self-conscious talks with Eddie had been pleasant in comparison. Young Eddie had been a trial to his father. He had spent his school and college days up to his neck in hot water. He liked night clubs better than classrooms. He admired dancing girls more than girl Phi Beta Kappas. During the summer vacation when his father had put him to work under Dave's supervision, he had painted each anniversary town a bright red. The town had always looked a lot older than its one or two hundred years after Eddie Merrill had torn through it.

At last the elder Merrill had thundered an ultimatum, an ultimatum tempered by a reward. He had given Eddie one year to prove that he was responsible and interested enough to remain with the Merrill Producing Company. If at the end of the year he had proved it, he would be made a junior partner as Dave was. If he failed, his father would change his plans, drastically and finally. Eddie would be on his own, without the security of a prosperous future.

Dave, on orders from headquarters, had kept his eye on Eddie. The past few months the young man had done well. He had worked hard, tried to drop his smart-aleck behavior. He and Dave had become almost good friends. But now the old hostility of a delinquent toward his sponsor was back in Eddie's attitude toward Dave.

"Eddie," Dave said. "Ross Anders has been murdered. That was a policeman talking to you back there, not a truant officer."

"Come on, Dave. What is it you want to say?"

"I walked to rehearsal tonight with Ross. He had his script with him."

Some of the belligerence went out of Eddie. "No," he said, "you're wrong."

"I think I know what happened. Sarah Cummings took Ross's room key from him after he was murdered."

Eddie turned to Dave with a jerk. "Sarah Cummings?" he said.

"I saw her tonight, Eddie, bending over Ross's body-- "

"You're not saying that she killed him?"

"No-- no. But I think she took his key and gave it to you. So that you could search his room before the police got to it."

"Search his room for what?"

"For whatever it was that Ross was using to blackmail-- "

"To blackmail who? Me? Sarah?"

"I don't know the answers. You know more than I do, I'm sure of that. You're in trouble, Eddie. Your lying to Winters proves that. And I think Sarah's in trouble, too. What's it all about?"

"It's all about nothing. I tell you I didn't lie-- "

"Eddie, are you trying to help Sarah?" Is that it?"

"Why should I try to help her? Sarah Cummings is a girl I met four weeks ago. She's nothing to me except a nice, pretty kid. Why should I stick my neck out for her?"

"I don't know why, Eddie. Maybe you've changed. A while back I'd have said you wouldn't stick your neck out to holler fire if the old ladies' home was in flames. But lately-- well, you've become fairly human."

"Thanks a lot. Look; if Sarah Cummings is in some kind of jam, I don't know about that, either."

"If there's nothing wrong, Eddie, there was no reason to lie to Winters."

"I didn't lie to anybody. You think Ross didn't forget his script. I know he did. I went back to his room and got it for him."

"Eddie-- "

"Dave, there's nothing more to discuss."

"Okay, Eddie."

"Okay, Uncle Dave."

Dave walked quickly away from Eddie Merrill. It was a matter of self-protection. It didn't pay to slug the boss's son, no matter how jeering and unpleasant he was.

The midmorning sun the next day apparently approved of what was going on in Ridgefield.   There was an extra enthusiasm in its glow, as if it enjoyed a rousing historical pageant. Dave Logan tried to close his eyes against it, but that was impossible. He dragged himself out of bed and discovered, to his concern, that it was nearly nine-thirty.

He had been unable to get to sleep before daybreak; since then he had slept like someone sandbagged. Now he tried to forget his nagging worry for Sarah Cummings, his impatient anger toward Eddie Merrill. He had a big job to do today; somehow he had to get it done.

In the hall downstairs Arch Steuben was sorting mail on the covered radiator. The old man glanced up the stairs at Dave. "Letter for you," he said.

"Thanks. Going to the parade, Mr Steuben?"

"No, sir, not me. I got some figurin' to do. About the murder. That pipsqueak chief of police! Why I was catching up with killers before Harry Winters was out of rompers."

"Do me a favor, Sheriff. Catch up with this killer."

"Maybe I will," Arch said slyly. "You know, I just might, at that."

"You know something we don't, Mr. Steuben?"

"Maybe. But I still got some thinkin' to do about it. That letter there looks personal. Aren't you going to read it?"

Dave looked at the envelope and recognized the handwriting of Mrs. Edward Merrill Sr. He smiled; nothing like a little irony to begin the day. Mother wanting to know if son Eddie was behaving himself and thanking Dave for keeping an eye on him. Mrs. Merrill averaged about one a week of these letters.

Dave moved out of the dim hall onto the sun-struck porch. He opened the letter, and inside the folded sheet of notepaper was a picture clipped from a newspaper. An attractive young couple, seated at a table, were enjoying a famous New York night club. The boy was Eddie Merrill Jr. of Chicago. The girl was Miss Joan Mason of Clarion, Michigan. Dave recogized the smiling young lady immediately. He knew her as Miss Sarah Cummings of Ridgefield, Ohio.

Arch Steuben spoke from behind the screen door: "Bad news?"

"I don't know," Dave said.

He read the letter. It seemed that Mrs. Merrill kept a scrapbook of her son's athletic, scholastic, and social career since he was a teen-ager. This picture was taken two years ago, during Eddie's last year at college. And it seemed that when Mrs. Merrill had been visiting Eddie here in Ridgefield two weeks ago, she had met Sarah Cummings. Sarah had been bewilderingly familiar to her. Yesterday, glancing through the scrapbook, Mrs. Merrill had discovered why. Now she was worried. What was going on? What was this girl doing in Ridgefield, using an assumed name? Why were she and Eddie pretending that they had never known each other before?

Mrs. Merrill hadn't bothered her husband about this yet. Perhaps Dave would discover for her that there was nothing to worry about. Perhaps she was even wrong about the picture. Dave looked at it again. Mrs. Merrill had not been wrong about it; there was no mistake. Miss Joan Mason, of Clarion, Michigan, was Sarah Cummings and Eddie Merrill was an old friend of hers....

The screen door slammed. Arch said, "Anything I can help you with?"

"No, no thanks, Mr. Steuben."

Dave headed for the street, across town to the old ball park, where the parade was forming. The parade route was already lined with happy, eager children and their smiling parents.

As Dave reached the ball park three motorcycle policemen came out of it in formation. Behind them, in a huge, open-topped touring car, came the Mayor, Admiral McKevin, Luther Dunning, and in his honorary position as the town's oldest citizen, Ed Freeley. More cars followed, filled with the town's lesser lights. Eddie Merrill had got the procession started on the dot, an almost impossible feat.

Inside the field, Dave watched Eddie at work. He was a busy boy, a smiling charming demon. He had what it took to handle people when he wanted to use it. At his direction, the high-school band swung out of its station and was on parade. Then he saw the first of the floats, donated by one of the service clubs, on its way, a mountain of flowers emblazoning the legend: Ridgefield, 1853-1953. Eddie saw Dave and gestured to him, grinning that everything was under control.

Dave left Eddie to his job. He walked out of the field beside the Little Theater float, sporting in tableau the scenes from its most successful productions. When he got to the Town Hall, Ridgefield's four leading citizens were already on the reviewing stand. He stood watching. He saw Sarah Cummings-- Joan Mason of Clarion, Michigan-- pass by in a float that amusingly depicted the history of the female bathing suit, from the voluminous garments of yesteryear to the brevities of today. Sarah was the modern girl, very modern and very pretty. With a charming tolerance she withstood the whistles of the juvenile wolves lining the sidewalks.

Then the parade was over and after the Mayor's introduction, the admiral's hearty voice was booming over the public-address system. Ridgefield was a great place...a great place to come back to...he was proud of Ridgefield....Well he remembered the day some forty years ago when he had left it on a freight train, running away to join the Navy...he was a boy of fifteen then, Luther Dunning barely nineteen, the Mayor was a baby...and Ridgefield was a sleepy little town. But now...

A hand touched Dave's elbow. It was Mrs. Carson, chairwoman of the pageant's costume committee. Mrs. Carson was upset. "Mr. Logan," she said, "have you seen Margot Durante?"

"No, I haven't. Not this morning."

"She was supposed to meet us at the high school for a last-minute checkup on the costumes for this afternoon. It's getting late now and-- well-- "

He quelled his annoyance at Margot. "Maybe I can help."

"Well, there is one thing. Midge Caldwell stumbled on some wonderful clothes of her great-grandmother's in a trunk in her grandmother's attic, and we wondered if we couldn't use them instead of the rented costumes. If we can, almost all the costumes will be real-- all of the women's anyway-- and we'd be so proud."

"I'm sure they're all right, Mrs. Carson."

"Yes, but it will take some shifting around, and we don't know the script well enough and it's getting late, Mr. Logan."

"All right, Mrs. Carson. I'll come over."

The admiral was receiving an ovation. The parade and its ceremonies over, the crowd was breaking up. Dave and Mrs. Carson fought their way to the high school. After he had solved the costume problem, Dave had some things to attend to at the high-school stadium concerning the pageant. It was noon before he got back to Arch Steuben's house.

He went at once down the hall and into the wing that led to Eddie's door. His hand was raised to knock when he heard sobbing, the low, helpless sound of someone protesting against life. Then he heard Eddie's voice, gentle and comforting, almost pleading.

"Darling," he was saying, "don't. It's going to be all right; it's all going to be over soon. We can tell everyone that we're married. I know what it's been like keeping it a secret--"

Dave's hand dropped to his side. There was no reason now to talk to Eddie Merrill, to show him the clipping that his mother had found. He knew why Joan Mason of Clarion was in Ridgefield pretending to be Sarah Cummings. Ed Merrill Senior would not have approved of his son's marriage to anyone, not during this year of probation.

The scream wrenched Dave away from the door. It pulled him down the hallway, through the dining room, into the little library beyond it. He found Arch Steuben's niece cowering in the doorway. Her hands were over her eyes, blotting out the sight before her. Arch Steuben lay sprawled on the floor. He had been savagely struck down by a blow on his temple. There was no doubt at all that he was dead.

Dave heard footsteps behind him, and voices. Eddie Merrill and Margot and Alice Knapp were converging upon him. He turned, blocking the doorway.

He said, "No, don't. Get Miss Steuben out of here. It's Arch. He's been murdered!"

There was a knock on his bedroom door. Dave crossed the room to it, opened it. Margot Durante stood in the hall. It was an effort for her to rise above her shock and fright to speak. Her voice was harsh with strain:

"Dave, Winters wants to see you now. He's through with me."

"What is it, Margot? Did he give you a tough time?"

"Nothing special, I guess. Eddie and Alice look as if they've both been through the wringer. Good luck to you, Dave."

"Thanks, Margot."

The Chief of Police was waiting for Dave in the living room. There was anger in the policeman's face now, an angry grief. This was no longer an impersonal murder case to him; an old man whom he had known all his life had been the second victim of Ross Anders' killer.

Winters said, "I gather from Miss Steuben that everyone had left the house for the parade this morning except you and Arch."

"That's right. I overslept."

"Did you see Arch?"

"Yes."

"Why wasn't he going to the parade? Did he tell you?"

"Well, he was in one of his sly cryptic moods. He said he had some figuring to do about Ross's murder."

"Oh? You think he was on to something we missed?"

"I didn't think anything of it at the time. I thought he was dramatizing himself, the way he always did. But now I think he must have known something. He must have confronted the murderer with it."

Winter's voice was thoughtful: "Arch was capable of that."

"I think he wanted to be a hero once more. He wanted to bring in the killer himself."

"That would be like Arch. And being here in the house with all of you, he might have found something, or overheard something. Yes, I guess there's no doubt that Arch knew who the killer was; his death proves that. All right, let's get on with it. What did you do after you talked with Arch-- until Miss Steuben found him?"

"You want my alibi?"

"Yes, and if you have one it'll be a nice change. Neither Eddie nor Miss Durante nor Miss Knapp has one. Each of them says they were alone in their room after the parade. Any one of them could have--"

Dave stopped listening. Eddie Merrill hadn't been alone in his room. Sarah had been with him. She must have been able to slip out of the house unnoticed in the confusion after the discovery of Arch's death.

"Tell me," Winters was saying, "just what you did."

"I checked to see if Eddie was having any trouble with the parade. He wasn't. Then I watched the parade and listened to the admiral's speech. After that I went to the high school with Mrs. Carson. There was a costume problem that needed solving."

"Couldn't Miss Durante have solved it? That's her job isn't it?"

"Well, she wasn't around and--"

"Was she supposed to be at the school?"

"Yes, but--"

"But what?" Winters interrupted brusquely. "Maybe the reason she wasn't there was because Arch Steuben wanted to see her. Maybe--"

"Wait," Dave said.

Winters strode to the door; he had given up politeness. He shouted, "Miss Durante! Miss Durante down here, please!"

The chief waited for her at the foot of the stairs. He motioned her into the living room and followed her in. She looked questioningly at Dave.

Winters spoke first: "Miss Durante you missed an appointment this morning. You were supposed to have been at the high school. What happened?" Margot looked again at Dave. Winters said, "No, your colleague didn't double-cross you. I dragged it out of him. All right, Miss Durante. What happened that was so important that you couldn't do your work this morning?"

"Nothing was so important," Margot said. "It was negligence, that's all."

"Negligence?"

"I started for the school and then I couldn't face all that crinoline and gingham and old lace. I was fed up. I came back here and went to my room."

"You picked this morning to get fed up," Winters said.

"Maybe," Dave said, "I can help, Margot--"

"I don't need any help, thanks. This was my last job with Merrill. I told Ross that last night. I was quitting."

Winters said, "You told Anders last night. Was that what the two of you were quarreling about?"

"Oh," Margot said. "So you know about that."

"Yes. Was Anders against you quitting?"

"Yes."

"Why? Why did he care?"

"Well, he got me the job, in the first place."

"You knew Anders before you came to work for Merrill," Winters said. His tone was accusing. "You and Anders were old friends, weren't you?"

"Friends? That's a little too strong. I knew Ross ten or twelve years ago, when I was trying to break into the theater in New York. For years I didn't even see him. Not until last spring in St. Louis. The road show that I had a bit in folded. I ran into Ross and he gave me this job. I was broke I needed it. But I never intended to make a career out of it."

"I see," Winters said. He rose abruptly. "I'd like to talk to you a little more, Miss Durante. If you'll come with me to headquarters now--"

A voice said, "Why are you taking Miss Durante to headquarters?"

Admiral McKevin and Luther Dunning were standing in the doorway. It was Luther who had asked the question. The two men moved into the room.

"Harry, is it true?" the admiral said. His robust voice was softened now with shock. "Is Arch Steuben dead? Has he been--?"

Luther interrupted him: "Why are you taking Miss Durante in, Harry?"

"Just for questioning, Luther."

"But why Miss Durante? Rather than any of the others?"

Winters hesitated for only a moment. "Miss Durante knew Ross Anders years ago. Anders was killed by someone he tried to blackmail, someone he had probably known a long time, and well enough to have discovered something about them."

"No," Margot said. "Ross didn't know anything about me. I

haven't anything to hide."

Winters went on as though she hadn't spoken: "Miss Durante has no alibi for her time after the parade-- when we know that Arch was killed."

"Just a moment," Luther said. He paused; he seemed to be making a decision. "I can account for Margot's time. She was with me."

"With you?"

"Yes. From right after the parade until--"

Winters turned to Margot: "You might have told me that, Miss Durante."

"Harry," Luther said, "I think it is my place to explain that to you. You may already have heard some talk about Margot and me."

"No, I've heard nothing."

"Well, perhaps there's been no gossip. I was afraid there might have been. We've probably given reason--"

"Luther," the admiral said stiffly, "if you'd rather, I'll wait--"

"No, you might as well hear about it now. In a short while there will be no secret about it. Margot and I have become very good friends these past few weeks, more than good friends. We-- neither of us wants this relationship to end." His face flushed painfully and it was with obvious effort that he continued. "This isn't an easy decision for either of us to reach. For me to ask my wife for my freedom to marry Margot, for Margot to give up her career and face the gossip and prejudice here that are inevitable."

"All right, Luther," Winters said. His voice, like the admiral's, was stiff with embarrassment. "All that matters is that Miss Durante was with you." He turned to Margot, and he was clipped and official again: "What time did you return here, Miss Durante?"

"I don't know exactly. I'd been in my room fifteen or twenty minutes when I heard Miss Steuben scream."

"Fifteen or twenty minutes," Winters repeated slowly. "Doc Kroll figures that Arch was killed sometime within the hour before his body was discovered."

"I see," Margot said. "You still think I might have-- you still don't think I have an alibi."

"Not quite. But we'll skip any more questioning for now. Since Luther has explained--"

"Margot," Luther said, "you shouldn't have done it for me. It wasn't worth involving yourself."

Margot looked at him and her eyes were warm and soft. Dave saw that she had found the answer to her discontent, the end of her restless roving, in Luther Dunning. She said, "I couldn't tell them, Luther. But it was good of you, it was--" She stopped and turned abruptly to Winters: "Then that's all for now?"

"Yes."

She turned and walked quietly out of the room.

Dave picked Ross's script up from his bureau. It was time to get to the football field. There was work that had to be done. In just about an hour the curtain would rise on the pageant. Then, this evening, the Centennial Ball and the crowning of the Queen would finish up Ridgefield's celebration. Usually the Merrill staff would take a night train on the last day of their commitment and be on their way to their next assignment before the ball was over. But here in Ridgefield there was some unfinished business. Two men had been murdered. The police had requested, and not politely, that the Merrill staff stay on a while.

Up in the press box of the high-school stadium the town boys who were handling the switchboard informed Dave that everything was under control, including the public-address system. The boys' changed attitude toward him was baffling until he realized, in an unpleasant flash, that they were considering the possibility that they were speaking to a murderer. He didn't stay there any longer than necessary.

He was halfway down the aisle of the empty stands, looking for Admiral McKevin, when the admiral called his name. He was coming toward Dave, walking along the benches of the sixteenth row.

"I'm a little late," the admiral said, "Sorry."

"I'm sorry that I have to bother you about this, sir. I tried to reach Luther Dunning, but I couldn't locate him."

"Glad to help. Just what was it you wanted?"

"I'd like you to go over the script," Dave said. "To make sure there aren't any lines in it about Arch Steuben that would be offensive, now that Arch is dead. I thought someone who knew him better than I should be the one to do it."

"I see. That the script?"

"Yes."

Dave handed it to him. The admiral sat down, opened the script on the bench before him, started leafing through it. Down on the field Dave saw Alice Knapp and the waiting actor-citizens of old Ridgefield, checking on last-minute details. He found himself looking for a girl who was not Sarah Cummings of Ridgefield, Ohio, whom he had been so pleased to meet that he had begun at once to change the plans for his future. He was looking for a girl whose name was no longer either Sarah Cummings or Joan Mason; it was Mrs. Eddie Merrill Jr.

The admiral spoke, his voice sharp with surprise: "What's this?" He rose, holding the script in his hands, Dave looked over his shoulder. Tucked into the snap binding of the notebook, between two pages of Ross's neat script, was a sheet of paper foreign to its neighbors. It was a piece of white stationery whose folds were still visible. It was a letter dated August 10, 1935.

The admiral slipped the letter from the binding and handed it to Dave. He read it, his eyes racing over the page:

"Dear Mr. Kingsley,

"I shall return at once to Clarion and be at your house as you have asked, tomorrow night at nine. I am fully prepared to make a confession and turn myself over to the police. I pray, though, that you will find it possible to show me mercy. I swear that I will find some way to repay every cent of the money, and you must know that I would die rather than repeat my crime. It was a crime, I know, but I am not a criminal. I beg your understanding, not for myself alone, but for the sake of my wife and Joan."

The letter was signed "Samuel Mason"

The admiral spoke; his tone was ironical: "Interesting, isn't it, Dave?"

Dave didn't answer. The letter had been written almost twenty years ago by Sarah's father, and somehow Ross Anders had got hold of it. This was what Sarah had been trying so desperately to find with Eddie Merrill's help. It was Sarah's father whom Ross had been blackmailing.

The admiral took the letter from Dave's hand. He said, "Winters must see this immediately. This Samuel Mason, whoever he is, murdered Anders and Arch Steuben."

"Wait," Dave said. "Don't go to Winters just yet."

"Dave, do you know something about this? Do you know who this Samuel Mason is?"

"Yes, I know. Don't ask me to tell you, not just now. There's someone involved in this who deserves a chance to explain."

"That person can explain to the police, Dave."

"But not right away. Give me a little while, a few hours."

The admiral looked at Dave for a moment in silence. He folded the letter, put it in his pocket. "All right Dave. After the pageant you and I will take this to Winters. Agreed?"

"Yes, sir."

Dave turned away from the admiral's puzzled eyes. He hurried out of the stadium, through the crowd that was converging upon it to watch the pageant, and headed over toward Sarah's apartment.

When Sarah let him in, Dave saw that somehow the apartment was changed. It took him a moment to realize what it was. The tables and chest-of-drawer tops had been swept clean of everything that was Sarah's. The place had the look of an uninhabited hotel room. Now Dave understood her delay in opening the door for him. He had interrupted her packing; she had made him wait while she got her luggage out of sight.

Sarah looked tired. Her greeting had been subdued, anxious, as if she had sensed that Dave's visit wasn't a social call. When Dave told her of the letter that Admiral McKevin had found, a letter written in 1935, she covered her face with her hands. As he went on to tell her what was in the letter, she turned away from him, her shoulders drooping hopelessly.

Dave said, "That letter was signed by Samuel Mason. He's your father, Sarah, isn't he?" She didn't answer, and he said softly, "Sarah,

I know that you're Joan Mason."

She turned back to him. "You knew--?"

"Eddie Merrill's mother sent me a picture of you and Eddie together. She was worried that you were here pretending to be someone else. And this letter explains that, doesn't it? Your father is Samuel Mason."

"Yes."

"Ross was using this letter to blackmail him."

"Dave, my father made a mistake when he was a very young man. He was in debt, and then I was born and-- he did repay every cent of that money to the company. Nobody except Mr. Kingsley ever knew he had taken it, and he managed to return it without anyone ever knowing. But he did pay it back. You must believe that, Dave."

"I do believe it, Sarah. That's why I don't understand why he let Ross blackmail him. A theft committed so long ago-- and all of it repaid."

"Because there's more to it than that. When my father went to Mr. Kingsley's house that night, he found him dead. He had fallen down a flight of stairs; the doctor said he had died instantly. Mr. Kinglsey was alone in the house when he fell. Do you understand, Dave? This letter that my father wrote, the fact that it was he who found the body and reported the accident-- it would be almost impossible to prove that Kingsley's death wasn't murder."

"I see," Dave said. "That was the hold Ross had over your father-- the possibility of a murder trial."

"Mrs. Kingsley is a bitter woman, strong and relentless. If she thought, even suspected, that her husband's death might have been murder, it would have been horrible, Dave. That's why my father paid Ross. It wasn't long before I realized something was worrying him to death. About two months ago I finally got him to tell me what it was."

"When did Ross get hold of this letter?"

"When the Merrill Company did a pageant in Clarion, two years ago last June. You weren't there, Dave."

"No, I was on another assignment. But how did he get his hands on the letter?"

"He told my father that he found it when he was doing research on Clarion in the Kingsley's library. It was tucked in an old book, one that Mr. Kingsley must have been reading when the letter arrived. No one had ever seen it, of course, except Mr. Kingsley."

"It was there all those years, waiting for Ross?"

"Yes."

"And you came here to try to get the letter back?"

Sarah nodded. "I was in school in New York during Clarion's Centennial. Ross and I had never met. So I could come here using another name and he wouldn't know who I was. I got here a few weeks before all of you. I found a place to live, got a job. Then I volunteered for every kind of work to help with the pageant. I tried to work with Ross, to get close to him. I think now he must have suspected me. Perhaps he even realized who I was. That must be why he had the letter in his script. I never would have thought of looking for it there, even if I could have got my hands on it. You know how he always hung on to his script. He made jokes about its being more valuable than a first quarto Shakespeare."

"With that letter in it, it probably was more valuable," Dave said grimly. "And Eddie-- he knew all about this, of course."

"Yes, everything. Eddie's been wonderful, Dave. After I found Ross's body I searched it for the letter." Her face whitened in horror at the memory. "When I couldn't find it, I took his key. I meant to search his room myself, but I couldn't do it. I took the key to Eddie, and he did it for me. He's helped me all along, through everything."

Dave got up, slowly walked to the window and back. "You know, I've said some nasty things to Eddie Merrill. I've misjudged him about all this."

"He's been wonderful, Dave. He did everything he possibly could for me. He didn't stop once to consider the trouble he might be getting himself into. Why he should have been so unmindful of himself I don't know."

"I know," Dave said. "He's in love with you."

She looked up at him in quick surprise. "Oh, no Dave. He used to be sort of a beau of mine, but that was back East, when we both were in school. I hadn't seen or heard of him since then. I didn't even know he was working for his father. When he popped up here with the rest of you, I had to explain to him why I was in Ridgefield, using another name. I had to trust him, and it turned out I could. He's changed, Dave. He isn't the selfish smart-aleck he used to be. He's been a real friend to me."

"Sarah," Dave said gently, "you're tired. Don't bother going through all this make-believe for me. I know about you and Eddie. I heard you two talking in his room this morning."

"In Eddie's room? But I wasn't--"

"I understand what's changed Eddie, why he was willing to risk himself for you. Sarah, I know that you and Eddie are married."

"Oh," she said quietly. "I see."

"Congratulations. Eddie's a good guy."

"Dave," she said. She put her hand on his arm. "Dave, this isn't my secret. I shouldn't be the one to tell you. But I want you to know. Eddie is married. He's married to Alice Knapp."

"To Alice--"

"They were married a few months ago, just a week after they'd met."

"Well!" Dave said.

"They were afraid to tell anyone. Eddie's father would be certain to consider their elopement another of Eddie's escapades."

"Well!" Dave said again. "Good news has been scarce around

here lately, but this is fine!"

"Then you approve?"

"Eddie and Alice-- yes! I like it much better than you and Eddie. Listen: Don't you ever go around getting married without letting me know. It's all right for Alice, but--"

"Alice and Eddie will be fine for each other, and somehow they'll make Eddie's father see that. They thought if they could only wait out this one year....Dave, what are you thinking about?"

"About a murder," Dave said. "A couple of murders. Sarah, did Ross Anders-- could he have known about Eddie and Alice?"

"I suppose so. Dave, you're not thinking that Eddie--"

Dave said slowly, "I'm thinking what the police might think about it. Suppose Ross had found out about their elopement. Suppose he threatened to tell Eddie's father that Eddie was still his old wild, impetuous self. Ross might have pointed out to Eddie and Alice that he could get Eddie disinherited unless they made it worth his while to keep quiet."

"But you can't believe that it was Eddie who murdered Ross, or that it was Alice--"

"I don't know. I'm wondering what the police might believe."

"They mustn't know. We won't tell them...."

Her voice trailed off, and Dave could see that she was no longer thinking of Eddie and Alice. She was thinking of the letter her father had written and what would happen when the police found out about it.

"Sarah," he said, "McKevin promised me that he wouldn't take the letter to the police for a couple of hours. He'll give us that much time."

Hopelessly, she said, "That much time-- to do what, Dave?"

He shook his head. "I don't know. I hoped you could tell me something that might help. Sarah, your father will be able to prove he didn't murder Ross. He can prove that he was in Clarion when--"

"Dave, will I be able to prove that I didn't murder Ross? Because of what he was doing to my father?"

"Sarah--"

"I wasn't sorry, Dave. When Ross was killed, I wasn't sorry."

"We'll prove it-- somehow."

"Yes, we might. But, Dave, what will the police do about my father now? When they see that letter will they look into the whole thing? Will they discover that Mr. Kingsley died that night?"

"The police mustn't see that letter. Then neither you nor your father--"

"Dave, what can we do in two hours?"

He didn't answer her.

"Could I talk to Admiral McKevin? Could I convince him not to turn the letter over?"

"No, there isn't a chance of that. Arch Steuben was his friend, he-- Sarah, let's not just sit here."

"Dave, when he goes to the police I'm going with him."

"You can't."

"Yes," she said firmly. "I'm going with him."

They had no plan; there was no direction in their wandering about the empty town. Then at last, without speaking of it, they were walking toward the stadium. When they came up the runway and stood in the back of the box on the fifty-yard line, they found that the pageant was half over. On the field a group of bearded men and bonneted women were dedicating the first public library in Ridgefield.

There were three men in the box: The admiral, Luther Dunning, and the town's oldest citizen, Ed Freeley. The chairs that had been reserved for Arch Steuben and his niece were empty.

The admiral nodded gravely toward Dave and Sarah. He motioned Dave to his side. "I've seen Winters," he whispered. "He's here. I told him to wait for us after the show is over. Have you found out anything new?"

Dave shook his head. "Nothing."

The admiral glanced questioningly at Sarah, but he said no more. He turned back to watch the performance. Dave drew Sarah into one of the empty chairs, sat beside her.

Luther Dunning said, "It's going great, Dave, great. You're a success."

"Thanks," Dave said.

"Dave," Sarah said quietly. "He hasn't changed his mind about it?"

"No. We're seeing Winters after this is over."

Her hand reached out to him in a quick, frightened gesture and he took it in his, held it tight. They sat, blindly watching Ridgefield's history smoothly repeat itself...the laying of the cornerstone of the Town Hall, the opening of the railroad's spur line, the first high-school football game. Now the Kiley boys were thundering up to the Drake Stockyards and in a minute Luther Dunning lay wounded, his cousin Tom Drake shot to death. Now the sheriff was pursuing the bandits, shooting it out with them.

"Dave," Sarah said desperately, "if we both talked to the admiral we might make him see that--"

"We couldn't. His mind's made up."

Ed Freeley's querulous, impatient voice crackled through the gunfire. He turned resentfully toward Dave. "Didn't happen that way," he said. "I know! That's me driving that Hupmobile! I was there! Them Kiley boys didn't ambush Arch. Didn't he tell you that?"

"Yes," Dave said. "Yes, he told us, but we weren't able to--"

"Arch picked everyone of them boys right off their horses. I'll bet he would not have liked to see it done this way, he--"

The admiral put his arm around Ed Freeley's shoulder. "They had to do it this way, Ed. I'll explain it to you later. You watch the show now." Gently he turned the old man back to the field. "You'll like this part, Ed."

The church bells chimed five in the distance, and the actors portraying Ed Freeley and the sheriff stood with their heads uncovered, listening to them. The curtain of steam rose, and now on the field behind it they were setting the stage for the next scene. In twenty minutes the pageant would be over.

Sarah's hand was on his arm again. "Dave," she said, "Dave--"

"Wait," he said shortly. "Wait, Sarah."

"Dave, what is it?"

He rose quickly and stepped down a step to crouch in the aisle beside Ed Freeley's chair. "Ed," he said softly, "Ed, are you sure you remember? It's been over forty years."

Ed Freeley turned to him sharply: "Remember what? About the Kiley boys? 'Course I remember. They never ambushed Arch Steuben. I tell you the sheriff picked them off one by one."

"What about the church clock, Ed? That's wrong, too, isn't it? It didn't happen that way, it couldn't have."

"It sure did! That clock was strikin' five just as Arch shot the last of them bandits. Who says it didn't?"

"Admiral McKevin says so." The admiral turned at the sound of his name.

"Isn't that right, sir? The robbery couldn't have taken place until five o'clock. Because you were with Tom Drake at the water tower when the clock struck five."

The admiral looked him with unconcealed impatience. "What difference can it possibly make?" he asked. "That scene is over and done with. I see no reason--"

"That's what you said, isn't it, sir?" Dave's lips felt tight; it was an effort to make the words he spoke clear and distinct.

The admiral shrugged his annoyance. "Yes, that's right." He turned placatingly to Ed Freeley: "You see, Ed, you and Arch are both wrong. You've both forgotten."

"I haven't forgotten nothin' and neither did Arch Steuben!" Ed Freeley was sputtering in his insulted rage, and people in nearby boxes turned to smile at him in amusement.

"Dave, what's the point of this?" Luther Dunning's voice was half irritated, half curious. "As the admiral says, that part of the show's over and done with. What can it matter?" He patted Ed Freeley gently on his back, and he was smiling. "It's all right, Ed. Forget it."

"I won't have nobody callin' me a liar!" Ed was still loudly unappeased. "That there clock struck five times. I remember turning to Arch and sayin', 'Just five o'clock in the mornin', Sheriff, and you already done yourself a pretty good day's work.' That's just what I says to him."

"But Admiral McKevin says--" Dave started.

"I don't give a hang what Dan McKevin says. You can go to the library if you want to and look it up in the newspapers! It's all there in black and white. They got a big account of it."

The rustling sounds in the boxes around them, the chuckles and snickers, grew louder. Luther Dunning leaned forward again, his face concerned. "Dave, people are watching us instead of the show. It's absurd, haggling like this. Neither Dan nor Ed will ever admit it, but one of them's got to be wrong, and it's useless--"

"That's what I thought, Luther. But not now." Dave lowered his voice so that only those in the box could hear: "Now I think that both of them are right. Tom Drake was at the water tower at five o'clock. And the Kiley boys were killed at five o'clock. That's what really happened."

The admiral said, "This is nonsense. Tom Drake was killed by the Kiley boys."

"No," Dave said. "How could they have killed him? Tom Drake didn't get back to the stockyard office until after the Kiley boys had left, until after they were dead." He turned to Luther Dunning: "But you were at the office, Luther. You were the only one there when Tom Drake got back. You'd been wounded by the bandits, but only by a bullet in one shoulder. You could still fire a gun. You were reaching for the one in the drawer, you said, when the Kiley Boys shot you. And after they'd gone, Tom Drake came back. You knew if you killed him then his death would be blamed on the Kileys, you knew you'd be safe."

Luther Dunning laughed softly. "Dave, it's ingenious of you, trying to plant a forty-year-old killing on me. But it doesn't work. Why should I have killed Tom Drake? We were friends, he was my cousin. Anyone can tell you--"

"The stockyards," Ed Freeley said. They hadn't known that he'd been following, or even listening to them until he spoke. "Tom's father owned them stockyards. And Luther inherited them, the whole works. Maybe he thought that was reason enough for murder."

"That's what Ross Anders found out about you, isn't it?" Dave said. He turned to the admiral: "That was Ross's racket, you know about that. Finding things in his research of a town that he could use for blackmail. He's done it before, when he did a pageant in Clarion. And so he tried it this time on Luther. But Luther wouldn't take it; he killed Ross."

Luther rose, his mouth opened in shocked protest. But Dave was on his feet, facing Dunning, beating him down with his words:

"And Arch Steuben. Arch figures out the truth. He knew that he was right about those church bells, he must have realized that the admiral was right, too. And he tried to bring Luther in-- and Luther killed him."

"Wait a minute, Dave." Luther Dunning's voice was rising. "Haven't you forgotten something? That I couldn't have killed Arch, that I--"

"That you were with Margot? But you weren't. When you found she was in trouble with Winters because she didn't have an alibi, you lied and gave her one. You said the two of you were together. You gambled that she'd think you were protecting her with your life, and you won. She was grateful, so she played along with you. But when she learns that it was yourself you were protecting, that you were using her to give yourself an alibi, what will she do then? She's down there on the field. Shall I get her, Luther?"

"No." Luther's voice was expressionless. "No, don't bother."

"Luther," the admiral said.

"It's true, Dan," he said. "I killed them." He turned slowly and started to walk out of the box. The admiral spoke his name again and he turned back. "You come with me, Dan," he said. "We'll go to Winters."

"Yes."

Dave followed the admiral onto the runway. "Admiral Mc-Kevin."

"What is it, Dave? Oh, yes." He reached in his pocket, handed Dave a folded sheet of paper.

Dave watched the men until they were out of sight. When he turned he was looking into Sarah's eyes. Without speaking, he handed her the letter.

"Dave," she said.

"No, let's not talk until we are on the train, and I've got my arm around you."

"All right, Dave. That will be better. I'll even like that."

A cautious killer was deliberately sabotaging the Top Secret project. Which of the seven suspects had struck twice and was waiting to strike again?

the JET PLANE MURDERS

by Richard Storrs

COMPLETE AMERICAN MYSTERY NOVEL

Only the flapping of the plane's ailerons broke the dead silence of the hangar. The body beneath it was still

121

Born in Fresno, California, in 1915 and a Harvard graduate, Richard Martin Stern is an Edgar-award winner, a past president of Mystery Writers of America, and the author of numerous successful novels both in and out of the crime/mystery genre. He is perhaps best known for The Tower (1973), one of the two novels on which the film The Towering Inferno was based. In the fifties, he was one of the most prominent writers of slick magazine novelettes, four of which were gathered in Suspense (Ballantine, 1959), but the tale that follows, originally published as by Richard Stern in September 1954, is his one contribution to the American mystery novel series. Its unique background is based at least partly on first-hand experience, Stern having worked as an engineer for Lockheed Aircraft between 1940 and 1945.

THE JET PLANE MURDERS by Richard Martin Stern

It was five years since Matt Holmes had seen Holmes Aircraft, an enormous and sprawling factory. He could remember when there had been only the one small shed and the grass field, and, of course, the old man, his father, Bert Holmes, big and loud and dominant, filled with a dream that had become reality. Now that he was dead, everything seemed changed.

In the lobby of the Administration Building there was a tall girl, cool-seeming, who led him up the stairs and down the well-remembered hallway to the big office. "I'm Myra King. I was your father's secretary." She smiled then for the first time. "Welcome home."

There were memories in this office, too many memories. Here he had sat-- how many times?-- summoned and waiting, dancing attendance like a puppet on the old man's string. "Was it you who cabled me?" Matt said.

She nodded and smiled. "A cable to Cairo, one to Madrid, one to Morroco-- nobody really knew where you were, flying whose airplanes, building whose pipe lines."

"I was building an airfield. Not that it matters. Now I'm here." And he watched her, waiting for what he had come to find out. "What happened to my father?" he finally said.

"An accident in the plant," she said flatly. "A wing fell on him. A hoist let go, and he was under it."

"Go on."

"That's all there is. Fifteen hundred men work in final assembly, and only one wing has ever dropped off, and he was under it when it fell."

"Thanks," Matt said.

"Quite a few people have been waiting to see you," she said. "Colonel Armitage, the Air Force representative--" She stopped there, and cocked her head to the footsteps in the hallway. "The colonel wants to know who's running this railroad."

The colonel was short and sturdy, with a command pilot's wings over three rows of ribbons. "Good to have you here." The corners of his eyes crinkled as he smiled. "You're taking over?" the colonel asked.

"I doubt it," Matt said. And he saw the change in the colonel's face.

"Why not? You're the son, aren't you? Own part of the factory, don't you? Then what's all this nonsense?" The colonel paused. "If you aren't, who is? Palmer? Haller? Conklin? Brown? Who's the boss?"

"I don't know that, either."

"Then you'd better find out," the colonel said brusquely. "Quick. While there's still a factory." He wheeled and walked briskly out.

"We have all kinds of characters," Myra said. There were more footsteps in the hall. "They come and go."

This man was big, as large as Matt. He wore flannels and a leather jacket, and his hair was red.

Myra said, "Barney White, Mr. Holmes."

"Well, well," Barney White said. "The crown prince." His eyes were blue, bright. "I've heard a lot about you."

"Have you?"

"The word is that you were coming, but that you wouldn't stick around long. Too much like work." He dropped a sheaf of papers on Myra's desk and then turned to her: "Progress report, as ordered, even though you haven't got a boss any more." And to Matt: "Nice to have had a look at you, at last." He walked out, big and cocky.

Myra sighed. "Like I said-- characters."

Matt said, "There used to be a man here named Hazeltine, John Hazeltine."

"There still is. Everybody knows Johnny Hazeltine. You want him? I'll get him on the telephone for you."

"I'll see him out in the shop," Matt said, "wherever he is."

He came out of the Administration Building and into the main alleyway, familiar, unchanged. He opened the door of the sheet metal department, and the remembered sounds and smells flowed around him with almost physical force-- the shriek of shaper and saw, the solemn clank of punch press, the whine of the giant hydro

bearing down with enormous force; the muttered distant thud of the
drop hammers; and above it all the warm smell of metal and oil.

And Johnny was there, in his horn-rimmed glasses and his crew
cut, unchanged in five years. His smile spread slowly. "Well, well.
The wandering boy's come home."

"More or less." Beyond Johnny a great drop-hammer die for
stamping out metal sections of a plane fuselage moved toward the
melting pot, began to disappear.

"Still at it," Matt said. "Destroying perfectly good tooling."

"I'm a hard man to please." Johnny took a shop order from his
pocket, initialed it, and handed it to one of the foundry men. Matt
glanced at it idly. Across its face in red letters had been stamped:
EXPERIMENTAL, RUSH.

"Coffee?" Johnny said.

They sat on a wooden bench in the canteen area, the paper cups
between them. "It was the old man that brought you back," Johnny
said. "Sorry about that. It was-- one of those things. He got--
careless."

"Did he?" Matt said. "The old man? After forty years of
building planes, he just got careless. Is that how it was, Johnny?"
They were old friends, long ago school friends. To Johnny he could
talk, ask.

"I wasn't there. I-- heard it; not a sound, a silence. The riveting
stopped as if the shift had ended. My boss was there, just walking
through final assembly, Barney White--"

"He's your boss? Big fellow? Red hair? Cocky?"

Johnny's smile was quick, wry. "That's the one. The executive
type, not like me; he's the ambitious type. And now--" He stopped
there.

"Go on," Matt said.

Johnny set his cup down slowly. "It isn't anything."

"I want to hear it," Matt said.

Johnny said slowly, "Barney and the old man had some arguments, Matt. Barney's in charge of the Experimental Lab. We're
doing a job for the Air Force. The old man didn't think the job was
moving, that's all." He looked up again, smiling.

"The old man was going to fire him?"

"Maybe. Look, Matt; the old man had arguments with lots of
people. At one time or another, he chewed out half the factory. He
used to pick on you; that's why you never stuck around."

Matt said, "This job you're doing for the Air Force-- is it going
the way it should go?"

"I'm just hired help," Johnny said. "And that's just the way I like
it-- no responsibility." The grin faded slowly. "But, since you ask,
the answer is no. We're behind schedule."

"And who is running the factory? Palmer? Haller? Conklin?
Brown?"

"My guess is nobody. The joint's staggering along by itself."

Johnny stood up. "Well, back to work, boy."

Matt sat alone for a time, astride the wooden bench, while the coffee went cold in his cup. The old man had walked under a hoist, and a wing had dropped on him. Barney White was due to be fired; now he was not. The colonel wanted to know who was running the factory, and the answer was that nobody ran it, nobody had seated himself in the old man's chair. And the new Air Force project in Experimental, Barney White's project, wasn't going as it should. These were cold hard facts. He stood up at last and headed for Plant Protection, the security department.

Simmons was in, small and neat, studiously polite, ex-FBI. He shook Matt's hand. "I heard you were back."

Matt said, "After forty years, the old man just got careless. Is that it?"

"Could be." Simmons folded his hands on his desk, looked at him. "The wings are carried over the safety lane. The operator controls the hoist with a switch box in his hands. He was new-- maybe he pushed the wrong button. He denied it, of course." Simmons looked up then. "There was an inquest-- accidental death."

"And where is the hoist operator now?"

"Why?"

"I think I'd like to talk to him."

"You can do it better than the police? Than I can?"

Matt had, really, expected no other action. He said, "Is it just-- forgotten? The old man and I didn't get along, that's true, but--"

"But you're still the son," Simmons said. He studied his hands again. "The operator's name is Traub, Harold Traub. He likes to play the horses. He's dropped pretty close to a thousand dollars at the track in the last ten days. When he came to work here he was broke." He looked up. "I'm telling you this to show that we're still working on it. It's in competent hands."

"In other words," Matt said, "it's none of my business."

"You said it. I didn't." Simmons shrugged. "Just passing through? As I remember it, you never liked it here."

Matt was silent. He had one more fact, now. "So he was murdered?" he finally said. He pulled the telephone across the desk and dialed his office.

"Myra," Matt said, "this is Matt Holmes. I want to see Ben Palmer, Paul Haller, Jim Conklin, and Mark Brown in my office. You have that?"

She sounded amused: "Which one first?"

"All together. In my office. Now."

"I'll round them up," she said. "By the way, there's a Miss Sue Kinkaid here to see you-- old family friend, she says."

"I'll be right over," he snapped. "Call the others." He hung up and looked at Simmons: "We'll talk later." He saw the slight change, the beginning of respect in Simmons' face.

Myra was on the telephone when he came in. He could see Sue on the sofa in the inner office, and he went to her, closing the door behind him. "Surprise," he said. He found himself reaching for her hand with awkward, stiff formality.

"Is it?" Sue said. She was smiling. "I thought that if I waited for you to call me, I might be old and gray and haggard."

"You know better." He sat down, for the first time behind the big desk that had been the old man's. "I had to come here--"

"Business first." Her smile seemed to spread. "But I'm part of it, too, Matt. You hadn't heard? Your father left me some of his stock, not as big a part as yours, but big enough." Her expression took him back a long, long time, teasing him. "He hoped, I think, that he was keeping it in the family-- your family."

"I see."

Suddenly she was serious. "He didn't even know you, Matt. I do. He thought that when he was gone, you'd be anxious to come back here, and stay. I know better."

He was silent.

She said then, "Will you sell your stock, Matt?"

"Why?"

"I want to help-- someone."

"Who?"

"You don't know him, Matt. He works here. He started out with nothing, the way your father did, and some day he'll go as far. I want to help. His name is White, Barney White." She paused. "Will you sell, Matt?"

He shook his head slowly. The intercommunication box buzzed, and he leaned forward to flip the switch. Myra's voice said, "Everybody's here-- Boss."

"Send them in," Matt said as he closed the switch. To Sue, "This concerns you, too."

The door opened and four men filed in. Myra followed with her notebook.

These four were the factory, each a king in his own domain. Matt sat there studying them, choosing his words.

"In a sense," Matt said, "I've been pushed into this. The old man built this place. He started with a little shed out where the final assembly line is now." He glanced at Jim Conklin, head of the Sales Department, who was the oldest. "You remember that. So do I. I wasn't even as high as this desk. You wore breeches and riding boots and a leather helmet and goggles." A hero to a small boy.

"They wear baseball caps now, and dark glasses," Conklin said.

"Later on, you taught me to fly-- in between tearing down engines and putting fabric patches on torn wings."

Then he looked at Paul Haller, the engineer now. "It was already a factory when you brought your ideas here, Paul, and sold the old man on them. And I listened and watched and saw what came of them, and then went off to college to get an engineering degree because you and the old man thought it was best, and so did I."

"I remember," Haller said. "Get on with it."

Matt looked at Ben Palmer, big, solid, the production man. "You put us in the big time, Ben-- you and the war, together. You were trained to think in thousands of parts, all alike, interchangeable; we thought in terms of making parts up as we needed them, because that was the way airplanes had always been built. You gave us mass production."

"We?" Haller said. "Us?" There was no question in what he meant.

"Yes," Matt said. "I was here, on vacation from college, when Ben arrived. I was here when all of you came"-- he turned to look at the fourth man, Mark Brown-- "except you. I wasn't here when the old man brought you over from Thorndike."

"Leave me out of this," Brown said. "I'm the new one."

"Well," Matt said, "there's the background, most of it. There was always the old man. Now there isn't. When I was a kid I resented him. He kept me around him like a dog on a leash, but he'd let me off the leash sometimes, but never very far. I was a monkey on his string. Even during those vacations from school and college, I didn't have a job. I trailed him, and ran errands for him, and sat and listened while he settled your fights. I didn't like it. I hated it."

Myra King's head came up, and her eyes went to Matt's and held there briefly. Then she bent over her notebook again.

"After the war," Matt said, "I came back. I stayed almost three years. I wanted a piece of work of my own, but all I got was a little piece of his, and I didn't think it was enough. But he said it was, and he was the boss." He put his hands flat on the table. "Now I see why. He didn't want me to be a design engineer." He looked at Haller. "They think in terms of design, and only that." Everything he said had been leading to this. He waited.

Jim Conklin said, "Amen." Ben Palmer's big head nodded gravely.

"He didn't want me to be a production man, either," Matt said. "Or a materiel man, or--" he looked again at Conklin-- "or your understudy in Sales."

"He had ulcers," Conklin said. "I don't. I sleep nights, too." His old eyes were bright and a grin softened his hard face.

"This morning," Matt said, "I was asked who was running this factory. It's a good question." He went from face to face this time. "Who is?" And in the silence he pushed back his chair and stood up. "I'm going outside. Think it over and talk it over. I've had my say."

Haller's voice sounded angrily as Matt closed the door.

He stood at the window of the outer office thinking of the old man, heavy-handed, pounding his lessons home. Matt had learned, whether he had wanted to learn or not, and in the end the entire process had become as familiar as the back of his own hand.

But it was more than that which held him here. What he had said to Simmons was true: He and the old man had never gotten along together. On the other hand, he was the son, and so the facts, the little bits and pieces he had accumulated during the morning, especially the ones which implied murder, could not be ignored. He had no name for the force or quality which made this so, but it existed, nonetheless. So he was here, and so he would stay.

Behind him the door of the inner office opened and Jim Conklin walked out, his old eyes bright. "Quite a show, bub. You've got yourself a job. You had it from the moment you put your finger on the sore spot. This place can't operate without a referee." He paused. "We all know it. Paul Haller's the one who doesn't want to admit it."

Behind him Haller said, "That's not accurate. I recognize the need. But I don't think he's big enough to handle it."

"You're outnumbered, Paul," Conklin said.

"I realize that, too."

Then Sue came out of the office. She seemed to look through Matt as she went by. She didn't speak.

There was only Myra King left, with her notebook and pencils. She was smiling. "When you get started," she said, "you really go to town, don't you? Who's next-- the colonel?"

"You guessed it," Matt said, smiling.

"One colonel," Myra said, "coming up"

The colonel sat in the visitor's chair. "I apologize for this morning. My job is to get along with this factory." He lighted a cigar, short, thin, black. "How much do you know?"

"Nothing. Let's start on that assumption," Matt said.

"All right." The cigar punctuated his talk. "Half the factory builds commercial transports. I don't care about those. The other half builds fighters for us. The contract calls for a new model-- new armament, new gunsight, a whole new nose. Your Experimental Department's building the first of the new ones-- what you call the 'prototype.' It's supposed to be done in time to let us test it and let you get ready to go into production on it-- all of this before you finish the last of the current models." The colonel paused. "It isn't going to be ready in time."

Matt had guessed as much already. "Will you let us build more of the old model, until we are ready for production on the new?"

"No," the colonel snapped. "You've heard of budgets, economy, Congress? In a way, it's none of my business until the prototype fails to be delivered at the deadline. On the other hand there's a file in the Pentagon with my name on it. So far, I've got a pretty clean record."

Matt nodded. "You wouldn't like us to fail to deliver."

"Exactly." The colonel stood up. "It would go on the record that I was here when it happened; and before that time I'll cover myself with a report recommending cancellation of the whole contract. We don't want a stink in Congress, somebody asking why the Air Force goes along with a factory that can't produce. You'd better find out what's going on, and you'd better find out quick."

He sat for a little time after the colonel had gone. He had more facts now, and they all seemed to point in one direction.

He called Myra. "Now Barney White," he said. "And some lunch for you. Call him and then beat it."

He thought of Sue, who wanted to help this man. He was still thinking of Sue when Barney arrived.

"Colonel Armitage doesn't like the way the new model is going," Matt said.

"His privilege," Barney said. "He listens to his inspectors, and you know what Air Force inspectors are like. Or, do you?"

"I do." Matt paused. "You were born with red hair, but there's nothing that says you have to spend your life living up to it." There was silence. "You're behind schedule. Why? Parts? Tooling? Manpower?" He hesitated. "Or is it something else?"

"Like what?"

"I don't know. Maybe I'm seeing things. Was the old man?"

Barney shrugged his shoulders. "What do you want me to say? That he rode me-- yes. But I didn't drop a wing on him. This morning I called you the crown prince-- now you're the boss. You can make it tough on me, fire me, and no kickbacks. Is that what you're after?"

"Sue and I grew up together--" Matt began.

"I don't hide behind Sue. Let's get that straight."

"All right," Matt said, forcing himself to relax. "Begin at the beginning."

As Matt listened, Barney's tenseness disappeared and he warmed up to a subject he knew well. In other circumstances, Matt thought, they might have liked each other, respected each other. Now there was Sue, subtle and not mentioned, but still between them.

"We had troubles," Barney said. "Every new model does-- engineering troubles, shop troubles, parts spoiled, parts lost. I took chances; sometimes they worked, sometimes they didn't."

"And when they didn't, the old man jumped you. I've been there."

"But you could walk out on it," Barney said. "So we had a blowoff. It was no secret-- those things never are. Two days later a wing fell on him." He waited, but Matt said nothing. "I'm three weeks behind," Barney said. "The progress report doesn't show that, but I know the job better than the people who scheduled it."

"Can you catch up?"

"I don't know."

Matt said, "Johnny Hazeltine's your assistant, isn't he?"

"Yes," Barney said. "Old friend of yours, isn't he? I thought of putting him on nights to jack up the swing shift. Or do you have other plans? Like maybe giving him my job?"

"Are you tired of it?"

The tenseness had returned. "Meaning what?"

"The old man was going to fire you." This was why Matt was here, in this chair, to make decisions. "I'm not. I'll ask Ben Palmer to transfer you to one of the production lines, fighters or transports, if you want."

Barney said slowly, "And if I don't want?" His eyes had altered.

Matt said, "I may be wrong and the old man may have been right, but I'll leave it to you."

The flat muscles worked in Barney's cheeks. "I don't beg."

"No," Matt said. "You didn't beg. I made the decision." He paused thoughtfully. "Put Johnny on nights, if you want, if you think it'll help."

After Barney had left, Matt sat for a time staring at the wall and trying to examine his motives, and finding them obscure. The phone rang, and he picked it up.

Myra said, "Miss Kinkaid phoned and wants you to stop by her place after work. And Mark Brown would like to see you."

"All right," Matt said. "And send Brown in."

The door opened and Mark Brown walked in.

He was not as big a man as Ben Palmer nor as Barney White, and yet there was a force in him and assurance, the impression of power under strict control. He was smiling, but his eyes were steady with appraisal, reserved. "I didn't offer my congratulations this morning. As the new man I didn't want to push. I offer them now; you did the job neatly." He sat down and leaned back in the chair.

"I didn't particularly want to do it," Matt said.

"I know. It was evident; and all that I had heard about you tended to indicate that you had never liked the factory, never wanted to stay." Again he smiled. "And now, because it had to be done, you're here. You face reality; few men do. I admire that."

After the colonel, after Barney White, this was satisfying. "Thanks."

"Paul Haller," Brown said, "is skeptical of your ability. You know that. Ben Palmer is hopeful; Ben recognizes his own limitations. Jim Conklin, who is the most capable of the three, is also the oldest, and is beyond the age of wanting additional responsibility; Jim will support you; Jim is willing to be shown that you can do the job."

Matt was interested now, no longer relaxed. "That leaves you," he said.

"Yes. I will help, any way that I can." And the smile came and went once more. "Your father brought me here from the Thorndike company and put me in charge of materiel, essentially a purchasing and storekeeping job. At Thorndike I was what your father was here, what you are now-- general manager. I am not unacquainted with engineering; I have been a mechanic and a production man; I know selling and marketing." He paused. "I tell you this so you'll realize that I appreciate the problems you're going to encounter, or perhaps already have. You've talked with Colonel Armitage? Good." For the first time the eyes lost their quality of appraisal; they were approving now. "Then you know the gravity of the situation."

"More or less," Matt said. "I'll talk to Ben Palmer tomorrow."

"That, certainly, is the next step. In the meantime, if you approve, I'll take one of my best men and assign him directly to the experimental project with orders to do whatever needs to be done to eliminate any shortages of purchased parts, purchased equipment, sub-contracted items, anything that falls within my jurisdiction."

"I not only approve," Matt said. "I applaud."

Brown smiled. "And if at any time I can help you--" He was standing now. "This is a big compnay. It can be enormously successful-- it has been. The loss of your father was serious, but now you're here."

He felt alone when Brown had gone, and he sat quietly for a time, thinking that loneliness was something which any man in this job had to learn to accept-- as the old man had done. At last, he got up and walked out, pausing at Myra's desk. "I'm going to prowl in the shop."

It was solid darkness when he returned to the office, tired, and yet refreshed. Myra was still at her desk.

He said, "There was no need to wait."

"A matter of viewpoint," she said. "Your father put me on salary. I cost the company the same whether I'm here or in my bathtub." She glanced at her note pad. "Nothing important, nothing that won't keep."

He got his hat from the tree. "You have a car?"

"They run busses for people like me," she joked.

Matt smiled then. "I'll give you a ride."

Her eyebrows rose. "Nothing in the conditions of employment says that the boss--" She stopped, and her eyebrows lowered. "Thanks." She stood up, all in one graceful movement. "I keep asking myself why I have to be flip sometimes. I haven't found the answer."

In the big car, with only the dim light of the instruments, she finally relaxed. "You're about his size," she said, "but you don't roar quite so loud."

"The old man?" He smiled. "My bellow is off key. It embarrasses me." He reached for the radio switch; the humming began and then the music.

"Johnny Hazeltine thinks you're a sort of oversized superman."

"We were kids together at school-- we worked in the shop together."

Myra said, "We turn here, past the Corners. Johnny's probably in there now, baring his soul to the bartender."

"Gus--" Matt mused. "He's tended bar there since I was a kid. It was a speak-easy in those days. The fliers hung out there. Jim Conklin and most of the others."

She said, "I don't want just pieces. I want the whole story, right from the cradle."

Something in her voice made him turn to study her. "You collect biographies?"

"Only sometimes." And there was silence to her apartment house.

"I make a wicked shish kebab and a divine salad," Myra said suddenly. "Care to try it?"

Matt said, "Maybe another time, if the offer holds."

"Just remember that I asked." And she had the door partially open, when the music stopped and an announcer's voice began:

"We bring you now our Valley news program....A man was killed by a hit-and-run driver less than half an hour ago in the parking lot of the Corners Cafe on Valley Boulevard. He has been identified as Harold Traub, a recent employee of the Holmes Aircraft Company. Police are searching for the hit-and-run car, though no description was available. There were no eyewitnesses to the accident....And, coincidentally, Matthew Holmes came home today to take over the duties of his father, Bert Holmes, one of the valley's leading industrial pioneers, who was killed recently in an accident at his factory."

Matt switched off the radio and sat motionless. Myra hadn't moved from her seat.

She said, "Isn't that the one? Traub, I mean?"

"Yes," he muttered. "The hoist operator, the horse player." He was thinking of Simmons, and of the competent authorities who had been watching Traub.

"Another accident-- or, was it?" she said softly.

"Good night," Matt said. "Forget it."

She hesitated. "You take care of yourself, you hear? I lost one boss and two would be too many. You stay out from under wings, and away from dark parking lots." Her voice altered suddenly: "Please."

"Good night," Matt said.

He drove slowly, thoughtfully, back out to Valley Boulevard, along it, and then up the hill to Sue's house.

Sue was waiting in the big living room. "A little late," she said. "But then, you're a busy man."

"I am."

"A tycoon, yet," she bantered.

He sat and stretched his legs, watching her face, thinking that this was the way it should be. "The girl next door," he said, "the daughter the old man never had." He smiled. "Speak up. What's on your little mind?"

"I'm that transparent? Maybe I am," she said thoughtfully. "I was wrong about you, Matt. I didn't think you'd stay, ever. You're changed. I can't see inside of you any more. I could once."

"Maybe that's good."

"What changed you?"

He stood up abruptly, the relaxation all gone. Through the large window he could see the valley, the squares and lines of lights that were houses, stores, the irregular mass of lights that was the factory. Faintly he could hear a transport engine revving up, the deep, settling thunder. First the old man: now Traub-- he wondered who might be next.

Sue broke in suddenly: "Has Barney anything to do with-- whatever the trouble is , Matt?"

"Barney White? I don't really know."

"Am I wrong about him, Matt? Have I been fooling myself because I was-- lonely?"

"I don't know," Matt said.

"Bert was going to fire him." She hesitated. "I-- even talked to Bert, hoping he would change his mind. And then--"

"A wing fell on him," Matt said. There was silence. "The old man was going to fire him. I'm not. I told him this afternoon, gave him his choice. I don't know if it was right, or not."

She had risen from her chair, and she was smiling again, with her lips and with her eyes, as she came toward him at the window. "You'll have to bend down," she said. And he did: her lips were soft, warm. She stepped back, smiling still. "You're quite a person, Matt. I've never said that before, have I? I've never really thought it before, not in the same way." And the smile began to glow. "You'd better wipe the lipstick off."

"Maybe I like it," Matt said. He was smiling as he left.

He ate alone in the big empty house-- his, now, with only Anne, the old man's housekeeper, to fuss over him. And he went to bed early and lay in the darkness thinking of Barney White and Sue, of Johnny Hazeltine and the colonel and Mark Brown, of Traub, whom he had never seen, and now would never see, and of Myra King, who had told him to be careful. He could make no order, no pattern, of the facts, the personalities, none at all. He knew only that two men had died, violently; and the last thing in his mind as he went to sleep was the conviction that this was not the end.

He went first to the plant protection office the next morning. To Simmons he said, "You're the professionals, you and the police. Now Traub is dead."

"We made a mistake, a bad one," Simmons said frankly.

"You did." He let it go, then. Recriminations would not bring Traub back, just as wishing would not alter facts. He said, instead, "Have you thought why the old man might have been killed?" Matt said. "That was the beginning." He was the boss now, and Simmons listened patiently. Matt took the advantage: "He was lonely. No real friends, and that means no real enemies; nobody close enough to him to be either one." He paused "Profit, then? Only one man benefited, as far as I know."

"Who?" Simmons' face was attentive now.

Matt had made his judgment on Barney White; for the time being, he would abide by that. "Maybe later," he said. "The old man was in a funny position here; you may not have seen that. He held this factory together. No man is indispensable," Matt said grimly. "But some jobs are, and the old man's was one of them. It has to be filled or the whole machine runs down-- not all at once, of course, because it will go for a while on momentum alone. But sooner or later it stops. And then no more planes come out of the door."

He stood up. "You don't have Traub to follow to the race track any more, you and the police. You might start thinking who could want the factory to run down. And why."

He went next to Ben Palmer's office. "I've talked to Colonel Armitage and to Barney White. It seems we're in trouble."

Palmer said, "The Experimental Department was Bert's basement workshop. He played around in there with things like this project, things he wanted done fast. He treated us, my production shops, the way a man with the basement workbench treats a machine shop down the street-- having it make the things he hasn't the equipment to make himself, only that. And when he was finished with something, this new fighter model, for example, he'd come to me and say, 'Here it is, and this is how we made it. Now go ahead and make five hundred of them.'"

"And engineering?" Matt said. "Who did the design work?"

"Paul Haller's boys. There are four of them working down there right now."

Matt was silent a moment. "Suppose we're not ready for production with the next model and the Air Force cancels the contract, what do we have to fill in with?"

"We don't," Palmer said. "Two or three months ago we might have made other plans. Now--" He shook his head. "Did Armitage threaten cancellation?"

"It was mentioned," Matt said; and he saw, then, the first beginnings of fear in Palmer's face, where he had never seen fear before.

With Haller, the engineer, the artist, he trod softly: "We're in trouble, Paul, on the fighter modification. The only engineering changes we can afford are those that have to be made for safety or function. Refinements can come later, maybe, after we're in production."

"Those have been standing orders," Haller said, his eyes behind the rimless glasses as hot-seeming as ever.

"Then you're 'way ahead of me," Matt said. "I'll pass the word along to Barney White, on the project."

And Barney would bring straight to Matt any engineering changes he considered superfluous; but it was unnecessary to say this aloud. Haller didn't like it, but he understood, and he sat quietly as Matt walked away.

Back in his office, Myra followed him inside. "All dusted and polished." She sighed. "What a housewife was lost in me-- so far."

Matt was smiling as he sat down at his desk. "You and the old man must have been quite a pair."

"We got along. He was quite a guy."

"Most people seemed to think so," Matt said.

"But you didn't." She had her notebook in her hand; she poked at it idly with the point of her pencil. "Did you ever wonder why, Boss? Why you and he didn't get along, I mean?"

"There were lots of reasons," Matt said feebly.

"No. There was only one. When he looked at you, it was like looking in the mirror. And there wasn't room for two like himself." She arched an eyebrow suddenly. "That's my good word for today." She looked down at the notebook. "A dozen people want to see you. I've weeded them out-- those, anyway, that just wanted to present red apples."

"Something else first," Matt said. He dictated a memo, then, to Ben Palmer, with copies to Paul Haller and Mark Brown, Colonel Armitage and Barney White, giving highest priority and unlimited overtime as required to all shop and tool orders of the fighter modification.

"Now," he smiled, "you can schedule whatever you think best." He had done all that he could do to help the fighter project, and he doubted that it was enough, but he could only wait and see.

Later that morning Myra appeared in the doorway as a visitor left. "Johnny Hazeltine called. He's at home, and he wanted to talk to you."

"About what?"

"He didn't say. Do you want me to guess?"

"No," Matt said. "Call him."

Johnny was quick: "Barney the White has stuck me on the night shift. He has an idea I can stir the crew up a little for him. But you know me; I'm the lazy type. And I don't like nights."

Matt said, "I won't interfere, Johnny. Did you really think I would?"

"Frankly," Johnny said, "no, I didn't. But a man can hope, can't he? It's going to play havoc with my social life."

He had never been able to get angry with Johnny. "I feel for you."

"Thanks. And nuts to you, too, you captain of industry," Johnny said as he hung up.

For the rest of the day Matt sat, and listened, made his notes and asked his questions, made decisions. When he left the factory that night he carried an attache case that had been the old man's, filled with papers and reports, and he sat late after dinner studying them, digesting them. And in bed, just before sleep came, he thought of what Myra had said about him and the old man-- mirror images. He had never seen it that way before.

The following afternoon Jim Conklin called. "I hear you're

cutting a swathe. Ben Palmer's happy; you've taken a load off his mind. Paul Haller's mad because you told him off. Doing any good?"

Jim was like a breath of fresh air. "I wish I knew," Matt said.

"Mark Brown thinks you're doing just fine, and he's a deep one, boy. He made a monkey of us while he was at Thorndike. There was a hydraulic gadget Haller's boys thought they'd dreamed up-- ask Brown about it some time." Conklin chuckled. "Ever have a yen to fly one of your own planes, son?"

"I'm desk-borne," Matt said. "A transport, you mean?"

"A truck? No, I mean a fighter, son."

"Wait a minute. You're flying jets, at your age?" Matt asked.

The chuckle sounded strangely out of the past, bringing to Matt's mind a picture of Jim Conklin, not old then, in breeches and riding boots, flying contraptions made of fabric and wood and whirling light, and Matt, a small boy, watching in awe.

"What's the good of being a wheel, tell me that," Conklin said, "if a man can't have some fun. We stretched a fighter, made it a two-seater. We call it the Droop. It looks like the dickens and flies sort of like a brick, but it's fun. Goes whoosh and everything. Tomorrow afternoon? About five? Or is Friday better?"

Matt looked at his calendar covered with Myra's handwriting. "Friday," he said, making a note.

"We'll see if you've forgotten what I taught you-- if you ever learned it."

"I'll make you eat that," Matt said.

The chuckle sounded again. "That'll be the day," Conklin said as he hung up.

Matt buzzed for Myra. She came to the doorway. "Next one," he said. "Trundle him in."

She had the door closed, and she leaned against it. "You look, for the first time, like you're enjoying it."

"Maybe I am."

She nodded. "It's where you belong."

"Is that your word for today?" Matt grinned.

"Could be." She was smiling, too. She started to turn away.

"Wait a minute," Matt said. "You offered me a dinner once."

"So I did."

"I'd like to take you up on it. How about Friday? It's a good day."

"Fine," she said; and then she was gone, and the next visitor came, bearing his problem.

It was late when Matt finshed up. Myra, in the doorway, said, "That's it, for today."

"I've earned my salary?" Matt questioned.

"You surely have," Myra said. "Simmons called. He said it could wait."

Matt frowned. "No. I'll call him."

"I'll get him for you." She crossed the office and picked up the telephone, dialed, spoke, handed it to him. He watched her walk out and close the door.

Simmons said, "It isn't much, but I thought you'd want to know. A right front fender turned up in an auto wrecker's yard this afternoon. It was banged up, and the headlight was broken and on the glass there was something that could have been blood, and was. And there were a few threads-- not much, but enough-- from the suit Traub was wearing when they found him in the parking lot."

"The first break," Matt said.

"Maybe. It may lead nowhere. It'll take a long time to check all the garages that could have changed the fender. And somebody may have been paid to keep his mouth shut. That's not unusual in hit-and-run cases. But we're not just sitting on our hands."

"All right," Matt said. "Let me know what happens."

"Right." Simmons hesitated. "I've been thinking as you suggested, about who might want the factory to slow down, and why."

"And?"

"Oh, I can't answer it," Simmons said. "What I have is a sort of corollary-- if there's anything to your idea, then you'd better take into account that you're in the same position your father was when Traub dropped that wing on him."

"I suppose so," Matt said. "I hadn't thought about it."

"You'd better," Simmons replied.

"All right. I won't walk under any wings."

Simmons' voice sharpened a trifle. "There are other ways accidents can happen. It might be well if you stayed out of the shops."

"You keep after that fender," Matt said. "I'll look after myself." He put the phone in its cradle and then looked up.

Myra was standing in the doorway, her coat already on. She said, "I didn't mean to eavesdrop. I just wanted to say good night."

"It doesn't matter," he muttered.

"I think maybe it does. He was-- warning you about something."

"Just general precautions-- don't get my feet wet; stay out of drafts." He stood up, stretched his arms until they cracked. "I used to have calluses on my hands. Now I'm getting them somewhere else. Sitting is--"

"Boss." Her voice was urgent. "I told you once I didn't want anything to happen to you."

"You told me to stay out from under wings, and out of dark parking lots. I have and I will. Look; nothing's going to happen to me."

She shook her head slowly. "You won't take orders, will you? Well, good night, Boss."

"I'll give you a ride," Matt said casually.

"No," she said softly. "I don't want it to be a habit, something you do without even thinking about it. Besides"-- even her eyes were laughing at him-- "I know some of the bus drivers, and I don't like to disappoint them." She paused. "I've set my sights on Friday."

She was gone, and the office suddenly seemed quiet, and lonely.

The hallway was dim, almost dark, the offices deserted-- except one: Mark Brown's office still showed a light. On impulse Matt walked down to it.

Brown was on the telephone. He hung up as Matt came in, and he sat, smiling, at the big, uncluttered desk.

Matt said, "You and I seem to be the last. Everyone else quits by the clock."

"Maybe that's indicative," Brown said. "One of the differences between us and the rest of the factory. Anything special on your mind?"

"No." He was thinking of Jim Conklin and what Jim had told him. "I hear you made us look silly over a hydraulic gadget when you were at Thorndike."

"In a manner of speaking. It was largely because of that coup that your father brought me here." His smile came and went. "Your Engineering Department was developing a hydraulic control. So was ours, an instance of parallel thought. We got there first, patented the design, manufactured it, and sold it with considerable success."

Matt was smiling. "And Paul Haller--"

"Paul wasn't happy," Brown said. "He even cried 'foul.'"

"But the old man was impressed," Matt continued.

"Yes," Brown said, "I think he was. He asked me to come here." He hesitated. "How's the fighter project? I had your memo. Sounds like a good idea."

"I haven't been down to the shop yet," Matt said. Barney White would have gone home. But Johnny would be there representing Barney. Matt hadn't thought of it before. "I think I'll take a look right now."

Johnny was working at a desk against a wall of the hangar. Matt walked over and perched on a corner.

"Slumming?" Johnny asked. "Seeing how the other half lives-- the moles who never see the daylight?"

Matt grinned. "Feeling sorry for yourself?"

"Oh, well. It's all work, no matter how you slice it. On the other hand, I could be stomping out a few dances with my girl right now." He shook his head, and his eyes, through the glasses, were bright, intelligent. "You didn't come down to hold my hand. You want to know how things are going?"

"That was the general idea," Matt said.

Johnny nodded. "Better, I'd say. You seem to have put a burr under Barney White's saddle. When I told him I didn't want to go on nights he got real mean." He paused. "And your memo has helped. Mark Brown gave us Dick Reinhardt, who's just about as good a man as he's got. All in all, we're picking up."

"Enough?" Matt said. "Can you get back on schedule?"

Johnny hesitated. "Between you and me, no. But Barney's the boss, and you better talk to him."

"I will," Matt said. "Maybe tomorrow." He slid off the desk and stood there, grinning down at Johnny. "When it's over, and you're back on days in circulation again, I'll buy you a steak and we'll talk over old times."

"I'll hold you to that, boy," Johnny said.

The big house was lonelier than ever tonight. Matt ate his solitary dinner, under Anne's fussing, and afterwards, over coffee, he tried to concentrate on the papers he had carried home. But it was no good. He was tired, unable to concentrate. He went, at last, to the telephone, and Sue herself answered. "If I came over--" he began, then stopped quickly. "This is Matt." He heard her soft laugh. "It's a nice night--"

"It's foggy."

"Is it?" He looked out of the window. It was. "All right, it's still a nice night. I thought maybe a ride."

Again the soft laughter. "Give me five minutes," Sue said.

They drove out Valley Boulevard, toward the pass and the sea. "Long time," Matt said. It was, in a way, like talking aloud to himself. "There used to be a country club here somewhere."

"You gave me an orchid for the dance," she said softly.

"And there went my week's allowance," he said, and was silent.

They climbed through the pass, dropped down to the coast highway. The salt taste was strong in the air, and pleasant.

She suddenly turned and said. "Why did you call me, Matt?"

"I don't know. Lonesome, maybe. Restless. Do I have to explain?" He slowed, pulled off the highway to the tip of the headland, parked, and switched off the lights. The deep muttering of the sea reached them.

"Barney--" Sue began.

"Let's not talk about Barney. Or the factory."

She said, "We aren't kids any more, Matt, with orchids and weekly allowances. We're supposed to be grown-up now."

He took his hands from the wheel and reached for her and drew her across the seat to him. She came, unresisting. His left hand found her chin and lifted it. Her lips, as before, were warm, but they lacked what he had hoped to find. He released her, and after a moment she moved quietly back to her own side of the seat. She said, "Do you know what you want, Matt?"

He was silent while he started the engine, turned on the lights again. "Do you?" he murmured.

Her voice was quiet, almost subdued: "I'm not sure."

He spent Thursday morning with Ben Palmer, Paul Haller, Colonel Armitage, and three Air Force experts from Washington. The subject was guided missiles. The colonel stayed when the meeting broke up. "No need to talk about it in front of everybody," the colonel said. "But all that we discussed here is contingent, of course. You understand that."

"Go on," Matt urged.

The colonel said, "We don't put guided missile and pilotless aircraft contracts into a factory where there is the slightest possibility of-- trouble. I'm talking about security. If you haven't considered that, you should. Parts, tooling, for fighter modification are still being lost, spoiled. Do you know why?"

"Speed," Matt said. "When you're in a hurry, it happens. Always."

"But you can't be sure that's the only reason," the colonel snapped.

It was true, and Matt thought of Barney White, whom the old man had judged unfit. He thought of Sue, too. It was difficult to separate judgment and emotion.

Myra came in as the colonel left. "If you don't need me, I have a lunch date," she said. "With Johnny. He eats late these days."

"Go ahead," Matt replied. "I'll be out in the shop."

It was time, it was maybe past time, that he saw Barney White. He started for the Experimental Lab.

Matt sat beside Barney's desk, the desk Johnny occupied last night. He listened to the big man telling him what, in substance, Johnny had told him: Things were better. But there was something in Barney's voice that had not been there before. Matt tried to isolate it, and failed. He said, "Can you get back on schedule?"

"I don't know," Barney replied. "We're gaining, but we're three weeks behind."

"Parts and tooling are still being lost and spoiled. Why?" Matt asked. He could see anger now, easy to identify; but there was something else, too, a reluctance that was puzzling.

"Why does it ever happen?" Barney snapped. "Everything has to be done yesterday, so there are mistakes; somebody guesses and doesn't bother to check. This isn't Production, where everything is set up, systematized, and there's no excuse for mistakes."

"You're satisfied those are the only reasons?" Matt asked. He watched, and saw again the hesitation, faint, but there.

"What are you getting at?" Barney asked. "I'm trying to remember that this is my job and you're the boss." He looked down at his hands, and then looked up again. "I had lunch with Sue today--"

"Forget Sue," Matt said. "That's neither here nor there." He stood up, puzzled at this thing, this attitude of Barney's which he could not identify.

Barney said softly, "Sometime, outside of the plant, we'll have a long talk about Sue, about where you fit in. Anything else on your mind?"

"That's all for now," Matt said, and walked back toward the

office.

He didn't see Myra until the last of the afternoon's visitors had gone. She said, "Enough for you today. I've reserved a table for two at my place tomorrow. Dress is optional."

She had something of the quality of Jim Conklin, the ability to loosen him, make him smile. And that made him think of Johnny, who had that quality, too. "Have a good lunch?" he asked.

"More or less." And then, unexpectedly, she said, "I used to be in love with Johnny, or thought I was."

He leaned back in his big chair. "And now?"

She hesitated. "Johnny is-- well, Johnny. Against the real thing, he doesn't measure up." She smiled. "Good night, Boss."

"No." Until this moment he had not realized that he had decided this. "Tonight I give you a ride. No habit. Because I want to."

"Do you?" She hesitated. "So do I."

They did not speak during the ride. In front of her apartment they stopped, and her voice then, in the half-darkness, was solemn, quiet: "You're flying tomorrow with Jim Conklin. Is it a good idea? Flying machines? Especially that one?"

He said nothing.

"You like to make your own way alone, don't you, Matt?" There was no censure in her voice, only solemnity. "But doesn't it ever get lonely?" she asked.

"Sometimes," he said slowly. He was thinking of last night, of the emptiness of the big house, of Sue, who had sat where Myra was sitting now.

Myra said softly, "Don't."

"Don't what?" Although, vaguely, he did understand.

She said, "Don't ever kiss me, touch me-- unless you mean it." And then she was out of the car, and her voice was jaunty again: "Good night, Boss. Thanks for the ride. Take care of youself-- hear?" And she was gone, tall and straight and proud.

Matt drove slowly home.

At noon on Friday, Barney White asked to see him. Myra brought the word in, closing the door behind her. "If somebody were to ask me, I'd say that he's embarrassed-- if you can picture that. You want him?"

Matt nodded and she opened the door and ushered Barney White in.

"Usually I kill my own snakes," Barney said. "But yesterday you asked me some questions." He took a piece of paper from his pocket, held it in his fist. "There was a piece of tooling overdue, a big drop-hammer die for stamping out fuselages. We needed it."

"Go on," Matt said.

"I put one of my boys on it, told him to run it down, find out what the delay was, do something about it. Yesterday, not long before you came down, he brought me this and asked me if I was crazy or something." He held out the paper.

Matt unfolded it. It was a shop order. In overprinting across its face it read: EXPERIMENTAL, RUSH. The order was to scrap the die. In the corner were penciled initials. He stared at it dumbly.

"The reason he couldn't find the die," Barney said, "was because it had been melted up, scrapped, by that order. The initials are mine. But I didn't sign them."

This, then, explained Barney's reluctance, his hesitation, yesterday. "There have been others?" Matt said. He stared at the order.

"Some. Not many, but important ones, things we needed."

"You told the old man about it? Simmons? Anybody?" He looked up.

"It was my baby--"

"And you didn't want to cry, so you kept it to yourself." He could see it; he could even understand it. "You're a fool, White." And there was neither softness or sympathy in his voice.

Barney stood up slowly. He held himself tight; his shoulders, beneath the leather jacket, were stiff, tense. He whirled and walked out.

Matt sat where he was, looking again at the order, staring at it, thinking of Johnny that first day, in the foundry, and of the big drop-hammer die sinking into the melting pot, remembering the order Johnny had initialed and handed to the foundryman. Johnny. It was the same order; of that, he was sure.

He rang for Myra, and when she came in, he studied her, too. "What time does Johnny come in?" he asked curtly.

"Three-thirty, more or less." Her eyes asked a question, which he ignored.

Barney would stay on, then, to overlap, to pass on to Johnny anything of importance from the day, to give him any special instructions. And he, Matt, wanted to see Johnny alone; out of the past he owed him that much.

"All right." Even his voice had changed. "That's all."

He stood up with a weariness he had not felt before, something deeper and harsher, a pain that reached far down into the secret place where a man kept his faith and his pride and his affections. If he couldn't trust Johnny, he thought, whom could he trust? And he walked past Myra as if she were not there.

He passed people in the hall, but he saw none of them. Then someone spoke his name, and he stopped, and looked. It was Mark Brown, calm, controlled, watching him steadily. Brown said, "Anything wrong?"

Matt was silent for a moment. "I don't know," he said. He still had the shop order in his hand. He folded it and shoved it in his pocket. "But I'm going to find out."

"Can I help?"

He shook his head. "Thanks." Unconsciously he echoed Barney

422 American Murders

White: "I'll kill my own snakes." He walked on, just walking without a destination.

The other afternoons had been long; this one was endless. The problems that were brought to him seemed stupid, mere indecisions. He dealt with them swiftly, almost brutally, but still they came, visitor after visitor. Then, at last, Myra appeared in the doorway. "It's quarter of five. Time for you to leave for the field, if you're still going flying."

"I am. Why wouldn't I?"

"Why take unnecessary chances?" She watched him quietly, seeing the change, not understanding it. "You asked about Johnny. You're going to see him?"

"Later," he said curtly.

"I see."

He faced her, frowning. "What do you mean by that?" And then, remembering: "Oh. We have a date, haven't we? I'd forgotten."

"It's not important," she replied.

"Now, look." He did not know how they had reached this point. Nor, at the moment, did he care. They faced each other. And it was then, in the silence, that the telephone rang. Matt picked it up.

Johnny's voice said, "Matt? I hoped I'd catch you." He went on smoothly, almost as if the words were rehearsed: "I'm in the shop, Barney the White's gone, and I've got something to show you."

The folded shop order was in Matt's pocket. And deep within his mind something was beginning to stir. "It's important?" he asked.

"If you're interested in this botched-up job we're doing."

"I'll come down." Myra was still there, still watching him. To her he said, "Call the field. Tell Jim Conklin I can't come." He saw the relief in her face, her eyes. "I'll see you at seven."

"You still want to?" She waited, but he said nothing, and she finally nodded. "I'll be ready."

Johnny was at Barney's White's desk, a blueprint spread in front of him. His eyes, through his glasses, were almost gay. "Take a look, boy. You still able to read a drawing? This is the new nose assembly, just as complicated as the engineer's little minds could make it." He had a pencil. It moved surely, pointing, and the voice went on: "...there was the problem, how to hold all the pieces in place while they're being riveted together. We've ordered a jig, the most complicated thing you ever saw, with arms that go in all directions to hold all these parts that make up the assembly. It won't be done for three-four weeks."

"Go on," Matt said.

"The Hazeltine triumph." Johnny touched the blueprint with the pencil. "Nobody else seems to have seen it. But by three minor engineering changes, reversing these three flanges, this great, big, complicated assembly breaks down into three simple assemblies that can be put together separately without any jig to hold the parts in place. So we save maybe three weeks." He leaned back. "Like it?"

Matt said, "You've showed this to Barney?" This was his first reaction.

Johnny grinned. "He told me it wouldn't work and to stop dreaming." He watched Matt's face and he shook his head. "Why he doesn't want to save three weeks is between you and him. He's the boss. I'm hired to help."

"Yes," Matt said. But there was more to it than this. "When did you show it to him, Johnny?"

"Quite a while ago. I--" He stopped there, and the brightness went out of his eyes; the smile disappeared.

"Go on, Johnny," Matt said. "You showed it to him quite a while ago, days, maybe weeks."

He waited. Johnny said nothing.

Matt said, "But night before last I was down here, and you didn't show it to me."

"I-- forgot."

"You can do better than that," Matt said. He was sure now; it had to be like this, because, otherwise, the timing was too coincidental, too exact. He reached for the telephone. His eyes did not leave Johnny's face. To the operator he said, "This is Matt Holmes. Get me Simmons, of Plant Protection, here or at home, wherever he is. I'll be here."

Johnny said, "What's up?" But there was only silence.

The phone rang, and Matt picked it up. To Simmons he said, "I want the Experimental airplane called the Droop grounded, as of now. And I want it hauled into the final assembly hangar and roped off, under guard. Tomorrow I want it torn down, piece by piece."

Simmons said, "You don't mind telling me what--"

"I do mind." There were pressures inside of him, building, stifling. "I've told you what to do. Now do it." He hung up, and then, at last, he took the shop order from his pocket and tossed it on the desk. "Why, Johnny? Why?"

And he watched Johnny read, and read again, and then looked up, trying to smile, shaking his head.

"In the foundry," Matt said, "the first day I was here, when you didn't know I was staying, and neither did I, and so it didn't matter whether I saw you sign the order or not."

Johnny said, "You think that, Matt?"

Matt tapped the blueprint with his finger. "You've known about this for quite a while. But you saved it until now, right now. Why, Johnny? Was it because you had to have something important to show me, something important enough to get me down here and keep me from flying? Because whatever else you might have done, like sabotaging the project, you still couldn't stomach the idea of letting me get killed in an airplane that's been doctored?"

Johhny's head shook, slowly, automatically.

"You're not cut out for villainly," Matt said. "You're weak. If you're going to try something like this-- sabotaging-- you can't afford to let anything-- friendship, squeamishness, anything-- get in the way."

"There isn't--" Johnny said. "I don't know--" He stopped.

"We'll find out about the Droop when we tear it down," Matt said. He was standing now. "I'll be in my office tomorrow, Johnny. I'll see you whenever you decide to come in and talk."

He wanted to say more, but in his mind there were no words, only dull emptiness. He went out of the hangar and closed the door behind him. He walked, but afterwards he couldn't remember where. It was dark when he got in his car and drove home.

He had showered, shaved, and just finished dressing when the telephone rang. It was Simmons.

"I'm at the field," Simmons said. Behind his voice there were factory sounds, unidentifiable. "There's been an accident. A man walked under a propeller. Or was pushed. The night man on the fighter project-- Hazeltine."

Matt said, "Johnny." And that was all. He stood motionless, and in his throat there was a sudden, sour taste, sharp and strong.

"He never knew what hit him," Simmons said.

Matt hung up then, and stared out the window at the valley lights below. Then, because the words had to be spoken aloud, he said, "I've just killed a man, a man who used to be my friend." And he walked out of the house, to his car. Myra King first, he thought; she was, she had to be, the starting place.

He drove slowly, past Sue's house, down the curving hill road. He had one more fact now-- first the old man, then Traub, now Johnny; all of them tied together because that was the only way it made sense. Add to that, because there was no longer any doubt, some sort of tampering with the Droop. Tomorrow, when they tore the ship down, piece by piece-- He stopped, thinking that there was another, better way than that. But it would keep, until the end of the night shift and the beginning of the silent period, the six hours and a half before Saturday's day shift came on. First, now, there was Myra.

When she opened the door she was radiant in a dark dress with white at the neck, simple and sleek. "Hello, Matt," she said, and let him inside.

"Yesterday," Matt said, "you saw my calendar. You knew I was going flying with Jim Conklin, in the Droop."

"Of course." Her eyes were faintly puzzled.

Matt said, "And then you had lunch with Johnny. You told him?"

"I-- may have. Yes, I think I did. Was it a secret?"

"Last night you tried to talk me out of going. And again today-- it was in your mind, but I didn't give you the chance. Isn't that true?"

"Matt--" She hesitated. "Yes. I-- didn't want you to go."

"And you were standing, talking to me, when Johnny called-- maybe even talking until Johnny called--"

"Matt, I'm not even sure what you're talking about."

"And then he called and I cancelled the flight," Matt continued.

She only watched him, her eyes wide and round.

"I had the Droop hauled in off the field, Myra. We'll tear it down tomorrow and find out what was done to it, find out why both you and Johnny tried so hard to keep me from flying in it. I owe you that," he said.

"What's happened?" It was only a whisper.

"You shouldn't have told Johnny. Or you should have let me go. But not both."

She had no words; she shook her head dumbly, her eyes, enormous, dark, never leaving his face.

Matt said, "Johnny's dead. He walked into a propeller-- walked, or else he was pushed--"

"Oh, no!" she moaned, and her hands half rose and hung there, motionless. Then, abruptly, she turned, and went, almost running, through the doorway and away from his sight. A door slammed, and that was all.

He sat where he was. He felt no pity, merely regret and blame against himself that this final, ugly stage had been reached. Had he done otherwise, not left Johnny alone, for example-- but there was no way of knowing what might have been. He knew now what he had to do, step by step, and this was all that was important. Mark Brown had told him once that he faced facts, reality; it would have surprised him to find that most people did not. He was still sitting, still waiting, when Myra came back.

She had washed her face. Her eyes were red, a trifle puffy, but she held herself straight and tall. "You took me apart. You meant to. It wasn't pleasant. Maybe it was necessary." She paused. "I'm back together now. I'm not the same. I think when you go that far down into fear or hurt you're never the same. Johnny's dead. You imply that I-- killed him."

"No," Matt said. "I did." And he watched, uncomprehending, as a new, gentle expression came into her face.

"Now I understand," she said. "Boss. Matt." And she shook her head slowly. "For the record, I tried to stop you from flying for the same reason that I'm sitting here now, like this, with my pride unbuttoned. I'm not devious; I'm not even a good liar; I was afraid something would happen to you, yes, but only because I'll always be afraid something will happen to you. You don't believe that, not yet."

He said nothing.

"And you wouldn't believe me if I told you that I had a picture of you in my mind for a long time before I ever saw you. I got it from Johnny and from your father, and I built it up into quite a thing. And I haven't changed it. But you're not ready to believe that yet, either."

"You--"

"I'm not through," she said quickly "You're learning. You're softening up, finding holes in your armor. You're blaming yourself for

Johnny. Because you tried to do too much, all by yourself."

He stared at her then. "How do you know that?"

"Because I know you....There. I've had my say." She could even smile. "Where are you going? To the plant?"

"Eventually. After a while."

She finally said, "I'll be there, Matt. In the office. If you want me." She looked up and shook her head as he started to speak. "Just-- be careful. Please." And she made a small motion with one hand, turning him around and sending him to the door without looking back.

The street was dark and silent, deserted. He stopped at a drugstore and called the plant. From personnel files he got Barney White's home address and phone number. He called; there was no answer. There was one more place-- Sue's house-- and he headed there.

There was a car in the drive. He looked at it carefully, tried to judge if the right front fender had been replaced, but in the dark it was a wasted effort. He should, at least, have asked Simmons the make of the car from which the fender had come. But he had not.

He rang the doorbell and waited, conscious of the sound of a transport engine at run-up in the valley below. This would have been the last sound that Johnny had heard. His anger rose, and then steadied.

She opened the door. She seemed to hesitate, watching him. Then, "Come in, Matt. We were-- talking about you."

And Barney's voice, soft, somehow eager: "We were, indeed." He wore a suit now in place of the leather jacket and the flannels; but the solid, hard look of him was unchanged.

In the living room Matt said, "Been here long?"

"What's that to you?"

Sue said, "We've been-- talking. I don't know how long."

"I got here a little after six," Barney said. "That prove anything?"

He couldn't know if it was important. There was too much that he didn't know. "I had a talk with Johnny Hazeltine."

"About me, I suppose?" Barney said. "He had tales, did he? Running to his old chum with little tidbits?"

Sue said, "Barney."

But Barney was beyond that. He said, "At first I thought you were a punk, the old man's son, taking a big job just to play for a while. And I thought that Sue had the same idea. Then I began to wonder. You took me in, I admit it, with your big gesture, giving me my choice, even making motions of front-office cooperation, jerking Engineering around, writing those memos. But after the big gesture, you couldn't wait to get here, tell Sue what a magnanimous fellow you'd been, could you?"

Sue said, "It wasn't like that. I asked him, made him tell me."

"Go on," Matt said. The anger was under steady control.

"And after the memos were out, so that the whole factory could see that you were doing everything to help, down you came, like the old man, to climb me, starting the build-up for the firing act. Wasn't that it?"

Matt had not seen it this way before; it hadn't occurred to him that Barney would see it this way. Myra had been right; he was learning some things about himself on this night.

"You're in the driver's seat," Barney said. "You've been here from the start." He looked at both of them now. "Maybe I'm out of my league, maybe I've just been kidding myself, or somebody has been kidding me." He looked at Sue, and she sat silent, stiff, unmoving. He looked again at Matt. "And how about that dish in your office? You playing in that direction, too? Is that how you people do it on this side of the tracks?"

"No." Matt was silent for a moment, thinking hard. "Sit down," he suddenly snapped; "you've had your say. Johnny called me down to the shop to show me a way to break the nose assembly into three parts so you don't have to wait for the jig."

"He did, did he? Why didn't he show me?" Barney's voice lifted almost to a roar. "Why?"

"He said he had," Matt said softly. Once before he had watched, and admired, the mastery of the man over himself. Barney's mouth opened and then closed again, and his shoulders moved gently beneath his coat, and that was all.

Matt said, "I didn't fly today. We've pulled the Droop into final assembly. We'll tear it down tomorrow."

The frown of puzzlement on Barney's face seemed real enough. "What does that have to do with it? I think we'd better have a talk with your pal Johnny." And this, too, seemed genuine.

Matt was suddenly blunt, brutal, as he had been with Myra; "He's dead." And he saw the shock in Sue's face, the incredulity in Barney's; but still he could not be sure. "He walked into a propeller. Or was pushed. I think he was pushed." Matt stood up. "I'll use your phone, Sue." He walked down the hall. There was only silence behind him.

He reached Simmons at home: "I want you to call the plant. There's no need to go down. I want the guard pulled off the Droop at the close of the swing shift."

Simmons said, "That's an order?"

"It is," Matt snapped, and hung up. He went back to the living room.

Barney was gone. Sue was still in her chair. She watched him fully. "I'll go along," he said.

"No." She stirred, roused herself. "Please, Matt. I don't think I could stand being alone right now."

He had left Johnny alone; he blamed himself for this. And his voice now surprised him with its gentleness: "All right, Sue."

"Have you eaten?" Sue asked. "We were going out to dinner, and then we got talking, arguing really, about you, and me--" She stopped there, and caught her lower lip in her teeth and held it for a moment. "I'll make us some sandwiches." She stood up and headed for the kitchen.

Matt paced the living room for a few minutes, then walked to the kitchen.

She turned and said, "I've known better sandwich makers. Mine always come out sort of raggedy. Does the girl in your office make a good sandwich?"

"I wouldn't know," he said quietly.

"I can make biscuits. And I can knit-- dresses, sweaters. But not socks, I never tried socks." Then she was quiet.

Matt suddenly crossed the kitchen in three long steps. She turned to him, burying her face against his shoulder, and he held her awkwardly, her head small beneath his hand. She made no sound, but her entire body trembled. And after a time the tembling stopped. She stepped back then and took the handkerchief from his breast pocket, wiped her eyes, blew her nose. "Silly, isn't it?"

"No. Not silly, Sue."

She watched him soberly. "In five years you've changed. In less than a week you've changed even more. Barney doesn't understand you, or won't, and I'm not sure that I do. Does the girl in your office?"

He was silent, considering this. He didn't know the answer.

"Matt-- don't let anything more happen. Do you understand? It's all mixed up, frightening. Bert, Johnny Hazeltine, you and Barney--"

"Particularly Barney," Matt said. "Isn't that it?"

She hesitated. "Yes. Am I wrong about him?"

"I don't know, Sue. I can't be sure-- yet," he said.

She turned back to the sandwiches. Over her shoulder she said "Bert always thought that some day you and I--"

"The time for that," Matt said clearly, "came and went when we were about eighteen." He had not seen it so clearly before. "Because he was what he was, and that I was, maybe, too much like him--"

She turned around then. "You are, you know. Although I've never seen it before. And he was sort of a second father."

"And that makes me your brother," Matt said. He could even smile. It was strange how easily their relationship fell into place "Those sandwiches-- I don't have much time."

"For what?" She whirled around. "You're going to the factor again?"

"Yes."

This time there was no tremble in her voice. She watched him "It has to do with Barney? Does it, Matt?"

"I don't know."

"That's what you're going to find out?"

"Yes."

She said slowly, "You told me, even though you know I coul

phone the factory, tell him you're coming?"

"Yes. But you won't, Sue, because you have to find out about him, too-- whether the old man was right in deciding to fire him--" He paused. "Or whether the old man was wrong. It comes right down to that."

She was silent a moment, then suddenly said, "Here's your sandwich." And at the door, as he was leaving, "Good luck, Matt."

He touched her cheek with two fingers in the old, long-ago familiar gesture as he walked past her and out.

The swing shift was not yet gone. As he reached the main gate, the public address came on. The girl's voice said, "Mr. Holmes, call your office; Mr. Holmes, call your office." The speakers shut off with a click.

One of the guards said, "Every five minutes for the last half-hour."

"Thanks," Matt said. Myra had said that she was coming down; he wondered what she wanted. He turned into the Administration Building, quiet, deserted on night shift. He climbed the darkened stairs.

The outer door of his own office was open, lighted; he could see it as he turned the corner. It was strange, he thought, that he had never doubted that Myra would come down, even at night and alone. There was that about her, a quality of dependability.

He stopped suddenly, and half turned, hearing the sound in the darkness of the long hallway behind him. He was silhouetted against the open doorway; this thought came first (or was it later?) and he jumped, automatically, reflexively; and he heard a soft, muffled shot. His shoulder stung sharply and he heard the bullet slam against the door panel. Then he was inside the office, and from the hallway he heard light, running steps, fading away.

Myra had half risen in her chair-- she stared at him. He crossed the office in two long strides and reached for the telephone, and then, slowly, withdrew his hand. The footsteps were already gone; the hallway was long, with three, no, four, stairways, each with its own exit, and by the time he could summon guards, it would be too late. Already outside he could hear the sounds of the night shift flowing toward the gates, two or three thousand people amongst whom a search would be, clearly, impossible.

Myra said, "You're dripping on the rug!" Her voice was tight, too loud, and she was still in the half-risen position, suspended there.

He looked down, then. The back of his left hand was red, and the blood dripped slowly from his fingers. There was no pain yet, merely a numbness in his upper arm, and he stared at the stain that was spreading in the material of his coat.

"Get it off," Myra said. Her voice was under control. "Sit down."

He obeyed, and her hands were swift and sure, easing the coat off, tearing away the sleeve of his shirt, and pressing a wad of shirt material against the wound. She brought his own right hand around to hold it. "Wait here. There's a first-aid station near Sheet Metal." She was gone, running.

He sat where he was, and the pain began now, only a burning sensation at first. He ignored it. The door of the office opened in; the upper panel was split, the cracks fanning out raggedly from the single hole. He studied it and waited for Myra to return.

She had bandages and she was breathing hard, but her hands were steady and firm as she strapped a pad into place. He watched her face as she worked, but it told him nothing. Finally, she was done, and her fierce concentration fell away, and her voice was tight and unsteady again. "Shall I-- call a doctor?"

"No." The arm was beginning to throb now, but he ignored this, as he had ignored the burning pain. He got his coat back on. "You called me. Why?"

"I found something I had remembered," Myra said. "It was about Johnny--" Her eyes began to widen. "I set you up, didn't I? I told the whole factory you'd be coming here, and so anybody could wait out there--"

"Yes," Matt said. It had been in his mind. But there was another possibility, too, although it was not pleasant to consider: Sue could have called Barney, told him that he, Matt, was coming to the plant.

"Never mind," Matt said tensely. "About Johnny-- tell me. Sit down."

She went slowly around the desk and sat down. Her eyes did not leave his face. "You think that I meant to--"

"Johnny," Matt said. He made his voice sharp, a command.

She picked up a paper from the desk. "It may not mean anything. I don't know." She hesitated. "This-- it's a year and a half ago now." She shook her head. "I told you I thought I was in love with him."

"Yes," Matt said. "Go on."

"He-- didn't, wasn't-- I wanted to help him."

She faced her facts, too, he thought, her own realities.

She said, "He asked me to get him a gate pass-- for blueprints. He said he wanted to study them at home, try to find better production methods--" She stopped. "It wasn't like Johnny. But i convinced me-- then." She hesitated. "Your father signed whatever I gave him to sign, without even looking. He trusted me."

"So Johnny got his gate pass," Matt said. For someone she loved or thought she loved, there were no limits, ever.

"We had our first squabble over it," she said. "But I did it. This is the carbon of the application. Is it important, Matt? Does it help?"

The throbbing in the arm was stronger now; he could no longer ignore it. "I don't know." He slid from the desk, flexing the arm gently. There was no hampering of movement, but there was weakness and the throbbing. Outside, the sounds of the factory had died; the low-pitched, scarcely audible pulse and hum was gone. In the shops the lights would be turned down, the machines stilled, the benches quiet and deserted; only here and there a maintenance man, or a janitor, or a watchman making his quiet rounds. From now until the beginning of Saturday's day shift-- six hours and a half-- the factory would lie dormant; it was for this that he had waited. But he had not counted on the arm, and now he had to take it into account.

"Suppose," Myra said, "that he wanted that pass because--"

"Not now," Matt said. This could wait; the other could not, and he had his decision to make. Watching her face he tried to marshal the facts, and the possibilities.

Myra said, "I'm being judged?"

"Yes," he said slowly. It was a small thing-- and yet it was not; the placement of trust was never a small thing. He had trusted Johnny, and he had been betrayed. He had made his judgment on Barney White, and the results were not yet in; he had trusted Sue not to telephone. Myra's public address calls could have been the lure, and the gate-pass carbon the excuse-- as Johnny's blueprint had been the excuse to call him down to the shop. He couldn't know, but he had to decide.

He said slowly, "Call Simmons. He's probably at home. Tell him I need him." He should have planned all along to have Simmons in on this. But he had not.

She was already reaching for the telephone. "Here? In the office?"

"No." He hesitated. "I'll be out in Final Assembly, I'll need him there. He'll understand."

Her hand stopped, rested on the phone. "No."

"No what?"

"Wait here for him. Or let me call some guards, somebody. Or--" She stopped there. "No," she said, "you won't stop now, for me, or for anybody." And her voice was changed; it was quiet now, and gentle, a tone he had not heard before. "And the funny thing is, I don't think I'd want you to." She picked up the phone. She was already dialing when he went out.

He waited until he was out of her sight, and then he tucked his left hand in his coat pocket to take the weight off his shoulder and reduce the throbbing. A half-hour ago he had been whole, and confident; now-- he wiggled his fingers, closed the fist and tightened it, and felt the weakness and the pain through his entire arm-- now he had one side left. But she had been right; although he could not have explained why, he couldn't have stopped now if he had wanted to.

There was a light in the glass door of the Plant Protection office. He went in. To the clerk he said, "I'm Matt Holmes." It was on his badge, but he wanted no mistakes, no argument.

"Yes, sir."

"I want a gun, a handgun."

The clerk's eyes grew round; his mouth opened and then shut again. He looked at Matt's face, at the badge, at the left arm and the blood.

"You heard me? I'll sign a receipt for it. Now get it," Matt snapped.

It came from a locked cupboard. Matt dropped it in his pocket, scribbled a receipt.

The clerk said to him, "Your-- your arm?"

"I hurt it." Matt turned away and closed the door behind him.

Outside, in the main plant alleyway, it was cool and dark. The lights had been turned off in groups, three dark, one lighted-- and the shadows between were heavy. Matt kept against the walls of the buildings, doing this from a sense of rudimentary precaution, no more. He met no one.

He skirted the plant Engineering Building and cut across a corner of the field where the transports stood buttoned up for the night, and the fighters, the ships vaguely lighted by standlights, watched by a guard probably already dozing somewhere. In wartime it had been different, but this was not wartime-- and yet, in a way, it was. Now, there was the same feeling of urgency, of tautness, a sense of strain, a realization that whatever happened, or was going to happen, held within it a finality that was no part of normal peacetime.

He picked his way across the field well out of range of the standlights. He passed Barney's hangar, and, for a moment, he thought that he saw a light inside. But when he looked again, sidewise, no light was there. He went on.

There was a small door at the head of the Final Assembly hangar. He went through this door and closed it silently behind him, and then paused while his eyes adjusted to the heavier darkness. Here, where sound and movement were the essence, there was only silence, stillness, as if life itself had ceased with the whistle.

There was, really, no need to see; he had walked along the fighter final assembly line perhaps twice during the last week, and a plan of it was in his head, as firmly fixed as if he had known it all his life. Here the tail assemblies were joined to the fuselage; here the outer wings were installed; here the ships came down from their platforms and stood upon their own landing gear; here the cockpit fittings, the control stands, the plumbing and the wiring and the cables, here the guns, the radios, the pilot seats, the cockpit canopies-- all of it he knew without conscious memory. This assembly line was familiar to him because it had been a part of him for as long as he could remember.

He had fought against it. He had hated it. But the feeling he had now, walking slowly past each station with a sense of knowing guiding himself by a knowledge that came from depths long since covered over but never, never unreachable-- the feeling he had now was of being home, where he belonged.

The gun in his pocket was a comforting weight. In the other

pocket his hand, and the arm it supported, felt as if they did not belong to him, had no connection except through the linkage of pain.

Toward the end of the hangar, the ships were a double line, wing-tip to wing-tip, with only room for a person to slide sidewise between them. He threaded his way toward the one open spot in the whole great hangar where the Droop had been hauled and roped off; where, in the morning, there would be room to work at the disassembling.

It was for this that he had told Simmons to pull off the guard at the close if the swing shift. The airplane was here; he had told Simmons and Johnny, he had told Myra, he had told Barney and Sue that tomorrow the plane would be torn down, piece by piece. And the word would have spread from other sources, too; from the guard who had watched on swing shift, from the hull gang who had hauled the ship in from the field-- and somebody, listening, would have heard. He had no doubt of this; it had to be.

Tonight then, now, the somebody, knowing what he was looking for, because he had put it into the ship or taken it away, or broken it in some way to make the plane inoperable or susceptible to failure, and seeing no guards, no witnesses, and having much to win and very little to lose, and having killed one, two, three people, and having tried to kill the fourth-- the somebody would almost certainly be tempted to remove the evidence-- and why not? In the somebody's place, Matt thought, it was what he would do, and he knew no better criterion to apply.

He stopped short of the last pair of airplanes, and he searched for and found beneath the trailing edge of one wing, a low wooden stand. He sat down to wait, resting his shoulders and head there against the sleek metal of the plane's fuselage, relaxing his left arm as best he could.

It was bad now; he admitted this. The throbbing had spread until it extended from his shoulder to his finger tips, the pulse beating powerfully. Slowly, silently, he tried a new position, found it no better, tried yet a third, and then gave up and sat still. The bandage was too tight, but with one hand, in the dark and with the need for silence, there was nothing he could do about it. The pain grew, until by its very sharpness, it seemed to clarify his mind, to free it as sometimes, it freed itself during the lucid period that preceded sleep. And the silence, and the darkness helped.

He thought of what Myra had told him about Johnny and the gate pass for blueprints, and he examined this new fact. Johnny had been lazy, and brilliant, and weak. He would never have taken blueprints home to study them. But he might have taken them home for other reasons. Matt began to see it now and fit it into the entire pattern.

He closed his eyes for a moment and concentrated all of his will on listening. The silence in the great hangar was absolute-- almost. He let out his breath soundlessly, drew in another, and concentrated again. He heard a sound, a mere, faint whisper of a sound. It seemed to come from the head of the hangar. Then there was only silence again. He slipped the gun from his pocket and rested it on his thigh. The pain of his arm was steady now, strong, but he forced himself to sit still and wait. He could not expect Simmons soon; he had no assurance that he could expect Simmons ever. So he dismissed it.

He closed his eyes and opened his mouth and concentrated again on listening. This time the sound was no longer a whisper. It was plain, a gentle stirring. But it came from the other direction, from beyond him. He got his feet beneath him, soundlessly, and shifted his weight.

He had forgotten the arm. He bent forward to rise, straining his shoulders to balance, and the pain he had felt before was nothing compared to this. It reached into his chest and caught at his breath, seemed to shake him and throw him back against the smooth fuselage. And he remained there, knowing that he had made a noise but, for the moment, unable to care. The pain subsided slowly, and his mind cleared again.

He helped himself with his good hand this time, holding the gun loosely and pushing against the wooden stand with his finger tips. He braced himself for the fresh pain which would come with the movement. It came, and passed, and he was standing now, not quite erect, listening again, but no longer sure of himself, no longer trusting his mind to separate the real from the fancied, to interpret correctly what his ears and his eyes conveyed.

The entire vast hangar, so silent only a few moments before, seemed filled with sound now, a low-pitched, hollow roaring that swelled and subsided in a sort of rhythm inside his head.

And there were other sounds, too, and he isolated these with huge effort. They were closer, and they seemed to have lost some of their secretive quality, taken on an inexorability, real, or imagined.

He had not really felt fear before, which, to his mind, meant panic. It had been, rather, as when you rode in an automobile that was going too fast, or when, in the air, you heard an engine miss a beat, falter. But you did not change your life to avoid automobiles or airplanes, because this process, once begun, had no ending except in the grave, where there was no longer fear-- or anything else. But what he felt now was the beginning of a deeper fear which came from a realization of weakness, and he fought it down, tasting its sourness in his throat. He moved away from the fuselage, lurching, really, and ducked beneath the trailing edge of the plane's wing.

The moving sounds were close; he located them beyond the nose of the airplane. He felt his back touch the underside of the wing, which seemed, ridiculously, to move with the pressure. And then he realized that the wing was moving, that it was the aileron he had brushed, and that the movement of this aileron caused a reciprocal movement of the other one, on the far wing, and that by this he had exposed his position as surely as if he had struck a match. The realization unnerved him, and it was no longer possible to quiet the real fear that caught at him now and shook him as the pain had. He

moved toward the nose of the plane, wavering, still trying desperately to keep himself erect and to look in all directions at once.

He heard a new sound, something falling and rolling, and he
swung his head in this new direction, and then tried to swing his head
back again, knowing that he had been fooled, but it was already too
late.   He felt the blow on the side of his head only as a sudden,
brilliant explosion, and the gun dropped from his good hand and
clattered on the concrete floor, and he went down, too.   He felt
himself hit, blindingly, on the bad arm. And that was all he knew.

He was lying face down.   The concrete was cold against his
cheek, and the waves of pain flowed up through his arm and into his
body, in an endless succession. He didn't know how long he had been
there; for a few agonized moments he couldn't remember where he
was. The hangar was still dark, but it was no longer quiet. On all
sides he heard the sounds of movement, hurried sounds, loud sounds,
unconcealed.

He got to his knees, and he spent precious time locating his gun.
When he finally found it, he began to crawl toward the fuselage, the
panic forgotten, only the pain and the determination remaining. Then
the lights went out, all at once; in his concentration, it was difficult
to comprehend the change. There were voices, raised, shouting, and
the hurry of running footsteps from behind him. But ahead, beyond
the airplane, there was Barney White. He was crouched and he was
moving fast, as a cat moves, his whole body flowing, poised and
purposeful.

Matt tried to lift the gun, but it was no good. He could only
watch, and not understand. And then he saw the other man, toward
whom Barney was moving, the man who stood by the ugly, elongated
Droop, and comprehension, complete and vivid, seemed almost to
explode in his mind. He tried to shout, "Look out! He has a gun!"
But his lips only moved, and no sound came out. And he watched
Mark Brown, calm, possessed, settle himself. The hand with the gun
swung up, waist-high, and steadied.

It happened quickly, and afterwards it was difficult for Matt to
remember the sequence. There was the noise of the gun, the same
soft, hollow sound Matt had heard in the hallway. And there was the
movement of Barney's foot and the solid sound as it landed, and
then-- or was it before?-- the movement, short and chopping, of his
hand, and the skittering clatter of the gun on the concrete; and then
the flurry of punches as Barney drove in, the red banner of his hair
waving above the field of battle.

Then there was comparative silence, and peace, with Brown lying
where he had fallen beneath the wing of the ugly airplane. Barney
stood, his legs wide-spread and his breathing deep and solid, looking
down, waiting. Slowly Barney raised one hand and began to suck at
the knuckles.

Simmons appeared, running, and then slowed to a walk, his mouth
drawn tight, disapproving, and he, too, had a gun. He slipped it into

the holster beneath his coat. He stopped to look down at Matt. "Satisfied?" he said. And then he walked on to where Barney stood, where Brown lay.

But Matt was not looking. Still on his knees, he had turned his head, supporting himself with his good arm. Myra King was there, and she sank on her knees beside him, looking hard into his face as if searching for something, her eyes deep and solemn, unfathomable.

Matt rolled over to a sitting position. He let his shoulders go back against the underbody of the fuselage. His mind seemed to have divorced itself from his body, to have moved away far enough to be able to look back dispassionately. It did not like what it saw. He could remember the panic he had felt, the weak helplessness, the way in which the bottom had dropped out of his confidence. And he remembered, too, something that Myra had told him-- that when you went far down into fear, or hurt, you were never quite the same again.

He said slowly, "I lost my nerve."

"It didn't look like it," Myra said. "You were pointed in the right direction."

Matt shook his head. The pain flowed strongly. "Bandage is too tight." It didn't seem to be his voice saying it.

"Is it?" Myra said. Her eyes were calm now, satisfied. She hunched forward on her knees and pulled his head down to her shoulder, to the softness of her breast. "I'll fix it."

"Yes," he whispered.

"I'll fix everything," Myra said. But Matt didn't hear.

It was later in Matt's office. Matt sat in his big chair. The bandage had been changed; the pain was, again, merely a dull throbbing which a man could ignore. But the memory of the other, the weakness and the panic, remained strong, and he looked around the room and saw the faces as he had not seen them before-- Simmons and Barney White; Colonel Armitage, roused from his bed; a short, square, sleepy-looking man named Andrews, Lieutenant Andrews, from the police. And, of course, Myra, sitting at the corner of his desk, her notebook spread in front of her.

Barney's hands were dirty-- large mechanic's hands, useful hands, one of them closed now. He looked at Matt with a curious expression from which the truculence was all gone. "I found it-- them," Barney said. "It wasn't hard. Brown only had a little time, so it had to be simple." He opened his hand now. They all looked at the two bolts that lay in his palm. "One in each intake scoop," Barney said, "taped there. When that engine really began to turn over, or take-off, probably, they would have pulled loose, into the impeller." He paused. "You would have had hunks of jet engine scattered all over the county."

Colonel Armitage made a short, angry sound, then turned to Myra. "I apologize," he said. "Forgetting my manners."

Myra smiled.

Matt looked at Simmons. "You were already here, in the plant."

"Of course. It was perfectly clear why you wanted the guard pulled off. Unfortunately"-- Simmons hesitated there-- "I could be in only one place at a time, and somebody had to turn on the lights."

Lieutenant Andrews opened his eyes. "You've got how many guards here? And none of them can throw a light switch?"

"All right," Simmons said. "I'll admit it. I thought that two of us was enough. I even gave orders that no janitors or watchmen were to go into the hangar. I didn't know you had been hurt until Miss King found me and told me."

Barney said, "I was in my own shop looking at a blueprint." He saw the question in Matt's face and he nodded. "It works, just the way Johnny said it would. I should have seen it, but I didn't." Barney hesitated. "I came out onto the field, just as you sneaked past, in the shadows. I followed to see what you were up to." He looked at his hands, at the bruised knuckles, then looked up and grinned. "I went in looking for a fight."

Matt smiled. "You found it, although it was no contest."

In the silence, they all looked at Matt. Myra said, "Your turn now." And then her eyes smiling, held his for just a moment.

Matt said, "It will have to be checked, but I think most of it figures." He paused. "There was a gate pass for blueprints issued to Johnny Hazeltine a year and a half ago. That was the beginning. I'm guessing, but I think it fits. Our engineering people were working on a hydraulic control. Jim Conklin told me about it; Mark Brown mentioned it, too. Thorndike, while Brown was running it, turned up with an identical design, patented it, and manufactured it profitably. Johnny always liked the easy way-- he knew everything that went on here-- and he had a gate pass for blueprints. I think there's a connection."

Colonel Armitage said, "Seems plain enough."

"Then," Matt continued, "my father hired Brown from Thorndike. He came here, from a little company which he ran, to a big one which he didn't. Consider it. He's capable of running an entire manufacturing company. He's worked up, as most people do these days." He glanced at Barney. "It can be done; you don't have to start in the driver's seat."

Barney said nothing. He nodded.

Matt said, "This man is ambitious, or he wouldn't be where he is. He's ruthless-- witness the hydraulic control. And he comes to a big company which is, essentially, a one-man business. It shouldn't be, but it is, or was."

"You told me," Simmons said, "but it was too-- intangible."

Matt said, "Look at it. Ben Palmer, Paul Haller, Jim Conklin. Brown told me himself, listed them. Ben is the only production man, Haller an engineer, and Jim is too old and too lazy. So it was a one-man business-- look at it through Brown's eyes."

"Big project," the colonel said, "trying to take over here."

Matt said, "No. It was easy, too easy. You showed me that. The fighter modification was urgent, so the old man took the best man he had, you, Barney, and he mothered the project himself."

"I'm beginning to see it now," the colonel said.

Matt nodded. "Brown saw it, too. So things began to happen. Brown had Johnny right there on the project. He had the club of theft to hold over Johnny's head, and Johnny couldn't stand pressure. It wasn't necessary to do much; Johnny knew what would slow the project down. And if the project failed--" He looked again at the colonel. "You told me what would happen-- cancellation for nonperformance; and because everything the Air Force does is on page one these days, it would be a long time before there would be another contract for a factory which had failed once. And we have to have military contracts. Every big aircraft plant does."

The colonel nodded.

"But suppose, after this failure," Matt said, "the factory were to have new management? The Air Force needs production facilities; you've even financed new plants. So we failed once, but Holmes Aircraft is being run by a new man now-- Brown-- who had no real part in that failure and whose whole production record is a success. Would he get contracts?"

"Almost certainly," the colonel said. "Neat idea."

Matt shrugged. "But as long as the old man is here the project might still succeed, despite Johnny Hazeltine. So-- a wing fell, and Traub, the hoist operator, had a thousand dollars for the horses."

He shifted his arm, eased it. "Traub lost the money on the races, and wanted more. So he put pressure on Brown, arranged to meet him in the Corners. But Brown didn't keep the date. He waited in the parking lot until Traub came out. Technically, Brown had already committed murder. Killing Traub didn't increase the crime."

Lieutenant Andrews said, "We've got the fender to match up."

Matt was tired, and the arm hurt, and his head ached where Brown had clubbed him. But it was not finished yet. "Johnny was my friend. I doubt if he knew about the wing beforehand. But when it happened, he must have guessed why. He probably guessed about the airplane, too. Knowing what Brown was up to, he could predict that something would happen to the airplane I was going to fly in." He felt no anger toward Johnny, only regret, emptiness, a sense of loss. "So he called me down into the shop. It was important, he said, and it couldn't wait. But he could have told me about it before, and hadn't. So I was suspicious."

"But it was important," Barney said. "He gave us back the three weeks he'd taken away from us." Barney, too, was changed, subdued.

"By then," Matt said, "I suspected-- everybody." He smiled at Myra. "Maybe Brown saw me with Johnny. And when he found that the Droop was being hauled off the field for disassembly, it was too much. Johnny was dangerous and so was I. And so, in the dark-- the standlights leave shadows, and it must have been easy-- Johnny was pushed into a propeller."

"And you were shot," Myra said. Her eyes were on him, deep and proud and gentle.

Matt said, "That's all I know, all I can guess. The way it worked out was luck, main force and awkwardness-- mine, I mean."

Lieutenant Andrews said, "We'll take it from here." He turned to Simmons as they stood up: "We're supposed to be the pros."

"Supposed to be," Simmons said. He even smiled.

Colonel Armitage looked embarrassed. "Apologize for what I said that first day. Good job." He marched out.

Barney said, "It's been quite a day. Some sleep now--"

"No," Matt said. There were times, he thought, when truth could be stretched. "I made a promise to Sue." And he saw the frown on Barney's face, quickly gone. "I promised her that I'd send you back to her, all in one piece. She made me promise." In Barney's face the struggle between desire and disbelief was plain. Matt said, "You'd better go find out. That's an order."

The grin began slowly, lighting Barney's eyes, his entire face. "Okay, Boss. If you say so." He was whistling as he walked out, and then he reappeared, grinned, and closed the door.

Myra put down her pencil. She watched Matt shift a little in his chair, reach out his good arm for her. In his face there was fatigue and pain, and a softness which had not been there before. The fatigue and the pain would pass. The other would not; this she knew. His arm reached her shoulders.

She said, "I told you not to do that, not to touch me-- unless you meant it."

"I heard you," Matt said. "I obey."

She was smiling as she moved toward him.

THE AMERICAN MAGAZINE MYSTERY NOVEL SERIES:
A CHRONOLOGICAL CHECKLIST

Following the author and title, the following information appears in parentheses when applicable: name of series detective (if not identified in the story's title); specialized or unusual background; and subsequent book publication. If the story was expanded to book length without any title change, the word "novel" and the date appear. If it appeared under a changed title, the new title and date are given. If it appeared in a collection of the author's works, the words "included in" appear, followed by the collection title and date. Appearances in other periodicals and in multi-author anthologies are not noted here.

1934

March	Mrs. Wilson Woodrow, "Eyes at the Window"
May	Leslie Ford, "The Strangled Witness" (novel, 1934)
July	Philip Wylie, "Death Flies East" (passenger flight)
August	Clarence Budington Kelland, "A Closed Room" (Scattergood Baines)
September	Leslie Charteris, "The Saint in New York" (novel, 1935)
November	Rex Stout, "Point of Death" (Nero Wolfe; Fer-de-Lance, 1934)

1935

January	Frederic Arnold Kummer, "Eight Bells" (shipboard; Death at Eight Bells, 1937)
March	Philip Wylie, "The Mystery of Galleon Key" (Florida keys)
May	Leslie Ford, "The Clock Strikes" (Col. Primrose; U. S. Supreme Court)
July	Frederic Arnold Kummer, "The Twisted Face" (novel, 1938)
September	Philip Wylie, "The Trial of Mark Adams" (shipboard)

November   Leslie Charteris, "The Pirate Saint" (treasure hunting;
                The Saint Overboard, 1936)

                                    1936

January   Leonard Falkner, "The Silent Staircase"
February   Mary Norman, "The Beauty Mask"
March   John F. Goodrich, "Crack-up" (aviation)
April   Leslie Ford, "Death Stops at a Tourist Camp" (motel)
May   Charles J. Kenny (Erle Stanley Gardner), "Come-on
                Girl" (This is Murder, 1935)
June   Max Brand, "Masquerade" (Mexican party)
July   Philip Wylie, "The Paradise Canyon Mystery" (desert
                resort)
August   Irvin S. Cobb, "The Widow Arrives" (Judge Priest)
September   Channing Pollock, "The Professor's Alibi"
October   David Frome, "Mr. Pinkerton is Present" (Mr. Pinker-
                ton Has the Clue, 1936)
November   Q. Patrick, "The Jack of Diamonds"

                                    1937

January   Wilson Collison, "There's Always a Woman"
February   George Harmon Coxe, "The Camera Clue" (Kent Mur-
                dock; novel, 1937)
March   Clyde B. Clason, "The Purple Parrot" (Theocritus
                Westborough; novel, 1937)
April   Alexandra Brown, "Curtain for an Actress"
May   Leslie Charteris, "Thieves' Picnic" (The Saint; novel,
                1937)
June   Philip Wylie, "Puzzle in Snow" (blizzard)
July   David Frome, "The Black Envelope" (Mr. Pinkerton)
August   Q. Patrick, "The Lady Had Nine Lives" (Timothy
                Trant; Death for Dear Clara, 1937)
September   Timothy Fuller, "The Second Visitor" (Jupiter Jones;
                nightclub)
October   Q. Patrick, "Exit Before Midnight" (skyscraper)
November   Arthur Tuckerman, "Death Goes Down Hill" (skiiing)
December   Philip Wylie, "Danger Mansion" (novel, 1940)

                                    1938

January   Theodora DuBois, "Crime in White" (Jeffrey and Anne
                McNeill; medical laboratory; Death Wears a White
                Coat, 1938)

February	David Frome, "Passage for One" (Mr. Pinkerton)
October	Mignon G. Eberhart, "Bermuda Grapevine" (included in Five of My Best, 1949; Deadly is the Diamond, 1958)
November	Drexel Drake, "The Falcon Strikes"
December	Rex Stout, "The Red Bull" (Nero Wolfe; cattle breeding; Some Buried Caesar, 1939)

1939

January	Leslie Ford, "Reno Rendevous" (Col. Primrose; novel, 1939)
February	Mignon G. Eberhart, "Express to Danger" (Susan Dare; Chicago el train; included in Five of My Best, 1949)
April	Phoebe Atwood Taylor, "Mystery of the Wander Bird" (Asey Mayo; included as "The Wander Bird Plot" in Three Plots for Asey Mayo, 1942)
June	Rex Stout, "Dark Revenge" (Mountain Cat, 1939)
July	David Frome, "Visitor in the Night" (Mr. Pinkerton; Mr. Pinkerton at the Old Angel, 1939)
August	Edward Hope, "Don't Tell the Police" (French Riviera)
September	Rex Stout, "Over My Dead Body" (Nero Wolfe; novel, 1940)
October	George Harmon Coxe, "Death is a Gamble" (theatre; Venturous Lady, 1948)
November	Eustace L. Adams, "Calamity Cay" (Bahamas)

1940

January	Q. Patrick, "Another Man's Poison" (hospital)
March	Kathleen Moore Knight, "Death Came Dancing" (Elisha Macomber; carnival in Panama; novel, 1940)
May	Rex Stout, "Sisters in Trouble" (Nero Wolfe; Where There's a Will, 1940)
August	Constance and Gwenyth Little, "Dark Corridor" (hospital; Black Corridors, 1940)
September	Dana Chambers, "She'll Be Dead by Morning" (Jim Steele; novel, 1940)
October	Hugh Pentecost, "Two Were Missing" (Luke Bradley; Madison Square Garden horse show; The 24th Horse, 1940)
November	Rex Stout, "Bitter End" (Nero Wolfe; as novel with Tecumseh Fox instead of Wolfe, Bad for Business, 1940; included in Corsage, 1977)

1941

February	George F. Worts, "After Midnight"
March	Charles L. Clifford, "While the Bells Rang" (U. S. Army; novel, 1941)
April	Q. Patrick, "Death Rides the Ski-Tow" (Peter Duluth; skiing)
June	Elisabeth Sanxay Holding, "The Fearful Night" (Caribbean resort hotel; Speak of the Devil, 1941)
July	Phoebe Atwood Taylor, "The Headacre Plot" (Asey Mayo; included in Three Plots for Asey Mayo, 1942)
August	Rex Stout, "Death Wears an Orchid" (Nero Wolfe; flower show; included as title story in Black Orchids, 1942)
September	Kelley Roos, "Death Waits in the Darkroom" (Jeff and Haila Troy; If the Shroud Fits, 1941)
November	David Garth, "Manila Masquerade" (Philippines; included in the story collection Manila Masquerade, 1942)
December	Q. Patrick, "Murder with Flowers" (Peter Duluth; circus; Puzzle for Puppets, 1944, as by Patrick Quentin)

1942

February	Frederick C. Davis, "Death at Cockcrow" (cock fight; The Shroud Off Her Back, 1953, as by Stephen Ransome)
April	Rex Stout, "Invitation to Murder" (Nero Wolfe; as "Cordially Invited to Meet Death" in Black Orchids, 1942)
May	Hugh Pentecost, "The Corpse Was Beautiful" (World War II air-raid spotting)
June	Mignon G. Eberhart, "Deadly is the Diamond" (Bland; diamond-cutting; included in Deadly is the Diamond, 1958)
July	Dorothy B. Hughes, "The Wobblefoot" (Kit McKitrick; The Blackbirder, 1943)
August	Kelley Roos, "The Body in the Garden" (Jeff and Haila Troy; The Frightened Stiff, 1942)
September	Lawrence G. Blochman, "Death Walks in Marble Halls" (New York Public Library; Dell 10¢ series, 1951)
October	Phoebe Atwood Taylor, "The Swan-Boat Murder" (Asey Mayo; Boston Public Garden; included as "The Swan Boat Plot" in Three Plots for Asey Mayo, 1942)
November	Clements Ripley, "As High as My Heart" (Civil War New Orleans)

December   Rex Stout, "Not Quite Dead Enough" (Nero Wolfe; as
                title story in Not Quite Dead Enough, 1944)

1943

January   Hugh Pentecost, "Mission to Murder" (Luke Bradley;
                U.S. Navy ship in Pacific; The Brass Chills, 1943)
April   Kelley Roos, "The Case of the Beautiful Body" (Jeff
                and Haila Troy; included as "She'd Make a Lovely
                Corpse" in Triple Threat, 1949)
May   Phoebe Atwood Taylor, "The Stars Spell Death" (Asey
                Mayo; astronomy; included in The Asey Mayo Trio,
                1946)
June   George Harmon Coxe, "Murder in Havana" (novel,
                1943)
July   Mignon G. Eberhart, "Murder Goes to Market" (Bland;
                supermarket; included in Five of My Best, 1949)
September   Hugh Pentecost, "The Dead Man's Tale" (novelet re-
                printed in book form, 1945)
October   Philip Wylie, "Stab in the Back" (island off Florida)
November   Kelley Roos, "The Toy-Boat Murder" (Jeff and Haila
                Troy; lake in Central Park; Sailor Take Warning, 1944)
December   Vera Caspary, "Sugar and Spice"

1944

January   Baynard Kendrick, "The Murderer Who Wanted More"
                (Captain Duncan Maclain; included in Make Mine Mac-
                lain, 1947)
February   Philip Wylie, "Ten Thousand Blunt Instruments" (New
                York Museum of Natural History)
March   Richard Powell, "Death Talks Out of Turn" (Arab and
                Andy Blake; Washington, D. C.; All Over But the
                Shooting, 1944; separate reprint of the novelet, U. S.
                Government Printing Office, 1944)
April   George Harmon Coxe, "The Groom Lay Dead" (novel,
                1944)
May   Phoebe Atwood Taylor, "Murder Rides the Gale" (Asey
                Mayo; girls' school; included in The Asey Mayo Trio,
                1946)
June   Abraham Polonsky, "No Neutral Ground"
July   Virginia Faulkner and Hugh Pentecost, "Murder on the
                Fred Allen Program" (radio show)
August   Rex Stout, "Booby Trap" (Nero Wolfe; included in Not
                Quite Dead Enough, 1944)
September   Kelley Roos, "Murder by Degrees" (Jeff and Haila

Troy; Columbia University Library; <u>There was a Crooked Man</u>, 1945)

October   George Harmon Coxe, "The Jade Venus" (Kent Murdock; novel, 1945)

November   Hugh Pentecost, "Death Wears a Copper Necktie" (aircraft factory)

December   Muriel Stafford, "The Case of the Vicious 'R'" (graphology)

1945

January   Erle Stanley Gardner, "Death Rides a Boxcar" (railroad freight yard; included in <u>The Case of the Murderer's Bride</u>, 1969)

February   Hugh Pentecost, "Death at the Whistling Buoy" (refugee ship)

March   Phoebe Atwood Taylor, "The Third Murderer" (Asey Mayo; included in <u>The Asey Mayo Trio</u>, 1946)

April   Kelley Roos, "Lady About to Die" (Jeff and Haila Troy; <u>Ghost of a Chance</u>, 1947)

May   Mignon G. Eberhart and Grantland Rice, "Murder in the Garden" (Bland; boxing at Madison Square Garden)

June   Baynard Kendrick, "Melody in Death" (Captain Duncan Maclain; opera house; included in <u>Make Mine Maclain</u>, 1947)

July   Hugh Pentecost, "Secret Corridors" (Luke Bradley, Dr. John Smith; included in <u>Memory of Murder</u>, 1947)

August   Rex Stout, "Help Wanted, Male" (Nero Wolfe; included in <u>Trouble in Triplicate</u>, 1949)

September   Eric Hatch, "Murder in the Blue Mist" (night club)

October   George Harmon Coxe, "The Fifth Key" (Kent Murdock; radio soap operas; novel, 1947)

November   Jean Z. Owen, "A Stranger's House"

December   Hugh Pentecost, "Volcano" (Dr. John Smith; included in <u>Memory of Murder</u>, 1947)

1946

January   Betty Baur, "The Doll Collector"

February   Roger Garis, "Birds of a Feather" (zoo)

March   Michael Blankfort, "The Widow Makers" (novel, 1946)

April   Phoebe Atwood Taylor, "The Disappearing Hermit" (Asey Mayo)

May   Rex Stout, "Murder on Tuesday" (Nero Wolfe; as "Instead of Evidence" in <u>Trouble in Triplicate</u>, 1949)

June   Veronica Johns, "The Boy is Handsome"

July	Edmund Ware, "The Lion Call" (north woods)
August	Hugh Pentecost, "Memory of Murder" (Dr. John Smith; included in <u>Memory of Murder</u>, 1947))
September	Dorothee Carousso, "The Unforsaken"
October	Kenneth Fearing, "The Judas Picture" (<u>The Big Clock</u>, 1946)
November	Erle Stanley Gardner, "A Man is Missing" (mountains; included in <u>The Case of the Irate Witness</u>, 1972)
December	Kelley Roos, "Death is a Trouper" (Jeff and Haila Troy; show boat; included in <u>Triple Threat</u>, 1949)

1947

January	Marjorie Carleton, "Dreadful Strangers" (<u>The Swan Sang Once</u>, 1947)
February	H. W. Roden, "Crime on the Pegasus" (luxury train)
March	Nancy Rutledge, "The Preying Mantis" (novel, 1947)
April	Rex Stout, "Before I Die" (Nero Wolfe; included in <u>Trouble in Triplicate</u>, 1949)
May	Leslie Charteris, "King of the Beggars" (The Saint; included in <u>Call for the Saint</u>, 1948)
June	George Harmon Coxe, "Speak No Evil" (Kent Murdock; <u>An Easy Way to Go</u>, 1969)
July	Anne Wormser and Jess Oppenheimer, "Murder in Black and White"
August	Erle Stanley Gardner, "The Case of the Crying Swallow" (Perry Mason; included in <u>The Case of the Crying Swallow</u>, 1971))
September	Donald Hamilton, "The Black Cross" (included in <u>Murder Twice Told</u>, 1950)
October	Hugh Pentecost, "The Cassandra Club" (Alan Quist)
November	Roger Garis, "Straight, Place, and Show" (greyhound racing)
Vacation	Hugh Pentecost, "Chinese Nightmare" (Dell 10¢ series, 1951)
December	Rex Stout, "Man Alive" (Nero Wolfe; included in <u>Three Doors to Death</u>, 1950)

1948

January	George Harmon Coxe, "The Hollow Needle" (Kent Murdock; novel, 1948)
February	Kelley Roos, "Dancing Death" (Jeff and Haila Troy; dance studio; without the Troys, <u>The Blonde Died Dancing</u>, 1956)
March	Phoebe Atwood Taylor, "Deadly Festival" (Asey Mayo;

village fair)

April   Sylvia Tate, "Man on the Run"
May   Hugh Pentecost, "An Element of Risk" (carnival)
June   Erle Stanley Gardner, "The Case of the Crimson Kiss"
            (Perry Mason; included in The Case of the Crimson
            Kiss, 1970)
July   Rex Stout, "Bullet for One" (Nero Wolfe; included in
            Curtains for Three, 1951)
August   Kelley Roos, "Beauty Marks the Spot" (Jeff and Haila
            Troy; charm school; included in Triple Threat, 1949)
September   George Harmon Coxe, "Lady Killer" (Kent Murdock;
            novel, 1949)
October   Kenneth Millar, "The Bearded Lady" (included in The
            Name is Archer, 1955, as by John Ross Macdonald)
November   Rex Stout, "Omit Flowers" (Nero Wolfe; included in
            Three Doors to Death, 1950)
December   Jack Iams, "Death Draws the Line" (comic strips;
            novel, 1949)

                              1949

January   Philip Clark, "Wife of the Victim"
February   Hugh Pentecost and Blake Cabot, "Murder in the Dark"
            (Lt. Pascal; included in Lieutenant Pascal's Taste in
            Homicides)
March   Graham Greene, "The Third Man" (novel, 1950)
April   Peter Ordway, "Invitation to Murder" (masquerade
            party)
May   George Harmon Coxe, "The Hidden Witness" (Kent
            Murdock; advice column; Eye Witness, 1950)
June   Rex Stout, "Door to Death" (Nero Wolfe; included in
            Three Doors to Death, 1950)
July   Elisabeth Sanxay Holding, "The Stranger in the Car"
August   Hugh Pentecost, "Murder for the President's Purse"
            (harness racing)
September   Helen McCloy, "Better Off Dead" (Dell 10¢ series,
            1951)
October   Philip Clark, "Three Strikes and Dead" (baseball)
November   Herbert Brean, "The Hooded Hawk" (auto dealership)
December   Rex Stout, "The Gun With Wings" (Nero Wolfe; in-
            cluded in Curtains for Three, 1951)

                              1950

January   Josephine Bentham, "The Trial of Steven Kent" (court-
            room)

February	Hugh Pentecost, "Eager Victim" (Lt. Pascal; included in Lieutenant Pascal's Taste in Homicides, 1954)
March	Patrick Quentin, "Passport for Murder" (European tour)
April	Helen McCloy, "Shake Hands with Death"
May	George Harmon Coxe, "The Widow Had a Gun" (Kent Murdock; novel, 1951)
June	Kelley Roos, "Murder Among Ladies" (Jeff and Haila Troy; Smithsonian Institution)
July	Hugh Pentecost, "The Murder Machine" (Lt. Pascal; quarry; included in Lieutenant Pascal's Taste in Homicides, 1954)
August	Edmund Ware, "The Singing Trees Murder" (north woods)
September	Rex Stout, "The Twisted Scarf" (Nero Wolfe; included as "Disguise for Murder" in Curtains for Three, 1951)
October	Robert B. Sinclair, "Design for Death"
November	Hugh Pentecost, "Deadly Friend" (military school; novel, 1961)
December	Lew Dietz, "Cry Wolf, Cry Death" (north woods)

1951

January	Patrick Quentin, "Death Freight" (freighter)
February	Rex Stout, "The Cop Killer" (Nero Wolfe; barber shop; included in Triple Jeapordy, 1952)
March	George Harmon Coxe, "Black Target" (Dr. Paul Standish; The Ring of Truth, 1966)
April	Gordon Gaskill, "The Glass Mask" (treasure diving)
May	Kelley Roos, "Final Performance" (Jeff and Haila Troy; Broadway reunion; without the Troys, Requiem for a Blonde, 1958)
June	Hugh Pentecost, "Death in Studio 2" (television studio)
July	Helen McCloy, "The Man Who Talked"
August	Rex Stout, "See No Evil" (Nero Wolfe; comic strips; as "The Squirt and the Monkey" in Triple Jeapordy, 1952)
September	Baynard Kendrick, "Room for Murder" (Atlantic City)
October	Lew Dietz, "Murder on Merry Mountain" (north woods)
November	George Harmon Coxe, "The Fatal Hour" (One Hour to Kill, 1963)
December	Patrick Quentin, "The Scarlet Box" (Rome)

1952

January	Rex Stout, "Nero Wolfe and the Communist Killer" (as "Home to Roost" in Triple Jeapordy, 1952)

February	Hugh Pentecost, "Murder in Manhattan"
March	Margaret Scherf, "The Man with Nine Toes" (Rev. Martin Buell; train; The Elk and the Evidence, 1952)
April	Hugh Pentecost, "The Talking Calf Murders" (cattle auction)
May	George Harmon Coxe, "Weapon of Fear" (Florida motel; Never Bet Your Life, 1952)
June	Helen McCloy, "The Waiting Shadow"
July	Hugh Pentecost, "Murder Plays Through" (golf tournament)
August	Kelley Roos, "Deadly Detour" (antique car museum)
September	Rex Stout, "This Will Kill You" (Nero Wolfe; World Series; included as "This Won't Kill You" in Three Men Out, 1954)
October	Mignon G. Eberhart, "The Crimson Paw" (poodle kennel; included in Deadly is the Diamond, 1958)
November	Gordon Gaskill, "The Blurred Killer" (Monte Cristo Island)
December	Lew Dietz, "Murder by Moonlight"

1953

January	Oscar Schisgall, "The Blonde in the Closet"
February	Hugh Pentecost, "The Dagger" (Civil War historical)
March	Patrick Quentin, "The Laughing Man"
April	Kelley Roos, "A Scream in the Night"
May	Mignon G. Eberhart, "Murder in Waltz Time" (Florida resort hotel; included in Deadly is the Diamond, 1958)
June	The Gordons, "Case File-F. B. I.: The Faceless Killer" (John Ripley)
July	George Harmon Coxe, "The Captive-Bride Murders" (island; Slack Tide, 1959)
August	Rex Stout, "Will to Murder" (Nero Wolfe; included as "Invitation to Murder" in Three Men Out, 1954)
September	Kelley Roos, "One Victim Too Many" (small town centennial)
October	Hugh Pentecost, "Murder Goes Underground" (coal mine)
November	Wyatt Blassingame, "The Body in the Bayou" (Bayou country)
December	Rex Stout, "Scared to Death" (Nero Wolfe; included as "The Zero Clue" in Three Men Out, 1954)

1954

January	Gordon Gaskill, "Murder East of Cairo" (Egypt)

February	Stuart Palmer, "A Valentine for the Victim" (Hildegarde Withers; comic strips; <u>Cold Poison</u>, 1954)
March	Hugh Pentecost, "Murder Comes to the Fair" (country fair boxing)
April	Wyatt Blassingame, "Make Believe It's Murder" (little theatre)
May	Rex Stout, "When a Man Murders" (Nero Wolfe; included in <u>Three Witnesses</u>, 1956)
June	Peter Ordway, "The Accidental Murders"
July	Kelley Roos, "The Case of the Hanging Gardens" (cavern tours)
August	Hugh Pentecost, "Blackmailer's Bluff"
September	Richard Stern, "The Jet Plane Murders" (aircraft factory)
October	Doris Miles Disney, "Ghost of a Chance" (Jeff DiMarco; Hallowe'en; <u>Trick or Treat</u>, 1955)
November	Scott Young, "Dead <u>Duck</u>" (duck hunting)
December	Rex Stout, "The Body in the Hall" (Nero Wolfe; included as "Die Like a Dog" in <u>Three Witnesses</u>, 1956)

1955

January	Hugh Pentecost, "Oval of Death" (stock car racing)
February	The Gordons, "The Case of the Talking Bug" (novel, 1955)
March	Gordon Gaskill, "The Curse of Sablier Island" (location filming)
April	John Rhodes Sturdy, "A Bullet for the Purser" (shipboard)
May	Rex Stout, "The Last Witness" (Nero Wolfe; courtroom; included as "The Next Witness" in <u>Three Witnesses</u>, 1956)
June	Stuart Palmer, "The Murder Mask" (Howard Rook; circus; <u>Unhappy Hooligan</u>, 1956)
July	Hugh Pentecost, "Murder Preferred"
August	Charlotte Armstrong, "Ride with the Executioner" (included in <u>The Albatross</u>, 1957)
September	Gordon Gaskill, "Heiress to Murder" (Italy)
October	Lew Dietz, "Killer in Town" (seaside resort)
November	Rex Stout, "Immune to Murder" (Nero Wolfe; trout fishing; included in <u>Three for the Chair</u>, 1957)
December	Mignon G. Eberhart, "Terror Trap"

1956

| January | Hugh Pentecost, "The Smiling Victim" |

February   Baynard Kendrick, "The Cloth-of-Gold Murders" (Flor-
                ida island)
March   John Rhodes Sturdy, "The Waiting Bullet" (island)
April   Peter Ordway, "Essence of Murder" (French perfume
                factory)
May   Rex Stout, "Nero Wolfe and the Vanishing Clue" (in-
                cluded as "A Window for Death" in Three for the
                Chair, 1957)
June   Hugh Pentecost, "Trail of the Vulture" (Alan Quist;
                Mexico)
July   H. Vernor Dixon, "Murder Flies High" (jet aviation)
August   Holly Roth, "The Girl Who Saw Too Much"